D1493228

THE
LIFE OF ALEXANDER WHYTE, D.D.

Yours truly,

Alexander Wylie

THE LIFE OF
ALEXANDER WHYTE
D.D.

BY

G. F. BARBOUR

SEVENTH EDITION, REVISED

HODDER AND STOUGHTON
LIMITED   LONDON

First Edition . . . . printed October 1923
Second Edition . . . . printed December 1923
Third Edition . . . . printed January 1924
Fourth Edition . . . . . . printed January 1924
Fifth Edition . . . . printed May 1924
Sixth Edition . . . . printed November 1924
and this the Seventh Edition . printed June 1925

MADE AND PRINTED IN GREAT BRITAIN BY MORRISON AND GIBB LTD., EDINBURGH

PREFACE TO THE FIRST EDITION

In the opening sentences of the Introductory Chapter I have sought to express the objects which have been before me in writing this record of Dr. Whyte's life and ministry. Thus it is only needful here to set down the names of some who have helped most in my task, and to whom my indebtedness is greatest. First I would acknowledge what I owe to Mrs. Whyte, Sir Frederick Whyte, and other members of Dr. Whyte's family, not only for the unrestricted access which they have given to all the material in their hands, but for much constructive assistance both in regard to wider issues and on points of detail.

The circle of those who contributed generously to this book out of their stores of memory and affection has grievously narrowed during late months. Since last December Dr. John Sutherland Black, Sir William Robertson Nicoll, Dr. John W. Ballantyne, the Rev. J. C. B. Geddes and the Rev. Harry M. Ross have all passed away; and I would thankfully acknowledge their interest in the progress of a task which none of them has lived to see completed. In particular, the intimate knowledge of Dr. Whyte's thought gained by Dr. Sutherland Black during an unbroken friendship of forty-five years, and his exact memory for fact and impression were of great service in shaping the earlier portion of the memoir.

The reader will gather both from text and footnotes to how many others my indebtedness extends.

It is impossible to name all those who have placed letters at my disposal or given help in other ways, but certain more specific acknowledgements must not be passed over here. For help in proof-reading my thanks are due to Professor A. B. Macaulay (who also read a large part of the manuscript) and the Rev. Hubert L. Simpson; for valuable advice and suggestion at more than one stage of the work, to Dr. John Kelman, Dr. A. H. F. Barbour, and the Rev. J. M. E. and Mrs. Ross; for material bearing on the first five chapters, to Mr. A. N. Dickson, Mr. Robert Gardiner, Mr. W. Keith Leask, and Mr. A. D. Wallace; and for assistance in other ways to Mr. C. Forbes Ridland, and to Miss Agnes J. Young, who has spent much care upon the preparation of the Index.

I desire also to acknowledge the courtesy of Sir James Guthrie and of the Senatus of New College, Edinburgh, in granting permission for the reproduction of the Frontispiece. . . .

Where so many have co-operated willingly, it is clear that faults both of omission and commission can lie only at the author's door. Of these I am far from unconscious; yet I send this *Life* forth in the hope that in some measure a living personality may shine through the imperfections of the record.

G. F. BARBOUR.

FINCASTLE, PERTHSHIRE.

new material, except that at two or three points I have borrowed from a vivid and informing sketch of Dr. Whyte's early ministry by Professor Robert Mackintosh, published under the title, " Dr. Whyte as I remember him," in the *Congregational Quarterly* for April, 1924.

G. F. BARBOUR.

March 22, 1925.

ERRATUM

Page vii, line 18, *for* "two are reproduced now," *read*
"four are reproduced now, including."

PREFACE TO THE SEVENTH EDITION

Less than eighteen months have passed since the
publication of this book in the late autumn of 1923 ;
but even the earlier months of this period fully showed
how widespread and how keen was the desire on the
part of those who acknowledged a great debt to
Dr. Whyte to learn more of his personal history, and
to hear his message in a new form.   The fact that this
Life has been welcomed wherever the English tongue
is spoken would itself have pointed to the desirability
of its reissue in a less expensive form ; and the desire
for this has, in fact, been definitely expressed both
in Britain and overseas.   The publishers have co-
operated heartily in making this possible without
too marked a change in the outward form of the book.
But some changes had to be made ; and, out of
fifteen illustrations and facsimiles which appeared in
the earlier editions, only two are reproduced now—
Sir James Guthrie's portrait of Dr. Whyte as frontispiece, and, at p. 384, the photograph in his study with
his son, Robert.

In a note to the Third Edition I acknowledged the
kindness of various correspondents who had pointed
out inaccuracies which I then corrected.   I have
taken the present opportunity to revise the text
throughout, making such changes in words or phrases
as the lapse of time or my own more considered
judgment made needful.   It has not been possible
to make more extensive changes or to introduce

CONTENTS

PART ONE.—THE PREPARATION—1836–1866

CONTENTS

PART FOUR.—THE LABOUR OF LATER YEARS— 1892–1907

life under a misapprehension
he was born ; but his neglect
ite sufficiently pronounced to
ces into the path of the bio-
never went beyond the briefest
read or places visited. He
etter, while his own letters were
ith only the day of the week.
nd his intentness on the actual
of living made him careless of
rd of his life : we owe what has
irely to the care of others. Thus
ces of the typical biography are
ent here ; yet the loss is less because
lived so largely in a sphere which,
owne's phrase, " owes no homage

the object which the compiler of
has primarily kept in view ? To
ing of place and circumstance that
outward current of this life—a life
much for the Kirk in Scotland and,
ter years, for the unity and charity
atholic ; to trace, as far as can now be
nces which helped to carry this working
wide fields of imagination and thought
; to bring to light such of the more
of his labours as pastor and friend as
wn without the betrayal of confidence
be made public. This book aims at
record and a picture : first for those who
and then for those who will come after in
and his Church.
main interest of the story must, then, be
Yet Alexander Whyte contributed not a
the life of his time, and followed its history
singularly watchful eye. Many men of action
lad to claim his friendship ; and even in exit was no ordinary life which began in a two-
Forfarshire cottage in the decade of the
Bill, when the Ten Years' Conflict in Scotland

CONTENTS

2

PART

CHAPTER I

" O the braw, braw t
    And I winna see
I'd be greetin' like
    Lookin' down upo

" BUTLER," says
the great moralis
books are his whol
in a real sense tru
Like all those who
thought and inspirat
life was less significar
his spirit. His messa
—a message preserved
its true essence and gre
duced in new forms of
whom his word brough
Thus the record of his
sense be written, for it is
It is still being written to-d
in the memory and life of
many lands.

     Moreover, the life of ev
in whose nature there is any
cism refuses to be exhausti
forms of strict chronology.
of philosophical mystics that
or of set purpose concealed,
Dr. Whyte did not carry his dis
reckoning of life as far as this—

I

and the Oxford Movement in England were changing the face of the religious world ; and which reached its quiet close in Hampstead amid the menacing ground-swell which has followed the storm of the Great War, but also amid new and far-reaching movements towards a wider Christian unity. Yet, as in the design of a great arch, the very width of the gulf to be spanned makes it but the more imperative that the curve should show a perfect unity, so this life was marked by unity of purpose even more than by length of days and range of interests. The same character and ideal, which appeared in the little lad herding in Glen Clova when he spoke of being a minister some day, showed itself as clearly seventy years later, when the old preacher slipped out in despite of doctors and guardians to give his message once more in the Methodist Chapel at Penn. From first to last, in this career of many interests, all was subordinated to the one form of service to which it had been so early dedicated. From the first conscious page to the last, the volume of Alexander Whyte's life bore the Pauline injunction, " Covet to prophesy," and the Pauline aspiration, " That I may know Him."

Alexander Whyte was born in the Southmuir of Kirriemuir on 13th January 1836. Twenty-four years later there was born in a house at the north-eastern extremity of the straggling, dull-red town a boy who, before the century passed, made " Thrums " one of the best loved and most familiar places in all modern fiction. The town and the ways and interests of its inhabitants have been made so real and vivid by Sir James Barrie in his books, from *Auld Licht Idylls* onward, that no subsequent writer need attempt, or would desire, to go over the ground again in the commonplace prose of our daily use. It is, however, worth while to refer more particularly to the second chapter of *Margaret Ogilvy*, in which the author describes the sudden coming, during his early boyhood, of a giant which transformed Thrums into a new

town, replacing " the click of the shuttle by the roar
of ' power.' " But he goes on to tell how it was
that, though this change took place when he was little
more than a child, and the old race of the hand-loom
weavers were already adapting themselves—or sending their children—to the new duties of the factories,
yet his imagination habitually dwelt in the older
time. " Though the new town is to me a glass
through which I look at the old, the people I see
passing up and down these wynds, sitting, night-
capped, on their barrow-shafts, hobbling in their
blacks to church on Sunday, are less those I saw in
my childhood than their fathers and mothers who did
these things in the same way when my mother was
young." The " Thrums " that all the world knows
is the home of Margaret Ogilvy's girlhood.

So it came about that Dr. Whyte testified in his
later years that Barrie's " Thrums " was a true picture
of his native town as he had known it. For not
many years before 1836 Margaret Ogilvy, who as
a child of eight became housekeeper as well as companion to her widowed father, might have been
seen swinging his dinner in a flagon, as she walked
through the long parks of Kinnordy towards the
place where he worked as a stone-mason ; and while
Alec Whyte was first observing the world around him,
she was storing up those impressions which stand
permanently engraven in the books of her son. So
those who would form a picture of the lanes of
Kirriemuir, and of the weavers who dwelt in them
about the year 1830, may find what they seek in
Auld Licht Idylls. Or, if the reader would explore
the Den that winds to the west, let him do so in the
inimitable company of *Sentimental Tommy*. If he
would breast the Hill and enter Caddam Woods, he
will find a guide in *The Little Minister* ; while, if he
leaves the Square by the southward road, he will find
himself dipping suddenly into the valley of the
Gairie, which divides the Southmuir from the older
town, and as he climbs the opposite slope, he will
pass " the bend on the brae " where Joey met his

early death almost within sight of Jess's Window. Long after, Dr. Whyte said of this spot that, "though he had passed it daily during his years of apprenticeship, yet his poor blind eyes saw nothing of the things that were to be seen in Mr. Barrie's books."

Yet there are some facts which cannot find a place in the imaginative history of "Thrums," but which have their own importance as bearing on Alexander Whyte's early life and spiritual history. The novelist has made the old town live for his readers, and, working in a different medium, a daughter of one of the most ancient and honoured houses of Angus has reproduced with singular skill the spirit of the country-side.[1] But it still remains for the biographer to set his subject in its prosaic geographical relations ; for "Thrums" is not to be found in any atlas, and even the ancient designation of the Sheriffdom or County of Angus might long be looked for without success.

Kirriemuir lies within the modern County of Forfar, and is not the least beautifully situated of a succession of small towns on the slope of the eastern Grampians, where they meet the fertile lands of Strathmore. No stranger who has had the fortune in the glow of a June day to climb the hill up which the steep lanes of the old town struggle, is ever likely to forget the wide sweep and varied beauty of the view, stretching from Ben Lawers in the far west to the low hills of Kincardine-shire where they fall to the sea beyond Montrose ; while the gently sloping common ground to the north is all aflame with golden broom, and beyond the woods of Caddam there rises the nobly moulded form of Catlaw. Through these woods there may be traced the line of a Roman military road, and the standing-stones and prehistoric forts in the neighbour-hood show how fully the importance, both for defence and for worship, of this commanding site was recog-

[1] *Songs of Angus*, and *More Songs of Angus*, by Violet Jacob.

nised in very early times.[1]   The story dimly suggested
by these and other prehistoric relics of the district
is carried a stage further by several small and rudely
sculptured stones which bear as their chief symbol
the Cross cut in low relief.

When the great Earls of Angus came in semi-royal
state during the fifteenth and sixteenth centuries to
visit their wide possessions north of the Tay, " the
Regality of Kirriemuir " was one of their chief
objectives, and the " Court of Regality," held on a
rounded eminence just to the west of the town, must
have been a scene of no mean feudal splendour.   In
the more democratic century which followed, the
fighting spirit had descended to the burghers of
Kirriemuir, who found themselves obliged to maintain their position and trading rights against the
growing importance of Forfar;   and the rivalry
between the " town of the knowe " and the " town of
the howe " six miles away was contested not only
with the weapons of economic boycott (as it would
now be called) but on occasion by hard blows.

Till the middle of the eighteenth century the
Court of Regality continued to dispense justice,
though with greatly limited powers, in the tolbooth
of Kirriemuir.   More than a century later the " baron
bailie," originally the powerful deputy of the Earl
of Angus but now shorn of ancient glories, continued
to play his part in the public life of the town.   Latterly his duties were chiefly of a ceremonial kind,
such as the picturesque " fencing " of the annual
market or fair on the town's common land on the
hill.[2]   It might seem that these half-medieval echoes
and survivals have little importance for our subject ;
yet they helped to give colour and substance to that
local patriotism which was strong in Kirriemuir.

[1] The facts in the following paragraphs are mainly drawn from the
exhaustive local history published in 1909 by Alan Reid, F.S.A.Scot.,
entitled *The Regality of Kirriemuir*.   Dr. Whyte contributed to it a
characteristic introduction, beginning, " Simply to read the proof sheets
of this remarkable book is like having a good holiday in dear old
Thrums."

[2] *Op. cit.*, pp. 95, 116, 160 ff., 185, 192.

As early as 1640, when the great Marquis of Montrose passed that way, we are informed that the village of Kirriemuir was almost entirely inhabited by weavers. Thus by 1836 there had grown up an uninterrupted tradition of over two centuries, formed by that type of industry which more, perhaps, than any other developed the powers of criticism and discussion in the older Scottish democracy. The discovery, about the year 1738, that Scottish weavers could compete successfully with the weavers of Holland in the production of " osnaburghs " ushered in half a century of expansion and prosperity ; and at the beginning of the nineteenth century Kirriemuir, with a population of about four thousand five hundred, produced annually " 25,000 pieces, or webs, of various sorts of linen." But things did not always go smoothly, and the town's history contains records of more than one conflict. In 1783 a disastrous harvest had rendered corn scarce and dear, and it was reported that the surrounding farmers were holding back supplies which were urgently needed by other sections of the community. So the weavers were stung to bitter anger, and organised raids on the farmers' granaries, commandeering supplies of grain, which was then brought in triumph to the Square of Kirriemuir, there to be sold at " reasonable " prices, the proceeds being duly handed over to the farmers who had involuntarily surrendered their stocks. " The honesty of this," as Sir James Barrie remarks, " is worth thinking about, but it seems only to have incensed the farmers the more." For they gathered a force of rudely armed irregulars and advanced to chastise the offending town. Then followed the " Battle of Cloisterbank," in which the farmers were routed, horse and foot, by the defending force of weavers and their wives.[1]

The last conflict was a more serious and tragic

[1] *Op. cit.*, chapter xii. ; cf. pp. 55, 153 ; *Auld Licht Idylls*, chapter v. (" The Auld Lichts in Arms "). Two leaders of the weavers were sentenced to transportation for their share in this affray, and a third to a public whipping.

one. The period following the Napoleonic wars was one of hard struggle for the weavers, and on the threshold of "the hungry Forties" the manufacturers, who acted rather as dealers or agents than as factory owners (the development of factories came later), announced a considerable reduction in the price paid for each web. A riot of some violence ensued, and an appeal to the Sheriff instead of to the forces of reason and conciliation did not mend matters, for he and his force of seventy police were practically besieged in the Town House, and after a few hours felt it more prudent to disappear quietly. But the triumph of the weavers was short-lived; for the cry soon passed round, "The sojers is comin'!" and they could not face a conflict with regular troops. So their leaders were soon taken to Edinburgh for trial, followed by sentences of from four to ten months' imprisonment. The earliest memory of the little Alec Whyte, then in his fourth year, was that of awakening in the night, and hearing the noise as his fellow-townsmen were carried off to prison. After this Kirriemuir saw no more violence, but the sense of injustice left behind added fuel to the ardent Chartism of the years which immediately followed.

Weaving, as practised in Scotland down to the middle of the nineteenth century, provided a singularly effective balance of individualism with the more social qualities. The weaving communities were compact and self-contained, and thus readily attained to a sense of common interest. From an early period the quality and measure produced by individual weavers were strictly regulated both by law and custom; yet the work of each lay to a great extent apart from that of others, and its success depended on his own skill and patience. Some worked in one of the two or three rooms of their own narrow dwellings; others shared a loom-shop with two or more fellow-craftsmen. But all had scope for reflection while they worked, and opportunity for free and constant discussion in the intervals of their labour. Many of them were keen readers, but they

could not have gained all that they did from the
scanty literature within their reach, apart from their
use of the dinner-hour and the leisure of the evening
for informal, but constant and searching, debate.
There are still a few aged people who recall the keenness and thoroughness with which the Chartist programme, or the " Voluntary controversy " and the
challenge to the liberties of the Kirk during the Ten
Years' Conflict, were debated and redebated in the
Kirriemuir of the " forties." Hence there arose a
general love of knowledge and capacity for criticism
exceptional even in weaving towns. Nor is it fanciful
to suppose that the union of a degree of poverty
hardly conceivable in these days with high and
vigorous thinking, which marked Kirriemuir in the
middle of last century, contributed much to the
intellectual development of her two famous sons.
The coming of genius cannot, indeed, be predicted or
explained ; yet we can see that it was a singularly
austere but fruitful soil into which the seed of genius
fell.

Of the weaving society of his boyhood, Dr. Whyte
gave the following account :

" There were rows and rows of weavers' shops
in the Newtown " (the Southmuir) " where I
was brought up ; generally comprised of a ' but '
and a ' ben '—the ' but ' being the kitchen with
maybe a little room as a bedroom or sitting-
room. Then at the other end there were four
weaving looms. The father would have one,
and perhaps two daughters would have one each,
and the son would have one ; if he had not, then
some other person would have it. It has always
amazed me how these people managed to live.
The father might make twelve or fourteen
shillings a week, and with a little extra work he
would perhaps make sixteen shillings, while the
others would have perhaps only five or six or
seven shillings. It is amazing to think of the
way they turned out, and always had a little to

give to a good cause, and sometimes—who would believe it ?—were able to send their sons to college. But it was done ! " [1]

From the Reformation onward, the study of the Bible, and its application both in theology and ecclesiastical polity, provided the great educative discipline of the Scottish people, greater even than the political discussions just referred to. In its religious history, Kirriemuir appears to have reflected on a small scale the main tendencies at work in the country as a whole.[2] At the Reformation few districts took their stand more decisively on the side of the reformed faith than the region of Angus.

North-eastern Scotland was perhaps less deeply stirred by the contendings of Covenanting days than by the Reformation ; but during the period of the Jacobite risings, when great parts of the country had sunk into religious and ecclesiastical quiescence, the clash of Presbyterianism and Episcopacy was loudly heard in Kirriemuir. In the main the Burgh stood on the Presbyterian side, while the Jacobites were strong in the country immediately around ; for, out of sixty men from the Parish of Kirriemuir who marched with Lord Ogilvy of Airlie in support of Prince Charlie in the '45, only twelve belonged to the town and only three were weavers.

If religious conviction may be judged by certain external tests, the minister and kirk-session of Kirriemuir in the eighteenth century showed a praiseworthy zeal. Sabbath-breaking and non-attendance at ordinances gave exercise to the disciplinary power of the " Beddal " and the Town's Officer. Offences against public morals were faithfully dealt with, and the vehemence of a notorious scold occasioned an admonition from the Session " to live more Chris-

[1] The address in which this passage occurred, delivered in Edinburgh, was fully reported in the *Kirriemuir Observer* of 9th Feb., 1907.
[2] For the following paragraphs, cf. *The Regality of Kirriemuir*, chapters ix., x., xiii., and xiv., and Appendix vi., vii. Dr. Whyte gave special praise to Mr. Reid's sketches in these chapters of the ministers of Kirriemuir.

tianly in time coming." In quite another direction, the piety of Kirriemuir was called into generous and surely most praiseworthy action by an appeal for help from " distressed Protestants in the Dukedom of Lithuania "—an appeal which has a strangely modern sound.

But, whatever achievements stand to the credit of the Church of Scotland in the mid-eighteenth century, there were those in Angus as elsewhere who were far from satisfied. They felt that the Patronage Act of 1711, and the Church's subsequent acquiescence in the annexation of spiritual functions by the civil power, fettered and shackled the exercise of those Christian liberties which had been so dearly bought during the previous century. They felt not less that their soul's health demanded a keener atmosphere than that which was furnished by the somewhat facile moralism of the time. They felt impelled to a closer study of Scripture than was fashionable in a politely sceptical age. Thus bodies of earnest men—few at first, but steadily increasing—left the Established Church, to form the Churches of the Secession. Soon they began to divide among themselves on narrow issues of Church polity, and before the end of the century one denomination had emerged whose members always stated the claim to spiritual independence in its most exacting form, and who thus formed the left wing of the whole movement. They were the " Auld Licht Anti-Burghers," and their double name was due to their steady refusal to compromise. They stood by the old testimony, refusing to admit any " new light " on the relation of Church and State, or to take the Burgess oath demanded of the citizens in certain Scottish towns.

The leader of this cause in Kirriemuir for fifty-five years, from 1779 till 1834, was the Rev. James Aitken, who did more than any other man to create the religious atmosphere of the circle into which Alexander Whyte was born. Mr. Aitken is described as a man of noble presence and great dignity, possessing a deep and melodious voice which rose in moments

of emotion into a kind of solemn chant. He opened
a week-day school, and laboured in other ways for
the education of his people, while among other fruits
of his labour were many household prayer-meetings
conducted by members of his congregation in turn.
It was during his ministry that the stone-mason
already referred to came under the influences which
made Margaret Ogilvy's early home a centre of that
strong and serious type of piety which, long after,
was unforgettably depicted by her son. But the
minister's intensity of conviction placed at times too
severe a strain upon the unity of his own flock and
the patience of his brethren in the Secession ; and in
1806 Mr. Aitken was deposed from his charge. Although his congregation thereby lost the church which
they had built in the Glengate, the great majority
followed their pastor out into the open fields. They
did not long remain there, however ; for out of their
deep poverty they set themselves, for the second time
within forty years, to provide a new place of worship.
This was the Auld Licht Church in Bank Street,
of which Sentimental Tommy heard such glowing
accounts in his childhood in London that he assured
his trustful sister that it was "bigger and lovelier
than St. Paul's," but which, when the children at
length saw it, proved to be "of a different style of
architecture."

Mr. Aitken's last controversy was over what now
appears a very trivial matter—the abolition of the
custom by which the precentor intoned each line of
the psalm before the congregation joined in singing
it. The reformers carried the day, and " the run
line " was abolished. But there remained a faithful
remnant—in this case finally reduced to one—whose
testimony is described at length in *Auld Licht Idylls*,
and more briefly by Dr. Whyte in these words :

> " I remember well how an old lady was so
> great an opponent to anything in the nature of
> an innovation that she would not worship unless
> the ' line ' was given out, and . . . when the

minister gave out a psalm after reading the
lesson or offering a prayer, she rose and went out
regularly as a protest."

On another occasion he recalled the eagerness with
which the boys of the community waited for and
watched her exit.

But we should do a great injustice to the memory
of the " Auld Lichts " if we concluded that their
chief interest lay in perpetually protesting against
the encroachments of the State or the defections of
the Church. They had a real and vital, if in some
ways an unduly narrow, experience of religion, and
they did the work which was most needed in the
Scotland of their day by re-establishing the tradition
of personal piety, and bringing it close to the lives
of the common people. Not a little that was ennobling in the surrounding of Alexander Whyte's
boyhood was due to the brave shining of the " Auld
Licht " in a dark place.

There were other notable factors in the religious
history of Kirriemuir a hundred years ago, such as
the visit of the Haldanes. But enough has been said
to show that strong and deep, if at times turbulent,
religious currents had flowed for long in the little
community. Like the citizens of most other Scottish
towns, they neither gained nor sought inspiration
from the architecture of their churches. But they
were fortunate—or wise—at least in this, that they
allowed the past to live on in the names of not a few
streets and lanes in the older portion of the town.
To the north of the Square, the following are still to
be found within little more than a stone's-throw:
the Roods, St. Malcolm's Wynd, St. Mary's Close,
Elders' Close, Seceders' Close; and the passer-by, as
he reads these names, may see in imagination the
successive ages of the religion of Kirriemuir, and of
Scotland. But it was from another quarter of the
town—a quarter without a history—that the boy came
who was destined to make " the old Regality " a
sacred place in the annals of the Kirk in Scotland.

" Our Lord's first humiliation on earth was His being born, and that in a low condition. Now, all His followers do not have that forerunning humiliation of His ordained to them. It is only some specially chosen men who have that eminent opportunity ordained and offered to them."—ALEXANDER WHYTE, *The Spiritual Life* (1917).

Two glens run deep into the heart of the Grampians behind Kirriemuir, Glen Prosen and Glen Clova; and the streams that flow from them meet to form the lower reach of the River Southesk under the walls of Inverquharity, the old castle of the Ogilvys, an hour's walk from the town. It was from Glen Prosen, the western of the two glens, that the family of Whyte originally came to Kirriemuir. This glen was the scene of an early experiment in co-operation between the Churches. In it there stood an old chapel, built in 1602, of which James Duncan, wright at Dalearn, who helped to rebuild it two hundred years later, records that "she was very loe of the walls, and had a pivilling roof on her (pavilion roof), and was all thacked over with heth, or what we call heder." When this primitive sanctuary was restored and enlarged, it was arranged that the Episcopalians, who were strongly represented in Glen Prosen, and the Presbyterians should share its use, and the ministers of either church were given the right to preach in it when they came from Kirriemuir "to deliver the word of God in this place." [1] One must in candour add that, by Dr. Whyte's own testimony, nothing was further from the thoughts of the Auld Licht and Free Kirk people among whom his own youth was spent than co-operation with Episcopalians. Much remained to be done before that point was again reached.

[1] Cited by Reid, *The Regality of Kirriemuir*, p. 341 f.

Thomas Whyte, grandfather of Alexander Whyte, was born in 1785 and spent a great part of his life in Kirriemuir, following the trade of sawyer, when sawing was still done by hand, in the West Roods. He and three of his twelve children reached the age of fourscore, so that Dr. Whyte clearly inherited something of his great strength of constitution from his father's family. A faded photograph of Thomas Whyte, which has been preserved by a kinswoman in Kirriemuir, shows a face of the type not uncommon among Scotsmen of the older generation—keen and worn, with high cheekbones and firmly set lips, but with a real kindliness of expression; and a letter, also dating from his old age when he had returned to Dalearn in Glen Prosen, shows in its small and legible handwriting and vigour of expression that the old sawyer still possessed more than the common measure of intellectual force. The archaisms in spelling in the letter are amply covered by the quaint apology with which it ends: "Excuse blunders and misaplyed words as I never learned Gramer."

Of Thomas Whyte's children, two only have a place in this record, the third and the fourth. John Whyte, the father of Alexander Whyte, was born on 4th June 1812; and David, who will be referred to later, in 1814. The central fact regarding the home into which the future preacher was born is that it was the home of his mother, Janet Thomson, only, for his parents were never married. Many Scottish boys have risen from the poorest surroundings to high distinction in the most various fields; but in few cases were their early years overcast, not only by straitening poverty, but by this other shadow.

No one now alive in Kirriemuir can remember John Whyte, for he left his native town soon after his son was born. But from the story of his later life, and in particular from the part which he played in the American Civil War,[1] it is clear that he possessed a high degree of self-reliance and of the courage

[1] See Chapter VIII.

which can devote itself to a great cause—qualities which have so often equipped the wandering Scot to face adversity. With these were doubtless combined in his youth that restless disposition and impatience of discipline which often form the reverse side of a naturally adventurous temper ; and his instinct for companionship was always strong. It was placed beyond doubt in later years by more than one trustworthy witness that he was ready, and even eager, to marry Janet Thomson ; but she very firmly refused, feeling that this marriage would have added to an initial error another which must have involved her whole life in falsehood. All who knew her in her later years are at one in their testimony to the very remarkable strength and tenacity of her character ; and, when she had once determined to carry unaided the burden of her child's upbringing, she gave every power of her vigorous mind and body to her lonely task.

When Dr. Whyte said, long years afterward, " In God's providence I was born in a poor rank of life," his thought must have travelled back to a cottage on the edge of the Southmuir, the westmost of a short row locally known as the " Fore Raw." Here he was born on 13th January 1836.[1] The Fore Row was part of the " new town "—an extension of Kirriemuir dating from the prosperous days of the weaving industry. Hence the cottages were relatively newly built in 1836, but they were of the single-storey type, with two rooms and sometimes an attic or bed-closet, familiar throughout rural Scotland. The cottage, as it now stands, has comparatively large windows and a slated roof, but there are others near by which still show the low-pitched roof of grey flags which commonly took the place of thatch in the district of Angus. The ' but,' or kitchen, is to

[1] There has been some doubt on both points. As regards the *place*, this is due to the fact that his mother more than once moved house during his boyhood, though always within the limits of the Southmuir ; and as regards the *year*, to the haphazard way in which parochial records were then kept.

the left on entering; and here Dr. Whyte was born. His mother and grandmother kept their looms in the 'ben' to the right, the floor being hollowed, according to the Kirriemuir custom, to make room for the treadle of the loom. From the cottages in the Fore Row the ground slopes gently down to the fertile levels of Strathmore, with its broad fields and belts of woodland; and there is nothing to bar the view until the eye rests on the line of the Sidlaw Hills.

The first task—and it was no light one—that awaited Janet Thomson was to provide the bare necessities of life for her boy and herself. So the anecdotes remaining from the years that follow deal with her work—not, indeed, at the loom, for there was nothing to distinguish one day's weaving from another—but in the harvest field, where the labour of an active woman was more in demand and more remunerative than in weaving. That she went out to field-work while her child was still very young, was shown by an incident nearly three-quarters of a century later. When the Old Age Pensions Act came into force a claim was made by an old inhabitant of the Southmuir, who could give no documentary evidence as to her age. She could, however, state that she was of the same age as Dr. Whyte, since her mother had been left in charge of both infants when his mother went to the harvest. Dr. Whyte was appealed to, and his reply as to his own age was accepted as satisfactory evidence in support of his old friend's claim.

The earliest distinct memory which Dr. Whyte retained throughout life was that of being awakened at night by the noise and shouting as the leaders in the weavers' riot were carried off to serve their harsh sentences in prison; and the earliest authentic tale regarding the boy himself is connected with Dr. Easton, the dignified and broad-minded Parish minister of Kirriemuir, who won the esteem of the community during a long ministry, and at one time occupied the Moderator's chair of his Church. Thus the incident

belongs to the years before 1843.   One Sunday, as
Alec Whyte and his mother were returning to the
Southmuir after church, she missed him, and realised
that he had lingered behind.   When he rejoined her he
explained in reply to her questions that he had seen
the Doctor, who had stopped and given him some
sweets.   " And did he say anything to you ? "   " He
said he hoped I was a guid boy."   " I hope you told
him what was true."   " Na ; if I'd done that, I was
feared he would ha' ta'en back the sweeties."   Evidently the habit of severe self-judgment began early
with Alec Whyte.   Another incident, slight in itself,
was told by his mother in later years.   She had sent
the boy out with a shilling to make some purchases,
but he returned empty-handed, with the somewhat
unsatisfying explanation that he had accidentally
swallowed the shilling.   " And," she gravely added,
" I could ill want it."   The loss of a shilling was
a real calamity in Thrums during "the hungry
forties "; and it is told on good authority that Janet
Thomson was once obliged to sell some of her few
blankets in order to keep her boy and herself fed and
clad.

Before many years had passed the boy could
accompany his mother, who was thus able to go
farther afield, to Torrybuckle or other farms ten or
more miles up Glen Clova.   In the summer of 1921
the present writer had the privilege of a short talk in a
cottage far up the Glen with a retired farmer of over
ninety who had seen two sons enter the ministry of
the Church of Scotland.   He told that his wife had
known Alec Whyte when both were " wee toddlers,"
playing at the side of the field while their mothers
worked.   Later still, Alec himself was able to gain
employment in herding at a farm, now demolished,
on the east side of the Glen.   Beyond securing keep
for the summer months, this work cannot have done
much to support the family finances, for the wages of
a herd laddie at that time were only about twenty or
thirty shillings for the season.   The boy's thoughts
were already rather with the books which he so

earnestly desired to read than with the cattle which he was engaged to watch. On one occasion, like a second and youthful King Alfred, his dreams of his future kingdom had made him forget his immediate task ; and the farmer's wife, seeing the cattle stray into the corn, ran out " raging him "—" I dinna ken fat ye're gaen to dae, or foo in the hale warld ye'll ever earn an honest living." The delinquent appears to have met this onslaught calmly—" What wad ye think if ae day I was to wag my pow in a poopit ? " " You, ye feckless cratur !——" But unhappily the rest of the justly angered dame's retort was couched in Forfarshire speech so racy as to elude the present chronicler. The truth of this story gains some confirmation from another regarding a harvest scene in the Parish of Airlie, where Janet Thomson acted as a forewoman among the harvesters. Finding her son's well-meant efforts rather a hindrance than a help, she broke out, " Get oot o' my road, laddie ; ye may be guid at yer buiks : ye'll never mak' a sharer " (shearer). But, even among those who felt that the boy had little aptitude for agriculture, the more sympathetic observers could see that he had a vocation for the pulpit " a'maist frae infancy."

One incident of Alec Whyte's boyhood was described by himself sixty years later. He was preaching on Psalm ciii. in a church in one of the poorest districts in Dundee, and was enlarging upon the blessed results of that pain and anguish of soul which the true penitent suffers. To illustrate this he told how his arm had been caught in the machinery of a threshing-mill, and so crushed that the marks still remained.

" In my boyhood in Kirriemuir," he said, " I met with a bad accident. This arm "—holding up his right arm—" was severely injured. It was thought, at first, that I would have to be taken to the Dundee Infirmary, and lose my arm ; but "—holding it up again—" it's there still. A

neighbour woman, a friend of my mother's—
Margaret was her name—skilled in dealing with
aches and bruises, when she had examined the
arm, said, ' We'll wait and see : we'll not let
them take the boy to Dundee yet.' The next
day, because of the pain I was suffering, my
mother was still more anxious about me ; but,
when Margaret came in, she greatly comforted
her by saying, ' I like the pain, Janet ; I like
the pain ! ' "

It was only in the intervals of such work as offered
in town or country—and when his mother had the
few shillings to spare that were needed for school fees
in those days—that Alec Whyte received any regular
schooling. But here we have the advantage of his
own reminiscences, which show that he went for a
time to the Free Church School and for a time to
Webster's Seminary, a handsome building at the
highest point of the Southmuir, which was built and
endowed by the trustees of Baron-bailie John Webster,
a Kirriemuir banker who died in 1829.[1]

"Kirriemuir has always been a town of
considerable intelligence, and the schools played
a great part in my early days. There were four
schools as I remember. There was the Parish
school, admirably equipped with teachers, and
there was another school, Webster's Seminary,
where I went myself as a little boy. You will,
no doubt, sometimes have noticed that the
Rector of Webster's Seminary has presided at an
Educational Institute meeting.[2] I am always
proud when I see such a reference, because it
leads me back to those days when I learned my
A B C and played in the playground of that
school. I did not get much education—any
more than John Bunyan did—in my young days,

[1] Reid, *The Regality of Kirriemuir*, pp. 175 ff. In the middle of
last century the fees charged ranged from 1s. 6d. a quarter for reading
alone to 6s. for all subjects.

[2] Alexander Menzies, LL.D., who was Rector for many years until
1908, was at one time President of the Educational Institute of Scotland.

and most of what I got was in the Free Church
Schools. They had admirable teachers there,
for the teachers came animated with the sweet
and warm spirit of the Disruption, and carried
it into the educational methods and treatment of
their children."

But the outward and financial hindrances to
learning were not the only obstacles in the boy's way.
He felt already, as he continued to feel throughout
life, that his defective verbal memory was no small
handicap. At one of the schools which he attended
for a time he was so severely chastised for his failure
in the memorising, which formed a very large part of
the school work of those days, that he returned to
his mother with marks of blood on his shirt, and with
a rankling sense of injustice in his heart. He felt
that he had done his best, and that he could not be
held chargeable with the weakness of his memory.
All the more remarkable was his early and passionate
devotion to reading—the characteristic to which the
few contemporaries who remember his boyhood most
constantly recur. So much information did he gather
that he was sometimes placed on the beam of a loom
in the evening, to expound to a group of weavers the
cartoon in the last copy of *Punch* that had found its
way to Kirriemuir. It is also told that when he
obtained one of the Waverley Novels to read, in spite
of his mother's suspicion of such doubtful literature,
he was so entranced by the study that he stopped
strangers passing up the brae to ask if they had read
it also.

By far the most vital influence in Whyte's boyhood was the religious training which he received
from his mother, from his Sabbath-school teacher,
James Kennedy, and from his first minister, Daniel
Cormick. Other more passing influences also had
their place, as appears from an early recollection
preserved in Dr. Whyte's last book. Every July the
gardeners of the parish, gentlefolk, country people,
and weavers alike, joined in a floral display and

procession; and it may be to the accompanying
flower show that the following words refer :

"When I was a child of nine or ten years old,
a flower show was being held in his native town,
and Dr. Burns Thomson of the Cowgate Dispen-
sary had come north to open the show. I was
standing at his feet looking up reverently at the
great man, when, towards the end of his opening
speech, he waved his hand over the wide display
of beautiful flowers and fruits, and quoting
Cowper said : ' But the best of it all is this, that
our Heavenly Father made them all.' I have
never forgot that proclamation of his that day." [1]

Another memory which remained ineffaceable
was that of the Sabbath school connected with the
South Free Church and of James Kennedy's teaching
in it.

"I have a great debt," he said in 1907, "to
acknowledge to my Sabbath-school teachers in
Kirriemuir, especially to one man. Boys, you
know, are quick to see things, and though I
was a little chap, scarcely reaching up to his
knees, I could see quickly at first that he had
not much interest in his teaching. Kirriemuir
has always been hospitable to revival movements,
and about this time a revival movement visited
the town. I remember, for instance, getting a
tract from Mr. M'Cheyne when he visited Kirriemuir.[2] When the revival came it played upon
my teacher, and I saw some change had come
over him, and instead of showing little interest
in his work, he did not get enough of us now,
and was always ready to put himself to any
trouble to teach us."

[1] *The Spiritual Life*, p. 85.
[2] Robert Murray M'Cheyne, minister of St. Peter's, Dundee, died
in his thirtieth year in 1843, but his short ministry made a deep imprint
upon the evangelical movement in Scotland. Alexander Whyte was
in his seventh year when M'Cheyne visited Kirriemuir three months
before his death.

Later still, when Kennedy's sixty years of teaching had ended and his pupil's active ministry was within a few weeks of its close, Dr. Whyte was told of a meeting which had been arranged to celebrate the jubilee as a Sabbath-school teacher of his old friend Miss Mary Low, and sent the following message to be read at the gathering : " Tell the teachers that I often recall my Sabbath-school days in the old South Church : often. And tell them not to be weary in well-doing. For seventy years hence old men will call their names blessed, as I call the name of my old teacher—James Kennedy." [1]

But the Sabbath school was only one item, and not the most formidable, in the routine of a child's Sunday in the years after 1843. In the morning Alec Whyte unfailingly accompanied his mother to the South Free Church, for " she was a great Free Church woman." " My grannie," his narrative goes on, " would take me to the Relief Church in the afternoon, and proud I was of her, because I always thought she had the whitest ' mutch ' of any woman in the town and was best dressed. Then I was allowed to go to the Auld Licht Kirk in the evening." " Allowed " is surely a significant word, showing that the combined theology of Daniel Cormick and James Kennedy and James Stirling, the devoted minister of the Relief Church, had not exhausted the thirst of the insatiable boy. At the Auld Licht Church, during the years from 1843 to 1846, the minister was the Rev. James Dunlop Paxton, who appears to have been a man of unusual, though somewhat erratic, gifts, and it was from him that Whyte received his first sense of the spell and power of sacred oratory.

Over all Scotland at this time men and women followed with breathless and absorbed interest the closing stages of the " Ten Years' Conflict," through which the majority of the General Assembly of the Church of Scotland, under the great-hearted leadership of Thomas Chalmers, sought to place beyond possibility of question the right of the Church to control

[1] *Kirriemuir Free Press*, February 2, 1917.

her own action in spiritual affairs without interference from the civil courts. The crucial difficulty in the long controversy was—as it always is—to determine precisely where the boundary line between spiritual and temporal interests should be drawn. The Church's claim fell under two chief heads. The General Assembly's " Veto Act " had recognised the right of congregations to refuse to accept as their minister any licentiate " presented " by the lay patron if they felt conscientiously unable to profit by his ministry; and the " Chapel Act " claimed that the Church must determine the composition of her own Courts without secular interference. Its aim was to secure that the ministers of the extension or *quoad sacra* charges, which had been founded in large numbers to meet the needs of an expanding population, should have the same voice in the affairs of the Church as ministers of fully con- stituted parishes. It would be retelling an often- told tale to trace, even in briefest outline, the long conflict in the law courts, and later the fruitless negotiations between the Church's leaders and the Government of the day. But in the weaving com- munities, and not least in Kirriemuir, every step was followed and every point in the tangled controversy keenly debated. It is even reported that Dr. Whyte's mother gained the nickname, " non-intrusion Janet," by her strong support of the party who fought against the " intruding " on an unwilling congregation of an unpopular " presentee."

The Ten Years' Conflict, and the Disruption at its close, cannot be truly understood if they are looked on only as an episode in ecclesiastical history and a stage in the age-long effort to find an enduring basis for the relations of Church and State. Along with this external aspect of the movement there went an inner stirring of the spirits of men, which changed the lives of thousands throughout Scotland, as we have already seen that it changed the life and inspired the teaching of James Kennedy, merchant in the Southmuir. The personality of M'Cheyne was one of

the most noteworthy on this side of the movement ;
but Chalmers himself was by choice and conviction an
evangelical preacher and social reformer first of all,
and only perforce a leader in ecclesiastical controversy.

To the South Church of Kirriemuir, founded in
1836, there was ordained in 1839 the Rev. Daniel
Cormick, whose ministry of eight years, ending with
his death in his fortieth year, left an impression which
remained strong and vivid for more than a generation.
He was a spiritual force rather than a leader in
controversy ; but when, in May 1843, he, like some
other four hundred and seventy ministers of the
Church, decided to leave the security of the Establishment and to face a future without provision save that
of the loyalty and generosity of his people, almost
his whole congregation accompanied him. So the
South Free Church came into being. A site was
found on the south side of the Glamis road, and a
church was built, which stood until its place was taken
in 1902 by one of much greater beauty. Externally
it was typical of the hurried and unadorned architecture of the Disruption period, with low-pitched
roof in two parallel ridges ; and one of Dr. Whyte's
less solemn memories was that, when its walls
were only three or four feet high, he and his companions used to race round them, thrusting their bare
toes into the damp cement. But it became the home
of a singularly living community, in which both the
famous sons of Kirriemuir were brought up, and which
has been depicted by Dr. Whyte in vivid words:

> " No minister all round about had less
> strength of some kinds than Daniel Cormick ;
> but . . . he was by far the holiest man of them
> all, and by far the most successful minister of
> them all. Mr. Cormick used to say in his
> humility, that had it not been for the liberality
> of Lady Fowlis, he would never have got to
> college at all, and that had it not been for the
> leniency of his professors, he would never have
> got the length of being a minister. Be that as

it may, it will be to the everlasting salvation
of many that Daniel Cormick was ever sent to
college, was carried through his studies, and was
ordained a minister.   When I was a lad in Kirriemuir, our minister's name was widespread and
dear to multitudes, not so much for his pulpit
gifts as for his personal and pastoral graces.
The delightful stories of Mr. Cormick's unworld-
liness of mind, simplicity of heart, and beauty of
character crowd in upon me at this moment till
I can scarcely set them aside.   And it was such
things as these in Daniel Cormick that far more
than made up for the fewness of the talents his
Sovereign Master had seen good to commit to
the stewardship of His servant.

   " I see myself standing in the passage all
through the forenoon and afternoon services,
the church was so full.   I see Dr. Mill in his
crowded pew, a much-honoured man, who
largely shared in his minister's saintliness.   And
there sits Mr. Brand, the banker and writer
[solicitor], whose walk and conversation, like the
same things in Dr. Mill, influenced and edified
the whole country round about.   Mr. Brand's
copy of Halyburton's *Memoirs*, with his name
and my mother's name on it in his own handwriting, is always within reach of my chair, and
I am sure I have read it at least as often as Dr.
Jowett said to Lady Airlie he had read Boswell.
And dear old heavenly-minded, if somewhat
sad-hearted, Duncan Macpherson, the draper.   A
saint, if ever I knew one ; if, perhaps, a little too
much after the type of Mr. Fearing and Mr.
Wet-eyes.   There never was a kirk-session in
Kirriemuir, or anywhere else, like Daniel Cormick's kirk-session ; and the pillars of it were
almost all, and almost wholly, of their minister's
own quarrying, and hewing, and polishing, and
setting up.   When David White of Airlie "—of
whom we shall hear again—" became awakened
to see what he was, and what a minister ought to

be, he sought out Daniel Cormick for his counsellor. As Walter Marshall sought out Thomas
Goodwin, and as Thomas Scott sought out John
Newton, so did David White sit at Daniel
Cormick's feet. The two ministers used to tryst
to meet in the woods of Lindertis, where they
strolled and knelt, and spent hours and days
together, till Mr. Cormick was honoured of God
to lead one of the ablest men I ever knew into
that grace in which he himself stood with such
peace and such assurance of faith." [1]

It was to this church that Alexander Whyte was
taken by his mother, and to this minister that he listened until his twelfth year. We can picture them
on their way to church, the mother wearing a shawl
arranged with the peak falling behind—she was much
chaffed by the good Dr. Mill when in later years she
first appeared in a silk dress—and the boy in clothes
which were always neat, if sometimes in process of
being outgrown. More important than this, we know
that, during these years of Daniel Cormick's ministry,
Janet Thomson was acquiring in the school of suffering
that strength of character and maturity of experience
which are still spoken of with deep respect by some
of the older people of Kirriemuir, and which did
much to mould the character of her son. On Sunday
evenings mother and son would sit together, talking
over the services of the day. She believed in the
virtue of prayer as well as of work, and once told a
friend that from the first she had especially asked for
wisdom for her boy.

In some directions she had little scholarship, and
for a time she frowned on her son's ambition to read
Carlyle. But she read her Bible and a few religious
books to good purpose, and by the testimony both of
her friends in Kirriemuir and of strangers who talked
with her, she possessed that intellectual vigour and
grasp which are at times independent of scholarship,
and that accuracy of memory which conventional

[1] Cited by Reid, *op. cit.*, p. 138 f. ; cf. p. 79.

studies seem at times rather to blunt than to increase. Her wide information often surprised her neighbours, and, when the day's work on Monday was over, she would drop into a neighbour's cottage, and go over the sermons of the previous day point by point. At a later time she taught for many years in a small Sunday school in the Southmuir, always preferring to teach a class of boys if boys could be found. Some of her sayings long remained in the minds of her scholars. On one occasion she overheard one of the girls in her class use the phrase, " As sure's deith "; and at once turned to her with the words, " Never say that, lassie; for there's nothing as sure as death. . . ." The words were said with such solemn emphasis that the girl addressed remembered them all through her life.

These scattered indications and impressions of a distant time—distant in thought and custom, even more than in years—may help to build up some idea of the surroundings of Alexander Whyte's childhood, and of the quiet influences which were already preparing him for his life-work. The story of his early and final dedication to that life-work will be told in the next chapter in the most memorable fragment of autobiography which he has left to us.

" First he wroghte, and afterward he taughte."
CHAUCER.

" Yea, this in him was the peculiar grace
That before living he'd learn how to live—
No end to learning :
Earn the means first—God surely will contrive
Use for our earning."
BROWNING.

DR. WHYTE delivered his Inaugural Address as
Principal of the New College, Edinburgh, on 13th
October 1909, choosing as his subject, " Former
Principals of the New College." After describing
the character and work of his five predecessors in
the Principalship—Chalmers, Cunningham, Candlish,
Rainy, and Dods—he continued as follows :

" Your present Principal, gentlemen, has
often looked for a good opportunity of speaking
a word of hope and encouragement to the poorer
students among you : a word of hope and encouragement such as no other man in Scotland
can possibly speak. And now that such an
opportunity has come, let all those students
whose fathers came over with the Conqueror put
their fingers in their ears. For what I have now
to say is not suitable for them, and it will not
interest them.

" Well, gentlemen, your present Principal
has been told that there was a full and a kind-
hearted house on that Assembly night when he
was led in to receive his orders from the Moderator. It may have been so, only he did not see
the Assembly all that night. All that night his
eyes were away back sixty years before that

Assembly night. Sixty years exactly to this anniversary day, the thirteenth of October, at about this very hour in the afternoon. And what he then saw, and this moment sees and hears, was a poor little fellow of twelve years old who was saying to his mother : ' Don't cry, mother ; don't be afraid, for I will go and serve out my time ; but, mind you, I am going to be a minister.' At that a great smile of love and pity broke over her strong sorrow-seamed face, when she turned away home wiping her tears with her apron.

" The next time I see that little man he is sitting on a gravestone in the parish kirkyard in his diet-hour reading the *Paradise Lost* that Mary Macpherson, Mr. Fearing of Kirriemuir's gracious-hearted daughter, had given him for a birthday gift. And to this day he well remembers how John Milton's great visions and great dialogues held his head and his heart high and safe above the songs and stories of the workshop. Again I see him every Saturday night in old James Mills' kitchen, sitting among the Chartist weavers who were waiting the arrival of the Dundee carrier who brought to them their weekly parcel of Radical papers. When the much - looked - for parcel was opened your future Principal got the new number of John Cassell's *Popular Educator* for next week's study, and the new number of the same publisher's *Biblical Educator* for to-morrow's reading. And there was not a happier home all next day in all the old Regality."

In these vivid sentences the five strenuous years from October 1849 to the autumn of 1854 are summed up ; but it is possible to fill in some further detail of the picture from other reminiscences, Whyte's own, and those of one or two friends who were also learning their trade in the same years. One of these, Robert Gardiner, was associated with him first in the work-shop in the Square at Kirriemuir, then at Airlie, and

later in the revival work of 1859. The shop in which
they served their apprenticeship together was that of
James Ogilvy, who carried on business as a shoemaker, and whose workroom, which had a window
overlooking the Gairie Burn, was not far from the
gate of the old kirkyard, to which Whyte so eagerly
carried off his treasured copy of *Paradise Lost* in the
dinner-hour. Mr. Ogilvy was a man of high character
and strong religious conviction, who for long was
precentor of the North Free Church ; and the apprentices worked much under his direct control. They
numbered as a rule either three or four, the exact
number depending on whether one had been recently
promoted to join the journeymen in the shop below.
Few things regarding Alec Whyte's youth were longer
remembered in Kirriemuir than his efforts to study,
even during his hours of toil at the bench. The
bench, indeed, sometimes supported an open book,
and the indefatigable student would turn his eyes
back and forward between his prescribed and his self-
imposed task. At other times he would spare certain
of his far-from-plentiful coppers to induce a younger
lad to read aloud to him as he worked ; and long after
the reader confessed that, like John Milton's daughters,
he had understood almost nothing of the passages
set him to read. Of the two methods of combining
manual with intellectual toil, probably the latter did
least injury to Whyte's progress in the shoemaking
craft, and it is said that on some occasions at least,
his fellow-apprentices appreciated and discussed the
passages read ; but it is easy to imagine that this
division of interest may have been something of a trial
to the good Mr. Ogilvy. This impression is confirmed
by a reply said to have been given many years after
by old Mr. David Barrie, the father of Sir James
Barrie, to a lady connected with Dr. Whyte's congregation who asked if it were true that her minister had
once been a shoemaker—" Ay, and a gey puir shoemaker he was ; but he's been a fine preacher to many
folk in Edinburgh who were sair needing it ! "
Yet, whatever may have been the degree of

technical skill to which Alec Whyte attained, he
went steadily forward until he had " served his time "
and discharged his promise to his mother.   Even at
this time his concentration of purpose impressed his
companions.   To become a scholar and enter one of
the learned professions was a consuming ambition
with thousands of working lads in the Scotland of
those days, but it could be fulfilled only through the
sacrifice of much hard-earned leisure.   Part of this
went to the study of arithmetic, of which Whyte was
ignorant until his fifteenth year.   " Three young men
—John Dickson, Jemmy Hall, and John Wilkie—all
hand-loom weavers, agreed to meet with Whyte in
Hall's house three times a week to study this branch
of learning.   John Dickson, as the one best up in the
science, was teacher," and long after gave the following
account of his friend's progress : " Dr. Whyte when
a laddie had sic a thirst for reading, that it was wi'
great difficulty I could get him to fix his mind on any
figures. . . . But he was always a man with a mind
for considering first principles : he only needed to
have the rule explained to him thoroughly, when he
at once mastered the whole thing." [1]

One of his companions, who used to walk from
the Southmuir to the Square with him as they went
to their respective workshops, said with a smile to
the writer, " There were nae games wi' him : it was a'
wark."   But another, who perhaps knew him better,
spoke of the humour in his talk, and of his fondness
for fishing.   Because holidays were few, it was all
the more needful to use them to the full ; and he is
said on occasion to have walked up Glen Prosen for
a great part of the night in order to reach a favourite
pool by daybreak.

Thus the lad maintained the contact with Nature
which began in his summers of herding as a boy ; and

---

[1] *Caledonia*, April 1895, p. 294.   *Caledonia* was a short-lived
magazine, edited by Alexander Lowson of Forfar, who drew largely
in his sketch of Dr. Whyte's early life on material supplied by John
Dickson.   To Dickson and his son, as will appear in the sequel, we
owe the preservation of more than half of the letters which are extant
from the first thirty years of Whyte's life.

his love of the hills lasted through life. For forty years the Alps, the mountains of Strathspey or Atholl or the West Coast, and the gentler summits round St. Mary's Loch, shared his allegiance. We may well believe that the very situation of Kirriemuir, between Lowlands and Highlands, helped to foster that singular union of thoroughness and determination with keenness of imaginative power and mystical enthusiasm which marked his character. The outlook of the town is over fertile Strathmore, and the general temper and occupation of its people were those of the Lowland Scot; but the hills are near by, and there may well have been a Highland strain in Whyte's immediate ancestry.

One or two other incidents are on record regarding his leisure time. He once told of an exhibition of trick-horsemanship which delighted him, though it was only intended as an appetising preliminary to draw attention to a sale of woollen goods. This inspired him to undertake what was a great expedition in these days—to Perth, thirty miles away, to see the Perth races. He succeeded in saving 1s. 6d. for the purpose, and by some means unrecorded, but probably on foot with an occasional " lift " from a friendly carter, he accomplished the journey and saw the races. He then wandered into the town and noticed a museum with an inscription ending in the word *Grati*.[1] This he took to mean that admission was free, but a crushing blow fell when the doorkeeper asked for a shilling as entry money; for his provision was spent, and thus he had to re-traverse the long homeward road without having seen the treasures of the museum. He added in telling the story, " I was not one of those who got prizes for Latin syntax ! "

Whyte's first visit to Dundee was made in a different manner. Many of the finished webs from the looms of Kirriemuir were sent thither by the road

---

[1] The deceptive inscription may still be seen over the columned porch of the Old Museum in George Street, Perth. It records the virtue of a former citizen in the words, " T. H. MARSHALL CIVES GRATI."

which, after crossing Strathmore, climbs and winds
its way through the Sidlaw Hills. The journey was
often made through the night ; and it was no ordinary
treat for Alec Whyte when Mr. Barrie had a consign-
ment of cloth to dispatch, to wriggle in among the
webs, and so find a snug resting-place in the cart as
it jolted on its way towards the city. As a young man
Whyte made the same night journey, but this time
on foot, in order to be present at the Communion
services in St. Peter's, Dundee, the scene of M'Cheyne's
ministry twenty years before.

The place taken by the Barrie family in Whyte's
early and grateful recollection demands more than an
oblique and passing reference here. For the parents
of Sir James Barrie he had a very special regard.

> " David Barrie," he once said, " had all the
> clear-headedness of the Chartists . . . and be-
> came one of the saintliest men I ever knew. . . .
> Margaret Ogilvy, his wife—I can see her now ; a
> dear little, sweet, gracious, humorous, tender-
> hearted soul. I loved her, and I hoped some-
> times she loved me. I once asked Barrie if his
> mother read his stories. ' No,' he replied, ' we
> don't let her read them : it brings on her hoast '
> (cough). I can see my old mother and her
> drinking their kindly cup of tea together."

Such hours spent with Margaret Ogilvy brought much
of sympathy and encouragement to Janet Thomson
during these years of constant effort and a sorrow
which could never wholly pass away—which rather
became greater, as she followed her son's progress in
learning and influence, and realised that every upward
step he took carried him inevitably into a world of
experience which she could not share.

In the main the story of these five years is that
of an untiring pursuit of knowledge and quest for
good books. In this quest he was not without
helpers, among them the Rev. William Livingstone,
Daniel Cormick's successor. " Long before I had got
to college," Dr. Whyte's grateful reminiscence runs,

" my well-read and most kind minister in Kirriemuir had lent me, quarter by quarter, the *British and Foreign Evangelical Review*, of which Dr. Cunningham was editor, and in which all his best papers appeared." [1] There is also a tradition in Kirriemuir that, at an earlier date than this, the boy asked his minister for the loan of some weighty volume. Mr. Livingstone gave it somewhat doubtfully, but when it was returned and he questioned the reader on its contents, he was astonished at the grasp and penetration which the answers showed.

There was, too, a remarkable figure in the Thrums of those days whose portrait has been sketched in words which I cannot forbear to reproduce here. Sir James Barrie has told that, when he was beginning to dream dreams of an author's calling, he had only one person on his side,

> " an old tailor, one of the fullest men I have known, and quite the best talker. He was a bachelor (he told me all that is to be known about woman), a lean man, pallid of face, his legs drawn up when he walked as if he was ever carrying something in his lap ; his walks were of the shortest, from the teapot on the hob to the board on which he stitched, from the board to the hob, and so to bed. . . . This man had heard of my set of photographs of the poets and asked for a sight of them, which led to our first meeting. I remember how he spread them out on his board, and after looking long at them, turned his gaze on me and said solemnly,
>
> 'What can I do to be for ever known,
> And make the age to come my own ? '

These lines of Cowley were new to me, but the sentiment was not new, and I marvelled how the old tailor could see through me so well. So it was strange to me to discover presently that he had not been thinking of me at all, but of his own young days, when that couplet sang in his head,

[1] *Former Principals*, p. 19.

and he, too, had thirsted to set off for Grub Street, but was afraid, and while he hesitated old age came, and then Death, and found him grasping a box-iron." [1]

The portrait is that of David Whyte, a younger brother of John Whyte; and although the tailor's reputation as a free-thinker limited his nephew's sympathy with him at one essential point, yet the older man's enthusiasm and knowledge fired the younger. So David Whyte helped to nerve both Whyte and Barrie for the adventure from which he himself had drawn back.

At other times Alec Whyte would be found occupying a quiet corner in the workroom of a weaver who possessed a like love of reading.

"I remember sitting in one of these work-shops—Davie Broon's—and reading *Chambers's Journal*. Davie paid 1½d. a week for it, and the first article I read was, 'How they weighed the Sun in a Little Room in Edinburgh.' How some great astronomical geniuses had actually, as I thought, taken the sun into a little room and weighed it! I see they have still the instinct in *Chambers's* for admirable narratives on science and astronomy; and it was they who introduced me to such fascinating tales as that. From the workshops I come to the booksellers—but, like the snakes in Iceland, there were none. James Mills' kitchen fireside on a Saturday night was the only approach to a bookseller's shop in Kirriemuir in those days."

The owner of the kitchen was a working plasterer, but he had a sound sense for literature, and was a real friend to the eager lad from the day when he found him reading *Paradise Lost* in the kirkyard. The friendship was maintained through three generations; and in 1917 Dr. Whyte wrote to Mr. J. F. Mills, whose bookselling business still goes on within

[1] *Margaret Ogilvy*, pp. 51–53.

a stone's-throw of the site of the old kitchen : " I never can forget my indebtedness to your grandfather, who provided me with so much good literature, when books were rare and dear." He sometimes told of the Saturday evening scene, as the group of Chartists waited the arrival of David Ethart (*Anglice*, Edward), the carrier from Dundee, and Alec Whyte drank in their radical theories and admiration for Kossuth ; but one more point in his fuller reminiscences is too characteristic to pass by. At first he contributed a penny a month for John Cassell's *Educator* ; but later the *Educator* began to appear weekly, and it was a serious task for him to get his mother " screwed up a point " in order to meet this grave additional expense.

During these arduous years Whyte was not only laying up stores of information, or growing in knowledge of the world of books. He was not less steadily advancing, through unremitting effort and discipline of will, towards that power of ceaseless, concentrated work, and that jealous watchfulness over the passing moments, which were among the greatest sources of his strength in later life. Nor was discipline of other kinds lacking. Kirriemuir possessed not a few saints, some of whom have been already named. But it was no garden of virtue, secluded and enclosed. It had its rough revelry at the great annual fair of Muckle Friday, or " Muckley," vividly described in *Sentimental Tommy* ; and Dr. Whyte has told of " the sense of abhorrence " which came upon his mind when he looked at some of the other papers which accompanied *Cassell's Educator* in the carrier's cart, while his reference to " the songs and stories of the workshop " shows that the character of his master did not exempt the apprentices from the need to shape their own characters in the face of hostile influences. Assuredly the " garland " to which Alexander Whyte finally attained was " run for, not without dust and heat." His profound knowledge of human nature, in its weakness as well as its strength, had its first origin in these early years. His whole

message in later days told of a virtue won at the
sword's point; and, if his early friends bore witness,
as they did, to the purity and strength of purpose
which he always showed, these were gained and kept
by his own steadfastness of will, supported, as he has
himself told us, by the great writers to whose high
thoughts he had already learned to look for inspiration.

Thus the year 1854 was reached; and in more than
one respect it marked Alexander Whyte's entrance on
manhood. In June he was received into full membership of the Church as a young communicant. The
entry in the Roll of the South Free Church is as
follows: " White, Alexander, South Kirriemuir, Shoemaker, June 1854 "; and in the margin there is
added, also by Mr. Livingstone, but in the tremulous
hand of an old man, " Dr. Whyte, Minr. of Free
St. George's, Edinburgh."

Thus in the summer of 1854 Whyte was still
" learning his trade " in James Ogilvy's shop; but
in the autumn he was at last free to begin his real
apprenticeship, and to prepare directly for his life-work.
The first step was to take a post as a teacher, since
teaching was then the recognised path to the university for those whose means were too narrow to enable
them to go direct. Not a few Kirriemuir lads had
followed this path with success; and another source
of encouragement was found in the home of his friend
and fellow-apprentice, Alexander Doig, whose father,
William Doig, had served for seventeen years in India
with the 72nd Foot, and on leaving the army had
settled in Kirriemuir and started a school at the West-
muir. The school was a somewhat struggling venture,
but the ex-soldier possessed wide knowledge and
vigorous opinions, and in his cottage in the evenings
discussions, in which Whyte took a leading part,
went forward on books, and on such historic subjects
as the character of Napoleon and the Crimean War.
These sometimes resulted in heated controversy,
but they had the great advantage of introducing
Whyte to distant scenes described by one who
had himself lived amidst them. It is interesting

to know that his mind was thus early directed to those Indian questions which occupied his last conscious hour on earth. Among the books to which William Doig introduced him was *The Anatomy of Melancholy*, and his imagination must indeed have been kindled by Burton's stately English, by his pensive outlook on life, and by the world of strange and varied learning into which he conducts his readers.[1]

The impetus which carried Whyte into teaching probably came in part from the soldier-schoolmaster, but the actual opening was furnished by the Rev. William Livingstone. The sphere was Padanaram, a roadside hamlet between Kirriemuir and Forfar, but considerably nearer the latter. The name had a quaintly patriarchal sound ; but neither the salary of 7s. a week which was attached to the post, nor the size and character of the schoolroom would be approved by a modern educationist. The building may still be seen, either from the public road or from the Caledonian Railway ; and Dr. Whyte told how, in later life, when travelling from Perth towards Aberdeen, he habitually rose from his seat the better to see his first schoolhouse. It is an addition built on to one of the cottages, and is now used as a store by the owner of the village shop. The inside measurement is about 18 by 14 feet, and the floor is of beaten earth. The " dominie's desk " stood in one corner, and on either side of a narrow passage were the benches, which are said to have accommodated nearly fifty scholars, the most advanced of whom paid 3½d. a week in fees. The number seems incredible, but is hardly greater than that accommodated in those days in other Scottish rural schools but little larger.

The building was owned by a certain David Milne, thus described by an old acquaintance :

" David's contribution to the cause of education in his parish was that he gave this room rent

---

[1] Alexander Whyte and Alexander Doig maintained their friendship until the death of the latter in 1881. A younger brother, who well remembers these discussions, is our authority at this point.

free. David was a character, and he and his brother Willie lived in a room at the east end of the house, and their loom-shop was in the middle. . . . Among the litter with which every corner of the house was strewed I have often seen lying many valuable books, such as Chambers's *Information for the People*, Butler's *Analogy*, and *The Scots Worthies*. A more honest, innocent, God-fearing man than old David Milne never breathed God's air, but he was chock-full of the most extraordinary eccentricities." [1]

The young dominie's life was a strenuous one. Daily he had to walk four miles each way between the Southmuir and Padanaram. Often he was obliged to learn overnight the lesson which he had to teach the senior scholars next day. And the salary was less than he might have been earning at the loom or the shoemaker's bench. So it must have been a real relief when, towards the end of the following year, he was offered the post of teacher of the Free Church school at Airlie, five miles west of Kirriemuir, and not far from the " Bonnie Hoose " celebrated in a famous ballad. Here his remuneration is said to have been £10 a year, plus the scholars' fees—not a princely income, but one which allowed him to hire a modest room for his own use at the Craigton of Airlie, and so avoid the long daily tramp to and from his school. His lodging was an attic room in the cottage of the village tailor, and so warm a friendship sprang up between the teacher and his hosts that the following year a little boy was named after him.

At this point we may pick up once more the thread of reminiscence in Dr. Whyte's Inaugural Address to the students of New College :

" Years pass on, and he is promoted to teach the Free Church School in the Parish of Airlie. In those site-refusing days the rotten marsh of Moberty had been turned into the present beauti-

[1] *Caledonia, loc. cit.*

ful church and manse and manse garden by
the willing labours of the Free Church congregation. And they had their recompense in the
pulpit work and pastoral care of the Rev. David
White. His early ministerial days in the parish
were just Dr. Chalmers's early ministerial days
in Kilmany over again. But after many trysted
walks with the saintly Daniel Cormick of Kirriemuir in the woods of Lindertis, Bishop Butler's
sermons still lay open beside David White's
Bible on his desk ; but by this time . . . .
young Spurgeon's evangelical sermons lay on
his desk also, till David White was the best
preacher in all the County of Angus : able and
evangelical preachers as that favoured county
town and country had. The dear old minister
came into the school every afternoon and took
the geography class, and then when the school
closed for the day he would walk with his young
teacher to his lodgings at the Craigton, talking
all the way about Hugh Miller and the *Witness*,
and pointing out what was meant by a first-rate
English style as he stopped and read selected
passages from Miller's leading articles. Another
afternoon he would bring the *North British
Review* with him, and would enthral his young
friend by telling him all about the learned men
of Edinburgh who were making the *Review* so
famous in those days. And so on, through three
never-to-be-forgotten years." [1]

As this passage shows, David White played a part
in stimulating and guiding Alexander Whyte's intellectual development as essential as that played by
his mother and Cormick and Kennedy in awakening

---

[1] *Former Principals*, pp. 59-61 ; cf. *Thirteen Appreciations*, p. 376.
The *Witness* was a weekly newspaper and the *North British Review* a
quarterly, both largely devoted to the defence of the Free Church.
Dr. J. Aitken Wylie, Hugh Miller's colleague in editing the former,
and Alexander Campbell Fraser, who at this time edited the latter,
were both in after years members of Free St. George's under Dr.
Whyte.

his religious impulses, while he did more than all others combined to open Whyte's way to college, and so to the ministry. David White was born near Forfar, and gained distinction in Classics and Philosophy at Edinburgh University. He was also deeply impressed by the lectures of Chalmers in the Divinity class. For a time after leaving college he travelled as a tutor; and he maintained throughout his forty years' ministry in Airlie the wide interests and the scholarly temper which he had acquired in early manhood. He was "presented" to the parish in 1833 in face of some opposition from within the congregation.[1] This formed a strange beginning for one who, within a very few years, stood out as a consistent upholder of the "non-intrusion" cause in a "Moderate" presbytery; but the change which was worked in his inner life through his friendship with Daniel Cormick brought with it an altered view of the relation which a minister should bear to the conscientious desires of his people. After the Disruption and his departure from the parish manse, he lodged for a time in Kirriemuir, walking out to conduct services in a small wood near Lindertis for the portion of the congregation which had followed him, and which was soon increased by those of like sympathies from surrounding parishes. A photograph taken in later life shows him as a man of noble and benignant aspect, with a strikingly intellectual forehead. One who still remembers him speaks of the singular solemnity which marked his preaching and which was yet more notable in his prayers.

The service which David White rendered to the younger man was fourfold. He showed how a true and wide scholarship might be made the basis of a fervent ministry and a faithful pastorate; he pointed out the elements which go to form a good English style; he gave the teaching in Latin and Greek

[1] Cf. *Airlie, a Parish History*, by Rev. William Wilson, pp. 233 ff. The reminiscences which follow are chiefly due to the Rev. John F. Linn, Mr. White's successor, and to Mrs. Galloway, the pupil mentioned below.

without which a University course was then impossible ; and (perhaps the greatest service of all) he encouraged Whyte's own desire to enter the ministry by the warmth with which he spoke of his intellectual and spiritual powers. It is said that the young teacher had been for many months at Airlie before he confessed to the scholarly minister how little he knew of even the rudiments of the classics ; but once Mr. White had found out the position he constituted himself Alexander Whyte's tutor, and gave him no rest from the drudgery of that narrow way of grammar and composition which alone led to college. Not only did they discuss literature on those afternoon walks already described, but during the children's playhour at midday the minister and teacher were often closeted together in the little hall of the church where school was held, and the children knew that they were " busy wi' their books." Where study was concerned, the minister was a stern disciplinarian, for novels were placed under the ban as likely to interfere with a due concentration on Latin grammar ; and there is real humour in the tale of one occasion when Mr. White's daily visit was paid to the school at an earlier hour than usual, and the teacher, though he was already one of the most conscientious of men, was caught with a volume of the forbidden type lying open on the desk beside him.

The memories of a scholar who was only eight or nine years of age when Whyte went to Airlie, but who was impressed for life by his character and teaching, enable us to picture in more detail the day's routine in the Free Kirk School. It began with worship, conducted with great earnestness by the young teacher, after which the day's work followed, broken by the interval already referred to. He was sparing in rebuke, but when any fault such as untruthfulness came to his notice, his look and a few words of reproof meant more than severe punishment from another. The little girl in question was interested most of all in the lessons given in Latin roots. Whyte would give a Latin word, explain its original meaning, and then trace its reappearance in perhaps a dozen English words, which the class were afterwards encouraged to introduce into an English composition. On one occasion, in following out this exercise she had used the words, "the celestial city," and when the composition was returned it bore the words, "I am glad that you are reading the *Pilgrim* : strive to be a pilgrim yourself, Helen." Such "pithy comments" were often written on the margin of the exercises done in school ; but this has the special interest that it refers to a copy of the *Pilgrim's Progress* which Whyte had given shortly before as a prize. This was among the first of the many hundred—if not thousand—copies of the *Pilgrim* which he distributed during more than sixty years. The inscription was dated "*Airlie Free School*, March 18, '57," and signed "A. WHYTE, Teacher."

On occasion the keener scholars saw that the teacher had to contend with educational difficulties of his own, for, like others who have gained their knowledge almost entirely from books, he was at this time "backward in some of his pronunciations." He had taught them, for example, to pronounce the word "column" as col*ume*, and unluckily, when two or three members of the Free Church Presbytery arrived to conduct the yearly examination, this word occurred several times in one of the passages given. Each time that it was pronounced according to the teacher's directions, one of the visiting ministers, Ferguson by name, said sharply, "Column, column!" A day or two later the word again came up in the class's reading, and was pronounced in the new fashion insisted on by the examiner ; but Whyte broke in with, "Let it be col*ume* the day, Helen : Ferguson's no here!"

It is said that, to most of the folk of Airlie, the teacher seemed too absorbed in his studies to be very conscious of his neighbours, and a description of him survived in the parish as "the mannie that could never speak to you for readin'." But when his scholars showed keenness in their work he became a true friend both of theirs and of their families. To the mother of one he regularly gave the latest of Spurgeon's Sermons which he had himself received from the minister. There was, however, another aspect in Whyte's life in these three years, a phase of struggle and depression, reflected in the following letter to one of his companions of the shoemaker's stool, James Graham, afterwards of Carnoustie: [1]

AIRLIE, *December* 12, 1857.

" MY DEAR JAMES,—Being rather sickish to-night, . . . I am rather averse to grapple with my Latin and Greek studies ; therefore as a pleasant half-hour's relief I take pen in hand to scribble a line or two to you.

" But now what am I to speak of ? Uppermost in my mind, morning, noon, and night are my studies, and well they may, for right hard work do I feel them to be. And what have you to relieve you ? you may ask. In answer to the supposed inquiry, I say *Nothing*. Not one friend of congenial mind within five miles, and a paucity of them even there, as you will believe. Consequently, I am driven back to my old work, and such has been the hardness of my application for the past two months that I perceive symptoms of my health giving way. Now, James, don't laugh—for the matter is rather provocative of laughter when you call to mind my old system of omnivorous reading and entire abstinence from Latin Grammar. Never before did I know what it was to have to say, ' I have not time to read a book ' ; but *now* I can assure you it is a different state of matters. Scarcely have I looked into a ' book ' since harvest except on Saturday nights or Sunday. Now isn't it easy seeing what is uppermost in a person's mind ?

" I don't think that I have a single scrap of

---

[1] His father, Peter Graham, a working shoemaker of small income but wide reading, was another of those who helped to stimulate Alec Whyte's love of books.

news to communicate. May I inform you that I have this week received a first letter from my father containing solid assurances of assistance ? I think he has heard of me through some friend. On Sabbath night first George is to preach in Mr. M'Lean's church.[1] I intend to hear him, having an interest in him as a townsman and brother of a heartsman. Enough of *Ego* ! What are you doing ? I don't mean physically. I know that you are making or mending shoes, but what are *you* doing ? I don't mean the James Graham whose name is publicly read as the public's servant. While hoping and wishing *him* success in *that* capacity, I specially inquire for another James who lives farther *ben* than this one. The James whom *I* know, and knowing him, love him. Are you supporting the emotional by feeding the intellectual ? Are you balancing the fancy by ballasting the judgement ? In short, are you in Spiritual, Intellectual, and Social health ? I hope, I earnestly wish so. Lately from being vilely stung by that worse than poisonous viper, a false friend (are not the terms paradoxical ?), I have been taking a retrospective look of my intimacies, and occupying an honourable position among them is the friendship between us. And yet, James, it is enough to make me shudder, the simulated friendship I refer to was really as intimate as ours. And yet most basely have I been treated. But why chatter of my private sorrows to you ; you may say—Had you been what you should be. an enemy's treacherous arrow would glance off your glistening armour. True ! ! !

" Kindest regards to your partner, and need I say,—Yours truly, A. WHYTE.

" Write soon."

As this letter indicates, John Whyte now began directly to influence his son's life. He had set up

[1] James Graham's brother, afterwards a minister in Melbourne.

business, apparently with some success, in New York City, and had married ; but after a few years his wife died, leaving him with an only daughter, who from this time began to take a great place in the interest and affection of her half-brother. He had written six months earlier laying before his father his whole mind regarding his future career and his plans for college. He told, too, that he had been encouraged by Mr. White and other friends to hope for success in study if only he could find a means of pursuing it ; and in such sentences as the following there breathes a sensitive pride which is not far from humility :

> " Inheriting a head and a heart (allow me to say it) above my fellows, sad has been my life often in my wishes and struggles to give my aspiring mind free scope. . . . Had I been an ordinary youth I would have been past needing help from you or any one, but such is not the case, and I thank God for it ; for though it has entailed on me a good deal of thought, sometimes bordering on despair, yet He has given me a higher intellectual life than could have been contained in a shoemaker's shop."

John Whyte's response—a letter containing what in those days ranked as a substantial gift—reached him one morning in December 1857 as he sat in school. His reply, after thanks and some family references, went on to speak of his uncle, whom we have seen as portrayed by Sir James Barrie :

> " Specially do I like to visit your brother ; intellectually he is peerless among working men, and were it not for that painful aberration of heart of which he is the subject we should be almost inseparable.
> " I must close, for my Latin and Greek grammars are lying at my elbow scowling ominously because of a ten minutes' neglect, a ten minutes stolen from their appointed hours.

I am progressing pretty well with my studies, but I can assure you they are harder work than that of the ' Stool ' yet. But then the question is all summed up in this—I like them. Sometimes when borne down with difficulties I have with a sigh asked myself—why all this labour ? Though I were ready, where is the pecuniary readiness to come from to support me for five or six months in another town ? You have stifled this mistrust for a time by your kindness."

Three months later, on 22nd March 1858, Whyte wrote again to James Graham :

" MY VERY DEAR FRIEND,—I lift my pen, not that I have anything pressing to communicate but just to keep up remembrance and preserve that subtle current of sympathy and fellow-feeling which forms the very life-fluid of some hearts. Grossness and hard-heartedness are apt to predominate in my heart till I meet a soul that can dissipate them. Oh ! how few of such there are ! ! The men and the women one meets in the world, instead of acting on you sympathetically and purifying and softening, have (it is a sad truth) a diametrically opposite effect. How often when rising, for instance, from the perusal of a book or article in which the writer had exhibited his appreciation and sympathy for the beautiful and tender in Nature and Man, and by so doing had evoked and held for the time in solution the better, the holier, and the nobler parts of our nature, when you felt a desire to hug to your bosom any creature almost you met, just because they had an *eye* and *something* behind it and looking *through* it—how often when the heart was a little warm pool of feeling, odorous of love and tenderness, has the first contact with some neighbour frozen it into a mass of icy frigidity sparkling with spear-like points of satire and bitterness, when the warm hand you were stretching out to embrace your fellow was transformed into stone-like coldness chilling and *smiting* every one around you.

"Is not such the case—have *you* not felt it, ay, has it not caused you many a sigh and dumb self-communing hour? Verily Paul spoke the experience of thousands when he spoke of being tied to a body of death. But thanks! this body of death is not ourselves (in a sad sense it is), for does not Paul say, 'Deliver *me* from the body of this death!' There is a *me* behind and below it, and our life-work should be to disinter ourselves from the superincumbent load of selfishness and sin which chokes and stifles every heavenly and divine aspiration.

"But what am I grumbling and growling at? To-day I have been very dead and you are suffering an infliction of 'lamentations' growing out of this state. Is not this a strange, *uncoudy*, cynical scrawl? Will I burn it? no! for it might emit a sulphurous and choking odour during combustion.

"There are no news. Write immediately, for I am afraid that when you get this you will think I am *skeer* or possessed.

"I am one whose glands are secreting gall."

The writer of this letter, with its rhetorical wording and its somewhat misanthropic outlook, affords a strange contrast to the Alexander Whyte of later years—resolute, self-controlled, and above all generous in his individual judgments, however he might scourge the faults of human nature in his preaching. He would probably have dismissed it as a youthful outburst, begotten of physical depression, and unworthy to see the light after more than sixty years. Yet these Airlie letters are valuable since they show how manfully he strove against both inward depression and hindering circumstance, and how the self-command and the charity which began to impress his friends even in his student days were only won by constant self-discipline.

Another letter, showing how he winced under the serpent's tooth of detraction, was apparently written about this time. It is addressed to John Dickson, and refers to certain unspecified accusations which had been spread abroad in Kirriemuir.

" God and I both know that my heart is black, even hatefully so, as regards His holy character, but bad as I know it to be, yet need I assure *you* that it is incapable of that depth of moral turpitude. May such charges only make me more desirous to live more unspotted before God, and with His commendation and that of my conscience (which I have in the present matter), I will be impervious to the shafts of envy and malice even though they be tipped with the poison of *pseudo*-friendship."

But, as we have already seen, in the retrospect of later years, the sunlight in the years at Airlie was more conspicuous than the gloom. Some forty years after, he wrote to Mrs. Allan, an old friend in the neighbourhood :

" I often recall the old Airlie days. My life has been a chain of mercies : and the Airlie days were not the least golden link in it. Be assured of my constant regard and good will."

And in October 1917 he wrote to Mr. John F. Mills, who had sent him a copy of Mr. Wilson's *Parish History of Airlie* :

" Thank you warmly for *Airlie*. The parcel was delivered to me on my invalid bed this morning, and the book has not been out of my hands all day. I turned at once to the chapter on David White, to whom I owe more than I can ever tell. I have read the chapter again and again with admiration and with gratitude to the author. The book has given me a day of real refreshment and delight ; and I prophesy that it will be bought and read and cherished far beyond the bounds of Airlie. The portrait is excellent, and I see Bishop Butler lying open on the desk beside the study Bible."

During these years Whyte's activities were not entirely circumscribed by the school and his little attic room at the Craigton. He carried on the work as a Sabbath-school teacher in Kirriemuir which appears to have begun at an even earlier time; and a most emphatic tribute to the influence which he then exerted came from a survivor of his class, who was herself engaged in the same work for fifty years, and who said to the present writer : " No one could have come through his class without being influenced for their whole life — he was *so serious and so earnest.*" The emphasis with which the words were spoken was the best witness to the deep and lasting impression made by the young teacher.

Whyte's work in the Sabbath school opened the way for one of the first speeches which enabled his friends in Kirriemuir to realise that a future orator had arisen in their midst. At an annual meeting of teachers connected with the South Free Church he spoke on the reform of religious teaching with a grasp of thought and command of language which surprised his older friends, as coming from one whom they still looked on as almost a boy, and also, we are assured, with a boldness of idea which somewhat startled the more conservative. He also gained experience as a speaker in a debating society, one of whose members, William Lawson, afterwards obtained some distinction in a very different sphere, that of financial journalism in London. A member of this body, Whyte's senior by several years, wrote long after :

" He was a member in a debating club which met in Kirriemuir, and I remember that on one occasion, when a speaker who was expected did not appear, he took his place and held the meeting with a speech on Temperance for almost an hour."

The Saturdays spent in Kirriemuir seem to have given some relief at this time from the bondage to those " beggarly elements " of Latin grammar which weighed upon him so heavily for the greater part of the week. The friend last quoted, who was also a teacher, recalled Whyte's enthusiasm for books, his knowledge of such authors as Carlyle, Kingsley, and Charlotte Brontë, and the keenness with which he analysed their literary quality during these Saturday talks. At the same time his own library began slowly to grow, and the day which fulfilled his long-cherished desire to possess a copy of Carlyle was a red-letter day for him.

> " I had no chance of getting books in Thrums. I remember when I was reading the *Dundee Advertiser* I saw among the literary notices a cheap edition of Thomas Carlyle's works. I cannot tell you, who are flooded with books, what I felt when I saw that I could get a copy of Carlyle. But though you can get cheap editions for a few coppers, I had to pay six silver shillings for my first copy of Carlyle. I have it yet. I sometimes take off my hat to that volume, because it was the first time I saw Carlyle, and you cannot know how I carried that volume of essays near my heart."

The volume is one with small print, in which *Sartor* and *Heroes* are bound together in the somewhat dingy brown cover familiar to Carlyle's older students ; but to the owner it was a possession beyond price. It bears the inscription " A. W., Kirriemuir, 1857," and fifty-nine years later Dr. Whyte added the name of his youngest nephew, to whom it now belongs.

This volume was also notable as the occasion of a strangely prophetic dream, in which, after the volume was ordered, he saw it clearly in the very size, style, and binding which, on its arrival, it proved to have. Dr. Whyte's active imagination often gave rise to vivid dreams, but there was no other instance in his long life of a similar psychic experience.

One other memory from these years he has placed on record, relating to his first sight of his future colleague, Dr. Candlish of Free St. George's, who came to Forfar to introduce a new minister.

> " In some way I had heard that the great Church leader and great Edinburgh preacher was to be seen and heard in Forfar that Sabbath. And my dear old fellow-angler and wood-cutting friend, John Dickson, and I walked down to Forfar together that Sabbath morning. And both my friend and I were greatly regaled and uplifted by that sermon, as I well remember. The next time I saw Dr. Candlish was in the same town of Forfar, when he came to introduce Mr. Chalmers to the East Church. And my sermon-loving friend and I made the same Sabbath-day journey, and with the same result." [1]

In telling his son the story of these two journeys, John Dickson mentioned a further point of coincidence—that the great Doctor's sermon was the same on both occasions ! He added that he had then assured his companion that he, Alexander Whyte, would yet be Candlish's successor and Moderator of the Church. Another friend, Robert Gardiner, tells how Whyte's recapitulation and analysis of the sermon captivated his companions in Kirriemuir, and how he revelled not only in the great preacher's message, but in the mastery of style and close-knit argument with which it was expounded.

By this time Whyte's apprenticeship was about to pass from its second stage into its third. He hoped for a time that, after his second winter at Airlie, he might have been ready for the great venture of a college career ; but the Rev. David White very wisely restrained him, pointing out that,

[1] *Former Principals*, p. 29 f.   Rev. Richard Waterston was ordained in January 1858 ; so the incident belongs to Whyte's last winter in Airlie.

until he had a somewhat firmer grounding in the classics, he would merely waste time and invite failure by proceeding to Aberdeen. After another year he was more fully prepared, and in the summer of 1858 he set out from Kirriemuir, which was never again his settled home.

1858–1862

> " Shon Campbell went to College,
>   The pulpit was his aim,
> By day and night he ground,
>   For he was Hieland, dour and game."
>   W. A. MACKENZIE.

THE four years which Alexander Whyte spent in Aberdeen proved of great importance alike for his intellectual and his religious development. They are also the years of the first four decades of his life from which the fullest records have been preserved, and it may tend to clearness if we consider these two great interests separately. The present chapter will thus deal with his college life and his intellectual progress, while his first efforts as a preacher, and in particular his part in the Revival of 1859, will be described in that which follows.

In the fragment of autobiography already quoted, the passage regarding Airlie and David White is followed by a reference to the summer of 1858 :

> " When that ambitious youth had laid past money enough to take him to Aberdeen, to Aberdeen he set off along with Alexander Ogilvy and Alexander Barrie. A kindly cynic had once said that Alec Whyte would sooner get to the planet Jupiter than to Aberdeen. But it was not so. He really got to that splendid old seat : the planet Jupiter notwithstanding."

He was helped to go by a reserve fund formed from his savings while at Airlie, augmented by £12 which friends there collected to assist his college course. This sum could not have lasted long, even under the frugal, not to say Spartan, conditions that ruled in the Scottish universities of those days, and especially in Aberdeen. So all through his eight winters at college, Whyte drew his main support from his own efforts, first as a teacher, and later as a student-missionary.

Many of his fellow-students were engaged in the same double contest for learning and for daily bread; and not a few fell by the way. The work of a winter session in Aberdeen was often interrupted by the call to mourn for a classfellow, who had succumbed to the threefold pressure of privation, overwork, and the rigorous climate; and a brilliant son of that austere Alma Mater, who himself died in middle life, once said that to read the prize lists of thirty years before was like listening to the roll-call of a regiment at the close of a severe campaign.[1] It was afterwards said by Sir James Barrie that " there were among Dr. Whyte's classfellows men who endured greater hardships to get an education than a traveller suffers in Central Africa." It is true that Dr. Whyte himself denied that he had been among those who suffered actual privation; but the following pages will give some impression of the steady strain which tested even his strong frame during those years. As he went, he was followed by the thoughts of good friends in Kirriemuir; and it is said that the minister of his church used sometimes to be asked by the old folk before a prayer-meeting to " pit in a word for that laddie Whyte—he weel deserves heartenin'."

It was to Aberdeen, rather than to the nearer University of St. Andrews, that the studious lads of Kirriemuir commonly went at that time, attracted by the bursary system, which was, in Professor Masson's words, " as familiarly known over the whole region as the Aurora Borealis in its nightly sky "; and which " had generated and sustained there a habit of looking forward to a University education among

---

[1] R. A. Neil of Cambridge; cf. Sutherland Black and G. W. Chrystal, *The Life of William Robertson Smith*, pp. 51–53, 62 ; and the lines on the " tertians' " mourning in *Shon Campbell*, a poem which in a few verses expresses much of the tragic romance which marked this aspect of Scottish life in the nineteenth century.

classes in which otherwise such a habit could hardly have been possible." [1] The " Bursary " was a small open scholarship, just sufficient to carry a student through his four years in the Faculty of Arts. These bursaries, more numerous in Aberdeen than elsewhere, were awarded on a test consisting almost wholly in Latin Prose composition. Whyte had little hope of gaining one, owing to his backwardness in classics, but his companions went northward, and he went with them.

Aberdeen then possessed two universities — a number, its citizens had boasted a generation before, equal to that in the whole of England—each possessing full status and dignity, if not, according to modern ideas, full equipment. King's College in the Old Town was founded before the Reformation by Bishop Elphinstone, and Marischal College was the later foundation of the powerful Earls Marischal in the New Town. The splendid " seat " to which " the three Alecs " made their way was the university of the Old Town ; and, although its anti-Presbyterian character had long since passed away, it remained more deeply rooted in the past than its rival, and at this period drew nearly two-thirds of its students from the country districts.[2] Thus Whyte's Arts course was passed under the shadow of the venerable grey crown of King's College, which so fitly symbolises its sway over the affections of its alumni, and close to the Cathedral of St. Machar, which bears witness to the continuity of Scottish learning and piety since the raising of the first humble Columban church in the meadows by the Don.

In those days, too, there was a certain distinction

[1] *Memories of Two Cities*, pp. 243–6.
[2] Cf. Mr. Keith Leask's Notes to *Life at a Northern University*, by N. N. Maclean (p. 364 f., cf. p. 355). The students of the different years in the older Scottish universities were known by the old terms, borrowed from the University of Paris, *Bajans* (*Bageants*, or *Bejants*, said to be derived from *bec jaune*, descriptive of a young bird), *Semis*, *Tertians*, and *Magistrands*. The average age of the *Bajans* at King's about this time was $17\frac{3}{4}$—just five years less than Whyte's age ; but there were great variations, grown men being balanced by boys of 13 or 14. Of the forty-four *Magistrands* in 1857–58, twenty-one, or almost half, were preparing for the ministry.

in residence in the "Aulton," since its separate corporation and town drummer maintained its proper pride in face of the busy and growing city two miles away. During his whole course Whyte lodged either within the Old Town or on the way towards it, in the Spital, the winding street whose name tells of a medieval hospice. For a great part of these years he shared his rooms with his brilliant friend, Alexander Barrie, Sir James Barrie's elder brother. He was Whyte's junior by several years, and was in some sort commended to his care by Mr. David Barrie on their departure from Kirriemuir. The partnership in study between Whyte and Barrie was a fortunate one for both, since the older man's singleness of purpose and maturity of character found its complement in the ready wit and scholarly aptitude of the younger.

An impression of Whyte's appearance as he entered on his Arts course may be gained from the description of a classfellow, who remembers him as " a broad-shouldered, spare, alert young man, with reddish hair and light blue eyes." More than one of those who knew him at this, or a somewhat later, time say that strength and eagerness were the outstanding characteristics of his face in youth. The fine moulding of the forehead must have been a marked feature even then; but the refinement and spiritual beauty of his face in later years came gradually with years of thought and discipline. In the noble phrase of an old writer, they were " the outward passage of an inward greatness."

The summer vacation of the northern grammar schools was brief, and an autumn term began early in August for the benefit of those who required some further preparation in the classics before the college session. Whyte took this three months' course, on his first arrival in Aberdeen, at the small grammar school in School Road, as George Macdonald had done eighteen years before. The following letter does not place the discipline of this institution in a favourable light; but something may be set down to the natural impatience felt by a " muckle scholar " of twenty-two,

who had been forced to strive for knowledge as for
fine gold, with the high spirits of mere boys during
the first days of a new session.[1]

"MRS. MILNE'S,
ORCHARD COTTAGE, OLD ABERDEEN,
August 13, 1858.

" MY DEAR FRIEND,—I must fulfil my promise
and pen you a few lines—few they will be at
present for two reasons : first, nothing of great
importance to communicate; and secondly, *very
little time.*

" I landed safely here on Saturday forenoon,
secured comfortable lodgings, spent the day in
arranging matters, and being very tired slept
very soundly at night.   On Sabbath I went to
three of our churches here.   Heard Dr. Davidson
in the afternoon.   He is said to be the best
preacher north of the Tay.[2]   He preached a very
thoughtful and spiritual sermon from John vi. 63,
' It is the spirit that quickeneth.'   But I must
here remark on the deeply earnest tone of all the
discourses I heard ; they were very refreshing,
and they will be needed here, for the study
obtrudes on every corner of the mind and every
moment of time.

" Then on Monday came the tug-of-war ; by
9 a.m. I found myself in the Grammar School.
Imagine to yourself a small square house as plain
and unclassical as possible, with benches like a
church and a little desk in a corner, the place
altogether capable of holding forty or fifty

[1] It has sometimes been stated that Whyte attended the historic
Grammar School of the New Town in the Schoolhill, but the description
in the following letter and the reference to William Barrack both support the statement in the text, which is in accord with Dr. Whyte's
own statement to Dr. Morland Simpson, Rector of the Aberdeen
Grammar School, that it was the school in the Old Town which he attended for a term.   William Barrack was at the Old Town school
from 1858 to 1860, when he became Rector of the (New Town) Grammar School.

[2] Rev. Alex. Dyce Davidson, D.D., of the West Free Church, for
many years one of the leading preachers and citizens of Aberdeen.   *Cf.*
Dr. Whyte's tribute cited by Strahan, *Life of A. B. Davidson*, p. 35.

students. It was about two-thirds full on Monday, it is altogether full now. Seated in the desk is a young man, apparently about twenty-four or twenty-six years of age, thin, whiskerless, and spectacled; ranged before him are the students, young men, youths, and boys, from twelve up to double that age. I will in a few words give an epitome of a day's work. We enter, he is reading a chapter, the young men are some of them following him, others learning their lessons, some copying from their neighbour's written exercise, having spent the previous night idly, some testing the toughness of their neighbour's skin with a pin, some eating berries, some handing about written papers containing sham invitations to tea, or notices such as this : ' Students desiring of joining the Ciceronian Grinding Club meet at such-and-such a place with 7s. 3d. in their pocket.' Others sticking up bills on their neighbour's back, such as ' Sale of Spanish Asses, this is a specimen,' and this going on till the prayer be said. Then, perhaps, Virgil is read; we are in the VI. Enead at present, reading perhaps thirty lines a day. After it is read and parsed comes the Greek Grammar and Xenophon. Then it being about 12 o'clock we get out an hour, and go home and take lunch ; back by two and begin to Cicero, we are reading his oration against Cataline, about half a page a day. Then on Monday, Wednesday, and Friday we write versions (in school, none at home), Friday's being a trial version. That is, on Monday Mr. Barrack tells the number of errors in each, and assigns places in the class accordingly. Of course I do not know yet how I may do. . . .

" It is very hard work here, John. Virgil and Cicero are new acquaintances to me,[1] and yet I get on fine with them, indeed I will translate as well as two-thirds of the class, but they are far ahead of me in Greek and Versions. I must

[1] As might be inferred from the writer's spelling of their works !

close, for I have a great deal of work to-night,
yet to-morrow is a play-day, but not to me I
assure you.

"Read this to my mother, please. . . . Write
soon.—Yours very truly,   A. WHYTE."

The next letter is more cheerful, and it is easy to
imagine the joy experienced by one, who had found
good books so hard to come by, on his first entrance
into a great library :

"ORCHARD COTTAGE,
OLD ABERDEEN, *October* 8, 1858.

"MY DEAR FRIEND,—What has been the
matter with you this long time ? I expected a
line from you when you got back from your
harvest; you must be through with it long ago.
And you know you must have much more news
to communicate to me than I possibly can have
to you. Indeed I have nothing to say but the
old story, grinding away with more or less
progress ; another fortnight finishes the Grammar School and three weeks hence the real tug-of-
war will begin. There is a fierce struggle going
on among our higher scholars for the bursaries.
. . . For myself, I am only preparing for the
College classes. I am sometimes reading a little
too much ; through the kindness of the Greek
Professor I have got into the College Library
where there is a collection of above 70,000
volumes ! At present I have lying beside me a
few books which, though long anxious for, I never
saw before. They are Hare's *Life of Sterling* ;
Guesses at Truth ; and Coleridge's *Literaria
Biographia* ; and Lessing's *Education of the
Human Race*. First-class books all of them. . . .
Write immediately a long letter, for I have been
uneasy at your protracted silence.—Ever your
sincere friend,   A. W."

Very soon after this letter was written Whyte's
acute financial problem was solved, but solved in a

way that added to his work not less than to his income. Among the graduates of the year 1855 was David Stewart, afterwards Sir David Stewart, whose father was head of a comb factory—a not unimportant Aberdeen industry. Whyte soon came to know the family, and father and son together arranged that he should have the opportunity of conducting evening classes among their younger workers at a salary of £25 for the winter.

Although the College session was a short one, compressed into five months, the work was both hard and continuous, as the following letter shows. Indeed it was not until two years later that the Senatus, who showed a rigid economy in the matter of holidays, granted a petition from the students for an addition to the Christmas vacation by extending it from two to four days. The work of the first session consisted chiefly in the study of Latin and Greek on a standard which would now be considered more appropriate for a secondary school than for a University. "Rhetoric," or the introduction to the principles of literary style, was often included in the same year's study. The only one of his teachers who greatly impressed Whyte during his first or second year was Professor (afterwards Principal Sir William) Geddes, whose teaching of Greek left a deep mark on the minds of his students.

On Christmas Eve Whyte sent the following account of his progress to John Dickson :

"I was beginning to think ere you wrote that I was forgot, or if not forgot altogether, at least *neglected*. But the old kind voice spoke in your letter, and its echoes answered, He loves you still ! I have little to communicate of importance. I am studying very hard, the whole time is occupied. We often grind till two hours past midnight, but as this is too wasting, we will bed earlier and rise by cockcrow. I am *now suffering* for my devotion to literature and neglect of classics. In Latin I am now pretty good, indeed as good as one-half of our class ; the advantages of the majority thereof compared with mine have been as four to one. But I am making head fast, and though my name cannot appear on the prize list at the end of the session, yet I will then be an average Latin scholar, which perhaps will be *better*, for *me*, than prizes will, for those who get them. Gross Egoist ! ! ! ' "

After a reference to the books being read (Quintus Curtius, the *Cyropædia* and the *Fasti*) and to those in prospect (Euripides and HOMER, writ large), the letter continues :

" When the New Year is past we have to begin and revise all the work of the session preparatory for our examination. *This causes double work.* So much for Classics.

" I have just returned from the D(ebating) Society. I had the honour of being Chairman to-night, an almost unparalleled honour on a Bajan (first-year student). Last night I led the debate on Cromwell, opened by a speech of twenty minutes. A Magistrand (fourth-year student) replied in a speech of equal length, then followed eight speakers, ten minutes each. I carried, or rather Cromwell carried ! A grand subject ! ! Of course I can't say anything of my speech, only this : had you been present *you* would have been gratified with the reception it met with. . . .

" I still feel the want of a sympathetic companion. I know diligent and far-on students, but they are *nothing else*. I know *good* young men, but their *heads* are *light*. Their goodness has too narrow a basis for our age and the state of our intellectual life. A few of us have originated a prayer-meeting in the Greek classroom on Friday and Tuesday evenings, when we enter into devotions mutually. We, *I* at least, have much need of such. Oh that I could meet a young man

or woman of deep spiritual life and broad intellectual culture ! my heart and head ache for want
of living sympathy and intercourse.   Kirry was
better for this, and you'll agree it is not over-
prolific of such."

The Debating Society here referred to became an
important training-ground for Whyte.   It met on
Friday evenings in the Mathematical classroom in
King's College, and was open to all Arts students.
It would appear to have been less cumbered by detailed rules and by the transaction of private business
than some college societies ; but if rules were simple,
they seem to have been not ineffective, and there was
no lack of animation in speech or in applause.   Indeed,
when the burning question of the " fusion " of the
two colleges in a single University was the subject of
debate, the strength of the rude benches with which
the room was furnished was severely tested under the
cudgel-strokes with which members protested against
the sinking of the identity of their beloved college
in a larger whole.[1]   It does not appear whether Whyte
took any pronounced part in this controversy : in
view of his indifference to all questions of organisation
and machinery in comparison with the things of the
spirit, it cannot have stirred him deeply.   But it is
significant of his force and maturity of character and
his command of speech—greater, in all probability,
at this time than the rather rudimentary style of his
letters would suggest—that, within two months of his
enrolment at King's, he was chosen to lead in a debate ;
and it is yet more significant that his first success in
this field was won by the exposition and defence of a
character, and that the character of the great Puritan
statesman of England.

A fellow-student—the Rev. Duncan Ross of Appin
—has given an account of another occasion on which
Whyte intervened in a debate, but found himself in
a decided minority.   The subject was Theatre-going,
which he felt was not treated with due seriousness ;

[1] *Life in a Northern University*, pp. xxxiv ff., 82 ff.

and he threw special emphasis into the reminder how much the families of those there gathered had sacrificed to send them to college, urging that it would be in the last degree unworthy if they should waste either their time or the resources thus painfully gathered for their use. Whyte's own evenings were occupied in teaching and study, except for the Debating Society and for occasional Saturday evenings spent with friends or at the gatherings of Free Church students at the Divinity Hall.

The desire for a wider social horizon, and for friendship of a more satisfying kind, which finds expression in the letter last quoted, was already on the way to fulfilment. Friends came in increasing numbers, some of whom will be named later; but of all the friendships of these days none did more for Whyte than that of John Gibb, afterwards Professor at Westminster College, Cambridge. Gibb belonged to a well-known family [1] of engineers, but he himself had turned to theology. He was described by Marcus Dods not long after as " one of the best-read students I have met, an intelligent and lenient critic of men and things, a good deal chastened by bodily weakness and acute pain, and possessed of a faculty of clear and independent thinking." [2] In some ways the friends differed widely. Gibb had a critical and diffident vein in his nature, which contrasted with Whyte's ardent faith and decisiveness in action. But each saw much to admire in the other; and Whyte found himself for the first time made free of a good private library and made welcome in a cultured home. Thus his visits to Mr. Gibb's home, Willowbank, became points of refreshment in an otherwise grey existence. At first he went chiefly to his friend's little study, but before long he began to join in the family life, and to win the warm regard of the generous head of the house—a regard which the younger

---

[1] The family tradition is still maintained by Sir George Gibb, the younger brother, and Sir Alexander Gibb, the nephew, of Dr. Whyte's friend.

[2] *The Early Letters of Marcus Dods*, p. 267.

man fully returned until Mr. Gibb's death in 1867. Whyte's eager talk about books—poetry and fiction, as well as more serious works—is still remembered by a daughter of the house—afterwards Mrs. Milne Rae— to whom he wrote many years later : " Those evenings greatly helped to carry me through a time of labour and care that I can never forget." And when his friend passed away in 1915, he sent a tribute in which he told of the " wealth of the best literature, ancient and modern, that covered John Gibb's study table," and which concluded with these sentences :

" John Gibb was a beautiful example of his own favourite words : *Anima naturaliter Christiana* ; for he was a born gentleman. And then all his fine and refining scholarship, all his wide reading of the best books, all his foreign travel and study, and all his varied experience of life—all that combined to make John Gibb a man of great intellectual and moral and spiritual distinction. His loving heart, his sweet humility, his tender delicacy of spirit, and his mellow wisdom, all worked together to make John Gibb a man quite by himself : a rare man, whom to have for a friend was a privilege and opportunity of no ordinary kind. Yes, dear, dear John Gibb." [1]

Whyte had undergone a long and continuous strain during the eight months from August 1858 to the following March ; but a letter to John Dickson at the close of the session shows that no weariness could diminish his hunger for reading, for it contains these sentences : " The session is over and I am nearly over too. I have wrought very hard, too hard indeed. I have suffered now for my all-absorbing devotion to English literature. . . . I am reading like a famished wolf, five volumes since Friday."

A few days later he was back in Kirriemuir ; and some of the companions who had been wont to call him " Sandy " now recognised his new dignity by addressing him solemnly as " Sanders."

[1] *The Presbyterian Messenger*, June 1915.

On 12th April he wrote to his father from the South-muir :

> " I have again got back to my native town after eight months of intense application to, and I hope great success in, my studies. I worked very hard to make up leeway and succeeded in passing my examination honourably and got first-rate certificate. In the classes I had a fair standing, but more than a fair standing in the College Debating Society. There I was if not best yet almost so. There was no young man at College who had read or knew so much of books and literature generally ; none who had seemed to think so much or so deeply on the questions which are stirring in the minds of thinkers and writers of this country.
>
> " And now for a few weeks I am lounging about visiting and recruiting, but I have not yet heard of any situation for the summer months, and would require such both for the present and to provide for next session. I think by another session, if spared, and at Aberdeen I may be so well known and recommended that there will be no difficulty in securing teaching enough, at least for the summer. In other circumstances I would have been much better having all the time till next session preparing Mathematics, Chemistry, etc. for the second year."

The summer of 1859 was spent, partly in the visit to Logiealmond which will be referred to in the next chapter, but largely in preparing those scientific subjects which then required to be studied by candidates for the M.A. degree. Whyte's natural distaste for mathematical studies, combined with the excessive pressure of his work in other directions, prevented him from progressing far in Mathematics or Physics, and in Chemistry his position was even less favourable. His defective memory here formed a severe hindrance, and at one stage of his course the victims of an exceptionally wholesale " plough "

in this subject chose this " formidable red-haired
student " as their spokesman in a remonstrance to
the Senatus.   During this interview he hinted broadly
that the teaching of Chemistry left much to be desired.
A day or two later Principal Campbell met the outspoken student in the street, and said to him, " Mr.
Whyte, what you said about —— was quite true, but
all the same you ought not to have said it." [1]

But, while Whyte had no capacity for the
study of abstract science, he was open to the
appeal of science where it touches the imagination.
From the day when, as a boy, he had read of the
weighing of the sun by men of science, the wonder of
astronomy impressed him ; and it entered into his
preaching to the end of his life.   There is also a passage in the last chapter of the last book which he
published, which shows how the new vistas of thought
and knowledge opened by the theory of Evolution
laid hold upon his mind during his King's College
days.   His subject is the deep-rooted disease of human
nature, and after quoting two passages from *Paradise
Lost*, he continues :

> " Moses and Milton lived and wrote long
> before the days of Darwin and Herbert Spencer.
> For myself, I have read repeatedly and atten-
> tively all these four authors on the subject of
> this chapter.   And I find plenty of room for all
> four in my Gospel doctrine, and in my Gospel
> hope.   The *First Principles* was a great book
> with me in my student days.   And that truly
> great book opened my eyes on outward nature
> in very many ways.   But, with all that, I return
> continually to Moses, and to Paul, and to
> Milton." [2]

Whyte was a true Socratic in this, that all his
varied interest in the world about him centred and

---

[1] Dr. Whyte related the incident to the present Principal of Aberdeen University when receiving the Degree of LL.D. half a century
later.

[2] *The Spiritual Life*, p. 254 f.

converged upon the great ethical and religious problems of the right conduct of human life and the
divine purpose for mankind. The following letter,
written at the beginning of his second session, shows
another Socratic trait, for he appears in the closing
sentences as a propounder of searching questions
to those who might well have been his teachers in
philosophy. It is addressed to John Dickson from
" 45 Spital," and is dated " Saturday night, half-past
10 o'clock " :

" For the first ten days after I came up I
wrought very hard preparing for our examination.
The day before the Greek examination I sat all
night. Scarcely rose from tea-time the night
previous till I rose to go to college at nine next
morning. As soon as that hurry was over, my
teaching work began, and between it and preparing the work of three classes, I have literally
never had a spare hour. The only spare time
I can get is an hour or two in the public reading-
rooms on Saturday night."

Then follow particulars of the classes—Mathematics,
Greek, and Chemistry—meeting in all for four and a
half hours each day.

" Then the preparation for all these classes
and my two hours' teaching nightly. On Monday
I start a new class which will occupy me an
extra half-hour. The teaching is hard, wearing
work, but the salary is very good.
" I have scarcely got a book opened since I
came north. Only on Sabbaths I have read
Isaac Taylor's *Restoration of Belief*. A noble
book. But I get a rich intellectual treat on
Sabbath nights from Mr. Mee, a Baptist minister
here.[1] I assure you in all calmness that I have
heard sermons from him, that for *thought* and
beauty of expression leave Candlish far behind.

---

[1] Rev. George Samuel Mee, afterwards a journalist in Bradford,
was at this time pastor of the Baptist Chapel in John Street, Aberdeen.

Let me candidly confess that the first time I heard him I could not follow him. I felt my mind paralysed as it were with the loftiness of his thinking, and the purity and grandeur of his language. I have taken notes of some of his sermons. Imagine such a man preaching to some sixty or seventy people every Sabbath ! ! ! But his little chapel is packed in the evenings, principally with the intelligent young men and women in the city. Last Wednesday night there was a paper read at a meeting in connection with his church (a kind of essay class) on ' Revelation ' by a young man. All are welcome to go. After leaving the combmakers, I went." (In the discussion that followed, Mr. Mee invited Whyte to say something.) " I said nothing on the essay, except that I thought it had not touched the question at the point that is the point of defence and attack at the present day, referring to the controversy between Mansel and Maurice, and then put the question to Mr. Mee—' Can you tell me the point at which the system of Maurice impinges on that of Sir William Hamilton, as applied to Revelation by his disciple, Mansel ? I know where they join theologically, I wish to know where they disagree philosophically.' "

Mr. Mee did not know of the existence of the controversy referred to : Mr. M'Combie of the *Aberdeen Free Press*, who was present, had heard of it but did not know where the point of contention lay. Whyte adds, with some severity :

" I wondered, for had I had three days to spare I had read the books "; and concludes the letter : " I hope your spiritual and intellectual life is growing. Read, Pray, Think. And remember absent friends, specially such friends as
                                                            A. W."

The incident recorded in this letter shows how swift Whyte's instinct for any important theological development had already become.[1] The reply of Frederick Maurice to Mansel's once-famous *Bampton Lectures* of the previous year had hardly issued from the press when this Arts student, still three years away from the official commencement of his theological studies, was hot on its track.

During the two previous decades the great Sir William Hamilton, who died in 1856, had brought a new understanding of Kant's thought within the reach, not only of his students in Edinburgh, but of those who possessed a philosophical bent elsewhere. Hamilton's teaching, as interpreted by H. L. Mansel of Oxford, leaned somewhat heavily to the negative and dualistic side of Kant's thinking. As is indicated by the very title of the *Bampton Lectures*, their author was much concerned to lay down the limitations of human thought, and in particular its inability to pass beyond the finite world of ordinary experience to the Infinite. But he argued, somewhat as Butler had done, that since these limitations applied to human thought in all its manifestations, they could not be used to discredit the religious consciousness in particular. There was a sphere, he held, of faith as well as of knowledge ; and the ideas or principles which proved inconsistent when they were carried out in a *speculative* way, might have a *regulative* value for the moral and religious life.

All this, as well as Mansel's deductions in the sphere of theology, was challenged by Maurice in replies which far exceeded Mansel's own statements both in length and in vehemence, and which contained an impassioned, rather than a clearly expressed, vindication of the Christian Revelation as he understood it. The difference between the two thinkers was not unfairly expressed by Mansel in the following

---

[1] The books in question were (1) *The Bampton Lectures for 1858 on the Limits of Religious Thought*, by Rev. H. L. Mansel, afterwards Dean of St. Paul's ; (2) a criticism entitled *What is Revelation ?* by Rev. F. D. Maurice (Preface dated June 4, 1859) ; and (3) *An Examination of F. D. Maurice's Strictures on the Bampton Lectures*, by Mansel. In January, 1860, Maurice replied again in a *Sequel to the Inquiry, What is Revelation ?*

sentences towards the close of his *Examination of Maurice's Strictures* :

" I believe, with him, that God is revealed in Christ. But . . . I do not regard the manifestation of God in the flesh as a direct manifestation of the Absolute and Eternal Essence of the Deity ; but as the assumption of a nature in which the manifestation is adapted to human faculties and limited to a mode in which man is capable of receiving it."

In the original *Lectures* he had, apparently at least, gone further towards a virtual agnosticism, as when he said that " we must remain content with the belief that we have that knowledge of God which is best adapted to our wants and training. How far that knowledge represents God as He is, we know not and we have no need to know." On the strength of such passages Herbert Spencer (the *tertius gaudens* in this controversy) came in to claim in the *Prospectus* to his philosophical writings (March 1860) that his own doctrine of the Unknowable did but " carry a step further the doctrine put into shape by Hamilton and Mansel."

But Whyte ranged himself with those who placed the opposite, and constructive, interpretation on Mansel's thought, seeing in it chiefly a due recognition of the inevitable limitations of man's knowledge—a wise and humble answer to the question—Canst thou find out the Almighty to perfection ? In the spring of 1860 he bought the *Bampton Lectures*, and was soon in mid-stream, carried along by the author's wide knowledge, clear style, and well-ordered argument. He believed that he had here found a way of reconciling the older theology with the intellectual conception of the infinity of the Divine Nature. To the dangers of Mansel's sharp division of Faith from speculative Knowledge he does not seem to have been fully awake.

At a later period of his Arts course, Whyte read

a paper on Mansel's thought at the Saturday evening gathering of Free Church students already mentioned. One who was present says that it " not only excited the admiration of his fellow-students, but of the professors and other citizens who used to attend the meeting." It opened with a somewhat pessimistic survey of the theological thought of the time ; and Carlyle, Newman, Coleridge, Maurice, Kingsley, and Jowett were quickly reviewed, and then embraced in one comprehensive condemnation, with a youthful exuberance of epithet. But, more important than the somewhat headlong criticism of writers, several of whom he afterwards came to reverence, is the fact that he had thus early acquired a first-hand knowledge of their works.

From these thinkers he turns to Mansel's work with high commendation, and goes on to give an abstract of his argument. The following passage, based upon Mansel's Fifth Lecture, may be quoted as representing the style and reasoning of the essay :

" Truth and falsehood are not properties of things, but relations, and as such must be differentiated by or for the various orders of intelligences. But not only are we brought to this result by the stern necessities of Philosophy. The Scriptures themselves uniformly give evidence of an ever-present recognition of this principle. For on examining the systems of religious truth which have been the outcome of the human intellect, we see that the antinomies of the Infinite and the Personal are never found long together, as witness two of the hugest and most elaborated of mundane systems, the Hindoo and the Greek. In the former the Personality of the Godhead totally disappears in the all-embracing Pantheism ; while in the latter the infinity of God is lost in their Polytheistic Anthropology.[1] But in the Hebrew Scriptures the case is very different. In them language is

[1] Perhaps a slip for " Anthropomorphism."

felt to be inadequate to shew forth the greatness of God, just because the Human Mind fails to grasp that greatness ; yet there the grand truth stands towering far out of human ken, yet in that dim and indistinct cloudline in looking at which the eye quivers and quails with the height and the exceeding glory, we read the mystic words, *Infinite, Absolute*—terms common alike to the vocabularies of men and angels ; which being interpreted mean : ' Hitherto, and no farther.' And yet amid all this His personality is never lost for a moment. Yea, it is this which is the burden of the revelation. He is not only the Infinite One, but He is ' Our Father.' He makes us, He feeds us, He loves us, He yearns over us. He loves our good. He hates our evil."

In his last paragraph the writer notes and welcomes the measure of unity which underlies the controversies of the time :

" Amid all the heat and din of controversy raised by the publication of this book, it is cheering to see that all parties, even after the most hostile encounters, return to the cardinal doctrine of a personal, living Christ. For this is the rallying-point of all who bear the name of Christian, and let us thank God that in our day such men are neither few nor weak."

With an eloquent elaboration of this theme the essay closes.

The following letter to John Dickson belongs to the vacation at the close of Whyte's second session, and is written in the midst of his first plunge into the philosophy of Sir William Hamilton, and the theology which Mansel based upon it :

ORCHARD COTTAGE,
April 17, 1860.

" MY VERY DEAR FRIEND,—I hope you have rested in the assurance that, though I have been long silent, it has not been the silence of for-

getfulness or neglect. I've read somewhere—
'Never make a man your friend till you *know*
him, but having made him your friend let him
be so to the end.' A noble maxim, and well
worth our endeavour to realise the blessing it
implies. Well, the session is over, that is,
another step is taken onwards on the journey of
life. You'll have heard of the mishap that has
befallen me in my examination, my not having
passed my examination in Chemistry. It no
doubt looks a serious matter from the Kirry
point of view. To me, I assure you, it has no
such aspect. . . . Trouble not yourself, for it
troubles not me.

"And now that the harness is off, what are
you doing ? Do you ask ? Let me answer you
fully. I will be teaching at my usual place two
hours every night, and I have got another hour's
teaching in private, assisting two boys to get up
their lessons for the *Gymnasium*—a large school
where boys are prepared for college. The salary
for the last is not large, but it helps somewhat.
Tell my mother of this; she does not know. I
only got it on Saturday last. But now for the
most important part of my day's work. All my
teaching being after five o'clock, you see I have
a long day. Doing what ? Well, I came back
to Orchard Cottage last week, and have a room
alone. Last ten days I have walked about a
good deal ; I assure you I was requiring it. I
have gone daily and spent an hour or two in the
reading-room—all the papers and reviews. I
have now begun to read Sir William Hamilton's
works in Mental Philosophy. Reid's works also,
the Father of 'The Scotch Philosophy,' with
M. Cousin's, all lie on my table. I have also,
during these few days, read, and I hope I may
say mastered, *The Limits of Religious Thought
Examined, being the Bampton Lectures for 1858.*
The book of the season. Perhaps you have heard
me speak of it. A noble book, but a stiff one.

But for a bedding to these, I have not forgot fiction. You know it was always one of my canons that, in our later fiction, there is a very great deal of sound education for head and heart, held in solution. . . .

" Another I have read is *A Life for a Life*, by the author of *John Halifax*. You'll remember how you liked it ; let me just say of this, that it is a *riper book*. If you have not read it, try and get it, and I promise you a treat such as seldom comes to our share in this cross-grained life of ours.

" Have you seen *Macmillan's Magazine*, one of the finest, most scholarly, chaste, high-toned periodicals we possess ? . . . Or *The Cornhill*, edited by Thackeray ? A marvel of cheapness, with two capital novels publishing monthly in it, one by the editor, and the other by Trollope, entitled *Framley Parsonage*. A delightful story. I see all these in the reading-room. You see, if I want the society of friends—and to me it is a great want—I have the advantage of plenty of good reading.

" But it would enhance the pleasure if I knew that *Kirry friends* were enjoying the same.

" Ever, in the bonds of brotherly affection, yours,   A. WHYTE."

Another letter to the same friend, written apparently during Whyte's second session, gives a further glimpse of the pressure and strain of his work :

" *Thursday Morning*, 1.30 *a.m.*,
45 SPITAL.

" MY DEAR JOHN,—Your welcome note is to hand to-day. Thanks ; it has relieved my mind. I am happy to be assured that my mother is well and happy. . . .

" Concerning myself I have nothing to communicate. I am working very hard, as you may imagine, knowing what my duties are. I send you this note after a long and hard day's work.

I am sitting studying and in an hour or two I awaken Mr. L. He rises to his work and I go to bed from three till eight.

"No time for reading, or anything of that nature. Last Sabbath I was reading *Guido and Julius, or the Consecration of the Doubter*, a work of Tholuck's.[1] Get it. It'll only cost you 1s. or 1s. 6d.—do order it and read it prayerfully, and your soul must be stirred to deeper and deeper longings and quickenings. . . ."

The method of alternating nocturnal study disclosed in this letter is further described in a story of Alexander Barrie. He and Whyte only possessed one copy of a text-book which formed the chief subject of a forthcoming examination. As in the case above recorded, they agreed each to use it for half the night, Whyte sleeping during the early part while Barrie studied. In the comfortless chill of the early morning watch, Whyte awoke, rose and found the fire gone out and his friend sound asleep, his forehead resting on the table beside the open book. Dr. Whyte told, too, with great relish, how on one occasion both entered for some special examination for which he had prepared elaborately, making full notes. The evening before, Barrie, who had not prepared at all, asked for his friend's careful note-book, threw himself down on the sofa and read it two or three times through. Dr. Whyte concluded, " when the result was announced, Barrie was first, and I was nowhere." Barrie afterwards admitted that this story rested on a substratum of truth, but hinted that, like the stories of their joint fishing exploits which will be referred to later, Whyte's vivid imagination did not allow it to lose anything in the telling.

The next letter to John Dickson, dated from Orchard Cottage on 2nd June 1860, admits that the writer had been working too hard, to the temporary

[1] An early work (1823, twice translated into English at later dates) by one of the leading defenders of traditional Lutheranism against the Tübingen school of critics.

injury of his health, and begs his friend to spend a week with him, as he apparently did not expect to return home that summer. This urgent invitation was finally accepted, and the next, undated, letter gives directions for the journey :

" Get my *portmanteau* and bring it with you. Also in it the following books which I would like up—viz. 1. *Brimley's Essays*, 2. *Thomas à Kempis*, 3. All *Carlyle's Works* that are in the house or can be got. My uncle has a volume—if you were in town you might ask it, if he is done with it. Excuse all this trouble. I know you will. . . .

" Goodnight. I'll be at the station at 10 a.m. on Saturday.

" Till then,—Yours affectionately,

" A. W."

Dickson retained a lifelong memory of the visit which followed, and the chronicler in *Caledonia* has preserved some of his reminiscences of long walks round Aberdeen and " long talks about men and books and events." It is recorded that Dickson one day asked his friend " if he could now see that a collegiate course was indispensable to fit a man to be a teacher of the people " ; a point, it would appear, that young Whyte had in his callow days much doubted. " Yes, I think so now," replied our student, " for if I have been taught nothing else of great importance, I have been taught to think."

In the following winter (1860–61) this process received a powerful impetus, since it brought Whyte into contact with two of the strongest influences of his early life—first, the teaching of Alexander Bain, and, a few months later, the writings of Thomas Goodwin. Of these very divergent masters something must now be said.

After much controversy which only ended with an appeal to the Privy Council, Aberdeen's two universities were united on 15th September 1860 ; and a new chair of Logic and Psychology was established at King's, to which Bain was appointed in face of vigorous opposition on the ground of his markedly unorthodox views. His youth had been a hard one— harder in some respects than Whyte's own. His father, an ex-soldier and weaver, was in circumstances so poor that the son was forced to start work at the loom at an early age, and the greater part of his education was gained in his spare hours. During these years he steadily drifted away from the grim Calvinism which had overshadowed his home, and came to find full intellectual satisfaction, first in mathematical studies, and then in the Moral Philosophy and Psychology of the English "philosophical radicals." In 1842, at the age of twenty-four, he was already an assistant lecturer in Marischal College, and in that year he met John Stuart Mill in London. Not long after, he gained recognition as the ablest and most incisive of Mill's disciples, and indeed went beyond his master in the thoroughness with which he worked out the principles of the Associationist school in Psychology. His two monumental works, *The Senses and the Intellect* and *The Emotions and the Will*, represent the culmination of that mode of thought which had its beginnings in the work of Locke two centuries before ; and those who can speak of them with direct knowledge report that they contain much close and acute analysis which is not wholly superseded even now, and that, by emphasising the place of activity in the life of the mind, Bain did something to prepare for an advance towards a deeper psychological insight than that of the Associationist school.

It is certain that Bain's thorough and lucid teaching of Logic and Psychology left a strong and lasting imprint upon Whyte's mind. It might have been thought that the new professor's reputation as a sceptic would have prejudiced Whyte against him ; but it was a credit to both men that, if such a prejudice ever existed, it was quickly changed into admiration. Before being installed in the Chair, Bain was obliged to sign a test declaration, in which he promised never to " endeavour directly or indirectly to teach or inculcate any opinion opposed

to the Divine Authority of the Holy Scriptures or
to the Westminster Confession of Faith." Such an
undertaking can hardly have been congenial to him,
but there is strong evidence that, in his class-work,
he strictly observed it. The deductions which some
of his students might make from his general philosophical principles were another matter; but Whyte
at least seems to have found no difficulty in accepting
Bain's psychological contribution while holding firmly
to his own religious view of the origin and destiny of
Man.

Bain has told in his *Autobiography*,[1] as Dr. Whyte
in later years used to recall from the student's point
of view, the difficulty in which he found himself on
his appointment to the Chair; since in three months
he had to prepare courses in subjects as far apart
as Logic, Psychology, and English Literature. As
regards the two former, his plan was to take Mill's
Logic—copies of which had been generously supplied
for the class by the author—as the text-book for that
portion of the course, and his own book on *The
Senses and the Intellect* as the basis of his teaching in
Psychology. "The students by turns read selected
portions" of Mill's work, on which the professor
"made comments and gave additional illustrations."
As was natural in a follower of Mill, he devoted a good
deal of critical attention to the thought of Sir William
Hamilton.

Dr. Whyte was emphatic, when recalling Bain's
teaching, that this makeshift method had proved
most effective in training the students of this period
to read the works of a great thinker slowly, attentively,
critically. Bain was himself a master of clear though
unadorned statement and exact analysis, who gave
great thought even to the elocution of his lectures, and

[1] P. 271 f.; cf. chapters ii. and iii. for his earlier life. Cf. also J. S.
Black and Chrystal, *Life of Robertson Smith*, pp. 34 f., 56, for an estimate
of the early years of his professorship; and p. 443 of the same work
for Robertson Smith's remarkable tribute to Bain as " an excellent,
powerful, and conscientious teacher," who respected the intellectual
independence of his pupils. I am also indebted to Sir W. Leslie
Mackenzie for later recollections.

whose single-minded devotion to truth never failed to impress his more serious students. All these qualities made their mark on Whyte; but the cardinal point in his influence was that it did much to turn Whyte's thinking into psychological channels; or perhaps it should rather be said that Bain strengthened that inborn interest in the examination of motives and the study of character which in later years so largely shaped his preaching.

Thus Whyte was enabled for the first time to give sustained thought to those philosophic subjects in which his early training placed him at an advantage instead of at a grave disadvantage, and which gave the natural bent of his mind free play; and it was of no small importance that he now came under the sway of an intellect limited in many directions, but clear, penetrating, masterly in analysis, and unswerving in the pursuit of truth. The occupant of the other philosophical chair, Professor William Martin, was a man of a very different type, a former minister of the Church of Scotland, " whose course of instruction proceeded in a pre-established crescendo of rhetoric, strongly flavoured with reminiscences of the pulpit." [1] But any philosophical deficiences which the Professor of Moral Philosophy may have shown were out-weighed, in Dr. Whyte's view, by his devotion to Bishop Butler. In giving an account to an Aberdeen audience of Martin and his share in the Revival of '59, Dr. Whyte used these characteristic words :

" I am not sure that you Aberdonians ever gave Professor Martin his due. Perhaps if he had been less evangelical, he might have been counted more philosophical. At any rate, his greatest detractors had to admit that he could teach Butler. I look back with gratitude to his lectures on Butler, and his genuine insight into that thinker of thinkers." [2]

[1] Sutherland Black and Chrystal, *op. cit.*, p. 55.
[2] Address delivered in October 1909, published in *Reminiscences of the Revival of '59 and the Sixties* (Aberdeen University Press, 1910), p. 21. Bain had also a real appreciation of Butler; see Whyte, *Thirteen Appreciations*, p. 269.

6

Thus the work begun by David White of Airlie was continued by William Martin, and Alexander Whyte found himself thoroughly embarked on his lifelong study of that master of human motive, Bishop Butler. So in a not unimportant sense it may be said that Martin's influence seconded, instead of counteracting, that of Bain, by pointing Whyte towards an introspective, rather than a purely speculative, approach to the problems of the moral and spiritual life.

But during this winter of 1860–61 a star which Whyte considered even brighter than that of Butler rose above his horizon. The manner of its rising he described more than sixty years later in the following words to the students of New College, Edinburgh :

" On opening the *Witness* newspaper one propitious morning my eye fell on the announcement of a new edition of Thomas Goodwin's works. I entered my name at once as a subscriber to the series, and not long after the first volume of *Goodwin's Works* came into my hands. And I will here say with simple truth that his Works have never been out of my hands down to this day. In those far-off years I read my Goodwin every Sabbath morning and every Sabbath night. Goodwin was my every Sabbath-day meat and my every Sabbath-day drink. . . .

" It was a great time, gentlemen, when I was attending the University and New College. The works of Dickens and Thackeray were then appearing in monthly parts. The Brontë family were at their best. George Eliot was writing in *Blackwood*. Carlyle was at the height of his influence and renown. Ruskin, Macaulay, Tennyson, and Browning were in everybody's hands. And I read them all as I had time and opportunity. But I read none of them all as I read Goodwin. He is not to be named beside them as literature. No. But then they are not to be named beside him as religion." [1]

[1] *Thirteen Appreciations*, p. 157 f.

There were, however, interruptions during this winter which broke the course of this swift current of study and reading—interruptions from toothache and rheumatism (the only maladies which attacked Whyte's vigorous constitution until he had passed his seventieth year), and also from one of these elections to the office of Lord Rector, the students' representative on the governing body of the University, which sweep tumultuously across the surface of Scottish student life every third year. Both are referred to in the following letter, the last written during Whyte's college days which has escaped the destructive passage of the years :

"No. 1 COLLEGE BOUNDS,
January 11, 1861.

" MY DEAR MOTHER,—I feel I ought to have written you sooner, but there is little to write of beyond myself, and I was neither very well nor very cheerful ; these things kept me from writing when I otherwise would.

" Since I wrote you I have been a week at home from college, owing to toothache and rheumatism in the head and neck. I suffered very great pain for four or five days, and at last had a tooth pulled.

" Very shortly after, I was able to go out again, but it had weakened me greatly owing to want of sleep. Several nights spent sleepless with racking pain. But at present, I am as well as I have been all the session. I am at present very thin, but I hope to hold up till the end of the session, when I will get a little relaxing of my work. Eleven weeks to-night will finish it. You may have an idea how I am *enjoying* it when I know so well to a day when it will be over.

" Dear Mother, I am sick, sick tired of the work here, spending night and day and the spring of manhood in *grinding* Trigonometry and other trash, which if it was to be learned, ought in my case to have been over at fifteen instead of twenty-five. God willing, I will spend the summer on work more like a man's work, and bearing more on the future sphere of action which I hope under God yet to attain to. But I'll tell you of these things afterwards.

" We have had a terrible contest in the Election of a Lord Rector for the University. Sir A. L. Hay, a local landed proprietor, and Mr. Maitland, Solicitor-General for Scotland,[1] were the parties proposed. I, along with the great body of our (*i.e.* Arts) students, supported Maitland. The Medical Students, as a body, and a large number of the Divines, supported Hay.

" At a Public Meeting held for the nomination, I had the honour of seconding the motion for Maitland, but it was a frightful scene. I got myself well-nigh blinded with peas thrown, and latterly rotten eggs were had recourse to. I escaped as easily as any of the speakers. We carried the day, and I expect to see Maitland down shortly to be installed Rector. I assure you, he is a good deal beholden to your son for his seat !

" Now that the Election is over, and the New Year holidays, we are again working very hard. I have Logic in addition to other classes, which makes me doubly hard wrought. But it is a profitable study. Had I had time to get it up, I might have taken the First Prize in the class. As it is, I don't expect one. But I may tell *you* that my classfellows think me the best Logic Scholar amongst them. Though I don't get a Prize, I may (D.V.) grind it during the summer to pass an examination for *First Honours* in Logic—a much more honourable thing than taking a class prize.

" Should I be able, as I hope to be, to take *First Honours* in Logic and Moral Philosophy, it is the highest honour the University can confer

---

[1] Edward Francis Maitland, afterwards Lord Barcaple, was at this time a member of Palmerston's government.

on a student. I'll see how the summer finds me
as to health and time. . . ."

Whyte's own estimate of the part he played in
this Rectorial election was more than confirmed by
that of his friends. Now for the first time he had
shown his power to compel the attention and sway
the feelings of a large gathering. When he rose,
the tumult was at its height, and a student was heard
to ask whether " Whyte *the Tertian* " proposed to
second Maitland's nomination, indicating that only
Magistrands should be allowed to speak at so important a function. But soon Whyte was master of
his uproarious audience. Not only could his voice
be heard, but the hail of abuse and greengroceries
quickly subsided. " His oration carried with him all
the waverers, and thus secured the election of Mr.
Maitland." [1] Thus, more than a year before he
graduated, he had gained a position of unquestioned
leadership in this turbulent undergraduate democracy.

The ambition disclosed in the letter to his mother
was not wholly fulfilled. On 5th April 1862 the
annual graduation took place, and " the three Alecs "
all figured in the list of M.A.'s. Alexander Ogilvy
took a pass degree ; Alexander Barrie, received First
Class Honours in Classics ; Alexander Whyte was
awarded Second Class Honours in Mental Philosophy,
gaining fourth place in the Moral Philosophy class-
list. He himself always believed that his poor record
in the scientific part of the course was not without its
influence on the Honours degree assigned to him.

Alexander Barrie said in after years that it had
been an arduous task to " hoist Whyte " through his
examinations in languages, and more especially in
Mathematics ; and at times Whyte himself seems
almost to have lost heart in face of the difficulties in
his way. When one of his sons failed in a mathematical paper, he wrote to him as follows :

" With all my heart I feel for you in this
defeat. My own College time was a long-

[1] *Caledonia*, May 1895, p. 397 ; and Rev. D. C. Ross's reminiscences.

continued torture to me because of my examinations. I never had the memory for that kind of test : and I did not act wisely with the memory I had. As soon as I got to Aberdeen I let myself loose upon the College Library, to the neglect of my proper studies, and read English classics when I ought to have been grinding up Chemistry, etc. And I do not believe I would have taken, or rather got, my Degree at all, but for the kind treatment of my professors."

Another, somewhat unexpected, proof of the mental strain which the examination system involved for one of his training and temperament was found in the recurrence throughout the greater part of his life of an " exam nightmare," in which he found himself desperately appealing to or arguing with the examiners. After he was securely in possession of the degree of Doctor of Divinity he used, in the course of this evil dream, solemnly to urge upon his tormentors that it would be preposterous to " plough " one who was authorised to append the letters " D.D." to his name !

The severest struggle was, however, now happily over ; for the examinations of Whyte's theological course presented no such serious obstacle when once the disadvantage of his early lack of schooling had been overcome. At this time the four years' partnership in study between Whyte and Barrie came to an end, though it was succeeded by a fourteen years' partnership in holiday occupations—less constant, but not less cordial, and certainly not less happy. The two students had lived on Aberdonian fare, paying for lodgings, according to Mrs. Alexander Barrie's testimony, the sum of 3s. 6d. per week. But their landlady's provisions were supplemented, as was then customary, by the scones and oatcakes which accompanied the student's clean linen in the fortnightly box from home. When Whyte graduated, his friend gave him the four volumes of Alford's *Greek Testament,* with the following inscription on the fly-leaf of volume i. :

ALEXANDRO WHYTE, A.M.
Amico dilecto et magnopere æstimato
Hoc signum caritatis parvum
Donavit
A. O. BARRIE.

April 7, 1862.[1]

It was no *signum parvum* of Barrie's esteem that he should have found the £3 12s. needed to supply his friend with the best Greek Testament then to be obtained. Rather it was an example, when viewed in conjunction with the 3s. 6d. a week for lodgings, of the comparative estimate of bodily and spiritual needs which both men shared, and which Whyte showed the year before when he pledged his scanty earnings for months ahead in order to become a subscriber to the twelve-volume edition of Goodwin's Works. But neither ever regretted the expenditure, and nearly sixty years later, when Dr. Whyte passed away, the four volumes of Alford and the twelve of Goodwin stood close to his bedside.

[1] "Given by A. O. Barrie to Alexander Whyte, M.A., a dear and very greatly esteemed friend, as a small token of his affection."

" I will pour out My Spirit . . . and your young men shall see visions."
JOEL.

THE story told in the last two chapters has been, above all, one of the pursuit of knowledge. Its motto might well be, " With all thy getting, get understanding." But during these years, and above all during his time in Aberdeen, Alexander Whyte was gaining a deeper education, and a wider enlargement in his knowledge of the heart of man and of its response to the Spirit of God, than could be gained from Mansel or Bain, or even from Butler. In the midst of the constant activity of his days at college, his evenings of teaching, and his midnight studies, he was caught into the current of the great religious movement which swept over the North of Scotland during those years. Fifty years later, in an address given in the Free North Church, Aberdeen, he told how he first came into direct touch with the Revival of '59 :

" Mr. Chairman and dear Aberdeen friends, it was a sunny autumn evening, fifty years ago, when I first arrived in your beautiful city. I had long looked forward to that day and sometimes feared it would never come. But in God's great and singular goodness to me, I was at last permitted to step out of the train upon your beautiful streets with a swelling and grateful heart, and I remember it as it were but yesterday. All the way from Edinburgh this afternoon, as I was sitting alone in the carriage, it was all passing before my grateful eyes. I had long looked to become a student at dear old King's, and my heart swelled to God with great gladness, and it swells to-night. I was passing up King Street with all my earthly possessions in my portmanteau, when I came to the door of the North Church, and saw a great meeting filling the square and the adjoining streets. I felt at home at once; for I had been born and brought up in a town which had been blessed with an evangelical ministry, and with successive times of refreshing from the presence of the Lord. I had many fears in my heart in attempting to enter the gates of your great University, but I took a great cheer and a great hope as I saw that magnificent meeting. I think you have chosen the very best spot in Aberdeen for this meeting to-night. To me to-night it is full of the sweetest and brightest memories. . . .

" There were two students speaking one after another at that meeting—Stewart Salmond and George Cassie. I fell in love with both of them that evening, and they became lifelong friends of mine, and a source of great refreshing to me in the work of Christ. You know what a pillar of righteousness and power in the religious life of the community Principal Salmond was.[1] I do not need to eulogise him. George Cassie may not be so well known. But George Cassie had a splendid record, and for fifty years he held aloft the Gospel banner in the same pulpit and parish. He was preaching better and better till he was taken away. . . . When I came into the church . . . there were two pews running parallel with the wall and they were filled by little blackfaced boys from the combwork. John Gibb, whose name is now so fragrant at Cambridge, was teaching the two seats of those boys, and all that

[1] Rev. S. D. F. Salmond, D.D., became Principal of the Free (later United Free) Church College, Aberdeen. The Rev. George Cassie was for long minister of the Free Church at Hopeman, on the Moray Firth, and the Rev. George Campbell of the Free North Church took a leading part in the meetings in Aberdeen.

was a great delight to me to see. My memory awakens, as I go back to that happy meeting, which introduced me to those very dear friends. I can say 'Amen' to all that was said about Mr. Campbell's great meetings on the Broadhill. Many was the Sabbath evening he preached there when I sat at his feet. He was a gracious and genial soul full of the spirit of the Gospel.

"The names," Dr. Whyte continued, referring to the previous speeches, "of all those great men that you have heard were quite familiar to me— Reginald Radcliffe and the others. I would often steal away from my books and go home refreshed from their meetings. Then on the Saturday forenoons we had a missionary meeting over in old King's, when those eminent men came and spoke to us. It kept my head above water. Then there was the splendid preaching on the Sabbath, when I heard Dr. Davidson. Oh, what preaching! manly, sanctifying, edifying, heart-touching preaching. I thought I had never heard preaching like it. Dr. Davidson was a great citizen of Aberdeen, and one of the greatest evangelical preachers in Scotland. Indeed, it was the Revival atmosphere that kept some of us alive in those days. I hope Torry still thrives as a congregation. Many were the Sabbath evenings that John Gibb, George Angus, and I went over to Torry. We had splendid evenings with the fishermen. Get a fisherman once thoroughly converted, and you get a mystical depth and spirituality of life in him which is something wonderful and not to be found in commonplace people like you and me. Many were the Sabbath evenings that we refreshed our souls in Torry, and came back again strengthened for the next week's work." [1]

---

[1] *Reminiscences of the Revival of '59*, pp. 18-21. The Free Church in Torry was a simple wooden building by the Dee, erected after the Disruption at a cost of £40.

These memories of great gatherings in the city of
Aberdeen, and of smaller meetings among fellow-
students or in the fishing village (as it then was) of
Torry, across the Dee, represent an important phase
of Whyte's share in the work of the Revival. But
he also took part in the same movement amid the
different conditions of an agricultural countryside,
first in Perthshire and later in Aberdeenshire. We
have seen that the first notable book which he possessed as a boy was the copy of *Paradise Lost* given
him by Mary Macpherson; and the friend who had
divined thus early his future appreciation of great
literature was now the wife of Mr. Maxwell, the Free
Church minister of Logiealmond, some ten miles from
Perth. In the summer of 1859, she and her husband
asked Whyte to spend some weeks with them in
their manse, where he found himself in the full
stream of the religious awakening; and he afterwards related that it was at this time, in the little
schoolroom of Buchanty, farther up Glenalmond,
that he " first opened his mouth in preaching the
Gospel."

What the Revival meant in the valleys of Perthshire may be illustrated by the description of one who
witnessed it as a child in Strathtummel :

" There were meetings in that summer (1859)
which have helped me often since to realise what
the Apostle's first evangelistic visit to Galatia
must have been—a whole countryside met in
eager but orderly array on a great grassy sward,
rolling a psalm—the 66th, to *Torwood*, the 40th,
to *Coleshill*—to Heaven, that was like the many
waters of the Revelation, and then hanging rapt
on the preacher's prayer or the preacher's word.
That theme never ended without one word which
went home. It was that which asked every
hearer present whether he had come under
personal allegiance to the Great Captain, the
King of kings. I have seen strong men deeply
moved under such appeals. All the best men

and women I have known in the Highlands had
made a most definite response to them." [1]

These scenes were doubtless not unlike those in
Glenalmond, not far off. In a letter from the
" Study, Free Manse, Logiealmond," Whyte gives
John Dickson an account of his work, " just plodding
on," in preparation for the next session at the Univer-
sity, and continues :

" Are not these great days of the Son of Man ?
Are you getting any news of such work in Ireland
and the West of Scotland ? Kirry, I am afraid,
is not in a very hopeful state as far as prospective
blessings are concerned. . . . Mr. Maxwell had a
letter this morning from Brand, asking him to go
to Kirry and to bring the young converts with
him who are here at present. They are away to
address a Pullar's Meeting to-night in Perth.
They will speak again here on Sabbath. Eminently spiritual men. I think they will be
in Kirry on Monday night, and I hope I do not
need to urge you to go and hear them; and hear
them prayerfully, not, I beg of you, critically or
captiously, as you value gracious means. Oh,
there has been far too much of this with us both ;
God grant it may now cease. . . . If you have
read any account of the origin of the awakening
you will know that it had its origin, it is believed,
in answer to a prayer-meeting held in Kells
Schoolroom by four young men, and you will find
John Wallace the first of them.[2] Should he come,
he will give you an account of his own experience
and then a short account of the spread of the
work. Now, know what to expect. He is a
poor, uneducated, working Irishman—a few years
ago a wild, drunken, cock-fighting Irishman.
Now he is an eminently spiritual man of God—

---

[1] R. W. Barbour, *The Gift of the Celtic Race to Religion.*
[2] The Kells here referred to is a village in County Antrim—not the
Kells in County Meath, which was celebrated in the early history of
the Irish Church.

has, I think, the strongest hold on God's promises
and faithfulness of any man I ever met. He
mispronounces fearfully . . . is far from the
clerical type, but he is a jewel of the first water
though in rough setting. His kindness, humility,
sympathy, Christ-like walk, cheerfulness, and
quiet humour make him a most pleasant companion. Humility such as his is wonderful.
Think of it, the origin of the Irish Revival which
has brought tens of thousands to Christ and
is spreading through England, Scotland, and
Wales. Verily we are honoured in having him
under the same roof.

" But I must close. I am going to a district
prayer-meeting to-night. There is much prayer
here. We have very full meetings and great
earnestness displayed. God send His Spirit to
bless and save us! Let Prayer abound, John.
Seek Jesus. Let us emulate each other in the
race ! And that He may watch over you and
bless you is the prayer of—Your abiding friend,
                                     " A. W."

Already in these early meetings Whyte showed
unusual power as a preacher, and Mr. Maxwell
began to speak of him as one who would yet
do notable service in the Church in Scotland. From
this time began these preaching forays in the glens
of Forfarshire of which some account will be given
in the next chapter. Before the summer of '59
ended, he had the joy of hearing that the same wave
of living religious interest had reached his native
town. The visit of John Wallace to Kirriemuir
powerfully impressed a friend of his then working
at Craigton of Airlie ; and soon that district was
stirred by meetings of great solemnity, carried on
by a group of young workmen, counselled and
guided by the Rev. David White, who gave his
whole strength to forward this deeply penetrating
movement.[1]

[1] *Reminiscences of the Revival of '59*, pp. 75 ff.

It was nearly a year later, during the week which
John Dickson spent at Orchard Cottage, that Whyte
received his first offer of regular work as a preacher
in Aberdeen. At first he hesitated to undertake such
a responsibility, feeling his lack of experience, but,
as soon as his hesitation had been overcome and his
work had begun, the impression made by his preaching
was strong and enduring. In April 1861 a further
request came to him, from the leaders of the Congregational Church at Woodside, one of the northern
suburbs of Aberdeen, to occupy their pulpit during
the summer, preaching twice on Sunday and leading
the weekly prayer-meeting. The salary was only
15s. a week—no great amount for one of the gifts
that Whyte had already shown. But, although the
congregation, which had passed through a time of
much difficulty in previous years, was too small to
be lavish in the remuneration which they gave, they
appear to have given hearty support to their student-
minister, and they even sought to secure him at the
end of three months as their permanent pastor.[1]
Whyte declined these overtures, but carried away a
warm memory of his Congregational friends ; and it
is characteristic of him that, while he ever considered
first his duty to his own communion, yet, thus early
in his life, his sympathies had passed beyond its
boundaries. During these years in Aberdeen, he
acknowledged his deep indebtedness to the Baptist
preacher, Mr. Mee, and gave of his best to the Con-
gregationalists of Woodside.

Before his university course ended, a summons
came to work which, though it lasted only a few
months, formed a landmark in Whyte's life. He
was asked to occupy the Free Church mission station
which was erected by the Duchess of Gordon in 1860
at Kinnoir, some four miles north-east of Huntly.
He said long after that, when this call reached him
through the Free Church minister of Huntly, he
" thought it was a mistake " on Mr. Williamson's

[1] *Caledonia*, May 1895, p. 393 ; cf. *Aberdeen Free Press*, January 7
1921 ; September 1, 1921.

part ; but it proved to be no mistake, and he went to
the very focus and centre of the Revival.

Some of the leaders of this remarkable movement
in Aberdeenshire were ministers, but in the main it
was guided by laymen.[1] The young Irishmen who
came over in '59 have already been referred to ;
Reginald Radcliffe, who stood at the very centre of
the movement, was a Liverpool solicitor, a man
without natural eloquence, but possessed by an
unquestioning faith in the power of the Spirit.
Duncan Matheson, a stonecutter of Huntly, had
served as a soldiers' missionary in the trenches before
Sebastopol, and later had bought a derelict printing-
press and had learned to use it in order to provide
tracts for his meetings. Other leaders were fishermen, like James Turner, or men of means and leisure,
like the Hon. Brownlow North. In an age when the
various Presbyterian Churches were only beginning
to overcome their suspicions of lay preaching, this
element of lay leadership, drawn from the most
various ranks of society, brought its own freshness
and stimulus ; and in this, as in so many other great
religious movements, no small part of the attractive
power consisted in the rediscovery of the power of
sacred song. In the main, the Scottish metrical
psalms were used ; but hymns, until then unknown,
were also introduced, and one of the most highly
valued was " Just as I am," a hymn on which Dr.
Whyte used often to preach until the end of his life.

Still another break with the conventionalities of
the past was the release of religion from its customary
imprisonment within the walls of churches. The
great work of the Revival was done in the open air—
in Highland valleys, and in the squares of Aberdeen or
on the links near by ; but the chief scene of such
meetings during the four summers from 1860 to 1863
was the Castle Park, lying between the little town
of Huntly and the River Deveron, overlooked by

[1] For what follows, cf. the *Life of the Last Duchess of Gordon*, by
Dr. Moody Stuart ; and the *Life of Duncan Matheson*, by Rev. J.
Macpherson, as well as the *Reminiscences* already quoted.

the stately ruin of Huntly Castle. A deep, curving grassy bank formed a perfect natural auditorium, and here country people and fisher-folk gathered to the number, it is said, of seven thousand, or even ten thousand, coming long distances by road or rail. The ground was given, and the preparations made—including the provision of food for those who came farthest—by the Duchess of Gordon. She was a woman of much force of character, whose husband had died long before, and who had cast in her lot with the Free Church in the years following the Disruption. In her later years Huntly Lodge was the focus of the most living religious movements in the north-east of Scotland.

It was while these gatherings in the Castle Park were at the height of their power and influence that Whyte was appointed missionary at Kinnoir, and took up his abode in lodgings in Huntly.[1] The whole atmosphere of the place, the warmth with which he was received and the thoroughness with which his evangelistic work was supported and followed up by a group of young men and women in Kinnoir, gave a new uplift to his spirit, the effect of which remained with him throughout life. In later years he told the most ardent of his fellow-workers, John Lobban, that these meetings had made him what he afterwards became ; and the words of his Inaugural Address in the New College bear out this strong statement :

" Huntly, and its heavenly suburb, Kinnoir, will never be effaced from your present Principal's thankful heart. Jacob Behmen was wont to say that he had no books ; he had only himself.

[1] This does not agree with Dr. Whyte's statement in his Inaugural Address that he went to Huntly immediately after his first session at King's College (April 1859) ; but his memory for dates was not infallible, and letters quoted in the last chapter show that he was at Kirriemuir in that month, waiting to find work, and that in the summer of 1860 he was teaching in Aberdeen. It was in June 1860 that the wooden church at Kinnoir was opened (*Reminiscences of the Revival*, p. 99 ; *Life of the Duchess of Gordon*, under date 1860). Mr. Gordon Gray (afterwards of Rome) was the first missionary, and Whyte the second. That would indicate the summer of 1861 as the date of his appointment, which was renewed for the summer of 1862 after his graduation.

Well, that far-too-early-preaching student had few books ; but he was beginning to have himself. And besides himself he took Ellicott to Kinnoir with him to keep him right on the grammar of the Ephesians, and Thomas Goodwin to keep him right on the doctrine of that sweetest of Epistles. 'Thicken your exhortation with doctrine,' said the sometime President of Magdalen to his divinity students. The great President always did that himself, and out of his fine book it was so done at Kinnoir also. And, though he says it who should not say it, those were rare Sabbath evenings in that little wooden church. But thanks mostly to the '59 Revival which was still pulsing its new life through that richly favoured district, and to Thomas Goodwin, the greatest pulpit exegete of Paul that has ever lived." [1]

Dr. Whyte's fellow-worker has recorded that, on these summer evenings, " there was among us a joy exceeding any earthly joy, because it was the joy of the Lord. When the meeting closed those who had not found rest would hang about the doors, lest God's Spirit would leave them. The word was put to us that way—we must make haste." [2] And in the Aberdeen address already quoted, Dr. Whyte repeats the story of his evenings in Kinnoir with some fresh touches, and then describes other parts of his work :

" It is the audience that does the preaching. Farmers, shepherds, farm servants, and others gathered there, and we had rare evenings. Thanks to the Revival and Thomas Goodwin. Then on week-days we would set off to the feeing markets, where there would be an extemporised platform of deals and barrels. I see it at this moment. . . . Here is Mr. Williamson, one of the handsomest and best-groomed men in the

[1] *Former Principals*, p. 62 f.
[2] *Reminiscences of the Revival*, p. 100.

country. You would think of the House of Peers
when you saw him. The pink of a perfect
gentleman; just what . . . David Masson
called Robert Bruce in the days of James I.,
'that stately Presbyterian divine.' At the
opposite pole was the Glasgow Flesher,[1] with a
face you would have thought had been hewn
out by his own hatchet. And here is Mr.
Williamson not ashamed of the Flesher, nor was
the Flesher afraid of Mr. Williamson. The
Flesher had a voice that sounded like thunder,
and the ploughmen were greatly taken with him.
The fact that he had lost an eye in a 'Briggate'
fight made them draw near. Then there was
Duncan Matheson, with a voice like one of
the bulls of Bashan, but with gospel notes in
it as tender as a mother singing her child to
sleep."

A revolution had indeed taken place when religion
had broken loose from the " stated ordinances of the
sanctuary," and invaded the rough " feeing markets "
(hiring fairs) of Strathbogie in the person of the
" Briggate butcher "; and a fragment of conversation
overheard on such an occasion and recorded in the
Life of Duncan Matheson may be added here for the
sake of its local colour—" A wonderfu' change has
come over Jake Tamson : for there wasna a rocher
chiel in a' the countryside, an' noo he's as hairmless
as a stirk, and sings and prays instead of swearin' an'
fechtin' as he used to do."
In addition to his work at Kinnoir, Whyte carried
on his reading, borrowing books from William
Andrew, a watchmaker, who had gathered a library
of the old divines. He also gave considerable assistance at Gartly, five miles south of Huntly, where the
Free Church minister was in poor health: and one
who heard him there described to the writer the
solemnity of his preaching and his prayers. On one

---

[1] *Anglice*, butcher. Robert Cunningham, butcher and ex-pugilist,
spoke with great power at these meetings.

occasion his prayer began in a way singularly characteristic of his later life :

> " ' Remember me, Lord, with that love
> Which Thou to Thine dost bear ;
> With Thy salvation, O my God,
> To visit me draw near.'

" O Lord, may this be the prayer of every soul here before Thee this day ! "

At first Whyte walked from Gartly to Kinnoir (a distance of seven or eight miles) when he had to conduct services in both places on the same day. Hearing of this, the Duchess of Gordon gave instructions for a horse to be provided to save his strength and his time. Once he mounted the horse, but never again; and amid the solemn memories of Huntly and Kinnoir he retained the humorous recollection of his first and last ride—humorous, perhaps, in retrospect, rather than at the moment itself. It is not clear how much he saw of the Duchess personally ; for her activities were limited by a serious illness at this time. But one who was then a young visitor at Huntly Lodge recalls his coming to conduct family worship—a somewhat severe ordeal for a student, as the household and guests had been known to number as many as fifty when they were all assembled for morning or evening prayers.

Nor was Whyte's preaching confined during these months to Huntly and its neighbourhood. The great open-air gatherings held there drew together ministers of evangelical sympathies from all Aberdeenshire and Banffshire ; and these were unwilling to return without securing speakers from the centre to bring the same message to their own lonely flocks. One of these was Fullerton of Strathdon, who had been a parish schoolmaster before the Disruption, and had sacrificed his whole livelihood in order to join the Free Church, of which he afterwards became a minister. After years of quiet and often discouraging work he found a new source of power in the Revival, went to Huntly, and returned bringing the young evangelist from Kinnoir with him. There was a group of young men in Strathdon who had caught the same inspiration, and who often went miles across the moors in parties of two or three to hold a kitchen meeting in some remote township. A survivor of this group related to the writer, with an enthusiasm un-dimmed by the passing of sixty years, how profound an impression was made by Whyte's address when he accompanied Mr. Fullerton on his return from Huntly.

To this testimony we may add that of one who knew this district well at a later period :

" It was interesting to find in the Aberdeen-shire of 1900, memories still surviving of Dr. Whyte's evangelistic pilgrimages away back in the sixties during his student days. He himself records how he saw the work of God ' in Padan-aram, and in Airlie, and in Kirriemuir, and in Logiealmond, and in Huntly, and in Aberdeen, and in Hopeman.' . . . Some of the Aberdeen-shire folk were of the opinion that even Dr. Whyte of St. George's, the famous and eloquent divine, was not so impressive a preacher on sin and salvation as Alexander Whyte, the student-pilgrim with the flaming heart, who still lived among their early recollections." [1]

Or, in the homelier phrase of an Aberdeenshire farmer who heard him in after years : " Man, he's no bad yet, but no so guid as when he was up beside us."

It would be a hard task—and here it is a needless one—to estimate the value of the Revival of '59 for the religious life of those parts of Scotland which it most deeply stirred. The words in which the appeal was given, and some of the conceptions associated with it, have an unfamiliar sound to-day. It may be said that the message laid too much stress on the saving of individual souls and too little on the social aspects of the Gospel ; but none can deny that this

---

[1] *The Presbyterian Messenger*, February 1921. See also Dr. Whyte's *Bunyan Characters*, Fourth Series, p. 263.

great awakening to an intense conviction of spiritual
realities was abundantly justified by its fruits—the
dedication of thousands of changed lives to the
service of God and man.   Certain it is that the two
marks of the Revival which recur constantly in the
reminiscences of its survivors—a deep sense of sin
and an intense experience of the power of prayer—
became and remained most distinctive marks of
Dr. Whyte's own message.   Nor did the sense of sin
which became so keen at this time finally result in a
gloomy or morbid religious outlook ;   for we are told
that the spirit of joy and fellowship among those
who had passed through these experiences was not
less marked than the heart-searching with which they
began.

For Whyte himself, it was a great thing that this
experience met him thus early in his career.   It is
true that this was far from the beginning of his
personal religious life.   That beginning was due to
his mother and his first minister ;   and the influence
which he exerted upon the children whom he taught in
Kirriemuir and Airlie, proves beyond a doubt how
real and strong were his early convictions.   But
there is also much to suggest that these convictions
retained something of that austere and often painful
striving which was impressed on the whole life of his
early home.   But in '59 and the years that followed,
he found himself borne forward on a wave of religious
enthusiasm and power, which he described in memorable words towards the close of his address at the
meeting of commemoration fifty years after :

" A Revival quickens dead men, touches
men's imaginations, and sets loose their hearts.
. . . There is a Divine mystery about Revivals.
God's sovereignty is in them.   Just when His
time comes, ' a nation shall be born in a day,' and
it gives us a heart of hope to think of that.   It
is in His hand.   ' Thou hast ascended up on
high :   Thou hast led captivity captive.'   And
Thou hast the Holy Ghost to give to Thy Church

and people. I may not live to see it. But the day will come when there will be a great Revival over the whole earth. He has said : ' I come to give you life, and that more abundantly.' Go on and preach His Gospel, for He has it in His seven-sealed book that there will be a time of refreshing till all the ends of the earth shall see the salvation of God. See that you are doing your utmost to hasten on that kingdom. For whatever else is shipwrecked on the face of God's earth the kingdom of the Lord Jesus Christ is sure to come into harbour. . . .

> " ' For Thou art God that dost
> To me salvation send,
> And I upon Thee all the day
> Expecting do attend.' "

CHAPTER VI

1862–1866

" Beautiful for situation, the joy of the whole earth . . . on the sides of the north, the city of the great King."—Ps. xlviii. (often applied to Edinburgh by A. W.).

" TOWARDS the end of his Aberdeen time," so Dr. Whyte's Address to the students of New College continues, after his account of Kinnoir,

> " the subject of these remarks was toiling late one night for his imminent degree examination, when Alexander Barrie, his room-mate, burst in on him with this exclamation, ' I say, what do you think ! I have just seen an advertise-ment in the *Witness* of a presentation bursary in the New College for a student of the name of Whyte, the preference being given to the candi-date who spells his name with a " y " ' ! That being so, a year passes on, and that New College student of whom we are now speaking is sitting at his books in his little garret in Scotland Street in this city, when his old landlady came into his room and said to him that Dr. Moody Stuart [1] was standing on the landing and was asking to see her lodger. If she had said that the angel Gabriel was standing on her landing and was asking to see her lodger he would not have been more amazed. ' Oh yes ! ' she said, ' I assure you it is Dr. Moody Stuart. I know him quite well, for I often go to hear him preach.' And she

---

[1] Minister of Free St. Luke's Church, Edinburgh, and biographer of the Duchess of Gordon. Dr. Williamson of Huntly had " passed on " his assistant's name to this friend in Edinburgh, and offered to release the former from an engagement to return to Kinnoir in 1863.

was quite right.   It was really Dr. Moody Stuart.
William Law, that vainest of men, was wont to
say that when he looked out of his eastern window
every new morning at daybreak he always saw
Almighty God creating his shining sun anew
every morning and sending him up into the sky
in order to lighten him, William Law, to another
day of duty and devotion. Your Principal had
not discovered William Law in those days; but
he had some of that same vanity, though he
could not put it into such classical English. For
he always looked on Dr. Moody Stuart, and on
his deacons' court, and on his congregation, and
on his Sabbath services, and especially on Andrew
Fleming, his congregational treasurer, as all created
and kept in life and in prosperity for the sole advantage of their missionary. And so it was.
What with William Whyte's bursary and Andrew
Fleming's quarterly cheque, that New College
student was in clover, and by the goodness of God
he has never wanted a blade of that sweet herb
ever since. Three more truly blessed years so pass
to him in dear St. Luke's and in this dear college.
And they pass in a way that your Principal will
perhaps tell you about, one by one, when you
visit him in his study. And then his three years
in St. John's, Glasgow, and then Edinburgh
again. And then, after forty red-letter years
in Edinburgh—this to-day! Unless, indeed, this
is all a dream!"

.   .   .   .

The restrictions as to home or surname attached to
many of the presentation bursaries in the Scottish
colleges were both quaint and arbitrary; nor could
they be easily reconciled with modern ideas of uniformity in education. Yet this illogical arrangement
was often justified by its fruits, and never more so
than when the bursary referred to brought Alexander
Whyte to Edinburgh and the New College, and assisted
to maintain him there during the four winters of his

theological course. Thus the first link was formed
between him and the city with which his name will
always be associated.

Long after, Dr. Whyte received the freedom of
the city of his adoption, and took the occasion to
" salute the Lord Provost of this incomparable city "
—a city which, he said, even Scott and Stevenson
could not sufficiently praise, and which might be
described in the words used by Milton of Athens,
" the eye of Greece." He went on to name certain
of the great citizens of Edinburgh when he first knew
the city. There were the judges, like Lord Moncreiff
and Lord Ardmillan. There were the doctors who
had made the medical school of Edinburgh famous,
with " Simpson, that great genius at the head of
them, a noble figure and a remarkable man." The
authors also, including Hugh Miller and " Rab "
(Dr. John Brown) ; and the ministers, among whom
Candlish and Guthrie shone out as " stars of the
Church." " These," Dr. Whyte said, " were some of
the great figures that used to ornament and adorn
and strengthen the city in the days of my youth " ;
and he characteristically added that the resources of
the Kingdom of Heaven were not yet exhausted,
but that great men, true men, serviceable men,
would surely arise to follow in the footsteps of their
fathers.

Whyte's thoughts had turned to Edinburgh even
before the midnight irruption of Alexander Barrie
with his news of the fortunately named bursary.
Two of his closest friends in Aberdeen, Gibb and
Macphail, had already gone to the New College ;
and ever since Mr. Livingstone in Kirriemuir had
lent him certain of the theological writings of Dr.
William Cunningham, who succeeded Chalmers in
the Principalship, Whyte had earnestly looked forward to the day when he might sit at Dr. Cunningham's feet. To those of to-day who know Cunningham's name at all, the attraction is somewhat
hard to understand, for he was the sternest and most
dogmatic of the Disruption leaders, the last typical

systematic and controversial theologian of Scotland
in the old sense of the term. But Cunningham had
great historical knowledge, as well as a trenchant
intellect, and over the stronger minds of that time
in the Free Church his influence was profound. Dr.
Whyte has told how, when he heard of his death
during the winter of 1861–62, "it was almost as if
Edinburgh itself had been submerged that morning." [1]
When Whyte first arrived in the city of his adoption
in the autumn of 1862, Dr. Robert Candlish—of whom
we have already heard and shall hear more in the
following chapters—had been appointed Principal of
the New College ; and the minister of the Free High
Church, Robert Rainy, who was just ten years senior
to Whyte himself, had succeeded to Cunningham's
Chair of Church History. Another young scholar,
Andrew Bruce Davidson, son of a small farmer in
Aberdeenshire, had recently been appointed Tutor
and Assistant in Hebrew ; and for just forty years
Rainy and Davidson continued to influence profoundly, though in very different ways, the thought
and character of those who passed through that
widely known school of theology.

Davidson had been appointed to provide a substratum of sound scholarship in Old Testament studies,
while the Professorship of Hebrew was still held by
Dr. John Duncan. He also was the son of a poverty-
haunted home in the north-east of Scotland, who
had lived to be one of the most erudite men of his
time—"the Coleridge of the Free Church," one
called him ; and another said that "it seemed as if
Pascal had shuffled into the sandals of Socrates, and
walked up and down our Edinburgh streets, with
large utterance of response to the inquiring youth
around." [2] Dr. Whyte described "Rabbi Duncan"
in two settings. In his classroom "he taught nobody
Hebrew, but of all the men of my time he was most
truly a genius. He could not manage his class, but
gave it an impetus to thought with every word he

[1] *Former Principals*, p. 19.
[2] A. Taylor Innes, *Studies in Scottish History*, p. 183

uttered." And again, in Dr. Moody Stuart's church,
he might be seen, " sitting down below the pulpit,
slobbering with tears and sweat his Bible, unreadable
to any but to himself." Round this unkempt, unworldly figure, with his rapt gaze and flowing beard,
there had gathered a legend of fabulous learning in
the Oriental tongues, as well as of the strange intellectual wanderings and heart-shaking inner experiences through which he had reached his theological
resting-place. There had gathered also many of
those tales of an almost incredible absent-mindedness
which seem to find a point of attachment in every
centre of the higher learning, but which clung in
special profusion to the skirts of this almost medieval
scholar. The " Rabbi's " great learning and speculative bent were, however, combined with a vast
discursiveness in his teaching, and with a strait and
strict view of literal inspiration ; so it was well for
the students of New College that the younger colleague
in this remarkable partnership possessed all the gifts
as a teacher which the old scholar lacked. At this
time, indeed, Davidson was only beginning that
constructive work in the interpretation of the Old
Testament which was destined to make it a new book
for those who passed through his classes; for his
appointment as Dr. Duncan's colleague dated from
the middle of Whyte's course, and Whyte was one of
eighty-six students who signed a memorial in support
of his claims.[1]

Dr. Whyte's debt to Dr. Rainy was nobly acknowledged in his own Inaugural Address as Principal :

> " I am not sure that Dr. Rainy was always
> very easy to be known, and by everybody. And
> yet there was no man among us more simple,
> and more unstudied, and more natural, and less
> practised than was our dear and honoured Fourth
> Principal. The day that saw Dr. Candlish enter

---

[1] Strahan, *The Life of A. B. Davidson*, pp. 83 ff. Dr. Davidson's
widest influence was mediated through his pupils, especially Robertson
Smith, Elmslie, Harper, and George Adam Smith.

on his Principalship here, that same day saw
Dr. Rainy enter on his Professorship ; and I was
happy enough to enter on my student life here
that same day. It was a great day to me. I
had looked forward to it from afar, and here it
was come at last ! Dr. Rainy was wont to say
in his great humility that he owed a great deal
of debt to his first students. . . . They were so
patient with him, he said, they were so attentive
and so respectful and so reassuring to him. And
I well remember how all that came out, so sur-
prisingly to me, when he was making a speech of
welcome to me at the congregational meeting
that was held on the week of my induction into
St. George's. What he said that night took me
quite aback ; but . . . made me say in reply
that we would have been so many brute beasts
if we had been rude or disrespectful or in any
way unappreciative of such a man and of such
matchless work as he gave us from his chair. . . .
Dr. Rainy's depth, his insight, his power of
realisation, his philosophical grasp, and his
theological judgment—all combined to give me a
view of the sub-Apostolic Fathers that I had not
hitherto met with, and I do not know where there
is anything at all like it." [1]

These words were spoken in 1909 ; and in a still
later utterance Dr. Whyte named Rainy along with
Athanasius and Newman and Dorner as the masters
from whom he "learned his Christological Philosophy." [2] Such tributes become all the more noteworthy when it is recorded that, owing to the serious
illness of Dr. Rainy in the winter of 1865–66, the
students of Whyte's year missed much of his most
mature teaching in his advanced class.

[1] *Former Principals*, pp. 37–40.   Cf. the tributes to Rainy in *The
Early Letters of Marcus Dods*, pp. 253–56 (*e.g.* " A lecture he gave
the other day on Origen I never heard equalled ").   Dods also wrote
appreciatively of Rainy's unprofessorial bearing, and of his contribution to the social life of the College.
[2] *The Spiritual Life*, p. 86.

At the same time, Dr. Whyte once told one of the most intimate of his younger friends that he had learned more from his fellow-students at the New College than from his professors. Of these student-friends, John Gibb has already been described. Another fellow-student who did not less for Whyte was Simeon R. Macphail (afterwards of Liverpool), the youngest of three brothers who did notable service in the ministry. Macphail was a true Highlander in his open and affectionate nature and in his love of poetry. Not only had he the gift of attracting friends to himself, but he added thereto the hardly less valuable power of bringing his friends into touch with one another. It was to Gibb and Macphail that Whyte owed his introduction to Marcus Dods ; and through Macphail he came, before the end of his college course, to know the family of his future wife.

Dr. Marcus Dods was Dr. Whyte's immediate predecessor in the Principalship of the New College, and their friendship and co-operation in the ministry was unbroken for forty-six years. Dods was less than two years older than Whyte, but was eight years his senior in academic standing. He completed his theological course, and was admitted as a licentiate of the Free Church, in 1858. For six years thereafter he worked as assistant or as *locum tenens* in a church in Newcastle and in various Edinburgh churches, preaching to, and being passed over by, a long succession of vacant congregations the while. Towards the end of this time—such a time of hope deferred as few men of Dods' intellectual eminence and nobility of nature ever had to suffer—he wrote to his friend Taylor Innes, with a touch of ironic humour, that he was meditating a discourse on the sick man at the Pool of Bethesda, adding, " He, however, had thirty-eight disappointments, I only twenty-one as yet." [1] How Dods turned his necessity of waiting to glorious gain may best be told in the words of Alexander Whyte, whose admiration steadily grew in depth

[1] *Early Letters*, p. 312.

during the eighteen months that followed their introduction :

"When I came to Edinburgh . . . Simeon Macphail took me to Marcus Dods' lodgings to introduce me to his friend.   Simeon was always a pet friend of Dr. Dods, and he did me that and many other services, never to be forgotten by me. And from that day down to this day Marcus Dods has been a support, and an enrichment, and an ornament to my intellectual and spiritual life, such as it is.   For, both in Edinburgh, and in Glasgow, and back again in Edinburgh, what walks we had and what talks on every Saturday afternoon ! . . . For, whatever we started off with in our conversations, we soon made across country, somehow, to the Logos, to the Messiah, to Jesus of Nazareth, to His thirty years, and then to His three years, to His death, and His resurrection, and His indwelling.   And, after Jesus Christ, many were the uplifting and enlarging and exhilarating talks we had about Paul. . . . Between Christ and Paul, many were the Saturday afternoons on which I came home from my walk with Dr. Dods certified, and strengthened, and encouraged, and refreshed, and made more ready for my pulpit work next morning.

"The thing that struck me most in my new friend was his steady, punctual, untiring, and so fruitful industry. . . . I will tell you what Marcus Dods did while he waited so long for his call.   He worked at his desk every day and with all his might.   Let any student, or any still-uncalled probationer, take down the six volumes of Lange's *Life of Christ*, and let him master the able and mature preface, and then turn over the learned notes and the minute index that our probationer contributed to that delightful book.   And then no sooner was that piece of work finished than there began to come forth

from the same probationer's lodgings volume
after volume of his monumental edition of
Augustine. The editor of Lange and Augustine
had already purchased a right to hate and to
denounce the all-desolating and the always-
disgraceful vice of idleness in a Divinity student,
in a probationer, and in a minister. And to my
knowledge his lashing lecture on ' Mr. Fritter-
day ' made an epoch in more manses than one in
the Free Church of Scotland of that day."

Dr. Whyte then mentions some of the books
which his friend begged him to read and study,
especially Foster's *Essays*, and *Ecce Homo* (which,
like Newman's *Apologia*, appeared during his second
year at the New College), and tells how he used to
reproach Dods with the time which he spent on works
less solid than these.

"But then he would soon have his revenge
on me. For he never turned over the leaves of
the most ephemeral publication that he did not
take something or other out of it for his pulpit
and platform lectures, and for his incomparable
review articles. . . . Hunt, as the wise man says,
where Dr. Dods would, he always brought home
venison, and he always roasted what he hunted."[1]

From this impression, mellowed by years of
friendship, we may turn to the corresponding picture,
sketched by the other friend in letters from day to
day. The first reference, dated 29th January 1863,
is engagingly casual: " Simeon [Macphail] wants to
introduce me to a friend of John Gibb's, a fellow
Whyte, a student; so I intend giving a young
supper some night." The occurrence of " the young
supper "—the parent of many suppers and still more
lunches in after years—is not recorded ; but on
14th April Dods writes again: " I have a new friend,
a man Whyte, who is always at me to marry and
establish a barrack for students. He, poor chap,

[1] *Former Principals*, pp. 45 ff.

is supremely miserable in lodgings alone, and main-
tains that he is going to the dogs—a locality which
certainly has a byway from solitary apartments of
single gents." In the following month the writer
reports: "I fraternise considerably with . . . Whyte,
a fine, honest, doctrinal, outspoken, hearty fellow,
that knows what he is himself, and does not require
others to be much better, though he thinks they are."
This last was a characteristic throughout life, but
perhaps a query should be attached to the last clause of
a description sent at the same time to S. R. Macphail:
"Many thanks for Whyte. I think we'll get on
well. I like him for his honesty, his intelligence, his
goodness, and his real happiness of spirit. He has
sorrows, but they don't cut very deep, as how could
they in a fair-haired Scandinavian like him." [1]

Dods had much excuse for thinking that other
men's trials could hardly be comparable with his own;
but in spite of his tribute to his friend's " real happiness," he says about the same time: "Whyte moans
so about his loneliness that he makes me think more
of mine." Beside this statement we may place a
fugitive impression gained by a young friend from
near Kirriemuir, who was taken by a member of Free
St. Luke's to see Whyte in his rooms in Melbourne
Place, and who remembers a somewhat depressed
student, convalescent after a slight illness, in surroundings that were not of the most cheerful. Dr.
Whyte's reminiscences of this period, as of the years
at Airlie, are gilded by the passing of the years, and
still more by the alchemy of his own grateful spirit;
but these contemporary glimpses show how many
things without and within were still present to try
his courage, although the fear that haunted him, both
before and during his Aberdeen days, that he would
never complete his course and enter the ministry,
must ere now have passed away.

Other friendships also began in these years, of
which more will be told in later chapters. Through
Dods, Whyte came to know Alexander Taylor Innes,

[1] *Early Letters*, pp. 258, 276, 286 ff.

a law student preparing for the Scottish Bar, who added to legal knowledge a lifelong interest in theology and in the polity of the Church. George Webster Thomson was another member of the group, who, like Innes, possessed wide sympathies and great personal charm. Whyte's meeting in his last year with a younger student, John Sutherland Black, marked the completion of the fivefold friendship which enriched his life long afterwards. Another friend, in whose rooms the last-named introduction took place, was Alexander Miller, afterwards of Buckie, whose elder brother, William Miller, had recently sailed for India, where, as head of the Madras Christian College, he did a unique work for Christian education.

During Whyte's New College course his labours as assistant or missionary in Free St. Luke's continued to occupy much of his time and strength. St. Luke's was founded in 1837 to provide for the religious needs of a growing population in the eastern part of the Parish of St. George's. Its foundation was in great part due to the initiative of Dr. Candlish, and under Dr. Moody Stuart, its first minister, the congregation rapidly became a large and active one.[1] Both ministers adhered to the Free Church cause at the Disruption ; and the bond of interest between their churches became a link in the chain which ultimately drew the student-missionary in Free St. Luke's towards his life-work as minister in the parent congregation. Like many of his fellow-students in New College, Whyte was powerfully attracted to Dr. Candlish, and divided his church attendance between the two churches, boasting, as he tells us, at college on Monday mornings regarding the " incomparable preaching " that he had heard the day before.[2]

In Free St. Luke's Whyte assisted Dr. Moody

[1] *St. George's, Edinburgh, 1814–1843, and 1843–1873*, by David Maclagan (1876), pp. 57–60.
[2] *Former Principals*, p. 30. Mr. Maclagan mentions (*op. cit.*, p. 92) that forty-five New College students attached themselves to Free St. George's after the Disruption.

Stuart with many of the week-night meetings and much of the visiting of his charge.   He also frequently supplied the place of other ministers who were preaching for Dr. Moody Stuart, and during the first summer vacation of his theological course spent three months doing the work of a minister who had fallen into ill-health, at Auchtermuchty, in Fife.   The present minister of this church, when he went there in 1918, found that some of the older members of the congregation still thankfully remembered Whyte's short sojourn with them fifty-five years before.   Thus, during his years at New College he confirmed and developed the gifts which he had already shown at Aberdeen and Huntly, and his fellow-students recognised in him a preacher of unusual maturity and power, as well as a great lover of the Puritan divines.

To this period—or even perhaps to the end of his King's College course—belongs the incident in Whyte's student days which most strongly and lastingly impressed his fellow-townsmen—his first sermon in Kirriemuir.   It was preached in the old South Free Church, and so great was the crowd which assembled that, even after benches had been set along the passages, several score persons had to be turned away.   The text was, " I am the light of the world," and the sermon made a deep impression, by its force of expression as well as by its spiritual fervour.   It must have been no small ordeal for the young preacher to face an audience containing most of the friends of his boyhood ;   and, when it was over, he asked his old friend, the beadle, Peter Donald, " Did you hear my heart beating as I came in ? "   His former employer was there, and some of those who had been his mates in Mr. Ogilvy's workshop ;   and it is said that they expressed their appreciation afterwards, and were met by the reply, " Ye see what has come from your awls ! "   We do not know what the mother of the preacher felt or said, but she must have pondered many things in her heart as that Sabbath evening drew to its close.

There are still two or three people advanced in
years who remember the sermons that Whyte preached
in country places round Kirriemuir during the vacations of his Arts, or of his Divinity, course.   One
of these, Mr. Mackenzie of Glasslet, a farm in Glen
Clova, described to the writer the gatherings of those
far-off days.   There was no Free Church in the
Glen, but the smithy served as a meeting-house, and
ministers from neighbouring parishes used to preach
from time to time there, or in a farm-kitchen.   Sometimes Whyte took such a service.   " When he was
to preach anywhere in the Glen, almost the whole
inhabitants would come out to hear him.   His voice
was so fine, and his matter so fine, and so finely set
out—though he was but a student."
    He found his way farther afield, too, especially to
Glen Isla, where another farmer of the same Highland
name was his host.   John M'Kenzie of Alrick was a
man of strong conviction and deep religious experience, whose influence still lives on in the memories
of the folk in Glen Isla.   He had taken a great part
in the founding of the Free Churches in that district,
and had a deep knowledge of several of the Puritan
divines whose works Whyte used to discuss with him
for long hours.   He was a man of kindly feeling also,
who had encouraged Whyte's mother to bring her
son seventeen miles from Kirriemuir to Alrick, when
he was still almost a child.   Later, when he began
to lay his plans for college, she again took counsel
with her trusted friend at " the Alrick " ;   and on
more than one occasion Whyte spent part of a
vacation there, taking his books to a wooded knoll
some distance from the house after breakfast, and
remaining so absorbed in study that his host's boys,
who looked on him with some awe, had to be sent
to summon him loudly when the dinner-hour came.
In a schoolhouse near by he preached one of his
early sermons during the Revival days, on the
text, "What are these that are arrayed in white
robes ?";   and one of the sons of the house (afterwards an office-bearer in Free St. George's) re-

members his intense preoccupation for hours before the service, and the impressiveness of the service itself.

Mr. M'Kenzie was a man of over sixty at this time, yet he and his student friend felt their differing years no barrier to mutual understanding. Their long walks often passed in talk regarding religious experience. Dr. Whyte said in after years, "the old saint's memory still sanctifies the glen," and went on to give one especial recollection of him:

> " That Sabbath night after supper I asked my friend to read to me out of the manuscript volume of notes he had taken of John Duncan's sermons long ago when the future professor was still a probationer in the neighbourhood; and he was still reading in his rich manuscript when the bell rang for family worship. After the worship was offered I turned to my friend and said to him, ' Let us have some more of the Rabbi's remarkable sermons.' ' Pardon me,' said the wise old priest, ' but we always take our candles after family prayers.' If," Dr. Whyte added, " we all took our candles immediately after family worship every week night, and if we could carry to our own room the full impression of the public worship every Sabbath night, it would be the salvation of countless souls." [1]

With the year 1865, the informal diaries, or rather memorandum books, begin, which give a bare outline of Whyte's movements. In April he visited Marcus Dods in Glasgow, where the congregation of Renfield Free Church, to their great credit and yet greater advantage, had called the often-rejected probationer. On 16th June he left Edinburgh for five weeks in the north, visiting Kinnoir, and joining his friend George Cassie for some days in Strathdon. Cassie had remained in Aberdeen for his theological train-

---

[1] *Bunyan Characters*, iv. 23.

ing, and at this time was in charge of a Free Church station in the pleasantly situated town of Alford. The summer was a brilliantly fine one, and Cassie was holding services in the open air, in which his friend helped. Time was found too for walks through " the Howe of Alford," since celebrated in Charles Murray's poems. One of these walks led to the farm of Glenlogie, where Rev. Dr. MacGilvray of Aberdeen was staying, who noted in his diary, " Mr. Whyte is a clever and enthusiastic student. I liked his spirit and manner."

It is noteworthy that the first pages of Whyte's diary are filled chiefly by the titles of books which he had in mind to read or to consult. There is a list of the Fathers, from Tertullian to Ambrose, who have written on the Trinity. American theology is represented by Jonathan Edwards and by *Princeton Essays*; Anglican, by Pusey and by Mozley's *Bampton Lectures*; German, by Dods' translation of Lange ; Roman Catholic, by Manning's *Temporal Mission of the Holy Spirit*; Scottish theology, by Chalmers. Along with this truly Catholic, but somewhat ponderous, array of theologians, it is a relief to find the " Farringford " edition of Tennyson's poems.

But Whyte's chief master more and more came to be Thomas Goodwin. In Chapter IV. we have heard of the beginning of his discipleship, and now the quotation, there begun, may be completed, since it tells of the second stage of his study :

" During my succeeding years as a student, and as a young minister, I carried about a volume of Goodwin with me wherever I went. I read him in railway carriages and on steamboats. I read him at home and abroad. I read him on my holidays among the Scottish Grampians and among the Swiss Alps. I carried his volumes about with me till they fell out of their original cloth binding, and till I got my bookbinder to put them into his best morocco. I have read no author so much or so often." [1]

One reason why the cloth binding of Goodwin's Works gave way under the strain of incessant use is not mentioned in this passage. Much of Whyte's time during these four years was spent in preparing the index which appeared in 1866 in the twelfth and last volume of this edition—a labour in which he received some assistance from one or two friends, but which was in the main his own. There is an Index of Texts, with almost exactly ten thousand entries, and a full Subject Index, which bears witness by its uniformity of plan and execution to the work of a single and most painstaking hand. The latter is, indeed, almost unique in its elaboration : it affords a conspectus of Goodwin's thought, and many of his aphorisms are transcribed in full. Its preparation wrought both the style and matter of the great Puritan's thinking into the very fibre of his apt and devoted pupil's mind. One might, indeed, gain no mean understanding of Goodwin simply by the study of this masterly summary of his many discursive works.

Whyte's reputation among his fellow-students as an authority on the Puritans was probably based, in part at least, on rumours of this great labour of love on Thomas Goodwin. But Marcus Dods had more direct means of judging, and, before this work could have well begun, he described his friend as " a very high Calvinist, and a lover of the Puritans," who " would talk doctrine for a year on end." It may seem strange to find an unusually strict Calvinistic theology ascribed to one who had shown himself so fervent an evangelist, and whose message had so direct and searching an ethical tone. But in the school of thought to which Whyte belonged no acute difficulty was felt in combining these two elements, and, like his immediate masters in theology, he would

[1] *Thirteen Appreciations*, p. 157 f. ; cf. *The Spiritual Life—The Teaching of Thomas Goodwin* (1917), *passim*.

have claimed to be equally Calvinistic and evangelical, or rather he would have regarded the former term as including the latter. His thought moved with no sense of strain within the limits of the traditional Reformed Theology, and his outlook upon the Bible and its authority had been as yet but little affected by the change which was beginning in the 'sixties to stir the level surface of Scottish orthodoxy. But it may well be added that, of the doctrines grouped under the title of Calvinism, he instinctively dwelt on those with the most direct bearing on life and conduct. He had less to say about Election than about the inability of the human will to raise and redeem itself, and the need for, and sufficiency of, the divine work of Grace in the heart of man. And, while these early writings are often expressed in language remote from the religious speech of to-day, they are consistently modern in the dismissal of mere speculation, and the endeavour to bring all things to the test of experience. Two examples of this may be given.

As early as Whyte's second year at New College, in a thesis submitted to Dr. Rainy, he speaks of " God's way of dealing with my own soul being made the ultimate conditioning cause which gives its peculiar texture and hue to my theology." And again, in the " Lecture for Licence " which he had to prepare before entering the ministry of the Church in 1866, he finds himself confronted with the task of expounding a passage in the Book of Revelation. Almost at the outset he states emphatically that " this Book is always a revelation of the present rather than of the future," and contends that the predictive element in it must be treated as subordinate to that of permanent spiritual value.

> " By nature our eyes are blinded to the momentous import of *to-day*, our ears are stopped to its crying urgency. . . . To see Christ reigning *now* and *here*, to see Him gathering in that countless multitude one by one *now*, to believe that

amid the rude framework of daily life, from under
the crushing tread of sorrow and sickness and
death, in the cold and all-but-lifeless routine of
religious duties, He should be patiently following
out His eternal purpose of Grace towards *me*,
this makes a demand on daily faith such as no
Prophet's cry or Seer's vision approaches."

Among the manuscripts which survive from the
New College period are a Latin thesis, the composition
of which must have been an uncongenial and perhaps
not very fruitful labour ; and a " Popular Lecture "
on Ezek. xxxvii. 1–14, delivered by Whyte at the
end of his third year before Dr. Candlish as Principal.
The great preacher's criticism was, " Sir, that is not a
bad sermon, if it had only been a little more on the
text "—a judgment which gave rise to much good-
humoured banter between its author and its recipient
when they found themselves colleagues in Free
St. George's less than six years after.

No account of a course at New College could be
complete which failed to refer to the two societies
—the Theological and the Missionary—which, during
the whole history of the college, have played an
invaluable part in its life and in the training of their
members. Whyte's work in Free St. Luke's interfered with his attendance at the former, and he
seems instead to have concentrated on work for the
Missionary Society. It met then and for long after
on Saturday mornings for the discussion of the
more practical problems of the Church's work, and
it has carried on, since the early days of New College,
Home Mission work in a congested district of the
city—at that time in the Canongate. Whyte was
chosen as its President in his last year ; and a boy from
the Royal High School, who was taken by a student
brother to one of the meetings which he addressed,
still remembers the kindling earnestness of his bearing
and his words. His Presidential Address, delivered
on 18th November 1865, was characteristic even in the

subject chosen—" On Present Personal Consecration to Christ." It contains passages of strict, corporate self-examination: " *We are simply not* ' fighting the good fight of faith.' " " Our epitaph may be the motto of Grotius, fitted to sum up too many ministers' lives—*Vitam perdidi operose nihil agendo.*" [1] " Hurrying time will drift us onward. Soon men will call us to be ministers of Christ, and the name and thought shall gall us having naught to minister. It is true in this respect, however absurd it may be in others, that *a man must live into what he is to preach.*" [2] But, later, there are words of greater hopefulness: " If God's grace goes with us we may have the transcendent honour of extending and perpetuating that type of simple, manly, intelligent, enduring piety that has long signalised Scotland and her Church among the nations of the earth."

There follows a reference to the influences then drawing men's thoughts away from the older theology, including the newly baptized science of Sociology ; and Whyte defines his attitude towards them as follows :

" I am not prepared to say to any one— because I am not prepared to act on it—' Give less attention to these things,' but I am convinced that we all give *far too little* attention to the unparalleled literature of our own profession, and far too little scope in our lives for the more masculine virtues of a Christianity at once Catholic and severe."

These quotations show the element of severity in Whyte's thought at this time : how far it was already Catholic is shown by the fact that both the address just cited and the " valedictory " delivered at the end of the session close with quotations from *The Christian Year*. In the latter address, Whyte first surveys the work done during the winter in the

---

[1] " I lost my life laboriously doing nothing."
[2] The italics in this case are mine.

Society's mission district, and makes the practical suggestion that it might be made more effective if the workers in future met more often for social conference and counsel. This longing after an increase of fellowship runs through the whole of the later portion of the address, and comes near to implying that he had felt the general tone of life in New College chillingly intellectual after the ardent comradeship which he had known during the Revival in the north. On this subject his words are singularly outspoken : " It will need personal and combined and continued effort to raise the spiritual temperature of this Hall to the ordinary range of Christian life as it is exhibited in the families you now return to or the congregations you will soon be called to minister to." Once more, after speaking of " the crushing sense of unreality which makes us weary of ourselves and of life, with a weariness that ages a man's spirit," he goes on to plead for a greater openness and freedom in giving expression to the spiritual life which really exists but is too often concealed by an assumed insensibility and reserve. " I believe," he continues, " that the only specific for this evil is . . . that we meet each other more as fellow-workers and fellow-worshippers." Then, glancing at the grounds for hope held forth by growing interest in the practical tasks of the Society, he makes a direct appeal to the students of the years behind him in these kindling words :

" Oh, let not opportunities of Christian intercourse slip away with the commonplace current weeks, else when the last week comes on you as it has done on us, the least reflective will feel a pang that he has done so little and been so unlike his ideal of a New College student. . . .

" If our hearts fail us about our life and walk during the past winter, let us look to Him who can give us back the years the cankerworm has eaten. Let us seek to have a standing secured and a Friendship formed with Him, so that the sight of the wintry past may but make Him dearer to us, who is the Stay of our present and the alone Hope of our future.

"Fellow-students, farewell! Some of you will know this day twelve months with what truth and depth of emotion I now bid you *farewell*!

"May the God of Mercy and of Peace preserve you and me to His Heavenly Kingdom!

> "'Dread Searcher of our hearts—
> ... O help us in our parts,
> To learn and teach Thy Love!'"

PART TWO—"MAN GOETH FORTH"
1866–1881

1866–1870

" Now for my life, it is a miracle of thirty years, which to relate, were not a History, but a piece of Poetry, and would sound to common sense like a Fable."—Sir Thomas Browne.

THE words from the *Religio Medici* which stand at the head of this chapter were often quoted by Dr. Whyte in after years. And indeed they were more obviously appropriate to the first thirty years of his own life than to the early life of Sir Thomas Browne himself. For the year 1866 saw him not only complete his thirtieth year and finish his college course, but become assistant and then colleague to Dr. John Roxburgh, in Free St. John's, Glasgow. Thus twelve years had taken him from the cobbler's bench in Kirriemuir to a position of acknowledged and growing influence as joint-pastor of a church in the heart of Scotland's largest and most active community. And, though the preceding years had been occupied by an effort which must at the time have seemed as prosaic as it was unremitting, yet in the light of what followed, they cannot but be recognised as a true " piece of poetry."

The contrast between Whyte's experience and that of his close friend, Marcus Dods, was indeed strange. Dods had to endure six years of waiting and disappointment before a call came to him : Whyte passed straight from college into the full and responsible work of a city minister. The story of the three months after he completed his New College course is told in his diary with a most admirable brevity,

in entries which reach a total of eighty words; but
from this laconic and unadorned chronicle we can
follow his chief doings during this spring. On 2nd
April he was present in the Music Hall, in George
Street, Edinburgh, at the most celebrated of Carlyle's
public appearances, which was also perhaps the most
memorable hour in the history of Edinburgh University, when a great concourse of students listened in
unwonted silence to the high moral appeal which the
greatest Scotsman of the age addressed to them.
Whyte's impressions of this great speech have not
come down to us ; but although he had by this time
passed under the influence of teachers of a different
school, he must have listened with singular interest
and reverence to the man whose books had been as
fine gold to him in the years when he was a working
lad and a struggling teacher.

The next entry has an interest of a different kind :
" Apr. 13—Simpson from Glasgow about Free St.
John's ! ! " The exclamation marks here suggest
that the request, brought by this office-bearer of the
congregation of Free St. John's, that Whyte should
preach there with a view to becoming the assistant
of Dr. John Roxburgh, seemed to him as startling as
Mr. Williamson's invitation to Kinnoir had seemed
five years before. But the proposal was seriously
meant, for a fortnight later the diary records an interview with Dr. Roxburgh in Glasgow, and on 29th
April Whyte preached twice in Free St. John's, the
morning sermon being that on Rev. vii. 1, 3, from
which some sentences have already been quoted.

The custom of the Presbyterian Church is that,
when a student has completed his college course and
satisfied the examiners appointed by the College
Committee, he is required to undergo a further test
or " trial " of a more practical character by the local
Presbytery. He is then " licensed to preach the
Gospel," and becomes a " probationer," authorised
to do a minister's work, save that he cannot dispense
the sacraments. Ordination follows when he has
been called to the pastorate of a congregation. The

second of these three steps is recorded in Whyte's diary in these words: "June 7—Licensed by the Free Presbytery of Edinburgh to preach the Gospel. God help me so to do."

Successive entries during the fortnight that follows tell of an evening meeting, presumably in Free St. Luke's, and a presentation of a "desk and purse of 34 sovereigns"—probably the largest sum Whyte had yet possessed at any one time; of his moving to rooms in Bath Crescent, Glasgow; and of his first evening service as assistant in Free St. John's, when he characteristically chose his subject from the fifty-first Psalm. The series closes with a note on 21st June, "Subscribe for *Review* and *Spectator*." No part of the thirty-four sovereigns was expended to better effect than that which went to furnish his study table with the *Spectator*. Fifteen years later the first habit which he taught his young wife was to read it regularly, and Saturday evening was jealously kept free from other engagements for this purpose. Whyte's estimate of the *Spectator*, and in particular his sense of indebtedness to its literary editor, Richard Holt Hutton, found striking expression in a letter addressed in April 1908 to Mr. John Hogben of Edinburgh:

"My dear Sir,—I have only now read your fine little book on Hutton. The quiet reading of it has taken me back to the early 'sixties, when I first came under the influence of the *Spectator*. What a delight the paper was to me in those days! Week after week it came as an inspiration of truth and beauty and power to my life. In those days the paper was valued and leaned on by me, and by multitudes like me, as no other paper has ever been, or has deserved to be. I suppose I have thirty volumes of the *Spectator* bound and preserved in my study: and I used to take references to the articles as I read them, and often returned to them as I prepared for my classes and for my pulpit. To me your warmest words about Mr. Hutton only contain the simple truth. The paper held its full hold over me till it turned upon Mr. Gladstone. But the way it treated that great statesman can never be forgiven to it by any true and advancing Liberal. I would like to have a talk with you sometime about these old days and old men.

"Meantime, I thank you warmly for your delightful book.—Believe me,

"ALEXANDER WHYTE."

In Glasgow Whyte was spared the loneliness which is often involved in passing to a new sphere of work, for three of his closest friends were there to receive him. Marcus Dods was minister of Renfield Free Church, Taylor Innes was engaged in legal work in the city, and Alexander Barrie was a classical master in Glasgow Academy. The Saturday afternoon walks and discussions with Dods were resumed; and the direction generally taken was along Great Western Road, which then led quickly into open country. Late in September 1866, Whyte, Barrie, and two other friends spent an autumn day in a long expedition to Loch Lomond. They walked from Inversnaid to Loch Katrine and back, dining on the boat on their way home; and this expedition became a yearly event as long as the two friends remained in Glasgow.

In Free St. John's, too, Whyte found, not only a pulpit, but an open home. For Dr. and Mrs. Roxburgh were most hearty in their welcome, and twice during his first month in Glasgow Whyte visited them in their summer quarters at the Kyles of Bute. Nor was his indebtedness for guidance in his new work confined to the advice of his chief: he owed not less to the quiet hints on the social side of a minister's work and bearing which Mrs. Roxburgh gave, and which Whyte, who realised how little experience he possessed in this direction, was ready with characteristic humility to accept. One of the qualities which most impressed those who knew him at this time was

his forthrightness, and it was in part at least from
Mrs. Roxburgh that he learned how to blend with
it the wisdom and restraint which marked the
conversation of his mature years. Long after, the
late Mrs. Alexander Balfour, one of the daughters of
the manse, who was absent from Glasgow at this time,
became a warm friend in Free St. George's, and Dr.
Whyte told her often that Dr. and Mrs. Roxburgh
had been as a father and mother to him. To another
daughter (Mrs. Mellis), we owe the most vivid description of his early ministry :

" Although it is so long ago, a man of such
marked personality and power made an impression that cannot be forgotten. Vigour of mind
and body was written all over him.
" In accepting the invitation to be assistant
at St. John's, he was much impressed by the
fact that he would have to preach to the father of
' the Principal ' (of the New College, Edinburgh),
old Dr. Rainy, who had been an elder there for
many years. Very soon his power as a preacher
showed itself, and many people were drawn to
the church, even though it was becoming already
a ' down town ' church and the houses in the
neighbourhood that had formerly been occupied
by families had now become business offices or
hotels. The weekly prayer-meeting revived ;
Mr. Whyte soon gathered a large ladies' class,
the members of which worked with enthusiasm.
His characteristic gifts were conspicuous in this
branch of work. I remember his pleasure in the
essays of some modest and retiring young girls,
who became capable theologians and wrote excellent papers for him. Words and their deriva-
tions had a special interest for him, and his use
of this in illustrating his teaching was always
very fresh. The Shorter Catechism became a
mine of deeply interesting thought . . . sometimes searching the heart, as when he expounded
the passage, ' envying or grieving at the good of

our neighbour, and all inordinate motions and affections to anything that is his.' [1] He saw deeply into the evils of the heart and revealed them to hitherto unsuspecting and thoughtless young people. I have heard him say of the Shorter Catechism, ' You could take your spade and dig in it.'

" Our father and he were always on a most happy footing with each other, and as he felt his vigour declining the older man began to lean more and more on the strength of the younger. Mr. Whyte was naturally a great deal in our house and at our table during his years in Glasgow, and we much enjoyed his original conversation and striking way of expressing himself about men and things. No doubt he was at that time learning a good deal that was to be profitable to him later in his great career in Edinburgh.

" From time to time he visited us when we were enjoying our summer holidays in one of the charming places on the Clyde, and he thoroughly entered into the pleasures of climbing hills to see extensive views of sea and land, or rowing to some wild place where the whole company gathered sticks to light a fire and make a gipsy tea. . . .

" Mr. Whyte had the faculty of making warm friends. When he was ordained as colleague and successor in St. John's, a large company of fellow-students and other admirers came to be present. They all prophesied great things for him. The text of his first sermon after ordination was a striking one, and one to his own mind: Jer. i. 9, 10—' And the Lord said unto me, Behold, I have put My words in thy mouth. See, I have this day set thee over the nations and over the kingdoms, to root out, and to pull down, and to destroy, and to throw down, to build, and to plant.' "

---

[1] *Shorter Catechism*, Answer 81, on the Tenth Commandment. Nothing was more marked in Dr. Whyte's ethical teaching than his constant and searching exposure of the sin of Envy.

These sentences have already carried us on to the end of this year when Whyte was ordained as Dr. Roxburgh's colleague in the pastorate of Free St. John's.   There could be no stronger proof of the swiftness with which he won the confidence of the congregation than the fact that this step was taken so soon. He went to St. John's as assistant towards the end of June, on the eve of the holiday season, when many of the members were scattering for the summer ; but as soon as they reassembled they took steps to make the tie between assistant and congregation closer and more lasting.   On 3rd October Whyte notes in his diary : " Prayer meeting.   After it Doctor [Roxburgh] spoke to me of probable result of meeting. *Deus facit.*"   To the grateful spirit of the young minister, it was indeed " the Lord's doing " that he should so soon be called to the full exercise of the high vocation which he had recognised as a boy in Kirriemuir and followed after with so steady a devotion. On 27th December 1866 he was ordained—now fully launched on his great life-work, amid the confident good will of the friends whom as a student he had knit to his soul.

During the next three years Whyte's fame—the word is not too strong—as a preacher spread widely. Several calls, or less definite approaches, reached him from different quarters, including one from a large congregation in Melbourne.   The most definite and important was a request in the autumn of 1868 to become minister of Regent Square, London, at that time the leading congregation of the English Presbyterian Church.   He seems to have considered this seriously.   At all events, the people of Free St. John's felt themselves in danger of losing their junior pastor, and descended upon him with a series of deputations and resolutions from the Kirk-Session, Deacons' Court, Sabbath-school Association, Young Men's Association, and adherents of the congregational mission, which, backed by Dr. Roxburgh's weighty advice, prevented him from leaving Scotland for London.   These resolutions, and others passed eighteen months later when he was under call to Free St. George's, confirm the account already quoted of Whyte's ministry in St. John's. Special reference was made to the close friendship in which he worked with Dr. Roxburgh, the new life which he brought into the weekly prayer-meeting and the home mission work of Free St. John's, and the way in which young men and women valued his preaching and rallied round him as a friend. The Young Men's Association in particular laid stress on "the earnest and practical, and not less the personal note " of his preaching. His whole influence stood for a dynamic religion in closest contact with the needs of daily life.

The problems of the congested and often degraded life around Free St. John's struck home to Whyte's imagination as soon as he arrived in Glasgow. This could, indeed, hardly fail to be true of any young minister called to follow, even for a time, in the footsteps of Thomas Chalmers, through whose efforts the original parish of St. John's had been founded, and who had made it the scene of a great experiment in the application of the Church's energy to social tasks.[1] Whyte gave much of his energy to strengthening the home mission work of his congregation, and found time, even before his ordination, to take part in a wider movement then beginning in Glasgow. A prolonged epidemic of typhus fever had reached its climax in 1865, when there were 1177 deaths in the city from this cause alone. In the following year a new City Improvements Act was passed, and a movement for sanitary reform began under the leadership of the recently appointed medical officer, Dr. (afterwards Sir William) Gairdner, and his assistant, Dr. Russell.[2] In the autumn Whyte's diary contains

[1] Chalmers's ministry in St. John's Parish lasted from 1819 to 1823, and in those four years he superseded the system of Poor Law relief by that of organised congregational care for those in distress. His work not only resulted in the moral uplift of his people, but in the reduction of the expenditure on relief by four-fifths. (See N. Masterman, *Chalmers on Charity*, the biographies of Dr. Chalmers, and his *Christian and Civic Economy of Large Towns*.)

[2] *Public Health Administration in Glasgow*, a memorial volume of the writings of J. B. Russell, pp. 19 ff.

more than one entry regarding this urgent work for the public weal, and shows that he was seeking to enlist in it the active interest of the office-bearers and teachers of Free St. John's.

In his view the social problem was closely bound up with that of education. This was shown by an address given at the annual meeting of the Glasgow Sabbath - School Union in April 1867, in which he spoke of the many cases in Glasgow where " parents, or rather owners, are trafficking in the withering lives of their children," and showed how " this state of things is fast undoing the work of the missionary, the social and sanitary reformer." His own early experience as a teacher had quickened his interest in the whole problem of education, and in this address he looked forward with keen expectation to the assumption by Government of the responsibility for the education of the people as a whole, a measure which was carried out some three years later. While urging that the Bible and Catechism must maintain their traditional place in the day schools of Scotland, he pointed out that the work of voluntary religious education would always be needed as well, and that it might form a valuable source of mutual sympathy and understanding between different classes, between the west end and the east.

Two years later, in March 1869, several new office-bearers were ordained in St. John's, and Whyte's address to them and to the congregation shows how his conception of office in the Christian Church had been enriched by the practical experience of three years in the ministry. His counsel to the new elders has, in its concluding portion, a further and permanent value, and so may fitly be quoted here :

" *Visit your people regularly.* . . . I cannot lay down rules to you concerning the frequency of your calls, or even the way you are to conduct them. I am not to lay down rules even about prayer and Christian discourse in your visits, because I cannot see my way to lay down any

stringent inflexible rule for myself. But let us
be on our guard against letting our visits degener-
ate into mere calls of formality or courtesy. . . .
We are visiting as ministers and elders of
Christ's Church. We are to visit on a religious
errand, and it is to be done in a religious way.
The more this spirit rules us in our visits, the
better for the honour of our Master, and the
good of the people, and the well-being of our own
souls.

"And lastly : Seek to be the *guide* and
counsellor and *friend* of your ministers in their
walk and work among the flock. You will in
many cases necessarily know more about the
people than we can do. Come and consult con-
fidentially with us about cases of anxiety, or
conversion, or discipline, or sickness, or even
family troubles as they emerge. Few things can
befall the individual or the household that we
ought to be strangers to. Let us rejoice with
them in their joys, and sympathise with and
comfort them in their sorrows.

"Let us know when our presence is specially
needed or desired. Do not fail, I beseech you,
to do this. But protect us also from all unreasonable and absurd demands, as you best,
you only, can. All men do not know a minister's
life as you do. We look to you for guidance,
and not less for shelter. Quell the strife of
tongues when you meet it. Be servants of the
Prince of Peace among the flock."

The words addressed at the same time to the
newly ordained deacons show how strongly the
speaker felt the necessity of bringing as many men
in their first youth as might be into that form
of practical service which was represented by the
diaconate in the Free Church of Scotland. This
aim to have a large, and a youthful, Deacons'
Court was one which Dr. Whyte followed most consistently in Free St. George's in later years. His

advice to the deacons in St. John's may be summed up in two brief sentences: " Do not speak much about the work you are to do, but do it." " Never fall into arrears with your work, and never fail to connect it all with the Church's Living Head, your Master and Saviour."

Of Whyte's power of influencing individual men and women an instance may be quoted from Kirriemuir. On one occasion during his Glasgow ministry he was preaching at his old home; and after the service two girls came to speak to him, who had as children been pupils in the school at Airlie ten or twelve years before. He found out that they had walked in from Airlie to hear him and that they proposed to return after the afternoon service; so he offered to accompany them, and shared their walk for several miles. As they went, he pressed the claim of his Master to their personal allegiance so earnestly and persuasively upon them that, for one at least, that walk proved the beginning of a life-long and happy Christian experience.

CHAPTER VIII

PERSONAL EVENTS—DEATH
                                                    OF HIS FATHER

1861–1871

"If we reckon up only those days which God hath accepted of our Lives, a Life of good Years will hardly be a span long : the Son in this sense may outlive the Father, and none be climacterically old."— SIR THOMAS BROWNE.

DURING these years, while Alexander Whyte was steadily advancing in the calling to which he had given his life, events had taken place in the history of his family which make it needful to turn back to the spring of 1861. The bombardment of Fort Sumter on 12th April of that year is commonly taken as the beginning of the American Civil War ; and within the following fortnight John Whyte responded to Lincoln's appeal for volunteers on the side of the North. There can be no war, however bitter and destructive, which does not call out self-sacrifice and heroic virtue on the part of some whose earlier history has not shown these high qualities. This was assuredly true of John Whyte. He had almost completed his forty-ninth year, and had the care of his business in New Jersey and of a motherless daughter on his mind ; yet so promptly did he volunteer that on 27th April he was appointed " Comasary of the 79th Regiment, Highland Guard, New York State Militia." An old photograph shows him in a uniform which provokes a hardly avoidable smile—a bearded figure in black service cap (in shape not unlike the French *képi*), a kilt, and a colossal sporran, hanging far below his knees. But while the Highland uniform would astonish any kilted soldier of the present day, there was stern enough work waiting for its bearer, and the service cap still exists pierced by a bullet-hole through its crown. On 4th July he received a pass for himself and his

nephew—another Alexander Whyte, also in the Highland Guard—on military duty ; and a few days later
they were fighting together in the first battle of Bull
Run.   The issue is told in a letter from the uncle to
the nephew dated,

" RICHMOND PRISON,
November 27, 1861.

" . . . You know the last that I knew of
you was when the balance of the 79th was making
an attempt to rally in the field, when I called you
and said that Captain Farrish wished to see you
over at such a fence.   I had then my personal
idea that if we did rally and make another
attack after seeing every other regiment panic-
stricken and flying in every direction, that few
or none of us would be left alive to tell the
tale. . . . After all, an attempt was made to
form the balance into a square, until they, seeing
others, got panic-stricken also. . . . I made
search for you for a while, thinking you might
then be in search of water.   I then left the
woods reluctantly—as I had been the cause of
you being there, and wended my way as I say.
I had seen thousands, not many left the field
after me."

The account that follows of John Whyte's final
capture is somewhat confused, and need not be
quoted here ; but his son summarised, long after,
the tale as he had heard it.   " He remained to give
a drink of water to his wounded Colonel, and so
was taken prisoner, and went through the horrors
of Libby Prison.   He said they were indescribable,
soldiers actually bayonetting prisoners if they
looked out of the window."   The letter above quoted
is naturally silent on this topic, though much may
be read into the following sentence : " There were on
Monday 350 of us, prisoners, left here for Tuscaloosie
(Alabama), alas many of them half naked, but in the
best of spirits seeing they go to a warmer climate."
Another letter (which perhaps failed to reach its

destination) gains in significance from the sufferings of
the prisoners, though its most obvious peculiarity is
the unmilitary parlance which was characteristic of
the citizen armies in the Civil War :

" RICHMOND PRISON,
January 1, 1862.

" TO GENERAL WINDER.

" DEAR GENERAL,—I am sorry to trouble you,
but you will confer a very great favour by giving
heed to this. I am satisfied, Sir, to remain here,
in your charge until honourably exchanged by
my Government and yours. I have been a
prisoner of war since the 21st day of July, and
now find that some men have been exchanged
from here yesterday morning, the 31st—who
have only been imprisoned since the 1st of
October — and of the same rank as I hold,
First Lieutenant—and I am the oldest military
man taken. If influence is made to bear in
this matter—I can very soon furnish enough.
How is that, General ? — I am, with great
respect,

" JOHN WHYTE,
" Lieut. 79th Regt. N.Y.S.M.,
" New York."

Eventually John Whyte secured his exchange.
At the end of the war he visited Scotland, and his
son came to know him for the first time. Each seems
to have recognised and appreciated the high qualities
of the other ; and we may well believe that John
Whyte, aged beyond his actual years by the privations
he had endured in the prison at Richmond, had gained
through his devotion to a great cause a dignity and
strength which his character had lacked in his stormy
youth.

Not long after this brief visit from his father,
Alexander Whyte found himself settled in Glasgow,
and at once began to think seriously of inviting his
sister, now about nineteen years of age, to share his

dwelling, and so make it a true home. During his first year in Glasgow, Whyte wrote two letters, which give some insight into his own feelings and plans at this time, and show how anxious he was that his sister should share them. The first is dated three weeks before his ordination :

> " FREE CHURCH MANSE,
> LIVINGSTONE, MID-CALDER,
> *December* 3, 1866.

" MY DEAREST SISTER,—Your very sisterly and very welcome letter of date 19th ult. was forwarded to me from Glasgow this morning. I am rusticating for a week or two at present previous to my ordination. I return to Glasgow to-morrow to see my Mother, Grandfather, etc.

" I must explicitly thank you, Dear Sister, for your letter. It is so kind, so good, so sisterly. May God bless you, my Dear Child !

" You have good reason to complain at my negligent habit of writing. All my correspondents do so. I can only say *peccavi !* But they all admit I am a capital friend to converse with. I hope you will soon be able to homologate that opinion. You wish me to write a long letter now, which you hope to receive about Christmas. I hope you will receive this before that time, because I wish you to know and ' keep ' my *ordination day*. How to ' keep ' it I need not direct to a sister's loving and pious heart ! Need I ? I cannot state now definitely the day of my ordination, till I go to Glasgow to-morrow, but I shall keep this open, as I am keeping Father's, that you may both know the day. You say that you wish much to see it. Dear Sister, though you sometimes think I forget you, I must now frankly tell you this, that there is no human being I would more wish to be with me that day than a little Yankee girl I have never seen with my eyes. Can you guess who she is ? But as that cannot be, I'll tell you what I often

think of as next best, that at one of my *earliest
communions* she be with me to commemorate our
Elder Brother's love Who hath made Himself
known to us. (I have mentioned my wishes to
Father. Wait till he has revolved the matter
in his mind and heart.) But I do hope, yea I
know, that your heart will be with me that day.
The ordination will take place either at 12 o'clock
noon or at 3 p.m., I expect, and in the evening
there will be a congregational service when
friends of the congregation and of the young
minister will be invited. The details are not yet
arranged. Assuming that the smallest item of
news will interest you, I'll let you know all that
takes place. By the way, you might acknowledge any papers, etc., that contain personal
news, as I do not know whether you know the
steps the matter has taken. Did you and
Father get the ' Congregational Report ' and the
' List of Elders and Deacons ' I sent ? I thought
both would interest you. But you'll understand
St. John's work better yet, I hope.

" Of Father—I have written him a long letter.
I thank you very much for the extract from *his*
letter. I love him deeply and I pray God we
may yet love him in the Lord. So I read again
those words so characteristic of him in their
strong realism. I think I see him, and the
tears start to my eyes. You have done a good
deed in sending them, Dear Sister !

" You'll be returning from ' home ' to-day,
probably. You say ' Where is my home ? ' I
have told Father that at any time it may be the
Free Manse of St. John's, Glasgow. If a home
means *Love, comfort,* and *work,* they are all
waiting you as the sister of the colleague pastor
of Free St. John's. If Father permits you, you'll
surely not refuse to come and be my housekeeper for a time. You could help me greatly
in the opening years of my pastorate here. It
is a very onerous and honourable position, as

I have told you before, and the love and aid of a little, loving, working sister would greatly further me in my work.   I intend taking up house soon. I can't call it *home* till you come to consecrate and people it !

" But as was proper, I have spoken to Father about this.   *Let him speak first.*

" Ere I close, let me say again how much and how deeply I reciprocate your wish to be with me at my ordination.   But I'll think of you and I know you'll not forget me.—Your only and loving Brother."

The second letter incidentally records the beginning of the writer's close friendship with Dr. (afterwards Sir) Alexander Russell Simpson, who three years later succeeded his uncle, Sir James Young Simpson, the discoverer of chloroform as an anæsthetic, as Professor of Midwifery in Edinburgh University.   Both friends went from Glasgow to Edinburgh in the same month—October 1870.

" 14 SHAFTESBURY TERRACE,
GLASGOW, *May* 21, 1867.

" MY DEAREST SISTER,—I am just starting for the Free Assembly of our Church in Edinburgh.   It sits on Thursday first.   Dr. Roxburgh is Moderator.   I do not know how much or how little you know about Church matters in Scotland.   But if you know anything of the Old Presbyterian Church of America—the Princeton Divines—our Church is the same in doctrine, discipline, and government.

" The Assembly sits in May.   Ministers and Elders from all the Presbyteries in Scotland sit and vote in it.   It sits for ten days.   I am a member sent up from the Presbytery of Glasgow.

" I had a call on Saturday night from Dr. Simpson, a young medical man in Glasgow, whose sister married Mr. Wells.[1]   He had heard from his sister and she had told him that she had seen

[1] Later, Rev. James Wells, D.D., of Pollokshields.

you.   I was glad to hear it.   I hope soon to hear from them about you.

" But I wished to write a letter before the Assembly to ask you to write me on receipt, and for the following reason.   On the 17th June Mr. Barrie and I start for a holiday tour on the continent of Europe, and I would like to hear from you before we start.   We will be away six weeks.

" I have been working hard all winter and am much in want of rest. . . . Dr. Roxburgh has done little work all the spring.   He is not strong, and I try to relieve him as much as possible.

" Well, Barrie and I propose to go to the Continent for six weeks.   You'll know European geography, so I'll give you some notion of our proposed tour.   We start from Glasgow on Monday, the 17th June, pass through London, spend a day or two in Paris, and spend our first Sabbath in Geneva.   Walk through Switzerland and spend the next Sabbath in Milan, the next in Venice ;   then set our faces homeward by the Rhine.

" Won't that be a splendid tour ?

" Switzerland and the north of Italy, Milan, and Venice are splendid sights.   Hitherto, as you perhaps have some notion, I have neither had time nor means to travel, and I am anxious to see these places, now that I have a little time.

" My work is getting on well in St. John's ; the congregation is increasing. . . . Tell me specially about your plans for the next season. Are you going to school again, *or coming to Scotland ?* "

No record survives of the tour of the two college friends ; but in the following year it was repeated— as far at least as Geneva, the Rhone Valley, and the Rhine—by the brother and sister.   For, in the autumn of 1867, Elizabeth Whyte arrived in Scotland, and the

" little Yankee girl " found herself in the strange post
of mistress of a Scottish minister's household.   The
week before she came, her brother's diary contains
one of the constantly recurring lists of books to be
purchased ; only on this occasion it is headed by a
new rubric, " Books for drawing-room "—an apart-
ment for which Whyte had never hitherto found any
use.   Even now he seems to have confused its purpose with that of his study, since the list includes
Homer, Plato, and à Kempis, as well as Tennyson.

Elizabeth Whyte soon came to fill a very large
place in her brother's life, for she had a nimble brain
as well as a most affectionate nature.   She not only
helped him by her bright companionship, but did
much work as his secretary ; and it was no small loss
to him when, shortly before he left Glasgow, she left
his roof to become the wife of a college friend of his
own, the Rev. Thomas Macadam, then minister of
Chryston, not far from Glasgow.

By this time the reports which came from John
Whyte, who had now settled in New York, showed
that he was suffering from severe rheumatism, caused
by the privations he had endured in the field and in
prison eight years before.   In the summer and autumn
of 1870 he was busy winding up his affairs as a store-
keeper in New Jersey, and " making calculations to
go to Glasgow as soon as he could get all straitened
up."   But as the winter passed, his infirmities increased ; and the contemplated journey was never
made, though he lived long enough to congratulate
his daughter on her marriage, and his son on his
settlement as colleague to Dr. Candlish.   In April
1871 Whyte wrote to his sister, giving the news of
their father's death, and added :

" I know how much you leant on him : and
how hopeful you were again to see him.   It has
been otherwise appointed.   It is an irreparable
loss to us both, but ' it is the hand of God,'—and
He will not suffer it to be such a loss as to hurt

us if we look to Him in whom the fatherless
findeth mercy. . . . Keep a quiet, awed, trustful
heart.   Let no rebellion or flood of grief come to
hurt you, or to grieve the spirit of meekness and
resignation.   You will be always on my heart
till I see you."

When this letter was sent, a last message was on
its way across the Atlantic, written by John Whyte
ten days before he passed away on 31st March.   Even
at this distant time, and to readers of another generation, it has a singular and poignant interest.   Cicero
in his book on Old Age has represented the elder Cato
as describing that sad inversion of the wonted order
of nature, when a father is called upon to bury the
son who has passed away before him.   There is
pathos here also; but it awakens wonder rather than
sadness, as we read the request of a father for the
prayers of a son who had gone so far beyond him in
the spiritual life.

"NEW YORK,
March 21, 1871.

" MY DEAR SON,—After so long I shall now
write to you a few lines to let you know that my
health is pretty good at present, and in the hope
that you are in good health and strength in
the great position to which you are called and
chosen.   You say in your letter to me that
matters seem to prosper well with you in your
new sphere, and so does your sister.

" I hope that she and her husband are both
well and in good health, and that his congregation
will like him as a pastor.   He tells me that she
is a good helpmeet to him in his gospel services,
and that she is much respected amongst the
people.   I have no doubt that she will be glad
to have a call from you.

·   ·   ·   ·   ·

" I am glad to know that Dr. Candlish is so
kind and thoughtful, and hope that you give him

and the hearers the greatest satisfaction, and are a blessing to them in this world and also in that which is to come—is my prayer, and may you all do as well as I wish you to do. . . . Not to do as I have in this world, but to be up and doing while the day is, for the night cometh when no man can work. Do pray for me to the Heavenly Father, for Christ's sake, to take away my hard and backward heart, and give me a new heart and a new mind, and that He will draw me to look to Him who is the finisher of faith, and may I be led to believe in Christ who laid down His life for mankind. I pray that all our sins may be forgiven, and hope that we may all meet in the Heavenly Temple not made with hands, but eternal in the Hand of God. Pray that all my former sins are forgiven and that I shall hereafter trust in Him, the Saviour of the world. . . . I hope, as your sister has told me often, that you always mention me in your worship, and trust that your prayers will yet be heard and even yet be answered. Do ask your sister and her husband to forgive me and pray for me at the throne of grace, and you, my son, forgive me and pray from the heart that God will forgive me, a poor, unfortunate, ungodly creature. I do hope and trust that all your prayers will be heard and answered in their own time, and God's ways.— Your loving   FATHER."

The thoughts which this letter awakened in Alexander Whyte's heart found expression in a hastily penned note to his sister, in which these words occurred :

" Christ has given us Father, I believe, and we will see him where there are no separations. . . . It is as if Father had spoken to me out of Heaven."

And at the end his thanksgiving burst forth in these broken sentences :

" O my God, I thank thee !

" How good Thou art !   How ungrateful and mistrustful we are !

" My cup runneth over—if I have a lip to taste it aright."

"O my God, I faint day [...]
"Now may Thou self Thou [...] (thou?) afraid and
[...]
"My soul trembleth sore: thee [...]
(?) it night.

CHAPTER IX   CALL TO FREE ST. GEORGE'S—
COLLEAGUESHIP WITH DR. CANDLISH
1870–1873

" Let age approve of youth."—BROWNING.

ALEXANDER WHYTE'S Glasgow ministry, as assistant and colleague in Free St. John's, lasted just four years ; and we have seen that during this time more than one congregation at a distance sought to secure him as its minister.   But Dr. Roxburgh's advice to his junior colleague on these occasions was un-hesitating and definite—" This is not for you."   The spring of 1870, however, brought a call to become Dr. Candlish's colleague in Free St. George's, Edin-burgh, and on this Dr. Roxburgh looked in a different light, saying, " This is what I have been keeping you for, and you must go."   And, as his earlier advice to remain had been followed, so was this indication that the time for parting had come.

Dr. Roxburgh had a long-standing interest in St. George's ; for he had occupied the pulpit of the undivided church as *locum tenens* during the winter of 1833–34, a few months before Candlish was called to the pastorate.   Further, the two veteran ministers were close friends.   Yet it remains a signal instance of foresight and magnanimity that Dr. Roxburgh not only made no attempt to hold back a colleague who had proved so great a strength to his people and himself, but actively forwarded the step by which the names of Alexander Whyte and of Free St. George's were first linked together.   But if his name deserves to be remembered on account of this generous act, that of the first mover in the same transaction from the side of Free St. George's must not go unre-corded.   This was James Craufurd, Lord Ardmillan, who had been an influential elder in Dr. Candlish's congregation for nearly thirty years ; and who in the years that followed constantly encouraged his new minister both by his friendship and counsel and by his rapt attention as a hearer. Lord Ardmillan's duties as a judge had brought him not long before to preside over a Circuit Court in Glasgow, where he stayed with Dr. Harry Rainy. He went with his host to worship in Free St. John's; and it is told that, as the judge and the venerable physician talked over the sermon and the personality of the preacher, the latter said, " I often wonder where that boy gained all his knowledge of the human heart." When Lord Ardmillan returned to Edinburgh, he lost no time in persuading the Kirk-Session and congregation of Free St. George's that he had found in Glasgow the junior colleague of whom they had long been in search.

Dr. Whyte's memories of the call, and of his reluctance to undertake a heavy responsibility in " the fastidious city " of Edinburgh, were more than once expressed in his later years ; and one of his last letters, written less than two months before his death, at a time when Free St. George's was again vacant, contained these sentences :

" This recalls vividly to my mind my situation when the St. George's call came to me. No minister could be in a happier place than I was in St. John's. But the call came to me with such a weight that I felt it impossible to decline it. Dr. Roxburgh, my Senior Colleague in St. John's, told me that I must go to St. George's, and the whole situation was so pressing that I could not take the responsibility of refusing the call. Three or four men—Dr. Wilson of the Barclay, Dr. Laidlaw, and Dr. Dods, had all refused to look at St. George's ; and though I felt myself to be the most unlikely man in the Free Church to occupy such a post successfully, I risked all and went, and I never for a moment regretted my decision. . . ."

This decision was intimated to the waiting congregation in Edinburgh on 23rd June 1870, the call having been unanimously determined upon several weeks before.

Among those who had proved friends to Whyte during his days at the New College were two sisters, members of Free St. George's, Miss Wood and Miss Marion Wood; and he wrote at this time to the former :

" 99 HILL ST. [GLASGOW],
Tuesday.

" MY DEAR MISS WOOD,—I return Miss Cathcart's note with thanks for your consideration. Such things are cumulative, and enable me to *count* on a kind reception among the people. I get kind letters every day from friends up and down the land. I may well thank God for his wonderful ways with me.

" With my kindest regards and gratitude, Yours most truly,   A. WHYTE."

Dr. Candlish's letter of welcome to his newly chosen colleague has not been preserved, but its tenor may be gathered from a letter written on the following day to one of his tried friends in the Kirk-Session, Mr. David Maclagan. It is dated from Buxton, where Dr. Candlish had gone after a serious illness :

" The wire flashed to me yesterday about four o'clock most excellent news. . . . It set me up at once. . . . Now, I thank God, all is so far well. For the congregation, I cannot doubt that a signal spiritual good has been got, if only they receive it humbly, meekly, prayerfully, believingly. And with me, His poor, unworthy, unfaithful and unprofitable servant, how graciously has the Lord dealt ! I can now look forward to the closing years, if years be granted, of my earthly service and ministry, with some good hope of their being not burdensome to me, nor altogether useless to my beloved flock. . . .

" I have written to Mr. Whyte, taking him to my heart. And I have told him that I don't think he should be inducted till the beginning of October, when the congregation is decently gathered, and the Communion on the 30th is drawing near. I . . . have told him my reasons for letting him know all this immediately —namely, first, that he may not feel himself hurried in parting with my old and dear friend, Dr. Roxburgh, with whom I deeply sympathise ; and, secondly, that he may have as long an interval as possible between his two fields of labour. I have asked him, also, to pay us a visit here in July, when we can fully talk over the affairs of the congregation, and begin, at least, to mature plans for our winter campaign. May the Lord grant His blessing in connection with all that we may jointly propose and do ! "

During this summer of 1870, then, the future minister of Free St. George's was preparing in mind and heart to enter on the sphere of work to which he gave his strength, ceaselessly and unreservedly, for forty-seven years. For part of the time he was also preparing in body, by long walks round Braemar, where one of his chief companions was a brilliant scholar who had been appointed at the unusually early age of twenty-four to a chair in the Free Church College at Aberdeen. But of William Robertson Smith we shall hear more in the sequel.

At this point it is not unfitting to take a backward glance over the history of the congregation to which Whyte had now been called to minister. Two generations before, during the later years of the Napoleonic wars, the need had been felt for fuller religious provision for the dwellers in the New Town of Edinburgh, then fast extending to the north and west of the Old Town. Parliamentary sanction was obtained for the formation of a new parish ; and in June 1814 St. George's Church, whose classical façade and noble dome were designed by Robert Reid, was dedicated for divine service.   Dr. Andrew Thomson was inducted as its first minister—a man of dignity and eloquence, and a whole-hearted supporter of the evangelical party which was then becoming strong in the Church of Scotland.   In a controversial age, he was known for his unsparing use of great polemical gifts ; but a more attractive feature of his character was his talent as a musician, to which the tune, " St. George's, Edinburgh," remains as a witness.   Under Dr. Thomson, and still more under the Rev. Robert Smith Candlish, who became its minister as a young man of twenty-eight in 1834, the congregation steadily grew in numbers and influence.[1]

In 1843 St. George's was rent in twain by the Disruption, and seven elders and a large number of members followed their minister into the Free Church. For some months the congregation of Free St. George's worshipped in a temporary building, the " Brick Church " in Castle Terrace, and in January 1845 they found a home, which lasted for nearly a quarter of a century, in a newly erected church in Lothian Road. It was here that Whyte and many other New College students of his time used to worship, and here that the chief part of Dr. Candlish's work as a preacher was done.   But the Lothian Road church was only one degree more permanent than the " Brick Church " had been, and ultimately its site was required for an extension of the Caledonian Railway.   Thus the congregation found its final abode in the new " Free St. George's " in Shandwick Place, which was opened for worship by Dr. Candlish on 24th October 1869, just a year before Dr. Whyte's induction.

The later 'sixties had, indeed, been a time of

[1] This is indicated by the fact that within this period eleven judges of the Court of Session were elders or regular worshippers in St. George's, and that Dr. Chalmers was for a time a member of the Session.   St. George's had three ministers before the Disruption, and Free St. George's three others during the remainder of the nineteenth century.   It is somewhat remarkable that of the six, not one was over thirty-five years of age at the time of his induction, and three were under thirty.   It was a congregation first built up, and then reinforced, by a succession of young ministers.

transition and anxiety for the congregation in more than one sense. The brief colleagueship of the Rev. J. Oswald Dykes, afterwards Principal of Westminster College, Cambridge, had closed with the breakdown of his health more than five years before. Dr. Candlish himself had become prematurely old under the burden of his labours as preacher, author, and church-leader, and in later years as Principal of the New College ; and the letter just quoted expresses his joy in the prospect of sharing his burden with one of Whyte's vigour of body and spirit. Yet the warmth with which he took the younger man " to his heart " sprang less from weariness or fear for the future of his congregation than from the generosity of a singularly ardent nature.

Dr. Candlish's writings now rest undisturbed on their shelves ; yet his intellect, and his whole personality, profoundly impressed many of the strongest characters in the Scotland of his day. His portrait is striking, largely because of the contrast between the width and height of forehead and the smaller scale of the other features, while there is more than a suggestion of impetuosity in the sensitive mouth. The union of intellectual power with moral and emotional intensity which this remarkable face indicates is confirmed by the records of his life. It has been said that there was something *daimonic* in his personality, as the restless spirit drove the fragile frame ever forward. It was Principal Rainy's judgment that " he, above all others, represented the *vis viva* of the Free Church, and was the means of awaking and reinforcing it ; he, above any other, stood connected with its impulse, its activity, its energy." [1]

In theology Dr. Candlish was a son of his time ; yet in certain respects he showed a courage and a width of outlook foreign to many of his closest associates. Thus, in addressing the students of New College regarding those problems of biblical criticism

[1] Quoted, from a sermon preached after Candlish's death, by David Maclagan, *History of Free St George's* (1876), p. 189. Cf. the vivid descriptions in the *Memoir of W. G. Elmslie*, pp. 13, 17.

which were then becoming acute, he said boldly : " Any inclination to oppose or limit free inquiry, or free speculation, in any line fairly open to human research, should be resisted. Any dread — any jealousy or resentment of results should be repudiated." As regards doctrine, his counsel was summed up in the words : " Make it palpably plain that it is salvation in Christ, not salvation through Christ, that you preach." [1] The distinction may at first seem over-subtle ; but its object is to make clear that a personal relation, and not an external theory of the Atonement, lies at the heart of Christian experience. In this thought, as in their attitude to biblical inquiry and their essentially personal conception of the preacher's office, the two colleagues in Free St. George's were wholly at one.

Many old tales might be retold to illustrate the union in Dr. Candlish of various qualities not often found together. He was irascible and warm-hearted ; logical and impulsive ; a wise leader of men and singularly disinterested and unworldly where his own interests were concerned ; unsparing of his own strength and careful of the health of others. Thus this exponent of a highly elaborated theology was beloved by children, and provided a gymnasium for the New College students ; and all Dr. Whyte's eulogies of his kindness of heart were compatible, with the memory—recalled with his quiet smile—" It wasn't safe to speak to my colleague in the vestry before his sermon ! " Dr. Whyte's fullest tribute to his master, both as colleague and as preacher, was given in his own Inaugural Address in the New College :

" What a colleague Dr. Candlish was ! How Dr. Candlish thought for me ! How he planned for my comfort ! How he spared me too much work ! How he sent me off on frequent little

[1] Both passages belong to the session of 1871–72. See *The Gospel of Forgiveness*, Appendix, pp. 475, 460, and cf. the description of the preacher's work as an " ambassador of Christ " : " The transaction is personal throughout ; doubly personal ; personal in both its stages " (p. 464).

holidays ! And how we dined together and talked together, and how full of a high good humour and even rich fun he could be on occasion ! "

His tribute to Dr. Candlish goes on to speak of his skill in the exposition of Scripture and of his way of handling his text :

" He would set himself to unwind and un-weave its texture, filament by filament, and fibre by fibre, with the most minute analysis and the most practised exegetical skill. And then how he would address himself to the reweaving of it all again, and that into a rich web of evangelical doctrine. After which he would, as it were, shape and fashion out of it so many gospel garments wherewith to clothe and adorn his listening and believing people, till you can have no idea what a favoured and what a delighted and what an evangelised congregation Dr. Candlish had in the St. George's of those great days. And till men like Lord Cowan, and Lord Moncreiff, and Lord Ardmillan, and Murray Dunlop, and Sheriff Spiers, and Sheriff Jameson, and Dr. Bell, and David Maclagan, and Samuel Raleigh, and John M'Candlish, and scores of such-like Christian gentlemen, would all frankly tell you that they owed their own souls to Dr. Candlish's pulpit. And I did not wonder to hear them saying that, for I never heard such soaring, such winning, and such heart-consoling preaching as the third Principal of the New College preached to his privileged people." [1]

Beside this description of Dr. Candlish's preaching we may place a single sentence in which Dr. Taylor Innes said that, in prayer, he " made himself the mere mouthpiece, mind, and heart of that great multitude, and the overpowering burden became to him such a burden as wings are to an eagle."

[1] *Former Principals*, pp. 30–34.

Dr. Whyte's ministry in Free St. George's had its beginning on 9th October 1870, when Dr. Roxburgh preached in the morning, and he himself in the afternoon. He followed the example of Newman at the opening and the close of his ministry in St. Mary's, Oxford, in the choice of his subject—" Man goeth forth unto his work and to his labour until the evening "—a text which has helped to define the major divisions of this *Life*. Dr. George Steven has preserved this memory of the sermon, and of Whyte's influence as a preacher to young men in the early years of his Edinburgh ministry :

" I can see him, a young man, with long yellow hair which he flung back with his hand from time to time. His voice came to my ear as the sound of the North Sea breaking on the cliffs near my native place—a sound and memory that was always with me when I heard him preach. . . . We students came to know Dr. Whyte's preaching very well, and it was a strength and guidance to us at all times. We also came to know how heavily he leaned upon Newman, although it was always a Newman evangelised."

Years after, Dr. Whyte told this friend that, of many poor sermons which he had preached in Free St. George's, he looked on this opening sermon of his ministry there as the poorest. But in spite of this criticism the sermon has this interest even now, that it expresses with great clearness the purpose and ideal which he had in view when he first entered the pulpit where so great a part of his life-work was accomplished :

" Whatever I am enabled to bring here of strength or endowment or attainment or experience, be they great or small, by God's continued and increased grace, I shall consecrate myself to the instant pursuit of the one work of saving myself and them that hear me."

But the ministries of consolation and instruction also form a great part of the preacher's office, and the latter is described in these words :

" To interest the young in the Church, and in good men, and in good books, and in good works. . . . To teach you all how to read and use your Bibles wisely and with profit — to read with understanding, and to read often, the deepest parts of them. To press continually the sovereign and uncompromising place of prayer in the Christian life, and in a word to set Christ in His fullness, in His Person, and work, and rule—continually before you."

So did he conceive of the preacher's office.

The story of how he came to estimate the place occupied by pastoral work in a complete ministry was told some twenty years later in a sermon on Watchful, the shepherd on the Delectable Mountains. First he recounted an incident, which he sometimes referred to in his familiar talk, regarding the last hours of a well-known minister of those days, Dr. Fairbairn of Newhaven.

" Calling back to his bedside a young minister who had come to see him, the dying man said, ' Prepare for the pulpit ; above everything else you do, prepare for the pulpit. Let me again repeat it, should it at any time stand with you between visiting a deathbed and preparing for the pulpit, prepare for the pulpit.' I was immensely impressed with that dying injunction when it was repeated to me, but I have lived—I do not say to put my preparation for the pulpit, such as it is, second to my more pastoral work in my week's thoughts, but—to put my visiting in the very front rank and beside my pulpit. ' We were never accustomed to much visiting,' said my elders to me in their solicitude for their young minister when he was first left alone with this whole charge ; ' only appear in your own pulpit twice on Sabbath : keep as much at home as possible : we were never used to much visiting, and we do not look for it.' Well, that was most kindly intended ; but it was much more kind than wise. For I have lived to learn that no congregation will continue to prosper, or, if other more consolidated and less exacting congregations, at any rate not this congregation, without constant pastoral attention. And remember, I do not complain of that. Far, far from that. For I am as sure as I am of anything connected with a minister's life, that a minister's own soul will prosper largely in the measure that the souls of his people prosper through his pastoral work." [1]

Another counsel, given by the considerate elders of Free St. George's to their young minister, was this : " Take long holidays, but be regularly in your own pulpit when you are at home." They not only gave the advice but made it easy for him to follow it, and so helped to determine the use of his time during his whole ministry. From the very first, the strain of the ministry in St. George's was so great that generous intervals were needed, both for bodily recuperation and to give time for reading in preparation for the coming winter's work in pulpit and class ; for Dr. Candlish's health did not allow him to take as active a part as he would have wished in the work of the congregation. This was especially true of the winter of 1871–72, when prolonged illness withdrew him from all regular work and threw the whole burden upon the shoulders of his colleague. It was a time of great pressure for Whyte, and also of testing for the congregation, who lost six leading elders by death in less than a year.

Whyte's summer holiday in 1871 began and ended with quiet days—in the manse at Hopeman with his friends, Mr. and Mrs. Cassie, and at Chryston with the

---

[1] *Bunyan Characters*, i. 263. Cf. the passages which follow on Paul's pastoral visiting in Ephesus, and on a minister's use of his young communicants' roll.

Macadams. The latter was a true home to him during
these years, and the occasions were many on which
he lectured or preached there. At Hopeman he was
deep in a characteristic combination of authors,
Dante, and John Owen, whom he afterwards called
" the most massive of the Puritans." A year later
their place was taken by Herbert Spencer and
the American Calvinist, Hodge—an equally strange
pair of yoke-fellows ; and a year later still Dante
and Spencer were associated. The first two summers
introduced him to two of the holiday-grounds which
he loved most in later years, Lochalsh and Atholl.
In 1871 he went from Strome Ferry by Balmacara
to Glenelg, where Dr. Johnson passed so troubled a
night, and after three hours in bed left for Skye in
a small boat at 3.15 a.m. The whole west and north
of the island, from Loch Coruisk by Sligachan and
Loch Bracadale to the Quiraing, were covered by gig
or boat or on foot during the following days. A year
later, on his way south after a walking-tour with
Cassie in Ross-shire, he stopped at Blair-Atholl,
spending one day in exploring Glen Tilt and another
in climbing Ben-y-Gloe—" five hours up and down
and a splendid view," is the record in the diary. An
Edinburgh entry some months later shows the range
of his reading: " Rested after visiting, and read
Rabelais."

A short " supplementary holiday " in the early
autumn of 1872 was spent in rooms at Lochearnhead
Schoolhouse, with A. E. Scougal as companion. Dr.
Scougal, like Alexander Barrie, was one of the first
inspectors appointed under the Education Act of
1870 ; and he became in later years greatly honoured
for his religious work, as well as for his educational
services as Chief Inspector for Schools in Scotland.
On several occasions the three friends fished together
in Loch Earn and the lochs and burns around, and
there is a legend in the Whyte family that once for
three successive days they brought in nine dozen each.
On this visit Dr. Whyte records the more modest
basket of four dozen, caught one day at the Braes of

Balquhidder ; but he had the encouragement of the following charming letter from his senior colleague :

"EDINBURGH, *September* 28, 1872.

"MY DEAR PISCATOR,—It liketh me well to find by palpable, edible proof that thy right hand hath not lost its cunning, nor thy heart its loving loyalty in the gentle craft.   The fish have proved right savoury and delicious. *Perge Puer!* Go on and prosper.   And if thou usest vermicular or other living and sentient bait, see that thou dealest tenderly with whatever animal thou impalest on thy hook, and remember the counsel of thy great master in the art, make the process easy and pleasant for the creature thou usest for thy sport and handle him as though thou lovest him.

"We got home well and safely yesterday afternoon and are none the worse of our journey and our exposure to the very sad weather we have had to encounter during the past week. I hope you won't spoil your holiday by working. Rather get more fish.   I trust the weather will improve for you.   Write me a line, but don't let me see you till the 13th October.—Yours very truly,   ROBT. S. CANDLISH."

In the year that followed the writing of this letter, it is not too much to say that Alexander Whyte's history merges in that of his revered colleague.   All in Free St. George's, and Whyte most of all, were watching week by week the fluctuations in his bodily strength.   For some months his energy returned in part, and he was able once more to preach once each Sunday, his sermons being marked more than ever before by the pleading tenderness of their appeal. But with the spring two heavy blows fell upon the old man.   First, his old comrade in the leadership of the Free Church, Dr. Thomas Guthrie, passed away, and he nerved himself for the great effort of preaching the funeral sermon, which closed with a moving apostrophe : " Friend and Brother ! Comrade

in the fight ! Companion in tribulation !—Farewell !
But not for ever. May my soul, when my hour comes,
be with thine ! " [1]

An even greater trial soon followed. During the
period after the Disruption, the Free Church had
steadily drawn towards the United Presbyterian
Church, the heir of the seceding tradition described in
the Introductory Chapter. For ten years negotiations
for union were carried on, and the hope nearest
Dr. Candlish's heart was that he might have a share
in bringing them to fruition. But there was a strong
" constitutional " minority in the Free Church, who
were unwilling to depart from the theoretic advocacy
of church-establishment which was maintained at the
Disruption,[2] or to move towards the " voluntary "
position of the sister church. Slowly it became
apparent that to press the movement for union at this
stage—it was accomplished twenty-seven years later
—would mean division and disaster for the Free
Church. A crisis was reached in the Assembly of
1873. Dr. Candlish spoke for the last time, and
returned home much exhausted ; but he was followed
to his house in Melville Street by several trusted
friends, who felt that an indefinite postponement of
the Union was the only way of avoiding a fresh disruption.[3] Dr. Whyte used to describe the scene in
after years—the sense of sorrow in all hearts, and the
passion of disappointment in Dr. Candlish's gesture
as he threw down the paper after he had signed the
fatal amendment, for he felt that he was " signing
away the one hope of his life." He was only twice
able to preach in Free St. George's thereafter.

Another incident during the last months of Dr.
Candlish's ministry throws light on the Free Church of
the day from another angle, that of congregational
worship. The Scottish Church has always cherished
the custom of singing the psalms in metre ; and for

[1] Maclagan, *St. George's, Edinburgh*, p. 174.
[2] Expressed in the statement of Chalmers, " We quit a vitiated
Establishment, but should rejoice in returning to a pure one."
[3] Cf. P. Carnegie Simpson, *Life of Principal Rainy*, i. 196 f.

long the seventeenth-century version of Rous and others was the only form of praise allowed in her services. Gradually the collection of Scripture Paraphrases, compiled largely from the works of Watts and Doddridge, began to win a place beside it ; but it was only after much controversy in the years following 1870 that the use of a general hymnal was authorised in the Free Church. Dr. Candlish was personally in favour of the introduction of hymns, and the Session unanimously supported him. But the use of the new hymn-book was postponed by his own desire, until he himself was able to give out the first hymn in Free St. George's, for he had long wished that it should be " Rock of Ages." One of his most devoted elders said after his death that the most impressive of all his memories of Dr. Candlish was the intense solemnity of his reading of Toplady's famous hymn at this service.

As the autumn of 1873 passed into winter, Dr. Candlish became much more gravely ill. A letter from Whyte to Miss Wood spoke anxiously of him, and told how the writer dreaded the coming months ; and during part of October a daily meeting was held in the church for prayer on Dr. Candlish's behalf. Ten days before the end, which came on Sunday, the 19th, Whyte was summoned back from a short holiday at Chryston by a telegram from Dr. Rainy, who shared to the full the burden of these days. Whyte was often at his colleague's side during the week that followed, and sometimes in after years repeated his sayings, such as, " Oh, man ! I wish I had learned all the psalms by heart ! " Dr. Whyte would tell this to his children to drive home the importance of imprinting the psalms and other great religious utterances on the memory.

The last scene must be described in Dr. Whyte's own words :

" The dying Principal sent for me to bid me farewell, and I found Dr. Rainy already at Dr.

Candlish's bedside. I had no sooner entered the room than the dying man put out his hand to me and said : ' Good-bye. I had hoped to be spared to help you a little longer '—he was always my helper, the humble soul—' but it is not to be. Good-bye.' And then he motioned to Dr. Rainy to kneel down at his bedside, when he threw his withered arms around Rainy's neck and kissed him and said : ' I leave the congregation to Whyte and I leave the New College and the Assembly to you.' It was a scene never to be forgotten. And it was a dedication and a sanctification to have seen it and shared in it." [1]

When Dr. Whyte was Moderator of the Free Church, he told this story in a great gathering of Highland ministers, and then, turning to Dr. Rainy who sat beside him, and placing his hand on his shoulder, he added :

" Man, there was only one thing I ever envied ye for, Principal, and that was the kiss that Candlish gave you on his death-bed. . . . But I doubt not he had often kissed me in his heart ; and I cannot pass from this without saying that it is only born gentlemen and gentlemen born again who could have treated a poor nameless youth as Candlish treated me."

[1] *Former Principals*, p. 42 f.

"Where there is no vision, the people perish."—PROVERBS.

FROM the end of October in this year of 1873 Dr. Whyte was sole minister of Free St. George's. More than twenty-two years passed before he in his turn obtained a colleague ; and during the greater part of this time he had no regular assistant, though for several years the Rev. J. Grant Mackintosh, a retired minister, gave valuable help in pastoral work. We have already seen that, during the three preceding years, the part taken by Dr. Candlish in the work of the colleagueship had been only intermittent ; yet his presence and interest were in themselves a great moral reinforcement. Now, there was no other to share the responsibility. But Whyte's powers were already mature and he had never feared responsibility : indeed it may well be that the sole responsibility for Free St. George's drew out and developed these powers. Such, at least, was the opinion of one observer, who wrote some years after :

" How different Whyte was in his colleague days ! I remember him, massive, powerful, and conscience-striking as now, holding your intellect, winning your reverence. But what a difference ! *Then* he was like a half-trained lion going along in harness with another lion— older and mightier, and thoroughly trained— giving a lurch, shaking his shoulders, and raxing out the reins and other harness occasionally, as if there was something more in him, but then relapsing again into the becoming, eighteen-

forty-three [1] regulation-stride, to keep step with
the old lion; but never, almost never at least,
fairly breaking out and loose, and going all-fours
into the air, harness and chariot along with
him, in the way that some biblical animals,
Ezekiel's and John's, for example, are morally
bound to do."

And now, for the second time, Whyte felt the
breath of a great religious quickening at the very
moment when he was called to make a fresh beginning
in his own career.   In the month after Dr. Candlish
died, two American evangelists, then quite unknown
in Scotland, arrived to conduct a mission in Edinburgh.
But soon the names of D. L. Moody and Ira D. Sankey
were on all lips.   They had been invited to Edinburgh by the Rev. John Kelman of Leith (whose son
became Dr. Whyte's colleague a generation later)
and by the Rev. James Hood Wilson of the Barclay
Church ; and by the end of the year leaders of all the
churches, including Professors Cairns, Charteris, and
Rainy, had rallied to their support, and a deep impression was being made upon the life of the city, more
especially upon its young men.   Among the younger
ministers who took the most whole-hearted part in
the mission was Alexander Whyte ; for there was
much to attract him in its intensity, and in the
prayerfulness and the ethical temper which have been
named as its chief features.[2]

It is needless to describe the revival of 1874
with the same fulness as that of 1859.   It lies
nearer to our own time, and it is still a living
memory with many ; nor did it find Whyte's character
at the same plastic stage as the earlier movement.
In externals there were some resemblances amid
obvious differences.   Both were led by laymen, but
loyally supported by ministers.   Both drew largely

[1] 1843—the date of the Disruption and the birth year of the Free
Church.
[2] George Adam Smith, *The Life of Henry Drummond*, p. 58 ; cf. the
whole chapter.

upon the inspiration of song, and enlarged the place of praise in Scottish religion. But, while the earlier movement was carried on largely in the open air and powerfully affected the people of the country, the later gained its chief triumphs in the towns and cities. Yet the heart and the aim of the two movements were alike ; and Whyte gladly bore his share in the work which went on in Edinburgh during the winter of 1873–74. During the earlier part of February, an intensive campaign, as it would now be called, was carried on to follow up the work of Moody and Sankey ; and in this Whyte was engaged night by night with ministers like Dr. Hood Wilson and laymen like Professor Simpson. It was said of his addresses in the Free Assembly Hall during this winter that they represented the highest level of evangelical preaching, " awakening, arresting, interesting, scintillating with imaginative insight." The spiritual power which had thrilled the country folk of Huntly and Strathdon twelve years before was now fully felt in Edinburgh—as it was always felt when Whyte spoke in the tense and expectant atmosphere of such a time of quickening.

These fresh winds of the Spirit did much to fan the flame of enthusiasm in Free St. George's, where the result was seen in the unwontedly large Young Communicants' Classes of the year 1874. Since he first came to the church Whyte had sought to revitalise the congregational prayer - meeting, which had become somewhat half-hearted : as he told a friend at the very end of his ministry—" I put a lot of steam into it." After 1874 there was no further difficulty. The attendance on Tuesday evening became so great that the prayer-meeting adjourned from the hall of the church to the church itself. One of its frequenters tells how he came to Edinburgh, a shy lad from Ross-shire, and hesitated to press into the crowded church on Sunday, but found his weekly feast at this evening gathering. So warm did his attachment become that he and two other young men, of very different social stations, used to meet daily in the unfrequented churchyard below St. John's Episcopal Church to pray for their minister and his work. In the prayer-meeting Whyte's freshness in exposition and directness in appeal to the conscience and the will were set free from the trammels of manuscript, as he spoke from the heart on the Book of Job or on Bunyan's *Holy War*.

Of those in Scotland whose gifts were first drawn out by Mr. Moody by far the most notable was Henry Drummond, then in his twenty-third year. His biographer tells how for nearly two years he led missions and addressed great audiences in many parts of Great Britain and Ireland, and, after all this, quietly returned to Edinburgh in the autumn of 1875 to complete his theological course at the New College. But he continued to carry on the work in which he had shown such singular power by organising a series of meetings for young men on Sunday evenings in the unconventional surroundings of the "Gaiety Theatre." [1] Most of the speakers were Drummond's friends and contemporaries, but a few senior men were asked to take part. Among them was Whyte, who once spoke from the words, "The blood of Jesus Christ His Son cleanseth us from all sin." He already knew the value of an unexpected or even a startling opening, and the first words of the address were these : "There's no such text as this in the Bible—if you take it alone." He then showed the absolute dependence of these words on the condition which precedes them—"if we walk in the light"—and went on to emphasise the significance of the present tense "cleanseth," as referring to a process, not accomplished once only, but ever needing to be renewed. [2]

Such echoes from the early days of Whyte's Edinburgh ministry, as well as the account given in

[1] This small and unaristocratic place of entertainment, near the foot of Chambers Street, was afterwards re-christened the "Operetta House," and became familiar to generations of students from 1898 onwards as the scene of Dr. Kelman's meetings.

[2] From recollections communicated by Sheriff Scott Moncrieff penney.

Chapter VII. of his work in Glasgow, make it possible
to form an impression of certain characteristics of
his preaching during this period. While it appealed
to the men and women, experienced in life and in the
things of the Spirit, whom Candlish had gathered
round him, yet more especially he was known as a
young man's preacher. He was as faithful as ever
to the evangelical standpoint, but he showed at the
same time an ethical directness and an absorbing love
of good literature which were not universal in the
evangelical school—or perhaps in any other religious
school. The unflinching moral appeal in his teaching
was its outstanding mark. The same man who, as a
student, had been ready to " talk doctrine for a year
on end," now showed how powerfully he could bring
doctrine to bear on the sternest facts of life. His
teaching was strong, not only in the analysis of the
hidden sins of the heart, such as pride and envy, but
in its perpetual summons to work while the day lasts.
In this respect he enjoined no more than he habitually
practised. As Professor Robert Mackintosh has said :
" Whyte did nothing easily. He put every ounce of
his exceptional strength into each effort as it had to
be made. . . . He lived in the light of the eternities,
and struck home habitually to the deep places of the
conscience."

The forthrightness which is remembered as a
characteristic of Whyte's talk in those early days was
even more marked in his preaching. He had little
patience with the somewhat timid proprieties of
Victorian Edinburgh ; and, as he found elements
of shame in the life of the city which called for
attack and exposure, he set himself fearlessly to
expose and attack them. Even among the students
of the 'seventies there were some who felt that he
wielded the prophet's scourge too openly and
relentlessly ; and one such student has said that he
knew young men who were "shaken to the foundations of their being " by some of Whyte's addresses
on personal morality. Especially when he was
addressing gatherings of men, he used a directness of

speech very rare at that time ; and one of the most arresting of his appeals was conveyed in the question —" Young man, what will you think of this on your wedding morning ? "

In his own pulpit also, Whyte could speak with arresting power. Once, as he finished reading the grim passage in Proverbs regarding the ruin wrought by the " strange woman," his hearers caught their breath as his voice rang out,—" Stand up, young man, and say Amen to that ! " On another occasion Mr. Benjamin Bell, a well-known surgeon, who had been for many years an elder in Free St. George's, wrote thus to his minister :

> " I cannot help telling you how much I appreciated your discourse this forenoon on the seventh commandment. It was very *masterly*, and I know that it must have been the outcome of much prayer and consideration. . . . I write this, notwithstanding your warning this afternoon against flattery, to let you know what one, who does not stand alone, thought of it."

It must not be thought that these two appeals— the summons to work and the summons to purity— formed the only content of Whyte's preaching at this period. Now as always, other elements were present, of which some account will be given later ; but these qualities unquestionably made a profound impression on the young men who heard him, both within and without his congregation. Nor can it be forgotten that in his early days he had gained a knowledge of temptations from which many of those who pass into the ministry are guarded by the security of well-ordered homes. The very memory of the shadow which had rested upon his own home helped without doubt to lend directness to his words on moral issues, as it not less surely helped to impart the sympathy and understanding which he showed, throughout his ministry, towards those who came to him in perplexity or in remorse.

Whyte's early ministry showed its practical force in other ways also ; for the efforts of the congregation and its minister were never confined to the work carried on within its own borders. The " Sustentation Fund," organised through the foresight and wide sympathy of Dr. Chalmers for the support of the ministry of the Free Church throughout Scotland, had all along proved an efficient instrument in drawing out the help of the wealthier congregations towards their weaker fellows, and Free St. George's had all along taken the lead in its support. The root idea of this Fund was, and still is, the maintenance of a standard income (known as the " equal dividend ") for ministers in full charge. No congregation was allowed to pay a " supplement " to its minister until its contribution reached this standard ; and it was impressed on the wealthier congregations that they must look on it as a point of honour to support their weaker brethren. At the beginning of Whyte's ministry the congregation's yearly contribution to the Fund was somewhat over £3400 ; but eight years later, in spite of depression caused by the failure of the City of Glasgow Bank, it exceeded £5000, and this figure was maintained for over ten years. This was equivalent to the support of some thirty ministers in small charges. No man would have dismissed any mere statistical or financial criterion of a Christian ministry more resolutely than Whyte ; yet it is worth noting as a by-product of his work and teaching that his people showed so practical a concern for the well-being of others.[1]

They continued also to give generous backing to the Home Mission in Fountainbridge, and here their minister gave them a strong and consistent lead. Few Communion seasons came round when he was not present at one of the services there, and much of his time was given to supervising and encouraging

[1] Whyte also did his share of work at a distance, making at least one round of country presbyteries to arouse interest in the Sustentation Fund. It was a matter of justifiable pride that it could be said at a later date that less than one-third of the income of Free St. George's was applied to congregational purposes.

those who were engaged in building up a new congregation in that district.

Another most distinctive aspect of Whyte's ministry during these years undoubtedly was its outlook on religious education. This showed itself in three distinct spheres. First there was his immediate work among the young people of his own congregation, in his Classes and in the Young Men's Fellowship Meeting. Next came his lectures on Dante and other subjects, with their wider appeal. Finally he sought to bring new life into the educational work of the Free Church as a whole through the " Welfare of Youth " scheme.

1. From the day on which Whyte delivered his first sermon in Free St. George's, he entered into the labours of Dr. Candlish and found a great congregation awaiting him at the morning service ; but in his Bible Classes the early 'seventies were the day of small things. As I write, I have before me a small notebook, bound in faded red leather, which bears the same relation to the large manuscript volumes familiar to the members of Dr. Whyte's Class in later years as the classes of 1871 did to those of a generation later. Yet the small pocket volume has its own distinction, as the seed from which the great tree grew, which will be described in Chapter XVII. It bears the date November 1870, when it served both as the roll-book and lecturer's manuscript for the Young Women's Class, which started with thirty-five pioneer members, round whom twenty more gathered in the following weeks. The time of meeting was Wednesday evening (afterwards altered to four o'clock on Wednesday afternoon) ; and from the first, the class for Young Women was distinct from that for Young Men, which met after the second service on Sunday, although the subjects studied were in their main outlines the same.[1]

[1] The substitution, half-way through Dr. Whyte's ministry, of an evening for an afternoon service carried with it the alteration of the hour of the Young Men's class to 8.15 p.m. In the earlier period he remained in the vestry during the short interval between the two services.

In these first years, the time of the class was divided between the Shorter Catechism and a course on the Prophets and Kings of the Old Testament, in which the life of David was fully treated. That portion of the notebook of 1870 which deals with the Catechism contains not a few of the quotations and some of the comments and questions which Dr. Whyte built into his closely packed *Commentary* twelve years later. The questions, in particular, already formed an integral part of his method. At the close of each meeting he dictated three or four questions, to form the basis of thought and inquiry during the week which followed. Often these turned on the derivation or interpretation of words, for he never ceased to impress on the men and women attending his classes, as he had upon the school children of Airlie, that it is only through the exact and scrupulous use of words that we can attain to the accurate understanding of things and ideas. It is characteristic that the first of the thousands of questions which he thus dictated in Free St. George's dealt with a *word*, which occurs in the famous definition of " Man's chief end " : " What is the meaning of ' glorify ' ?—put it down in your own words." [1] On a later page we find him deriving and distinguishing *Religion, Righteousness, Holiness, Piety, Godliness, Spirituality, Saintliness.* Towards the end of the winter, he broke off his measured progress through the Catechism in order to take up its teaching on the Sacraments, for the sake of those who were preparing to join the Church as young communicants.

By the year 1874 the study of the Shorter Catechism in the classes had been completed, and the first portion of each hour was now given to a general survey of the Bible, extending over several sessions, while the later part was assigned to a more detailed study of a particular book. Such was the plan, but the lecturer's interest in his wider theme often made

---

[1] This question, elaborated, is the second on Answer 1 in his *Shorter Catechism*. While the classes remained small, Whyte encouraged members to submit written answers.

the former encroach far into the time assigned to the latter. In the winter of 1874–75 the books chosen for special study were the Epistles to the Galatians and the Hebrews; and the general survey had advanced as far as Isaiah.

Two years earlier Matthew Arnold had brought out in Macmillan's series of shilling primers, to which so many of the most distinguished English writers of the time contributed, a little book entitled *The Great Prophecy of Israel's Restoration*, and Whyte proceeded to recommend it to his class. This primer was an annotated reprint of the last twenty-seven chapters of the Book of Isaiah, in the language of the authorised version, with only a few alterations at points where that version is misleading or obscure. In the preface Matthew Arnold explained his object—to enable English readers to understand this prophecy as a whole, in the sense in which the *Agamemnon* or the Sixth Book of the *Iliad* is a whole, since " by virtue of the original it is a monument of the Hebrew genius at its best, and by virtue of the translation it is a monument of the English language at its best." Arnold went on to avow his own acceptance of what would now be recognised as conclusions of a moderate criticism, *i.e.*, that this portion of the Book of Isaiah is by a different author from the earlier chapters, that it dates from the time of Cyrus' deliverance of the Jews from exile, and that the fifty-third chapter has a collective as well as an individual reference. But he did not argue these positions at length, nor seek to impose them on the reader. His object was literary and religious, not critical.

Whyte's use of this book caused much protest among the more conservative of his congregation. The views referred to were not unfamiliar to the younger ministers of the day, but appeared new and startling to many of their people; nor did Matthew Arnold's general religious outlook commend his detailed conclusions regarding the Old Testament. The mere fact that he dwelt so eagerly on the literary supremacy of the English Bible was almost looked upon as undermining its sacred character ; and here at least Whyte fell under the same condemnation. The outcry seems in his case to have passed without serious consequence ; but at least it was a premonitory breeze, heralding the gale of " the Robertson Smith case," which broke over the Free Church two years later and put Whyte's courage to a most searching test.

In the years which are covered by this chapter, and for some time after, Whyte found further scope for his zeal on behalf of religious education in the Young Men's Fellowship Meeting which took place before the Sunday morning service in Free St. George's. He not only gave the Opening Address at this meeting year by year, but himself prepared its syllabus. Under his guidance, nothing was allowed to be desultory or to depend on the chance inspiration of the moment ; for these outlines of study show the same thoroughness as his preparation for his own classes, and are built up on the same plan. On alternate Sundays the subject was taken from the Shorter Catechism or the Westminster Confession, the intervening days being occupied by the consecutive study of a period of Biblical history. For each meeting Whyte supplied one or more quotations, or a note indicating the literature which he considered most helpful for the understanding of the morning's subject ; and two or three of these programmes, which were always in print by the beginning of the winter, bore the characteristic announcement that the minister's library would be open to those to whom the preparation of papers had been assigned. It was not Whyte's fault if that preparation was ever hurried or incomplete.

Already during these years Whyte's orders to his bookseller, of which more will be heard at a later stage, were on a prodigal scale. And not merely for the furnishing of his own growing library ; for he was constantly supplying the bookshelves of others. Hodge's *Systematic Theology* found its way into not a few Free Church manses at his expense, but less forbidding authors were provided for other readers. At this time the " Golden Treasury " Series proved a source of ever widening delight to those who loved literature, and Whyte gave many volumes to his younger friends, especially those containing the poems of Wordsworth and of Matthew Arnold. Among religious books his favourite gift was a volume of Newman's Selected Sermons or his University Sermons ; and here, as in the case of Matthew Arnold's *Isaiah*, Whyte's breadth of view brought him into occasional collision with those whose religious sympathies were more restricted than his own. On one occasion he gave a young friend a volume of Newman, with the words inscribed, " The finest of the wheat "—under which one of his more severely orthodox elders subsequently wrote, " The worst of the chaff ! "

Nor was it only the younger members of his congregation who found in Whyte a guide into the paths of good literature. A series of letters to Miss Wood and her sister show how he delighted to pass on books and articles from which he himself had profited to older friends, and how glad he was sometimes to receive an equivalent. The letters are undated, but belong to the very beginning of his ministry in Free St. George's.

> " Lest I should forget, let me ask your atten-
> tion to an article of great power, and intimate
> knowledge, on *The Vatican Council* in the
> October number of the *North British* [*Review*].
> . . . Probably it is written by Sir John Acton,
> the leader of liberal English Catholics.[1] It will
> repay *study*. A hurried reading will scarcely
> let you into its remarkable hold of the great
> questions at present moving among leading
> Catholics."

> " I send you Teresa and Mozley to test your

---

[1] Lord Acton, who edited the *North British Review* for a time, received a peerage from Mr. Gladstone in 1869.

catholicity and culture—and, I hope, to increase both. . . . I preach in the morning. Help me! " With much affection to you both."

" Look at *Nature*, herewith sent. Read repeatedly and reverently Clerk Maxwell's Lecture on ' Molecules.' . . . The science of our day should help to sanctify us ; *i.e.* make us humble, reverent, thoughtful. How far we are from that ! "

Another letter refers to a book published in 1872 and much discussed thereafter, W. R. Greg's *Enigmas of Life* :

" . . . I hoped when the book was announced that questions of a deeper kind : questions yet more pressing, for his solution and mine, would have been stated at least. But Greg has not met face to face with the deepest and darkest problems. There are worse evils than dyspepsia, and worse pain than gout, and ideals higher and more heart-breaking in their remoteness than that of an early marriage on a competency, or a refined home (with a *few* children) on a small salary. The Life that is ' enigmatic ' to Greg does not go very deep—it does not go so deep as to *strike sin*, as a Yankee critic might say. . . .

" In many minds, *Enigmas of Life* and *Middlemarch* are seething together. I hope many of our fellow-students add, ' the Gospels.' "

A later note, apparently written as the sisters were about to start on a journey, offers to lend them a supply of books by such authors as Stanley, Mozley, Gladstone, Dean Church, or Dr. A. B. Bruce, and concludes, " Say which or how many." And another note to Miss Marion Wood begins :

" I have never read Lockhart—but I will do so now. And I am glad that my first reading of the *Life* will be associated with two such friends of Sir Walter as Miss Wood and yourself. My best thanks for the kind gift."

2. Until far on in his life as a minister, Dr. Whyte gave no small part of his time to lecturing on biographical or literary subjects—but always on subjects with a definitely religious bearing. It would be impossible to estimate how many Scottish towns and villages he visited, or how many thousand miles he travelled on these errands of kindness—for most often he went in response to an appeal from a college friend, or, in later years, from some younger minister whom he wished to encourage. Even by the year 1875 two or three of his favourite lectures had been heard in many parts of Scotland. The lectures on Bunyan and on " A Day with William Law at King's Cliffe " had not yet been composed ; but he lectured on such subjects as " The Evangelist Mark," " The Life of Augustine," and " Erasmus." Such subjects would hardly be reckoned popular to-day, but they marked a somewhat new departure fifty years ago ; and at a time when there was but one orchestral concert in the year in Edinburgh, and when public lectures were as few as they have since become embarrassingly many, a lecturer could count on an eager as well as a patient audience. Whyte's more elaborate lectures cannot have occupied less than an hour and a half in delivery ; and the subjects of two in particular are of interest as dealing with periods somewhat apart from those which he studied in later life. These were on " Socrates," and on " The General Assembly of A.D. 325 ; or the Council of Nice : its Occasion, its Members, its Debates and Results." The latter in particular is written with great spirit, though not with the distinction of Dr. Whyte's fully developed style ; and the seriousness of the theological discussion is relieved by animated descriptions of the chief actors in the drama and of the miracles which the history of the age ascribed to them.

This lecture was originally delivered to the Young Men's Association of Free St. John's in the autumn of 1869, and was the first which Whyte gave to the young men of Free St. George's a year later ; but, often as he lectured at this time on Socrates or

Athanasius or the other great men named above, his chief work in widening the outlook of the Free Church in the 'seventies was accomplished through his lectures on Dante. He had first come to know the *Commedia* through the blank verse of Cary and the prose of John Carlyle at some point during his student years, and the copy of Thomas Carlyle's *Heroes*, of which we have already heard, may well have set him on the quest. Nor could such a watcher of the skies as he had already become fail to recognise the glory of this new planet when he first looked into the pages of Dante. The moral intensity and rigour of the *Commedia*, united to the soaring imagination which gives wings to its verse, infallibly carried him captive to the spell of " the sacred poem, to which both heaven and earth have set their hand." Nor could Dante well have found a more effective exponent in the Scotland of fifty years ago. It is true that Whyte's ignorance of Italian prevented him from taking his place among the original expositors of Dante—a place which he would have been the first to disclaim. But the time and circumstances were hardly ripe for Dante scholarship in the strict sense. What was needed to commend the *Commedia* to thoughtful Scottish people was the voice of one who was strong to recognise its poetical grandeur and moral insight, and quick to penetrate to the permanent religious truth contained in forms of thought belonging to a past age. This service Whyte's lectures most admirably performed.

At the mid-point of Whyte's Glasgow ministry he had already begun to lecture on Dante. One such lecture was given in Aberdeen on the invitation of a student's society, the secretary of which was William Robertson Nicoll, whom Whyte had first seen as a boy in his father's manse at Auchindoir—the little upland manse which contained 17,000 volumes— during one of his early preaching tours in Aberdeenshire. Whyte at this time greatly admired Dean Church's essay which had been published in an Anglican periodical; and shortly after, when the works of Symonds and Maria Rossetti appeared, they were as eagerly laid under contribution. By 1874 Whyte was provided with a succession of lectures on Dante, consisting of a general survey and appreciation, and separate expositions of the *Inferno, Purgatorio,* and *Paradiso.* He found in Free St. George's a Young Men's Literary Society, which already boasted a somewhat chequered history of just a quarter of a century ; and for more than one winter he both opened and closed its session with lectures on Dante.

It is related that on one occasion, when entering the church to deliver his lecture, he let his manuscript fall, and, in order to give time for its collection and rearrangement, asked the audience to begin singing Psalm cxix. A member of the audience recalls that, before many verses of the longest of the psalms had been sung, the lecturer gave up the attempt to restore his disintegrated manuscript, and the lecture was abandoned. As these manuscripts came into the present writer's hands they consisted of some six or eight batches of loose sheets inserted in the pages of a venerable copy of the *Contemporary Review.* They formed a strange contrast to the fastidious order which ruled among Dr. Whyte's books and manuscripts at a later time ; and the task of arranging them recalled on a small scale the description in the first part of *Sartor Resartus* of a green-spectacled editor delving in the paper bags which contained the confused medley of Herr Teufelsdröckh's literary remains. Some of the sheets were unnumbered, some numbered, and some renumbered; and it was obvious that the material had been used at different times, and arranged and rearranged to meet the needs of different audiences.

The most conspicuous of Whyte's lectures on Dante were given during the winter of 1876–77 to the Philosophical Institution of Edinburgh—a body which has little to do with philosophy in the strict sense, but which has for long done much to sustain the general intellectual life of the city by means of its library and the courses of lectures which are held in its hall. Whyte's two lectures appeared in the programme of the Institution in distinguished, though rather incongruous, company. They were preceded by a lecture on " The Uses of a Landed Gentry " by J. A. Froude, and followed by one on " Fielding and Smollett " by Justin M'Carthy ; and it was in no small degree due to Whyte's eloquence that the *Commedia* now began to find many students in Edinburgh for every one who read *Roderick Random* or *Tom Jones*. On this occasion so great was the interest awakened that, when a young member of Free St. George's went to the library of the Institution on the day after the first lecture to ask if she could secure a translation of Dante, she was met by an amused negative from the librarian : " Miss ——, I think you must be the hundred-and-fiftieth lady who has been here to ask for Dante this morning. We've had to pull dusty copies out from our farthest-off shelves, but they're all gone now ! "

That Whyte's endeavour to make Dante known to the reading people of Scotland in the 'seventies was the work of a true pioneer is attested by the half-apologetic tone in which he more than once introduced his subject. " Dante is so little read," he said on one occasion, " the few who have begun to read him have gone so short a way, and those who have read deeper have found him so hard to be understood, and demanding such patience, labour, and catholicity of temper, that I do not wonder to find little expectation awakened by a topic like this. I trust before I am done that the greatest stranger here to the work and worth of Dante will have learned something of a great man and a great book, and thus that the choice at least of the lecturer will be fully justified." Another lecture began with quotations from Hallam, Carlyle, Macaulay, and Lowell, all designed to justify the lecturer in his daring choice of an unfamiliar theme. What he had himself found in the *Commedia* is well shown by the use made of a simile used by Hallam, who said that to come to Dante from the crowd of common books " is as if, at some of the ancient games, a stranger had appeared upon the plain, and had thrown his quoit out among the marks of former casts, which tradition had ascribed to the demigods." " The figure," Whyte added, " is an original and striking one ; only it fails to bring out the solitariness and the supremacy of Dante's work. For what demigod's quoit had ever cut the ground where Dante's discus fell ? Who of the great players had made bare such an arm, or cast such a weight of metal to such a range ? *Not one.*"

3. By this time Whyte was deeply engaged in a work for religious education in Scotland which had wider bearings than either of those named. While his classes influenced scores, and his popular lectures reached hundreds, of young people, he was eager to bring the same ideals to bear on this whole side of his Church's work ; and his opportunity came when he was appointed by the General Assembly joint-convener of the " Committee on the Welfare of Youth." In a notable speech in the Assembly of 1876 he set forth the lines along which he sought to guide the Committee's advance. The movement for the extension of Young Men's and Young Women's Christian Associations had received a marked impetus from the Revival of two years before, and in particular from Mr. Moody's advocacy and wise counsel ; and members of the Youth Committee gave their earnest support to it. The Committee at the same time sought to increase the number of Young Men's Associations in the congregations of the Free Church, and prepared a scheme by which her sons and daughters, coming from the country to the great cities, might find friends ready to welcome and to help.

Another of their chief endeavours was to bring the best biblical scholarship of the day within hearing of the laity of the Church. In each of the three cities where the Free Church possessed a Theological College, this service was naturally entrusted to the professors of Divinity ; and among the courses of popular lectures thus arranged for, we find that in Edinburgh the Prophets were treated by Professor A. B. Davidson, and the New Testament by Principal Rainy,[1] while in Aberdeen lectures on " The Leading Features of Old Testament History " were given by Professor Robertson Smith, over whose head the shadow of the famous heresy trial was already beginning to spread.

Still another venture, referred to in this address in the General Assembly of 1876, continued to occupy Dr. Whyte during the forty-five remaining years of his life ; so the account of its origin which he then gave may well be reproduced, as it is given in the Official Report of the Assembly :

" There was another part of the report . . . which did not properly fall to the care of the Committee, but which he had set agoing and to some extent carried into effect. He had always studied what fresh interest and, if possible, fascination he could pour into his Bible Class. He made the Bible and Catechism always the basis of his teaching ; but still there were a thousand ways of teaching these ; and every man who taught to much purpose would find out his own way of impressing their lessons upon those who sat under him, either in the pulpit or classroom. He had read with pleasure the series of English classics published by the Clarendon Press containing selections from Chaucer, Spenser, Shakespeare, Bacon, Milton, and Bunyan. He had admired the taste, scholarship, and skill with which the work was executed, and it came to his mind that it would be a most valuable thing to have the books of the Bible

[1] This was not the first time that Whyte had stirred Rainy up to exercise his great gifts outside the walls of the New College. The part he played three years before in prompting Rainy's three lectures in reply to Dean Stanley (lectures whose fame resounded in Edinburgh for many years) is acknowledged by Dr. Carnegie Simpson in *The Life of Principal Rainy*, i. 226.

in a similar form for the benefit of our Bible classes. He had accordingly made this suggestion—as they invited hints—to the Clarendon Press, but they intimated that they had no intention of issuing such a work. They were, however, not dependent upon the Clarendon Press, as there was sufficient wealth of scholarship and intelligence among themselves to produce such a work as he had hinted at. He had spoken on the subject to Dr. Dods of Glasgow, and Mr. Clark, a publisher, a member of that House, and by this time the work was fairly under way. These works would put their cultivated young men on a level with technical scholars and in the front rank of all ascertained knowledge."

The series thus projected was given the title, "Handbooks for Bible Classes and Private Students." When its publication began it represented a definitely new departure; and although it has had many friendly rivals since then, it still keeps its place among aids to the interpretation of the Bible. For thirty years Marcus Dods and Alexander Whyte were its joint-editors,[1] and their responsibility for its development as well as their wide area of common literary and religious interest led to a constant exchange of letters and, still more frequently, post cards. One colleague would apply to the other for a lost reference or for his opinion on a new book, and a post card would bring the reply. Sometimes communications were longer, for, like other editors, they found difficulties in their path—as, for example, when some excellent contributors sent " copy " which had too obviously suffered an imperfect change from a previous existence in sermon- or lecture-shape. But on the whole their contributors served them well, and, as years passed on, the editors had the satisfac-

[1] After Dr. Dods's death, Dr. John Kelman, who was already Dr. Whyte's colleague in Free St. George's, took his place; and on his departure for America in 1919, Dr. Whyte asked Dr. James Moffatt to act as joint-editor of the series.

tion of knowing that they had helped to open the way to independent authorship for more than one scholar of promise. The most notable of these was Professor T. M. Lindsay of Glasgow, whose handbook on the Reformation in this series heralded the great history which he gave the world many years after. Professor A. B. Davidson wrote on the Epistle to the Hebrews, and Dr. Dods and Dr. Reith were among the contributors to the part of the series first planned—editions of the various books of the Bible with introductions and notes—while Dr. Whyte's *Shorter Catechism* appeared in 1883 in the more general section which was added later. Two other volumes which appeared early, and which after more than a generation continued to be the most valued, were *The Life of Christ* and *The Life of Paul*, by Dr. James Stalker. Nor would any account of the Handbooks and Dr. Whyte's part in their preparation be complete if it failed to take note of the warm personal friendship which grew up during the progress of this enterprise between him and Sir Thomas and Sir John M. Clark, the successive heads of the publishing house of Messrs. T. & T. Clark.

Another scheme ran parallel with this during the years following 1876, and claimed as large a part of Whyte's time and care. This was the " Welfare of Youth " scheme, which was developed by the Youth Committee under his guidance and that of Simeon Macphail. The two friends wished to secure that the new aids to study should not only exist, but be used to the full. A series of competitions was organised, graded according to age, and divided into sections. When it was fully developed, examinations were held yearly on prescribed periods of biblical history, and on the Shorter Catechism, and subjects in Scripture or Church History were set for essays. After nearly fifty years the scheme still awakens interest and encourages the study of the Bible among the young people of the Church, not only in the towns but in remote country places. At the outset its success was great ; and often, when the results for

the year were read out on the "Youth night" in
the General Assembly, which was filled to over-
flowing for this occasion, the names of girls or
boys from distant corners of Scotland, and even
from the farthest Hebrides, stood among the
highest.

Whyte was not merely content to launch the
scheme and see that it was heartily taken up in his
own congregation : for many years he, and later his
wife, took a large personal share in the reading of the
essays sent in from the Church as a whole, or in distributing them to scholarly friends to be judged and
classified. Such work as this may appear to experts
in religious education at the present time to belong to
a competitive order which is already passing away.
Even if this be so, there can be little question
that the "Welfare of Youth" played a most
useful part in the life of the Church, both before
and after the Union of 1900. It cannot be claimed
that Whyte foresaw in 1876 the new educational
methods which are but gradually being developed
to-day. His most marked originality lay in other
spheres.   But he was determined that the methods
which were considered most effective in the secular
education of his time should be applied not less
thoroughly to the study of Scripture and of Christian doctrine ; and he sought strenuously and not
without result to awaken enthusiasm and to fix a
like resolve in the mind of his Church.

The speech, already referred to, in which Whyte
unfolded these ideals and plans, was remembered as
one of the most eloquent of his utterances from the
platform; but the glowing passage with which it
ended referred so closely to the ecclesiastical controversies of the day, that it is hard to disentangle
the permanent from the temporary strands in its
texture. Its main purport was, however, to state
and answer the question how the young men and
women of the Church could be bound to her in faith
and loyalty. Not, the speaker contended, mainly
through controversy—though her central principles

must be upheld, and though he clearly avowed his own distrust of the too intimate association of Church and State. The bond must first of all be a personal one.

" He believed, after all the well-spent labour in discussing their principles, and making plain the truths of history, they would succeed best by attaching the growing youth to living persons, and it was through attachment to persons that they would also interest them in Free Church principles and evangelical religion. . . . They would effect far more by discharging their duty faithfully in the pulpit than by climbing a thousand platforms, and probably losing their character in the effort. He would far sooner hear of a servant lassie hurrying through her work to get to the prayer-meeting, or a ploughman lad in the obscurest corner of the land, whose voice thrilled as he spoke of his minister, than of a blare of trumpets and waving of banners, and a real prince coming to authorise a Church to open her Assembly. . . . There was a Church once in Scotland that, by the blow of her eagle wing, beat down a tyrant's throne, but that Church got her power with our fathers by her care for their children. . . . Let fathers and brethren labour and pray that the great Head of the Church might continue to say to our Scottish youth, ' Ye have seen how I bare you on eagles' wings, and brought you unto Myself ; now, therefore, ye shall be to Me a kingdom of priests and a holy nation.' "

Whyte's impassioned description of a Church that had won her hold on the loyalty of her people through her sufferings, and kept it by her care alike for the minds and for the souls of her children, not only aroused the Assembly to a storm of enthusiasm at the moment, but left deep and enduring impressions on many hearers. Seventeen years after, Robertson Nicoll wrote :

" It was the finest piece of pure, true, genuine eloquence I have ever heard, and the impression produced was electric and eternal. For the first time I felt that I had seen the real man. Always before he had been repressed from without and from within, disguised, restrained. For a moment he was himself."

" An Athenian's true holiday is the day on which he serves his
country best."—THUCYDIDES.

" The reaper is equally paid even for the time in which he sharpens
his sickle."—GOODWIN, quoted by A. W.

THE two preceding chapters have shown how many
forms of strenuous labour Whyte crowded into the
early years of his Edinburgh ministry. It was said
years afterwards by one who had been in service in
a house on the opposite side of Melville Street that
on winter mornings she was wont to see his study
lamp alight soon after six ; and the pressure under
which he worked even showed itself in his handwriting, which at this time was perhaps at its most
illegible. But he found time for relaxation as well,
and he was often a guest at the houses of his congregation or other friends, nor did he shirk those dinners
of formidable length in which Victorian society
delighted. Many of his hosts were members of the
medical and legal professions. Among his friends in
the former was Dr. John Brown, the author of *Rab
and His Friends* ; while in the legal profession, now
and always held by him, as by many of his fellow-
townsmen, in quite peculiar esteem, the literary
tradition still lingered which had come down from the
days of Scott through those of Cockburn and Jeffrey.
During the early 'seventies no name appears more
frequently in his diary than that of the judge who
had been the chief agent in bringing him to Free St.
George's, and who during the remaining six years of
his own life never failed to give his minister the wisest
counsel and the most constant support. Lord Ardmillan, it was said, belonged to " the great Society

of Encouragers"; and Whyte often testified to the benefit which he had derived from evenings spent at the richly intellectual table of this venerable friend, whom he afterwards described as "the most gracious and gentlemanly man I ever knew."[1] On his own part, he maintained the reputation which he had gained in Glasgow as a singularly stimulating talker, especially when his enthusiasm for literature found an opportunity to blaze forth. He also did his own share of entertaining, especially when his friends from country manses found themselves in Edinburgh.[2]

The more personal records of Whyte's life at this time exist chiefly in the form of holiday reminiscences preserved by others. These include more than one account of his preaching in country places, where, now as later, he spoke with a freedom and a homely originality scarcely possible in the pulpit of a great city church. If his holidays were long, they were far from being inactive, and a part of every vacation resolved itself into a pilgrimage or a preaching-tour. His passion for his calling so pervaded his nature that he might well have said that his best holiday was the day on which he had most helped his fellows by the message which he bore.

Sometimes he found himself taking part in one of those Sacrament seasons in the Highlands, to which men and women often travelled far across the hills or arms of the sea. For a week the services went on with little break. At Ullapool, in Wester Ross, during one such season Whyte found the congregation gather at seven every morning; and late in the evening the services of preparation still went on, conducted by the "Men," or senior elders, if the ministers were not present. The veneration

---

[1] See *Bible Characters*, iii. 167.
[2] He first lived in rooms at 1 Coates Place; and then, after a few months in a house in Manor Place lent by Mr. James Howden (for forty years an elder in Free St. George's), he moved to 52 Melville Street, where Dr. Candlish had spent his later years. Here he had a most efficient housekeeper, Marjory Hamilton, afterwards Mrs. Keddie.

for the Elements was so great that, out of a great
concourse gathered in the open air, only a handful
of the most deeply experienced believers went forward
to the Table itself. Whyte never approved of this
extreme reluctance to obey the Master's command,
" This do in remembrance of Me." But he sym-
pathised deeply with the reverence which underlay
it ; and the heart-searching preparation for, and
self-dedication in, the partaking of the Sacrament
appealed to his own deepest feeling. He valued the
Scottish observance of the Fast Day (usually the
Thursday before the Communion Sabbath) and of the
Thanksgiving service which followed ; and, as these
came to be less generally and solemnly observed, he
never ceased to deplore their passing and to seek
for some spiritual equivalent. Even from a less
exalted point of view, the Fast Day had one great
advantage, in that it allowed the great preachers of
the Church to be heard by crowded congregations at
a distance from their own homes ; and throughout
his first fifteen years in Free St. George's Whyte did
much of such Fast Day preaching.

The vacation of 1874 began with an evening
meeting in Logiealmond, where he had started his
career as a preacher fifteen years before. Then
followed four strenuous days in and near Inverness.
Whyte spoke nine times during a mission in pur-
suance of Moody and Sankey's campaign, three
of these meetings being in the open air. Whyte
then returned southward and spent several days in
his old haunt of Glen Isla. Long walks up Glen
Isla and Glenshee were combined with a further
series of addresses to gatherings of their scattered
inhabitants. Next he was joined by Simeon
Macphail, and the two friends made their way to
Appin, where they spent several days with Dr. and
Mrs. Laurie of Drumneil, one of the many places
of great beauty in the historic country bordering
Glencoe. One day was spent in a twenty-two-
mile walk up Glencoe, and Whyte's comment is that

of many pedestrians in that district before and since,
" Wet but grand!"

Whyte and Macphail were now joined by two other
college friends—George Low, then a minister in
Aberdeen, and Duncan Ross. The latter, who spent
nearly fifty years as minister in Appin, knew the
country well, and acted as the party's guide in a
pilgrimage to Iona, which he has lived to describe
in notes written since Dr. Whyte's death. On the
first day, they left Appin early by the *Chevalier*, and
trans-shipping at Oban reached Iona in time for a
long afternoon on that sacred soil. They walked over
the rough moor and bog which covers the southern
part of the island to Port-na-curraich, the lonely bay
where Columba first landed, and where, tradition
says, he buried his coracle lest he should be tempted to
return to his loved Erin. There the four friends lay
on the warm gravel by the boat-shaped mound which
the islanders believed to be the grave of Columba's
bark ; and as they idly threw pebbles into the summer
sea, Whyte led the talk, not to the great Celtic
missionary, but to the supreme Italian poet. Dante
was the master of his thought and imagination at
this time, and he spoke of what the *Divina Commedia*
had meant to him as the great epic of the sanctification of the human soul.

When the friends returned to the hamlet near the
ruined Cathedral, they found the little Free Church
filled in the gathering dusk by an expectant congregation, for word had gone round in the afternoon that
Candlish's successor was to be there. It was arranged
that Low and Macphail should speak first, that Whyte
should follow, and that Ross should conclude with a
few words in Gaelic.

" I don't remember," is the testimony of the
last-named after forty-seven years, " one word
of what they "—Low and Macphail—" said,
but I remember Whyte's address as if I had heard
it only yesterday. It was on the words, in
Ps. xvi., ' I have set the Lord always before

me ' [1] ; and after explaining how David and
David's Lord would do so, he became very practical in the application, and called upon the
crofters and tradesmen to set the Lord always
before them, for, if they did that, they would
do their work right well.   He called upon the
women to set the Lord always before them when
doing up the house, cooking the food, rocking the
cradle, for, if they did, their hearts would be
singing all the while.   And then, turning to us
ministers, he called upon us to set the Lord
always before us while engaged in our studies,
for, if we did that, then our preaching would be
so much the better.   And so it was that, not only
did his own piety grow warmer among the ruins
of Iona, but he helped to make the piety of the
residents grow warmer too."

The next day was no less crowded.   Another early
start, this time in a sailing boat which they had
chartered, took the friends round by Ulva, the home
of David Livingstone's father, and Gometra to Staffa.
Thus they entered Fingal's Cave, and sang the
hundredth psalm within that great cathedral whose
pillars were not built with hands, before the tourist
steamer arrived on her southward course.   They
returned with her to Iona, crossed the sound, and
walked eastward along the Ross of Mull to the Free
Church Manse.   The minister sent them on in his
dogcart to Bunessan, where they were to spend the
night, and where another audience was awaiting them.
The order of the Iona meeting was again followed ;
and again Mr. Ross records that, while he has forgotten the other addresses, he has a vivid impression
of Whyte, standing on the schoolhouse floor, unen-
cumbered by written notes, " pouring out a burning torrent of eloquence."   Next day a bathe in
Loch Scridan varied the eastward walk across Mull,

---

[1] A treatment of the same theme twenty years later will be found in
Lord, Teach us to Pray, pp. 90 ff.   This is typical of the way in which
Dr. Whyte often recurred to his favourite texts.

on the track that readers of *Kidnapped* were to follow breathlessly ten years later. Before the week ended, Whyte had spoken again at Port Appin and ascents had been made of Aird's Hill and Ben Scuillard, a mountain of over 3000 feet at the head of Loch Creran, where Whyte's diary records that he was first at the top.

On Sunday he preached in his friend's church on, " These are they which came out of great tribulation." Addressing the boys in the congregation who knew a little Latin, he said that the word " tribulation " came from the Latin, *tribulum.*

> " This," he said, " was a heavy platform of wood, the under side of which was studded with nails and flints, which the oxen dragged back and forward over the shining sheaves to separate the grain from the straw ; as God drives His *tribulum* over His people to separate them from their sins."

But Mr. Ross's memories of August 1874 show how Whyte could find illustrations close at hand as well as in his favourite study of etymology.

> " Sometimes," he said, " you see a steamer rounding the island in front of you, churning up the waters in its progress, and, long after it has disappeared round the next headland, raising waves which all but swamp the little boats which anchor in the creeks and bays ; and such may be the effect of our sins when we have passed out of sight, for they may be doing deadly injury to people that are unknown to us." Again—regarding the future, and the perspective of its events—" Such events seem to lie close to one another, but they may really be like the mountain-ranges, which, as you look, seem to lean the one on the other, whereas there are leagues of sea or broad valleys lying between them."

The chronicler to whom we owe these notes had heard Whyte speak in Glasgow six years before, but was impressed by the vastly increased power of his preaching during this Argyllshire holiday. His first years in Free St. George's had brought into full exercise powers which had formerly been but half developed.

A year later an account of his preaching to a Highland audience was set down by an observer trained in a very different school. Two young Englishmen, who had been friends at Eton and Trinity, Cambridge, were returning from a tour in Skye, and found themselves spending Sunday at Lochearnhead, Whyte's favourite fishing-ground. One was the Hon. Arthur Lyttelton, afterwards Bishop of Southampton. The other, the present Viscount Esher, long afterwards printed privately a volume of *Extracts from Journals*, from which I am permitted to transcribe the following passage. The date is 5th September 1875.

" To-night we had an impressive service in the hall from Mr. Whyte, minister of the Free Kirk, St. George's, in Edinburgh, successor to Dr. Candlish. He preached on the 103rd Psalm, the Communion psalm of the Presbyterian Church. It had been chosen, he said, because it was the only psalm of pure thanksgiving free from any petition. It was written by David when he was an old man, in communing with his heart, to which the psalm is addressed ; he compared this kind of meditation in private with that which an ordinary man would use lying awake at night or walking on the hills or along the stream. Then he worked out very carefully the different terms of the thanksgiving. He dwelt especially on the verse in which David speaks of the Lord crowning the head of the sinner with tender mercies and loving-kindness. Here his cultivation came out, and he was overcome by the beauty, the poetry of the expression. ' If Shakespeare had written it you would never have heard the end of it,' he burst out, ' but the English in which it is put is lost in the meaning,

the depth of truth in the fact.' His distinction
between the scholarly reading of the Bible and
that of the women up in the glens, solitary and
reft of their children, who had never been to
school except the elementary class, where they
learnt their alphabet, who turn to it as their only
book, was very elegant and touching. He told
us about an old woman of ninety-eight, his
parishioner, whose questions were always of
her neighbours' children : ' How about the
schools, or the boys at sea, or the lad away in
India '—never anxious about herself or grumbling. Then he turned to the last verse, the
summing up of the Lord's benefits, His granting
new life after sin, just as an eagle renews her
youth. This image, he said, David had borrowed from what he had observed on the hills,
when the eagle, after bringing up her young and
sending them away, retired with soiled plumes
and torn wings, torn and soiled in the struggles
for the food of her young, to a cleft in the rocks,
and after moulting and being sick unto death,
issued forth in full plumage and almost youthful
beauty. Then he described what he imagined
may have been the scene when David tottered
up to his palace wall to rest in the setting sun,
leaving the manuscript wet on the table, and
some servant passing looked at it, and then at
his master, and said : ' Look at him, the old
man; he does not look as if youth was renewed
in him.' And from this he drew the distinction
between the old and the youthful heart.

" His peroration was an address on the
peculiarity of the congregation, collected haphazard, never to meet again on this side of the
grave. It was a striking discourse in the low,
dim-lighted room amid the weeping congregation.
Sprung from the people, his use of the vernacular
and of Scottish expressions, and local images of
the moors and glens, made what he said very
impressive and deeply touching."

Towards the end of the following winter Whyte snatched ten days from his work in Edinburgh, and made the pilgrimage to which his later recollections returned most often.   On 14th March 1876 he visited Newman at the Oratory, Edgbaston.   In his later student days he had already begun to acknowledge the spell of Newman's literary and spiritual genius. During his Glasgow ministry we hear of his reading *Gerontius* with the members of Dr. Roxburgh's family.   At the same period, his friend, Ross of Appin, spent a night in his rooms and began to speak enthusiastically of Frederick Robertson's *Sermons.* In reply, Whyte pointed to four volumes on one of his shelves, saying, " These sermons are far more to me than Robertson's."   The volumes formed part of a new edition of Newman's works then appearing.   This judgment, given at a time when the thought of Robertson was setting a deep imprint on many of the ablest young minds in Scotland, tells much of Whyte's religious outlook.

We need not seek to trace fully the points at which the thought of Newman especially influenced Whyte, since he expressed his debt in the most elaborate of his " Appreciations " a quarter of a century later ; but three or four of these points of contact may be briefly indicated here.   Newman's constant and all-pervading conviction of the presence of God in the life of man, his awed sense of the insignificance of all earthly interests in comparison with the moral and religious issues which reach out into eternity, his delicate but searching analysis of the hidden processes of good and evil in the heart, his reverence of spirit, and the quiet perfection of his English style, which unfailingly conveyed to the reader the most resolute conviction or the subtlest shade of emotion—were all fitted to establish an effortless mastery over an ear and a conscience so sensitively attuned as those of Alexander Whyte.

In those days of entrenched Protestantism it needed no small courage for three Free Churchmen who were still young in the ministry to go on pilgrimage to the Oratory. But Whyte found that his friends, Marcus Dods and George Webster Thomson, were more than ready to join him. An interview was asked for, and Newman readily granted the request.

" He received us with all that captivating urbanity which has become proverbial ; and though we did not intrude ourselves long on the courteous old man, a good many points were touched on in our short interview—Rome, Oxford, Scotland, Abbotsford, Sir Walter Scott, Matthew Arnold, and so on—the old saint treating us in all that with a frankness and with a confidence as if we were old friends of his, as indeed we were. At one point in the delightful conversation he said, ' But, gentlemen, is not your Church a very learned and a very open-minded Church ? ' At that Dr. Dods looked round to me and smiled. But our sensitive host would not have it so. Taking off his biretta cap, which he took off and put on a dozen times during the short interview, he drew near his chair and said, ' Oh, believe me, I mean it ! And I will tell you how and why. It was my birthday ; and a friend of mine sent me a hundred-pound note to buy something for myself on that day. Some time before I had seen in Mr. Baker's catalogue a book advertised that had made my mouth water. It was a complete and splendid copy of the *Acta Sanctorum* of the Bollandist Fathers. And with my hundred-pound note in my pocket, I posted up to London like a schoolboy to get my great prize. But what was my consternation when the bookseller told me that a Dr. Cunningham of Edinburgh had telegraphed for the Bollandists that morning, and that the sixty volumes were well on their way by that time to the New College Library.' " [1]

Soon after, the three friends took their leave, and while a correspondence, to be described in Chapter

[1] *Former Principals*, p. 24 f.

XIII., renewed the friendship between Newman and Whyte during the last decade of the great Cardinal's life, they never again met face to face. All the more did Dr. Whyte keep as a fragrant memory the impression of this one meeting with the teacher to whom, in face of profound differences, he owed so much.

Two years after this, Whyte took part in a deputation to Mr. Gladstone which also deserves some record. In the early months of 1878 feeling was rapidly rising in Scotland in regard to the Near East, and men became more and more apprehensive whither the Disraelian policy of friendliness to the Turk and hostility to Russia might lead. At the end of April Whyte and Stalker, who had been working together on the "Handbooks for Bible Classes," met in Whyte's study, and called to their counsels three or four younger men, including Robert Barbour, then a theological student, and Patrick W. Campbell, a young lawyer and office-bearer in Free St. George's. Before the conclave broke up, it was decided to secure signatures for an address to Mr. Gladstone from the ministers of the Free and the United Presbyterian Churches, and from the smaller Protestant Churches in Scotland, expressing their gratitude for his firm stand on behalf of the oppressed Christian peoples in the Turkish Empire, and against the forces which were dragging Britain towards a second Crimean war. Campbell took the main part in preparing this address and obtaining signatures for it, and he and Whyte were in constant touch for a fortnight. At the end of this time, some sixteen hundred signatures had been appended, representing the overwhelming majority of ministers in the Churches concerned—a striking example of rapid organisation in the days before the coming of the telephone. A week later, on 23rd May, a small deputation, of whom Whyte was one, breakfasted with Gladstone at the Westminster Palace Hotel ; and, after the address had been handed to him, he acknowledged it in a speech which foreshadowed his great speeches on behalf of the Christians of the Near East a few months later. Indeed, the incident probably helped to turn the statesman's thoughts towards Midlothian, in more than a metaphorical sense. Whyte did not speak at the breakfast, but his fame as a student of Newman had preceded him; and he used to describe how, after the speeches were ended, Gladstone advanced across the room, pointing a long forefinger towards him, with the words, " I hear that you are a student of Newman— do you know *Gerontius* ? " After the great Midlothian campaign, on the eve of the General Election of 1880, Gladstone took the opportunity to worship in Free St. George's. Whyte's share in presenting this memorial not only strengthened his admiration for one whom he always regarded as, above all else, a great moral leader : it gave the first definite expression to that sympathy for the suffering Armenian people which was one of the permanent interests of his life.

In the year which intervened between Whyte's meetings with Newman and with Gladstone, the marriage of his friend Alexander Barrie ended the series of their holidays together. Before the marriage took place, the last of these expeditions carried them to the Rhone Glacier and the Furca, instead of to those Highland glens, where Whyte once said with a smile that his best sport had been enjoyed, " poaching wi' Barrie." During the same year Alexander Barrie's younger brother came up to study at Edinburgh University. Sir James Barrie has referred in *An Edinburgh Eleven* to the freshman's awe with which he approached its massive portals ; and he now adds the recollection that it was Whyte who first piloted him into " the Old Quad " and introduced him to the officials who controlled the " matriculation" of its successive generations of students.

Whyte's short spring expeditions with Marcus Dods, Webster Thomson, and Taylor Innes went on until the end of the 'seventies. On one or two occasions they went to London, seeing Henry Irving at

the Lyceum ; and on others they had walking tours
in the Lake District or in the Highlands. During
these tramps, discussions on theology were varied
by the comments of Taylor Innes on the geology of
the country traversed, or by the long passages from
the English poets which he and Webster Thomson
recited in place of marching songs.

There exists also—though in a somewhat inac-
cessible form—a full account of a pilgrimage which
Whyte undertook in the summer of 1878 with Simeon
Macphail. The latter, during a ministry of nine years
at Elgin, had become greatly interested in the beautiful priory church of Pluscardyn, some miles to the
south. It was the only pre-Reformation church in
Scotland used by a congregation of the Free Church,
and Macphail desired to learn all that he could
regarding the order of *Vallis Caulium* in Burgundy—
a small branch of the great Cistercian tree—to which
the monastery had belonged.[1] In 1881 the result of
his researches appeared in an elaborate quarto, *The
Religious House of Pluscardyn*.[2] The book was
dedicated to Alexander Whyte—" on the completion
of the twenty-first year of our friendship, as an
expression of deepening regard and admiration of
gifts and character consecrated to the work of Christ
and the noblest of the sciences." The introduction
tells how the friends set out together to find the
parent house of the Order. They were content with
a " very hasty survey " of the Paris Exhibition of
1878. Leaving the main line of the Lyons railway at
Nuits-sous-Ravières, they arrived in the late afternoon at the quaint, old-world town of Châtillon, on
the upper waters of the Seine. Its attractions are
fully described, from the Église Saint Vorle, founded
in A.D. 991, to the Hôtel Côte d'Or, where the travellers
stayed, and which struck them as " having dropped
almost intact from feudal times into the nineteenth

---

[1] As did the monasteries of Ardchattan and Beauly—both, like
Pluscardyn, founded in A.D. 1230. These were the only houses of the
Order outside France.

[2] Published by Oliphant, Anderson & Ferrier, Edinburgh.

century." The entrance led through a spacious
kitchen, presided over by a travelled and hospitable
genius, named Jacques, who seems to have combined
the characters of *patron* and *chef*, after the older
French manner. The narrative does full justice to
his professional skill, as shown by the sixteen items
which went to compose an early breakfast, and also
to his aid in setting on their way the two eccentric
Scotsmen who were determined to penetrate the
inmost recesses of the Forest of Châtillon in quest of
the *Val des Choux*, or, in their own tongue, the *Kale
Glen*.

It would take too long to follow in detail the fortunes of that memorable first of August under the
brilliant sunlight of the Côte d'Or—the drive at first
through cultivated country ; the plunge into the
depths of the *Forêt*, where the road gradually became
transformed into a series of steep ascents and descents
over grassy drives used by foresters or huntsmen only ;
the growing wonderment of the driver ; and the final
arrival in the fertile *Val des Choux*. Here the
travellers were courteously received by the proprietor
of the place, a certain M. Alker, who had gradually
bought the valley from six different proprietors, so
that everything possible might be done to preserve
those portions of the great monastery, now united
under one ownership, which time had spared. " We
told our errand," the narrative continues, " said we
understood he knew English, which he protested was
scarcely true—though it was so, very much more
truly than our efforts at his language could be said
to be French." At all events a sufficient ease of
communication was established to allow of M. Alker's
showing his unexpected visitors all that remained of
the monastery, the Guest House, the Refectory, the
Cemetery, and the not less indispensable fish-pond—
the great Church had been blown up, apparently of
set purpose, less than fifty years before. Much
information was also gained for Macphail's contemplated treatise, and further lines of research were
suggested.

" We parted," the story concludes, " from our new friend soon afterwards, full of gratitude and delight. Early in the evening we tasted our first Pommard in the arbour of the Côte d'Or Hotel, and later found ourselves settled for the night in Dijon, with bright prospects of a raid among the antiquities and libraries of that good city on the morrow. How these prospects were not realised, but instead the skill of a little French doctor and his powerful restoratives were fully tested, need not here be told, as they belong to another romance than that of the search for the *Val des Choux*."

The rest is silence ; and it is vain to inquire which of the friends was subjected to the unspecified remedies prescribed by an unnamed doctor for an undefined malady. Whyte's diary now ceases to give even the meagre help hitherto afforded ; for the only entry during the weeks that follow is " St. George's shut "—a statement more soothing to the mind of the traveller than informing to the biographer. The incident may, however, stand by itself —or rather may stand beside that of the visit to Newman at the Oratory—as showing how Whyte's interest and admiration had come to embrace regions of Church History and forms of religious thought far removed from the tradition of his own youth and education, faithful as he yet remained to what was central in that tradition.

" *Non sine scientia, sine necessitate, sine amore.*"—BENGEL.

" When God shakes a Kingdome with strong and healthfull com-
motions to a generall reforming, 'tis not untrue that many sectaries
and false teachers are then busiest in seducing ; but yet more true it
is, that God then raises to His own work men of rare abilities and
more than common industry not only to look back and revise what hath
bin taught heretofore, but to gain furder and goe on some new en-
lighten'd steps in the discovery of truth."—MILTON.

DURING the five years from 1876 to 1881 the Free
Church of Scotland passed through a conflict not less
acute, and even wider in its repercussions, than the
" Ten Years' Conflict " which ended in 1843.   The
subject at issue was again that of Christian liberty ;
but, whereas the earlier conflict had turned on the
liberty *of* the Church to carry on her spiritual work
unhindered by encroachments on the part of the State,
this new controversy was rather concerned with
liberty of thought and inquiry *within* the Church.
A generation before, the relation of the Church to
the Scriptures and the authority of the sacred text
were looked on as matters lying beyond the reach of
dispute.   Now, with apparent suddenness, the Church
was forced to consider anew these hitherto unexamined
principles.   Yet in one respect both conflicts were
alike.   As the range of the dispute widened and its
implications became clear, the whole mind of the
Scottish people was stirred to activity and interest.
The debates of Presbyteries or Assemblies on the
views of Robertson Smith were followed and reproduced in railway carriages and workshops and country
smithies ; and so among the laymen of Scotland a
true, though at times a violent, process of education
went on in the meaning of Criticism, the process by
which the Old Testament came into being, and the

nature of the Inspiration by which the Bible was formed and the Church is guided.[1]   In a real sense, the Robertson Smith case completed—or made an approach to completing—the liberating work begun at the Reformation.   Even when Gladstone's Midlothian Campaigns broke upon the Scottish people with such a wave of interest and emotion as only a small and compact nation can experience, they did not for a moment overshadow the other debate with which this chapter is concerned—a debate whose stages were followed with eager interest through a large part of Protestant Christendom, as it came to be realised that the example of this relatively small Church, grappling with a problem of universal urgency, might have far-spreading results for the extension of liberty or for the entrenchment of old tradition.

At the centre of all this turmoil was the small and eager figure of the young Professor of Hebrew in the Free Church College at Aberdeen, whom great German scholars were proud to claim as a pupil, and whose brilliance was hardly more marked than his amazing versatility.   The latter was illustrated by the fact that two of the greatest teachers of the day each sought to capture him for his own line of study— A. B. Davidson for the exposition of the Old Testament, and P. G. Tait for mathematical physics. Smith unhesitatingly chose the former as his lifework, in spite of the assurance of high distinction which was held out by those who urged him to take up a scientific career ; and some of his friends reflected afterwards how much smoother his course through life would have been had he devoted his powers to pure science.

Whyte's meeting with Robertson Smith in 1870 has been already recorded ; but this was the renewal of an earlier acquaintance.   During his student days in Aberdeen, Whyte had more than once visited

[1] Half the membership of Presbyteries and Assemblies is made up of elders.   " Laymen " should here be understood as including " laywomen," though the latter had no direct share in shaping Church polity in Scotland.

the Free Church Manse of Keig on Donside, and had
been arrested by the eager aspect of a group of boys
and girls, whose minds seemed even hungrier than
their bodies. William Robertson Smith was the
eldest son, and Whyte's first memory of him was that
of a boy extended on the study floor, devouring an
encyclopædia too bulky to be handled otherwise by
its young reader ; and of the questions regarding
King's College and the means of getting there with
which he was plied by the three eldest children—two
of whom died before their studies were complete.

In academic standing Smith was four years
junior to Whyte, and thus just missed being his
fellow-student, first at King's College, Aberdeen, and
then at New College, Edinburgh. Nor would their
main interests have been the same if they had met as
students, for Whyte did not then give his best thought
to the linguistic studies in which the younger man
was supreme. But during the early 'seventies Whyte's
experience in his pulpit, and perhaps still more in his
Bible Classes, brought him a steadily increasing sense
of the importance of a fearless and thorough study of
biblical origins—such a study as Robertson Smith had
in mind when he used these words in his inaugural
address :

> " The higher criticism does not mean negative
> criticism. It means the fair and honest looking
> at the Bible as a historical record, and the effort
> everywhere to reach the real meaning and histori-
> cal setting, not of individual passages of the
> Scripture, but of the Scripture records as a
> whole. . . . This process can be dangerous to
> faith only when it is begun without faith—when
> we forget that the Bible history is no profane
> history, but the story of God's saving self-
> manifestation." [1]

For over five years after his appointment in
1870 Smith quietly pursued his scholar's way in
Aberdeen. General statements as to the need for

[1] *Life of Robertson Smith*, p. 128 f.

unfettered historical study of the books of the Bible themselves, rather than of traditions regarding them, did not unduly alarm the orthodox, although the more thoughtful might have seen that the postulates of such a critical study were radically opposed to the traditional view of the Bible as of equal historical value in every part. Criticism and a theology based on the idea of literal inspiration could not long exist together. But it was when the young professor began to publish the results to which he and others had been led by these new principles of interpretation that the tempest of controversy first arose.

This occurred when, in December 1875, the article " Bible " appeared in volume iii. of the famous Ninth Edition of the *Encyclopædia Britannica*. It was significant that the writing of this important article should have been entrusted to a scholar just entering his thirtieth year. Its tone was scholarly and detached ; and it was in some ways unfortunate that Robertson Smith's first prominent attempt to give a connected view of the Bible, and especially of the Old Testament, in the light of the results of historical research and the guiding principle of historical evolution—then vehemently distrusted by the orthodox—should have been made in a form which did not admit of such statements of his positive faith as that just quoted. In the pages of the *Britannica*, the writer could show his mind as a scholar, but not his full belief as a Christian minister ; and thus an unduly negative impression was given to those for whom the whole structure of faith rested on foundations such as the unity and historicity of the Pentateuch.[1] Nor was the writer himself aware how farreaching was the reconstruction of traditional belief which his method involved. He himself applied it

[1] Cf. the cancelled opening paragraphs of the article, reproduced by Dr. Sutherland Black and Sir George Chrystal, *op. cit.*, p. 179 f., with their comments on p. 181. I have sought in the following pages to draw impartially on the elaborate account of the " case " given by Robertson Smith's biographers and on the complementary—not to say opposed—account in Dr. Carnegie Simpson's *Life of Principal Rainy*, vol. i. pp. 306–403. Happily it is not my duty to attempt an *eirenicon*.

only within the sphere of biblical literature and history, while in theology he remained a convinced evangelical, and even a Calvinist.[1] Nothing seems stranger to those of the present day who go back upon the records of that troubled time than the extent to which the protagonist of freedom in the interpretation of Scripture was content to rest his case on the *Westminster Confession*. The *Confession* did not, indeed, exclude views such as that of the composite character of the Pentateuch, or the relatively late date of Deuteronomy and many of the Psalms. These were not advanced till long after that formidable defence of Calvinism was framed ; and so Robertson Smith could confidently challenge his critics to prove that, in defending these positions, he had been unfaithful to his ordination vows. At first sight it seems unfortunate that the view of the Old Testament, which was destined to make it a new and more living book to many, should have been buttressed even for a time by an appeal to the authority of the *Confession*. Yet further thought may well modify this impression ; for, if the theological as well as the critical question had been formally debated in the 'seventies, the traditional views must have triumphed all along the line. The fact that Robertson Smith was not at this time interested in the restatement of dogma but only in the reinterpretation of the Bible, meant that the new outlook on Scripture had time to prepare the way for the reconstruction of belief. It also enabled men like Whyte to take their stand unhesitatingly at his side.

In the months which preceded the Assembly of 1876, the voice of alarm began to be heard in the Church, and it was discovered that an earlier article on " Angels " also threw doubt on the literal accuracy of Scripture. Dr. Begg, who had played the chief part in blocking the Union negotiations only three years before, again appeared as a sower of discord ; and Smith's friends began to feel an apprehension from which he himself was still free. They understood better

[1] Cf. *Life of Robertson Smith*, pp. 221 ff.

than he how little the Church as a whole was prepared
to accept, or even calmly to consider, his conclusions
regarding the slow development of the priestly code
contained in Exodus and Leviticus or his assignment
of Deuteronomy to the prophetic age.   The discussion
had not, however, gone far enough to allow of any
definite action when the Assembly met, so the whole
question was referred to the Committee which had
the oversight of the theological colleges of the Church.

With this reference of the case (for such it had now
become) to the College Committee, Whyte's definite
and official part in it began.   For he was a member
of this Committee, and the youngest of the eleven
ministers who were members of it, if not of the Committee as a whole.   The only one of his colleagues who
was definitely on the side of Robertson Smith was
Professor James S. Candlish, who inherited much of
his famous father's nobility of nature, and was greater
as a theologian, though not as an orator.   In
addition, Principals Rainy and Douglas and several
of the laymen on the Committee were believed to be
generally favourable to Robertson Smith.   Rainy,
indeed, was already convinced that a formal condemnation of the main contentions in the *Britannica*
article must at all costs be avoided, and that the date
of Deuteronomy could never be made a question of
faith.   So far he was on the side of free inquiry ;
but he was by no means satisfied that Smith had
sufficiently considered the wider bearings of certain
statements which he had used, or their effect on those
in the Church—the great majority—to whom the
whole method of the newer biblical scholarship was
unfamiliar and alarming.   Smith on his part was
naturally unwilling to make any statement which
could be interpreted as a recantation of the conclusions which he had deliberately reached.   He
did, however, make a statement to the Committee
in November which, in Dr. Rainy's opinion, would
" operate in a reassuring way." [1]

But in Dr. Rainy's judgment a further declaration

[1] *Life of Principal Rainy*, i. 321–3.

was required, and it was at this stage that Whyte made his first definite attempt to act as mediator. The position, as he saw it, was described in a letter to Miss Marion Wood, dated 2nd January 1877 :

> " My best thanks for your gift, and for all the friendly words that accompany it. And for all the true friendship I have all along found in Miss Wood and in yourself. It has often cheered and encouraged me when I had too much care and anxiety—and too little of such intercourse as ours has all along been. . . .
>
> " I have just come home from spending all the afternoon in the College Committee over Prof. Smith's case. . . . I cannot describe the scene to you : suffice it to say that two of us fought a stout and winning battle for scholarship and culture in the Church. I have had a walk with Rainy since—and have told him plainly how he is spoken of and looked to as a leader by men younger than himself. I think it has been a well-spent afternoon. Had you been here, I could have *told* you a great deal that I cannot write. . . ."

Whyte's attempt at mediation was carried out in a decidedly original way. Either on the walk just referred to, or during another interview at the same juncture, he suggested that Dr. Rainy should write a letter such as, if he were in Professor Smith's place, he might issue to calm the apprehensions of the conservative party in the Church. Dr. Rainy agreed, and handed to Whyte, to be forwarded to Robertson Smith, such a draft, or rather model, epistle.[1] Perhaps he hardly hoped that his impetuous friend would thus allow himself to be coached by Dr. Rainy in the art of soothing wounded susceptibilities. But both now and later Whyte was determined to leave no possible expedient untried for the restoring of peace with liberty. For this task he had unusual qualifications. His fearlessness in speech and fidelity to his

---

[1] Both biographies contain this literary curiosity, in which Robert Rainy speaks *sub persona* William Robertson Smith.

friends won and kept the confidence of the younger reformers, while his steadfastness in the old theological paths and his position as the successor of Candlish gained for him a hearing from those on the other side. Nor could either he or Dr. Rainy forget the link between them forged at Dr. Candlish's death-bed only three years before.

After Whyte's first endeavour as a peacemaker had failed, he was called on to give proof of his courage. By March 1877 the College Committee had prepared their Report, which bore on its face clear marks of compromise. It found no " sufficient ground for a process of heresy," but found and lamented certain elements in the article "Bible" which were " fitted to create apprehension " (especially the argument that Deuteronomy was attributed to Moses only by " a literary form "), and considered the article as a whole to be " of a dangerous and unsettling tendency." From these conclusions, or rather from the latter part of them, two members only, out of twenty, dissented.[1] Candlish and Whyte each entered an independent dissent, and the latter is so characteristic, and withal so concise, that it may well be given in full :

" 1. Because the Committee should have kept themselves to their instructions, and simply reported to the Assembly that they had ' not found in the article any ground sufficient to support a process for heresy against Professor Smith.' For as soon as the Committee begin to reason, and argue, and judge about the article generally, they immediately travel into matters which I have no ability to discuss.

" 2. Because if anything was to be said beyond an exact report on the legality of Professor Smith's teaching, the opportunity should

---

[1] Two others dissented in the opposite interest. Cf. *The Life of Robertson Smith*, pp. 208–11. The authors add : " Mr. Whyte's dissent does the greatest credit to his courage no less than to his common sense."

have been taken of relieving their brother of the
odium that has unfairly fallen upon him, and of
tracing home much of the present excitement to
its real cause—the published criticisms of his
article, and the current talk about it—the
motive and merit of which this is not the place
to characterise, but which the Committee might
righteously and usefully have given their mind
about.   The opportunity should also have been
taken to suggest to the Assembly, in connection
with this case, to instruct their people that
there are necessarily many questions in scholarship and theology that require the long and close
study of trained and able minds, and that such
questions as Professor Smith is compelled to
discuss in his article belong to the province of
specially equipped scholars.   Further, the Committee might well have recommended all our
professors and ministers to cultivate a close and
intelligent acquaintance with the labours of
contemporary scholarship as a sure means of
warding off all unreasonable panic on the one
hand, and also of escaping intellectual stagnation
in professional study on the other.

" 3. Because instead of the timid and cau-
tious tone of the Report, a hearty and grateful
acknowledgment should have been made of the
goodness of God to our Church in the succession
of eminent theologians and teachers He is raising up among us.   And especially recognition
should have been taken by the College Committee
of the fact that our professors are making first-rate
scholarship indigenous among us, and are compelling the eyes of men to look to us with envy,
because in our Colleges we are combining, and are
training our future ministers to combine, the most
loyal and affectionate devotion to our Church
polity, worship, and confessional position, with the
occupation and cultivation of a foremost place in
contemporary scholarship and biblical theology.

" 4. Because, while regretting that Professor

14

Smith did not enough consider that the perusal of his article would not be confined to the theological schools, the Report does not, at the same time, strenuously insist that the traditions and prepossessions of those who cannot be familiar with critical and scientific questions are not to be allowed to trammel the hands and brand the names of men who are doing some of the Church's selectest and most delicate work.

" For these and other reasons I dissent from the Report."

The whole outlook of this vigorous protest is determined by the writer's firm belief that the cause of religious truth has nothing to fear from single-minded inquiry in any field of knowledge. Whyte would have endorsed without question the saying of his friend, Marcus Dods, at a later time, that " the man who refuses to face facts doesn't believe in God." And this faith found its issue in a true intellectual humility. Whyte knew his mind as few men did regarding his own work—that of a preacher to heart and conscience—but regarding work done in other fields he was slow to express an opinion, and slow indeed to criticise. He was always ready to trust the scholar, the man of science, and the social reformer with the same freedom to choose the methods best adapted for their several spheres as he claimed for himself in his pulpit or among his congregation—on one condition only, that each did his work " as ever in his great Taskmaster's eye."

The Assembly of 1877, to which the report of the College Committee with the accompanying dissents was presented, gave the Robertson Smith case a new direction. Smith now " claimed a libel," *i.e.*, demanded that the charges against his teaching should be precisely formulated, and judged according to the regular law of the Church.[1] This implied that

---

[1] An ominous feature of this Assembly was the carrying by a majority of more than four to one of a motion suspending Smith from the duties of his professorship while the case ran its course. These duties he was never allowed to resume.

the case passed from the College Committee into the hands of the Presbytery of Aberdeen, the Church court to which he was immediately responsible. The charges were accordingly formulated in a document of great length and cumbrous terminology, under eight heads. These were discussed in detail during the following winter. The Scottish dailies, and especially the *Aberdeen Free Press*, devoted many columns to reporting these debates, in which Robertson Smith expounded and defended his views with remarkable lucidity and skill in debate. It was these reports which did more than anything else to make the laymen of Scotland familiar with the historical and religious issues involved in Old Testament criticism ; nor is it easy to name any country save Scotland in which intricate arguments on subjects such as the Deuteronomic code and the true character of prophecy would have been followed with so close and widespread an interest.

Point by point, Smith's defence carried the Presbytery with him, though the majorities were sometimes narrow. His opponents appealed to the Assembly of 1878, where, on several of the issues raised, their appeals were dismissed. But on the chief issue, that regarding the non-Mosaic authorship of Deuteronomy, the appeal was sustained by a majority of twenty-three, in face of a weighty argument by Principal Rainy, who defended, not, indeed, the views which had been called in question, but the right of a professor of the Church to hold them. The " libel " was then recommitted to the Presbytery of Aberdeen ; and, though shorn of some of its vertebræ, it yet, " like a wounded snake, dragged its slow length along " throughout the succeeding winter. More and more the prosecution, defeated in the attempt to prove Smith's teaching incompatible with the Confession of Faith, concentrated on the vague charge that his writings were " dangerous and unsettling." Yet, even so, the history of the previous year was repeated with curious exactness. Again the Presbytery consistently supported Smith, and the

Assembly of 1879 again reversed their judgment—
though now on a greatly narrowed issue. Again
Principal Rainy's counsel, which now took the form
that a special committee be appointed to confer
with Professor Smith, was rejected, this time by a
majority of one.

Whyte's contribution to the debate which ended
thus unfortunately was a brief but outspoken speech,
in which he said that to take Professor Smith's side
meant that the speaker took his own life and character in his hand; but he had risked them in the
same cause before, and still believed that " generous
construction, kindly treatment, and a spirit of love "
would bring the Church to a harmonious and just
finding. When he went on to speak of the methods
of the prosecution, his vigour of language seems to
have caused somewhat of a storm in the House. He
complained that, while he slept, a new clause had
been added to the Confession. He allowed that
Professor Smith had been " rash and precipitate,"
but he asserted that Smith was being prosecuted for
heresy " under an unheard-of law, and a manufac-
tured and illegitimate libel."

But Whyte's part in the controversy during the
three years from 1878 to 1880 was not limited to this
speech of five minutes' duration, in which indignation
and the appeal for charity were so strikingly mingled.
All the time he kept in touch with Smith and with his
leading supporters. It so happened that, while several
Edinburgh ministers were among the foremost in the
prosecution, the chief protagonists of liberty were
stationed at a distance—Professors Lindsay, Candlish,
and Bruce, and Dr. Marcus Dods in Glasgow, and
Professor Salmond in Aberdeen. Thus, when the
scene of action swung towards Edinburgh, the manse
of Free St. George's in Melville Street became a kind
of committee-room for the Robertson Smith party;
and many long and anxious consultations took place
in Whyte's study. As late as the summer of 1879 he
still hoped to bridge the growing gulf between Professor Smith and Dr. Rainy, and helped to arrange

an interview at which he himself was present. Two hours' hard controversy only served to emphasise the difference which had grown up, though Smith congratulated himself on having " practically broken " the Principal's " whole line of defence." [1]

Much turned during the succeeding months on Dr. Rainy's attitude. He became growingly convinced that Smith " was impossible," and that, for the sake of peace, he must either resign or be removed from his chair ; and his respect for precedent and for the decisions of the supreme court of the Church made him unwilling to try to reverse the decisions of 1878 and 1879. Before the Assembly of 1880 met, it was known that he intended on these grounds to transfer his support to the party of the Rev. Sir Henry Moncreiff, who led the moderate conservatives, as Dr. Begg led the implacables. But this time the unexpected happened, and Dr. Rainy, after seeing his own motions in defence of Smith defeated in two successive years, again found himself in a minority when he supported the motion proposed by Sir Henry that Smith should no longer act as a teacher of theology. The successful motion was framed by Dr. Beith, one of the most venerable ministers of the Church, who had been converted to a belief in liberty of criticism as the controversy ran its course. He had been a member of the Assembly which, forty-nine years before, deposed MacLeod Campbell, whose name is now honoured as the greatest Scottish theologian of the nineteenth century, for alleged heretical teaching regarding the Atonement. Dr. Beith thanked God in his old age that he had not shared in that fatal vote, and now, by his last public act, sought to protect his Church from a like error.

---

[1] *Life of Robertson Smith*, p. 329 ; *Life of Principal Rainy*, i. 358. Cf. the long letter from Rainy to Whyte the previous year, and that of February 13, 1880, to Dr. Adam, in which Rainy says : " I have taken an opportunity of saying to Whyte how difficult I find it to represent to myself the maintenance of Smith in his chair. He did not remonstrate much—only mourned over the loss of a man who might serve us so well. But Whyte is much more sensitively alive than most Smithites to the amount of injury to the Church under which we are suffering " (*Life of Principal Rainy*, i. 348, 363).

His motion—which withdrew the libel against Professor Robertson Smith, but instructed the Moderator to admonish him to use greater care and consideration in the future exposition of his views, and left the ultimate decision regarding them " to future inquiry in the spirit of patience, humility, and brotherly charity "—was carried, amid tense excitement, at the conclusion of a debate which lasted until after midnight, by 299 votes to 292. Robertson Smith was summoned to the bar of the House, and in two nobly expressed sentences accepted the Moderator's admonition, and gave the required undertaking for the future.

Unhappily " the minor peace of the Church " so secured was only measured by days. Early in June —ten days after this historic debate—a new volume of the *Encyclopædia Britannica* appeared. It contained an article by Robertson Smith on " Hebrew Language and Literature," in which many of the views complained of in the article " Bible " reappeared, and on some points the writer committed himself more definitely than before to the theories of Wellhausen and other continental scholars. At once a fresh hue and cry arose, and the accusation was now made that Robertson Smith had not only shown himself unguarded in the expression of his views on the Old Testament, but that his promise to the Assembly had been no sooner made than broken. The defence was obvious—that the article had been written during the previous year, and passed for the press long before the Assembly met. Why, it was then asked, had not the writer taken some means to prepare the Church for the shock of this new article ? It would have been difficult to find a suitable opportunity during the few days that intervened ; and it may well be doubted whether the explanation, even if it had been made before the article appeared, would have prevented the fresh onslaught that now took place. There is no need to describe the embittered controversy of the following months—the accusations of bad faith on one side and of irregularity of procedure on the other. But so great was the revulsion of feeling that, when the Assembly of 1881 met, and Whyte made his last, and by far his greatest, stand on behalf of his friend and all that his friend's work stood for, it was scarcely doubtful that he was leading a forlorn hope.

One important fact in the changed situation was that Dr. Rainy no longer hesitated. The " libel " had been finally killed by the proceedings in the Assembly of the previous year, and, so far as the Robertson Smith case was concerned, there was no longer any danger of a pronouncement binding on the ministers of the Church that the Mosaic author- ship of Deuteronomy was of the essence of faith. Thus Dr. Rainy felt that the ground was clear for the Assembly to exercise " the reserve power " which he believed it to possess in cases of crisis, and to remove Professor Smith from his chair, as one who could no longer be trusted to train students for the ministry. The elaborate motion which he proposed could be reduced to these simple terms.   The alternative motion which Dr. Whyte [1] brought forward was, in its main proposal, a repetition of Dr. Rainy's motion which had been defeated by a single vote two years before.   For it provided for the setting up of a strong special Committee to go into the more recent develop- ments of the case, and it even gave the proposed Com- mittee power, if they saw fit, to institute a fresh process before the Presbytery of Aberdeen.

" Nothing," Dr. Whyte said in moving his resolution, on 24th May 1881, " but a constraint of conscience I could not overcome would have been able to place me in the position I now occupy. Had it been possible, I would have shrunk from the performance of this duty, but I have not found it possible to do so. It is from no doubt of the righteousness, legality, or sound policy of my motion that I feel the pain of my position in moving it, but entirely from my want

[1] He had just received the Doctorate of Divinity.

of experience in this perilous kind of work, and from want of ability for it, and still more from the profound apprehension of that distressing breach of peace and love that too commonly follows on such controversies as this. . . . But all thoughts of our own private convenience and comfort . . . and all apprehensions whatsoever of what may come to oneself out of his performance of duty, all this must be put aside, scrupulously and totally put aside, except in so far as all these things may operate in securing the utmost wisdom and self-restraint, purity of motive and simplicity of aim in all we say and do."

The speaker proceeds to argue that the most difficult task of Churchmanship often lies in dealing, not with definite problems of doctrine or creed, but with the "floating, unformulated, undefined, un-authorised body of ideas and sentiments . . . that hangs around the mind and heart of the Church."

" And," he continues, " we must deal with it in ourselves and in others with the utmost reverence, solicitude, and caution, on the one hand, and with all attainable intelligence and thoroughness on the other. Speaking broadly, we have on the one side in this great controversy the conservative caution and sensitive reverence of the Church, and, on the other, the keen, restless, insatiable spirit of modern critical inquiry. . . . Principal Rainy's motion articulates this caution, the solicitude, the anxiety—may I not fairly say the timidity, the mistrust, and the panic that is so natural to the one state of mind . . . whereas the other motion claims that the devout sentiment and solicitude that is in the Church shall not persecute out of it the faithful and diligent student, or be a barrier in his way in seeking out the whole truth attainable concerning the past ways of God with His Church, and the work of the Spirit of God in the production, preservation, and transmission of the Word of God."

The speaker then examines the always recurring charge that the teaching of Professor Robertson Smith had proved " disadvantageous," " unsettling," " unsafe." First he gives his own testimony, and then turns with a mordant and telling irony on his opponents :

" Am I to say it has been ' unsafe ' for me ? I cannot, for it would not be true. My acquaintance with Professor Smith both as a friend and as a writer has been not only safe, but most reassuring to my personal faith and most advantageous to my professional equipment. And I would be astonished to hear that any injury or disadvantage has come to the Principal from the writings of Professor Smith. Sir, the thing is impossible. No one would believe it. . . . I can well believe, nay, one sees every day, that Professor Smith's work has been ' unsafe ' for many of Principal Rainy's followers to meddle with. Their leader's motion describes their case most plainly and literally, I will not say cynically. It has been most ' unsafe and disadvantageous ' for many of them that they ever heard of Professor Smith's writings ! . . .

" As to Professor Smith's work in his chair being ' disadvantageous ' to the Church, I will only ask, in these days of unsettlement and doubt, when all our halls from time to time have to lament the loss of some of their ablest students— Has the Church lost any of her students through Professor Smith's ' unsafe ' and ' unsettling ' teaching ?—or, retaining them, are the students of Aberdeen, who have most deeply taken on Professor Smith's impress, turning out incompetent, heterodox, or unevangelical ? Are they not rather conspicuous in their generation for scholarship, loyalty, and an earnest spirit ? . . . Surely, if such things can be said, and cannot be disproved—surely a generous hope might yet be entertained that some way, short of an indecent and unlawful violence, might be found of dealing with such a servant."

Dr. Whyte next turns to the statement that Robertson Smith had shown " a singular insensibility to his responsibilities as a theological professor."

" Why, sir," he breaks out, " it is the very opposite of that that is the simple and literal truth. I have often charged Professor Smith to his face with the opposite fault—an absolutely morbid sensibility to what he considers his responsibilities in your chair. Sir, had my learned and labour-loving friend had less sensibility to his responsibilities, we had not been in this trouble ; but, then, neither would we have had the noble opportunity we have this day of taking a foremost place among the free, learned, and evangelical Churches of modern Christendom."

A further charge in Principal Rainy's motion that Robertson Smith had shown " a culpable lack of sympathy with the reasonable anxieties of the Church " has, his defender allows, " much more superficial show of truth and accuracy about it. . . . He has not always had a bridle in his mouth when his opponents were before him. All that is no doubt true, but let him who has always shown sympathy with the anxieties of his foes cast the first stone at the inculpated professor. I cannot. No, nor will I keep the clothes of them who do ! "

After an enlargement on this theme and a brief exposition of the leading points in his own motion, the speaker rose to a peroration which deserves to hold a place among those impassioned pleas for the freedom of Christian thought, of which the *Areopagitica* is the most shining example in English prose :

" In conclusion, sir, I repeat my most solemn belief that the motion it is my honoured privilege to lay on your table this morning opens up to you the only safe, righteous, and lasting settlement of this great question. You cannot arrest the movement of mind in Christendom of which these inculpated writings are an outcome. Had this movement of the theological mind been confined to Professor Smith and a handful of German or Germanised scholars like himself, you might have ignored it or arrested its progress in your Church. But the movement is not of them ; they are rather of it. They are its children, and they cannot but be its servants. Fathers and brethren, the world of mind does not stand still. And the theological mind will stand still at its peril. No man who knows, or cares to know, anything of my personal sympathies and intellectual and religious leanings will accuse me of disloyalty to the Calvinistic, Puritan, and Presbyterian polity, or neglect of the noble body of literature we inherit from our fathers. But I find no disparity, no difficulty in carrying much of the best of our past with me in going out to meet and hail the new theological methods. Of all bodies of men on the earth the Church of Christ should be the most catholic-minded, the most hopeful, the most courageous, the most generous, sure that every movement of the human mind is ordered and overruled for her ultimate establishment, extension, and enriching. The Church of Christ of all institutions on the earth should be bold to bear all things, believe all things, hope all things, endure all things. And her divine wisdom is shown in times of trial like this when she has to meet foes, as they seem to her, and seek as long and lovingly as may be to reduce them to friends. And bear with me while I say it : whether you, fathers and brethren, have the courage of your faith or no, that remains to be seen—but your son and servant under you has that courage to a fault.

" Why, sir, does Professor Smith stand to-day accused before this house ? What has his error

or fault been ?   It has been this : He thought
he saw the opportunity, and perhaps too eagerly
and adventurously seized it, of outflanking your
great enemy, the unbelieving, disintegrating,
and unremorseful criticism of the great foreign
schools.   He went out in your service, if not at
your behest, and he seeks to return to serve you
still.   He is fitted by gifts, by learning, by saga-
city, by descent, and by personal piety, to serve
you as few men in any generation possibly can,
and you are sitting here deliberating how you
can most speedily cast him over your walls to
the scorn and rejoicing of the besieging enemy.
Surely, surely, the Free Church of Scotland will
not brand herself as such a hard-hearted, short-
sighted, panic-stricken mother to her loyal, if
adventurous, son.   I will continue to hope for
better things.   And I pray that grace and wisdom may be given to you and to your suspected
son, so that to him and to you may yet be fulfilled
the prophetic promise, ' That he and his brethren
may long live to carry in captives among you,
so that strangers shall stand and feed your
flocks, and the sons of the alien shall be your
plowmen and your vinedressers ! ' "

This eloquent appeal, even when reinforced by a
powerful speech in his own defence delivered by
Robertson Smith before the debate closed towards
midnight, failed to carry conviction to the majority
of the House.   Dr. Whyte's motion received only
245 votes against 423 for Dr. Rainy's.   Two days
later, after another debate in which Dr. Dods and
Professor A. B. Bruce fought a brilliant but unavailing
rear-guard action, the Hebrew Chair in the Aberdeen
College was declared vacant.   But the last word was
spoken two days later still, outside the precincts of
the Assembly Hall.   Three hundred friends and supporters of Robertson Smith met in the Freemasons'
Hall, George Street, on 28th May, under the presidency of Mr. Benjamin Bell, the veteran surgeon of

whom we have already heard, to protest against, and dissociate themselves from, the decisions of the Assembly. The gathering contained many men of deserved influence in the older generation of the Free Church, as well as the great majority of those who were destined to lead in the decades that followed.[1] Doctors Walter Smith, Whyte, and Bruce were among those who spoke ; but a new element was introduced when Professor Lindsay definitely committed himself to the main positions advocated by his friend, and challenged Dr. Adam, who had been prominent in the later stages of the prosecution, to take what action he cared on that declaration. The meeting did not break up until it had passed four resolutions, of which the last may be quoted here : " We declare that the decision of the Assembly leaves all Free Church ministers and office-bearers free to pursue the critical questions raised by Professor W. R. Smith, and we pledge ourselves to do our best to protect any man who pursues these studies legitimately." Thus the efforts of Whyte and his associates, though they failed of their immediate object, issued in the more secure establishment of that freedom of inquiry and teaching the exercise of which had been disallowed in the case of Robertson Smith. Professor Lindsay's challenge was never taken up ; and, although in the twenty years that followed, charges of heresy were brought against Professors Bruce, Dods, Henry Drummond, and George Adam Smith, each successive onslaught was feebler than that which went before, and Dr. Whyte never again needed to stand forth as one of the foremost defenders of intellectual liberty.

After Professor Robertson Smith went to reside in Cambridge, Dr. Whyte met him less frequently, but the intimacy was kept fresh through their mutual friend, Dr. Sutherland Black. Thirteen years later, just before the close of the long illness which carried off the great orientalist in his forty-eighth year, Mrs.

[1] See the particulars in the *Life of Robertson Smith*, pp. 447 ff.

Whyte wrote a letter which shows how the conflict appeared in retrospect.

" *Easter Monday.*

" DEAR DR. BLACK,—You and our dear friend are constantly in our thoughts. We sit beside you as you wait in that shaded room.

" Often have I wished it had been possible just once to thank him for the great things he did for us in those vivid years, 1878–80. It was little short of a *Vita Nuova* : intellectually it certainly was that. . . . It was a great time, and if your friend was sacrificed, and I know how cruelly you must feel it—more, probably, than he ever did—we can endure for ourselves what we cannot for others—his blood has been the seed of the truth. . . . I did not mean to write this, it is an intrusion in such an hour ; let us only say we do not forget you nor him.—Yours in sincere sympathy,   JANIE WHYTE."

Here it might seem natural for this chapter to close ; but there is a further question which inevitably suggests itself—What was Dr. Whyte's attitude in his later years to that critical treatment of biblical problems which he had so manfully defended in the years which we have now surveyed ? Or how can we reconcile the declarations in the great speech of 1881, with such an impression as that recorded by a whole-hearted admirer in another Church—that Dr. Whyte's sermons showed " a way of handling the Scriptures which owes nothing to modern criticism " ? [1]

The present writer does not claim to bring forward a complete reply to these questions ; but there are certain considerations which undoubtedly help to answer them. First and most important is the distinction between liberty of inquiry and the particular results reached by inquirers at any given time. It

[1] Professor George Jackson, *Reasonable Religion*, p. 202. The spirit of the short tribute in which these words occur is shown by its final sentence : " The present writer is one of many who count among the few unforgettable experiences of their lives hours spent at the feet of the great preacher of Free St. George's."

was the former that Whyte defended in the years before 1882, and on this defence he never went back. On this point the biographers of Robertson Smith are most emphatic: " As regards Mr. (now Principal) Whyte, it must not be forgotten that he has never publicly committed himself to any of the views of the critical school, and that, so far as is known to the present writers, he has never adopted them." [1] As one of the writers, Dr. Sutherland Black, knew Dr. Whyte's whole mind on biblical and theological questions over a longer period than any other of his friends, his testimony carries great weight. Even in the 'seventies, Dr. Whyte was concerned with the principle that inquiry should be free, and that the authority of Scripture should find a more secure basis than the old, rigid theory of literal inspiration, rather than with the special conclusions of the newer biblical scholarship at the stage which it had then reached. None the less, his use of Matthew Arnold's text-book on the Second Isaiah, and his statement in 1881 that he had found Robertson Smith's teaching " most reassuring " to his personal faith, make it clear that he recognised a new and valuable light both for the members of his classes and for himself in the fresh and daring methods of Old Testament scholar- ship. For forty years his counsel never varied : Let those in the Church—always the great majority— who have not the talent or the opportunity for exact scholarship, trust those who are carrying on, earnestly and believingly, " some of the Church's selectest and most delicate work." Even in his last years he welcomed the writings on the New Testament of such younger scholars as Professors H. A. A. Kennedy and James Moffatt not less eagerly than he had welcomed the Old Testament researches of Professor Robertson Smith forty years before, and he set no less a value on their friendship.

At the same time, it is true that he made less direct use of the results of modern scholarship in his later preaching. In the 'seventies, according to Dr.

[1] *Op. cit.*, p. 185.

Sutherland Black's testimony, he drew largely on Ewald's work upon the Old Testament and on Keim's exposition of the Gospels. But, as time passed, his preaching concentrated more and more on the study of *characters*, and his interpretation increasingly became intuitive and psychological rather than historical. His main interest was in the Revelation of God as shown in His dealing with the souls of individual men, rather than in His education of the chosen People as a whole. Dr. Whyte's method was to penetrate straight to some feature in the inner life of his subject, and he less often considered the slow processes of social development by which that life was shaped. He had more of the dramatic than of the historical sense ; and he would have found no reason to quarrel with the telescoping of sixteen centuries by which the greatest of dramatists carries the medieval " Dukes of Athens " back into classical times. This characteristic was reinforced in the early 'nineties by his study of the Mystics ; and, partly under their influence, questions of historical sequence, and consequently of the date and authorship of the several books of the Bible, fell more and more into the background of his thinking. Temptation and sin, penitence and the struggle after virtue, the " goodness and severity of God "—these formed Dr. Whyte's supreme interest ; and these had not changed with the centuries, save for the infinite enlargement of our apprehension of them which he saw in the work of Jesus Christ and its interpretation by St. Paul.

Nor was it of serious moment to him whether any experience, which he recognised as that of a kindred spirit, had its origin in the outward life of an historical character, or in the heart of a nameless seer or poet. Thus he began a sermon on Job by acknowledging the mystery which hangs over the authorship of that marvellous book, but within two paragraphs he went on to speak of its patriarchal hero in the most literal way.[1] Job *was* real to him, because in the Book of

[1] *Lord, Teach Us to Pray*, p. 78.

Job a human soul speaks out of a real, intense, agonising, and finally triumphant, religious experience. In the same way he instinctively connected the fifty-first psalm with the historic David, and the ninetieth psalm, as well as the thirty-fourth chapter of Exodus, with the historic Moses. Regarding the authorship of the Psalms he did once speak definitely, and in some detail. " We say the ' Psalms of David ' because he is *the* Psalmist, because he is called again and again the sweet singer of Israel, and because he has left such an impress upon the praise of God, both for the Old Testament Church and the New. Thus we say familiarly ' the Psalms of David,' meaning the whole Divine Hebrew Psaltery that has come down to us, though there may be other singers there." [1] The address goes on to give the traditional division of the Psalter—fifty-seven psalms being assigned to David, twelve to Asaph, and so on, with a most characteristic paragraph on " the Orphan psalms," as the Hebrews called them, which were fatherless and nameless, but now have as high a place as any in the whole Psalter.

Dr. Whyte's dramatic way of dealing with his authorities sometimes led to his counting too confidently on the literary knowledge of his hearers. At the outset of his long series of *Bible Characters* he preached a sermon on Eve, which called forth a letter of pained protest from an old friend in the country, who read it as implying that our Lord had " made a tremendous attack " on women. Dr. Whyte replied that his statement had reference to Jesus *the son of Sirach*, as he thought would have been plain from his reference in the immediate context to the Wisdom books, but he accepted the full blame for his failure to make his meaning perfectly clear.[2] A more remarkable case remains vividly in the

[1] This address was given to a men's meeting in the Wesleyan Central Hall, Edinburgh, on February 18, 1906, reported in the *Scottish Review* of March 1. He instances the parallel case of " the Wesleyan hymns," which are not all necessarily by the Wesleys.

[2] The correspondence was published in the *Expository Times*, January 1895; but when the sermon appeared in book form, this particular passage was withdrawn.

mind of the present writer, who looks back on the sermon on Lazarus in which it occurred as the most overpowering effort of the religious imagination which he ever heard from the pulpit of Free St. George's. Towards the close, Dr. Whyte spoke of what the later life of Lazarus must have been from the point at which the Fourth Evangelist breaks off; and said, "A post-canonical author has these entries in his Arabic diary, which I will faithfully copy out for your satisfaction about Lazarus." Then followed eleven brief quotations from Browning's *Epistle of Karshish*, woven into a prose paragraph which ended with these words, " You can construct for yourselves out of these authentic fragments what Lazarus's second life was as long as the chief priests let him alone." [1] Dr. Whyte was so impressed, and so satisfied, by the intuitive and sympathetic enlargement of the biblical narrative by the modern poet that he did not hesitate to use the word " authentic " of Browning's interpretation.

Dr. Whyte's preaching, especially his later preaching, was emphatically that of a seer and mystic rather than that of an historical student. It is remarkable that one whose mind habitually moved on the imaginative level, and who was not naturally endowed with the historical sense, should have cared so much for the maintenance of freedom in criticism and in research, and appreciated so keenly the work of the scholars whom he numbered among his friends. It is the biographer's task to make clear, so far as he may, the various facets of his subject's mind, rather than to attempt to reduce them to an unreal consistency. But one thing admits of no doubt : the strength of Dr. Whyte's own faith and his piercing vision of divine truth made him confident that no explorations in the field of history or science could ever undermine the foundations of the Temple.

[1] *Bible Characters*, iv. 84.

PART THREE—THE WORK OF NOONTIDE:
CHARACTERISTICS
1881–1892

CHAPTER XIII EARLY MARRIED LIFE :
CORRESPONDENCE WITH NEWMAN

1881–1884

" There is nothing mightier or nobler than where man and wife are one heart and mind in a house, a grief to their foes, and to their friends great joy, but their own hearts know it best."—*The Odyssey*.

THE year 1881 formed a happy turning-point in Alexander Whyte's life, for it saw his marriage to Jane Elizabeth Barbour. Her parents were accustomed to spend the winters in Edinburgh, and Whyte had been introduced to them at 11 George Square by Simeon Macphail while he was still a student at New College. In September 1879, and again a year later, he visited them at their summer home, Bonskeid, in the valley of the Tummel in the north of Perthshire. These two scenes had formed the background of his future wife's upbringing, and she had shared to the full in the intellectual quickening which came to many of the leisured girls of Edinburgh in the 'seventies. This was due in part to the classes in literature and philosophy conducted in Shandwick Place by teachers such as Professors Masson and Calderwood, before the University classes were thrown open to women, but hardly less to the influence of Whyte's own work described in Chapter X. She had also shared the interests of her two brothers, Robert and Hugh, who had recently completed their college courses in theology and medicine respectively. In 1875 Robert Barbour left Edinburgh University with a " double first " in Classics and Philosophy, and bearing the reputation of being, in his friend Henry

Drummond's words, "out of sight the ablest man of his time at college." During the four following years, while he pursued his course at the New College, he shared every interest in nature and literature, in philosophy, art, and religion as well as in education and social reform, with his younger sister. During one summer at Bonskeid they rose at six, in order to have two uninterrupted hours for study ; and a year's reading included the *Niebelungen Lied*, part of the *Divina Commedia*, the *Odyssey*, and part of the *Æneid*. In reading the classical poets, the sister read from a translation, the brother from the original, breaking in with frequent illustrations and comments from other spheres of knowledge.

All this enabled the young wife to bring into her new home an enthusiasm for the things of the mind comparable to that of her husband, and a sense for art which he had previously had little opportunity of cultivating. But, strong as were the mutual interests furnished by Dante and Wordsworth, a still stronger bond was their common enthusiasm for Robertson Smith and his cause. The letter quoted towards the close of the preceding chapter gives one proof of this, but it was shown in a different way at a less anxious moment. On the night of Robertson Smith's shortlived triumph in 1880, Janie Barbour sped along George IV. Bridge from the Free Assembly Hall to tell the great news to her mother, who had gone home three hours before, fearing the opposite result and unable to face the pain of it. That night at 11 George Square, Evening Prayers took the form of a brief thanksgiving service between 1 and 2 a.m. ; and next day the daughter of the house cabled the words, " Smith victorious," to her elder brother who was then in South Africa.

Her engagement to Alexander Whyte took place in December 1880, though the public announcement was deferred till the following spring. The spring brought him the degree of " Doctor of Divinity " from the University of Edinburgh. It is easy to lay too much stress on such distinctions ; yet this was not without significance, both as setting a final seal of academic approval on his own hard-won self-education, and as giving him the title by which for forty years he was best known—" Dr. Whyte of Free St. George's." It is said that before receiving the degree he was asked by the University authorities what contribution he had made to learning, and sent in reply the Free St. George's Congregational Year-book as the one publication which stood to his credit. Long after, when receiving the Freedom of his adopted city, he recalled with amusement being told that the degree was conferred rather on his congregation's account than on his own ; and he added that, for their sake, he would not have refused to take all the letters of the alphabet after his name !

Dr. and Mrs. Whyte were married on 9th September 1881. Forty years ago weddings in church were hardly known in Presbyterian Scotland ; and, owing to the illness of Mr. Barbour, the scene was 52 Queen Street, the home of the bride's sister and her husband, Professor A. R. Simpson. The house holds a notable place in medical history, for it was in the dining-room that Professor Simpson's uncle and predecessor, Sir James Simpson, made those experiments in the anæsthetic properties of chloroform which endangered his own life, but brought untold benefit to sufferers in many lands. The marriage ceremony took place in the room above, brightened with heather and autumn rowans from Bonskeid. It was performed by Principal Rainy, whose presence proved that the vigorous controversy which had passed less than four months before had left unbroken the personal friendship of the two men. At the wedding-breakfast, after the bride and bridegroom had left, he said that he knew no man who possessed a greater power of making friends than Whyte. Robert Barbour, the bride's elder brother, who was now under call to the Free Church of Cults, near Aberdeen, also took part in the service ; and his prayer that the newly wedded lives might be filled " to the full with mutual beauty, honour, and blessedness, and spared long for works of usefulness and services of love," assuredly did not fail of its answer.

Dr. and Mrs. Whyte went first to Bonskeid, where they passed the opening days of their married life in visiting old friends in the farms and cottages who had watched her grow up from childhood. On Sunday, 11th September, Dr. Whyte preached on his favourite passage in the thanksgiving Psalm ciii. in the chapel a mile from Bonskeid—a pulpit from which he spoke often during the thirty-five years which followed. From the Tummel valley Dr. and Mrs. Whyte went on to Glencoe and Loch Awe, and by the beginning of October they were installed in the manse at 52 Melville Street.

The winter which followed was a crowded one. Among the guests at one of their first dinner-parties was Professor James Bryce, who was already famous as an historian and jurist, but whose great career as a statesman still lay in the future ; and on another occasion a group of friends gathered to do honour to Professor Robertson Smith.

Another event of the autumn was the completion of the church buildings of Free St. George's, which had been left in some respects unfinished in 1869. Ten years later Dr. Whyte appealed to the congregation for a sum of £8000 to meet the cost of the tower, and of adding a vestry behind the church. The response was generous, and made possible the building of the *campanile*, which is without question the most successful part of the building from the architectural standpoint, and whose copper spire forms so fitting a complement to the green dome of the sister church when the fitful sun shines on the towers of " Auld Reekie." It was characteristic that the first congregational function which Dr. and Mrs. Whyte carried through together was a supper to the workmen who had built the tower. Body, soul, and spirit were all provided for, as the supper was followed by a concert, and by addresses from Principal Rainy, Mr. Taylor Innes, and Mr. T. R. Buchanan, who had recently been elected as Liberal Member for West Edinburgh.

In May 1882, Dr. Whyte's mother, whose health had begun to fail some time before, became gravely ill, and he was summoned to her bedside. Even after she ceased to be able to teach in her beloved Sabbath school or to attend church regularly, her interest in both remained. Her convictions were also strong on the question of temperance; and she flatly declined to send her contribution to the Sustentation Fund through the usual channel, since the collector was engaged in carrying on a licensed business in the Southmuir. So it was arranged that one of the office-bearers of the South Free Church should call for her subscription instead; and the last time he came to see her, although she was now very weak, she asked why he had delayed calling on her to contribute. It was no small joy to her in these last months to know that her son had so signally proved his power in the Christian ministry, and to welcome his bride when they went together to Kirriemuir.

For a time after her son's visit she rallied, and he returned to Edinburgh for the Assembly and other duties. Then, on 7th June, he learned by telegram that she had passed away early that morning. The following day he reached his old home; and the funeral took place on Saturday the 10th. The resting-place where her body was laid is close to the western wall of the new cemetery high on the Hill of Kirrie-muir—a point from which the whole sweep of Strath-more and the surrounding Grampians and Sidlaws lies open to the view, and only a few yards from the spot where, fourteen years later, her friend Margaret Ogilvy was laid to rest. Her faith in life and death was truly represented by the words inscribed beneath her name on the coffin:

> " Nothing in my hand I bring;
> Simply to Thy Cross I cling."

This parting was quickly followed by another. Sunday, the day after his mother's funeral, was spent by Dr. Whyte in the quiet retreat of Glen Prosen in the company of his sister. He returned to work

in Edinburgh for three days, but on the following
Friday, he saw her and her three children embark
for Canada, whither Mr. Macadam had preceded
them. Dr. Whyte never again saw Elizabeth Macadam, or her youngest child, the little Alec, who
had been called after him and to whom he was
tenderly attached. It was fortunate for him that,
after this double deprivation, when he could no
longer look to the manse at Chryston as a second
home, his own home was no longer solitary. There
in the following month his eldest daughter, Margaret,
was born.

Before the baby girl was three months old, an
accident happened which came very near to ending
Dr. Whyte's work in mid-career. On 9th October,
he and his friends, Mr. Webster Thomson and Mr.
Orrock Johnston, were driving by coach from Ballater
to Braemar. They had reached a point near Invercauld Bridge, when, owing to the slipping out of a
linchpin, the right fore-wheel suddenly came off, and
the coach was thrown violently on its side. Several of
the passengers were thrown to the side of the road, and
Dr. Whyte's head fell sharply against a wall. In the
end, his friends suffered perhaps more than he, since
they never quite threw off the effects of the nervous
shock which the accident caused ; but at the time his
injury was far the gravest. He lay unconscious on
a bank by the roadside bleeding from the wound in
his head, until arrangements were made to take the
injured to the Invercauld Arms Hotel at Braemar,
three miles away. The first news that reached his
wife was when she opened the *Scotsman* at Bonskeid
twenty-four hours later and saw that he was suffering from a serious scalp wound. She set off by
the first train with her child, and at Aberdeen was
met by her brother, who had already gone from
Cults to Braemar and had brought back a reassuring
report.

Never did the strength of Dr. Whyte's constitution
prove of more value than in this crisis. Four weeks of
slow return to health followed, amid the wealth of

colouring and the keen autumn air of the Braemar valley. Queen Victoria, who was still at Balmoral, noticed the little Margaret being carried by her nurse along the road below Braemar, and inquired more than once how Dr. Whyte progressed. On 2nd November the patient was able to move, and in a single day the drive of forty - five miles to Bonskeid was accomplished, though summits of 2200 and 1200 feet had to be passed on the way. As the carriage crossed the former—the highest point on any driving road in Britain, above the celebrated " Devil's Elbow "—the snow already lay deep on the road.

One day, as Dr. Whyte, who was now convalescent, walked with his wife on the hillside above the Pass of Killiecrankie, the thought came to them that, since he could not resume work for some months, this might prove a unique opportunity for a winter visit to Italy. A telegram soon brought Dr. Joseph Bell from Edinburgh, who, like his father, Mr. Benjamin Bell, was a greatly trusted elder in Free St. George's. For nearly forty years he proved himself the close friend, as well as the physician, of its minister ; and his acuteness of observation was so striking that he was commonly believed to have suggested to Sir Arthur Conan Doyle, when a medical student in Edinburgh, the character of Sherlock Holmes. He at once expressed his approval of the scheme for a southern journey, and before Christmas Dr. and Mrs. Whyte had seen the Palace of the Popes at Avignon, and the Roman amphitheatre and temple at Nimes. Thence they went on to the Riviera, where the convalescent showed the completeness of his recovery by bathing in the Mediterranean at Antibes on New Year's Day of 1883. A memorable visit to Dr. George Macdonald at Bordighera and a short stay in Venice brought the journey to a close.

Two other developments of these years deserve mention here. It was about this time that Dr. Whyte felt constrained to become an abstainer. In the middle of last century the moderate use of alcohol was

taken for granted in the ministry of the Free Church
as in other circles ; nor did it awaken any comment
if a minister was offered a glass of sherry in the vestry
before preaching for a friend, or provided an evening
glass of toddy for guests in his study. Dr. Guthrie
was the first leader of the Church to break away from
these customs ; and his becoming an abstainer was
greeted with much head-shaking amongst the devout,
since it was taken for granted that his motive for
doing so must have been that of personal prudence.
Only a man, it was assumed, who had found modera-
tion impossible could be forced back on abstinence.
But by the early 'eighties, sentiment was fast changing,
and men had begun to recognise that the true motive
was the Pauline one—concern for the safety and
welfare of others. Many things in Dr. Whyte's
ministry may have brought home to him the need for a
firm stand on this question, and doubtless his mother's
strong conviction played its part ; but the decisive
factor in his case, as in that of Dr. Rainy shortly
before,[1] was what he had seen within the circle of
his own friends. The first temperance meeting which
he addressed was in the church of his brother-in-law
at Cults. At this meeting he told most impressively
how he had been brought sternly up against the havoc
wrought by intemperance in the lives of more than
one of the ablest and most promising among his own
friends. For their sakes he had felt constrained
himself to give up the use of alcohol; and he pled
with the most solemn emphasis that his hearers
should join in the same renunciation. For him it
was a definite act of self-discipline, since no man of
forty-five years of age can change the habit of half
a lifetime, however strictly controlled it has been,
without a vigorous and continued effort of will.

The spirit in which he sought to lead others to
the step which he had thus deliberately taken—
especially those among his friends whom he knew to
stand in need of this safeguard—is best shown by a
letter to one of the most consistent advocates of

[1] *Life of Principal Rainy*, ii. 279.

temperance in his generation, Mr. Charles J. Guthrie, son of Dr. Thomas Guthrie, and afterwards one of the judges of the Court of Session :

" DEAR MR. GUTHRIE,—Could you spare an hour this evening to be present when a friend of mine takes the total abstinence pledge ? I wish that the step should be taken with as much seriousness, and, if I may say so, with as little loss of self-respect as possible ; and therefore I specially wish *you* to be with me. An hour from your house [and] back again would suffice. If you say Yes, I will send a cab to your house at any hour that suits you.

" It is a serious case. . . .—Truly yours,
" A. WHYTE."

One of Dr. Whyte's texts when speaking on temperance was Dr. Johnson's saying, " Drink water, and go in for a hundred " ; and another was the story of Daniel's refusal to accept a portion of the king's meat or of the wine which he drank. Commenting on the latter, he used these words :

" We are abstainers many of us, against our own hearts ; or, if our hearts are in our abstinence then it is our hard and self-righteous hearts. . . . And this makes one man peevish and melancholy in his abstinence, and another man fierce and intolerant. And thus our latter end is worse than our beginning ; and our self-denial than our self-indulgence. We must not only abstain, but we must make our abstinence genial and full of liberty and delight." [1]

Deeply as Dr. Whyte felt the urgent moral constraint of the temperance appeal, he felt more deeply still the need for naturalness and charity in our response to it.

The other new venture of the years between 1881 and 1884 was of a different kind, and links itself rather

[1] *Bible Characters*, Third Series, p. 166.

with the scheme for Bible-class handbooks, which made steady progress through these years. Before Dr. Whyte became an author himself, he had proved himself a " cause of authorship in others "—if one may thus adapt a Platonic phrase. Early in 1881 he approached a number of his more scholarly friends in the Free Church with a proposal for a series of lectures on *The Evangelical Succession*.[1] There were to be twenty-one lectures in all, delivered during the three succeeding winters in Free St. George's on Sunday evenings—in addition to, not as a substitute for, the regular services and the meetings of the Young Men's Class. " The special object of the scheme will be," so Whyte's preliminary letter ran, " to exhibit the genius of the Evangelical Principle, to trace its manifestation, development, and vicissitudes, in various ages of the Church and human history ; and to illustrate its ruling and moulding power over diverse types of national, intellectual, and spiritual character. The lectures to be biographical, historical, popular, and distinctively evangelical." Those who have carried through a scheme of this character will appreciate the added labour which it involved, beyond the already arduous work of these three winters. The first course of seven lectures extended from the Apostle Paul to Luther, the second from Calvin to Bunyan, and the third from Pascal to Chalmers. Many of the lectures had high qualities of style and treatment ; and as a sequence they showed a varied interest sustained by an underlying unity. Among the best were the opening lecture on the Apostle Paul by Principal Rainy, and those by Dr. Dods on Augustine, Professor Lindsay on Anselm, and Dr. Taylor Innes on Rutherford. The last-named lecture was afterwards described by Dr. Whyte as " the finest thing that had ever been written on Rutherford." [2] And in 1904 he wrote of another lecture in the series—

---

[1] The lectures were finally published in three volumes bearing this title—now unfortunately long out of print, though one or two of the lectures have been reissued in other forms.

[2] *Thirteen Appreciations*, p. 121.

" John Knox," by Robert Barbour—that " nothing more eloquent, or more heart-kindling " could be found for the Knox centenary the following year.

But modern books continued to find a place beside the classics of theology on Dr. Whyte's heavily laden study table. A letter to Dr. Sutherland Black, headed only " Sabbath night," but evidently written about this time, shows how ready he was to assimilate the best work in foreign theology when it was brought within his reach : " I have just finished a re-perusal of your Ritschl.[1] Accept the late thanks of an unscholarly preacher for your service in it. Is his second volume published ? If so, is there any chance of seeing it in English ? " Other letters from Dr. and Mrs. Whyte to the same friend show how much thought they both gave to correcting and classifying the essays sent in each spring under the Welfare of Youth scheme. The preparation of the final prize list was left to Dr. Black's scholarly judgment ; and on one occasion Mrs. Whyte applied to him, with something of the optimism of youth, for such a statement as would finally settle the delicate problem where allowable quotation passes over into plagiarism.[2]

In the early 'eighties Dr. Whyte was among the first to recognise two young Scotsmen of genius. In 1882 J. M. Barrie, who had frequented his Young Men's Classes in Free St. George's, graduated at Edinburgh University ; and when, a few months later, he went south to follow a journalistic career which soon led out into wider fields, he carried with him introductions to the editor of the *Nottingham Journal* from David Masson and Alexander Whyte. Later, when he went on to London, Dr. Whyte sent him an introduction to W. T. Stead.

In this case the background of an old family friend-

---

[1] *Justification and Reconciliation*, vol. i.
[2] For several years Dr. Black conducted a senior class in Free St. George's in preparation for the Welfare of Youth. More than twenty years later Dr. Whyte wrote : " We did splendidly when J. S. B. had the Welfare Class."

ship lay behind Dr. Whyte's interest in the younger man's success in authorship. But his admiration for Robert Louis Stevenson sprang wholly from his sense that a new voice of undoubted genius had begun to sound. It was shortly before this—perhaps in the early months of 1880, when Stevenson's published writings were still few and relatively slight—that Whyte began to speak of him as a writer of rare promise. An elder in St. George's, Mr. James Watson, once said to him, " I hear you are an admirer of Louis Stevenson ? " " Certainly." " Will you come and meet his father, who is very much worried about his son's Bohemian ways ? Tell him what you think of his son's writings ; it will help to reassure him." Whyte willingly agreed, and shortly after met Mr. Stevenson at dinner at the house of their mutual friend in Charlotte Square, telling the old engineer that his son's name would yet stand beside that of Swift or Sterne, high on the roll of the masters of English prose. " The old man," said Dr. Whyte in relating the incident long after, " pooh-poohed what I said—or affected to do so—but I stuck to my guns." [1]

In the summer of 1881 Stevenson was persuaded to stand for the Chair of Constitutional History in the Faculty of Law of Edinburgh University. The appointment was in the gift of the Faculty of Advocates, of which he was a member ; and, as the lectures were confined to the summer term, his friends believed that the work would be not uncongenial, and that his health would stand the strain. During June and July Mr. and Mrs. Stevenson were at Kinnaird Cottage above Pitlochry, and Dr. Whyte went from Bonskeid, six miles away, to see them. Unfortunately Stevenson was ill at the time and Whyte's stay at Bonskeid was brief, so they had little opportunity for talk and discussion ; but in the late autumn Stevenson wrote from Davos, acknowledging the

[1] Sheriff George Watson writes that he well remembers the dinner in his father's house, and the impression made on the young people there gathered by this prophecy of Stevenson's coming fame.

support which Whyte had given him in his candidature.[1]

> "THE CHALET, HOTEL BUOL,
>   DAVOS PLATZ, GRISONS,
>   SWITZERLAND.

"MY DEAR DR. WHYTE,—I have just received from my father a copy of my testimonials; and I shall leave you to imagine with what feelings I read your more than generous contribution. I question if this be one of the services for which thanks can, with propriety, be rendered; but, proper or not, I have to thank you. Yours is one of the most gratifying chapters of that, to me, most gratifying pamphlet. I am truly surprised how much people find it in their hearts to say for me.

" I am back again on my Patmos, or rather Pisgah, with five months of snow before me; not this time, however, in a crowded and gloomy hotel, but in a little house of our own, overlooking the valley and close to the pine-woods. This is a great alleviation; and I promise myself to be as happy as the day is long—though this is the case, if ever, to append a modest *D.V.*

" Will you present my regards to Mrs. Whyte, and believe me, with all gratitude and good wishes, Sincerely yours,

> "ROBERT LOUIS STEVENSON.

" P.S.—I dare say you can imagine what a HUMBUG I feel when face to face with these testimonials; antimonials, I used to call them; and when I reflect upon that career of imposition of which this is the crown, antimonial seems the better word. So I pass, at least, from blushes to disgust. Next time, I shall be more hardened.

> " R. L. S."

---

[1] At the election, Stevenson's nomination was seconded by an unknown junior, now Lord Shaw of Dunfermline, whose opinion of his fitness for the chair was entirely based on the reading of *Virginibus Puerisque*, then recently published. (Lord Shaw, *Letters to Isabel*, p. 139.) Stevenson received seven votes out of about two hundred, according to Lord Shaw; Sir Sidney Colvin gives the number as three!

In 1883, Dr. Whyte published his first book, *A Commentary on the Shorter Catechism*, and sent a copy to his exiled fellow-countryman, who acknowledged it in the following letter :

"LA SOLITUDE,
HYERES-LES-PALMIERS, VAR.

"DEAR DR. WHYTE,—An old friend indeed has come to visit me, and in a charming garb ; your Commentary is an enchiridion of a worthy strain ; I have remarked already many interesting plums, and I must refer at once to my favourite : 'Be careful of your health, but be careless of your life.' It would be hard to better that.

"What we all owe to the Shorter Catechism it were hard to limit. We must have learned more philosophy, perhaps above all more *style*, than we or our teachers dreamed of : a more eloquent book, with so much method in the eloquence, being difficult to find. I am partly its obliged admirer, partly its conscientious enemy. The first question and answer—I wish the whole were in that strain—are purely sublime. Thenceforward it is apt too much to dwell among cobwebs and split hairs, to forget the soul and its strong affections, to address itself to captious enemies rather than to young minds desiring guidance and requiring trumpet notes of encouragement. Not in this correct and somewhat leaden manner, but with a more communicative and engaging ardour, should religion, philosophy, and morals be presented. David, I find, was the man after God's own heart. The book smacks of the Long Parliament and the 'constitutional party' in religion.

"Pardon me this picking of faults. I am Scotch ; *que voulez vous ?* 'Aiblins, I'm no' verra shure of Davie'—you know the anecdote. Your book at least has not fallen on barren soil : it has already interested me, and already a friend who came to visit me and took it up from curiosity, has made a note of the title and publisher, determined to possess a copy. With many thanks, believe me, Yours very truly,

"ROBERT LOUIS STEVENSON."

At this time Dr. Whyte again came into communication with Cardinal Newman, who spent much time in answering requests for advice and sympathy from those in other churches who reverenced him.[1] The *Commentary on the Shorter Catechism* played its part here also, but the first step was taken by Mrs. Whyte. Soon after her marriage, she wrote asking for Dr. Newman's autograph to accompany a portrait which she intended to give her husband, and reminding him of his three visitors from Scotland five years before. He replied with all his wonted graciousness of spirit :

"BIRMINGHAM,
November 12, 1881.

" MY DEAR MADAM,—You pay me a very kind compliment in selecting my portrait for such a gift, and I gladly send you my autograph.

" I have to thank you also for what you say about the interest which Dr. Whyte takes in my writings, which suggests the hope and trust that, in spite of the sad divisions of Christendom, a great work is going on in the hearts of serious men, tending towards a restoration of the scattered members of Christ, even though not in our day, yet in the future, in ' the times and seasons which He has appointed.' Is it not hard and strange that they who have strong religious sympathies in common, should not enjoy that Unity, which He has made the outward token that they are His ?

" I well recollect the visit of the three gentlemen, though they were not long enough here for me to distinguish one from the other. As to their request, I will gladly remember my

[1] Father Ryder, quoted by Wilfred Ward, *Later Life of Cardinal Newman*, vol. ii. p. 359.

dear Scotch friends unknown when I say my daily Mass.

"Thank you for the Year-book.[1]   It is a very interesting memorial of work.   I fancied I found two or three misprints.   Is ' Pope ' right, p. 30, line 7 ?   I thought the lines were in Johnson's *Imitations of Juvenal*.

"With my best respects to Dr. Whyte, I am, Very truly yours,

"JOHN H. CARD. NEWMAN."

This letter was accompanied by a separate sheet containing not a single autograph, but four autographs in varying forms, including the simple *John Henry Newman* of his earlier days ; and was followed five days later by a further message : " I ought to have said in my letter to you the other day, that, if I have not, in my autographs, sent you what you wanted, I hope you will tell me.   In that case, I will follow your instructions, and send you what is more to the purpose."   Could the fine gold of Christian courtesy be further refined than this ?

The portrait to which this autograph was attached was Rajon's etching of the aged Cardinal from the painting by Ouless.   Along with Richmond's beautiful drawing of Newman in his Anglican days, it occupied a place of honour in Dr. Whyte's study during the remaining years of his ministry.   Thus Dr. Whyte had beside him a double reminder of the man whom he so greatly revered.

A year later, when he was slowly regaining strength after the coach accident, his wife again wrote to Cardinal Newman, asking whether they might hear him preach if they were to break the southward journey at Birmingham ; and she received the following reply :

---

[1] Mrs. Whyte had enclosed the Free St. George's Year-book for 1881–82.   The quotation occurs in the notes prepared by Dr. Whyte for the " Young Men's Sabbath Morning Fellowship Meeting " ; and the lines run :

"Still raise for good the supplicating voice,
But leave to Heaven the measure and the choice."

Dr. Newman was right in his ascription of the lines.

" BIRMINGHAM,
November 26, 1882.

" DEAR MRS. WHYTE,—I have to thank you for a very kind letter—also, for Dr. Whyte's message through you, for which, of course, I thank and praise God, not, however, if I may presume to use St. Paul's words, without ' great sadness and continual sorrow in my heart ' that there should not be One Body and One Spirit among those who profess One Lord and One Baptism.

" I think I shall never preach again, for my voice is gone, and I cannot speak without an effort. This Christmas will be the first, I think for thirty-five years, that I have not taken the Sermon in the Oratory Church.

" I am much concerned to hear of Dr. Whyte's bad accident.—Very truly yours,
" JOHN H. CARD. NEWMAN."

In the following year, Dr. Whyte sent Cardinal Newman a copy of his *Shorter Catechism*. The letters which he received in regard to his book throw great light on the character of both men.[1] But they can hardly be understood without a transcript of the sentence to which Newman took exception. In the first edition of Dr. Whyte's Handbook (pp. 184–5), his comment on the words of the Catechism, " not after a corporal or carnal manner, but by faith, made partakers of His body and blood," ran as follows : " This is directed against the Popish doctrine of transubstantiation. According to that doctrine the bread and wine are changed into the very flesh and blood of Christ, so that all communicants literally and physically eat the flesh and drink the blood of Christ." In the second edition, the second sentence was altered as follows, the words approved by Cardinal Newman appearing in inverted

---

[1] The six letters which follow were printed as an Appendix to Dr. Whyte's *Newman, an Appreciation*, which was published in 1901, but is now out of print.

commas, but without mention of his name : " According to this doctrine, 'the substance of the bread and wine is converted into the substance of the very flesh and blood of Christ, so that all communicants literally and substantially partake of His flesh and blood.' "

In the following letter, Cardinal Newman acknowledged Dr. Whyte's gift of his book :

" *December* 15, 1883.

" MY DEAR DR. WHYTE,—I thank you for your Commentary which you have sent me.   It has interested me greatly : it rejoices me to meet with so much in it which I can sympathise and concur in—and I thank you heartily for the kind references you make to me in the course of it and for the words you have written in its first page.

" But it pains me that so large a heart as yours should so little enter into the teaching of the Catholic Church, let alone agreeing to it. Thus you say that we consider that we *physically* eat our Lord's flesh and drink His blood in the Holy Eucharist.   It might quite as truly be said that in John vi. our Lord speaks of ' eating His flesh and drinking His blood ' physically as that we so speak.   We consider the *substance* of His body and blood to be in the Sacrament, and thereby to be given to us—and you truly say (p. 17), speaking of the holy Trinity, that the ' substance ' is that ' awful, mysterious essence of which the qualities are *not* [1] extension, or colour, or figure,' etc., that is, *not* the ' phenomena ' which we call physis or nature, and which we could only receive ' physically,' but that unknown reality to which sensible qualities attach themselves and belong, without being *it*.

" Excuse this outbreak of controversy, and believe me to be, Most truly yours,

" JOHN CARD. H. NEWMAN."

[1] The italics here are Newman's.

From the letters which follow we can infer the readiness with which Dr. Whyte met the Cardinal's criticism, by proposing that he should himself suggest such a form of words as he considered would give a true interpretation of the Eucharistic teaching of the Church of Rome ; and they also show how scrupulously each of the correspondents sought to avoid compromising or misrepresenting the position of the other.

" December 21, 1883.

" MY DEAR DR. WHYTE,—It is very kind of you to ask me to suggest an emendation in the passage I pointed out to you, now that a second edition is called for. I hope I shall propose nothing that you cannot accept. Anyhow, I shall quite understand any difficulty which may arise, and shall be sure that you grant me as much as you can. I quote some sentences from our authoritative documents as references, but of course only in justification of my changes in your text, not as if I wanted them introduced into it.—Very sincerely yours,

" JOHN H. CARD. NEWMAN.

" P.S.—I ought in my first letter to have expressed my sense of the service you are doing to the cause of Christian charity by your quotation from authors external to your own communion."

The letter concluded with a transcript of the sentence to which Dr. Newman objected, followed by the form which he suggested it might assume, and contained a separate sheet with the Latin text of the authorities referred to—all carefully copied by the aged Cardinal's own hand.

The three following letters explain themselves, and indicate how the point was finally adjusted :

" B'M., December 26, 1883.

" DEAR DR. WHYTE,—I am sorry to have given you the trouble of a correspondence, and feel I have to ask your pardon.

" As to your kind proposal to insert my letter into your second edition, I will not dream of consenting to it.

" It would be a poor return on my part to your courteous treatment of me in your book, to turn your catechism into a controversy. Nor will I do it. The two ideas are quite distinct. Nor would it be fair to myself, as if I felt sore *personally* when my faith was misconceived. What claim have I to introduce myself into your volume ? My only possible claim would be your thinking that I had made *a case*. To consider that I had *not*, yet to insert my letter, would be granting more than you had a right to grant, in justice to yourself.

" Nothing then can make me approve a course, which, though generous in you, does you harm without doing me good.—Your faithful servant,

" JOHN H. CARD. NEWMAN."

" B'M., *December* 31, 1883.

" MY DEAR DR. WHYTE,—You are treating me with extreme kindness, and if any word of mine to you implies annoyance in me, I assure you it misrepresents me, and the nearest approach I have had to any feeling of pain has been a great anxiety lest I should have quoted our profession of doctrine incompletely, and that I had left out any authoritative testimonies or popular beliefs which would give to our tenet a different aspect.

" But indeed I sincerely think such a different aspect cannot be found. Not the most ignorant or stupid Catholic thinks that he eats physically the body of our Lord. What we all believe is that we partake the Body or Blood that hung upon the Cross, and that, in the words of the Anglican service, ' that our sinful bodies may be made clean by His Body, and our souls washed through His most precious Blood,' but as to the *how* He brings this to pass, it is a mystery.

" To strengthen my feeling that I had acted quite fairly by you, I put my hands on a copy of our authoritative ' Penny Catechism ' taught in our schools, and I now send it, if you will kindly accept it. You will find the passages bearing on the point at pp. 42–44.

" Inverted commas are all that can be needed, and are a happy thought.—Most truly yours,
" J. H. CARD. NEWMAN."

" B'M., *January* 2, 1884.

" DEAR DR. WHYTE,—Since I sent to you my letter, agreeing to your printing ' substance,' etc., in inverted commas, I have been teazed with the thought I have not been fair to you, as I will explain.

" You say ' this is directed against the Popish doctrine.' I am right in saying that the ' Popish doctrine ' is *not* what you have stated it to be, but I am *not* fair to yourself when I allow you to propose to say that ' the Shorter Catechism ' directs its words against the doctrine (*really* ours) of ' the change of *substance.*' Is it not more likely that its writers knew little, or thought little, of the decrees of the Council of Trent, and were aiming at the extreme notions of the *multitude* who were in many places superstitious and sadly in want of instruction ?

" This doubt has made me quite miserable, since you have been so very kind to me ; and I so confide in that kindness, that I would rather put the matter entirely in your hands without me.

" Excuse this bad writing, but the power to hold a pen is going from me.—Very sincerely yours, JOHN H. CARD. NEWMAN."

Dr. Whyte did not apparently feel that the point raised by the Cardinal's sensitive regard for his correspondent was a serious one, since the passage finally stood as had been arranged in the previous letters. Nearly two years later he sent a friend's book to convey his Christmas greetings to Dr. Newman, and the expression of his unaltered regard. A letter came back in whose brief sentences the unmistakable music may still be heard :

" *December* 31, 1885.

" MY DEAR DR. WHYTE,—I am very glad that you give me the opportunity (as you do by your gift of Mr. Mackintosh's volume) of wishing you a happy New Year, which I do with all my heart.

" Your recommendation will go very far in making me take an interest in it—but you must recollect my age. I read and write very slowly, and the day is ended, ere it has well begun. And, though I do so little, I am soon tired, and am always ready for the indulgence of a sound sleep.

" I hope you will allow it, if I send to you and to all who are dear to you my Christmas blessing. —Most truly yours,

" J. H. CARD. NEWMAN."

" A little generous prudence, a little forbearance of one another,
and som grain of charity might win all these diligences to joyn and
unite in one generall and brotherly search after Truth."—Milton.

" Love is of no sect or party ; it neither makes nor admits of any
bounds ; you may as easily enclose the light, or shut up the air of the
world into one place, as confine love to a sect or party.   It lives in the
liberty, the universality, the impartiality of heaven."—William Law.

During the 'eighties Dr. Whyte's influence continued
to grow, and the circle of his interests to expand.
He had been known for more than a decade as the
most searching and powerful preacher of personal
morality in the Church to which he belonged ; and
at this period he was more ready than at a later time
to raise his voice on behalf of those public movements
which appealed to his judgment and his conscience.
His interventions in public affairs were not, indeed,
frequent.   He never used the pulpit for political
ends, and he always felt that it, rather than the platform, formed his true sphere.   But in these years he
carried his temperance convictions into the advocacy
of legislative control of the liquor trade as well as of
personal abstinence ; and he gave open expression to
his views regarding Disestablishment and Home Rule.
Regarding the position of the Church of Scotland,
he continued to hold—as the great majority of his
fellow-ministers in the Free Church then held—that
the most direct path towards the reunion of Scottish
Presbyterianism was through disestablishment and
disendowment.   He thus added his name to a disestablishment petition, signed by 1475 ministers in
Scotland, which was presented to the Government in
1885.[1]   But his mind was already open to the con-

[1] Cf. Carnegie Simpson, *Life of Principal Rainy*, ii. 30.

sideration of other lines of advance ; and in the early
'eighties a group of friends held a series of meetings
in his study to explore the possibility of a double
approach—to the Church of Scotland on the one
hand as well as to the United Presbyterian Church on
the other.   One of the most earnest participants in
these discussions was Mr. Thomas Nelson, then the
head of the well-known publishing house and a greatly
respected office-bearer of St. George's ; and, although
this effort led to no result at the time, it doubtless
helped to prepare the soil for a later sowing, the fruits
of which are still to be garnered.

Dr. Whyte's indication of his views on the Irish
question caused much more comment at this time.
During the year 1887 the outlook in Ireland was
stormy, and political feeling was correspondingly
embittered in Britain.   The trouble was at the
moment largely agrarian, and the acuteness of the
land question in the Highlands, where the first
Crofters Act had just come into force, brought the
Irish counterpart vividly before the Scottish mind.
Mr. John Dillon in particular was active in organising
the " Plan of Campaign," by which thousands of
crofters joined in a rent-strike to enforce attention
to their demand for the abolition of rack-renting and
for other reforms.   During the summer Mr. R. B.
Haldane, now Viscount Haldane of Cloan, brought
Mr. Dillon, who was passing through Edinburgh, to
52 Melville Street ; and the Irish leader spent several
hours in ardent talk in Dr. Whyte's study, carrying
away with him an invitation to meet several of the
leading men in the Free Church on his next visit.

The opportunity came in November, when Mr.
Dillon returned to Scotland, just after the Mitchels-
town riot had further inflamed opinion.   A letter
from Mrs. Whyte found him at Inverness, where he
was speaking to an audience familiar with crofting
problems ; and he wired that he would gladly come to
breakfast on the morning after his Edinburgh meeting.
This took place in the Music Hall on 21st November
1887, and Dr. Whyte's presence on the platform is

noted in the newspaper report, though he was not one of the speakers.   Mr. Dillon dwelt largely on the agrarian troubles in Ireland, describing the evictions and defending the " Plan of Campaign " ;   and a resolution of welcome, thanks, and sympathy with the speaker's aims was moved by Dr. John Carment, a veteran member of the legal profession and a singularly impressive personality, whom Dr. Whyte held in quite peculiar esteem now and for long after.

Among the friends who gathered to meet Mr. Dillon next morning were Principal Rainy, Dr. Carment, Mr. Taylor Innes, Professor Simpson, Mr. T. R. Buchanan, and Mr. Thomas Nelson.   The breakfast was a complete success, and the guest expressed his wonder not less than his gratification, that he should thus find himself the welcome guest of such a gathering in a Scottish Presbyterian Manse.

But, although the occasion was entirely private, it soon attracted attention and criticism outside. The most pointed expression of this criticism reached Dr. Whyte some three weeks later in the form of a long, reasoned remonstrance from thirteen prominent members of Free St. George's, eight of whom were elders,[1] and one or two, like Dr. Joseph Bell, especially intimate friends.   The letter first described " Mr. Dillon's opinions and projects as not merely unpatriotic and dangerous from a political point of view, but as contravening fundamental laws of public and private morals " ;   but soon passed on to argue the general, and without doubt most difficult, question how far a minister of religion ought to give active support to a political party in matters of acute public controversy.

" We think," the signatories said, " that he cannot take such a part without to a greater or less extent compromising the congregation ; he cannot divest himself in public estimation of his representative character, or fail to do something

---

[1] In an attack which appeared in the press eight elders and one deacon were magnified into " about thirty of his office-bearers " !

towards clothing his personal political opinions with the authority which belongs to his office ; and he has been invested with that character and office . . . for other objects and on other considerations than those of secular politics. No one would ever think of questioning your sacred right of individual opinion and of supporting that opinion by your vote, but we venture to submit to you that many considerations . . . point to the high expediency of our minister abstaining from identifying himself in so marked a manner as you have recently done with *either side* of any burning political controversy."

Dr. Whyte felt acutely that the position in which he was placed by this attempt to limit his freedom of action as a conscientious citizen was both difficult and unfair. The action which was chiefly complained of by the writers of the letter from which these sentences are quoted, as well as by other less responsible critics, was taken in the privacy of his own house, and not in any public gathering. Even after the passing of many years he spoke of the remonstrance with keen emotion to members of his family, especially to his eldest son, Fred, who has thus recorded the conflict which his father passed through :

" He soon felt that he must choose between his political opinion and his effectiveness as Minister of a great congregation. He showed no hesitation in his choice. His calling as a Minister had first claim on him then as always. Ardently as he cherished his political convictions, he felt that they must not be allowed to impair his mission as a Minister of Religion."

From this time forth he " scrupulously refrained from giving any public sign of his political faith "— unless it be counted an exception that he accepted an invitation to the platform when Mr. Gladstone addressed his last great meeting in the Edinburgh Corn Exchange. But so careful was he in later years to avoid wounding the political susceptibilities of any of those to whom he ministered in spiritual things, that his son had been for some months a Member of Parliament before Dr. Whyte even heard him speak in public.

Some later echoes of this incident may be mentioned here. On the eve of the general election of July, 1892, Dr. Whyte reached the passage regarding " Faithful in Vanity Fair " in his course of Sunday evening lectures on the characters of the *Pilgrim's Progress*, and took occasion to emphasise the difficulty, and the vital importance, of maintaining a strict regard for truth even during an election.

> " A general election is a trying time to all kinds of public men, but it is perhaps most trying of all to Christian ministers. Unless they are to disfranchise themselves and are to detach and shut themselves in from all interest in public affairs altogether, an election time is to our ministers, beyond any other class of citizens perhaps, a peculiarly trying time. How they are to escape the Scylla of cowardice and the contempt of all free and true men on the one hand, and the Charybdis of pride and self-will and scorn of other men's opinions and wishes on the other, is no easy dilemma to our ministers." [1]

We have seen how Dr. Whyte interpreted his own duty, but the self-denying ordinance which he accepted for his congregation's sake rested heavily upon his conscience as a citizen.

In 1909 Mr. Dillon again met Dr. and Mrs. Whyte in Edinburgh, and he more than once expressed his abiding sense of gratitude for the welcome offered him in 1887. These sentences are taken from a letter written to Mrs. Whyte from Dublin a few days after her husband's death :

> " Parting from those we love must always be very terrible. And yet, I suppose, one ought not to grieve over such a death as that of your

[1] *Bunyan Characters*, i. 209, 211.

husband—the triumphant ending of a very rich and splendid life.

" I have always treasured the memory of that time in 1887 [1] when he received me in his house in Edinburgh at a time when I was practically an outlaw in Ireland. I have always looked on Dr. Whyte's action on that occasion as one of the greatest examples of real Christian charity and moral courage that I have experienced in the course of a rather stormy life. Since that time I have always felt the greatest respect and affection for Dr. Whyte."

At this time Dr. Whyte was in close touch with a religious movement, which had a very definite social outlook, among the thousands of students gathered at Edinburgh University. Professor Henry Drummond was the guiding spirit of this movement, but its beginnings date back to the spring of 1884, when the tercentenary celebration of the University was held. In April, many of the most renowned scientists of the day gathered to do honour to the University, and literature found commanding representatives in Robert Browning and James Russell Lowell. Dr. and Mrs. Whyte were present at the great meetings of this celebration, and heard Pasteur and von Helmholtz, Count Saffi, the Italian patriot and jurist, and de Laveleye, the Belgian economist, give expression not only to their devotion to learning, but to their religious faith, while the last-named pointed to the teaching of Jesus as the one hope for the future of mankind. At a time when Science was still commonly supposed to spell Materialism, this testimony from men who stood in its foremost rank made a deep impression on the more thoughtful students. This was reinforced from a very different quarter during the following winter, when C. T. Studd, the Cambridge University and All-England cricketer, and Stanley Smith, who had been stroke of the Cambridge eight, conducted a series

[1] " 1888 " in the original.

of meetings among the students of Scotland, before they sailed as missionaries to the heart of China. Immediately after their visit, Henry Drummond began those meetings in the Oddfellows' Hall, which brought a new religious conviction to multitudes of Edinburgh students and which are impressively described in the twelfth chapter of his *Life*.

A year later these meetings were resumed with still greater effect ; and as the end of the session approached, a strong desire was expressed by the men themselves for a Communion service, at which many who had been indifferent to the claims of religion might make common profession of their new-found faith and love. On 28th March 1886 the Lord's Supper was first celebrated in the Oddfellows' Hall, and Dr. Charteris and Dr. Whyte were asked by Professor Drummond to conduct this memorable service.

The following autumn saw the establishment of the " Chalmers University Settlement " in the Fountainbridge district by a group of men, drawn largely from the Medical Faculty, who were closely associated with Professor Drummond's meetings in the Oddfellows' Hall. The first suggestion came from Mr. Charles M. Douglas, one of the most distinguished students of philosophy at the time,[1] and the work of organising the Settlement was largely accomplished by him in collaboration with Dr. Hugh Barbour. The ideal of social brotherhood, which had then begun to radiate out from Toynbee Hall, gave its central inspiration to the scheme ; and this, to the Scottish mind, connected itself readily with the far-reaching ideas of Thomas Chalmers. Professor Drummond and Dr. Whyte gave their powerful support from different sides—the former by appealing for workers from his great student audience, the latter by fostering co-operation between this new venture and the work already carried on in Fountainbridge by the congregation of Free St. George's. It was a genuine pleasure to him that, from the year 1882, the minister in charge

---

[1] Author of *The Ethics of J. S. Mill*, and afterwards M.P. for North-West Lanarkshire.

in Fountainbridge was his old friend, the Rev. George Low. Two years later, the " Chalmers Institute " in Ponton Street was bequeathed by Mr. Thomas Ivory for the extension of the work under Mr. Low's charge. A girls' club, evening classes, and other activities were soon in operation, manned chiefly by the younger members of Free St. George's ; but there was still room to spare, and in 1886 the Kirk-Session readily agreed that it should be used for the University Settlement. The Settlement was managed by an independent committee which included Dr. (afterwards Sir German) Sims Woodhead, then an assistant lecturer in the University, Dr. Barbour, and Mr. P. W. Campbell. The two bodies co-operated closely along their different lines of effort for the good of this crowded neighbourhood. Nor could a district have easily been found giving greater scope for the combined activities of the Fountainbridge Church and the Settlement ; for close by were the coal wharf at the terminus of the " Union Canal " and the municipal slaughterhouse, both of which have since been removed, and many of those who attended the clubs or lectures were engaged in the rough occupations there carried on. To all this work Dr. Whyte contributed less by initiating methods or supervising details than by his constant and large-hearted sympathy. Not infrequently he also gave a Saturday evening popular lecture, speaking with all the homely force and freshness of imagination which he brought to this congenial work on such topics as the *Pilgrim's Progress*—his favourite lecture-subject at this time.

As Drummond's work now began to extend from the Universities of Edinburgh and Glasgow to those of England and the United States, it brought a great widening of sympathy, as well as a deepening of personal conviction, to the most active among his fellow-workers ; and some of them became conscious that the appeal of the Christian message to the student-world was gravely hindered by the isolation in which the various Churches stood. Might not some advance be made, they asked, if representative students, and a

few of those to whom the students of the day most
looked for guidance, were drawn from different
churches and colleges, in order to discuss in free and
unhurried conference the problems which pressed
most heavily upon the student-mind ? Again the
initiative came from Dr. Barbour and Mr. Douglas,
and again Professor Drummond and Dr. and Mrs.
Whyte entered heartily into their plans as these
took shape.

The Conference met at Bonskeid in the late summer
of 1889. Dr. and Mrs. Whyte went north, the former
as one of the speakers, and Mrs. Whyte to assist her
now widowed mother in acting as hostess to twenty-
eight university men, drawn from four countries and
from many branches of the Christian Church. Their
signatures are still preserved under the legend written
in Drummond's flowing hand, " Conference of University Men, Aug. 24th–Sept. 6th." The list is headed
by the names of Whyte and Drummond himself; and
other senior men present were A. C. Headlam (now
Bishop of Gloucester), Thomas Raleigh of All Souls
College, Oxford, John Sinclair (afterwards Lord Pentland), Alexander Martin, and James Stalker. Among
the undergraduates who have attained distinction
since in varied spheres were Herbert Gray, then
warden of Edinburgh University Settlement, Halliday
Douglas, afterwards professor at Toronto, whose early
death closed a career of great promise, Percy Alden,
and Donald Fraser.[1]

The plan followed has been repeated on innumerable occasions since—often in gatherings much larger
and more widely representative—but it had all the
attraction of novelty in 1889. Morning and evening
sessions were held, the afternoons being kept free for
mountain-climbing and other outdoor occupations.
At each session a paper was read on some question

---

[1] Dr. Donald Fraser says that, in his view, this gathering, and
another which took place the following summer (when the late Dr.
Marcus Dods, the present Bishop of Durham, and Dr. Dearmer were
among those who took part), laid not a few stones in the foundation of the
British Student Christian Movement, of Mansfield House Settlement,
and of other social and religious movements of the following years.

17

of theological restatement, or on the relation of the Churches one to another, or more especially on the problems of religious work in the Colleges. Thus Dr. Headlam enlightened the Presbyterians present by an account of the Oxford Movement, and the Anglicans gained a new insight into the thought of the Free Churches. No minutes or records were kept, but those who took part bear unanimous testimony to the stimulating effect of these papers and of the frank discussions which followed, upon men whose aspirations were fully awake, but whose intellectual sympathies were still largely bounded by the limits of their own denomination or school. For Dr. Whyte the gathering represented a definite stage in the advance towards his later enthusiasm for Christian Unity.

An impression which the Conference, and Dr. Whyte's part in it, left on the mind of a young graduate of Yale was set down thirty years after by the late Mr. James B. Reynolds, President of the American Institute of Criminal Law and Criminology :

" In the summer of 1889 it was my privilege to be the sole American delegate at a conference of Scotch and English university men in Bonskeid, Pitlochry. Before I went there, I heard Dr. Whyte preach in his own church in Edinburgh. Both his sermon and prayer deeply stirred me, and I was very glad when, later, he became one of the leaders of the Bonskeid Conference. The others, Henry Drummond, Robert Barbour, and Marcus Dods, met our problems as students. The messages of each of these leaders stand out in memory, after more than thirty years, and gave cheer and inspiration to the group of university men present, who, standing on the threshold of life, had many questions along all lines of thought and action.

" The message of Dr. Whyte came to us students as that of a strong captain of men, who preached a faith wrought in the storms of life,

to help others who, like himself, suffered tempests
of the soul. He seemed then sailing in calm
waters ; his weather-stained experiences and his
note of victory through strong faith and hard
works were tempered by a warmth of sympathy
and an understanding mind that caused our
hearts to burn within us as we listened to him.
I cannot believe that any of those present that
summer have forgotten his impression of the soul
of the man or of his vibrant message."

Within a few weeks of the Conference just
described, Dr. Whyte was called upon to perform one
of the most grateful tasks which ever fell to his hand.
The General Assembly of 1889 appointed Dr. Marcus
Dods to the Chair of Greek and New Testament Exegesis in the New College ; and the Presbytery of
Edinburgh showed a fine discrimination in choosing
his intimate friend to give the address at the service of
Induction.   In this address Dr. Whyte expressed his
own conviction that, " the historical, exegetical, and
theological problems connected with New Testament
study in our day are not the ephemeral heresies of
restless and irreverent minds ; they are the provi-
dential result of that great awakening of serious
thought, and of scholarly and devout inquiry, which
began at the Reformation and has been in steady
progress in the best schools of Christendom ever
since."   He went on to indicate to the new professor what would be expected of him, while warning
him half playfully not to look for his own exalted
standard of industry or intellectual capacity from all
his students.   Yet Dr. Whyte added:

" We expect and demand that he shall show
all his students his secret: the secret, that is, of
how to work, a secret that is closer kept and less
divined than is commonly supposed. We expect
also that he shall teach his classes something of
his own open and opulent mind. We expect,
and insist, that he shall tell them that, as
preachers, they will soon run dry, and will be-

come a clog on the true progress of their Church, unless, to old age, they are still open to truth and always learning; growing all their days in breadth and grasp of mind, as also in docility of heart."

The following year gave further proofs of Dr. Whyte's hospitality of spirit, which increasingly found its reward in the high regard of Christian men outside his own Church. In 1890 the Rev. Robert F. Horton visited Edinburgh as a delegate from the English Congregational Union to the smaller Union in Scotland ; and he has recorded his memory of the warmth with which its members were welcomed by a group of the leaders of Presbyterianism in Edinburgh. In particular he refers to a meeting at which Principal Cairns, Principal Rainy, Dr. Walter Smith, and Dr. Whyte all spoke :

" Dr. Whyte gave a singular impression of authority. Afterwards I learned to sit at his feet, as the interpreter of William Law and St. Teresa, and the best exponent of John Henry Newman . . . but that first contact with a great practical Mystic marked, though I did not know it then, an epoch in my life. . . . It is not always that poets and writers seem personally as great as their books. . . . But in those four great Scotsmen I had an experience, not to be forgotten, of finding great writers greater than their writings. . . . I pass no judgment on Presbyterianism as a system, but of Presbyterians I unhesitatingly say this, the greatest men I have known are included in their ranks." [1]

It was about this time that a young Wesleyan minister, the Rev. George Jackson, now of Didsbury College, began work within a stone's-throw of Free St. George's, which aroused Dr. Whyte's admiration and sympathy in an especial degree. He gathered round him, by services and meetings in the Albert Hall in Shandwick Place, many young men and

[1] Dr. Horton's *Autobiography*, p. 107 f.

women whom the Presbyterian Church had failed to touch.   Later, as the success of Mr. Jackson's work became established, it was transferred to the Central Hall, Tollcross ; and in both stages, its small beginnings and its subsequent great extension, Dr. Whyte followed it with eager interest and help.   His later support of the Brotherhood Movement will be referred to in Chapter XXIV., but there may be quoted here an account by one of its representatives, the Rev. R. Moffat Gautrey, of a visit to his study :

> " He talked to me of my work in Nottingham, and referred especially to my activities as President of the National Brotherhood Movement. He insisted upon calling me a leader, who was nobody, and he the master in Israel whom I had revered and loved for years, though I had never seen him till then.   It is that kind of courtesy which, coming from a saint like Alexander Whyte, makes a man wish beyond words to grow in grace and spiritual stature."

In 1890 Dr. and Mrs. Whyte welcomed General Booth to their home, and on four other occasions during eleven years he was their guest.   He was then engaged on a great new social venture by the Salvation Army, which he called the " Darkest England " crusade.[1]   Several friends, including Lord Polwarth, one of the most active laymen in the Church of Scotland, were asked to meet him and to support him at a great meeting for the furtherance of his campaign.   After his return to London, he wrote to Dr. and Mrs. Whyte :

> " I am very tired and very busy.   But still I feel I must just express my gratitude for the kindly sympathy you so freely extended to me during the few hours I had the privilege of being in your home.   I left Scotland with a greatly increased affection for it. . . . May God reward and bless

[1] The title had reference to one of the most popular books of the day, H. M. Stanley's *Darkest Africa*.

you all, and may He enable us to fulfil the expecta-
tions which we have been the means of raising by
this plan for the helping of the poor people. . . .

"Believe me, dear Doctor and Mrs. Whyte,
Yours affectionately,   WILLIAM BOOTH."

On another occasion Dr. and Mrs. Whyte heard
from one of the Edinburgh officers of the Salvation
Army that General Booth was planning to visit
Edinburgh.   They were themselves to be absent on
the date named, but Dr. Whyte sent the message,
" Tell the General the house is entirely at his disposal
if he would care to come."   When this invitation
reached its destination, the General replied, " Tell
the Doctor it is *not* his house I want, *but him*."

In 1891 Dr. and Mrs. Whyte spent three days of
rare and varied interest in Oxford.   Their host at
Mansfield, where Dr. Whyte preached and also
gave a lecture on *The Dœmon of Socrates*, was
Dr. Fairbairn, an old friend, who had more than
once spoken in Free St. George's.   They were also
entertained at All Souls by Mr. (afterwards Sir
Thomas) Raleigh, who introduced them to Canons
Driver and Sanday and Dr. Max Müller, and at Christ
Church by Dean Paget, afterwards the Bishop of
Oxford.   Mrs. Paget was the daughter of Dean
Church, and thus Dr. Whyte found himself in personal
touch with the inmost circle of the Tractarian Movement, and saw with keen appreciation the memorials
of Newman preserved at Christ Church and Oriel.

Whenever an opportunity came, Dr. Whyte spent
a holiday Sunday in London, and went to hear the
great preachers of the day, both of the Free Churches
and of the Church of England.   At this time he was
most strongly drawn to Dr. Joseph Parker and the
City Temple.   A correspondence with Dr. Parker in
the early 'eighties regarding a proposed visit of the
great Congregationalist to Edinburgh had by this
time led up to a warm mutual regard.   The progress
of this friendship can be traced in the modes of address
of three out of a small packet of Dr. Parker's letters

which still remain. The first, dated " May 6, 1882,"
begins :

"MY DEAR SIR,—I little thought that my
first invitation to preach in the Free Church
would come thundering down from its highest
height. But here it is, and now I don't know
what to do with it " ; and ends on a similar note
of humorous humility : " I once fell asleep under
the afternoon eloquence of your great predecessor, so I feel I owe the Free Church an apology
and a sermon."

The second and third letters may be given here in
full, though the third belongs to a later time :

"21 DALEHAM GARDENS,
SOUTH HAMPSTEAD, N.W.,
February 4, 1885.

"MY DEAR DR. WHYTE,—I say to you what
I have said to Dr. Dods—I will gladly wait till
April for an answer. So let it stand. I want
you *both* to come, and you may presbyterianise
the whole church if you can. Thanks for this
word to ministers. It is very solemn and
rousing. Your ' Joseph and Mary ' is marked
by many a sentence like sweet briar, and is really
most helpful : that last touch about the ' nameless woman ' made me jump.[1] When you say
you have been so often in the City Temple you
do but heap up judgment against yourself, in-
asmuch as you did not come in to see me and
give me the fraternal grip.

"Three of you going off to the Perthshire
hills for rest—ah, me ! I will say of you, ' They
are not in trouble like other men, neither are they
plagued like other men,' but there the murmuring
quotation shall end.—Ever yours,

"JOSEPH PARKER."

---

[1] Cf. *Bible Characters*, iv. 9, and 266 below. Dr. Parker refers to an
earlier and fuller form of the sermon on " Joseph and Mary."

"TYNEHOLM,
SOUTH HAMPSTEAD, N.W.,
June 2, 1897.

"MY DEAR FRIEND,—The thoughtful courtesy of Mr. Innes has enabled me to see your reference to me in a recent lecture reported in the *British Weekly*. On Sunday evening I preached from this text:

"'I have likened the daughter of Zion to a comely and delicate woman.'

Next Sunday I could preach from a modern text:

"'I have likened the minister of Free St. George's to the king of hearts, at once royal and fearless and tender.'

Not a man in ten thousand would have had the courage even if he had had the generosity. Your tribute throws me into the deepest dust, and then lifts me to the Right Hand in which is all my strength. I have lived in the Bible. I love it. To me it is infinitely more than literature.

"What a pleasure it was to see Mr. Innes and to hear from him of your splendid condition. He was full of life and light himself, and he made me the stronger by his handgrasp. I am thinking of you all as gathered in the Assembly, burning with holy zeal in relation to the evercoming Kingdom of the Cross, and planning still greater campaigns in the holy war. The God of Ages make you younger day by day, and spare you to His Church as a strong tower to which troubled men may flee in the day of fear.

"With the love of a brother, Ever yours,
"JOSEPH PARKER."

These letters, and the paragraphs which precede them, show how Dr. Whyte's circle of friends had expanded beyond the bounds of Scotland, and how many ties of sympathy he now possessed with men of various outlook in other churches. It was characteristic of his appreciation of his own contemporaries that, in his Moderator's Address some years after, he ran over the names of great preachers—" from Paul to Luther ; and from Luther to Chalmers and Newman and Robertson ; and from Robertson to Spurgeon," and then interjected—" and why should I not say to Parker and M'Neill ? " To these years also belong the first beginnings of that influence through the printed word which afterwards marked the lives of thousands who had never listened to his voice. In the early 'eighties the weekly prayer-meeting in Free St. George's more than maintained the impetus which it received during the Revival of '74. Dr. Whyte spoke in it with the same freedom, force, and originality which characterised his work in his classes for young people, and it drew forth much of the same enthusiasm on the part of students and other hearers from beyond the limits of Free St. George's. In March 1884 an article appeared in the *Christian Leader*, a weekly paper of strongly evangelical outlook, published in Glasgow, giving an account of the lectures on the characters of the *Pilgrim's Progress* which were drawing large audiences every Tuesday evening. Dr. Whyte sent an appreciative note to the writer, Mr. R. Cochrane, expressing his gratification that strangers came to the meeting and found it interesting and profitable. Setting out from this small beginning, the editor of the *Christian Leader* went on to secure regular reports of the addresses on Bunyan and Rutherford, when some years later, at the desire of the Kirk-Session, they were remodelled and given afresh at the regular Sunday evening service.

During the same period Dr. Whyte followed with the most cordial interest the career of the friend whose journalistic talent opened a wide door for his own message in the following decade of his life. In 1886 the Rev. (afterwards Sir) William Robertson Nicoll resigned his ministry of Kelso Free Church after a serious failure in health, and within a few years he gained a secure position of influence in London as editor of the *Expositor*, and founder and editor of the *British Weekly*. In the summer of 1885, Dr. Whyte wrote to Mrs. Nicoll during her husband's serious illness :

> " Your husband is much on my mind. Assure my dear friend of my prayerful good wishes, and be good enough amid your many cares to send me a post card occasionally, with only one word upon it, such as ' much better,' ' almost well.' "

In September of the same year, Dr. Whyte wrote again, referring to the editorship of the *Expositor* and incidentally defined the difference as he saw it between the preacher's and the scholar's treatment of scriptural themes. He also referred to the sermon on the Virgin Mary which had awakened Dr. Parker's admiration :

> " 52 MELVILLE STREET, EDINBURGH,
> *September* 8.
>
> " MY DEAR NICOLL,—I had heard that you were to take the *Expositor* in hand, but had not had any assurance of the fact till I got your letter. I was very glad to get it, and to hear from yourself that you are to take up such an interesting and important piece of work. I feel sure you will make the *Expositor* far more interesting and useful than it has been. . . . It has neither been truly scientific and scholarly in its papers, nor truly popular. I hope in your hands to see it both—and at the same time deeply and richly evangelical. There is no theological journal known to me that approaches pleasing me in this respect.
>
> " I do not feel that my sketch of Mary would help you on the popular side, but, if you wish it, I cannot refuse to put it into your hands. Should it appear as a kind of study, or, what I would prefer, just what it is, a regular lecture in course on the opening scenes of Mary's life ? I think sermons should appear frankly as what they

are : and real studies as such.   Believe me, my
dear friend, I wish and expect that this may be a
great success and means of good in your hands.—
Most truly,   A. WHYTE."

The *British Weekly* was not yet in sight when these
words were written, and the story of how Dr. Whyte
found a wide platform in it must be told later.   Here,
however, we may note that, although he had now
passed the age of fifty, he was still unknown to the
readers of his day, save for his *Commentary on the
Shorter Catechism*, which he himself described as
rather a *catena* or chain of extracts than an original
work, and for such reports of his addresses as appeared
in the *Christian Leader* during the years covered by
this chapter.

" ' How is he, Lord, to-night ? ' I said.
' Safe asleep in his little bed.'
But not the sight of the narrow tomb,
Nor the bitter blight of an opening bloom—
Not these can trouble the heart's deep rest,
When I see him clasped to his Saviour's breast."
R. W. BARBOUR.

THE years which were filled by the enlarging contact with men and movements described in the last chapter, and still more closely by unremitting work for pulpit, classes, and congregation, saw also a succession of sunlit spaces interspersed with deep shadow in the life of Dr. and Mrs. Whyte's home.

The month of August 1885 was spent in a cottage on Loch Fyne, and the children were left for a few days there while their mother was busy in the home in Edinburgh. During this short absence the little George, who was just six months old, became gravely ill. The doctor of the place delayed to summon the parents, and took a less serious view of the illness than the faithful nurse. A message was then sent, but failed to reach its destination ; and Dr. and Mrs. Whyte heard nothing until the 19th, when a telegram announced that the little child had passed away early that morning. A long and sad journey to and from Argyllshire followed, and on the 21st the body was laid to rest in Edinburgh, in the Dean Cemetery. Few friends could be present at that season, but among those who gathered to take part in the service of committal were two brothers-in-law, Alexander Simpson and Robert Barbour, and the venerable church-officer of Free St. George's, Charles Mitchell. Robert Barbour, who had passed through the same trial not many months before, conducted the brief service ; and in the evening, as the parents and he talked together in the study, Dr. Whyte said, " Do you know, I somehow don't feel myself to-night—it seems as if I had one foot here, and one foot were where he is." Three days later, he and his wife received the brief poem of which one verse stands at the head of this chapter.

Twenty years after, Dr. Whyte wrote to a young minister whose little boy had just died :

> " DEAR FRIEND,—I have been thinking of you all morning and of the funeral day of our little George. I stepped in before the under-taker's man, and could scarcely let him screw down the little coffin lid. By these things men live and ministers preach. I go out far from home alone this afternoon. You may be sure I will not forget you.
> " Tenderest sympathy for your dear wife :
> " ALEXANDER WHYTE."

Three years after the death of his infant boy, Dr. Whyte heard that his sister had passed away in Ontario, where her husband was now a minister. The early ending of her strenuous and devoted life came as a sharp sorrow to the brother whose home she had crossed the Atlantic to share twenty-one years before ; and he wrote regarding it to Mrs. Robert Barbour :

> " My sister's death has bereft me of the best of friends. She loved me above measure. And I feel her death all the more that she is the last, I may say, of my near kindred. But I have one here who is both wife and sister to me : the wisest of friends and the best of wives."

Many years later he wrote to Mrs. Macadam's elder daughter : " I often, often remember your mother. She was *the* friend of all friends to me. God bless you all for her sake ! "

In the early summer of 1891 Dr. Whyte travelled with his wife to Aix-les-Bains, and they were present when Robert Barbour passed away after many months of illness. His death and that of Mrs. Whyte's mother early in 1892 meant the loss of two near friends who were possessed by a glowing religious conviction and a devotion to the work of the Evangel not unlike Dr. Whyte's own. When a volume of Robert Barbour's poems and letters was printed not long after, he wrote of it as " a worthy tribute to a beautiful mind and heart."

Among others who passed away during these years was Dr. Whyte's former host and helper in the things both of the body and the spirit—Mr. John M'Kenzie of Alrick, Glen Isla ; and the following letter to a member of his family bears witness to the place which this old friend never ceased to fill in Dr. Whyte's regard :

> " I have received the sad intimation of the death of my very dear and honoured friend. He never knew, and I cannot convey to you, how much I loved and revered him. I mourn with you his departure—but why should we ? He was full of years, and his years had done for him their best work—they had by God's grace made him very ripe for his place among the glorified."

But these years also brought new joys in their train, as the children in the home began to take a larger part in their parents' life. One of Dr. Whyte's letters to his eldest child, Margaret, tells of a long winter journey, undertaken to preach for his friend, the late Dr. Miller of Buckie, on the Moray Firth :

> " At a quarter to five this morning Nurse's alarm clock went off and blew me out of bed while it was yet dark, and Mamma was very good. Though tired and sleepy, she rose and came downstairs and gave me breakfast and brushed my hat and looked out her best rug for me, and opened the door for me and said ' Good-bye.' Give Mamma a kiss, and tell her she was very good.

" The morning was dark and wet, but I got quite comfortably to the station and took my ticket to Buckie *via* Forres. It was dark for some time in the carriage, and till the sun rose I wrapped myself in Mamma's rug and talked to myself. . . .

" At Perth I got a cup of tea and a roll, and took my seat in the Highland train. I was alone all the way to Buckie. The hills of Perthshire were covered with snow, and were very beautiful —where they had not a coat of snow they wore a russet brown garment very beautiful to look at."

In a somewhat later letter, Dr. Whyte tells his eldest boy of the brief winter expedition to Perthshire with Mr. Taylor Innes and Professor Drummond, which, as we saw in the preceding chapter, awakened Dr. Joseph Parker's envy. It is headed " Aberfoyle, Feb. 12, '89 "; and begins with an account of the curlers whom the writer had seen engaged in " the roaring game."

" Tell Mother," he continues, " that Mr. Innes came this morning, and we have had an excellent walk up past the head of Loch Ard. We expect Mr. Drummond to-morrow: the gentleman who called you a ` wag.'

" My dear Fred, I am sure you remember your prayers night and morning. Jesus says, ' Ask and it shall be given unto you : seek and ye shall find : knock and it shall be opened unto you.' Margaret and you will perhaps find out where these words are, and learn them, to say to me the Sabbath after I come back."

Some time after he wrote to one of his children who had been ill: " I have been asking the Divine Physician speedily to heal you and to spare you to be a noble and good woman. And I have had some very happy times with Him in this empty and silent house." It may have been during the same childish illness that the dialogue described in the following letter took

place between the lonely father and the children's
canary :

"DEAR JANET,—I was out beyond Corstorphine visiting this afternoon and had to telegraph
this—'Douglas, 7 Charlotte Square.   Home at 8.
Dr. Whyte.'

"On my way home I got some nice chickweed
for Dick, and when I took it in to him, he was just
saying his prayers before going to bed. 'How
are Janet and Aird ? ' he asked, as he nibbled a
little fibre of grass. 'Better, I hope, Richard,'
I said. 'Tell them,' he said, 'that I whistle to
Jesus every morning to ask Him to make them
better.' 'My dear Bird,' I said, ' I did not know
that you could speak to Jesus.' 'O! Dr.
Whyte,' he said, ' are you a minister, and have
you forgotten the 148th Psalm ? ' [1] 'I shall read
it when I go upstairs,' I said. 'Very well,' he
said; 'good-night, thank you for this nice chickweed, and remember my love to Janet and the
Moderator.' [2] And as I shut his door, he said,
'The Lord's my Shepherd,' and popped his head
under his wing. And I came up and read the
148th Psalm. And, sure enough, David must
have had a canary like us.—With Dick's love and
"FATHER'S."

In the same year (1892), the little "Moderator"
received a post card in similar vein, regarding a large
black half-Persian cat, Dante, who for many years
maintained a dignified place in the household economy.

"*Thursday night.*
"Dante came up to prayers to-night, and
when he heard it was the Psalms I was reading
he winked with delight and lay down at my feet.
And then when Jeannie left the door open for him

---

[1] Ps. cxlviii. 10: "Praise Him, . . . creeping things, and flying
fowl."

[2] The pet name of the younger boy, Aird, who was born during the
sittings of the General Assembly.

to leave the room after prayers, he purred and
said, ' No : thank you ! ' And then when we
were left alone he whispered to me how much
he missed Aird and Rhoda, and asked when they
were coming back. He leaped up on my knee
and stroked my face with his soft tail when I
said ' Monday.' A. W."

Finally, another post card says to a little maid in
her seventh year : " Your welcome little letter came
in on my tray this morning, and it was much sweeter
than my mammoth pear " ; and concludes with the
invitation : " Come to be company to your
" FATHER."

The summers of this period were times of singularly
varied companionship. Craig Dhu, where the vacation of 1888 was spent, was situated on a wooded
knoll overlooking the Spey between Newtonmore and
Laggan. Cluny Castle, which had been rented that
year by Mr. Andrew Carnegie, was within an afternoon's drive ; and the two parties met several
times, and joined on at least one long expedition, as
distances were then reckoned. It was an especial
interest to Dr. Whyte to meet Mr. John Morley at
this time, for their common interest in books, and
their devotion to Mr. Gladstone, gave ground for
much friendly talk. Some months later Dr. Whyte
called at Mr. Morley's house in London, and was
greeted *in limine* with the words, " Why, you are
the first parson that ever crossed my threshold ! "
An old comradeship of the rod was also renewed
this summer, when Whyte's four angling friends,
Simeon Macphail, Alexander Barrie, A. E. Scougal,
and John Sutherland Black all gathered at Craig Dhu.
" We have fished daily," one letter reports, " all the
week : we breakfast at 7.30, go off for the day, and dine
at 9 ! Barrie and I took ten dozen in two and a half
hours in a small loch belonging to Cluny." Another
welcome guest during these years was the Rev.
W. W. Peyton, whose knowledge of geology and other

branches of natural science added interest to the long
walks among the hills which alternated with fishing
expeditions. Mr. Peyton's chief book, *The Memor-
abilia of Jesus*, showed a union of science and mysticism, fused in the crucible of a glowing and scintillating imagination—a union too rare to bring popular
recognition to the writer, but profoundly stimulating
to the minds of his friends.

During 1888 and the four following years one
member of the angling fellowship, Dr. Sutherland
Black, received invitations from Dr. Whyte to fish
in points so far apart as a remote loch in Galloway,
when elaborate directions were given for the finding of
a cross-country track from the nearest station ; " the
best stream in the South of Scotland," whose name
must not be divulged here ; the Perthshire Highlands ; and the region bordering on Glencoe. Two
urgent post cards may be quoted, from a series dispatched from the shores of Loch Linnhe in August
1890, even though the first may diminish the writer's
credit with the severer professors of the gentle art.

" Thanks for card. Have not yet tried the
loch or the stream. The deep-sea fishing holds
me in strong lines. I took five dozen capital fish
last evening. The sport is not so high-class as
fly-fishing ; but it has delights of its own—the
sea : the hills : the fish : and the talk.
" One day will bring you here : I look for it.
                                        " A. W."

" ' *The twelfth*,' 6 o'c.
" Just home from Loch Lundavra with three
dozen and a half, and a wet skin. I have engaged
the boat for you and me. ' Red body and gray
wing.'   A. W."

A year later Henry Drummond felt that his friends
needed a complete change of scene and occupation
after the long strain of anxiety during the last illness
of Mrs. Whyte's brother, and made a most characteristic plan to secure this. The objective was the

extreme north-west corner of Scotland, and the means of travel was a carriage, accompanied by a small pony, to be ridden alternately by the two boys who went with the party—Dr. Whyte's son, Fred, and nephew, Hubert Simpson. The carriage was occupied by Dr. and Mrs. Whyte, Professor Drummond, Mr. Taylor Innes, and whichever boy was not at the moment on the pony. The route led from Lairg to Lochinver, back to Inchnadamff, and then north to Rhiconich and Cape Wrath. The intervals of travel were taken up by fishing, and by discussions on religion and many things beside. From Rhiconich the travellers walked over to Kinlochbervie one Sunday, and found the little church there half filled by a large party who had landed from their friend Mr. Peter Mackinnon's yacht. " A tremendous storm shook the building before the service ended, and the valiant minister and his wife outdid even the best traditions of Highland hospitality by taking in the whole of both parties for a meal at the manse, and producing a series of dogcarts and other vehicles to convey them home." It was not the last time that Dr. Whyte found out the unlooked-for resources of lonely Highland manses, or experienced the generosity of the ladies who dwell in them.

After the rest of the party had returned south, Professor Drummond took Dr. Whyte to his own favourite fishing-ground on the Laxford River and Loch Stack ; and the latter had his chief—almost his only—experience of salmon-fishing, under the instruction of a master in the art. It is said that the ghillies named after him the pool where he landed his first salmon. From the Lodge at Achfarrie, before his first salmon was secured, he wrote to his son, who had now gone with Mrs. Whyte to Bonskeid :

" MY DEAR FRED,—Mr. Drummond and I have had another delightful day on the Laxford and Loch Stack. Read what the *Sportsman's Guide* says about both waters. The forenoon was slow work ; but mother knows, and you have not forgotten, how noble the hills are all round the Loch. In the afternoon we had a capital take of sea-trout. I took one of four pounds' weight—my biggest fish. When it was hooked it started down the loch with a rush that made my reel spin and skirl. He plunged and dived and rushed and pulled till I thought I must lose him, but the hook held, and after a lively fight with him, David at last reached out the net and lifted him into the boat. A great big spotted fellow. ' David ' is my man : Mr. Drummond's man is ' Neil,' from Kinlochbervie. David is a great, strong, kindly crofter with a lot of children in Durness, and his pay this week as my ' ghillie ' will get shoes and stockings for his children for next winter. . . .

" When I am sitting in the boat waiting for the fish to come I fill up the time thinking of mother and grandmother and you all ; and I often pray for you that you may be all good and happy. To-day when I was waiting for a big fish, I said to myself the prologue to John's Gospel, and ' The Shepherd-boy's Song ' in the *Pilgrim*. Will you all learn it for me this week and let us have it at our little church next Sabbath ? . . .

" Tell grandmama that our *menu* is tea and *salmon* at breakfast ; *salmon* sandwiches for lunch ; and fresh *salmon* for dinner.

" The Salmon-fisher's Love to all."

One change must be noted which took place in the outward setting of Dr. Whyte's life during the period covered by this chapter. Late in the year 1889 he and his family left the manse of Free St. George's and went to reside at No. 7 Charlotte Square, which continued to be their home for twenty-eight years. It stands on the north side of the Square, which was the only part completed according to Robert Adam's original design, and which is recognised as the finest example of the Brothers Adam's

art on its domestic side.   As at 52 Melville Street,
the study was a room with three high windows occupying the front of the house above the doorway ; but in
Charlotte Square the windows looked out on a garden
studded with trees, and over these to the left there
rose the noble mass of the Castle rock.

Fifteen years earlier, when Whyte was preparing
to succeed Dr. Candlish in the former house, he had
called in the aid of his lifelong friend, William Scott
Morton, who designed the furniture of the study, and
in particular, the massive bookcases which in course
of time came to fill all the available wall-space.
Many a talk the preacher and the designer had on
life and art, on books and personal religion, as the
work went forward.   In 1889 the same gifted friend
was again called in, for the new study was more
spacious than the old, and the already large library
could be extended further.   When all was complete,
the high bookcases were surmounted by busts of
Homer, Plato, Dante, and other masters of knowledge
and imagination, while a lower bookcase, standing
close to Dr. Whyte's desk and containing many of the
books to which he most constantly referred, supported
a small cast of the full-length statue of Thackeray.
On the walls on either side of the hearth, portraits of
Carlyle and Herschel found a place beside those of
Newman already described.

The study thus furnished became a place apart to
many men and women of the most varied intellectual
outlook—not only a place where great sermons were
fashioned, but a confessional, where their questions
and perplexities were met with the most patient
sympathy and wisdom.   To those who came thus,
the door of the study was always open ; but against
intruders on trivial or business errands it was fast
closed during the hours when Dr. Whyte was busy at
his desk.   His pulpit owed much to the wise and un-
relenting watchfulness of his family and household in
this respect.   This gave his study an atmosphere of
quiet ; but its still more striking characteristic of
order was due to its master.   At whatever hour one

entered, the same order reigned. Dr. Whyte might be writing at his desk, or reading in a chair by the fire ; but in either case, save for half a dozen letters addressed for the post lying on a small table near the door, and for another table with weekly and monthly magazines, and a small pile of correspondence under a letter weight at the side of his desk, there was not a paper nor a loose sheet of manuscript to be seen in the room. " He is a remarkable combination of order and enthusiasm," a younger preacher once said, adding somewhat wistfully, " I envy him his gift of order." This love of order may have been in some measure inborn, but it had been strengthened and established by long self-discipline ; until finally an untidy room or any slovenliness in attire, or lack of the most scrupulous personal cleanliness, affected him with an almost physical distress. Yet in his hours of visiting at Fountainbridge at least he must have seen much of these things. Nor did he share the indifference to the externals of worship shown by many men of great inwardness and mystical fervour. He laid no small stress on the wearing of the dignified, though sombre, pulpit robes prescribed by long usage in the Presbyterian Church. But, when he spoke on this subject, he would sometimes add with a twinkling eye, " Yet my heart warms to the red jersey of the Salvation Army ! "

Such were the surroundings in which Dr. Whyte's work was done for nearly thirty years : to give even an imperfect description of that work itself will demand more than one of the chapters that follow.

" The pulpit is a jealous mistress, and will not brook a divided allegiance."—A. W.

" He failed in no activity, but the pulpit was his throne."—W. R. NICOLL regarding A. W.

IT may be well at this central point in Dr. Whyte's ministry to disregard chronology for a time, and in this and the two following chapters to take a wider survey of the work which he did in study and pulpit, in his classes, and among his congregation. The materials for this survey will be drawn from various points of his ministry, those already surveyed and those still lying ahead. The aim of the present chapter is not to convey to those who never heard Dr. Whyte any sense of his greatness as a preacher—it is granted to very few writers to preserve the thrill of sacred oratory as Dr. John Brown has done towards the close of his essay on Dr. Chalmers—but rather to describe his methods of preparation, and to set down in his own words his conception of the preacher's office. Certain characteristics of his preaching may also be recalled to his former hearers ; and in this regard the present chapter may be read in conjunction with, or as a supplement to, the admirable study contributed by the editors of the Sermons on Prayer which have been gathered and published since his death.[1]

Few preachers can have taken their hearers so fully into their confidence as Dr. Whyte did. The difficulties which confront a minister in preaching or as a pastor, and the opportunities of his calling ; his disappointments and his rewards ; the ceaselessness of his duties, and the great " compensations " which they bring in leading him to constant meditation on the

[1] Preface to *Lord, Teach Us to Pray*, edited by the Rev. J. M. E. Ross and Mrs. Ross.

greatest of all themes ; the pitfalls surrounding his path, and its high and glorious goal—all these formed the theme of passages in many a sermon and address. Thus in the 'seventies Dr. Whyte wrote a paper entitled " A Minister's Compensations," in which the greatest of these compensations is thus described : " What is occasional with another is or may be continual with me. Morning, noon, and night my Bible must be in my hands."

Nor did his congregation alone obtain such flashes of insight into their minister's ideal of his work on their behalf ; when he was given an opportunity of addressing the Church as a whole, he most often chose to speak on the same subject. During the sittings of the General Assembly, certain preachers are chosen to conduct services on Sunday in the Assembly Hall. In 1884 this duty fell to Dr. Whyte, who chose as his subject, " Ministerial Efficiency " ; and as his text, " Mine own vineyard have I not kept " (Cant. i. 6). It was not to be looked for that he would wield lightly a weapon so formidable as these words supplied, and the sermon must have made many ears tingle. It was undoubtedly remembered and spoken of for long, and it is said to have left its mark on the practice of the Free Church. After a few opening sentences on the vineyard metaphor here and in Psalm lxxx., the preacher recalls the condition of the Scottish Kirk in the years immediately following the Reformation, and in particular the care taken by the reformers to provide for the oversight and encouragement of its ministers throughout the land. He praises the order of " Superintendents " then instituted, as preserving the strongest element in the episcopal system, the rest of which had been swept away ; and indicates how their functions gradually passed over into the hands of Presbyteries. Coming to the famous Assembly of 1638, he quotes the Act providing for a yearly visitation of each congregation and specifying the thoroughness with which it was to be carried out. Then, passing on to the actual practice of the Church, he indicates a " weak point in the system . . .

the very point with which our Presbyterian reformers took such special pains. The link is wanting that should bind the individual minister and the individual congregation more closely to the whole Church." For, " unless a Church zealously sees to it that there is the utmost ministerial efficiency and devotion among her office-bearers, no glory in her past history and no generosity in her people will avail her long, or will save her from barrenness and death."

Next he calls his hearers to " consider how our slack and oblivious system works," and contrasts the care taken by the Church for the training of the student with her lack of care for him when he has become a minister. " His failures or successes, his helps or hindrances, she knows nothing of. He may have a hard, uphill, cross-bearing life, but she knows it not." How different if he had lived in the six-teenth century, and " John Knox or Robert Bruce, with two or three like-minded elders, had gone down periodically to visit that minister, and his remote congregation. Can you not see what power, courage, and hope would thereby be given to that lonely pastor ? "—a power, courage, and hope, it may here be said, which the speaker brought to very many of his scattered brethren in after years.

The preacher then turns to the remedy. He does not propose that the Church should appoint a new order of Superintendents, though it may be read between the lines that he regards that system as the ideal : he does urge that a regular yearly visitation of congregations should be entrusted to the strongest and ablest men at the Church's command, that so all her parts may be drawn more closely together. And such a regular, stringent visitation would, he argues, have the most beneficial effect in preventing those " ministerial shipwrecks," with which he next deals in a scathing passage. A minister would no longer feel that he was settled peacefully in his charge for life, unless he were to commit some scandalous fault. " What have been called the rights of ministers have sometimes been pled in bar of such a discharge of discipline. But let it never be forgotten that in the best days of our party in Scotland our ministers were more taken up with their people's rights than with their own." But, he continues, if the visitation recommended were strenuously carried out—"the very fact that my work was to be inquired into by my brethren would help to put me on my mettle. It would keep a healthy fear alive in my heart. I should be taught to look on my charge not as a field I could work in as much or as little as I chose, but rather as a stewardship, an account of which I had to render from time to time even to my fellow-men." Finally, if cases of ministerial inefficiency were vigorously dealt with, the people of the Church would respond at last to the summons to provide an adequate maintenance for an active and zealous ministry.

To those who knew Dr. Whyte in his later years only it may seem strange that he should have passed so rigorous a judgment upon the minority of ministers who had lost keenness and conscience in their work. But this drastic utterance does not stand alone. Twenty years later he said: "I would have all lazy students drummed out of the college, and all lazy ministers out of the Assembly. And all the churches will have to take steps to do that soon, if they are to live and thrive in this hard-working world of ours." [1] Tolerant and forbearing as Dr. Whyte was—ever willing to believe the best of every man provided only he found evidences of real endeavour, however imperfect the result—yet there was one failure for which even his charity found no excuse, since he regarded it as the betrayal of an infinitely sacred trust. "I would have laziness held to be the one unpardonable sin in all our students and in all our ministers."

But it was not chiefly in this negative way, through the denunciation of idleness, that Dr. Whyte revealed his own conception of the ministerial office and influenced the practice of his brethren. He did so yet more by his glowing praise, and still more

[1] *Bunyan Characters*, iv. p. 5 f.

glowing example, of industry. Not long after the
sermon on " Efficiency " was preached before the
Assembly, he was asked to address the students of
the New College, and chose as his subject Quintilian's
Institutes of Oratory, and especially the rules laid
down by the great Latin teacher and critic for the
Education of an Orator. Quintilian's insistence in
the *Institutes* that the orator must be a man of noble
character as well as of intellectual endowment, that
he must be trained in virtue even from infancy, and
that he must use the greatest diligence in the study
of the best books ; his analysis of the literature of
the ancient world, in order so to guide the reading of
his aspiring pupils, and his advice regarding the
cultivation of style—all these, Dr. Whyte argued,
made Quintilian an unmatched companion for the
theological student who was resolved to fit himself in
all respects for his arduous calling ; and he concluded
by urging that such students should undertake for
themselves " the translation of his precepts into the
language of the Christian school."

In 1898, Dr. Whyte was called to the Moderatorship of his Church. In choosing a theme for his
Opening Address he went past the great Christian
classics which he had done so much to make familiar,
back to this Spaniard who taught rhetoric in Rome
in the days of Domitian. The definition of an orator
adopted by Quintilian from Cato, " A good man
skilled in speaking," formed the text of his address ;
and only after giving a full summary of Quintilian's
treatment of this theme did he set it in the frame of
an evangelical ministry in modern Scotland. In this
address, as in that which closed the same Assembly,
Dr. Whyte seemed almost to forget the presence of
the elders who formed half its number, so bent was
he on counselling and encouraging his fellow-ministers,
and those who had not yet entered on their ministry.

" Oh ! " he broke out, " not so much my
fathers or my brethren, but my sons in the
Gospel ministry. My heart is full of you and of

your people, and has now for a long time been.
I would fain leave this seat and appoint to meet
with you all apart. I would fain confess to you
some of the shipwrecks of my own ministerial
life ; some of the sunken rocks I have foundered
on, and some of the whirlpools that have well-
nigh swirled and sucked down my soul. Only
there is no use. I need not speak about such
things to you. You would not believe me.
You would not know what I was saying. . . .
Fathers and Brethren, did not Augustine and
Calvin speak to the point when they said :
' First, second, and third—humility ' ? And
especially in you and me ? . . .

" Prayer and work. All great and true and
eminently successful ministers from Paul's day
downward bear the same testimony : prayer
and work. . . . Let us pray and work, my
brethren, in what remains to us of our time
on earth, with all our might."

This exhortation to humility, prayer, and work may
well stand as the speaker's final and conclusive
summary of the duty of a Christian minister.

The Closing Address resumed the same theme.
One passage deals with the excuse that the minister
lacks time for his manifold duties. Again Quintilian
is at the speaker's side with an apt quotation : " We
shroud our indolence under the pretext of a difficulty.
The truth is, it is lack of real love for our work." And
the address goes on :

" We have plenty of time for all our work,
did we husband our time and hoard it up aright
. . . were we only sufficiently jealous of every
man and of every thing that comes to steal our
time. Did we work as many hours every day,
and as hard, as the people who support us work ?
As early in the morning, and as late at night, and
as hard all the livelong day ? Oh no ! We
cannot look seriously in one another's faces and
say it is want of time. It is want of intention.

It is want of determination. It is want of method. It is want of motive. It is want of conscience. It is want of heart. It is want of anything and everything but time."

From this summons to the most careful and jealous husbandry of time, we naturally pass to an account of the speaker's use of his own time. But first we may hear the testimony of Dr. G. H. Morrison, one of his earlier assistants :

" No man has ever enjoyed his fellowship, and been admitted to his intimacy, without awaking to the tremendous strength of his will. Along the line of duty he is one of the most determined, I would venture to say one of the most dogged, persons whom God ever created. It would seem as if nothing—no mood, no listlessness, no lack of present inspiration—could keep him from his appointed task in its appointed hour, or prevent him from carrying it through, no matter how heavily the chariot wheels might drive. . . . And yet with this so grim determination—and at times it can be very grim—with this will, built up through a thousand minute victories into strength and liberty, there is a certain tenderness about him, a large sympathy, a sweet and gracious courtesy, that are infinitely attractive and endearing."

The " thousand minute victories " here spoken of had built up, among other qualities, a great power of concentration, of which one instance may be given. The time was August 1901, when Dr. Whyte was deep in the preparation of his essay on Newman ; and the place the sitting-room at Inverdruie, a house on the border of Rothiemurchus Forest which more than once formed the family's summer home. The long, somewhat narrow, room served both as study and drawing-room, and a whole library of Newman literature occupied a long shelf down one side. At the far end was Dr. Whyte's desk, and near the door on this occasion was a tea-table, round which a party was gathered in animated discussion. But the intent figure at the desk remained motionless, as deeply absorbed in Newman as if the whole range of the Cairngorms had guarded his privacy. In this respect Dr. Whyte practised what to most men is a mere counsel of perfection, and fulfilled to the letter the precept of Quintilian that concentration must vanquish all hindrances to study:

" For, if you bend to your task with your whole mind, none of the stimuli which play upon the eyes or ears will penetrate to your spirit. . . . Nor must we ever give in to reasons for indolence. For if we consider that we should only study when we are fresh in mind, glad in spirit, and free from every other care, there will be always some reason for excusing ourselves. Wherefore, in the midst of a crowd, or when travelling, or even during a feast, let thought make its own solitude." [1]

Dr. Whyte's allotment of his time had both a yearly and a weekly aspect. The former depended on the provision already noted of a generous summer holiday. Never less than two, and in later years three, summer months were spent away from Edinburgh, and shorter times at Christmas and Easter. But these weeks or months were not in the ordinary sense vacations, for they were closely packed with reading, meditation, and sometimes writing. The first claim on the summer vacation was preparation for the following winter's classes—a subject of which more will be said in the following chapter—but through all these times of leisure went the thought, the observation, and the free play of imagination which gave freshness and amplitude to the preaching of the months that followed ; while often an incident, an experience, a remembered gleam of natural beauty, from the time of leisure illuminated a sermon preached in Free St. George's after the holiday's end.

[1] *Inst. Orat.*, x. iii. 28–30.

For more than forty years Dr. Whyte's weekly round of work scarcely varied by an hour. In the early years of his ministry he had already reached the paradoxical conclusion that one of a minister's " compensations " lay in this—that the frequent breaks in his working time compelled him to start as early in the day and the week as might be, so that interruptions should always find him ahead of the clock. So too, when his ministry had come very near its end, he told a gathering of brother ministers : " As a rule, and even when I was most tempted to procrastinate, as Dr. Johnson taught me, I 'sat down doggedly' to my desk. Ay, and that, sometimes, on the Sabbath night, and always on the Monday morning."

But in fact, as has been indicated already, interruptions in the morning were jealously guarded against, and the four hours following nine o'clock were kept sacred for study. Nor was the time too long, especially during the crowded years when he had no colleague, and during a great part of which he spoke five times each week to large audiences *in the church*, the only address which was repeated in substance being that to the Young Women's and Young Men's Classes. Unless there were guests at the midday meal whose presence called for Dr. Whyte's, he commonly had a very light lunch in his study. Soon after, he set out on his pastoral rounds, and visiting along with other congregational work went on till about six, though he returned earlier when he had an evening engagement. Other evenings were spent at his desk or among his books.

There were only two variations in his normal working week. On Wednesday afternoon the Young Women's Class took up part of the time assigned to pastoral work ; and Saturday brought the one break in the steady round of toil. On that day both sermons were finished by one o'clock, and the afternoon was spent in the company of Dr. Taylor Innes and as many other of the group of friends as were in Edinburgh at the time. The evening was devoted to the weeklies, the *Spectator*, *Saturday Review* (afterwards replaced by the *Nation*), *Athenæum*, and *Academy*; and from its first numbers, the *New Statesman* joined this goodly array. The same evening, new books or pamphlets were ordered to which Dr. Whyte's attention had been drawn by the weekly reviews. By 9.45 (the hour of evening prayers) the reviews were readdressed, ready for dispatch to friends at a distance. In later years the young people of the household secured some relaxation of this rule, but they often complained that the current of periodicals flowed through the house so swiftly that it was hard to do more than catch sight of them as they passed.

But all this carefully ordered effort was concentrated upon the first day of the week. When Dr. Whyte was approaching fourscore, he used these words : " I can testify, and with the most entire integrity, that from my childhood, down to this hour, I have greatly loved and greatly valued the seclusion, and the silence, and the rest, and, especially, the reading proper to the Lord's day." [1]   For him, the day began early. He was called at six, and a devoted member of the household brought his porridge to the study before seven. Thus he secured two or three quiet hours before breakfast for prayer and for revision of the day's work in pulpit and class. By 10.30 he was in the vestry, with everything in order— half an hour before the hour of morning service.

To sum up the impression of this unhasting, unresting life, we might well borrow a chapter-heading from Lord Morley—" The Day's Work of a Giant " ; and those who watched Dr. Whyte at work might truly apply to him a remark regarding Mr. Gladstone which he often quoted with high appreciation—" His industry was more than half his genius."

The *method* of Dr. Whyte's preparation was based on systematic note-taking, and on the constant use of a large, interleaved Bible. The defective memory for fact and detail, which had troubled his childhood

[1] "Newness of Life: A New-Year Exhortation," *British Weekly*, January 9, 1913.

and caused his downfall in the Chemistry examination at King's College, remained a handicap throughout life, although his memory responded swiftly to stimulus from his imagination when his emotions were kindled. At other times it was neither ready nor trustworthy. He used to complain that he had the worst memory in Edinburgh, and to tell his student-friends, " No one knows the labour that my memory has cost me ! " The moral which he drew, for others as well as himself, was, " Always read with your pencil in your hand." His children gradually discovered that, while ordinary presents had little attraction for him—he never learned to use a fountain-pen—he had an insatiable appetite for notebooks, small and large. Such a small notebook was always in his pocket to capture and preserve ideas which came at unexpected times. But these were only aids and extensions of the central instrument of his study, the interleaved Bible, of which the pages became densely crowded with references. When they would hold no more, Dr. Whyte fell back on his other method of the subject-index.

His own use of this method is fully set out in a series of letters to his nephew, Hubert Simpson, who was about to begin his studies for the ministry :

" 7 CHARLOTTE SQUARE,
EDINBURGH, *May* 13, 1901.

" DEAR HUBERT,—I send for your acceptance to-day an Interleaved Study Bible. I have used such a Bible ever since I was at your stage of study, and the use it has been to me is past all telling. For more than forty years, I think I can say, never a week, scarcely a day, has passed, that I have not entered some note or notes into my Bible : and, then, I never preach or speak in any way that I do not consult my Interleaved Bible. I never read a book without taking notes for preservation one way or other. And I never come in my reading on anything that sheds light on any passage of Scripture that I do not set the reference down in my Bible over against the passage it illustrates. And, as time has gone on, my Bible has become filled with illustrative and suggestive matter *of my own collecting* ; and, therefore, sure to be suggestive and helpful to me in my work. *All* true students have their own methods of collecting and husbanding the results of their reading. But an Interleaved Bible is specially suitable and repaying to a preacher. The Bible deserves all our labour and all our fidelity ; and we are repaid with usury for all the student-like industry we lay out upon it. If you wish a talk, and have anything to ask me about this method,—come and let us have a talk.

" Praying that you may be the most industrious, prayerful, and successful of ministers.— With high regard, ALEXANDER WHYTE."

Six weeks later, Dr. Whyte wrote to ask if the vacant pages had begun to be filled, and added :

" I have this week, and this day, got so much help out of reference to books I entered in my Bible years and years ago, that I am jealous lest you lose a day. You wonder at my solicitude, but I will be vindicated by your gratitude when I am no longer here to urge you. Take a volume of first-rate sermons—Newman, or Robertson, or Parker, or Spurgeon, etc.—and enter the texts of a whole volume at once, and go on till the habit will work automatically."

A later communication to the same student, undated, and with the rubric, " With 5 books, A. W.," on the envelope, runs as follows :

" I send you some ' imagination ' literature. Take a careful note of it all in your Bible under ' Imagination,' and in your *Index Rerum*. I hope your Bible is filling up. This case of ' Imagination ' is a good illustration of the need and use of a Reference Bible or Notebooks conscientiously, religiously, faithfully kept. 'Nulla dies,' etc.[1]   A. W."

No treatment of Dr. Whyte's conception of preaching can pass over the tremendous importance which he attached to the work of the imagination referred to in this letter ; but first, some paragraphs must be given to his view of *Style* and *Delivery*. These may seem lesser matters ; but to him nothing was trivial, and nothing could safely be neglected or left to chance, which might serve to wing or to barb the preacher's word. As in the case of imagination, the inborn power and the delight in its use were present from his early years, while that power came but slowly into its fullest exercise—so it was in regard to style. The companions of Alexander Whyte in the shoemaker's shop were already impressed with his love of words and command over them. "The Study of Words " was both practised and enjoined by him from his days in Airlie onward. Later, Archbishop Trench's book with that title became one of his prime favourites, which he distributed liberally and went through in his Young People's Classes. In the early 'eighties he wrote to a friend : " I cannot write good English, but I flatter myself I know it when I see it." Twenty years later he again avowed that he fell short of his own ideal as a writer of English, but added, " A good style, especially in sacred composition, is one of the purest delectations of my daily life." [2] More and more as the years passed, his ear and his mind found that refreshment in English prose which in youth he had gained from Milton or Wordsworth or Shelley. Not long before his death, he told his eldest son that in his view the best pages in his elaborate essay on Newman were those which dealt with Newman's style ; and one of the few fragments of

---

[1] *Nulla dies sine linea*—" No day without its line "—the motto of the Greek artist, Apelles.
[2] *Bunyan Characters*, iv. p. 7.

his table-talk which were successfully captured and preserved by his children ran as follows : " Style !— it's the march of language : it's the way one word is married to another, the way the words lean upon one another, the way they walk together. Style is the wings of a book that carry it down from generation to generation."

It is charitable to suppose that the writer in a journal of some intellectual pretensions who said that Dr. Whyte had no sense of style had only known him afar off, and had never heard how he foretold the renown of the still obscure Robert Louis Stevenson. A very different judgment was that of a writer in the *Nation* : " The only living preacher we can think of who talks outdoor English is Dr. Alexander Whyte of Edinburgh." Dr. Whyte's feeling for style is clearly seen in his delicately discriminated eulogies of the English of Hooker and Bunyan, Law and Newman, and his not less delicately tempered and half-reluctant criticism of the style of Bishop Butler. Thus he speaks, with a characteristic choice of epithet, of the " somewhat unsunned and severe spaces of the *Analogy*," but adds, " The more I read Butler, and the better I understand him, the more I enjoy his peculiar style." The occasional humour of his own writing is well illustrated in his description of the cobbler Behmen setting to work, " as with his awl and rosin-end, to sew together a sentence, and hammer together a page of the most incongruous and unheard-of phraseology, till . . . we continually exclaim, O for a chapter of John Bunyan's clear, and sweet, and beautiful English." [1]

This delight in style was instinctive, but was deliberately sharpened and burnished as part of the preacher's armoury. One of the friends who best knew his mind in regard to preaching says that he was little troubled by the search for ideas (he once said, " I have more ideas than I know what to do with "), but that he suffered great travail in finding the most arresting form in which to express his ideas. To

[1] *Thirteen Appreciations*, pp. 44, 82, 250, 274, 358 f.

cleave a way for the truth, as he himself saw it, into the mind dulled by the repetition of conventional religious language and into the apathetic heart—such was his ever-present problem. Nor did he grudge any labour in order to do so. He always kept a copy of Roget's *Thesaurus of English Words and Phrases* on his desk, and only by long and severe effort did he attain that " happy daring in the use of words," and especially in the choice of telling and unexpected epithets, which marked his style in later years.[1] As far as the present writer can judge, it was only in the sixth decade of Dr. Whyte's life that his characteristic style reached its full development ; and his letters grew in grace of expression and in a certain combined economy and originality of phrase until he had passed threescore and ten. In his later books, a purist might perhaps point to characteristics which tended to pass into mannerism—his use of favourite adjectives like " incomparable," his repetitions, often with an added epithet prefacing the word repeated and emphasised ; his way of beginning sentences with " And " or " Till," and his fondness for the intensive " so "—but to those who knew him, these turns of style were so steeped in his own personality that no one of them could be removed without loss.

The deliberate craftsmanship with which Dr. Whyte chiselled his style for the enforcement of his message may well be studied in the conclusion of his address on *Mrs. Timorous*. The second last paragraph ends by quoting the resolve of Christiana, " Yet I must venture," and this gives its *motif* to the last. Sixteen times in that page is the word " venture " introduced as noun or verb ; and with every recurrence it sounds a more insistent trumpet-note of summons, up to the crash of the closing phrase, " *Make that tremendous venture now !* " Or, in the same volume, we may turn to the magnificent apostrophe which closes the characterisation of Great-heart—" Go back, then,

---

[1] *Verbis felicissime audax*, Quintilian. In his copy of Roget, Dr. Whyte noted such facts as that Gladstone never allowed himself to use the word " endorse."

from thy well-earned rest, O brave Great-heart! go back to thy waiting task." [1]   But the reader of Dr. Whyte's sermons will find proof on every page of the way in which the writer's pen was disciplined to the preacher's task.

Dr. Whyte's generosity in estimating the work of others was known to all ; yet when he felt it a duty to criticise, he could do so with great point and incisiveness.   Especially was this the case regarding faults of expression.   He once wrote to a young minister :

> " I am better pleased with your teaching than with your style.   You should rewrite this discourse, and ask as you write—would Newman have used this and that expression in a sermon ? Really attentive, and intelligent, and spiritually refined hearers will feel a jar and a distaste at a good many of your expressions : and that oftentimes spoils the effect of a sermon full as much as thin and defective doctrine.   Excuse the freedom of an old pulpit hand."

A note to Miss Innes, the sister of his lifelong friend, shows how even his Saturday afternoons— jealously guarded as they were for the uses of friendship and of intellectual recreation—were on occasion sacrificed to his exacting conscience regarding the *form* of his sermons.   It is headed, " Friday afternoon," and runs :

> " I got your kind message ; 'but not before I had resolved to tear up the second draft of my sermon for Sabbath, and write a third.   This will nail me down to my desk all day to-morrow. But for that, I would have been with you."

Nor was this effort after adequacy of expression ever relaxed.   When Dr. Whyte was in his seventieth year he said in a letter to one of his children, who had undertaken a piece of literary work at his

[1] *Bunyan Characters*, ii. pp. 90, 187.

suggestion : " I wrote my last forenoon sermon three times over. And that is the only thing in which I resemble Newman. He wrote *all* his sermons as often as I wrote mine last week."

Yet, while Dr. Whyte made Newman his model in the care which he lavished on the writing of his sermons, and suggested that that great writer's English would provide a touchstone by which any lapse from dignity and purity of diction might at once be detected, he himself followed lines of appeal too daring and unclassical to be paralleled in the works of his great exemplar. At times in Free St. George's and more frequently in addressing smaller audiences without the restraint of manuscript, his inborn dramatic talent broke through his conception of the austerity of the pulpit, and his hearers held their breath while he acted out some impassioned scene of spiritual conflict. Sometimes his "attack" (to borrow a musical term) was so unconventional that his congregation wondered for a time whither the preacher meant to lead them. Many will remember a sermon on the True Vine, preached after a journey to Southern France, which began as follows, with no introduction other than the announcement of the text :

"BOUQUÈRON, ABOVE GRENOBLE,
Sabbath forenoon, April 19, 1903.
"MY DEAR ROBERT,—After breakfast and family worship this morning, we each took our own favourite book and separated for the forenoon. I selected for my retreat the great vineyard that covers the sunny slope above Grenoble."

Then followed the remainder of a long letter to his fourth son, describing the apparently hopeless barrenness of a vineyard before the life of the spring-time had begun to touch it with green, and forecasting the change that would shortly pass over it. Thus a vivid introduction was given to the spiritual message enshrined in a metaphor, which too often we wholly fail to visualise.[1]

Another instance of the unpredictable element in Dr. Whyte's preaching is recorded by Mr. Alfred Hollins. When he first came as organist to Free St. George's he found that the slowness of the pneumatic action in the organ caused an appreciable interval between the pressing of the key and the giving forth of the sound. He mentioned on one occasion that this made it difficult to lead the singing effectively or to play rapid passages—never imagining that Dr. Whyte would take note. But he had overheard the organist's remark, and some years after, when preaching on the perfect conditions to which we may look forward in heaven for the prosecution of work or art, he suddenly added as an illustration—" And Mr. Hollins will have an organ which will answer to the slightest touch of his fingers." At times, also, sudden flashes of humour—often too quaint or too grim even to cause a smile—played like summer lightning over the surface of his preaching.

So far we have touched on the preparation of the study; but the more formal side of the preacher's equipment extends to the pulpit as well, and Dr. Whyte laid hardly less stress on Delivery than on Style. When one of his assistants was about to be ordained, he wrote to him at unusual length, dealing plainly with this matter :

"... I pray that you may have a happy day : and may both get good and do good. And that it may be so—will you take a word from an old pulpit hand ? Your sermon has been long ready : but be up earlier than usual to meditate and pray over it. Steep every sentence of it in the Spirit. Take the title of one of Newman's sermons as your prayer and aim all the day : 'The salvation of the hearer, the motive of the preacher.' Preach as if it were your last

[1] *The Walk, Conversation, and Character of our Lord*, pp. 324–6.

sermon, and your first will be memorable, both to you and to the people. Beseech for a special blessing on your first sermon in that pulpit. And throw all you are into it : into the *delivery* of it. I am not afraid for its matter or its language—but I am not without some fear as to its delivery . . . Do not despise delivery, falling back upon matter. The matter is dead without delivery. Delivery ! Delivery ! Delivery ! said Demosthenes to the aspirant. You able fellows are tempted to despise delivery as being ' popular.' I implore you to rise above that delusion, and to do your very best by your message by delivering it in your best possible. *And pray after it.* We are tempted to pray *before preaching*, because we are afraid at the people and at our work ; but prayer for ourselves and the people *after* preaching is much neglected. Do not neglect either. And go on. Your own heart will tell you more and better.—With great regard, A. W."

So truly did the writer hold the balance between the external and the spiritual in preaching. Delivery to him was an essential element ; thus preaching always remained distinct from literature. Even after his own sermons had begun to sell by tens of thousands he held to this distinction ; for he advised the same friend to beware of requests to publish his sermons, adding, " Preaching is one thing : literature is another. Only Newman has both in one. Not A. W."

Of his own delivery it is impossible to write with any adequacy. The quality of his thought and the intensity of his imagination may be gathered from his books. One aspect of his presence and bearing is preserved for future generations in Sir James Guthrie's noble portrait, reproduced as frontispiece of this volume. But no description can convey to those who never heard it how much of the effect of his speaking was due to the living voice. Sometimes, indeed, his voice fell so low that a few words or a clause were indistinctly heard by those farthest from the preacher. But how great was its range! How the devoutness of his nature found expression in it! How the first words of the service carried with them the sense of the very Presence of God! How it fell low in contrition or warning, and rose and swelled and thrilled in the urgency of appeal! How fitting an instrument it was for the proclamation of his message —nay, rather, how message and instrument are indissolubly joined as its tones still " vibrate in the memory "! One hearer, looking back, has often recalled the words in which R. H. Hutton described the preaching of Frederick Maurice :

> " There was intensity—almost too thrilling— and something, too, of sad exultation in every tone. . . . This was what made his character present itself so strongly to the mind as almost embodied in a *voice*."

Nothing was more characteristic in Dr. Whyte's teaching than his emphasis on the right exercise of the *Imagination*. In his view it was an essential instrument for the preacher because it was an essential organ of the spiritual life. This was a topic to which he frequently returned, and which he treated from varying angles, and with a constantly changing wealth of illustration. Sometimes he approached it through psychology and by examples borrowed from science and literature. He began one such address by pointing out that all our powers of understanding, memory, conscience, and heart—" all that is within me," in the Psalmist's words—help to constitute the imagination. Then he told the story of the driftwood, picked up by Columbus on the shores of Spain, awaking in the explorer's imagination the vision of the New World. Other discoverers from Galileo to Lord Kelvin were cited to bear witness to its supreme value, and then followed instances from the great imaginative writers from Dante, through Shakespeare, Milton, Bunyan, and Gibbon to Carlyle. The Religious Imagination was treated under four heads : the Reading of Scripture, the Sacramental Principle, Prayer, and Praise. Dr.

Whyte sometimes closed his treatment of the imagination by enlarging on its use in praise, and by pointing
out how every verse in Psalm xxiii. is a distinct and
vivid picture, or tracing the imagery in such hymns
as " Rock of Ages " and " When I survey the
wondrous Cross." When addressing a Conference
of Sabbath-school teachers, his closing appeal was to
consider what the children in their classes would be
ten, twenty, thirty years after, that so they might
gain a fresh sense of the living import of their work.

The counsel so given on the use of the Imagination
formed the centre of Dr. Whyte's own practice both in
his inner life and in his preparation for the pulpit.
Even study and reading, highly as he esteemed these,
were only preliminary to the preacher's task. For,
while the thoughts of the great religious teachers upon
the nature and destiny of man might be found in
books, and all the mechanism of study which has been
described might help to weave them into the fabric of
the preacher's message, yet if that message were to
be living and powerful, they must be fused by the
glow of personal experience and lit up by the flash of
imagination. And, during the long, solitary walks
of his holiday seasons, not less than in the silence of
his study, Dr. Whyte of set purpose let his imagination
pierce through and through the subjects or the characters regarding which he had in mind to preach.
This deliberate and conscious cultivation of that
which he regarded as " nothing less than the noblest
intellectual attribute of the human mind " brought
its abundant reward. For long years he carried out
his own precept, " Let your imagination sweep up
through the whole visible heavens, up to the heaven of
heavens. Let her sweep and soar on her shining wing,
up past sun, moon, and stars." [1] And year by year, till
he was far past middle life, the wings of his " sanctified
and soaring imagination " grew ever stronger.

If space allowed, it would be possible to show
how his imagination had its interior and cosmic aspects,

[1] From the sermon on " Imagination in Prayer " (*Lord, Teach
Us to Pray*, p. 243 f.).

now penetrating, as Dante penetrated, into the hidden origins of conduct and laying bare the utmost consequences of sin, and now rising, as Dante rose, into the sphere of unchanging light. It might be shown, too, how his imaginative power passed into more gracious forms as the years went on. But such an account can only be very brief, and the examples here given must be few.

In Dr. Whyte's earlier ministry it was the unflinching directness of his preaching, his often startling exposure of sin, and his urgent and repeated summons to repentance that most deeply impressed his hearers. In keeping with this was the stern—even lurid and terrifying—use to which he sometimes turned his imagination. Of this side of his preaching Principal George Adam Smith spoke from Dr. Whyte's own pulpit three days after he passed away :

> " In Scottish preaching of the 'seventies, sin had either with the more evangelical preachers tended to become something abstract or formal, or with others was elegantly left alone. But Dr. Whyte faced it, and made us face it, as fact, ugly, fatal fact—made us feel its reality and hideousness, and follow its course to its wages in death. He did this not only by his rich use of the realism of poetry, and fiction, and biography, but as we could feel through his experimental treatment of it, out of his own experience of its temptations and insidiousness, and of the warfare with it to which every honest man is conscript."

There were two passages which became wellnigh legendary in Free St. George's for their impassioned and terrifying vehemence. Once he was preaching on the Rich Young Ruler, whom he followed right out of the Gospel story. The preacher, we are told,

> " watched him and made his congregation see him wheeling blindly down the black depths of the inferno, circle after circle, until just as he disappeared on his way down its bottomless

abyss, he, who had been bending over the pulpit, watching him with blazing eye, shouted : ' I hear it ! It's the mocking laughter of the universe, and it's shouting at him over the edge, " Ha ha ! Kept the commandments ! " ' " [1]

The other passage is still referred to with bated breath by a few who heard it forty or fifty years ago. It told of the hell-hounds of remorse in pursuit of a man who had come to see the horror of his sin. At night he could not sleep for the baying of these hounds of vengeance, nor would he ever shake them off as long as he lived. And what of the end ? " You may be saved," the preacher exclaimed, " but they will pursue you up to the very gates of heaven, and leave the bloody slaver of their jaws upon the golden bars ! "

At other times, the power of the preacher's imagination lay largely in this—that in his experience " the terror of the Lord " and the joy of His Presence were separated by so narrow a space. " What will it be to be there ! " he exclaimed at the close of a rapturous passage on the bliss of the redeemed ; and then, suddenly and solemnly, he added, " And what will it be NOT to be there ! " Or we may recall a passage in his Closing Address as Moderator in which he advised his brethren to reread their pastoral visitation book, " continually, systematically, deliberately, slowly, imaginatively," calling up as they did so the face and history and character which belonged to every name entered there. Then he described the humbling memories that would flock into the minister's heart as he read—memories of the young man whom he had failed to invite to his house, the dying member whom he had left unvisited, the family in deep trouble for whom he had delayed to

---

[1] I borrow this, and several incidents and descriptions later, from Dr. Kelman's memorial address, *Whyte of St. George's*. This grim passage must have been an improvisation. It does not occur in the MSS. of the sermon (preached in 1878), but it may have been introduced after some sentences on the later life of the young ruler, which conclude, " One trembles to think of the career and end of this once so promising youth."

seek help. And so on through a closely packed page of instances ; until he broke out :

> " Oh ! the shame, and the pain, and the absolute agony of reading page after page of a pastor's old visitation book ! At any rate, of my reading of mine ! Till this is sent of God into our hearts; that He who gave us that book to go by, oh! so many years ago, has taken it also, with all the rest, and has nailed it to His cross."

Again, there were gleams of singularly beautiful and tender imagination, even in the earlier years in Free St. George's, as when he asked regarding the Annunciation, depicted " on a thousand sacred canvases throughout Christendom, . . . why no spiritual artist has stained the whiteness of the lily with the red blood of a broken heart." So too, in the same sermon, he follows in imagination the Virgin Mary's journey to the hill country of Judea—" She may have crossed Olivet as the sun was setting. She may have knelt even in Gethsemane. She may have turned aside to look on the city from Calvary." [1]

In its most typical exercise, Dr. Whyte's imagination was always an unveiling—now of the human heart, and now—especially in his later years—of the glories of that future world of which most preachers of the day almost hesitated to speak. Yet the two were inseparably linked ; for the greatest glory of the world of the redeemed was, he often repeated, that its denizens had been such men and women as we now are. One such sermon closed with an account of " a three-cornered contest in heaven " between William Cowper, the preacher, and one of his hearers, who all challenged Paul's claim to be the greatest example of the redeeming power of Christ. " I think I know," he said, " who will carry away the prize from you both. Nay, I am sure I know ! "— dropping his voice to a whisper, as he closed the Bible —" Of whom *I* am chief ! "

---

[1] *Bible Characters*, Fourth Series, pp. 1, 3. The sermon in its original and longer form belongs to 1883 (cf. pp. 263, 266 above).

Closely connected with his use of imagination was Dr. Whyte's varied power of illustration. Some of his literary analogies were very apt and striking, but as a rule his simplest illustrations were the most effective, especially those drawn from his own experience. On one occasion he was preaching on the words, " He hath laid help upon one that is mighty," and illustrated the work of the Redeemer by the canon laid down in Horace's *Ars Poetica* that, in tragedy, a god should never be introduced save to untie a knot which had baffled all human skill. The analogy was singularly apposite ; yet it probably left most of the congregation cold. Very different was the effect of the next illustration. Dr. Whyte told how, in a lonely walk at the head of Loch Rannoch a few days before, he had found by the roadside a helpless and struggling sheep which had become entangled in a loose end of barbed wire. He set to work to release it, but the terrified animal only struggled the more, and the whole result of his endeavour was to enmesh it more firmly in the wire and to pierce his own hands with the barbs. When he had begun to despair he saw a figure coming towards him—the shepherd, who, with one or two skilful turns, swiftly set the foolish and frightened creature free.

Similarly in a sermon in Dr. Whyte's volume on St. Paul we may contrast his elaborate use of a somewhat frigid metaphor from Goodwin, with the simple and heart-searching passage in which he returns to actual life. " Just go home to-night, and do that deed of love, and truth, and humility, and brotherly kindness, and self-denial, in His name, and already Christ is dwelling in you, and working in you, as well as in Paul." [1] In such a passage, when he brought his hearers face to face with the Character and Work of Jesus Christ, his power was unfailing. Many are the sacred memories in Free St. George's of sermons at Communion seasons when he preached on the Passion of our Lord. It was in a passage on the crown of thorns in one such sermon that he suddenly said

[1] *The Apostle Paul*, p. 157 ; cf. pp. 151, 155.

with arresting emphasis, " I wonder in what slug-
gard's garden they grew ! "

Dr. Whyte's preaching was personal, ethical, inward, and it dealt but sparingly with speculative or
social problems. In his later years he seemed to
stand at a distance from many of the intellectual
problems which most persistently confronted the
young minds of his time. He was once asked by an
interviewer if he found much scepticism among young
men, and replied, " I hardly know that I am com-
petent to say. Certainly, sceptical young men do
not come my way. Perhaps they know my line of
work and do not seek my advice." He characteristically added that what he feared most among young
men and women was " indifference, and indolence,
and neglect of spiritual things." But this limitation
in the scope of his work carried with it no loss of
intellectual quality, nor did his personality ever lose
its influence over young and eager spirits. He did
not directly meet our difficulties, as other teachers
of the day in great measure met them. But he did
something higher and rarer. He stood through all
that he said and all that he was, as a living proof of
the unquestionable reality and final importance of
the spiritual life. It might be hard to reconcile our
apprehension of this with the theories of science or
philosophy, or with the disorders of the social life
around us ; but the testimony itself could not be set
aside. In face of all unsolved enigmas we felt that
the experiences of which Alexander Whyte spoke,
and the Power which had made him what he was,
were no fantasies of the imagination, but must in the
long-run prove to be the unshakable foundations of
the deepest life and the truest knowledge. Others
might defend Christianity by the weapons of the
intellect : he did so by the evidence of an inspired
personality—by vision, not by argument.

If theology is something separable from life, then
he was no theologian. His strength lay in his union
of a lofty spiritual imagination with a deep and searching knowledge of human character. In the middle

region of abstract thought the wings of his genius drooped. *Generalia non pungunt*—" Generalities do not pierce deep "—was a favourite quotation ; and if his denunciations of the depravity of the human heart ever seemed exaggerated and unconvincing, or even provoked an instinctive opposition in the minds of some hearers, it was when they were most general. When he came to speak of particulars, to track down instances of envy or pride or lack of consideration for others, the conscience of the hearer at once awoke.

It was Dr. Whyte's lifelong aim to be a preacher of righteousness, and, since he would not heal the wound of his people slightly, a preacher, first, of sin. The school of religious thought in which he was brought up, with its emphasis on strict self-examination, and perhaps also the entail of suffering in his early home, had given a sharper edge to a naturally sensitive conscience. This characteristic appears in the following recollection spoken in his fiftieth year :

" The first text I ever heard a sermon from was that great text in Zechariah, ' Is not this a brand plucked out of the fire ? ' ' It is I, Lord,' my young heart answered ; and my heart is making the same answer here to-day."

Self-knowledge was a great part of the burden of his teaching, but not self-knowledge with a view to self-reform. He was, indeed, ready to address the most urgent and telling appeals to the will of his hearers, especially in the earlier years. At a later time, he sometimes, under the influence of Paul's saying, " What I would, that do I not ; but what I hate, that do I," appeared to pass almost too disparaging a judgment upon the capacity for good of man's *Will*.[1]

[1] For a time in Dr. Whyte's ministry the account of the divided self in Romans vii. seemed to colour his whole interpretation of the New Testament. He always insisted that it represented St. Paul's Christian, not his pre-Christian, experience ; and when the opposite view was set forth by scholars like Dr. Denney, to whom he was most ready to defer on other points, he held to his own view. (Cf. *The Apostle Paul*, p. 127.) At an earlier time he told his people : "You'll never get out of the seventh of Romans while I'm your minister."

But we have seen how he exalted the faculty of *Imagination*; and he would have found much to agree with in the dictum, lately become fashionable, " The imagination is stronger than the will." To exercise the imagination upon great and ennobling themes was in his view a mighty safeguard of the spiritual life, and its highest use was directed to Jesus Christ. But the final truth, as he expressed it in his old age, was of a yet more mystical order :

> " Many serious-minded men take an infinitude of pains to produce a true holiness for themselves out of their own corrupt hearts; squeezing, all the time, oil out of a flint. Whereas, the true way, and the only possible way for them to get the mastery over the indwelling sin is by receiving into their hearts a new spiritual nature out of the fulness of that new spiritual nature that is in Christ." [1]

It was by no accident that two-thirds of the volumes of sermons which Dr. Whyte published contained in their titles the word, " Character." The conflict of good and evil, not as abstract principles, but as forces contending for the lordship of human lives, formed the chief subject of his preaching. In this wide sense he was from first to last an ethical preacher; and telling instances were recorded of old enmities which were brought to an end through the influence of his preaching. He came, also, to grapple very closely with certain concrete moral problems ; but he approached them always from the side of disposition, never from that of organisation. When he spoke of the temptations of a business life, he treated these temptations as direct tests of Christian character, and never inquired how far they were due to the accepted organisation of industry. Few preachers can have spoken so often or so trenchantly of the home as an arena of moral discipline, and the home is essentially the sphere of individual character.

[1] *The Spiritual Life*, p. 146 f. ; cf. pp. 196 ff.

Like his predecessor, he refused to "reckon on any gregarious and collective regeneration of humanity," addressing himself to the conscience of men one by one, " that so the kingdom may at last come, whose citizens are all holy." [1]

He never failed to distinguish the God-ward from the man-ward aspect of religion. No spiritual teacher of his time and land preached with the same insight on penitence or on prayer. Much as he valued the privilege of public worship—carefully as he prepared his own share in it—yet to him the typical and the highest form of devotion was secret prayer. This came out in his startling reply to the question of a young minister whether he advised the preparation of prayers for the pulpit : " Certainly I do ; but public prayer is an unnatural act." The same thought is developed in the sermon on " The Secret Burden," based on one of his favourite passages in the prophets—that in Zechariah, in which the word *apart* occurs eleven times in three verses. [2] Discipline, Prayer, the Interior Motive, Humility before God and man, Purity attained through Suffering—these were among the master-notes of his preaching.

Dr. Whyte set forth his ideals as a preacher in occasional letters as well as in public utterances. One such was addressed in 1908 to a Methodist pastor, the Rev. E. Jenkins, who had written to ask his counsel. He replied by return of post from Switzerland :

" Never think of giving up preaching ! The angels around the throne envy you your great work. You ' scarcely know how or what to preach.' Look into your own sinful heart, and back into your sinful life, and around on the world full of sin and misery, and open your New Testament, and make application of Christ to

[1] From an Address by Principal Candlish to the students of the New College (*The Gospel of Forgiveness*, p. 482).
[2] *Lord, Teach Us to Pray*, pp. 267 ff.

yourself and your people ; and, like Goodwin, you will preach more freshly and more powerfully every day till you are eighty. . . .

" Don't hunger for books. Get a few of the very best, such as you already have, and read them and your own heart continually : and no fear of your preaching. For generations Rutherford has inspired the best preaching in Scotland. Behmen ' had no books, but he had himself,' and, though you had the whole Bodleian Library, and did not know yourself, you would not preach a sermon worth hearing.

" Go on and grow in grace and power as a Gospel preacher.—Warmly yours,   A. W."

Regarding two sermons afterwards printed in the volume on *The Apostle Paul*, Dr. Whyte wrote to the Rev. A. B. Macaulay (the letter is headed, " Sabbath afternoon ") :

" How have you got on to-day ? I never got on—to my feeling—worse. . . . But, I have often been eloquent, and puffed up, and no good done : and, who knows, but my text may be illustrated in me to-day—' to him that worketh not, but believeth.' Somehow, unaccountably, a great gospel text is always the most difficult text to me to preach on, so as to make it fresh and interesting. But, difficult or easy, I must preach more on such texts. And so must you. It is for such texts, above all else, that we have our pulpits committed to us. In William Law's day, he complains, all the ministers round about preached on such subjects as ' Euroclydon,' or on ' The times when the Gospels were writ.' And a great deal of my preaching must come under the same scornful condemnation. As also, much of my visiting. In Law's day the pastors spent their visits ' cursing the weather,' and ' telling and hearing of the approaching marriages.'

" Did you ever grapple with ' the Blood of God ' ? I am to try that soon.   A. W."

Close to the subject of Dr. Whyte's preaching lies that of his prayers. Intensely subjective they often were, yet how many are still treasured in the sacred storehouse of memory. One who was a student in the early 'nineties has spoken of the days when " every sermon in Free St. George's was a volcano, and every opening prayer a revelation." The humility of his prayers, their unexpectedness, the " pleading note " of which he himself spoke, led all of his congregation who had the power to follow into a place apart. One of his former assistants, Professor J. M. Shaw, applied to him the words used by William Penn of George Fox :

> " The inwardness and weight of his spirit, the reverence and solemnity of his address and behaviour, and the fewness and fulness of his words, have often struck even strangers with admiration as they used to reach others with consolation."

His prayers at the graveside can never be forgotten, from the opening sentence taken from the Shorter Catechism—" The souls of believers are at their death made perfect in holiness, and do immediately pass into glory "—on to the triumphant close. At one Communion season in Free St. George's, it was known that an elder of the congregation was passing away, and part of Dr. Whyte's prayer at the Table ran thus :

> " We shall not again see him here carrying a Communion cup, but Thou hast a cup waiting to be carried by him at the great Communion. . . . We envy him : with holy sanctified envy we envy him. We envy him his life, and we envy him his death, and we envy him so soon to find his work at Thine own Communion Table above."

The tributes, also, in which he commemorated the earthly service of those who had passed to a higher service, showed a characteristic glow of feeling and dignity of phrase.[1]

Throughout the services which he conducted,

[1] Cf. his tribute to Mr. Gladstone, reproduced in Appendix III., p. 656, below.

whether in his own pulpit or elsewhere, everything was thought out, yet nothing was stereotyped. His advice about the preparation of prayer has already been quoted ; but he would hardly have laid it down as a rigid rule, for late in his life he wrote to Dr. Kelman of "the point and power that belong rather to spontaneous than to prepared prayer." His services showed a variety and originality which a lesser man could not have attempted without disaster, but which were extraordinarily impressive in his hands. Even to the customary Presbyterian formula at the conclusion of a passage of Scripture, he would give an unwonted freshness by the addition of one or two words, as thus: "May the Lord add His blessing to the reading of His *gracious and beautiful* Word." Who but he would have read, at the grave of an aged and saintly lady, the account of Christiana's passing, from the close of the *Pilgrim's Progress* ? In the Communion service there appeared the same desire to awaken the heart and conscience of his fellow-worshippers by varying the familiar order. More than once, when he came to the words of institution, " After the same manner also He took the cup," he broke off, with the cup in his right hand, and told how once " Rabbi " Duncan, when distributing the elements, saw a woman in a seat near the front of the church pass the cup untasted while the tears coursed down her cheeks ; and how the great scholar, leaving his place at the Table, stepped down into the aisle, and, taking a cup from the elder who held it, gave it himself to the weeping communicant, with the words, " Tak' it, woman : it's for sinners."

The closing act of each service was as characteristic as all that went before. Most often it included one of the benedictions or doxologies from the Epistles; but it might begin with the words, "*Sursum Corda*," and end with the lines which in a very special sense he made his own :

> " O may we stand before the Lamb,
>   When earth and seas are fled,
> And hear the Judge pronounce our name,
>   With blessings on our head."

It remains to say something of Dr. Whyte's preaching to smaller gatherings or on special occasions, when he dispensed with manuscript and spoke out of the fulness of his heart. Many of those who knew him well felt that, powerful and memorable as were many of his sermons in Free St. George's, his high-water mark both of oratory and inspiration was reached in these less formal sermons and addresses. The wish was sometimes expressed that he would speak with the same spontaneity from his own pulpit ; but in his later years he never departed from his chosen method there. Once, in discussing the alternative of reading as against *extempore* speech with Dr. A. B. Macaulay, Dr. Whyte said that some of his best addresses had been delivered without paper—and some of his worst. He may have feared that, if he began to speak *extempore* Sunday by Sunday, after a time his preaching would lose in substance and in grasp. However this may be, it seems certain that the extraordinary richness of idea and imagination and spiritual experience which marked his spoken word was maintained, even to the age of four-score, largely by his persistent study and care in composition.

There were indeed certain all-too-rare occasions when he spoke without manuscript in his own pulpit —his sermons to children. For long he conducted such a service three or four times a year, after each Communion season. Later, when he obtained first an assistant, and then a colleague, the children's service became more frequent, but Dr. Whyte conducted it less often. But when he did so, his addresses were full of a homely point and tenderness. Sometimes he chose a hymn as his text—" Gentle Jesus, meek and mild," or, before a baptismal service, " A little child the Saviour came "—and then the allotted time was apt to run out and find him still expounding the first verse. Once when baptizing his colleague's child he said to the father, " He'll teach you more, sir, than any of your college professors did."

Part of a children's address, on the right use of

holidays, was described to the writer by one who joined the church under Dr. Candlish and who beguiled the tedium of an invalid life by recalling her ministers' sermons of twenty, forty, or fifty years before.

" When you are in the train, starting for your holidays," Dr. Whyte said to his young hearers, " don't sit with a sour face at the window, or say, ' No room here,' when people who are late pass along looking for a seat ; lean out and say, ' Plenty of room here ! ' " Then followed counsels for the holiday itself, and at the close— " When you are starting to come home, don't forget old John, the coachman, who helped you to catch your first trout, but give him a packet of tobacco. And leave half a pound of tea for that old saint in the village.'

Another such memory has been recorded in *Conference*, an Indian missionary journal, edited by Dr. Macphail :

" One of the most characteristic addresses we ever heard from Dr. Whyte was delivered to a small meeting of children at St. George's which we were once asked to address while on furlough. Dr. Whyte presided, and Mr. A. B. Macaulay, who was at that time Dr. Whyte's assistant, and Dr. George Smith were present. Dr. Whyte read from the Gospels the story of the widow who cast her mite into the treasury, and went on to say : ' This woman was a washerwoman. She washed the dirty linen of Simon the Pharisee and other Pharisees round about Jerusalem. We shall all see this woman, children, when we get to heaven. The Lord will come in with this woman on His arm, and He'll say, " Come here, Dr. Whyte; come here, Dr. Smith; come here, Mr. Macaulay. Do you see this woman here ? She has done more than any of you." And I shall go up to her and say, " Woman, I used to preach about you, down in Edinburgh." ' "

Of the sermons preached in his earlier days in country places—in Glen Clova and Kinnoir, at Lochearnhead and in Iona—records have been given in earlier chapters, and much of what was there said applies to similar gatherings up to the end of his active ministry. Sometimes the place of meeting was a schoolroom in the Border country or in the far North or West ; sometimes a mission-hall or small chapel, like that near Bonskeid. Other buildings were even humbler. Of two used successively at Balmacara, one was a hall, hardly more than a shed, roughly built of undressed boards, the other an empty granary on the upper floor of an outbuilding near the house. But rude and informal as the surroundings sometimes were, these scattered buildings became to hundreds the very Gate of Heaven—so convincingly did the preacher open up the great realities of the spiritual life.

Even the outward setting of these informal services helped to bring speaker and hearers close together. His gown was laid aside and he wore a closely buttoned frock coat ; but more important than any detail of dress was the fact that his audience were near enough to follow every gleam of the clear blue eyes, and every passing light and shade upon the expressive face. For some, the memory of the smile which so wonderfully lit up its strong lines is that which abides most enduringly. At such a service, especially if it were held in the evening, Dr. Whyte commonly chose only three singings and a very brief passage of scripture, in order to leave time and scope for the address ; but the exposition of the opening Psalm, giving its spiritual meaning line by line in brief, home-coming touches, played the same part as the stately music of a cathedral in striking the keynote of the whole service, and raising and attuning the congregation's spirit.

The subjects which he chose for such gatherings varied little in forty years, but no address was ever exactly repeated. In the later period, he preached often on the hymns, " Just as I am " and " The sands of time are sinking," on Psalms

xxiii. and ciii., or on the words, " These are they which came out of great tribulation " ; but most of all on the three texts to which he returned with unabated freshness year after year—" The Lord, the Lord God, merciful and gracious " ; " Who is a God like unto Thee ? " and " Lord, teach us to pray." [1] It is a cause for no small gratitude that we now possess, in the volume of sermons on Prayer, more of the material which went to the making of those great addresses than was contained in any of the books published within Dr. Whyte's own lifetime. At other times, especially when he preached on several occasions to the same country audience, he chose subjects which he had recently treated in his own pulpit, such as " Luther on the Galatians " or " Paul's thorn in the flesh " ; but these were always adapted and brought near to the lives and needs of the men and women before him.

No preacher in Scotland was so eagerly welcomed as Dr. Whyte at a distance from his own home, or maintained for so long a hold upon the affection of congregations in every corner of the land. The scene outside a church in which he had been announced to preach was thus described by a minister of great devotion and original genius, the late Rev. J. P. Struthers, of the Reformed Presbyterian Church, Greenock :

" Owing to another meeting of which I had charge, I was nearly an hour late when I got to the church where Dr. Whyte was preaching. But the doors were shut, and barred from the inside. A lad who was standing there told me the building was crammed full and hundreds had gone away. Well, I thought, if the building is so full as that, somebody will be sure to turn faint . . . and then will be my chance ! And

---

[1] Ex. xxxiv. 6–9 ; Mic. vii. 18, 19 ; Luke xi. 1. See *Lord, Teach Us to Pray*, pp. 52 ff. *et passim* ; and on Dr. Whyte's early and lifelong debt to Goodwin's exposition of Ex. xxxiv., cf. *Thirteen Appreciations*, p. 167.

I kept running round and round the building,
watching the different doors, hearing the sound
of the preacher's voice, but unable to make out
what he said ; and then at last a door opened,
and out came a lady, conveyed by two friends,
and in I went, and heard such words from Dr.
Whyte as I trust I shall never forget."

His own early experience gave a special directness
and intimacy to his preaching when his audience was
chiefly composed of those who lived by the work of
their own hands. Nor were there any congregations
that awaited his coming more expectantly than those
of Fountainbridge and the Pleasance, where he spoke
with the same homely force as in a Highland schoolhouse. It was a very poor old woman in the latter
district who said there was no preacher whom she
would so willingly hear as Dr. Whyte, " for he aye
gars me greet." Sometimes, too, he addressed the
large company of the poorest in Edinburgh who came
to the Sabbath Free Breakfast Mission, of which he
was a director. On one such morning he had asked
that Newton's hymn, " Come, my soul, thy suit
prepare " (one of those which he chose most often),
should be sung ; but as the hymn-book in use did not
contain it, he then chose, " There is a fountain filled
with blood." The chairman of the gathering [1] has
described how, at the close of the hymn, Dr. Whyte
was called on to speak. Springing from his seat
on the platform, he called out in a loud voice :

" Say, ' I ! ' We have just been singing in
that hymn of Cowper's :

> ' The dying thief rejoiced to see
> That fountain in his day ;
> And there have I, as vile as he,
> Washed all my sins away.'

Cowper wrote these words ; they expressed his
experience : he put himself alongside the dying

---

[1] Mr. James M'Kerrell Brown, C.A., an elder in St. George's
Parish Church, who was an ally of Dr. Whyte's in much religious
and philanthropic work.

thief, and like him received cleansing and pardon. Say '*I !*' *My* name is Alexander Whyte, and I can put my name in that verse, alongside the name of the dying thief, and of William Cowper. Can you put *your* name there ? Can you say, ' I ! ' ? Don't look at your neighbour and wonder if he can say, ' I ! ', but see that your own name is written down there.''

The attention of that large meeting was gained by the first words of the address and held to the end. On another occasion he was addressing a smaller but equally poor audience, whom he astonished by saying that he had found out the name of the wickedest man in Edinburgh, and had come to tell them. Then, bending forward, he whispered, " His name is Alexander Whyte ! "

There was a special note of sympathy in his preaching to people with whom life had dealt hardly. Not that he was ignorant of the temptations and sins of the mean streets in the cities or of secluded country places. He of all men could not have preached on, " Just as I am ! " or on, " The Lord God, . . . forgiving iniquity and transgression and sin," without dealing searchingly with the consciences of his hearers. But there was less of sternness than sometimes in his own pulpit ; and the smile of rapturous contemplation broke more often over his features, as his imagination took wing, and for a short space the material surroundings of his hearers fell away into forgetfulness, as they caught some reflection of the preacher's vision of the consummated and triumphant " Joy of his Lord."

Of these sermons, none was more memorable than that on " Who is a God like unto Thee ? " In its course, the preacher used to tell of an incident which occurred at the end of Dr. John Carment's life. Dr. Whyte had occasion to call on business at the office of his friend, who was then far over eighty years of age. After their business was completed, the noble old lawyer thrust his papers and writing materials on one side, and looking straight across the cleared desk at his visitor, said with great intensity, "Have ye any word for an old sinner ? " Dr. Whyte described his amazement at the abrupt question, coming from one whom he revered as a saint on the very verge of glory. For a moment he was too nonplussed to answer ; but then the words came into his heart which he had given to one and another in the course of his visiting that afternoon, and he stammered out, " *He delighteth in mercy* "—and so took his leave. Next morning he received a letter from Dr. Carment, telling that he had been passing through a season of profound inward darkness, but that the four words left with him by his friend had sent a flood of light into his spirit. The light never again faded until, a very few days later, he passed into the perfect day.

The story seems simple, perhaps even bald, in the coldness of print ; but the thrill of it lay in the telling, and most of all in the preacher's invocation of the spirit of his departed friend, whom he pictured as looking down on the conflicts and failures of those who were still on earth, and as bearing anew his testimony to Him who " delighteth in mercy."

Once, after a singularly solemn New Year's sermon, a devoted member of Free St. George's went to the vestry to thank his minister. He ended with the words, " It went to my heart as if you had come straight from the Audience-chamber." "And perhaps I did," was the quiet and grave reply.

" He fanned intelligence."—*Epitaph on Richard Baxter.*
" Brutus never read a book but to make himself a better man."

No part of Dr. Whyte's work was more characteristic than that which he carried on for forty years in his Classes for Young Women and Young Men. Many in his own church and beyond it have since sought to follow in the way which he opened up by treating religious experience in vital connection with great literature ; yet it may confidently be said that no one else has conducted classes in a manner comparable to his, or maintained the same freshness and power over so long a time. His Classes may not, indeed, have occupied the very first place in his thought and endeavour ; yet they stood close to his pulpit in his estimate of his own work. He was by instinct a teacher as well as a prophet, and he found in his class-teaching opportunity for a twofold appeal, to the conscience as well as to the intellect of the hundreds of men and women who came week by week to learn from him. In the power that springs from spontaneity his work in the Classes even surpassed his preaching. In the latter he was at times oppressed by the " Burden of the Lord." His sermons then bore the mark of the travail of mind and spirit which had gone to their making. But his teaching in the Classes was always a delight—to himself first, and hence to his audience—so freshly and lavishly did he give of his store of knowledge and wisdom and faith.

In Chapter X. some account was given of the modest beginnings of Dr. Whyte's Classes after the second service on Sunday for Young Men, and on Wednesday afternoon for Young Women. These continued for some years to be " Bible Classes," as

the term was understood in the evangelical churches
of Scotland, although from 1875 onwards they were
simply announced as " Young Men's " and " Young
Women's Class." The subjects chosen were biblical
and doctrinal, not historical or literary ; yet the
teacher's passion for great books, and his keen
interest in the history of language, even then gave
his expositions a width of outlook and a humanistic setting which were unlooked-for in the Free
Church of that day. Already he was opening many
new doors of beauty and interest to the young minds
around him.

After ten years in Free St. George's, he had begun
to move farther from the traditional paths. The
authoress of *Pro Christo et Ecclesia* attended the
Young Women's Class at this time, and bore witness
long after to the deep impression made by the
singular union of delight in great thoughts greatly
expressed with the most searching analysis of motive
and conduct which marked Dr. Whyte's lectures on
Milton and Butler. " The delight in beauty," she
wrote, " seemed to act as a chisel upon the moral
granite, shaping a character of splendid proportions."

For more than ten years thereafter the division of
the class-work into two sections—biblical or theological, and literary or philosophical—was maintained. Under the latter, more humanistic, division
of the programme there were included topics such as
" The Trial and Death of Socrates " and Trench's
" Study of Words " ; and the other course until 1890
comprised studies in the Westminster Confession and
the Shorter Catechism. Two years before, Dr. Whyte
entered on a course which some who had long experience of his classes thought the greatest of all—
that on the *Divina Commedia*. It extended over four
sessions, and was combined during the two last with
an introductory study of the New Testament. The
next winter (1892–93) was devoted to Butler as a
theological and ethical classic, and to William Law
as a master in literature and in the devotional life.
Thereafter, the division of subjects disappeared, and

theology, devotion, and literature were conjoined in a series of widely sweeping surveys, each of which extended over more than one session of the Classes. Their successive subjects were " The Mystics " (1893–96) ; " The Great Autobiographies " (1896–1902) ; " The Stoics " (1902–4) ; and " The Makers of Scotland " (1904–7). Three shorter courses followed, and a pencilled programme among Dr. Whyte's papers shows that he planned for the year 1911–12 " A Rapid Review of Forty Years' Congregational Class-work." This memorandum is headed by the symbol *Deo Volente* ; but, while he received strength to do much other work in the six years that followed, he was not permitted to give, or his expectant Classes to hear, this summary of all his long intellectual and spiritual pilgrimage with them.[1]

In this great achievement, by which such varied treasures were placed within the reach of thousands of men and women, of whom only a minority were " students " in the narrower sense, it is hard to know whether to admire more the teacher's industry or his catholicity. In the main, he moved from the more ethical and theological to the more mystical and interior presentation of Christianity ; and perhaps it is not fanciful to see in his study of Dante the watershed from which streams flow in either direction. Yet there was a unity of conception and treatment throughout, though the emphasis may have shifted somewhat as the years passed ; nor did the ethical insight or the power of practical application which marked Dr. Whyte's earlier ministry ever fail.

Much that was recorded in the preceding chapter regarding Dr. Whyte's preparation for the pulpit applies to his class-work as well. The three months of his long vacation (July to September) were kept in the main for the great amount of reading which

[1] The titles of all the courses from 1883 onwards, and the complete programme issued at the outset of the most extensive of these—that on " The Great Autobiographies "—will be found in Appendix I., along with the outline of the course planned but never delivered.

he undertook. Specially constructed boxes, closely packed with books, and designed to serve as temporary bookcases when the journey's end was reached, preceded or accompanied him to Aviemore or Balmacara, or even to the distant Christianiafjord. The short Christmas vacation was used in the same way to complete his preparation for the latter part of the winter. His conception of repose as only a change of activity comes out in a letter from Bonskeid at Christmas, 1896 : " I am working some hours every day in my room for my omnivorous Classes. The rest is doing me great good." Four years later he writes from Aberdour: "I am busy over Cowper. My Classes go with me wherever I go."

The same short holiday is chronicled in a letter to Dr. Taylor Innes, in which he characteristically presses his reluctant friend to undertake an article for one of Dr. Hastings's dictionaries, and as characteristically sets on one side some suggestion made by Dr. Innes for his own work as not in line with his special methods :

"I wish you were here for a walk and a talk about many things. The roads and the sands are fine, though the day is short. I am working at Cowper with great benefit and great delight.

"As to Hastings—you are the man. And it would lengthen and crown your life to do something in that line. Not, perhaps, to his plan or order : but to your own genius and taste. I wish you would. For myself, my mind and my hands are full of present and prospective work, should this tree be spared by the Husbandman. My Sabbath work is as you know it, and I will do my best at it for such time as I am permitted. My Class-work is before my mind, and to some extent already in hand, for the next two years, D.V.—and your sketch-plan for me would not suit me nor my Classes. I have hit the vein for them, and for myself, in the meantime, and I must not be seduced from it, even by the attractions of authorship.

"If I am in town next week we must have as long a walk some afternoon as the short days will allow.

"In your early and less fastidious days did you ever read the *Cardiphonia*? I intend Newton and Scott, a day each, after Cowper.

"Ever yours, with a love and regard you cannot know; also Miss Innes.   A. W."

Another letter, sent in December 1902, from the same winter retreat to one of his daughters, then studying in Paris, gives a more detailed picture of his preparation for the prospective meetings of his Classes:

"We have been in this most restful place for ten days, and we return home to-morrow. . . . We have been twice back in Edinburgh, once to be present at Fred's ordination as a deacon, and again for the Christmas service and the Christmas Tree. . . . I had Dr. Dods and Dr. Thomson and Mr. Innes here for two days. We had a fine time, as we always have, over books, and men, and movements, literary and theological.

"I have given all my reading time to Cicero. I had intended to finish my Stoic studies in the Classes with this session, but when the Christmas recess came, I found I had so much material on my hands, and such interesting men and authors still to discuss, that it would not be possible to finish the subject this session. One result of this resolution is that I hope to do something like justice to Cicero. That great man was as far as possible from being a Stoic in his public life; but he is one of the foremost, if not the very foremost, of the Stoic writers. And I am looking forward with the greatest interest and hope to taking both Cicero the man, and Cicero the orator and the writer, up during what remains of this session: leaving Epictetus, and Seneca, and Marcus Aurelius for another session, *D.V.*

Cicero's Letters, his Orations, and his moral writings are so rich that I do not think I can wholly fail to make the end of the session both interesting and profitable to the Classes.

" I read, and hear read, your letters with great pleasure. You are working hard, and that is one of the sure sources of happiness both to yourself and to all who love you. Hard work, and a life of faith and prayer."

But the most striking proof of Dr. Whyte's concentration upon his work for the Classes was given when he refused—not for the only time—a pressing invitation to cross the Atlantic in order to preach and lecture at Northfield, on the ground that he could not spare sufficient time from the task which so absorbed his energies.   In the autumn of 1897 he was speaking to his Men's Class on the words, " Whatsoever thy hand findeth to do, do it with thy might."   He threw out a warning to the students of Divinity present that, when they became ministers, they must not allow themselves to be drawn aside from a minister's main work, and added :

" I've tried, in my own way, to keep to my own way.   An American deputation waited upon me the other day and said some very flattering things of me, and asked me to come across to preach to five hundred students. I said to myself that I had five hundred students every Sabbath night, and that I wouldn't have had them if I had been going all over the country to preach to five hundred students here and there. So I refused."

Some of Dr. Whyte's friends, British as well as American, regretted the decision recorded in these words ; but no faithful account of his life could omit to record it as a proof of his devotion to his " omnivorous Classes."

The mechanical side of the preparation to which Dr. Whyte attached so paramount an importance can be described in brief. When a subject had been decided on for his next course, or when he approached another stage in one of his longer courses, he began to collect and arrange notes on his wide reading. These were made in pencil, as a rule on half sheets of note-paper, which were lodged in a large envelope, along with cuttings from newspapers and magazines illustrating the subject in view. When the envelope had begun to fill up, its contents were summarised in a small index-volume ; and when it in turn had become crowded with references, a substantial octavo manuscript book was begun, containing the actual notes used in the Classes. Both the small and the large notebooks were strongly bound in black calf. In addition to references, the former also contained brief jottings for future amplification. Thus that on " The Makers of Scotland " contained under the heading, " Knox," three pages of such notes, followed by references to nearly forty works on the Reformation and the Renaissance—an indication of the labour which Dr. Whyte spent upon his preliminary reading.

If he never spared himself in preparing for his Classes, and was ever willing to advise others about books—sending, now a post card to a former assistant, and now a reply to an inquiry from a lay preacher in one of the English Free Churches—he claimed a like generosity on the part of his friends. One of his first steps when finding his way to the heart of a great thinker's message was to obtain from some expert a summary of the most recent literature on the author. Sometimes the request must have arrived at an inconvenient time. Thus we find Professor Calderwood apologising for delay in sending some notes on the eighteenth-century moralists, since Dr. Whyte's request for guidance in his reading on Butler had found him " breasting waves of manuscript " ; and, years after, Dr. George Adam Smith, then in uneasy process of transition from his professor's chair in Glasgow to the Principalship of Aberdeen University, makes a similar apology before setting down several closely packed pages of references to the latest works on Isaiah. Dr. T. M. Lindsay begins a letter on Luther's

writings by disclaiming the typical bookman's interest
in books as such. He explains that he " cares little
for what a man has said, compared with what a man
has done," and adds that " Luther's strong, smiting
words " were "not so much books as trumpet
blasts." Bishop Dowden acknowledges a copy of
one of Dr. Whyte's class programmes by saying,
" Happy are the men and women who are brought to
make the acquaintance of such distinguished writers
as have a place in your syllabus " ; and adds some
notes on leaders in the Oxford Movement, among them
this *obiter dictum* : " There is more true poetry in
four or five of Newman's lyrics than in all the *Christian
Year*." On another occasion Mr. Augustine Birrell
sends some recollections of Mr. Gladstone's talk on
Cromwell. In addition, the members of Dr. Whyte's
own circle, especially Dr. Dods, Dr. Taylor Innes, and
Dr. Sutherland Black, were called upon to contribute
from their wide stores of reading ; and the two latter
often undertook to unearth facts or track quotations
in the Advocates' Library or the British Museum
when nearer resources failed.

The harvest of this wide research was finally
gathered and arranged in one of the octavo manuscript books already referred to. Only at long intervals was a paragraph written out fully—for example,
at the opening of the winter's course, or when an
important author was first introduced. For the
rest, Dr. Whyte expanded, in the act of speaking,
the facts and memoranda with which his notebook
was crowded, giving life, colour, and harmony to his
theme as he passed swiftly on.

The main features of both classes were alike.
In both, Dr. Whyte always aimed at securing that
as many as possible of those attending should be
definitely enrolled ; [1] but a large number remained on

---

[1] One of Dr. Whyte's MS. books contains this note at the end of
his first lecture for the winter—" *Cards* ; with names and addresses.
You are committed to nothing, not even to regular attendance. Only,
a favour and a strength to me."

the margin, as occasional students, coming to the classes whenever they could, without giving in their names as members. Very commonly from five to six hundred gathered at the Young Men's Class ; but sometimes there was a marked increase, as at the beginning of the course on " The Makers of Scotland." The attendance at the Young Women's Class, which met at four on Wednesday afternoon, was very similar. In both cases, the term " young " was most generously interpreted, for there were always some present whose hair was already turning grey.

Many of those present belonged to Free St. George's ; but a large proportion came from other churches in all parts of the city—just as had been the case in the Prayer Meeting in the years round 1880— and a few came from other lands, and even from the Far East. In this sense the statement holds good, that Dr. Whyte's Classes were less a congregational organisation than a service to the community. Yet it is not less true that he could never have rendered this service without the hearty and continuous support of his Kirk-Session and Deacons' Court.

There was an elusive Somewhat in the spirit and atmosphere of " the Class " which makes the attempt to draw an adequate picture venturesome, if not hopeless. The Men's Class met after the second Sunday service in Free St. George's which for thirty years has begun at seven o'clock, and many of its members came direct from other services or occupations. Just before eight o'clock struck, groups of these began to gather opposite the side door of the church in Stafford Street, seeking what shelter they could from the wind or rain of the winter evening. Then, as the muffled notes of the organ within were heard in the dismission hymn, those who were nearest the side door pressed up the steps and the crowd in the street below grew thicker. Those first admitted found that perhaps three-fourths of the evening congregation had already left the church. Other members of the Class pressed eagerly in to join those who had remained from the service, until the area was occupied, save for the extreme corners of the building.   As one looked round the audience it was clear that they differed in occupation even more than in age.   Many were clearly students from the University or other colleges of the city, but others came from business or warehouse, or from the legal offices in which Edinburgh abounds, while yet others were artisans.

At 8.15, the door in the apse behind the pulpit opened ; and Mitchell, the church-officer, emerged from the vestry bearing a pile of books, with projecting slips of paper marking the quotations which were to be read during the evening's " rapid conversation," as Dr. Whyte called it, but which were seldom all overtaken before the inexorable stroke of nine o'clock.   Then Dr. Whyte came quietly in, and, instead of advancing to the pulpit, descended the steps to the platform immediately below it, from which he spoke, notebook in hand, except when he took up a volume from the table beside him or the broad balustrade in front.   His gown was laid aside, and his whole manner and speech were more intimate and informal than when he occupied the pulpit ; and as he was slightly nearer his audience, they could the better catch every changing expression of his face. These apparently trivial factors helped to form a singularly close *rapport* between speaker and hearers, and thus his classes resembled those services in the smaller and humbler places of worship which have been referred to at the close of the preceding chapter.

On entering, Dr. Whyte gave out two or three verses of a psalm or hymn.   The singing was led from 1897 onward by Mr. Hollins at the organ. After engaging shortly in prayer, Dr. Whyte took up the thread of his discourse.   He spoke for nearly forty minutes with great range of expression—varying from a quiet yet racy humour to the most intense solemnity of moral warning or spiritual appeal.   His gestures reinforced the impression of the spoken word.   Thus, when he was speaking of the treasures which he had found in some half-forgotten work by one of the Puritans or the Mystics and urging his

hearers to " sell their beds and buy it," he would hold
up the battered old volume for all to see, or thrust
his hand, still clasping it, into the breast of his coat
next to his heart.   One former member of the Young
Men's Class has said that " to see him *handling* a
book was a lesson in itself, so reverently and lovingly
did he do it."   Then, as nine o'clock drew near, he
broke off suddenly, and dictated a series of questions—
never less than three or more than four—which were
intended to form the basis of the week's study and to
provide heads for the succeeding lecture.   Then
Mr. Hollins was asked to play the verse, " O may we
stand before the Lamb," and the benediction brought
the Class to an end.

The stress laid on these questions and the extreme
care with which they were dictated showed Dr.
Whyte's anxiety that those who came to his Class
should themselves follow in the trail which he had
blazed for them, and not be content merely to listen to
his graphic account of it ; nor did anything delight him
more than to know of members of the Classes who were
thus following him.   To one such, the late Mr. G. S.
Aitken, he replied : " It is a great delight to me to
discover from time to time men like yourself, who are
accompanying me in the work of the Class.   And,
sometimes, going before me ! "   Such conscientious
members of the Classes were often found among those
whose daily work was quite unconnected with literature.

There was a group of three or four friends, one
of whom was a warehouseman and another a commercial traveller, who attended the Class for some
fifteen years.   They lived near Leith Links, and,
after attending the services and teaching in the
Sabbath school of their own congregation, they
walked to and from Free St. George's in the evening
—about five miles in all.   More than this, they met
regularly on Saturday evening during the sessions of
the Class to prepare for the following night, by
reading over the passages which Dr. Whyte had
prescribed, marking the arresting phrases or sentences which came into them, and discussing the

questions which he had dictated. In this way they followed, closely and unitedly, his courses on Dante, the Mystics, the Great Autobiographies, and the Stoics. At this point they dropped off reluctantly, one by one, as the responsibilities of the eldership and a change in the hour of service in their own church made it more and more difficult for them to go so far from home ; but one of the group still conducts a Bible class, using much of the material and following as far as may be the lines marked out by Dr. Whyte.

A proof of the way in which Dr. Whyte's class-teaching gripped the student-mind also may be found in the frequency with which he spoke pointedly to the students, and not least to the divinity students, in his audience. Another was afforded in 1897, when Mr. J. M. Hogge, then editor of the University magazine, gave his leading pages to a character-sketch of Dr. Whyte, and replied to some who criticised his choice of subject that the issue had sold out in two days. This article contained the words, " Men look forward to ' taking out ' Whyte as our predecessors looked forward to taking out Masson." The two names were also linked together by Sir James Barrie when he said, after Dr. Whyte's death, that the names of Masson and Whyte had certainly been to him in his student days " the two great names in Edinburgh." And a few weeks later the same comparison was made in far-off Vancouver :

> " What Professor Masson did in some part for Milton in book form, Dr. Whyte did with living voice. Probably many a student could say with the writer that, influenced by Dr. Whyte's expositions, he read through Milton—finding the great story in his sonorous verse as arresting and delightful as that of any novel, and mentally much more enriching." [1]

[1] From a tribute in the *British Columbia Monthly*, by Mr. D. A. Chalmers, the editor, who had attended Dr. Whyte's Young Men's Class for seven years.

Those will understand the weight of the comparison who have noted the reverence with which students of the 'seventies and 'eighties speak of Masson—of his rugged personality and his power of inspiring a lifelong devotion to the great English classics, and most of all to Milton.

In the Classes, it has been said, Dr. Whyte spoke, not as a divine but as a man. All was natural and direct—the unforced flow of an ardent nature and a richly stored mind; and this directness and humanity won the hearts of men and women of the most widely differing ages and mental attainments. One member of the Young Women's Class (now Mrs. E. J. Sanderson) who began attending it at the most unusual age of eleven, thus records her first impression :

> " I remember the shock of acute joy as my mind suddenly woke, and ' Trench on the Study of Words ' under Dr. Whyte's wonderful teaching opened a new world. I remember going home through the lighted streets, breathless and dazed, and determined that I would read every word of Max Müller, hopefully suggested for our Christmas holiday reading ! Alas, its many pages of Sanscrit were as much over my head then as they are now !
>
> " What treasures of learning and wisdom were spread before us. There was something very royal in the greatness of his knowledge, and the absolute selfless humility with which it was laid at the feet of his ' Young Women's Class.' He himself was nothing : the masters he interpreted to us were all. . . . I am glad to remember that I did a little realise something of the enormous labour which lay behind it."

If Dr. Whyte sometimes flattered the capacity of his hearers by the reading which he asked them to undertake—as in the case of Max Müller on philology, or of some of the weightier Puritan divines whom he so pressed upon their attention — yet he well knew that one secret of the successful teacher is to ensure that his class follows the progress of his own thought. Indeed, in the earlier days of the Young Women's Class some of its members used to complain humorously that he seemed to think that they could neither punctuate nor spell, so minutely and meticulously did he dictate the questions at the end of the hour—a process which was referred to as " Jeremiah, comma ! " But, while this excess of care disappeared at a later time, he never lost the art of carrying his Classes with him at every point of his exposition. This was in part due to his insistence on the close study of language, and on penetrating to the bed-rock of the author's meaning or to the " visual image " behind the words that he used. He never tired of emphasising the difference between the two opposite methods of reading—" reading on a sofa " and " reading with pencil in hand." Like Ruskin, he held that the careful reader will never pass rapidly over an unfamiliar word, but will always track down its derivation and find out its exact significance. Another characteristic of his teaching was his keen delight in a penetrating or memorable phrase, and the way in which his favourite quotations formed a recurrent note in his talk. " The perseverance of the saints is made up of ever new beginnings " ; " Brutus never read a book but to make himself a better man " ; " The arrow seen beforehand slacks its flight "—these and many more spring to mind. Or he would depict the special gift of a writer in a phrase, as, that Bengel " touched the matter with a needle " (*rem acu*), quoting in proof Bengel's description of the Christian life as a way " to be walked in, not to be loitered in." [1]

But, in Dr. Whyte's hands, all this care for verbal accuracy, and this delight in felicities of style, were subordinated to practical ends. He had the power of sketching the life-history of a thinker or reformer in a few vivid paragraphs ; and the insight was unerring with which he emphasised those aspects of his subject which could most surely be brought to

---

[1] *Via, in qua ambulandum non otiandum* (on Acts ix. 2).

bear upon his hearer's conscience and life. For, strong as was the intellectual interest of the Classes, their teacher's first care was for the moral and spiritual issues involved. Many could testify to this, but few with more knowledge than one who attended the Young Women's Class for many years, and who wrote as follows :

> " Most memorable of all, perhaps, the great Dante studies brought a wonderful insight into the mysteries of the *Commedia*, and our teacher led us where we learned that Hell is not only the future state of punishment for sin, but is sin itself, and its evil consequences here and now; and that Purgatory stands for the undoing of the effects of sin in this life, and formation of habits of virtue and the practice of holiness which shall be consummated in the Beatific Vision of the Paradise."

At times Dr. Whyte found in his author some phrase or idea which led out and up to one of his great flights into the purely spiritual region. Thus, when expounding Epictetus, he paused on the phrase, *Nomina debita,* " Names are debts." First he indicated how the Stoic teacher had applied the principle to the characters and lives of his own hearers, and then he linked it with his favourite text regarding the Name of the Lord (Ex. xxxiv.), and the Class listened breathlessly as he pressed home the message that the Almighty Himself has come under obligation to do and to be to us all that is implied in the great words, " Merciful, Gracious, Longsuffering, Abundant in Goodness and Truth."

Even the questions dictated at the end of the hour were seldom merely theoretic : at times they were given a startling personal point and urgency. Some years after his systematic treatment of Dante, Dr. Whyte returned to the poet during his course on " The Great Autobiographies." On this occasion three of the questions dictated on the *Inferno* were as follows : [1]

[1] Dr. Whyte's interjected comments are placed in brackets.

" Vindicate the employment of the passion of fear in personal religion, and illustrate from Scripture. (Dante was led through the *Inferno* that he might be terrified.) "

" Write out your own name and present address in your notebook, and beside it the number and the name of the Circle in Hell where your bed will be, unless the *Puissant One* (Canto IV. 50) draws you forth of it. (We've all made our bed in Hell, every one of us ; and it may become our sanctification. . . . ' He hath not dealt with us after our sins.') "

" Read almost nothing else, all these weeks, but your Dante, and they will be memorable weeks all your life to you. (All these sacred weeks, ' eschew impertinent books.') "

Later, when the Class reached the passage in which St. John examines Dante on Love, asking him what were the cords which had drawn him to God, and Dante begins his reply with the words, " The being of the world, and mine own being," [1] Dr. Whyte suddenly broke in with—" The bigness in few words of the thinking ! Do you *think* of these things, gentlemen ? "

Another instance of the way in which he gave a personal edge to a question based on an incident in Church History may be drawn from his account of the Covenanters. He quoted from Wodrow the narrative of an English merchant who told how, during a journey in Scotland, he heard three preachers (Blair, Rutherford, and Dickson) :

" In St. Andrews I heard a tall, stately man preach, and he showed me the majesty of God. I afterwards heard a little fair man preach, and he showed me the loveliness of Christ. I then went to Irvine, where I heard preach a well-favoured, proper old man, with a long beard, and that man showed me all my heart."

[1] *Paradiso,* Canto XXVI.

Whereon Dr. Whyte put the two questions that follow:

> " Give the names of those three preachers if you can, and say which of them you would have chosen for your minister."
>
> " A good Bible-lesson—Can you guess what scriptures those ministers would have read oftenest in the pulpit, and what psalms and paraphrases "—Dr. Whyte never feared an anachronism—" they would oftenest have given out to be sung ? "

This course on " The Makers of Scotland " contained more history than most of the subjects which Dr. Whyte chose ; but on that very account it gave special scope for varied and home-coming practical application. He recurred at intervals to the thought that the Making of Scotland, as it was conceived in the divine plan, was far from complete, and that until the nation were cleansed from the dark stains on her social and moral life, Makers of Scotland would still be needed. Perchance, he said, some of those in the Class before him had already been called to take no mean part in carrying forward this great work. His first lecture on Knox, delivered on 5th November 1905, opened with a paragraph on God's instruments and how they are fashioned, and closed with a personal appeal, launched in a series of searching inquiries :

> " The end of all is—ourselves. Are we, in anything, God's instruments ? Has He appointed us any work ? What is it ? And how has He prepared us for it—through our birth and upbringing, through our trials and our crosses ? "

Then he turned to the students of theology present, saying, " A congregation is waiting you : to be made by you, after you are made by God." Statesmen, too, would be needed in the future, as in the past. Reformers, theologians, preachers would all be needed, until the Making of Scotland was indeed complete.

A fortnight later, he spoke of the nine months of agony through which Russia had then passed during the First Revolution, and of his deep disappointment that no call to personal and spiritual freedom had come during these terror-filled months from his hero, Father John of Cronstadt. He then suggested—a suggestion to which the Class responded warmly—that he should have the *Life of Knox* bound in the best binding which his bookseller could supply, and should send it in name of the Class to the Russian preacher and saint, in the hope that it might help to rouse him to do a work for liberty in Russia comparable to that which Knox had done in Scotland.

With the end of the following winter—the winter of Principal Rainy's death—Dr. Whyte brought his studies of the Makers of Scotland to a close. The last lecture described the character and work of three men with whom he himself had been closely associated, and one of whom had passed away only three months before—Robert Buchanan, Robert Candlish, and Robert Rainy. He traced their efforts for Presbyterian re-union in the generation then closing, and ended by urging those who heard him to look towards and work for a wider union. " I do not envy any man who seeks to prevent or delay such a movement. Be *you* on that side ; it is Christ's side." [1]

But practical and personal issues of another order were also treated with a most solemnising directness. It was largely the fear of losing this freedom of speech that led Dr. Whyte to discourage, and, indeed, to forbid, any reporting of his talks in his Classes.[2] In 1901, he wrote from Aviemore to a member of the Young Men's Class who had asked him if he might take notes for publication during the ensuing winter :

" DEAR MR. MACKAY,—Thank you for your letter. It would greatly embarrass me in my work if I thought there were any one in the Class taking notes for the Press. Speakers greatly

---

[1] *Scottish Review*, March 28, 1907.
[2] For an exception to this rule see Appendix II.

differ in this respect ; but I would not do my
work with the proper freedom if I felt I was
speaking to an audience other than my own Class.
For many reasons that is so with me. Were I
to address the public on any of the subjects
taken up in the Class, I would prepare myself
specially for that public, and it would be a very
different product from the friendly and confiding
talk of my Class.

" I am delighted to think that you found the
class-talks worthy of your notebook, but that
does not prove that they are worthy of the
British Weekly.

" Preserve your notes for your own use :
and look in on me when you are in Edinburgh.
It is a great reward to know that I have had such
a fellow-student as yourself.—With warm regard,

" A. WHYTE."

This prohibition of reporting in the Classes, and
its honourable observance by their members, allowed
Dr. Whyte to withdraw the veil—in his Men's Class at
least—from certain of the more intimate and tragic
experiences of his own ministry. Thus he once told
of a college friend, a man of earnest spirit, who
entered the ministry, but after a time was deposed
for a grave fault. He was left penniless and resource-
less until Dr. Whyte found him clerical work in a
business house. After a time he was able to go to
another university to prepare for another profession,
but he had scarcely entered on his new field of action
when he died. " I went to his funeral," Dr. Whyte
concluded, " and there was nobody there to let down
the coffin. The gravediggers had to take the cords
along with me. He was absolutely friendless."

This story of a minister's shipwrecked life led up
to an urgent invitation : " Come to the Class and
read the books of the Class. Come to me, when
your back is against the wall : I will never shut
my door against you ! " Thus, in the Class, Dr.
Whyte offered the same welcome to those in moral

extremity as he had once offered when preaching
on Esau, in a passage which was overpowering to
those who heard it in its mingling of urgency and
tenderness, and which cannot be read without a
thrill of emotion to-day.[1]

On another occasion he was speaking in the Young
Men's Class of William Dunbar, the greatest poet
among the early " Makers of Scotland," and referred
to that strange inconsistency—due to the manners of
an age in which grossness was considered no reproach
—which allowed the author of two of the most perfect
religious lyrics in either Scottish or English literature
to include much that was foul in his longer poems,
Then he broke off, leaving, to all appearance, the
track of his prepared notes, and for the rest of the
hour he spoke of the dangers of impure books with a
weight of warning and an unflinching directness that
kept the pencils of his hearers idle, and their heads
bent, and that sent them out—on the testimony of a
doctor of wide experience who was present—firmly
resolved never again to open a book for any impure
interest that it might contain.

Thus, while most of those who followed Dr.
Whyte's teaching may dwell most often in retrospect
on the widening of horizons, intellectual and religious,
which the Classes brought, and on the kindling of
their love for the best books at the ever-glowing
hearth of his own enthusiasm, there are some who
remember with a gratitude not untouched by awe
the warning-posts erected against paths that lead to
moral destruction, and the help given as they sought
to return to the way of safety.

Enough has been said to show how much thought
and labour Dr. Whyte spent in his constant endeavour
to bring intellectual freshness and variety to the
meetings of his Classes, as well as to make these
hours stimulating to conscience and life. But his
efforts did not end with these stated meetings on

---

[1] *Bible Characters*, i. p. 171 ; there is a not less striking appeal in
the sermon on Hagar in the same volume, p. 148 f.

22

Wednesday afternoon or Sunday evening. Around them revolved a minor planetary system of other activities, in which he had the unwearied assistance of his wife, and of a little band of friends, chief of whom for many years was Dr. Sutherland Black.

Much trouble was taken to secure leaders of religious thought to address the social gathering of the Classes which took place soon after the Christmas vacation. In one typical programme, the central feature was a speech by Principal Fairbairn of Oxford on " Religion as the Romance of Scotland "; and the Prelude to *Parsifal* gave the key to the sacred music rendered by Mr. Hollins and Miss Isabel MacDougall.

On at least one occasion (March 1907), the members of the Classes were taken into partnership in their teacher's plans, by being asked to determine by plebiscite what subject should be taken up during the following winter. The choice given was—(*a*) " A great Greek Father (Athanasius), a great Latin Father (Augustine), five great Anglicans, and five great Puritans " ; or (*b*) " Some great Authors and some great Books that have greatly influenced me for good." The latter was chosen, and the course outlined by Dr. Whyte ranged from the Psalms, through Dante, Pascal, Andrewes, Bunyan, and the Shorter Catechism, to Butler and " the Hymn-book, noting the hymns, and their authors who have most influenced me." At other times, the members received a slip or a booklet containing a bibliography, or quotations bearing on the subject of study to which they could not readily have found access. Dr. Whyte's care for the form and appearance of these is witnessed by a note, asking Dr. Black to arrange for the printing of one such leaflet :

" Would you give orders, in terms you best understand, for 800 little slips of our recommended books, neat slips, that could be carried home in a class-book without crushing. There is no use in printing the whole big page. You

might ask a proof to-morrow of the slip to make
sure it is neat and fit."

The same care for small details is shown in a draft
advertisement of the course on " The Great Autobiographies of Scotland," written in Dr. Whyte's
own hand, for insertion in the Edinburgh University
magazine, which concludes : " Students are specially
invited to take part in this patriotic, intellectual,
and spiritual enterprise."

The story of another leaflet issued to the Class
was told by the late Dr. J. W. Ballantyne in a letter
written during the week before he died :

> " The first night of ' The Makers of Scot-
> land ' I went home, wrote what Whyte after-
> wards called ' Miltonic ' (!) lines on the ' Makers,'
> and dropped them into the letter-box at 7
> Charlotte Square before 11 o'clock. To my
> amazement I got a proof on Tuesday morning
> of my ' Miltonic ' lines printed as a broadsheet,
> and next Sunday evening Whyte gave a copy to
> each member of the Class ! "

At other times his efforts to bring the experience
of other minds to bear was more deliberate, and
during the summer he would arm himself with intimate expressions from one or more scholarly friends
of their debt to some great writer whose works were
to be studied. Thus one August he wrote from
Balmacara to Dr. Macaulay, then a young minister
in his first charge :

> " I ask you to do me a favour. I am to take
> ' Authors who have done me good, and in what
> way,' for the Classes next year, D.V. And, to
> brighten up my monotonous talks, I am to ask
> letters from my friends who have made some
> of my authors their special study, stating in
> what way, and to what degree, such authors
> have done them good. Will you take half an
> hour of your holiday to write me such a letter
> about Augustine ? You know how a thing like

that quickens the interest of a class, and sheds fresh light even on the most worn of subjects. Do this for me, like a good fellow. If you would come to us for a week and bring your letter with you, the favour to me would be increased a hundredfold."

Dr. Dods was also asked to contribute a similar appreciation, and not a few still remember the impressiveness of these tributes as Dr. Whyte read them to his Class. The following post card is in acknowledgment of Mr. Macaulay's: "First-rate. It was an inspiration from above that led me to ask for such appreciations as those of Dods and yourself." So also, when Dr. Whyte returned to Dante for the third time, he obtained a similar glowing tribute from Dr. Sutherland Black, and acknowledged it with typical brevity: " A first-rate paper. It should be in print that many might see it. Great thanks. A. W."

But it was during his earlier and more systematic study of Dante in the four winters from 1888–92 that these ancillary schemes were most elaborate. At this time Dr. Black's help was called in at every turn, while on several occasions he conducted the Classes in Dr. Whyte's absence. In one such emergency, when the subjects were the *Paradiso* and a Survey of the New Testament, Dr. Whyte wrote :

" I am ashamed to set you such a task as the accompanying. All the more that you take so much closer a grip of Dante and of Scripture than I do. But take entirely your own way, and talk as you choose in any part of the Classes."

In 1885, and again in 1889, Dr. and Mrs. Whyte visited Florence, and brought home many impressions which afterwards enriched this part of his work. In the spring of 1889 one of their party was Mrs. Traquair, a friend who was just beginning to secure leisure for the development of that rare imaginative genius, which has since found expression in her frescoes in the Catholic Apostolic Church in Edinburgh and in many churches elsewhere, as well as in enamels and illuminated manuscripts of great richness and beauty. To one of her sensitive insight, the work of the early Tuscan painters and sculptors, which she now saw for the first time, came as a true revelation; and her companions found their appreciation heightened by her enthusiasm. While they were in Florence, it came into their minds that this experience might be used to enrich the study of Dante then proceeding in the Classes. So plans took shape for a volume with delicate line drawings by Mrs. Traquair and a frontispiece of the meeting of Dante and Beatrice (*Purgatorio*, Canto xxx.), to which were added illuminating notes on the Chronology of the *Commedia* and on Dante's Library by Dr. Sutherland Black. At first it was hoped that the volume might be ready in the autumn of 1889 for use during the following winter; but the scheme was too far from the beaten track, and the collaborators in the work had too exacting an artistic conscience, to achieve such rapid progress. In September, Mrs. Whyte wrote to Dr. Black regarding a first approximation to the volume:

"Dummy is an interesting creature (*No: he is not, A. W.—I meant as a specimen of a peculiar race, J. E. W.*), but we distinctly feel he needs further evolving (it may mean devolving) before he will reach the ideal." After some suggestions for improvement the letter concludes: "After reading the above, A. W. says, 'Say he is wooden and commonplace!' Alas, poor dummy."

But under the care of Dr. Walter Blaikie, the distinguished head of Messrs. T. & A. Constable, who took a keen personal interest in the volume, "Dummy" gradually assumed a form which not only gratified his first originators, but has given delight to as many lovers of Dante and of beautiful books as have obtained possession of it. To this volume, which was privately printed, and which won the commendation of an authority so distinguished as Dr. Paget Toynbee, Dr. Whyte's only direct contribution was a Foreword of two sentences expressing his appreciation of the contributions made by Mrs. Traquair and Dr. Black. In view of all this, it is not surprising to hear of compositors who eagerly followed the work of Dr. Whyte's Class ; and of a bookbinder who delighted him by confessing that he had gained his first introduction to Dante by reading snatches of the poem as he bound up the sheets.

During the same winter which saw the appearance of *Dante Notes and Illustrations* an impressive recital was held in Free St. George's. The psalms and canticles referred to in the *Purgatorio* and *Paradiso* were sung by the choir, led by the late Mr. Walter Hately, who rendered the medieval music in so far as it could be traced. Several letters, written from Bonskeid in the days before Christmas 1890, show Dr. Whyte's keen interest in the project, which, incidentally, caused the one cloud in the history of a forty years' friendship. When the draft programme came into his hands, he suddenly realised that the singing of the *Salve Regina* [1] in Free St. George's would place too great a strain on the catholicity of spirit towards which he had begun to lead his people, and he sent Dr. Sutherland Black instructions that it should be omitted. The letter expressed great penitence for his neglect to impose his veto sooner ; but its tone was decisive, and his friend, though reluctant and protesting, had no choice but to comply. On the following day, Dr. Whyte heard that Dr. Black had fallen into the dentist's hands, and so was unable to join him at Bonskeid ; and the fellow-feeling for his friend's misfortune manifest in his next letter quickly dispersed the transient shadow of misunderstanding :

[1] " Hail, Queen of Heaven ! "

" MY DEAR BLACK,—We read your telegram and letter this morning with deep and keen regret. First for the *so painful* cause of your detention. Hell of all diseases : and remedies ! I wish you soon and well and always out of that *Inferno !* What plans we had laid : and how noble the hills are looking to-night. But, a Higher Will and Heart than ours lives and rules ! Amen !

" On the Programme :

" 1. Don't call it *Programme* but *Book of Words*.

" 2. Print Latin or Greek and English in parallel columns—if you can and approve—throughout, instead of merely references."

But the chief of these supplements to the Classes certainly consisted in the distribution of books. It was natural that Dr. Whyte should have found warm friends and steady allies in all branches of the book-producing and book-selling industry which holds so honourable a place in the life of Edinburgh. Sir Thomas Clark, his son, and Dr. Blaikie have already been named. Another friend on whose help in many directions he greatly relied was Mr. J. Scott Ferrier, whose firm, Messrs. Oliphant, Anderson, & Ferrier, published the great majority of his own writings. Among Edinburgh booksellers, Mr. John Macniven, Mr. A. D. Wallace, and Mr. John Molyneaux, the head of the Religious Tract Society's depot, were valued allies.[1] The last-named stated that, during the years when Dr. Whyte was deep in the study and exposition of William Law and the Mystics, his firm alone sold some five thousand copies of the *Serious Call*—a book till then almost unknown in Presbyterian Scotland. There is also a story, probably based on truth, of a second-hand bookseller in London who asked a visitor from Edinburgh if he knew anything of " a man named Whyte " who

---

[1] Mr. Ferrier was an elder in Free St. George's for thirty-five years and Mr. Molyneaux for eight years, before his early death in 1901.

appeared to be able to secure purchasers for any old and unsaleable remnant if he once took up the author in question. In later years Dr. Whyte used to send Messrs. Macniven and Wallace five hundred copies of his visiting-card at one time for insertion in the books which he ordered to be sent—sometimes to individuals and sometimes broadcast, as, for example, to every student in the New College or to every member of some remote Presbytery in the Highlands.

Thus his constant and urgent injunctions to his Classes that their members should *buy* the books which were worth more than fine gold to him— injunctions which were often, though not invariably, obeyed—were sometimes varied, after this fashion :

" If any reading apprentice-boy wishes to know about Behmen, and his poor mother cannot spare a shilling—if he will send me his name and address, he will get Behmen by return, on condition that he will send me a post card when he has read the little book, telling me about the good he has got from Jacob Behmen, the working shoemaker, but all the same the founder of German philosophy, and one of the saintliest of men."

On another occasion he gave this self-depreciating summary of his life-work : " If I were not a preacher, I would be a colporteur. Indeed, if I have been of any use at all to my generation, it has been more as a kind of colporteur than as a preacher." [1]

It is the way of colporteurs to offer no books which they cannot heartily recommend, and in this respect the comparison may hold good. But it was not always possible for those of Dr. Whyte's Classes who followed him into the byways of Puritan theology to agree with his judgment of such introspective and " intricate " authors as Fraser of Brea. In this region there often remained a definite difference of outlook between teacher and students, but

[1] From the " Undelivered Speech " on Church Union (1912) referred to in Chapter XXVI. below.

a difference which only made his intellectual and
spiritual mastery stand out in bolder relief. Dr.
Whyte's reluctance to treat his authors critically was
due to the fact that in public speech he applied the
maxim *nil nisi bonum* to books as well as to men,
and to the living even more than to the dead. His
favourite term " appreciation " meant on his lips
praise rather than appraisement. Only the few, to
whom he opened his mind in quiet talk in his study
or on long country walks, knew how shrewd and
pithy his critical judgments could be ; but if the
members of his Classes lost something of intellectual
stimulus through his refusal to criticise the authors
with whom he dealt, they learned all the more effectively a lesson which he was far more concerned to
teach—that of charity at all times, toward all men.

The materials for this chapter have come from
places as far separated as Western Canada and the
Australian Commonwealth ; and it may be said
confidently that in every part of the English-speaking
world there are those who remember Dr. Whyte's
Classes with gratitude. Nor is this less true of the
homeland. Some twenty years ago, two Edinburgh
students set out southwards for an Easter vacation.
They found the night train crowded by enthusiasts
on the way to an International football match in
London, and soon had to give up thought of sleep.
But in one corner of their compartment there was a
commercial traveller who maintained his sobriety and
intelligence amid the surrounding babel of tongues,
and they naturally fell into talk with him. After discussing the drinking habits of Scottish cities he went on
to compare Glasgow and Edinburgh in other respects.
His preference leant strongly to the former, but he
added, " There's one man I admire in Edinburgh."
The students wondered what civic or commercial
magnate was to be looked on as redeeming the medioc-
rity of their city ; but the information soon followed—
" That's Dr. Whyte of Free St. George's." After a
most vigorous tribute of appreciation, he wound up—

" Old Whyte's grand. There's no humbug about old Whyte! And that class of his on Sunday night—— ! "

In February 1905 an Edinburgh minister was in South Wales, attending meetings connected with the Revival which so stirred the life of the country during that winter. In a restaurant in Cardiff he found himself lunching at a table with several commercial travellers ; and the circumstances of the time led the conversation naturally to religious subjects and movements. His new acquaintances, seeing that he came from Scotland, asked if he knew Edinburgh and Dr. Whyte. On hearing that he did, one of them told how he and several companions always arranged, when on their northern round, to spend a Sunday in Edinburgh in order that they might attend Dr. Whyte's Class. They never came away, he added, without feeling that they had received a very real measure of help, and what they heard on these evenings gave them food for thought and discussion for weeks thereafter.

Later still, Dr. Whyte's fourth son, Robert, wrote to his father from Balliol College, Oxford :

" I was giving my bookseller to-day my Edinburgh address, and when I said, ' 7 Charlotte Square,' he said, ' Then you are a son of Principal Whyte.' I told him, and then came the usual reply, ' I was in his Class many years ago.' It was a pleasure to hear that reply in Oxford for the first time."

But in addition to these chance expressions of gratitude, heard in unlikely places, there were other tributes paid, more or less formal, at the close of each winter's Classes. If no one else rose to express the thanks of the Young Men's Class, the duty was effectively performed by Mr. James Stewart, an old man of distinguished aspect—a friend of Mrs. Sellar and her literary circle—whose figure was familiar to the citizens of Edinburgh twenty or thirty years ago, as he looked out from his place of business as a cab proprietor in the crow-stepped and turreted house at the southern end of the Dean Bridge. Mr. Stewart was credited with the almost fabulous feat of having read every book recommended to the Class; and it is certain that he comforted his own soul, and rejoiced the spirit of his minister, by his devotion to Marshall's *Gospel Mystery of Sanctification* during his last days on earth. Dr. Whyte's regard for his friend, and gratitude for the words of appreciation spoken on behalf of the Class, are shown by the following letter :

" DEAR MR. STEWART,—I thank you for your generous and loving intention toward me on Sabbath night. And I value your intention as it deserves. To me you are one of the pillars of the Congregation and the Class. I lean upon you and regard you more than you can know. I have a sure instinct that there is no one in the Class or the Congregation who is more loyal both to the truth and to him who bears it than you are. You have a living head and a loving heart : and I honour and love you for both.— Believe me,   A. WHYTE."

At first the expression of appreciation from those who had attended the Class took the form of a simple letter with several hundred signatures. Later it was sometimes presented, by Mr. Stewart or another, in the more elaborate shape of an illuminated address. The presentation which took place at the end of the Session of 1899–1900 had an especial and a lasting interest ; for the Class then gave Dr. Whyte his portrait painted by Sir James Guthrie, afterwards President of the Royal Scottish Academy.[1] It is recognised as one of the artist's noblest works ; but it is told that, when he first began to paint it, he had much difficulty in catching the animated expression

---

[1] Sir James Guthrie painted two portraits of Dr. Whyte during this winter. That which is now in the New College, and which is repro duced as the frontispiece of this volume, was a gift from many friends in the Church in commemoration of his year as Moderator.

which he desired.   Then a friend, Mr. John Warrack, had the happy inspiration to take him to the Young Men's Class, where he was so impressed by Dr. Whyte's alert pose and vigorous manner that next morning he made a fresh beginning, and carried through his work to a successful issue.   The story does but confirm the impression of many hearers that Dr. Whyte's powers never came into fuller or happier play than when he addressed his Class.

Six hundred former and present members of the Class in all parts of the world had joined in subscribing for the portrait ; and the words used on their behalf by the Rev. A. B. Macaulay, who had been Dr. Whyte's assistant twelve months before, may fittingly bring this chapter to a close :

" Your Class, Sir, consists of all kinds of men — students, clerks, tradesmen, artisans, teachers, lawyers, doctors, and business men. It would therefore be impossible even to indicate in any final way what your teaching has accomplished.   Varied appetites have been variously satisfied ; but none has ever received half-rations.

" But I venture to say this, which, though a bold statement, is nevertheless in the judgment of many observers a true one.   We believe that, under God, you have been able to influence, to a greater extent than any one else in this generation, men and women in three respects : First, in communicating an enthusiasm for books, and these the best in the English language (you know you have told us to sell our beds and buy them) ; second, in imparting by your own zeal a belief in the unseen world and in the substantiality of ideas ; and, third, in creating a passion for pure and lofty and spiritual objects.   Many have gone away from the meetings of your Class with a fresh interest in literature and a new delight in the truest thoughts, and many a man has returned to his home or lodgings armed in heart and purpose for another week's battle with temptation.

" But, Sir, while we ask you to accept this gift as a symbol of our gratitude and respect we do not confess that gratitude and respect exhaust our feelings. Because with all your giving—instruction, guidance, and advice—you have not refrained from giving us yourself . . . and we ask you to receive this portrait as a symbol of the esteem we entertain towards you as our teacher, and the love we bear to you as our friend."

" Therefore to thee it was given
Many to save with thyself ;
And, at the end of the day,
O faithful shepherd, to come,
Bringing thy sheep in thy hand."

M. ARNOLD.

DR. WHYTE's ministry in his pulpit and classes was
open to the world, and made a visible imprint upon
the life of his time ; but in this chapter we have to
do with the more personal and intimate side of his
work, whose records are locked up in the archives
of many grateful spirits. Thus what is here set
down must be of a more fragmentary nature, indicating, rather than expressing fully, what he was
as a pastor and a friend.

Something must first be said regarding Dr.
Whyte's care for the welfare of his congregation as
a whole. He was not by instinct or temperament
an organiser ; yet, unlike some who live much in
meditation on things inward and eternal, he never
failed to appreciate the importance of precision
and promptitude in the transaction of the Church's
temporal business, or to support those who were
charged to carry it on. His relations with the
officials of Free St. George's were those of the closest
association in a task of common concern, as successive session-clerks were ready to testify. But an
even more eloquent, because less formal, witness
might have been borne by the younger Mitchell,
who succeeded his father as church-officer in 1892.
Few men had better opportunity of knowing their
minister, and no one in Free St. George's felt a greater
reverence for him. During more than twenty years
they met daily if Dr. Whyte was in Edinburgh, and
sometimes in holiday seasons as well, when Mitchell's

skill as a photographer and an artist was much in request. There was at times a touch of humour in the relation ; and a pleasant tale is told of a children's gathering in the hall of Free St. George's when a whisper went round that Mitchell had been known to sing a humorous song. That stately functionary, who was watching the children from near the door, fled forthwith ; but Dr. Whyte gave chase, and, being the more active man, soon returned in triumph with his captive, who was compelled to perform, to the great delight of his youthful audience. But at the end the bond between the two friends became a very sacred one. Mitchell's last months were spent in a nursing home, as he sank under a slow and painful illness ; and many were the visits which his minister, then approaching his eightieth year, paid to bring comfort to the spirit of this devoted servant of the Church. Among other names worthy of commemoration—some of which will be mentioned later—is that of William Fletcher, for some years Clerk of Deacons' Court in Free St. George's, whose career of great activity and usefulness, closed by his death in early middle life, was commemorated in one of the most glowing of Dr. Whyte's pulpit tributes.

There was no duty which Dr. Whyte performed more regularly than that of presiding over the meetings of his Kirk-Session and Deacons' Court. Even when the appointment of a colleague might have been taken as relieving him from much of this work he still maintained it—in the words of one letter— as " a strict rule " to be present at these meetings, or, if he were compelled to break it, notified his colleague in advance. In the financial affairs which largely occupy the Deacons' Court, and in the more formal portion of the Session's business, he was slow to intervene directly, since he preferred to trust the judgment of other men. But his presence, even when he kept silence, constantly served to keep before his fellow office-bearers the spiritual aim which governed all their proceedings ; and his own self-effacing temper was an unfailing rebuke to the spirit of controversy. An elder supplies this typical reminiscence : " There was the meeting at which our chairman checked an incipient vote, which would have divided us, with a word of praise to one man and an appealing smile to the other." Beside it we may set a recollection by one of the younger office-bearers of the 'eighties : [1]

"For ten years I was one of his deacons; and nobody who can look back on those days will ever forget the inimitable way Dr. Whyte had of making every Deacons' Court meeting a little feast of the soul to every man of the twenty or thirty of us who gathered month by month in the session-house of St. George's."

Dr. Whyte always remained faithful to the custom adopted in his early ministry of securing the ordination of deacons at an earlier age and in larger numbers than was usual in the Free Church. Some of the younger office-bearers so appointed may have shown a lack of " staying-power," and a few found that they had no real vocation for the work, and fell away. But Dr. Whyte was willing to face the risk of a failure here and there, if only he could bring as many as possible of his young men to bear an active part in the Church's work; and not a few ministers and elders of the Church to-day are thankful that he gave them thus early an opportunity of doing her definite service. Nor could any minister have pressed the duty of acceptance more affectionately on those whom the congregation had chosen for office, or done more by personal talk to encourage any who were held back by difficulties of belief or by a sense of unworthiness. In spite of the firmness of his own beliefs, he laid no heavy theological burdens on other men's shoulders, but always stood for the greatest liberty and the widest comprehensiveness in the eldership of the Church not less than in her ministry.

[1] The late Rev. J. C. B. Geddes of Largs.

For the theological students in Free St. George's he had a special concern that, in accordance with a wise regulation of the Church, they should understand something of congregational business before going forth to preside over congregations of their own. So from time to time he invited such students to meet at his house, and accompany him to the Deacons' Court, obtaining explanations for their benefit of different points of procedure from the Clerk or the congregational Treasurer.

The business of the Session and Deacons' Court was by no means confined to the interests of the congregation itself. Throughout Dr. Whyte's long ministry the Sustentation Fund (later, the Central Fund) of the Church continued to be generously supported, and in later years the contribution to Foreign Missions was substantially increased. In addition to the share taken in maintaining the Home Mission work in Fountainbridge, the congregation also helped for a number of years to support a Church situated in the crowded working-class district of Dalry, farther to the west. Dalry Free Church had, indeed, an especially warm place in Dr. Whyte's large heart. He preached or addressed a week-night meeting there as often as he had opportunity, and gave ungrudgingly of his counsel and friendship to its minister. The spirit in which he approached the subject of giving was shown when an attempt was made in the Jubilee year of the Free Church to raise the stipend of all her ministers to £200 and a manse. He told his congregation that it had been arranged for the elders and deacons to go round their districts together, in order more effectively to bring home to every member the needs of the poorer ministers ; and added these words :

" Most men, it is to be feared, have no principle and no method in their givings. They dole out their contributions and subscriptions as if it were a cruel intrusion and a real injury they suffer just to be invited to give. And

23

thus life goes on, and wastes away, and they neither get the good nor do the good that intelligent, conscientious, methodical giving always brings with it."

When Dr. Whyte dealt with any question which might raise controversy in the Kirk-Session he always showed the greatest regard for the views of others and readiness to subordinate his own judgment. This is illustrated by a letter to Mr. John Morton, a friend in the congregation who was anxious that unfermented wine should be used at the Lord's Supper.

"DEAR MR. MORTON,—I feel all that you say; and, were the matter in my hands, you would get what you wish. But I know the opposition that would arise in the Session were the change you wish brought before them. And I am convinced the proposal made and pressed, even by myself, at present, would cause a division far more injurious than any hurt that comes to any one from the way of providing the elements. Anything you say goes far with me: but do not let this matter weigh too much on your mind.— With the greatest regard and love,

"A. WHYTE."

Letters which have been preserved by more than one elder in Free St. George's show the forethought with which Dr. Whyte planned the congregational prayer-meetings, that they might be at once united and comprehensive in the scope of the prayers offered. He was wont to suggest special lines of petition—for children and young people, or for Missions and missionaries—or of thanksgiving for national blessings and privileges. Thus, in 1889, when he was already oppressed by the burden of sixteen years as sole pastor of Free St. George's, he wrote to Dr. Sutherland Black:

"Will you take the second prayer . . . at our Colleagueship Prayer-meeting? Do. Do.

Pray for the schools and colleges and theological halls ; for the scholarship of the land and the Church ; for talented and devout and devoted ministers ; and for a good minister of Jesus Christ for ourselves."

His attitude to his people showed a characteristic alternation of searching, or even scathing, criticism with passages of unmingled praise. But his severest criticism was hurled at his congregation as a whole— as when he closed a sermon on God's Comfort by asking suddenly, " What's the use of speaking of comfort to people like you ? " or emphasised a passage on the Fall by sweeping his hand round the area and the galleries, and exclaiming, " These are the ruins of it ! "—while, in dealing with individuals, the note of encouragement was uppermost. Certain special examples of his genius for encouragement may be quoted, apart from his periodic references to his " incomparable " Session or Deacons' Court. One of these occurred at a meeting of office-bearers during a Presbyterial visitation. The older office-bearers were first asked to describe the spiritual state of the congregation.

" One after another they told of the great days of prayer and of revival long ago, and deplored that there was so little of the work of the Holy Spirit visible now. This went on until the minister could sit still no longer : he rose to his feet and said that he was deeply sensible of his own failings, and no doubt he and his congregation fell far short, but every year he lived he felt more and more that day by day he was going in and out among a spiritually minded people." [1]

Another incident belongs to a later time. The two colleagues and one or two office-bearers were gathered in the side-room before a prayer-meeting. The late Dr. J. W. Ballantyne was asked by Dr. Whyte to engage briefly in prayer, and felt himself

[1] *Memories*, by Rev. Thomas Gregory of Kilmacolm, p. 23.

led to pray especially that the Spirit of Love might rule in their midst. Then, as the ministers passed out, Dr. Whyte paused for a moment, and said so that only his friend who had prayed could hear : " You asked for the loving heart : *but you've got it !* " In the same vein is a parenthesis of four words in a note to one who had been long a member of Free St. George's : " When you are near God, as you always are, sometimes remember me and mine."

More than one reference has been made to the fact that, for many years after Dr. Candlish's death, his successor had neither colleague nor assistant. But this does not imply that no help was given ; for, during the 'eighties, the Rev. J. Grant Mackintosh, who acted as Joint-Session-clerk, gave much of his time to helping Dr. Whyte in his pastoral work, while invaluable help of other kinds was given by Dr. Sutherland Black, whose labours in connection with the Welfare of Youth Scheme and the study of Dante have already been recorded. These, indeed, lay in the line of his great attainments as a scholar. But, not content with these ways of assisting his friend, he laid lowlier duties on himself—the most notable being that for about eight years he edited the " Monthly Notes " of Free St. George's. Dr. Whyte was hardly less minute and exacting in his directions regarding these—as to their type and appearance as well as their contents—than in respect of the leaflets prepared for his Classes ; but his gratitude for his learned friend's labour of love is shown in such a note as the following, headed, " New Year's Day, 1890 " :

> " I send you Newman to-day as a mark of how much I love you and value your friendship and your invaluable counsel and help.
> " Read *Gerontius* to your mother on Sabbath night : and assure her of my honour and affection."

Another note to the same friend ends with " filial love

to your mother, and pastoral and brotherly love to your sister."

From these aspects of congregational administration, which only here and there touch the deeper levels, we turn to the main part of a minister's pastoral activity—that of personal contact with his flock. In this regard the part played by Dr. Whyte's assistants was of no small value. From 1889 onward the assistant was as a rule a young minister who had just completed his course at the New College. One of the first was the late Rev. J. C. B. Geddes, of Largs, the son of two greatly esteemed members of Free St. George's and afterwards the husband of a lady whose power of sympathy and unconquerable brightness of spirit made her visits to 7 Charlotte Square a source of unfailing delight to every member of the circle there, from Dr. Whyte to his youngest boy. Mr. Geddes thus described his two years' experience of assistantship to Dr. Whyte, as he watched his chief,

> " out on the vast field of his congregation, which stretched without geographical limit right across Edinburgh and beyond even its suburbs ; all the homes of which he knew so amazingly well :— out visiting his people—it took us two years of constant work to do that. He began at one end of the thirty districts, I at the other ; and after just about a year we met in the middle. I had the honour and inspiration of seeing how he did that without ceasing ; and in his study, and in his church I have seen him. . . . I cannot remember a single idle moment of his. . . . It was an indescribably inspiring spectacle of what work really is."

Dr. Whyte's own estimate of his pastoral work was far less flattering than that of those who shared it with him. A post card to the Rev. A. B. Macaulay ended with the words : " Never fall behind with your pastoral work when you are a pastor.

The remorse is indescribable." A series of letters addressed to the same friend, when he took up the assistantship in the spring of 1898, show how thoroughly Dr. Whyte trained those who worked under him. The first letter tells that Dr. Whyte had been going over the congregational roll with the Session-clerk, Mr. Robert Simson, whose brother, Mr. James Simson, followed him in this post ; and asks his new assistant to obtain from the clerk the names of members in three districts. It concludes : "Then dine here, say on Friday night, and bring your book : and I will give you some private jottings to guide you in your first visits to the people." Further instructions follow in a letter from Balmacara on 8th April :

" This is my first letter from this place ; and I write it because I left so much of my work in your hands. Take from two to three hours five days a week among the sick, etc., and your other visiting ; and be good enough to send me as full a report as you can of whom you have seen, and how they all are. Let me have your report once a week, or so. All my men have done this when I was from home. But Mr. Davidson beat them all in the business-like way he kept his book and kept me up in everything.[1] I felt as if I visited every afternoon when I read his diary."

A fortnight later a third letter begins : " Thank you for your pastoral memoranda. As I read them, I see the households, and am with you in spirit." These general counsels were followed by a succession of notes regarding cases of special urgency or difficulty. One such ends with a request to Mr. Macaulay that he should keep in close touch with an adherent of Free St. George's, not yet a communicant :

" Do not rest till he sits beside you at the Lord's Table : and bring him some Sabbath or

[1] Rev. A. P. Davidson, afterwards of Skirling.

Saturday night to ours. Keep these memos. in your book and let us go over them some time."

A letter on another subject, probably conveyed by the faithful Mitchell from Dr. Whyte's hands to his assistant's lodgings, has a characteristic note on the envelope: "Find out what Sabbath Mr. ——'s son is home from Glasgow, and bring father and son to supper that night. Call on the mother and ask about the son."

Students whose health had broken down, or who were stranded friendless in Edinburgh, also come into view. Especially when their aim was the ministry, Dr. Whyte would give lavish help in the form of books, and sometimes unrequested financial help as well. Often his first step was to send the original letter either to his assistant for investigation or to his colleague for consultation, with such a note as, "Have a talk with him and advise me if I can do anything for him." One such note, forwarding an appeal from a New College student, formerly in the ministry of another church, who had reached the end of his resources, ended, "Do your wisest and kindest, and let me hear." A somewhat similar story of a theological course arrested by family misfortunes prompted the following comment :

"This is a case to be talked over rather than treated in writing ; and talked over by such as yourself rather than by an old fossil like me. Send for ——, and have an hour with him, and let me have the result."

Still another brief note to Mr. Macaulay runs thus : "Get a hold for good of this widow's student son, and you will earn her blessing.—A. W." A post card bears the following : "Keep one of your hundred eyes on the ——s, Buccleuch Place. I found the Medical son had been working too hard, and was in need of a holiday.—A. W." On another occasion Dr. Whyte forwards a letter from a mother in Free St. George's, warmly appreciative of his work in the Young Women's Class, but explaining that a book which he had counselled the members to " sell their beds and buy " proved to be out of print.   In this case his appended note is brief : " Take note of the postscript," which ran—" Do remember our sons in prayer.   C. is beginning his medical course at the University."   Thus Dr. Whyte sought his assistants' fellowship in the ministry of intercession, which played so great a part in his own life, as well as in that of active effort.

This initiation into the secret places of Dr. Whyte's life as a minister won the reverence and affection of his long succession of assistants in no common degree.   True, when he had once impressed on them the paramount need of methodical, in-cessant, prayerful work, he was slow to give detailed advice, for he believed in the virtue of finding one's own way through the practical problems of life.   To one who asked for advice on the choice of subjects on which to preach, he said with a Johnsonian finality, " Sir, I have enough difficulty to find my own texts without finding yours ! "   Long after, when the same former assistant said that the only advice he remembered receiving from Dr. Whyte was to take good holidays, the old man replied with a smile, " Well, sir, and if you have followed my advice, have you or your congregation ever seen reason to regret it ? " [1]

In other instances, those whom Dr. Whyte found in trouble were commended for further sympathy and help to his wife—especially if any question of education were involved—or to one or other of his most experienced elders, several of whom he trusted greatly to deal with particular types of difficulty. But his personal interest was always maintained until the time of difficulty was over.   The following notes to different friends illustrate this side of his work :

" In my visiting yesterday I came on a poor body who makes her living by selling potatoes

[1] Dr. G. H. Morrison in the *British Weekly*, December 8, 1910.

and oranges. A thief came in the other day and bought a halfpenny orange and stole the five-pound note she had saved up for her rent at the term. Will you send me a pound for her ? "

" Can you spare me a pound or two for a bad case ? I am sending out to Canada an ill-doing and a heart-breaking youth, a son of a heart-broken mother : I am sending him out in the prayer and hope that he may turn over a new leaf in a new land. You are always giving, but it is only those who are always giving who always give more."

If Dr. Whyte could ask persuasively, he could also give graciously, as is proved by a brief note, written in reply to a request for a subscription : " You have done me a real kindness in your letter. I most gladly send you the small cheque." He could also thank his friends for making other demands on him, as a post card to his brother-in-law, Professor A. R. Simpson, shows : " Thank you for sending me down into your district this afternoon. I have had a royal time among your people. They worship you, and I do not reprove them."

We have already seen how closely Dr. Whyte restricted his activity to the direct work of the Church. In many other movements he showed a keen interest, but he wisely refrained, at least during his later ministry, from attending the committees by which they were controlled.[1] Yet, in spite of his avoidance of outside claims upon his time and strength, there are many indications that Dr. Whyte never ceased to feel the weight of his pastoral work. Not seldom he reproached himself with failure to discharge it as he would have wished to do. As long as he had to carry the burden unaided, the task

[1] Exceptions were the Edinburgh Committee of the Indigent Gentlewomen's Fund, which lay in the line of his pastoral work and to which he gave of his strength for many years ; the Association for the Inspection of Religious Instruction ; and the Edinburgh Free Breakfast Mission.

was beyond even his powers of accomplishment; though at times in his earlier ministry he would arrange a series of pulpit exchanges in order to give undivided time to visitation. The induction in 1896 of the Rev. Hugh Black as his colleague—of which Chapter XX. will tell—gave him relief by dividing the responsibility; but one difficulty remained. His innate reserve of nature and that lack of the smaller change of conversation which often marks those whose thoughts dwell habitually on the greatest themes, made it harder for him than for many others to establish an easy contact with the younger members of his congregation. Yet his. fellow-workers have witnessed to his remarkable knowledge both of young and old. Indeed, as the years passed, the children of the congregation came to love their senior minister more and more. In their case, his smile took the place of ready speech as a passport to their affection —and that smile never ceased to grow in gracious beauty. " I think," says a close and sympathetic observer, " the children were very much in awe of him at the beginning, but all grew up to love and reverence him; and it was their old Minister who was the magnet that drew them back to St. George's when they returned home from all parts of the world in after life." When he spoke to the children, either at one of the children's services already referred to or at a less formal gathering, he especially impressed two rules upon them : " Always look at the Minister when he preaches "; " Never pass your Minister in the street without smiling to him." Sometimes he was too absorbed to notice the smile ; but when he did, a proud child returned home to report that Dr. Whyte had smiled in return. A letter, written about 1892, to one of his congregation, tells charmingly how he was received by a little maiden of perhaps ten years old on one of his pastoral rounds :

" I much missed the father and mother yesterday, but if anything could have made up for their absence it would have been the good sense and good manners and tact of your daughter. She made me feel that I had made a real pastoral visit. You would hear that I had ' The Mouse ' also, excellently rendered."

His visits were often as brief as those of Dr. Chalmers in his great Glasgow parish, yet such a visit from him meant more than he knew—more, often, than a long talk with any other.

" He could not accomplish all he would have liked, but many of us know what his visits meant to us. He did not stay long, he never said much, but what he did say—how concise, how true, how much to the point, how full of strengthening and comfort ! One visit I shall never forget : he came in and stood at the couch and repeated :

> ' He gives the conquest to the *weak*,
> Supports the fainting heart,
> And courage in the evil hour
> His heavenly aids impart.'

Then a word of prayer, and he was gone. No doubt to several others that afternoon he brought strength and comfort by those words." [1]

It was his custom to carry round to one and another of the stricken among his people a text or the verse of a hymn which had lately brought healing to his own spirit ; and the twenty-second paraphrase, on which his friend Margaret Ogilvy had rested in her last days, was one that he often used in his pastoral work. One letter runs : " Had I seen you when I called, I would have given you the prophet's word when he was visiting the sick in Jerusalem—' He gives the conquest to the weak.' " On another occasion he had visited an elder's wife who was laid low by a lingering and incurable malady, and before leaving her bedside quoted the last verse, " On eagles' wings they mount, they soar." Then, at the door, he turned and added as an afterthought

[1] Mrs. Robert Simson, in the Memorial Booklet issued early in 1921.

—dropping into the homely Scots, as he was wont to do in moments of intimacy—" Put that under your tongue and suck it like a sweetie ! "

There was a little group of lonely women who gained a large portion of Dr. Whyte's pastoral care; for he did not wholly disregard his own preference in his visiting, and a strong attraction drew him to such dwellings as theirs. To one of these, occupied by Miss Mary Grant, who had many memories of Dr. Candlish, he used to send his children, and his successive new assistants, in order that they might profit by her racy wisdom as they took a message or a gift of flowers from her minister. Some of these faithful members could recall long passages from his sermons, and unconsciously reproduced his phraseology in talking of spiritual things. Throughout his ministry it was his custom to keep such members, who were prevented from joining in the outward fellowship of the Church, especially in remembrance at the time of the quarterly Communion in Free St. George's. On the Friday before each Communion Sunday he would send them post cards, generally written out in his own hand, giving the full order of service, including praise, scripture, and the subjects of the Action Sermon and Table Address, that so, beginning at eleven o'clock, they might follow from their own rooms each successive act of the service. And for those whose illness was very long-continued or dangerous he would hold a simple Communion service by the sickbed, accompanied by one of his elders, according to the Presbyterian usage.

Another feature of his work at these seasons was that he tried, as far as possible, to be present at preparatory gatherings which were held in three of the congregational districts—in one case in a boarding-school for girls, and in the others in the elder's house. One of these had begun very simply by the meeting of two or three members for prayer in view of the Communion ; then others gathered in, until the whole membership of the district was represented.

Dr. Whyte was singularly happy in the informal fellowship of the earlier part of these evenings, and singularly impressive in conducting the worship with which they closed. One who did much to arrange these gatherings speaks of the sense of unity that pervaded them—a sense not so readily attained in a large congregation—as those present realised with great clearness their oneness with Christ and with one another.

Family partings, too, brought Dr. Whyte thus into the homes of his people. He always endeavoured to be present to conduct Family Worship on Sunday evening in any household where death had entered during the preceding week. Or, if a daughter were sailing for the mission field, or a son setting out to take up work in the Indian Civil Service or in a business house in the Far East, a post card telling him of the approaching departure would bring him to the house on the evening before. Those who remember the originality, the tenderness, and the deep sense of the presence of God which marked his conducting of Family Worship on such occasions as these, can readily believe that his words travelled far, and remained long as a safeguard and an inspiration in the hearts of those who went forth to work in distant lands.

Two other stories of his pastoral work may best be told in the words of Dr. Kelman :

"One poor old woman whom he visited had complained during the whole of twenty minutes about everybody and everything, and he had sat silent. Then he lifted his gloves and hat, and shook hands with her to bid her good-bye, saying only, 'And, mind you, forget not all His benefits!'

"On another occasion, visiting one who had more cause for complaint, and whose heart was well-nigh broken, he kneeled down with her in her poor room, and said simply, 'O Lord, here's two poor old folk needing you sorely. You won't be hard upon us!'"

Resolute as was Dr. Whyte's character, he had seasons of deep depression regarding the results of his work in the pulpit or among his people ; and at such times a message of gratitude from one of them —sometimes from a retiring and little-known member — brought great refreshment to his spirit. On one occasion the sense of failure in his ministry coloured his evening sermon, and prompted one of his hearers to write and tell him something of what that ministry meant to her. She posted the letter before midnight, in order that it might reach him on Monday morning, and that afternoon's post brought his reply :

"Your letter is a cup of wine to me this morning.—Believe me,
"ALEXANDER WHYTE."

If he at times accepted with gratitude the consolations which others brought, he himself was a minister of comfort to many. Little can be said regarding this intimate and sacred part of his work ; but a letter may be quoted, addressed in 1895 to a friend whose daughter had died :

"I have been much touched by your bereavement. The best way to get one's heart touched by our brother's trials is to put ourselves in his place. When I do that, and look on my own girls, my heart goes out to you. God bless you and your house.—With great regard and sympathy, A. WHYTE."

A yet briefer letter was called forth by the death of Dr. Whyte's tried friend, Sir Thomas Clark, who passed away on Christmas Eve, 1901. This single sentence brought greater comfort to his widow than anything else could have done :

"DEAR LADY CLARK, — What a glorious Christmas morning this is for Sir Thomas.
"ALEX. WHYTE."

To a friend who asked his advice on a difficult life-problem, Dr. Whyte replied in these words:

" If any man should testify to the power and the goodness of God in his life, I think I am that man. And my testimony to you is this: trust in God. Still trust in God. And though He slays you, still trust in Him. All things are in His hand. All the keys are at His girdle. And we have His oath that all things shall work together for good to them that love Him. Thou knowest all things: Thou knowest that I love Thee !

" Let me hear from you soon. And never hesitate to tell my wife and me what concerns you. I think I can say that nowhere have you friends who love you more than we do."

To another young friend who was faced with a sudden break in his work he wrote :

" This arrest makes me all the more distressed on account of the work. But He who has laid this arrest on you, and on your work, does all things well. Not a hair of our head falls to the ground without Him. We repeat this, and do not disbelieve it at other times : but it is at times of sore personal tribulation that we come to *know it experimentally and unchallengeably.* He has His eye on you to make you a great servant of His : and this is one of His ways.

" May you have a victorious and joyous sense of His Presence and Peace."

Dr. Whyte did not write long letters of spiritual counsel, nor did he enter in his letters into elaborate argument on religious truth. When he wrote at all, his words were few and weighty, summoning, as in the instances just quoted, to a trustful acceptance of the divine guidance. But, if it were possible, he preferred that the seeker for his help should come to his study for a quiet talk. One who had such a conversation in a time of deep religious perplexity, in his study in Melville Street towards the close of the first decade of his Edinburgh ministry, preserved these notes of the counsel which he gave :

" Draw nigh to God and He will draw nigh to you. *Act* faith if you do not feel it. If you cannot think spiritually about Christ, think naturally of His work, a passage in His history, a word of His sayings. Better think thus than not at all. Though cold and faithless at first, love and faith will come. Do not wait for a surge of feeling, think of Him at once. His Holy Spirit works with what the old divines call ' concurrent grace,' not violently, or with external movement, but when we feel a softening on our knees, or at the reading of His word—a gentleness in our dealings with others—a sweetness in the frame of our minds—that is the Spirit working in our natures, moulding the dispositions we have. Gabriel is said to have come swiftly to Daniel ' whiles he was speaking and praying.' He would need to come very swiftly indeed to most of us, if he is to catch us on our knees ! How generally does the spirit of prayer find us in this attitude ?

.   .   .   .

" There is nothing more that I can say. Christ is before you to take freely ; accept Him, trust Him, believe what He says, *assume* that you are His, and behave as if you were. Do your part, and will God fail on His ? This will not bear to be stated. . . . Think of Jesus and let Him fill your thoughts, and love and faith will come. He offers Himself to the lost, not to the saved. If you were not utterly helpless why did He come ? *Throw yourself in His direction*, even though you cannot reach Him. Even if you die doing this, He will take care of you. He does not say ' See ' : He only says ' Look '— that is all you have to do with, He will take care of the rest. Go about your daily duties, your

reading, your praying, *assuming* that you are
God's child, acting in all things as if you were.
He will make it all right : He *is* making it all
right. You are incapable and helpless—use
Augustine's prayers, the prayers of a man who
had been for eleven years one of the greatest of
the Fathers. 'Take me, Lord, for I cannot give
myself; keep me, Lord, for I cannot keep myself.'
You did not rest in your hurry to see me to-day,
you knew where to find me. Do so with Him.
He is with you. Do not hang your head like a
bulrush.

" It would be better if you had more sense
of sin, but God's dealings with each soul are
different, and that will come as you get nearer
to Christ. Some ministers preach much about a
sense of sin—perhaps I do so more than most, but
do not expect to have all your feelings like other
people's. *Surrender* yourself to Christ ; say,
' Lord, I give myself up to Thee here and now,'
and go your way doing *your* part, He will not fail
to do His.

" Many a time I feel so cold and dead that I
might doubt if I had ever come to Him at all ;
but I go about my work notwithstanding, looking
in His *direction*, and my heart fills by and by
with His love to me. I was many years before
I was aware that I was over the boundary line,
so it may be with you. It is very simple—keep
looking ; He will take care of the *seeing*."

The study at 7 Charlotte Square became in later
years a place of not less sacred associations to many,
who brought to it perplexities of the most varying
kinds, and records of past failure in every degree.
This was the spot, it has been well said,

" where this great master of the human heart
perfected his sermons, where this great physician
of souls met his patients. His library has been
dispersed ; his working-books adorn to-day the
New College Library, and his various com-

24

mentaries rest in Highland manses. But the chief objects in that study were, after all, the two deep arm-chairs that rested, one on either side, by the spacious fireplace. In one of them sat this great specialist in sin, in the other a long succession of men who believed that no other doctor could understand their case. Here broken hearts were mended, here despairing souls got their glimpse of a new hope, here the chief of sinners saw the prospect of his final triumph through grace. The stories told in that sacred chamber are buried now with the physician." [1]

To most men Dr. Whyte would have seemed not altogether easy to approach regarding any trivial or everyday problem of conduct. Some, indeed, who had seen his genial mood as he discussed books and events with friends whom he knew well, knew how accessible he was and how interested in many of the small things of life ; but as a rule he gave the impression of a certain remoteness, or even austerity. Yet something in his face and bearing attracted those who were passing through deep waters. Here, they felt, was one who would take no shallow view of their case, and his very detachment from some of the things that absorb the thoughts of others helped to confirm this impression. And when they had made the effort needed to enter his study, they found that they were right. He listened, quietly, patiently, with no parade of sympathy, the clear blue eyes fixed on the speaker and the strong mouth firmly set ; yet the quiet attitude of this man, who had seen and suffered much, told alike of sympathy and of wisdom, and made it easy in talk with him to

" Cleanse the stuffed bosom of that perilous stuff
Which weighs upon the heart."

One of those who knew him best has described how he but very rarely broke silence on certain of the most

[1] Rev. R. Godfrey in the *Christian Express* (now the *South African Outlook*), March 1, 1921.

intimate and perplexing problems of human relationship—" but then he spoke with such wisdom as only
comes of experience passed through the refining of a
great mind."

He was a man of deep and various silences. " The
silence which overwhelmed one with shyness and
took away all one's power of speech," has been spoken
of by one who knew him both in dark days and
bright ; but there were also " the silence which was
suddenly broken by a remark which showed how he
had heard and noticed everything that had been said
and done, and the silence of his sympathy, summed
up in half a dozen meaningful words at the end."
This power of silent observation was one great source
of his strength as a counsellor and as a pastor. At
first it might have appeared that his generosity to
men whom others were disposed to judge harshly
was due to lack of knowledge, but those who were
most closely identified with him in pastoral work
found that it was far otherwise. He often startled
them by his acquaintance with the actual facts, yet
he was charitable and generous above all others.

This moral magnanimity was but another facet
of that largeness of nature which elsewhere appeared
in his width of religious sympathy. " Few men,"
it has been aptly said by a minister of the sister
church, " with such firm, clear views have had such a
genuine tolerance, love, and understanding for others
whose views were very different. He had it because
he knew the things that matter, and had an instinct
for discerning his brothers under sometimes strange
guises." Another gifted pen in the same church
described on the morrow of Dr. Whyte's death the
union in him of an apparent remoteness with a rare
power of encouraging others :

" Walking along Princes Street he was
isolated in his own atmosphere—in the world, yet
not of it. In the General Assembly he sat day
by day—silent, wrapped in meditation, while the
endless talk went on. He was there in the midst

of it; but his soul dwelt apart. . . . He had a great gift of silence. A young minister fresh from Keswick came into his study and spoke of his experiences with rapture, just as if the New Jerusalem had come. 'Ay,' said Dr. Whyte, 'it's a sair fecht up to the very last!' But he could be very human at times. And none could be more generous in praise. Many can remember a day when a letter came from Dr. Whyte. He had read that article or that book— and then the warm-hearted words. Surely a day to be marked with a white stone." [1]

Such letters at times conveyed much in half a dozen words : he once wrote after he and his wife had read a friend's article :

> "7 CHARLOTTE SQUARE,
> EDINBURGH.
> "A. W.: That's extraordinarily well written!
> "J. E. W.: Yes!   A. W."

Allied with this contrast was that between Dr. Whyte's frequent austerity, both in his bearing and in his attitude to human nature in the mass, and his wonderful gentleness and courtesy. The latter often passed into an old-world courtliness which remains in the memory of his friends, but cannot readily be described. At one time it became known to him that a friend, then an Anglican, but now a member of a Benedictine order, was making a serious study of the position of women in the Early Church. He invited her to make free use of his library, and arranged a table for her work near his own desk.

"He was never too engaged himself," she writes, "to turn and ask, with a smile which gave you the completest confidence in telling him all your perplexities, whether he could help

[1] "A Prince in Israel," by Rev. Norman Maclean, D.D. (*Scotsman*, January 8, 1921).

you, and with gentle courtesy he would get up to hunt for some book he thought might be of use. His presence was in itself an inspiration to thought and work, but it was his humility, the humility of a great mind, which impressed me more than all else."

The apparent contradiction between Dr. Whyte's scourgings of the depraved human heart in the pulpit, and his readiness elsewhere to believe the best, and to say the best, about individual men and women, struck all who knew him, and was not seldom discussed by his friends. Perhaps some light may be thrown upon it by two incidents, separated by a full generation of time. At Lord Ardmillan's table in the 'seventies, Whyte once found himself near Professor John Stuart Blackie, that figure of somewhat eccentric genius yet of abounding vitality and charm, who taught little Greek syntax to the students of his day, but brought a welcome ray of the brighter side of Hellenism into the grey streets of Edinburgh. The talk turned on epitaphs, and Blackie, turning to Whyte, said, with a swift flash of insight that brought the character of both men into bold relief: " If you have the writing of my epitaph, I know what it will be. It will be this—' Here lies a man who had every virtue but a sense of sin.' " [1] Long after, Dr. Whyte was with his eldest daughter and one of his nephews, and the talk turned to a young friend, of whose considerateness and unselfishness Dr. Whyte spoke with the very warmest appreciation. He ended his eulogy by saying, " I should apply to him, as fully as to any one I know, the phrase *anima naturaliter Christiana.* But," he added, after a pause, with an unusual measured emphasis, " I have observed that such characters seldom gain an experience of the deepest evangelical religion."

[1] Dr. Whyte told the story in his pulpit tribute after Professor Blackie's death in 1895, adding, " Could Socrates himself have said it better ? "

Dr. Whyte rejoiced in every form of goodness and in the ideal of Christian charity—ever to see and to proclaim the best in others—while his fondness for Tertullian's famous phrase showed his delight in the spontaneous virtue of those who

> " In love and truth,
> Where no misgiving is, rely
> Upon the genial sense of youth."

Yet, unaffected as was his appreciation of the " once-born " type of goodness, it was towards the " twice-born " that the whole bent of his spirit lay, and the whole strength of his preaching and his pastoral care of souls was directed. This represented to him the full fruit and perfection of the Christian order, and his highest hope for others was that they might attain the character which springs from a penitent spirit.

The one fault which strained his own charity to breaking-point was the lack of charity in others. On the rare occasions when a severe judgment of a man or a book escaped him, this was almost invariably the ground of his stricture. One couplet which he impressed on the conscience of his Classes was :

> " He that is wont to slander absent men
> May never at my table sit again ! "

And one motto which he had printed on a small card was—" Is it *true* ? Is it *kind* to repeat it ? Is it *necessary* to repeat it ? " Few men have known more of the weakness of human nature, and have yet so consistently practised the precept, " Judge not ! " or shown forth the charity that " thinketh no evil."

The humility and generosity of his later years, manifest in his constant practice of attributing to others the finest fruit of their common work and claiming neither reward nor recognition for himself, was built up on the foundation of a nature naturally proud and sensitive, with that " honest haughtiness " which Milton recollected in his own youth as having kept him " above those low descents of mind." He

began life with the pride which fortifies many who
have to fight their way forward against merciless
retarding forces. Yet in later days even this honest
pride had dissolved in a humility which pervaded
his whole nature, and served both as a rebuke and
as a standard to his friends. That it was almost
instinctively taken as a standard is shown by a phrase
in one of Dr. Denney's letters, in which he spoke of
Dr. Smellie as the humblest man he knew, " except
Dr. Whyte." [1] If the kindred sin of envy, which
he tracked with his most persistent and searching
spiritual analysis and of which in many sermons he
accused himself, had ever possessed any lodgement in
his heart, it had for long given place to a generosity
which at times even verged upon excess. The
secret of this victory, which was so complete as in
the end to seem effortless, may be gathered from
his own definition of " the truly humble man,"
as he " who has gone down deep into himself, and
who abides there, and walks with God there." [2]

Such were some of the characteristics which made
Dr. Whyte not only the preacher, but the revered
pastor and the healer of wounded spirits which he
increasingly became. By the early 'nineties his outward appearance had become venerable as well as
striking. It might have been said of him that the
epic of his life " had made him lean through many a
year " [3]—though that epic was written not in verse,
but in a ceaseless striving after the ideal in his own
life and in all the lives which his ever-widening
influence could reach. It is true that nearly twenty
years were to pass before the energy of his spare and
active frame showed any failure; but his face was
deeply lined, and the abundant fair hair, which had
turned to grey years before, had now acquired the
silvery whiteness which is seen in his most familiar
portraits. Yet no portrait can fully represent the
smile which often lit up his face. To those who

[1] *Letters to his Family and Friends*, p. 66.
[2] " The Melancholy Temperament " (*The Four Temperaments*, p. 92).
[3] Dante, *Paradiso*, xxv. 3.

knew him best it spoke of that steady habit of retirement and of meditation on eternal things, which he pursued amid the most varied surroundings, and which gave him his power both to speak the word of faith and to bring hope into broken lives. " Towards this contemplation all the currents of his outward service in sermon and congregational worship now converged, as into one central stream, and the perfect smile was perhaps its only outward expression."

PART FOUR—THE LABOUR OF
LATER YEARS
1892–1907

CHAPTER
XIX

STUDY OF THE MYSTICS—PUBLICATION
OF APPRECIATIONS AND SERMONS

1892–1901

" By all of Him we have in thee,—
Leave nothing of myself in me.
Let me so read thy life, that I
Unto all life of mine may die!"
R. CRASHAW, *On St. Teresa.*

" *Il a ôté les épines du Protestantisme.*"—L'ABBÉ BREMOND,
regarding A. W.

THE year 1892 gave a new direction to the current of
Dr. Whyte's theological—or, to use his own word,
experimental—reading and thought, and thus the
outward circumstances of the year are more than
commonly worthy of record. The long summer
vacation was spent at Bonskeid, where a son was
born on 8th August, and was named Robert Barbour
in memory of Mrs. Whyte's brother who had passed
away fourteen months before. It is this little boy
who appears with his father in the serene and
beautiful portrait afterwards taken in the study at
Charlotte Square ; and it was he who laid down
his life in his twenty-fourth year in the battle of
Loos.

During later summers at Bonskeid Dr. Whyte
was accustomed to work in the library at a writing-
table placed close to a window looking westward,
with the bound volumes of the *North British Review*
and other favourite books not far away ; but on this
occasion his study was a room at the top of the house,
whose oriel window commands the whole sweep of
the valley south-eastward, with the gleam of the

river Tummel visible through the shimmering birches below. Here he established himself with the complete works of William Law in the 1830 edition, and with other material for the study of Law and Butler in his classes during the following winter. He wrote in the middle of July that his chief reading was Law and Macaulay ; and as the weeks passed he became more and more absorbed in the former, as his second book, the *Characters and Characteristics of William Law*, began to take shape. Almost ten years had passed since the publication of his *Shorter Catechism* ; and, if the two books were different in almost all else, they were alike in this, that Dr. Whyte's own contribution was less in bulk, and in his own eyes far less in importance, than the quotations which the two volumes contained. The great aim of his work during this summer was to induce others to read Law by providing a careful selection of his best passages, and by an introductory appreciation, setting forth what Dr. Whyte himself had gained from the great Anglican—a debt which was summed up in a single sentence of the Preface : " The study of this quite incomparable writer has been nothing less than an epoch in my life." At a later date he wrote in the same ardent strain : " It was a red-letter day in my life when I first opened William Law, and I feel his hand on my heart and on my mind and on my conscience and on my whole inner man literally every day I live."

The volume on William Law was published, in a form of real attractiveness and beauty, in December 1892. But before we follow its fortunes further, it may be well to turn to a deeper subject—the influence on his own mind of the systematic study of the Mystics, which was the background of his whole life during the next five years. For from Law he passed on to Behmen,[1] and from Behmen to Teresa, Brother

---

[1] Dr. Whyte followed the older English translators in using the form " Behmen," now almost obsolete, rather than " Boehme." A letter to Mr. H. R. Allenson, the publisher, on this question ends : " I may be wrong. Anyhow, circulate him."

Lawrence, and many more.   It would, indeed, be an error to suggest that he now came under the influence of the great devotional mystics for the first time. Long before, he had drunk in Goodwin's teaching regarding the indwelling Christ ; for long he had known and valued à Kempis ; nor could any man of his intensity have steeped his spirit in Dante's *Paradiso* during many years, without apprehending the mystical elements with which it is shot through and through.   But the study of the Mystics which Dr. Whyte now began was more intensive and wider in range ; and in William Law he found a guide after his own heart, in whose writings a singularly devout spirit and penetrating intelligence found expression in English prose not less flexible and musical than Berkeley's or Newman's.

There was another aspect also in this new discovery.   Dr. Whyte was never in the strict sense a philosopher ; but in his student days he had been attracted, as we saw in Chapter IV., by the semi-agnostic theory of knowledge with which Hamilton and Mansel sought to reinforce the religious consciousness.   Now, however, he found in the writings of " the illuminated Behmen," as Law gratefully called him, a daring and unflinchingly idealistic view of the world as a whole allied with an equally penetrating and original exposition of the deep experiences of the Christian soul.   Dr. Whyte's estimates of Behmen, Teresa, and Law have a fervour that marks them out even among his many glowing " Appreciations," and in the first there is distinct evidence that the far-reaching thoughts of the shoemaker of Görlitz on Nature as well as on Man had awakened an answering chord in the spirit of his Scottish disciple, remote and obscure as he acknowledged some of these speculations to be.[1]

Yet it was the practical and experimental side of Behmen's thinking rather than his wanderings amid " the primitive and unfrequented roots of things," which riveted Dr. Whyte's attention and won his

[1] *Thirteen Appreciations*, 42 f., 50 ff.

gratitude. He would never have admitted that true
Mysticism was remote from, far less opposed to, the
great ideals of the moral life. In other words, his
interest lay not at all in Mysticism in its narrower
philosophical sense—in the neo-Platonist doctrine
of the all-embracing, all-absorbing Unity, in which
moral and personal distinctions disappear—but in
Mysticism as linked at every point with the Christian
experience of redemption. It was, indeed, a criticism
made by one of his oldest friends, Professor John
Gibb, that his essay on William Law failed to furnish
a definition of Mysticism. For a perfect definition
students are waiting still ; but in this essay Dr.
Whyte did attempt to define this great type of
thought, not in any formal way, but as his manner
was, by naming certain of the thinkers who stand
out as its exponents. His list began with Plato,
and ended with a contemporary poet—George
Macdonald—and with two scientists, one a fellow-
citizen of his own—" Stewart and Tait in their *Unseen
Universe*." Next he pointed out the mystical strain
in certain of the New Testament writings ; and
finally he thus summarised the message which Law
had found in Behmen :

> " Seek above every other search the one
> noble knowledge of thyself. For, only in the
> ever-deepening knowledge of thyself shalt thou
> come to know sin, and only in the knowledge
> of thyself and thy sinfulness shalt thou ever
> know aught aright of God. . . . The kingdom
> of heaven, the throne of grace, the Son of God,
> the Holy Ghost, are all within thee." [1]

It was this doctrine of Man as the moral microcosm
in whose breast all the qualities of the universe are
latent, in whose life all its strivings come to an issue,
and whose regenerated character may become a true
reflection of the divine image—which laid hold of Dr.
Whyte most firmly and made him rejoice in the name
of mystic. " Mysticism," he told his classes later,

---

[1] *Op. cit.*, pp. 224–7.

" means spirituality of the deepest kind " ; and this spirituality he now increasingly found in authors who differed widely both from one another, and from the Puritan tradition on which his faith had first been nourished.

Dr. Whyte set a high value on the extracts contained in the volume on William Law, and he and his wife gave away not less than one hundred and fifty copies. Of many letters of acknowledgment, two, coming from men of opposite intellectual outlook, may be quoted here. The first is from the author of *A History of English Thought in the Eighteenth Century*, and is dated 29th December 1892 :

" DEAR SIR,—Allow me to thank you very sincerely for your *William Law*. In spite of all differences of opinion, I heartily admire Law's intellectual power and am, I hope, sensible of the great beauty of his character. I hope that I may take your gift as a proof that, in your judgment, I did something like justice to him in the book which you quote. Of course there would be many points on which a defect of sympathy would show itself ; but at least I endeavoured to be fair and you encourage me to hope that I did not fail.

" I heartily return your expression of good-will, and am, Yours sincerely,

" LESLIE STEPHEN."

A week later a letter followed, expressive of a very different personality :

" MY DEAR DR. WHYTE,—' I was an hungered and ye gave unto me.' I just pined for some such reading as you have sent me. It is full of vision and music and strong tenderness. It is really ' very good ' in the Genesis sense—good where it ends, good in all its possibilities. I envy you the social solitude—the thronged loneliness—which you must have enjoyed in doing this book. . . .

" I have much to say but it cannot be written. Ink is a mistake.

" All as usual. Fire full of fire-views. Friends kind. The Lord often very near.— Ever yours, JOSEPH PARKER."

Dr. Whyte's friend, the Rev. W. W. Peyton, wrote on receiving the same volume : " I have had an idea that scientific conceptions can be translated into the poetic and the philosophic, and that they have been anticipated by the poet and the philosopher "—an idea which his own books sought to work out. Looking back nearly thirty years after, the same friend said of the tie that bound him to Dr. Whyte :

" A mystic sympathy seemed to lie between us, though we did not belong to the same school of thought. He was a large man with all the schools in him. I have in my library three volumes of the *Life and Letters of Darwin*, which he sent me as a New Year's gift—and Darwin was [then] the scare of the religious schools."

From this time onward William Law became perhaps Dr. Whyte's most favourite subject for popular lectures. He visited King's Cliffe near Northampton, the village where Law was born and where he spent his later years in an ascetic and strictly ordered life of prayer and good works. The resulting lecture, " A Day in King's Cliffe," soon rivalled that on " John Bunyan and the *Pilgrim's Progress* " in winning the breathless and enthralled attention of audiences in many parts of Scotland. It provided, indeed, a more signal proof of Dr. Whyte's power ; for Scottish hearers have a hereditary—and a generation ago had a personal—interest in the " Pilgrim," whereas to the great majority William Law was only a name, if even so much as a name, when the speaker began. But before he had gone far, King's Cliffe and its old Manor House, the endowed schools which Law founded and the rules which he drew up for the children attending them, but especially his study and his

hours of prayer, had gained an interest hardly second
to that of the prison of Bedford. Dr. Whyte's visit
to King's Cliffe, in company with Dr. Sutherland
Black, brought him the friendship of the Rector,
the Rev. R. F. Gould, and of an aged lady, Miss
Sarah Law, who was descended from the family of
William Law. Not long after, she sent Dr. Whyte
a fine panel of old oak, which had formed part of
William Law's pew in the village church, and which
from that time became one of the chief treasures of
his home—first at 7 Charlotte Square and then at
Hampstead.

One practical point in the writings of Law which
sank deeply into Dr. Whyte's thought and lastingly
affected his practice was the stress there laid on the
danger of controversy, and the almost invariable sins
of temper which controversy involves. Here also,
Law did but underline and emphasise an impression
that had long held its place in Dr. Whyte's mind.
Throughout his career he was slow to plunge into
controversy, and his originally impetuous temper
had long before this been curbed with a strong hand.
Even his great fighting speech at the conclusion of
the Robertson Smith Case opened with an expression
of his deep reluctance to face " the distressing breach
of peace and love that too commonly follows upon
such controversies." But from the time that he
passed under the spell of William Law, this sense of
the peril of controversy became one of the governing
principles of his life, alike in the home, in the affairs
of his congregation, and in the wider discussions of
the whole Church. When he spoke on this danger,
and pointed out the better way of forbearance and
patient love, he commonly reinforced his appeal by a
quotation from William Law; and it was characteristic
that he drew the same conclusion as one of the chief
lessons in the tremendous story of the Book of Job.[1]

---

[1] *Bible Characters*, iii. p. 123 f. For the influence of Law on this
side of his thinking, see especially the sermon on " Valiant-for-Truth,"
preached not long after he began the systematic study of Law's works
(*Bunyan Characters*, ii. pp. 203–9).

Dr. Whyte never accepted the full Quaker doctrine that war is always wrong and that physical force should not be used even for moral ends ; but he reached an analogous conclusion in another sphere, where it is less often applied. The maxim, " Force is no remedy," was true for him — or true with only the rarest exceptions—in regard to those conflicts in which the force used is that of brain and tongue. For this also can wound ; and hence arise many of those breaches of charity among those who ought to work together, which so gravely hinder the progress of every noble cause. But all his warnings as to the danger of controversy had their positive counterpart in the firm conviction that a better way may always be found, and that all differences of opinion may be made to issue in harmony if men will only follow the threefold path of prayer, of faith, and of love.

Yet it was not given to Dr. Whyte at this time to make his final escape from controversy. He had more than once been bitterly attacked in the press, and in 1896 he had to face an attack arising out of a prayer which he had offered at the meeting of the Disestablishment Council on the eve of the General Assemblies. Two or three phrases from this prayer were reported — in itself a proceeding of questionable propriety—and one in particular, " Bless the Queen, and make her a godly woman," was bitterly criticised, as implying that she had not already attained that character. Dr. Whyte was accused of the most extreme Pharisaism both in a leader in the *Scotsman* and in letters to the same newspaper from two anonymous correspondents, one of whom gave a grotesquely distorted account of the visit to Newman at the Oratory twenty years before. The incident is only referred to here because the letter to the editor, in which Dr. Whyte met the criticism of his assailants, shows better, perhaps, than any other extant document the spirit which he himself manifested in controversy :

R. S. Webster, Photographer, Edinburgh

WITH ROBERT, 1897

" *May* 22, 1896.

" Sir,—Our Lord has said that it is impossible but that offences will come ; but woe unto him through whom they come ! Now I see from some very severe strictures on my character, and on some reported words of mine, that I have been an offence to you again, and I fear to many others. No man living has more woe than I have at myself because of my unadvised and offending words. And, however often I keep silent, and however much I prepare myself before I speak, my feet will sometimes so go from under me that I suffer some sore falls, and am an offence to my best and most patient friends. At the same time, I cannot but think that, if you will read over again what you have sent out about me this morning, and will read it with justice and with love, you will feel that you have let yourself be provoked to put the very worst possible construction on my unhappy words. An impossible construction. Put the same construction on any prayer you ever heard offered for our Queen, and I cannot but believe that you will admit to-morrow that you have been much too cruel to me. God save the Queen. God bless the Queen. May God establish the Queen's throne in righteousness. May the Queen's sceptre be a right sceptre. May the Queen be a mother in Israel. May all the Queen's children rise up and call her blessed. Had I been led to put one or all of these petitions into my prayer that night, would you still have said that the opposite was clearly implied ? What was in my mind and in my heart for the Queen at that moment was a desire and a petition. That, before God, as He knows, implied, covered, and embraced all these several desires and petitions. What else—in the name of all that is just, and good, and true—what else could I have implied ? But, however unadvised, unusual, misleading, and open to evil constructions my words in that prayer of mine may

25

have been, you will surely believe me when I say it, that, bad as I know myself to be, I do not recognise myself in your vituperative portrait of me. I bow to your severe judgment of me in other respects and in other matters. But you will surely let me protest, with great pain and sorrow, at what has gone abroad about me at your hands this morning ; as also to express my lasting regret if there was anything in my words when fairly treated that so belied what alone was in my heart.

" As to the Newman matter, on which one of your correspondents comments with so much bitterness and ill-nature, I lay under such a debt to Dr. Newman that I had a great wish for once to see his face in this world. And when my two friends and I were passing through Birmingham on one occasion, that great man gave us this interview that we had, perhaps too intrusively, asked for. And our short visit will always be remembered by us for the sweetness and the exquisite courtesy with which we were treated. Your correspondent ' J. C. C.' and Dr. Newman's many admirers among your readers may rest assured that even under the arrogance of our interruption that urbanest of men did not ' forget himself.' He only won our reverence and love, if possible, more than before.

" As to ' Observer's ' so crisp and so pungent letter, it brought to my mind these words, ' Judge not that ye be not judged,' with Bengel's comment upon them, *sine scientia, amore, necessitate*. My only feeling towards ' Observer ' at this moment is a great regret that anything in me should have provoked him to cast abroad such opprobrious language at a man he does not know, and who would not hurt a hair of his head. I hope, sir, I have said nothing in these lines to increase the offence. If I have, you will throw them into the fire.—With all goodwill,

" ALEXANDER WHYTE."

To those who remember Dr. Whyte only in his serene old age, surrounded on all sides by unbroken reverence and love, these words, wrung from a sensitive spirit, may well give a new idea of the conflict through which that serenity was finally attained and of the self-mastery which went to the making of it.

The studies of these years strengthened his witness on behalf of Christian charity in another and more positive way, as other authors from beyond the pale of Protestantism came to share Newman's place in his esteem. The *Appreciations* of Law and Behmen were followed during the next six years by tributes to St. Teresa, Bishop Andrewes, Sir Thomas Browne, and Father John of Cronstadt, or, as Dr. Whyte preferred to call him, " Father John of the Greek Church." Of these— and, indeed, of all Dr. Whyte's many volumes—none travelled farther than the little volume on Teresa, which was read and valued in circles to which the writings of Scottish theologians seldom penetrate, and won the warm praise of the *Tablet* and the *Catholic Times.* By the end of the decade, the writer's correspondents included several Roman Catholics, both priests and laymen. One of the former, Father Humphrey, was by origin a Free Churchman, whose family were for long connected with Free St. George's. Dr. Whyte already knew one of his works on ethics, *Conscience and Law* ; and during the year 1897 chanced to meet his sisters, who had left Edinburgh some time before. They referred to a recent letter from Father Humphrey, who told that a book was commonly read aloud by one of the Fathers in the refectory during meals, and that of late the book chosen had been Dr. Whyte's *St. Teresa.* He at once said heartily, " I'll send him a copy from his mother's minister," and the copy so sent brought a letter of thanks telling how the gift had been appreciated, and how " some fifty Fathers and Scholastics " in a Jesuit college were following the author's thought, and praying

that he might come to see the full truth of the
divine revelation as they understood it.

Those who had known Dr. Whyte for a lifetime,
and who thought of him primarily as the most loyal
of evangelicals—as the greatest expositor of the
Puritan divines left in a Scotland which was fast
losing its Puritanism—might well feel surprise at the
welcome given to these writings by ardent Catholics.
Yet there were several factors which helped to
account for it. Baron von Hügel, whose personal
friendship with Dr. Whyte belongs to a later time,
tells how about this date he was strongly advised
by the Benedictine, Dom Cuthbert Butler, afterwards
Abbot of Downside, to read a remarkable appreciation of St. Teresa by a Scottish minister. He did
so, and was attracted by the writer's literary sense,
the fineness of his appreciation, and his avoidance
of the preacher's snare—the temptation to let his
own style fall into the merely rhetorical. More
important was the approach to religious truth, not
through reasoning, but through a sympathetic study
of personality. As Baron von Hügel came to know
Dr. Whyte's writings better, he felt an inconsistency
between the deep appreciation of many aspects of
Catholic belief which they showed on the one hand,
and on the other, the not less conspicuous loyalty
to what a Catholic considered as the divisive action
of the Reformers; but he recognised throughout
that no such inconsistency was felt by Dr. Whyte
himself.

Again, it has often been held — how far the
criticism is justified we need not stay to inquire—
that evangelical preaching has concentrated on the
beginning of the Christian life to the neglect of its
later growth; that it has tried unduly to simplify
Christian experience, and has thus been less fitted
to give guidance in the vicissitudes of its further
development. But no such charge could be laid
against Dr. Whyte. Here was a teacher who had
made the slow and often arrested working of
sanctification his daily and nightly study, for

whom growth in grace was a strangely involved process, and who never grew weary of emphasising the need of prayer and of discipline in the Christian life — the need of humility and of " ever-new beginnings."

Not less important in securing readers in churches far removed from his own was the openness of mind with which Dr. Whyte approached the story of the Virgin Mary, or the ecstatic writings of the great Spanish saint. No paragraph better sets forth what he understood by the habit of " appreciation " than that in which he tells how he himself came to appreciate St. Teresa; and a few pages later he adds :

> " A great saint of God is more worthy of our study and admiration and imitation and love than any other study or admiration or imitation or love on the face of the earth. And the further away such a saint is from ourselves the better she is fitted for our study and admiration and imitation and love, if we only have the sense and the grace to see it." [1]

This, then, was Dr. Whyte's great aim—to exercise the charity that " rejoices in the truth," wherever the truth is found, and however unfamiliar its garb. And the conclusion of the whole matter, as he came to see it, was expressed in the paradox that " the true Catholic, as his name implies, is the well-read, the open-minded, the hospitable-hearted, the spiritually exercised Evangelical " ; for " he belongs to all sects, and all sects belong to him." [2] These words, written in 1901, occur in the essay on Newman, a longer, more balanced, and more critical work than the writings of which we have hitherto taken account. In it, Dr. Whyte takes special pains to state his own convictions, even when they traverse and contradict those of the teacher

---

[1] *Thirteen Appreciations*, pp. 20, 27; cf. the noble quotation from Goodwin, *ibid.*, p. 169.

[2] *Op. cit.*, p. 314 ; cf. pp. 308, 359.

from whom he had learned so much. Yet certain even
of its more critical passages have been judged worthy
of careful consideration by a distinguished Roman
Catholic writer. The Abbé Bremond, in discussing
the question whether Newman ever really escaped
from the sway of *fear* in religion, quotes at length
from Dr. Whyte's book, and concludes : " Thus
speaks Mr. Whyte, an admirer and a friend. The
passages I have cited seem to show that he is right." [1]

Dr. Whyte's interest in the remarkable personality
of Father John, the preacher and healer of Cronstadt,
led him on to the study of the thought and ritual
of the Eastern Church. His short " Appreciation "
awakened widespread interest in Russia. On the
one hand, the *Anglo-Russian* took the view that his
pages on the Orthodox Church did full justice to
its virtues, but ignored its defects. On the other,
Mr. W. T. Stead, who was then in Russia seeking
to support the Czar's initiative in summoning the
first Hague Conference, wrote to tell Dr. Whyte
of a visit which he had just paid to the Countess
Tolstoi at Tsarskoe Selo. " I was very much pleased
to hear from her," he said, " a very enthusiastic
eulogy of your little book on Father John." And,
earlier in the same year (1898), Father John himself
had sent his greeting and benediction to the General
Assembly of the Free Church, over which Dr. Whyte
was presiding as Moderator.

During the decade from 1892 to 1901, Dr. Whyte
published books dealing with seven authors—St.
Teresa, Behmen, Sir Thomas Browne, Rutherford,
Law, Newman, and Father John. It is a selection of
singular catholicity, yet it forms but a small fraction
of the programme, embracing the Mystics and the
Great Autobiographies, which he dealt with orally
in his Classes during these years. Yet even among
writers so diverse certain common features may be
traced which won his admiration. Among these
were *Penitence, Perseverance in Prayer,* and *The
Practice of the Presence of God.* To these a fourth

[1] *The Mystery of Newman* (Eng. Trans.), p. 208, but cf. pp. 210 ff.

might be added—the mystical doctrine that the human heart contains the reflection, or in Behmen's phrase the *signature*, of all moral qualities and forces. These four marks were not equally present in all Dr. Whyte's chosen masters ; but if one were absent or inconspicuous, it was made up for by the overplus of the rest. There was, indeed, a strongly selective aspect in his great power of appreciation. A friendly critic (Mr. Hector Macpherson), surveying his published works at a later time, said that, like William James, he dealt with " the Varieties of Religious Experience " ; but that, while the great psychologist had left them " as confused as they were varied," Dr. Whyte's deep and broad spiritual experience enabled him to weld them into a unity. The centre of this unity in Dr. Whyte's teaching has been finely expressed in the words : " All these heroes were unveiled as interpreters of our Lord. He accepted their differences, and recommended the universality of their spirit." [1]

But this constructive and unifying work of interpretation had also its negative side, for no man could more entirely disregard uncongenial aspects in the thought of those to whom he acknowledged an immense debt. Sometimes he expressed his dissent, but more often he simply left on one side the beliefs which did not bring nourishment to his own spirit. It was said that he could read William Law and Newman with intense admiration, but remain entirely untouched by the High Church doctrine of the one and the emphasis on Authority in the other. It might have been added that he could learn much from authors who exalted the function of the Church, and yet retain the conviction that Christ's presence should be sought most of all in solitude.[2] His early training set the bent of his mind away from all sacerdotal and authoritarian teaching, and the study of the Mystics in his later middle life confirmed this bent. As regards the *sacramental* teaching of

[1] Sir George Newman, K.C.B., M.D., in *The Friend*, January 21, 1921.
[2] *The Spiritual Life*, p. 196 f.

such writers as William Law, the question is more complex. Here, undoubtedly, Dr. Whyte was influenced, but chiefly in one specific way. For from this time he taught, following Behmen and Sir Thomas Browne not less than William Law,[1] that every common action of life, from first awakening till the day's end, might be made sacramental; and he often drove this lesson home with a daring and arresting simplicity, especially when he dealt with the everyday actions of washing and eating which form the basis of the Christian sacraments. As to the understanding of the Communion, his indebtedness is summed up in a sentence which is typical of his whole outlook:

> " For myself I may say that the two best books by far I have ever read on the Lord's Supper are that of our own Calvinistic and Presbyterian Robert Bruce and that of the Anglican and Behmenite William Law." [2]

So he verified in his broad experience the saying that " the saints do not contradict one another."

At almost the same time as the publication of the *Characteristics* of William Law, the first of Dr. Whyte's volumes of sermons issued from the press. Along with its successor, published a year later, it contained his Sunday evening addresses on the characters of the *Pilgrim's Progress*, and both speedily gained a very wide circulation. Thereafter, for more than twenty years, all his evening sermons in Free St. George's were printed in the *British Weekly*, and afterwards appeared in book form. He had waited long before committing his sermons to the press; but he reaped the reward that comes to the author who has long passed his apprentice years, and has gained full mastery of his craft. During the ten years covered by this chapter, his published works

---

[1] *Thirteen Appreciations*, pp. 60, 197, 216.

[2] *Op. cit.*, p. 229.   Cf. Dr. Whyte's eulogy of Robert Bruce's book in the *Appreciation of Bishop Andrewes* (*ibid.*, p. 83), and his final exhortation to a wide charity regarding the different ways of celebrating the Sacrament in *The Spiritual Life*, p. 247.

increased in number from one to sixteen. The first two volumes of *Bunyan Characters* were followed by *Samuel Rutherford and some of his Correspondents*, by a third volume of *Bunyan Characters* (on "the Municipal and Military Characters in the *Holy War*"), and by the five volumes of *Bible Characters*.[1] Parallel with the publication of these sermons ran that of the series of *Appreciations* already named; but both were equally prepared for audiences in Free St. George's—the former for the evening congregation, and the latter for the two Classes. Neither now nor later did Dr. Whyte write a single book for direct publication. During these years also he published his little book on *The Four Temperaments*, and preached in the morning the great series of sermons on Prayer which have been given to the world since his death.

The various books of this period drew out many reviews, some from beyond the Atlantic. Most were favourable, and many enthusiastic; but there were exceptions. The *National Observer*, under the title *Gentis Priscæ fortissime Ductor*, poured two columns of its most scathing wit and rhetoric on the heads of Samuel Rutherford and his interpreter, finding a crude exaggeration in their view of sin and accusing them of a morbid "coquetting with death."[2] It was not to be expected that a review edited by Mr. W. E. Henley would look with any favour on Dr. Whyte's elaboration of the maxim, "Forefancy your death-bed!" Indeed, the authorship of the following sentence may well be the same as that of the line, "My head is bloody, but unbowed,"—"No healthy man believes that he is going to die; when the inevitable sword falls upon him he bows his head with the best grace he can muster and says nothing about it." This debate, in truth, is no new one. Some thinkers have always held with Plato, as Dr.

---

[1] The concluding volume of either series (*Our Lord's Characters*, and *Bunyan Characters—Grace Abounding*) belong to the following decade.

[2] *The National Observer*, December 29, 1894.

Whyte did, that the truest wisdom consists in " a meditation of death " ; while others have echoed Spinoza's reply—" not of death, but of life." Yet all depends on the understanding of the mysterious words employed. If " Life " is more than the present life, then " Death " becomes its portal—*Mors Janua Vitæ*—and the " meditation of death " may become the intuition of a life beyond.

It was not through his published volumes alone that Dr. Whyte became the spiritual guide of many thousands who seldom or never heard his voice. Week by week during each winter and spring, the *British Weekly* took his sermon of the Sunday evening before into an increasing number of homes, not a few of which were almost as humble as that of his own boyhood. If his volumes on the Mystics made him known to scholars in churches far removed from his own, his evening addresses carried his message to readers who made no claim to scholarship but found in it the sustenance of which their souls stood in need. These sermons were to many the choicest part of the journal in which they appeared ; but, on the other hand, it carried them to innumerable places which they would not otherwise have reached, and Dr. Whyte gratefully acknowledged this in such letters to Sir William Robertson Nicoll as the following :

" *Monday Morning*.

" MY DEAR NICOLL,—This morning I have sent off my last *Bunyan* to your printers. I shall never be able to tell you what I owe you for taking me up into your unparalleled pulpit. Your influence is immense, and you have given me some share of it. God bless you and yours. You and Spender are my favourite editors.— Yours,   A. WHYTE."

So it came about that Dr. Whyte's writings had, by the end of the century, found a welcome in many different circles, outside Scotland as well as within, and not least in the English Free Churches. One friend, when visiting the scenes of John Bunyan's life in the district around Bedford, found a framed portrait of Dr. Whyte in a place of honour over the mantelpiece of a cottager there.   Another student of his writings in East Anglia, who never saw him but has for long treasured his portrait, tells how he often found inspiration and hope in them when the heavens seemed to be brass above him, " as though all Dr. Whyte did was mixed with prayer, which was answered while his books were read." And when, in 1921, his eldest son arrived in India to act as President of the Indian Legislative Assembly, he met a long succession of men, including leaders of Indian political life not themselves Christians, who spoke with grateful recognition of the interest and benefit that his father's books had brought to them.

"Two are better than one ; because they have a good reward for their labour."—The Preacher.

"A new Salvation demands a new Song."—St. Augustine, quoted by A. W.

During the early 'nineties, when Dr. Whyte's influence outside his own city was fast being extended by the books named in the preceding chapter, there was an ever-present preoccupation and anxiety nearer home. This was caused by the endeavour, for several years unsuccessful, to find a colleague who would share with him the constant burden of his work, and so save him, in Dr. Robert Mackintosh's words, from "grappling single-handed with duties which might have taxed to the utmost a pair of robust colleagues." By the year 1890 Dr. Whyte's own thoughts and hopes and those of the great majority of his congregation turned increasingly towards Aberdeen, whence had come striking reports of the way in which students and many other young men were gripped and held by the preaching of the Rev. George Adam Smith, then of Queen's Cross Free Church, and now Principal of Aberdeen University. Mr. Smith was still a young man, and had himself been connected with Free St. George's, where his father, Dr. George Smith, C.I.E., the author of many missionary biographies, was a greatly honoured elder. As a scholar, he stood in the direct succession to Professor Robertson Smith ; and his first volume, on *The Book of Isaiah*, had recently proved that his gifts as an author were not less outstanding than his power in the pulpit. For all these reasons, and for others more intimate, Dr. Whyte cherished the earnest hope that he might see his way to come to Free St. George's as junior colleague. At first there was some shaking of heads among the rigidly orthodox in the congregation. These men could not easily reconcile themselves to the prospect of having a minister who explicitly maintained that the latter portion of the Book of Isaiah dated from the period of the Exile. Such timidities, however, received no countenance from Dr. Whyte, since it was certain that the friend and defender of Robertson Smith would not disown the critical views of one who combined them with so ardently evangelical a message. The congregation then proceeded to a call, and in January 1891 a strong deputation went to prosecute it before the Presbytery of Aberdeen. The leading statement in favour of the call was made by Principal Rainy, who represented the Presbytery of Edinburgh ; and several of the Kirk-Session of Free St. George's, including Dr. Taylor Innes and Professor J. P. Wood, gave support from the congregation. Mr. Smith's statement showed how the difficulty of the situation weighed upon him, but left no doubt that, strongly as he felt the claims of Free St. George's and the attraction of a call to work beside Dr. Whyte, he felt the call of the young men who had gathered round him in Queen's Cross more strongly still. Since this was his deliberate judgment, the Presbytery naturally supported him in it.

The decision was no small disappointment to Dr. Whyte ; but it cast no cloud on his friendship for the young preacher, nor did it diminish the appreciation with which he followed Dr. Smith's subsequent work as an interpreter of the Old Testament by voice and pen from the Chair of Old Testament Exegesis in the Glasgow Free Church College. The next step taken was to approach the Rev. Alexander Martin, then minister of Morningside Free Church, Edinburgh, and now Dr. Whyte's successor in the principalship of New College ; but the congregation received no encouragement to proceed in that direction. So, early in 1892, they began

to look to the West, where the Rev. Hugh Black
was rapidly drawing together a large and attached
congregation in the newly founded Sherwood Free
Church, Paisley. Again Dr. Whyte's trusted and
tireless friends, Dr. Taylor Innes and Dr. Sutherland
Black, did important service in opening the way for
a new call. It was taken up with great heartiness,
and signed by 901 communicants of Free St. George's.
Early in May the matter was ripe for discussion in
the Presbytery of Paisley, where proceedings bore a
strong likeness to those in Aberdeen fifteen months
before. Here also the young minister left himself
in the hands of the Presbytery, while indicating his
own sense of duty to his first charge ; indeed, in
this case the argument against transference was
unusually strong, since Mr. Black had not yet completed his first year of work in Sherwood. On the
other hand, Dr. Joseph Bell, who spoke not only
as a leading elder of Free St. George's, but as Dr.
Whyte's physician and intimate friend, said, " with
a very distinct sense of responsibility," that the
high pressure at which his minister had been working
could not go on. When the Presbytery unanimously
declined to place the call in Mr. Black's hands, its
promoters took the unusual step of intimating an
appeal to the General Assembly.

The days that followed were full of anxiety for
Dr. Whyte, but, now as always, he found relief in
hard reading. A letter regarding the prospective
decision of the Assembly, addressed to Dr. Sutherland
Black, ends with a reference to the author of *The
Fable of the Bees,* whose ethical scepticism lay in the
historical line of approach to the writings of Law
and Butler : " How are matters looking ? I am more
taken up almost with Mandeville than with aught
else. What a powerful writer he is of his kind."

The motion in the General Assembly, that the
decision of the Presbytery of Paisley should be
reversed and that Mr. Black should be translated
to Free St. George's, came up for discussion on
23rd May 1892. It was proposed and seconded by

two of Dr. Whyte's most loyal friends, Dr. T. M. Lindsay and Mr. Charles Guthrie; but their arguments did not convince the House, which endorsed the Presbytery's action by a large majority. As soon as the decision was reached, Principal Rainy sent from the Assembly Hall a brief expression of sympathy to Dr. Whyte. A longer letter which followed next day shows conclusively how real was the anxiety then felt by his friends lest his health should give way under the prolonged strain of his sole pastorate :

> " 23 Douglas Crescent,
> Edinburgh, *Sabbath*.

" Dear Whyte,—Yesterday I tried to write to you, but amid great interruption, and I had to break off in a hurry. I cannot have adequately told you how much thought and talk about you there has been, and how wistful and earnest. Many feel that you are called to carry a very heavy burden of anxiety, and that it does not look like early removal of it.

" Yet I have a strong impression that we shall see sooner or later some good reason for the turn things have providentially taken. But whether that be so or not, at least I hope that you will not feel tempted to take the burden more heavily than it needs, or to dream of submitting to increased strain during the further period of waiting. Rather, I should say, if you could at all bring your mind to it, you should ask the Presbytery for a long leave and go off resolutely for a long leisure. That would do more to impress the imagination of the Church with the idea that the ' need be ' is serious and pressing than any other course ; it would rather rally than injure the congregation, for it would put them on their mettle : and if you have further work to do, as we all believe and count upon it, in aiding the Church and the good cause through St. George's, you will come back to it with a stronger heart and a fresher head.

" In any case be cheered. *Reparabit cornua Phœbe.*[1] Or, which is a more religious way of it, He will turn the shadow of death into the morning. The things that try us most are experiences which are the most indispensable of all for us. There is more love in them, and more sympathetic care and thought for us, than in any others. We simply can't do without them. And the good they lead to shall be seen yet — not believed merely — in the land of the living. . . .— Yours ever affectionately,

" ROBERT RAINY."

The advice thus thoughtfully given did not commend itself to Dr. Whyte. We saw in the last chapter that he took his usual vacation in the summer of 1892—and made an even more than usually strenuous and fruitful use of it. Yet there was one clear gain from these events. They laid the foundation of his friendship with Mr. Hugh Black, and he lost no time in cementing it by sending his new friend two theological books, one being a volume of Wendt's *Teaching of Jesus*, then fresh from the press. Early in July, Mr. Black paid a short visit to Dr. and Mrs. Whyte at Bonskeid : and this was repeated in Arran at Easter two years later. At the latter meeting Dr. Whyte reopened the question of Free St. George's, but found that the work in Paisley had lost none of its hold on Mr. Black's allegiance. After he left, Dr. Whyte disburdened his heart to Dr. Sutherland Black, then resident in Cambridge, in these words :

" You may believe that this has not left me in the best of spirits this afternoon, and I wish you had been here for a long walk. I often and greatly miss you : and miss you this afternoon, with the future so dark before me."

Two years later, Dr. Whyte and his people reached the turning of this long lane, and the happy con-

[1] " Phœbe will replenish her horns of plenty."

clusion of their seven years' quest for a colleague.
Mr. Black was again called. This time he felt
free to leave his first charge, and he came among
them in the freshness of his youthful power, for
he was still under thirty. Early in February 1896
he was inducted as junior minister of Free St.
George's.

In many ways the period that followed was a
singularly happy one for Dr. Whyte. His children
were beginning to grow up around him and to share
his interests. He had recently entered upon two of
the largest and most congenial enterprises of his long
ministry, each of which occupied six years—the
course of evening sermons on *Bible Characters*, and
the study of *The Great Autobiographies* in his Classes.
His work in Free St. George's was now shared by a
colleague whose gifts as a preacher made an instant
and widespread impression ; and so a larger portion
of his own energy than heretofore was set free for
the wider work of the Church, especially for the
duties which fell to him in his year of office as
Moderator. But the best feature of this new order,
for which he had waited so long, was his relation
to his successive associates in the ministry. This
cannot be better described than in the words of
Dr. Kelman's memorial address :

" We would have laid down our lives for him,
Hugh Black and I. The only difference we ever
had with him was that by all sorts of subtle
ways he thrust us forward into any prominent
or desirable position which he himself was expected to take, and we had to watch him for this,
and circumvent his too great generosity. . . .
In the vestry, after one had preached, he
almost always had some kind thing to say,
and in the strength of a couple of sentences we
went out into the street taller and more erect
and feeling that life was worth living, when a
man like him should speak that way to one
of us."

During the months from October to May the arrangement commonly followed was that the colleagues took morning and evening service alternately, while Dr. Whyte's Classes on Wednesday and on Sunday evening remained in his own hands. Thus, on every second Sunday evening, his Young Men's Class immediately followed a service conducted by his junior colleague. On one such occasion, not long after Mr. Black came to Edinburgh he had preached an impressive sermon to a great congregation, and Dr. Whyte opened his Class with words which ran somewhat as follows :

> " After such a discourse as we have just heard, many of us would rather go home and think over what we have heard in the quiet of our own rooms. But I suppose that is impossible, and that we must just go on with the business of the Class in the usual way."

When Mr. Black was called to Free St. George's, there were those who said that the thoroughly modern outlook and method of the younger man would never harmonise with Dr. Whyte's stern and searching analysis of the dark places of the human heart. Never was an apprehension more signally disproved. The two messages did not coalesce : they could and did prove complementary. No man recognised this more clearly than Dr. Whyte himself, as appears from an incident recorded by Dr. Kelman :

> " I remember well on one occasion, under the sense that my own preaching had been of recent Sundays rather far removed from his region, trying to speak through an afternoon service in his own vein. All that he said to me afterward in the vestry was :
> " ' Deliver your own message.' "

We have seen how gratefully Dr. Whyte looked back upon the consideration and encouragement which he had received from Dr. Roxburgh and

Dr. Candlish. All this he now lavished in his turn upon his own junior colleagues. But there was this difference—that his early experience of colleague-ship lasted seven years, while his association with Mr. Black and Dr. Kelman extended happily to a period just three times as long. It is sometimes said that colleagueships, like partnerships in another sphere of action, are the mother of strife. Dr. Whyte showed during more than half of his long ministry that they may bring forth the most effective co-operation and the most gracious goodwill.

The years during which the quest of a colleague proceeded towards its long-delayed but satisfactory ending were also years of wider contact with other forms of Christian life and thought. Especially was this true of the year 1894. In February, General Booth was again a guest at 7 Charlotte Square, and on this visit he brought with him a unique per-sonality who became for several succeeding years a greatly beloved member of the circle there. Prince Nicholas Galitzin, who had come to Great Britain to study the social work of the Salvation Army, was a voluntary exile from his home in South Russia. He was only distantly related to the conservative Russian statesman of the same name ; but he had the ear of the Government sufficiently to be allowed to cross Siberia in the year 1897, organising committees of medical and other relief at each main centre where the exiles rested on their eastward journey before the railway was built. His emaciated figure, long beard, and intense expression at once arrested the attention ; he had lost his right arm, and he walked with more than a scholar's stoop, yet he could endure great fatigue in case of need. Still under fifty years of age, he already looked an old man—at least in the eyes of Dr. Whyte's children and their cousins, to whom his unpractical ways, his eccentric English, and his quaint generosity made him an intensely attractive figure. Prince Galitzin lived often during the next two years in rooms at

20 Charlotte Square, Edinburgh, and his friendship gave Dr. Whyte a new insight into the spiritual problems of modern Russia and the spiritual possibilities latent in the Orthodox communions of the East, while the mystical strain in his own religious outlook harmonised with Dr. Whyte's dominant interest at the time. He possessed the deep religious faith for which his countrymen have so notable a capacity ; and his detachment from the ties of ordinary life was, perhaps, also a typically Russian trait. These two aspects of his character are reflected in the words which he wrote in the visitors' book after his first two visits to Dr. and Mrs. Whyte : " All things are accomplished by God " ; " I was a stranger and ye took me in."

During the following summer the Whytes were at Aviemore, where on one memorable Sunday Dr. M'Laren of Manchester preached to a little congregation which included Dr. Martineau and Dr. Whyte. Here Prince Galitzin suddenly appeared again—in his comings and goings he was hardly less wraithlike than Shelley in Trelawny's description. Professor Drummond was also a guest, and they began to discuss the prospect of a new religious movement in the universities and among the *intelligentsia* of Russia. The talk, of which Dr. and Mrs. Whyte were deeply sympathetic hearers, on one occasion lasted till long after midnight. But the mission to Russian students which Prince Galitzin urged Drummond to undertake never became possible for him—the first warnings of his long illness were already arousing the anxiety of his friends—though it was carried through by his successors in the World Student Christian Movement after he himself had passed away.

In July 1894, Dr. and Mrs. Whyte carried out the most memorable of their pilgrimages together. Its chief objective was Bayreuth, but Dr. Whyte's heart was also set on visiting the homes of Thomas à Kempis and Jacob Behmen. The latter (Görlitz, in distant Silesia) proved too far off, and his ambition to see the home of the inspired shoemaker, whose craft he himself had shared in youth, remained unfulfilled. Much thought was spent both on forming a party for the journey, and on mental preparation, especially in the study of the *Parsifal* legend. Dr. Whyte wrote at this time to Miss Innes :

> " I think it is a pity that you should be so near Bayreuth and not hear and see *Parsifal*. I am not able to speak yet at first hand, but the *Parsifal literature* has moved me much. I shall send you something to read on the subject to-morrow."

A large group of friends left Edinburgh on July 13, but on reaching Holland they divided; and a select party of four—Dr. and Mrs. Whyte, Mrs. Traquair, and Dr. Sutherland Black—turned aside to the seldom visited town of Zwolle. Not far off, by the eastern shore of the Zuider Zee, lie Kempen, from which Thomas gained the name by which he is familiarly known, and the monastery of Mount St. Agnes, where his outwardly uneventful life was passed. In the quiet of this secluded place a Sunday was spent rich in memories of the author of the *Imitation*. Mrs. Whyte asked her companions each to set down an impression on the fly-leaf of her copy, and they wrote as follows :

> " *Cogitavi dies antiquos, et annos eternos in mente habui.*—J. S. B." (I meditated on ancient days, and had in mind the years of the Eternal.)
> " *Ama nesceri.*—A. W." (Love to be unknown.)
> " The peace of God which passeth all knowledge.—P. A. T." (Phœbe Anna Traquair.)
> " Agnetenberg, Zwolle, where Thomas lived for 64 years, and departed in peace, 1471."

A long day's travel to Bingen, followed by a day amid the noble battlements and churches of Nürnberg, brought the travellers, who now numbered

eleven, to the goal of their journey.[1]   Their lodgings
were on the outskirts of the little Bavarian town,
and the doors opened upon sunlit fields.   *Parsifal*
was heard on Friday, July 20, and again on the
following Monday, and *Lohengrin* on Saturday.   Dr.
Whyte was, now as ever, deep in the literature of
the subject, and eager to penetrate to the inmost
meaning of Wagner's mystical play.   The surroundings of the *Festhaus*, where all was directed and inspired by Wagner's widow, the daughter of Liszt; the
serious intention of singers and audience ; the sense
that the performance was the chief event of a day,
and not a mere evening's recreation, and that the
theatre was also a temple ; the absence of applause—
all these, as well as the artistic quality of the rendering
of both operas, impressed the party deeply.   Dr. Black
wrote after the first performance of *Parsifal* to his
mother, who had accompanied him on an earlier visit
to Bayreuth : " Dr. Whyte was much struck, especially with the sacramental scene at the end of the first
act.   For myself, the whole of the third act assumed
deeper meanings than I had ever seen before."

Dr. Whyte's love for *Parsifal*, as a great musical
interpretation of the drama of redemption and of the
process of purification by suffering in the human
soul, remained as a permanent enrichment of his life.
Three years after this visit to Bayreuth, a pipe-organ
was installed in Free St. George's, and Mr. (now Dr.)
Alfred Hollins, the well-known blind organist and
composer, came as leader of praise.   At a recital soon
after his arrival in Edinburgh, he played the Prelude to
Parsifal ; and from that time onward the Prelude was
played as the opening voluntary on every Communion
Sunday morning—a choice which had Dr. Whyte's
warm approval.

The introduction of instrumental music marked
an epoch in the worship of Free St. George's ; but

[1] The other members of the party were Miss Charlotte Rainy (the
translator of extracts from Behmen's works); Dr. and Mrs. A. H. F.
Barbour ; Miss Brown ; Dr. and Mrs. Carnegie Simpson ; and Dr.
J. C. Webster (a close friend during these years—afterwards Professor
of Gynecology in Montreal and Chicago).

it made no change in the close relation of friendship
between Dr. Whyte and the leader of the congregational praise—unless to intensify its warmth. During
the years between 1870 and 1897 two precentors held
office—Walter Strang, who had been Dr. Candlish's
loyal friend and fellow-worker, and Walter Hately.
When Mr. Hately died, some years after his precentor-
ship had come to an end, Dr. Whyte thus spoke of
his character and work :

> " He was a scholarly, a cultivated, and a
> refined Christian gentleman, full of Christian
> humility, Christian meekness, Christian rever-
> ence, and Christian sweetness of mind and heart.
> For myself, I have lost a true and a helpful
> friend in Mr. Hately's removal. When he was
> the leader of our praise, I always felt on the
> Sabbath morning that I had a true fellow-
> worshipper alongside of me. Full of interest in
> his holy art, he was still more full of the worship
> of God within the art."

How this relation was maintained in the new
form demanded by the changing musical standards of
a later time may best be told in Mr. Hollins' words :

> " I am frequently asked if Dr. Whyte was
> musical. If by that one means a musical ear
> and a technical knowledge of music, I would
> say no, for he had neither ; but this lack was
> more than compensated for by his keen interest,
> especially in music as related to sacred words.
> When he heard that Sir Edward Elgar had set
> one of his favourite poems — *The Dream of
> Gerontius*—to music, he insisted that we should
> go to the 1902 Sheffield Festival together. So
> much impressed was he with that wonderful
> work, that he arranged for me to hear it again
> with him at Westminster Cathedral : a circum-
> stance which showed me afresh his great-hearted-
> ness and wide sympathy. When the organ in
> St. George's was opened, he preached from the

text—' Singing and making melody in your hearts to the Lord.' In the course of his sermon he said that as far as he personally was concerned, he would have been quite content to have gone on worshipping *without* the aid of an instrument, for it was not so much the *music* he thought about, as the *words*. His interest in musical matters, however, increased during the years of my most happy association with him.

" Dr. Whyte's method of choosing the Praise differed from that generally adopted. His choice showed enormous care, the dominant idea being to make the entire preliminary portion of the service centre round his sermon, to impress it the more vividly on the congregation. On one occasion, his subject was ' Meditation,' and having seen a piece of mine on a recital pro-gramme called *Meditation*, he asked me to play it during the service—*not* as a voluntary, but a special item, previously announcing that I would now *play* a Meditation. I have known him choose a hymn because the text preceding it had a bearing on the sermon : and a favourite device was to read a psalm or scripture passage, then have it sung either as a Metrical Psalm or Paraphrase. In most cases this system might, I think, lead to monotony, but in Dr. Whyte's hands it hardly ever did ; and the more I became accustomed to it, the more I felt how thoroughly it harmonised with his particular style of preaching. He was very regular and methodical in preparation for the service, and his praise-list never failed to reach me in good time for the Friday choir-practice. I never had a praise-list from Dr. Whyte which was not written in the form of a letter : ' Dear Fellow-Servant,' ' Dear Colleague,' or ' Dear Leader, Help me to interpret this text with the following Praise.'

" I greatly enjoyed and always looked for-ward to the quiet quarter of an hour in the vestry with him before service. I always thought he had a beautiful hand, and though he rarely shook hands, he always had a kindly greeting: ' Come away in to the fire, sir; I knew your knock. Many people have their own characteristic knocks.' He seldom sat before going into the pulpit, but would walk up and down, occasionally stopping in front of the table to verify or jot down something which had occurred to him. He would draw up the big easy-chair in front of the fire for me, and keep me to the last minute, especially on cold days, saying, ' Now be sure your feet are warm before you go in.' Often he would talk books to me, or ask about musical matters : at other times, he seemed much occupied with the coming service, and spoke very little, yet even then one felt the restfulness and quiet dignity of his presence."

How rapid was the growth of this friendship on Dr. Whyte's side as well as on that of Mr. Hollins is shown by a note written in October 1898, the month in which the *Church Hymnary* was published.

" Will you accept an interleaved copy of the *Hymnary*, as a small mark of my thankfulness that we have you for our organist, and also as a token of my great regard for you ? I find my interleaved Bible to be simply invaluable : and I hope your interleaved *Hymnary* may be of some like use to you. I use my Bible for all kinds of notes and memoranda useful for illustrating the text, and you may find this volume of the same use in your department."

A post card from Bonskeid at a later time shows how ready Dr. Whyte was to share with others the benefit of Mr. Hollins' musical gifts : " Yes : go to your friends. We would be dogs in the manger to grudge you to those who need and desire you."

Dr. Whyte's interest in hymnology was keen and

constant, and Julian's work on that subject was seldom far from his hand. On one occasion an office-bearer in St. George's (the son of his old friend, Mr. M'Kenzie of Alrick) wrote to ask his opinion on the authorship of " O God of Bethel " ; and he replied :

" No end of disputes have arisen around Logan's name. You will see in the well-studied volume I send you what I believe to have been the facts about the Second Paraphrase. Dr. Julian, our greatest authority, sets the Paraphrase down to Doddridge, while he shows that Logan and others had made variations on it. If you care to see Julian I can send the volume to you."

On one matter in the conduct of Church worship he expressed himself with almost startling vehemence in a letter to Sir William Robertson Nicoll. Referring to those ministers who remain seated in the pulpit while the congregation sing, he quoted with approval the saying of Sir J. M. Barrie that " they seemed to think that the people stood up to sing praise to *them* " ; and then added : " Quote that again, and rub it in, till this bad habit is banished from every pulpit. What a power for every kind of good you have ! "

Perhaps in this regard he hardly took account of the more limited physical strength of some of his brethren in the ministry ; but none could deny that he practised his own injunction most strictly. So strong was his desire for a pervading unity throughout every service that he would never delegate even the reading of the lessons when he was himself the preacher. Even when he was over eighty years of age, he continued to conduct the whole service, which sometimes exceeded an hour and a half in length, and to stand throughout, save for the few minutes while a voluntary was played during the taking of the offertory. For him, the preaching of the Evangel —to use the old Scots phrase—was the centre of all the worship of the Church; but he never forgot, as his countrymen have at times been apt to do, that there can be no worthy service without fore-thought and reverence in every part.

During these years, Dr. and Mrs. Whyte shared in the deep anxiety of many friends, as they were slowly forced to recognise how serious was the painful illness which shadowed the last two years of Henry Drummond's radiant life. By the summer of 1894, as we have seen, there were indications of the oncoming of that illness. Drummond then sought refreshment at his old fishing-ground in Sutherland, and sent a humorous reply to the invitation which reached him to join the Bayreuth party, with a half-veiled reference to his last book, *The Ascent of Man,* which had appeared that spring :

> " The Savage has prevailed.   There are other reasons, but the main one is that I am only a half-evolved being.   It is sad to give up so much good fellowship, for there is enough beyond the Savage to make me know what I am losing— and this shall be my punishment."

By the end of the following year the full gravity of the illness had become apparent, and at Christmas Dr. Whyte wrote to Dr. Barbour, who was with his friend at Tunbridge Wells :

> " Say to Drummond that it is worth all his suffering to have so much tender and prayerful love poured out upon him.   Tell him that he cannot know how much his illness has endeared him to multitudes I meet.   ' It was good for me to be afflicted,' said David.   God bless Drummond, and you all."

Two years later, towards the end of the year in which Henry Drummond died, Dr. Whyte wrote to Mrs. Robert Barbour :

> " Thank you, Very Dear and True Charlotte, for your beautiful letter.   Yes : though it is

neither in as many words in Scripture nor in the Catholic Creed—I believe that they see and love all that is good in their dear ones on earth. Be sure the General Assembly and Church of the First-born in Heaven are not denied the news of what goes on in the Church of Christ on earth. At any rate, I am to believe it.—Your rich brother,   A. W."

1898–1899

" Blessings be with ye, both now and aye,
 Dear human creatures ;
Yours is the love that no gold can buy,
 Nor Time can wither.
Peace be to thee and thy children, O Skye,
 Dearest of islands ! "

         ALEXANDER NICOLSON.

By the end of the year 1895 Dr. Whyte had completed twenty-five years of his ministry in Free St.
George's ; and during the following year the congregation decided to mark their regard for his character
and appreciation of his work among them by giving
him a presentation of considerable value. A portrait
was first suggested ;[1] but the use to which he finally
put the fruit of their generosity may best be gathered
from a letter which was received a few months later
by the students of divinity in the Free Church.

" 7 CHARLOTTE SQUARE, EDINBURGH,
March 25, 1897.

" *To the Theological Students of the*
 Free Church Colleges of Edinburgh,
  Glasgow, and Aberdeen.

  " GENTLEMEN,—Last year, on the occasion
of my Semi-jubilee as their minister, my large-
hearted people raised a sum of money which, at
my special request, has been devoted to the
founding of a Theological Literature Prize in
our Three Colleges. My object in this foundation is to do what in me lies to promote among
our students and young Ministers the study of

[1] The gift of a portrait followed three years later, as has already been
stated, p. 347 f. above.

the great authors in Theology and in Practical Religion. Augustine naturally heads the succession of the authors which I hope will be taken up as time goes on : Luther, Calvin, Knox, Rutherford, Hooker, Taylor, Goodwin, Owen, Howe, Baxter, Bunyan, Butler, Pascal, Leighton, Edwards, Law. How great are the sources of lifelong interest, edification, and every kind of benefit that lie open to us, and through us to our people, in the works of these great masters of our Divine Science ! And it is my prayer, Gentlemen, in putting this message into your hands, that our foundation may be accepted and owned of God to accomplish in some measure the great ends for which it has been set up.— With the greatest regard and love,

"ALEXANDER WHYTE."

The "Alexander Whyte Theological Literature Prize" has continued to be given to students, or to those who have recently been students, in the three colleges during the twenty-five years that have passed since it was instituted ; and in the main the subjects prescribed for essays have been those suggested by Dr. Whyte at the outset. It gave him great satisfaction that the first successful essay—an elaborate study of the works of Augustine—was written by his friend and former assistant, the Rev. A. B. Macaulay.

But this has already carried us beyond 1898, the year in which Dr. Whyte was called to the Moderator's chair of his Church. In the Presbyterian Churches of Scotland, the Moderator holds office for a year, and his primary duty is to preside over the deliberations of the General Assembly, meeting in Edinburgh during the last ten days of May. May 19, 1898, the day on which Dr. Whyte's moderatorship began, was one of those days of brilliant sunshine and clear air which sometimes visit the old city in early summer, and flood its grey buildings and wide green spaces with light and colour. On the opening day of the General Assemblies, Princes Street is always gay with

flags in preparation for the coming of the Lord High
Commissioner, His Majesty's representative to the
Assembly of the Church of Scotland. But on this
occasion the flags waved at half-mast, and the
brilliance of the outward scene contrasted with the
sorrow of those who made their way to hear Dr.
Whyte's opening address to the Fathers and Brethren
of the Free Church; for early that morning Mr.
Gladstone had passed away, and the city with
which he had been so closely associated was plunged
in mourning. Of the many tributes which were
paid during the following days to Mr. Gladstone's
character as a Christian statesman, there can have
been none nobler than that which Dr. Whyte gave at
the close of his address that morning, and which will
be found in Appendix III. It must have been
written in the first hour after the news of Mr. Gladstone's death arrived, and it reflected the keen
emotion of that hour. Many still remember the
reverent hush that passed over the crowded hall as
Dr. Whyte repeated in tones tense and vibrant with
feeling the familiar words from *Samson Agonistes*,
beginning, " Nothing is here for tears." These
formed the opening of his tribute, and the closing
passage was yet more impressive, as he repeated
Dante's lines regarding the unembodied Light of the
supreme Heaven :

> " Light intellectual, replete with love,
> Love of true happiness, replete with joy,
> Joy that transcends all sweetness of delight ; "

and added :

> " With these heavenly words, out of his own
> ' Paradise,' Dante must surely have been sent to
> meet and welcome Gladstone at the gate of THE
> CITY this glorious morning ! "

The Assembly was still in session when Mr. Gladstone's body was laid in its last resting-place ; and
at the hour of his funeral, a Memorial Service was
held in the Free High Church, close to the Assembly
Hall. Dr. Whyte presided, and led the devotion of

the congregation in a prayer as solemn and moving as his tribute a few days before.

Reference was made in an earlier chapter to Dr. Whyte's opening address. Striking as it was in substance, it hardly ranked as one of the signal triumphs of his oratory ; for it was closely read, and at some points indistinctly heard, and he obviously spoke under a sense of unusual strain. But the fact that so practised a speaker should have felt this strain only confirmed the evidence of the singular humility which appeared in the first words which he spoke, before addressing the members of the Assembly :

" Whence is this to me ? And who am I, O Lord God, that thou hast brought me hitherto ? Is this the manner of man, O Lord God ? Who is a God like unto Thee ? " [1]

Such was the spirit in which Dr. Whyte took his place in a chair on which—according to the general judgment of others — he conferred a distinction at least as great as that which he received.

In addition to his more serious duties at the opening and close of the Assembly, the Moderator is called on to express, at different points in the proceedings, the greetings and goodwill of his Church to representatives of other evangelical churches at home, in the Dominions, or in foreign lands. The tact and delicacy of Dr. Whyte's mind, and his occasional flashes of kindly humour, came out clearly in these short addresses of greeting. A reference to his Dante studies by a deputy from the Evangelical Church of Italy awakened an especially warm response, and prompted him to speak of " the treasure-house of truth and beauty " which the Italians possess in " that great master of the human mind," and of the source of hope which the works of Dante afford for the future religious life of his land.

Several passing incidents of the Assembly renewed links with the Moderator's early and struggling

[1] 2 Sam. vii. 18, 19 ; Mic. vii. 18.

years. His friend, Dr. Salmond, was appointed Principal of the Free Church College in Aberdeen, and Dr. Whyte, in welcoming him to his new office, told what their early association, and especially the Saturday evening prayer-meetings during the days of revival, had meant to his own spiritual life. Then, in more playful vein, he told how they had fought out the Mansel-Maurice controversy over again in the student arena. Another reunion took place at one of the large breakfasts, at which in pre-war days the Moderator entertained the ministers and elders who had come from all parts of Scotland. The " Moderator's breakfasts " of the Free Church were held in the Music Hall in George Street, and before those present adjourned to the Assembly three or four of the guests were asked to make short speeches. One morning Dr. Whyte announced that he was about to introduce a guest, whose presence—if it had been known beforehand—would, he said, have brought the citizens of Edinburgh out in queues stretching far along George Street ! He turned to his right, and called on " the father of J. M. Barrie " to speak. Mr. David Barrie rose and, in a few sentences, told how, forty years before, he had accompanied to the station on their first journey to Aberdeen " the three Alecs," one of whom now sat in the Moderator's chair.

Another old Kirriemuir friend, John Dickson, of whom we last heard when he visited Whyte's lodgings in Aberdeen in '61, was also borne in mind, though he could not be persuaded to come to Edinburgh. The following note was sent to him two days before the Assembly began :

" DEAR JOHN,—I was just about to send you your ticket for Thursday when your telegram came in. It disappointed me much. I had been planning how to have an hour alone with you amid the multitudinous engagements of Thursday : but your wire upset all that. Be good enough to tell me what of my little books you

27

have : and I will fill up your set at this time. Write soon. I cannot tell you how much I would have liked to see your dear old face on Thursday.—God bless you, dear Jack.

"A. WHYTE."

John Dickson had never followed his friend into a professional or learned career, but he always remained a great reader ; and in these later years Dr. Whyte not only supplied him with Marshall and Behmen, Father John and the *Dream of Gerontius*, but sought for his judgment as one versed in the deep subjects of which they treat—and also as a judge of good preaching. When he heard some years later that his old comrade in angling and in the study of " experimental religion " was about to apply for the post of caretaker of a Y.M.C.A. Institute, he wrote in these terms :

"DEAR OLD FRIEND,—There is nothing I would like so much as to see you settled in some such office as that. Your knowledge of books : your love of everything that is noble and true : your love for young men : your loyalty to truth and to the Church of Christ—these, and many other gifts, and graces, and experiences of yours, to my mind eminently and conspicuously fit you for such an office as this.—Your lifelong friend, ALEXANDER WHYTE."

A Moderator's duties are many, and Dr. Whyte in particular was called on to address audiences of the most various size and outlook. Two records remain of addresses delivered during July 1898. In the latter part of the month, the British Medical Association held its annual meeting in Edinburgh ; and the fame both of the city and of its Medical School drew together a very large gathering of doctors and scientists from both sides of the Channel and of the Atlantic. A service was held in St. Giles' Cathedral during the meeting of the Congress to which its members were invited, and the office of preaching to this notable congregation in the old cathedral was laid upon Dr. Whyte. For this occasion he prepared his Appreciation of Sir Thomas Browne, feeling that no religious subject would more readily appeal to a great concourse of doctors than a study of the physician whose learning and piety were only equalled by the glamour of his style. Yet, congenial as the subject was to the speaker, there were those who questioned whether he had rightly gauged the main interest of his audience, for he sometimes drew upon his literary knowledge when he might well have spoken direct out of his searching experience of human life. On this occasion one of his most loyal friends exclaimed, " If only he had told them what a doctor may be and may do ! " Yet *Sir Thomas Browne* remains as one of his most interesting and most finished Appreciations.

The other address was given in very different surroundings. Dr. Whyte went for a few hours to Lochearnhead to open a sale for the Free Church congregation there ; and the audience so completely overflowed the little schoolhouse that they were glad to adjourn to the hillside before he spoke. In the quiet afternoon sunshine, with the loch to the eastward and the Braes of Balquhidder behind, he talked familiarly of the holidays which he had spent there a quarter of a century before—of the kindness of the people and the abundance of the trout—but refrained from giving the numbers that he and his friends had caught, lest they should think he was casting a fisher's long line ! Then he spoke of the services in the hotel close by, of which we have heard in an earlier chapter ; and, coming to the actual situation of the Church, enlarged on a theme which lay very near his heart, the approaching Union of the Free and United Presbyterian Churches. Looking to a larger Union beyond, he foretold that in thirty years these Churches would form part of a reunited Presbyterian Church in Scotland ; for. he said :

" ' The things which divide are temporal, ephemeral, passing—fast passing—away ; the things that unite are eternal.' Then, ' not in my own name, nor even in the name of the General Assembly, but in the name of the Lord Jesus Christ, the Redeemer of His Church, do I declare this sale open.' Then he beautifully added, ' May it be acceptable to Him who saw the widow's mite, so that her name is remembered with His.' " [1]

It was in such. Highland scenes, and still more among the scattered crofting townships of the far North and West, that the most striking work of Dr. Whyte's moderatorship was accomplished. His generous friends, Mr. and Mrs. Peter Mackinnon of Ronachan, hearing of the widespread desire that he should visit the churches of the Hebrides, lent their steam yacht, the *Oriental*, for the purpose, and so made possible a pastoral journey which could hardly have been accomplished by the slow and difficult means of transit which the West Coast commonly affords. On successive Sundays during August 1898, Dr. Whyte preached at Tain, Dingwall, and the great fishing-stations of Fraserburgh and Peterhead. At Stornoway on Sunday, the 28th, the mission to the Outer Islands began with a Communion gathering, to which men and women had walked great distances. The most striking of the three services at which Dr. Whyte preached was the Gaelic Communion, held in the open air, when an audience, many of whom had little knowledge of English, hung upon his words. This sermon struck the keynote of much of his preaching during these weeks ; and one of his colleagues described how, as the preacher spoke of " the Church of the First-born " :

"Their life-story became our own. That ' the greatest of all tribulation is indwelling

[1] From an account by Rev. Dr. Burford Hooke, of the English Congregational Union.

sin ' was assented to by visible and audible signs on the part of the rapt listeners ; but as we were asked, ' What better use could God put the believer's indwelling sin to than to use it for his sanctification ? ', I could see a half-startled reaching - forward of souls looking through watery eyes to lay hold of and treasure up a note which will, doubtless, henceforth, enrich the religious thought of the island."

Two busy days followed in Stornoway. The post-Communion Service of Thanksgiving was followed by a conference with ministers and church workers from the different parts of Lewis ; and in this and other private conferences Dr. Whyte was brought into very close touch with the difficulties of men and women labouring for the spiritual—and in some degree for the physical — welfare of the dwellers in remote and outwardly inhospitable townships. It may well have been that his sympathy and wise counsel in these smaller gatherings did even more than his public addresses to hearten such lonely workers, and through them the people for whom they worked. Nor was education forgotten. Dr. Whyte was present at the opening of the new Secondary School at Stornoway—the Nicolson Institute, which has probably sent a larger number of students to the universities in recent years than any other Scottish school serving so small an area. His address to teachers and scholars " electrified " his hearers, as did a lecture the following evening to a crowded gathering on " Bunyan and the Religious Use of the Imagination." He found time, too, to present prizes under his own " Welfare of Youth Scheme " at Garrabost, when he found one of the prize-winners, who had gained over ninety per cent. in the paper on the " Shorter Catechism," was a bare-legged and bare-headed boy of twelve.

On Tuesday evening the party rowed out to the *Oriental*, where the Rev. D. F. Mackenzie acted as their host in Mr. and Mrs. Mackinnon's absence, and also as courier, guide, and (on occasion) coxswain. Two other Gaelic-speaking ministers, the Rev. John Mackay and the Rev. Alexander Lee, also formed part of the company; and Dr. Whyte's three "curates," as they called themselves, supplemented his sermons in English by speaking and preaching in "the other language." Mrs. Whyte and the four eldest children made up the party at this stage, and at the end of the week it was joined by the Rev. John A. Duke and the present writer. Neither the strenuous work of its older members, who visited fifteen congregations and delivered seventy addresses in ten days, nor the boisterousness of the Hebridean weather, could damp the cheerfulness of the company. Dr. Whyte's achievements during these days were all the more remarkable that he was one of the worst of sailors. This had been shown three years before, when, after crossing to Norway, he cabled home, "Rev. 21. 1, last clause"; and the recipient of the telegram, on looking up the reference, found the words, "And there was no more sea!"

The first day of the *Oriental's* cruise was devoted to Harris. Nowhere else in Great Britain can the attempt be witnessed to raise crops on such small and shallow strips of soil. Even with the combined resources of fishing, weaving, and such agriculture as is possible among the rocks, the people are very poor; and this is especially true of the population, then about six hundred, of the little island of Scalpay, in East Loch Tarbert, which was first visited. They had almost all crowded into their primitive meeting-house to welcome the Moderator. They followed with intense delight his address on "A Saint's Soliloquy" (Ps. ciii.)—those who could, in English, and the rest in Mr. Mackenzie's translation; and they went away refreshed by the greeting which the Moderator brought from the whole Church, and by his hand-grasp after the service was over.

Scenes like this were repeated during each of the following days, and Dr. Whyte always shook hands with every member of the dispersing congregation.

Time would fail to tell of the visit to Rodel with its ancient church, of the storm which prevented the yacht from approaching the islands in the Sound of Harris, and of the fog two days later which caused the skilful Captain Kirkwood, to whom the travellers were indebted in many ways, to reverse his engines and head for the open sea. This prevented an eagerly looked for visit to the home of " Father John of the Hebrides," as one of the party called him; but this noble old Highland minister, the Rev. John S. Macphail, brother of Dr. Whyte's college friend, joined the party for a short time a day or two later.

A paragraph must, however, be spared for the events of the following Sunday, when the yacht lay in Lochmaddy, and the party scattered over North Uist, and as far as the neighbouring island of Berneray. In all ten services were held. Dr. Whyte preached three times, and spent five hours on the road, in addition to the long crossing to Berneray and back. The fishing-boat which carried him could only make a slow return passage, and the company of twenty-five on board sang Gaelic Psalms and English hymns alternately, while Dr. Whyte enlarged on one of his favourite quotations :

> " When the shore is won at last,
> Who will count the billows past ! "

By evening the words were altered to run, " When the *yacht* is won at last " ; for the slow return from Berneray delayed the services at Sollas and Lochmaddy, and, while Dr. Whyte was preaching on Psalm xxiii. in the little church at the latter place, the south-west wind which had delayed the crossing in the afternoon freshened to a gale. We found the yacht's gig awaiting us in partial shelter, while the *Oriental* lay nearly a mile away to windward in the open loch. It was then decided to divide the party, leaving four to be brought off later, and to this wise decision the last twenty years of Dr. Whyte's ministry were in all probability due.

For, if all had gone on board the gig, she could never have reached the yacht. Even with the lightened load, the first trip was an anxious one, especially for those who understood the danger of facing an angry sea in a boat too long to rise easily to the short waves, which were lashed by the wind sweeping down from Ben Lee. Once out of shelter it was clear that we must go on, for the gig could not have survived an attempt to turn back. Mr. Mackenzie was at the tiller, and the four Highland sailors bent stoutly to their hard task. For a time it seemed doubtful if they could win through, for the mail-steamer *Flowerdale*, not far from us, could be seen by the fitful moonlight slowly dragging her anchor before the gale. Dr. and Mrs. Whyte sat calmly, and he at least seemed hardly conscious of the danger; but when the sailors' intense effort finally brought us alongside the yacht, the captain was waiting on deck with a strained and anxious face, and curtly forbade a second journey. By midnight the wind moderated and the gig was able to return for those who had remained behind.

The following day formed a strange contrast. We made an early crossing, and found the Minch still vexed by the gale of Sunday night; but we anchored for breakfast in the complete calm of Dunvegan Loch, opposite the venerable grey castle of the Macleods. Two hours later we passed Vaternish Point and entered the Bay of Uig, where Dr. Whyte preached at a midday service. One passage in his sermon—addressed to a congregation holding strict Highland ideas regarding church music—gave an imaginative account of the antiphonal singing of Psalm cxxxvi. in the Temple, and pictured two long lines of singers, each of whom chanted one verse, while all joined in the refrain, " For His mercy endureth for ever." The description reached its climax in the words :

" And then an old prophet, far down the line, would lift up his voice and say, *He hath remem-*

bered us in our low estate ; and the whole congregation would join in the response, *For His
mercy endureth for ever.*"

As the voyage was resumed, we bore in our ears
as well as in our hearts the melody of Sheriff Nicolson's
Skye—most hauntingly beautiful of modern Scottish
songs—and the verse, " Where the sun sinks beyond
Hunish Head . . . Would I were sailing," was an
aspiration realised ; for we rounded Rua Hunish in
the late afternoon, sailed under the basaltic pinnacles
of the Quiraing, and in the gathering dusk reached
Portree harbour. We there heard, after several days
without newspapers, of Kitchener's capture of Khar-
toum, and we took part in an evening service, at
which Dr. Whyte preached on the text, " What are
these that are arrayed in white robes ? "
Conferences with the Presbyteries of Skye and
Lochcarron on the two days that followed brought
this missionary journey to an end ; but a week later
a Convention was held in Inverness to which ministers
and elders of the Free Church assembled from all
over the Highlands. Dr. Whyte spoke three times
to this gathering. His opening sermon, on the words,
" For their sakes I sanctify Myself," sent not a few
ministers back to their scattered parishes with a new
resolve to devote themselves heart and mind to the
work entrusted to them ; and he also gave addresses
on the Personal Life of Prayer, and on the Evangelical
Pulpit in Scotland. The latter, which is described
as one of his most thrilling utterances, began with
the early Celtic missionaries, and ended with the
ministry and character of Dr. Candlish. His own
experiences of the previous fortnight gave point and
actuality to his reference to " those ancient men,"
the followers of Columba, who " went about very
much like our Highland catechists of to-day, threading
the wild lochs of the west, and treading the northern
valleys and moors and mountains, carrying with them
the evangelical message."
So ended three weeks of remarkable effort. Dr.

Whyte's preaching had stimulated many consciences, and the touch of his personal sympathy had warmed many discouraged spirits. No other could have done these things quite as he did. Yet the question arises whether this unique journey might not have accomplished yet greater things, if he had conjoined a message regarding the wider need of the hour, and the duty of the Church as a whole, with his message to individual hearts. For the whole position of the Free Church in the Highlands was a critical one. Some six years before, a secession (the Free Presbyterian Church) had followed the passing of the " Declaratory Act," which gave a measure of much-needed relief from the rigours of the Westminster Confession; but many who still remained in the Free Church in the Highlands were wholly out of sympathy with the newer attitude in Christian scholarship, and there was much misrepresentation as to what Dr. Dods, Dr. George Adam Smith, and their colleagues really taught. It was one of the ironies of Church History that much of the weight of this misrepresentation fell on the shoulders of Principal Rainy, who had been bitterly attacked by the liberal school for his action in sacrificing Professor Robertson Smith, and was now attacked still more bitterly by the orthodox in the North. If Dr. Whyte had set himself to explain the meaning of " a believing scholarship," to use his own phrase, he might well have received a hearing more sympathetic than would have been granted to any other man, and done something to dissipate a dangerous misunderstanding.

The growing estrangement in regard to ecclesiastical policy was yet more serious. The " Establishment principle " which had been carried by Dr. Chalmers into the Free Church had long ceased to be held in the South, but in the Highlands represented at least a strongly held opinion. The opposition which wrecked the earlier negotiations for union between the Free and the United Presbyterian Churches was largely Highland in origin.[1] Now, after

[1] Cf. p. 159 above.

a quarter of a century, these negotiations had been resumed, largely under pressure of lay opinion in the cities, and were steadily advancing towards the consummation of 1900. But here also misrepre sentation, always aided by the language difficulty in the more remote Gaelic-speaking areas, had been at work ; and many earnest people came to believe that the " Voluntary principle " of the United Presby-terian Church stood for a denial of national religious duty, or even for a betrayal of the doctrine of the Headship of Christ over the nations. To these matters Dr. Whyte did not once refer—so far as I have been able to ascertain—during his moderatorial tour. It is true that, in concentrating on the religion of heart and conscience and especially on the great theme of sanctification, he spoke on that which was deepest in his own thought as well as most congenial to the thought and experience of his hearers. Yet the absence from his speaking, both in the islands and when he stood beside Dr. Rainy on the Convention platform at Inverness, of any such ardent appeal for union as he had made at Lochearnhead only a few weeks before, indicates that both leaders had been misinformed as to the state of opinion in the North. They clearly believed that opposition to union was crumbling, and that their words should deal not with the controversies of the hour, but with the abiding realities of faith.[1]

So much it seems needful to say in explanation of Dr. Whyte's silence on a subject which so engaged his thought and prayer and effort during the rest of his ministry. But it is idle to speculate as to the result, had he adopted the other course, and made the duty of union a central theme during these weeks. We cannot tell whether in so short a time he could have drawn the Free Church in the Highlands out of the current which was setting towards the rocks

[1] Dr. Rainy's two addresses at Inverness were of the same inward and spiritual character as Dr. Whyte's, and a correspondent present said that they " spoke as to the immediate future in a tone of con-fident independence."

of 1900 and 1904.   Seven years later he returned to
the North—and this time with a double message to
Church and individual, as the next chapter will show.
But before this later visit the main opportunity had
passed, and the schism in the Highlands was an
accomplished fact.

Yet our account of Dr. Whyte's moderatorship
must not end on this note of uncertainty.   The last
weeks of his year of office were again given largely
to the West Highlands, where he attended a conference at Oban, and preached in various churches in
the surrounding district of Argyllshire.   His sermon
at the opening of the Assembly of 1899 dealt with
the Work of the Holy Spirit ;   and then followed
what he called the last and best act of his term as
Moderator—when he nominated as his successor
Dr. James Stewart, of Lovedale, doctor, educational
pioneer, missionary statesman, and the friend and
companion of David Livingstone.   In welcoming
Dr. Stewart as his " dear friend " to the Moderator's
chair, he told the House that he was only repaying
the good turn done to him just a generation before,
when Dr. Stewart had handed over to him the
assistantship to Dr. Roxburgh in Free St. John's.

CHAPTER XXII

THE UNION OF 1900 AND THE
CHURCH CRISIS
1900–1905

" Who, through the heat of conflict, keeps the law
In calmness made, and sees what he foresaw."

WORDSWORTH.

THE bond of sympathy between Dr. Whyte and his
Highland brethren, which the events of his moderatorship had so greatly strengthened, was not in any
degree relaxed when he ceased to act as the representative of his Church. During the years that
followed, the Highlands were continually in his own
thoughts, and, as far as his influence extended, in the
thoughts of his people as well. It is told that, on
a Sunday of drenching rain in Edinburgh, he included
this realistic passage in his prayer : " Lord, we would
remember our Highland ministers. We think of
many of them on this wet day, going along a wet
road, to a wet church, to preach to a few wet people."
And when a missionary, who was about to preach
in St. George's and found Dr. Whyte in the vestry
" pacing to and fro like a lion in his den," asked if
any particular order of service should be followed,
the quick reply came : " No, no—do as you like—
only remember to pray for our Highland ministers."

Nor was his interest limited to the Gaelic-speaking
regions. In the summer of 1900, the hardy folk of
Scandinavian descent in the Orkney and Shetland
Islands found him as ready to face the discomforts
of the Pentland Firth as he had been to cross and
recross the Minch two years before. He wrote
regarding this journey to one of his most faithful
office-bearers :

" KIRKWALL, *Monday.*

" DEAR MR. DAVIE,—Here I am in your
native spot, and you not here ! How I miss

your expected presence and guidance ! At the same time, there is room in my week here for nothing but work. Since I left Edinburgh, I have never drawn bridle, as the word is. We gave as hard-worked a week to Shetland as ever I had, and we were compelled to leave the Island before all the charges were overtaken : and it will be the same here. I preached at Firth on Friday night, and went up to your old home after service and saw your loved and honoured Mother. We had a most friendly talk together, and much of it about you and yours. I was greatly pleased to have been in your old home and to think of you as brought up among such beautiful surroundings for body and soul. Your brother and his wife also, I was delighted to meet. Yesterday I preached three times : at St. Andrew's in the forenoon : in the Free Church here in the afternoon : and I gave my sermon on ' The Marrow ' to the sons of the Erskines in the U.P. Church in the evening. The day was a profitable one to myself.

" Mr. Lee and Mr. Mackenzie are away at their duties elsewhere. I go to Mr. Whyte's church this afternoon and to other appointments all Tuesday and Wednesday : Presbytery meeting here on Thursday, and I lecture on ' The Literary and Religious Employment of the Imagination ' in the evening : returning home on Friday.

" Our visit, thus far, has been all and more than we could have expected. The hospitality and kindness of the Shetland people were unbounded : and it is the same here.—With great regard, and affection, A. WHYTE."

The union of the two Churches, which had formed the goal of so much hope and endeavour, was consummated in Edinburgh in October 1900. Neither the Synod Hall of the United Presbyterians nor the Assembly Hall of the Free Church was large enough

to contain the uniting bodies ; so a great temporary
hall was erected under the wide roof of the Waverley
Market.   Here the first General Assembly of the
United Free Church was held, and Dr. Rainy, the
one prominent survivor of the earlier union negotiations and the unquestioned leader of the later, was
called with acclamation to the Chair.   While he
delivered his address as Moderator, Lord Rosebery,
Dr. Joseph Parker, and Dr. Whyte formed a striking
group immediately on his left.

The great concourse which greeted the consummation of the Union forgot for a time that a small
minority, including at this stage less than thirty
ministers of the Free Church, had remained outside
and were carrying on what they claimed to be the
true Assembly of that Church.   In the ecclesiastical
events and decisions that followed, Dr. Whyte bore
no direct part ; hence it would be purposeless to
discuss the question whether the calamities that
followed might have been averted by an immediate
and generous recognition of the claim of the residuary
Free Church to a share of the properties in which
they had formerly had an interest.   At all events,
it soon became apparent that it was their intention
to test in the Courts of Law their claim not only to a
proportion but to the whole of the funds and properties which were held by the Free Church at the
time of the Union.   The sequel to this claim need
only be described here in so far as will make clear
Dr. Whyte's view of the final decision given in the
House of Lords nearly four years later ; [1] but it
may be well to indicate the points on which the long
argument chiefly turned.   Two questions were involved—a wider and a narrower.   Has the Church
power to modify and to change articles of belief or
opinions on Church polity which do not enter into
the substance of her faith, in order that she may
adapt herself to the changing needs and duties which

---

[1] A full treatment will be found in Dr. Carnegie Simpson's *Life of
Principal Rainy*, vol. ii. chaps. xxv.–xxviii.   For the legal proceedings
see *The Free Church Appeals* (ed. R. L. Orr, 1904).

confront her in each new epoch ? This was the wider and permanent issue, and that which depended on it was—Had the Free Church, by abandoning the " Establishment principle " and entering into union with a Church holding " Voluntary " views, severed her identity with the Free Church of 1843 ? The crucial point in the Minority's case may be found in a single sentence of their original plea :

> " The contract of association or constitution of the said Free Church of Scotland under which it was first associated contains no provision for any alteration being made in the essential principles of the said constitution and standard of belief, or for union with any other Church or association of Christians holding different principles or recognising a different standard of belief, by any mere majority, however large. . . ." [1]

When the implications of this contention are examined, it becomes clear that, if it were once admitted, any reunion of the several branches of the Christian Church would become impossible, since in every union some tenets must be modified on one side or both ; and, apart from the question of unity, no power would remain to follow the leading of the Spirit into new regions of truth. To adapt a phrase of Plato's, the Church would be held in " complete immobility, an everlasting fixture."

The first judgment was given by Lord Low in the Outer House of the Court of Session in Edinburgh on 9th August 1901. It unhesitatingly recognised the right of the Majority to enter the United Church. An appeal was taken to the Second Division, where, nearly a year later, Lords Kingsburgh, Trayner, and Young reaffirmed the decision. But a careful examination of their judgments showed a difference of outlook which gave some warning of difficulties lying ahead. For Lord Young argued roundly that

[1] *The Free Church Appeals*, p. 8.

two non-established churches had always power to unite, being themselves final judges of the religious and doctrinal issues involved; while the two other judges took the more guarded ground, as Lord Low had previously done, that the Majority had not in point of fact departed from the principles of the original Free Church, since the duty of the State to establish the Christian Religion, while widely held as a subordinate opinion in the Free Church in its early days, had never been treated as a test or as a fundamental and unalterable article of belief.

The case was then carried to the House of Lords, but the hearing did not take place till the closing months of 1903. It became known that the six judges who heard the appeal were equally divided in regard to it; and that thus the appeal was likely to be dismissed, the unanimous judgment of the Court of Session reaffirmed, and the United Free Church confirmed in the use of her buildings and endowments. But before judgment was delivered, Lord Shand, who was believed to take the side of the United Free Church, died, and the case was ordered to be heard *de novo* by an enlarged bench. Finally, judgment was given on 1st August 1904; and Dr. Whyte with other leading Free Churchmen listened intently in the gallery of the House of Lords during a long summer day while the opinions of the seven judges were read. Long before the seventh opinion was reached it became clear that the case had gone against the United Free Church, that the decision of the judges in Scotland had been overturned, and that the Church's property was not to be held by the 643 members of the Assembly who had entered the Union, but was to be handed over to the 27 who had remained outside. This famous decision was supported by five judges—Lord Chancellor Halsbury, and Lords Alverstone, Davey, James, and Robertson; and was opposed by two, Lords Lindley and Macnaghten. The last-named closed his judgment by describing the position of the Free, and now United, Church in memorable words:

28

LIFE OF ALEXANDER WHYTE

"I do not think she has forfeited any of her rights by receiving into her bosom a reformed and Presbyterian Church, one with her in faith, in baptism, and all essential points of doctrine. And, for my part, I should hesitate long before I could give my voice for a decision which will, I fear, compel, or at any rate direct, her to subordinate the Scriptures to the Westminster Confession of Faith."

The distinction here indicated proved to be a real and vital one; for it soon appeared that, while the United Free Church might, in effect, be *directed* by the House of Lords to dissolve the Union, nothing could *compel* her either to do so, or to retrace the steps already taken in modifying the relation of her ministers to the Confession of Faith. This was made clear at the August meeting of the "Commission of Assembly" which took place ten days later in Edinburgh. This is usually a brief, lifeless, and thinly attended gathering for the transaction of routine business; but in 1904, under Dr. Rainy's leadership, it became a large and resolute convocation. Those who belonged to the United Presbyterian section of the Church, and who had no kind of responsibility for the disaster which had overtaken her, showed themselves not less determined than their brethren to vindicate the Church's right to guide her course according to the light of conscience, whatever material loss might follow. Dr. Whyte attended the Commission, and met many of those who gathered during these stirring days in Edinburgh, including Mr. Stead, who wrote a glowing account of what he saw for the *Review of Reviews*, and the aged Professor David Masson, who recounted his memories of Chalmers and the Disruption sixty years before. But in the main, Dr. Whyte's part was that of a listener; nor did he take part in the earliest of the protest meetings which were soon organised all over Scotland, and which helped to add volume to a wave of public interest as widespread and intense as the Ten Years'

Conflict amid which he was born, or the Robertson Smith Case in which he played so vigorous a part in his prime.

For nearly a month he kept silence, and in the first days of the crisis he confessed to friends who questioned him that he had not yet obtained any clear light upon it. Between the visits to London and Edinburgh already described, he and his family were at the Dell of Rothiemurchus, near Aviemore; and he was deeply immersed in preparing for his Classes that part of his course on "The Makers of Scotland" which dealt with the life and work of John Knox. As he read Knox's *History of the Reformation* with his children, the bearing of the earlier struggles of the Scottish Kirk upon this latest crisis became more and more clear to his mind. Day by day he also followed closely what eminent men of different schools had to say regarding "the Judgment," and he was greatly encouraged when leaders in other branches of the Christian Church, such as Dr. Thomas Hodgkin, the Quaker historian, came forward chivalrously to defend the United Free Church. Visits from Dr. McLaren of Manchester, Dr. Cameron Lees, and Dr. James Paton showed him how widespread was the sympathy felt in her time of misfortune; but his gratification was yet greater when an article on the same side by his eldest son (now the President of the Indian Legislative Assembly) appeared in the *Westminster Gazette*. In September he wrote from Aviemore regarding it:

"DEAR FRED,—I see your paper has been printed both in the weekly edition of the *Westminster* and in the edition for Saturday evening. Both by telegram and letter the word 'first-rate' is conveyed to me about it, and I agree with those who so characterise your paper. . . .

"Robert is out in the sunshine, and all looks well as regards weather to-day. See the *Nineteenth Century*—Wemyss Reid—for a true and beautiful paper on the Case."

Before this letter was written, Dr. Whyte had spoken at Grantown-on-Spey the word for which many had been eagerly waiting. His address fell into two portions, in both of which he took a line entirely different from that which defenders of the United Free Church were following on a hundred platforms elsewhere. While the younger theologians in particular were seeking to show how urgent was the need to loosen the bonds of the Westminster Confession, he took occasion to reaffirm the Calvinistic belief which he had never ceased to hold. He valued this belief for the assurance which it gave that, however weak the will of man and however deep the corruption of his nature, the work of divine grace must finally achieve its end.

" Predestination," he said, " is not for the platform. Predestination is not for the pulpit, except on very special and very exalted occasions. At the same time, I will take it upon me to say that both the sovereign predestination and the sovereign election of Almighty God are far too little preached on in these slight and surface days of ours."

He thus expressed his own adherence to the central convictions of the Scottish reformers regarding the sovereign grace of God. Next he went on to show how the intolerance which John Knox shared with the religious leaders of his day, Catholic and Protestant alike, had marred his great work, and how tragic had been the failure of the reformers to rise to the height of Dante's warning against " the grafting of the sword upon the crook." [1] From the evil of intolerance he passed on to speak of the duty of brotherly forbearance ; and in the concluding and most memorable portion of his speech he made his own characteristic suggestion for the appeasement of the strife which was daily growing in bitterness between the successful minority and the despoiled majority of the former Free Church. It

[1] *Purg.*, xvi. 113.

referred to a round-table conference which was in prospect between them, and its author brought it forward knowing that it would appear to many, " ' a devout imagination,' as Secretary Lethington called John Knox's *Book of Discipline.*"

" Let the two consultation committees meet beforehand for prayer and for the Lord's Supper. You start back at the bare idea, but try to put in words worthy of a Christian man why you do so. Were they not all till the other day fellow-ministers, and fellow-elders, and fellow-communicants, and do they not all look forward to sitting down together before long at the Table above ? In their Lord's name, then, let His Table be spread, and let the seat at the head of the Table be left empty to the eye of sense, but filled to the eye of faith and love. And as they communicate on His body and His blood, He will say over them and for them, ' Father, the hour is come, I pray for them, for they are Thine. . . .' And then in the strength of that meat, and in answer to that prayer, they would all be of one mind and of one heart. They would not know themselves, nor one another, as they blamed themselves and excused their neighbours, made nothing of the injurious words and deeds they had suffered, and made much of all the evil they themselves had all along said and done ; the Holy Ghost sitting on them in tongues of truth and love, as visibly as it was at the day of Pentecost. Till the reporters waiting at the door would tell to their dying day how they felt as they saw those who went in enemies coming out friends. . . . They went in, it would be reported, alienated and enemies, and they came out made one in mind and heart in Christ, who is the Master of them all." [1]

Unhappily for Scotland, and for the Churches then at issue, the nobly Christian advice thus given

[1] *The Scotsman*, August 30, 1904.

by Dr. Whyte was not followed : instead, the chance of a harmonious settlement grew steadily less.[1] Yet he continued to bear his own witness. In his first sermon to his own people after his return to Edinburgh, he spoke—as he had often done before, but with a new urgency—on the spiritual danger of controversy, and added :

> " For my part, I feel, and I freely confess to you, that there is scarcely any doctrinal or governmental or administrative difference between the several Churches in Scotland—no ! nor scarcely in all Christendom—that I could not submit to if only you would let me continue to preach more and more the forgiveness of sin, and the life everlasting. For the restraint of controversy, and for the reign of peace, and for the life of love, for my part, I would willingly become almost all things to all men. But you will say to me in triumph that truth is truth. And so it is. But I say also—and I more and more deeply feel it—that love is love. And I have the highest authority for it, that love is the fulfilling of every law ; the law of truth, and the law of duty, and every other law." [2]

At a public meeting in Aberdeen on 20th October, he again pled for Reconciliation ; but, knowing how strongly and how adversely the turbid current of controversy was running, he added this alternative plea : " Let us look forward to the day when we shall be one, being led on to that oneness by the movements of His grace and providence ; . . . and, if we must part, let us part like brethren."

As the autumn passed, it became more and more clear that legislative action must ultimately be taken to remedy the more outstanding injuries done by the House of Lords' decision. For, in name of the

[1] When the Conference met on 28th September, the suggestion of the United Free Church that the destination of the disputed properties should be submitted to arbitration was declined outright by the Free Church representatives.

[2] *Our Personal Part in the Present Church Distress* (Edinburgh, 1904).

sacred obligation of Trusts, it had deprived a Church, which was seeking to follow the twofold ideal of Christian freedom and of unity, of her instruments for the accomplishment of her appointed work, and had entrusted these to one which could neither use nor maintain the larger portion and which had neither ministers nor congregations over great tracts of Scotland. At this point a special Convocation was called to meet in Edinburgh. On 15th November, over fourteen hundred ministers and a slightly smaller number of elders gathered for an all-day session in the Synod Hall. The earlier part of the day was given to statements regarding the negotiations with the legal Free Church, and to the prospect of intervention by the Government. Resolutions were also passed expressing gratitude for the steadfastness of the Church's members in face of the crisis, and for the support of other religious bodies shown in fifty-six addresses received from outside Scotland. A special message of sympathy was sent to the foreign missionaries of the Church who were in a position of extreme uncertainty and difficulty.

Late in the afternoon Dr. Whyte rose to move the approval of a " Pastoral Letter to the People of the Church " which had been laid before the Convocation. The speech in which he did so was, by the unanimous testimony of those who heard it, the most overwhelming in its effect of all his platform utterances. It was, indeed, less closely argued than his great speech at the conclusion of the Robertson Smith case, but it combined in a unique degree the imaginative intensity of his earlier speaking with the spiritual glow of his later years. It had, inevitably, less of the chivalrous courage of one who knows that he is leading a forlorn hope, but it gained from the complete unity of thought and purpose which bound the whole great audience to the speaker.

" Moderator, beloved and honoured Fathers in the Lord,—I rise for a moment to move that this truly apostolic message shall be accepted by the Convocation, and sent out in the name of our Moderator to our dear and dutiful people. And the only addition I would suggest to be made to the letter is that the burning bush should be stamped on the head of it.[1] For sixty years the burning bush has been an ornament on the walls and windows of our churches, on our Assembly Acts, and on our Missionary Records; but since that sad Monday in London the burning bush has been brought home to our own firesides. It is burning with a fierce flame to-day in many families and in many congregations. It is a very real, and a very pungent, and a very testing experience to many of our beloved people, and in some parts of the country it is burning with a very malignant flame. Now, sir, we have the advantage of Moses and his mountain in this respect. All that Moses is able to record of his burning bush is that it burned, but was not consumed.

" But the half had not been revealed to him, for with us the bush is not only not consumed, but it is budding, and blossoming, and flourishing more vigorously than ever. The burning bush with us is drinking in the very flame like life, and transmuting it into strength, and sweetness, and fruitfulness. Look at the congregations, and see the new vitality, the new interest in things, the new devotion, the new liberality that have all been awakened since that unprecedented decision in London. The bush is burning indeed. But, instead of being consumed, it is striking its roots deeper than ever, and it is extending its branches further than ever, and it is promising fruit richer and sweeter than ever. The burning bush is a perfect miracle, and we will hand that old symbol down to our children with new associations and with a new testimony

[1] The Burning Bush, with the words *Nec Tamen Consumebatur* (" Nevertheless it was not consumed "), was the emblem of the Free Church, as it still is of the United Free Church.

to Him who dwelt and who still dwelleth in the bush. Now, sir, I will give you a few illustrations about how our congregations are thriving. I will tell you about my own congregation, or rather it is not mine, nor Mr. Black's, nor even Principal Dykes's ; it is Dr. Candlish's congregation. Well, we had our Deacons' Court last night, and a report of the Emergency Fund was given in for the last few weeks. Before this vitalising judgment was given, my colleague and I often had to lay our heads together to get a few more hundred pounds for something. . . . Well, the Emergency call came round. We issued it, as we all did to our congregations, and at our Deacons' Court last night a report was laid on the table, and the treasurer of that fund said that up till yesterday he had got £10,000. . . . We see the same thing all around. Our Highland collection was three times yesterday what it ever was ; and at the close of an afternoon meeting of ladies, in connection with foreign missions, the report was, ' We asked £40, and on the spot we got £90.' All hail ! such judgments ! There are two sides to everything, and there is a great and blessed side to this. . . .

" But this business, Moderator, has many sides, and I will tell you one side that sometimes pierces my heart and weighs me down to the very dust ; and that is the way in which God Almighty is making our Church a touchstone for the souls of men all round the world. I say it is a very solemnising thought to think that God Himself is taking our Church and is testing men's most secret hearts with her troubles and her sorrows. He is trying men to see what their hearts are made of, when a great and serviceable Church of Christ is being tried, and broken, and torn in this way. Our Church has been used for many ends ; but to my mind it has been put to its most solemn end and use when it is made the test of the hearts of all men who see her great necessities. I sat up in the gallery of the House of Lords when the judgment was being given, and there were various ways of looking at that judgment. I will tell you the way I looked at it. There was not a man in the House of Lords that knew the case as I knew it. Why! they were speaking in absolute ignorance or worse about our Church—the Church at whose breast I was suckled, on whose knees I was dandled, at whose feet I learned ' Man's chief End ' and ' The Lord's my Shepherd ' ; and when in His great and gracious kindness to me He sent me to preach the Gospel, it was in that Church. And I felt as I looked down there that there was not a man in the House of Lords who loved, and therefore knew, the Free Church of Scotland as I knew her. I sat and watched them, not measuring our Church, but measuring themselves. I saw the evangelical, free, living, progressive, Church of Scotland—I saw her, I say, as in a vision standing in the middle of that House, and I saw an invisible hand take judge after judge, and lead him up and measure him against that Church ; and some when they were measured went down, and some when they were measured went up. My heart trembled within me as I saw men who ought to have known better brought close to that touchstone. When I was sitting there with my heart hot within me, a figure seemed to rise from the benches of the House of Lords. It was Butler, and he lifted up his finger to me and said, ' Avoid giving of characters.' I held my breath as well as I could, and tried not to give characters, and I shall try not to give characters now. But in my eyes that day it was not we who were being weighed in the balance and found wanting, it was justice in our land ; it was the law of the land that was measured beside the law of God and found wanting. My Church is being made an engine of test, fuller's soap, and a refiner's fire, so that no man can hear of her trial without himself being tested. It breaks my heart to think that my Church has been made such a searching fire that no man can escape the test. Every man and woman in Scotland is being tried, as Christ touches their hearts and their minds with His great touchstone in this time of our great tribulation. . . .

"I want to say a word to my Highland friends. Hold you on, gentlemen. Go you back to your work ; and so long as there is a loaf in Edinburgh you will get your share of it. We want to tell these brethren that their wives and children are not altogether their own just now, but are the care of the Church, and that there-fore they need not fear to stand true. Just you hold on to the end in hope and patience and forgiveness. Refuse to be brought into quarrels, and bear yourselves as in the sight of your Master. He will set you in the place of honour, and one day a voice will ask, ' Who are these that are clothed with white robes, and whence came they ? ' And it will be said, ' These are they that came out of great tribulation, and have washed their robes and made them white in the blood of the Lamb.' And our faithful Highland ministers will tell their story to saints and angels.

"When I staggered down that fatal stair, and came out into the lobby in the House of Lords, I found my friend here—shall I call him my father or my brother ? I am getting so old now I will call him my brother—there he was walking about the lobby with his splendid serenity. Men said, ' Have you seen Rainy ? How is he taking it ? ' And the answer was, ' As smiling and happy as ever.' And why ? Because he has been long years rooted in God ; he is an experienced, Christian man. And just as Luther's policy and Knox's policy were the

fruit of their personal religion, so his statesmanship, and all his patience and forbearance,
spring out of this—that he is a living, praying,
godly man. None of you know him as I do;
and I will sit down by saying this, that as I think
of him every day and many times a day, I
rejoice at the grace of God towards our beloved
friend; and I often hear a voice saying in my
heart concerning him—and it is a voice that
comes down from Heaven:

> " ' Because on Me he set his love,
>   I'll save and set him free;
> Because My great Name he hath known,
>   I will him set on high.
>
> He'll call on Me; I'll answer him,
>   I will be with him still
> In trouble, to deliver him
>   And honour him I will.
>
> With length of days unto his mind
>   I will him satisfy;
> I also My salvation
>   Will cause his eyes to see.' "

Those who heard this speech have exhausted the
resources of metaphor in describing the accumulating
emotion which grew more tense with every step of
the orator's progress, and finally, as he sat down,
drew the whole audience to their feet in wave
upon wave of tumultuous applause.

" We were all sitting," Principal Cairns
writes, " in the dusty old United Presbyterian
Hall—a couple of thousand determined but
gloomy and savage men—when he came forward
on the platform and lit everything up. I have
never, I think, seen public speaking do so much
to lift the heart. I remember almost nothing
else of the meeting except that one speech, with
its closing exhortation to Rainy, as he laid his
hand on his shoulder, ' Hold you fast, my
brother ! ' I have always associated that speech
with what Queen Elizabeth's ambassador, Sir
Ralph Sadler, said of John Knox, ' The voice

of this single man can put more heart in us than five hundred trumpets continually blustering in our ears ! ' ''

Nor was the effect confined to the thousands who filled the Synod Hall on that autumn afternoon : before the week was ended men and women all over Scotland were quoting the phrase in which Dr. Whyte hailed " this vitalising judgment," and the passage in which he pictured the judges as themselves coming up to be judged by their attitude towards the Church and towards her demand for unity and freedom in her Master's service.

At night, the Waverley Market was thronged by a public meeting of over eight thousand persons ; but only one sentence of the speeches given need be recorded here. Principal Rainy mentioned his friend's tribute a few hours before to the serenity with which he had received the shattering decision of the Lords, and added in his calm, almost matter-of-fact, way : " I hope I am set in the belief—I ask you all to be set in the belief—that when trouble happens to us in the path of performing duty, we have no reason to be discouraged or cast down."

Throughout the two succeeding years Dr. Whyte followed keenly every development of the Church's fortunes—the favourable response of Mr. Balfour's Government to her appeal, the passing of the Churches Act, and the division of the properties of the former Free Church between the two claimants which was carried through by the Elgin Commission. It was during this long and troubled process that Dr. Whyte addressed a typically brief and undated letter to Mr. Thomas Shaw, M.P. (now Lord Shaw of Dunfermline), expressing appreciation of one of his statements on behalf of the United Free Church :

" DEAR MR. SHAW,—First-rate, conclusive, and unanswerable. — With high and warm regard,   ALEXANDER WHYTE."

Dr. Whyte's greatest service to his Church during these troubled months was given during a tour in the Highlands which began on 28th June 1905, and continued during the month that followed. In some respects it resembled his journey as Moderator seven years before. Again, he received a welcome of amazing heartiness, and again he conducted Communion Services, as well as addressed meetings, at many different points. But there was also a marked distinction between this journey and the earlier one. Addressing the office-bearers and members of a now broken Church, Dr. Whyte dwelt less on the inner problems of the heart and more on the duties which bind men to one another and to the body of which they are severally members. Several of the services were held in strange surroundings. At Burghead, where Dr. Whyte's old friend, Mr. Cassie, presided, a disused granary was the place of meeting ; and at Bruan in Caithness the dispossessed congregation were found worshipping in a temporary wooden building which had been built in two days during the depth of the preceding winter by willing hands under the direction of an aged minister.

Sir Frederick Whyte, who accompanied his father on this journey, has described it in these words :

" He was sent as the messenger of the Church to rally the Highlands after the shock of the judgment of the House of Lords. Never have I heard him deliver an appeal so powerful in its simplicity, so racy in its manner, so moving in its effect. His theme was always the same : that the Church was greater than the Law by which it had been smitten, and that the mission of the Church was greater than the Church itself. With an infinite variety of illustration, drawn from Scripture, from Bunyan, from the daily paper, and from the hillsides and lochs that spread their coloured panorama like a vast amphitheatre round his open-air pulpit, he delivered a message which his own congregation in Edinburgh was hardly ever privileged to hear. During the Highland tour of 1905 the power and freedom of his address exceeded anything before or since. It was a spoken word *in excelsis*, and could hardly be transferred to the written page.

" The tour itself covered the counties of Moray, Nairn, Inverness, Ross and Cromarty, Caithness, parts of Argyll, and ended in Arran. By rail, motor, and wagonette we travelled from place to place ; starting out at 8 o'clock in the morning, stopping about 11 at a wayside church or to meet a vast concourse on a heathered hillside, moving on again, an hour later, to lunch with a selected body of ministers who came in from all parts to greet him ; and pressing on again in the afternoon to repeat at least twice before sunset the experiences of the morning. He was in his seventieth year, yet neither in body nor in spirit did he show signs of fatigue. No great political leader ever underwent a greater strain in popular work, or was received with greater devotion. I remember, before we had proceeded far on the tour, he used to say to me every morning, ' Now, Fred, you have heard all this before : you had better go off and fish ; you can come back in the evening, and we shall see whether your basket is better than mine.' The remarkable thing about the whole tour was that, though he was really delivering the same message on each occasion, it never emerged from his ardent mind twice in the same form."

After this time of intense effort lightly borne, Dr. Whyte spent several quiet weeks with his wife and children on the small Island of Hankö in the Christianiafjord ; and soon after his return he was one of a little group of friends who stood on the platform of Waverley Station, Edinburgh, and saw Principal Rainy start on his last long journey to Australia. This farewell marked the close of a friendship which had begun with the beginning of

Dr. Rainy's professorship forty years earlier, and had been sealed by the memorable scene beside Dr. Candlish's death-bed. The two veterans had defended their Church together in these later days of her trial, but the strongest bond between them was one of a deeper kind. Its nature appears in a letter, written by Dr. Whyte two or three years before, at the end of the New College session :

> " Rainy closed the session this forenoon with an address on pulpit prayer. All the time I was listening to it myself, I was wishing that all our ministers could have heard it. . . . I need not characterise it : power, wisdom, devoutness, beauty, authority."

On 22nd December, a message reached Dr. Whyte that his friend had passed away at Melbourne. In his tribute in Free St. George's on the following day he emphasised, as did many others, Dr. Rainy's great qualities of mind and will—his wisdom, his courage, and his " uncomplaining endurance " ; but it was on other qualities, less recognised by the world at large, that Dr. Whyte dwelt with especial thankfulness :

> " I must not omit to mention here his extraordinary elevation of mind and heart and very appearance, when he was engaged in serving the Lord's Table. I never saw any man so wrapt in mind, and heart, and manner, as I have seen our friend on a Communion day in this very house." " Nothing in this life," he concluded, " is so enriching and so ennobling as to know intimately, and to love devotedly, a truly great and a truly good man : such as, by the grace of God to him, and to us, Dr. Rainy was."

AT BALMACARA

" From the lone shieling on the misty island
  Mountains divide us, and the waste of seas—
Yet still the blood is strong, the heart is Highland,
  And we in dreams behold the Hebrides."

THE last two chapters have made it clear how much of Dr. Whyte's thought and energy, during the period which they cover, was devoted to the good of the Highlands. This work was largely made easier by his spending most of his summer vacations in the North or the West, while in seven out of ten years he was in the Highlands at Easter as well. He and his wife thus came to know the people of more than one Highland district, not only as passing visitors may know them, but as neighbours and as friends.

From the summer of 1897, which was spent at Java Lodge on the farther shore of the Sound of Mull, two incidents have been recalled, one illustrating a new and the other an old friendship. It was at this time that Mr. and Mrs. Hollins were for the first time Dr. and Mrs. Whyte's guests. Dr. Whyte knew the difficulties of landing from the small boat to which passengers are transferred from the steamer at most ports of call on the West Coast, and he feared that his friend's blindness would make it hard for him to make his way up the rough little pier and across the stony beach beyond ; so he arranged for a farm cart to drive into the water, close alongside of the boat, that Mr. Hollins might land safely and with as little discomfort as possible. Among the other visitors at Java Lodge this autumn was the Rev. Duncan Ross of Appin, who had acted as guide in the Iona expedition a generation before. As the two college friends stood together on a rocky head-

29   449

land, looking across the shining waters of the Sound towards Ben Cruachan and the noble array of surrounding mountains, Dr. Whyte's thoughts were carried upward from the glory of the visible scene to a yet higher glory, and he asked wistfully: " Is it not a wonder that the Maker of all that beauty does not show Himself to us as He did to John in Patmos, knowing how we long to see Him ? "

For some years Dr. Whyte's two nieces, Elizabeth and Margaret Macadam, who had returned from Canada after the death of their father, found a home under his roof, spending part of each year with his family in Edinburgh or during their Highland holidays. It was a great joy to Dr. Whyte that in 1897 the younger sister married the Rev. J. M. E. Ross of Alford, one of his former assistants, and the son of his friend " Ross of Cowcaddens," of whom we shall hear in the following chapter.

Easter of 1898 was spent at Balmacara, on the landlocked waters of Lochalsh, which separates Skye from the mainland ; and as this became a second home to Dr. Whyte and his family for a dozen years, it deserves some description here.[1] Yet any description must seem inadequate to those who know that charmed country of sea-loch and infinitely varied mountain, and especially to those who knew Balmacara before most of the sheltering woods—its special glory in a country which supports little fine timber—had been stripped from the hill behind. At that time there stretched in front of the house a shallow salt-water pond, separated from the sea by a long bank of sand, over which the spring tides made their way. To the east rises the beautiful heather-covered peak of Scour Mhor ; to the south, in the distance, the scarped ridge of Ben Screel appears over Kyle Rhea and the hills of Glenelg ; and straight across the loch is Ben-na-Caillich, " the Old Woman of Skye." A short walk up the slopes behind opens a view of yet grander hills—the Coolins,

[1] The months spent there were April 1898 ; and August and September of the years 1898, 1899, 1902, 1906, 1907, and 1909.

these " mountains of God," as a Hebrew poet would have called them, in the far west, and to the south-east Ben Attow and Scour Ouran, in whose deep shadow lies Loch Duich, perhaps the most beautiful of all the Scottish sea-lochs.

Here the younger members of the family found a true paradise, though, as in all earthly paradises, the serpent had left his trail in the form of superabundant rain and midges. A small cutter, of which the eldest son was commander and navigator, merited her name, the *Hazard*, when she was out in face of the sudden squalls which sweep down from the mountains, or beating up against the four-knot tidal current which sets through the two entrances to Lochalsh, Kyle Rhea, and Kyle Akin. There was climbing, too, and fishing, though Dr. Whyte took little part in either sport : his angling career had reached its culmination and its close three years before in Norway, when he and Dr. Sutherland Black left their companions at Mandal, drove seventy miles up the Saetersdal behind two stalwart Norse ponies, picnicked for several days in a fishing " saeter," and caught trout of which they could keep no account, so great was their multitude. But after Dr. Whyte passed his sixtieth birthday he generally left the opportunities of fishing to be exploited by his boys, whose eyesight was keener than his own. To his other pursuit of walking he remained faithful for many years more. His longer walks often extended to about twenty miles ; but there was also an institution which cannot pass without mention in any account of his holidays. His children called it " Papa's quarter-deck." At Balmacara it was a stretch of gravel before and at the end of the house; at Inverdruie, the short drive leading down to the triangular village green of Rothiemurchus ; at Bonskeid, the lawn at the south-west angle of the house, looking down the wooded valley. But all were used in the same way—for a steady four-miles-an-hour walk, back and forward, often maintained for an hour or more, during which he meditated deeply on the truths which he gave forth to his people during the months that followed.

His long hours of meditation and of hard reading did not complete the tale of Dr. Whyte's industry during these summers at Balmacara. There were the services already referred to on Sunday evenings ; and there were expeditions to preach for neighbouring ministers, especially before the Union of 1900 and its divisive consequences (a sad irony !) closed certain of their pulpits against him. His wife also led the way in other schemes for the widening of interests and the awakening of latent spiritual faculties among the people of the West Coast. Their silver wedding day (9th September 1906) was passed at Balmacara, and his present to her consisted of the two noble volumes of *Carmina Gadelica*, in which the late Dr. Alexander Carmichael preserved much of the folk-song and the religious poetry of the islands, with translations often of haunting beauty and notes illustrative of the union of faith and music in the spirit of a gifted race. She took the keenest delight in the continuance of this work of recovery and interpretation by her friends, Mrs. Kennedy Fraser and Mr. Kenneth MacLeod; and also took counsel with artist-craftsmen, such as Mr. John Duncan, who believed that the Celtic tradition might readily be reawakened in other regions than those of music and song. She never ceased to hope that the Church might yet become the interpreter of all that is noblest in the Celtic vision ; and, in more immediately practical ways, she sought to recover old methods and models in such arts as tapestry and rug-weaving, to point to the fuller use of singing as a means of education, and to encourage the teaching of gardening and of Gaelic in the schools of the West.

To all such movements Dr. Whyte gave his genial and indulgent protection. In particular he took a sympathetic part in efforts for the good of a little community of railwaymen and others which had been planted among the rocky ridges at Kyle of Lochalsh by the extension of the Highland Railway thither

in 1897. Largely through the efforts which he and
his wife made on their behalf, a small church was
erected—the nearest place of worship had previously
been eight miles distant over a hilly road—and an
institute was opened which, under the charge of Miss
Anita Firth, proved a centre of interest and craftsmanship for this isolated community. Two years
after its opening, Dr. Whyte wrote to one of his
children that Miss Firth had " worked a perfect
revolution at Kyle."

But these activities outside the home were never
allowed to interfere with the family readings which
formed a central feature of each successive holiday.
Few desires lay nearer Dr. Whyte's heart than that
his children should inherit his own passion for good
books ; and he sometimes quoted a saying of Seneca's
—which might not be applauded in every family—
that Stoic fathers did not suffer their children to be
idle even during their holidays.

"I select," he said in the summer of 1904,
" some genuine English classic for each returning summer. I get copies of the most attractive
editions of our selected classic, and I put their
own copy into the hands of each one of my
children. And I get my stationer to prepare as
many neat and tasteful and attractive little notebooks as I have children. The notebooks are cut
and lettered down the margin so as to make the
entry of our notes methodical, and correct, and
easy to be recovered when they are wanted.
Our notebooks for several years past are now
before me, and I find them labelled in gold
letters to this effect : ' St. Quay, 1900—Milton ' ;
' Inverdruie, 1901—Homer ' ; ' Balmacara, 1902
—Cæsar and Some of his Contemporaries ' ;
' Bonskeid, 1903—Quintilian, and his Education
of an Orator.' And the notebook for 1904 is
in the stationer's hands at this moment, with
instructions to stamp on its cover this motto in
gold—' The Makers of Scotland.' For ' Cæsar

and his Contemporaries' we read Thomas North's *Plutarch*, that never-to-be-enough-praised English classic; and for 'The Makers of Scotland' we are intending to read Sheriff Charles Guthrie's edition of John Knox's monumental *History of the Reformation*, Mr. Taylor Innes's *John Knox*, and some other things on Knox if we have time."

In a letter to his eldest son, who was then in France, Dr. Whyte gave a picture of similar readings during an Easter holiday at Oban, when the party was made up by a Swedish friend (the late Dr. Harry Kellgren), Mr. Godfrey, and two nephews of Mrs. Whyte's.

"My dear Fred,—You cannot think what a disappointment it was to us all when we learned that you were not to visit us here. And to no one so much as myself, I think. It is so long since I have seen you, and you have so much to tell me. We have been ten days here, and you can picture to yourself our life. We have had the extremes of weather, one day perfect beauty and peace, and the next day a hurricane of wind and rain. But indoors there is so much interest that, when we cannot get out, we almost more enjoy ourselves. . . . After breakfast and prayers we have an hour of Smellie's *Men of the Covenant*, and then a few minutes entering mems of our reading into our notebooks, and then the day is free. Mr. Godfrey is in an adjoining house with Georgy Barbour and Henry Simpson, and they all come in to reading, and then spend the day together among birds, and books, and games, and boats."

A letter to the same son, written during another spring holiday, begins:

"I have just finished Gardiner's great *History*, and I have often thought of you as I read it. Gardiner is a masterly writer, of the profoundest knowledge and the noblest prin-

ciples. His knowledge of the period—James
and Charles—is most minute and correct, and
the *reflections* are full of truth and wisdom, and
are most impressive and profitable to read. Set
three crosses beside Gardiner's name in your
mind, and read him at your earliest opportunity :
this summer, perhaps."

At a later time, a holiday in Switzerland was
devoted to Stanley's *Eastern Church* and Tyndall's
Switzerland, and during the last summer vacation
before the war several mornings were given to Lord
Hugh Cecil's *Conservatism.* There were examinations, too, on the reading done—not necessarily of
the hurried order, for on one occasion four days were
allowed for the attempt to trace the references to the
Roman " Cæsar " in the New Testament and to relate
them to Shakespeare's play. A Sunday afternoon
near Christiania in 1905 was occupied with the
following task :

> " Lay down a map of the Patriarchal world
> containing Eden, Ur of the Chaldees, ' the Flood,'
> Egypt, and Canaan, with arrows on the margin
> pointing to Rome, London, Christiania, New
> York, and Tokio.
> " Lay down a roomy map of Egypt and
> Canaan, and trace on it all the journeys described
> in the Book of Genesis."

But, while Biblical and Church History filled a
large part in these programmes of reading, contemporary interests were not forgotten. At Balmacara
in 1899 the party was joined for some weeks by
Monsieur A. Nicole—now a pastor in the Swiss Jura
—who had studied during the previous winter in
Edinburgh, and had found in Dr. Whyte's Class for
Young Men the influence which, as he said afterwards,
" providentially sealed his vocation as a preacher."
Advantage was taken of his presence to study with
minute care the proceedings in the Dreyfus Case,
which was then tearing France asunder and holding the

attention of all Europe. All the evidence before the court-martial at Rennes, much of it highly technical, filling many columns of the British dailies, was read aloud; and on one evening the neighbours were invited to share in this study, as the following announcement, preserved in the family guest-book, records :

THE DREYFUS CASE

PASTOR NICOLE, B.D. of GENEVA, will deliver a Lecture on "The History and the Lessons of the Dreyfus Case" at Balmacara House, Lochalsh, on Friday evening, 25th August, at 7 o'clock.

ALEXANDER TAYLOR INNES, Esq., Advocate, Edinburgh, in the Chair.

Collection for the Funds of the Ardelve Library.

Nature-study found its place also. Though Dr. Whyte was no naturalist, it gave him keen satisfaction that his children had the privilege of doing some field-work with Professor J. Arthur Thomson during a holiday at Balmacara, and that at a later date his boys developed an intense interest in bird-life under the guidance of their friend, Mr. Robert Godfrey. A post card to his son, Robert, runs : "Saw a splendid eagle sweeping and swooping which made me think of you." Nor had he ever lost his early interest in astronomy, especially in its bearing on that great problem of religion, the place of Man in the Universe. He often chose Sir Robert Ball's books for reading aloud, and he would look towards the sun, repeating to himself how long its light takes to reach the earth. This interest received a fresh impetus from the presence on various holidays of Dr. Sutherland Black. Both were fascinated by Professor Lowell's theory of the artificial origin of the "canals" in Mars, and during one holiday a post card from Balmacara reached the present writer, who was at the moment away from home :

"Have taken the liberty of sending to your housekeeper to send on *Mars*.[1] Dr. Black is

[1] The volume by Professor Lowell was originally a gift from Dr. Whyte.

here, and we are deep in astronomical matters, and especially in the habitable parts of the heavens. Again, if you come to Balmacara direct from Bonskeid put vol. xxi. of the *North British* [*Review*] in your portmanteau for

"A. W."

But there was a deeper interest underlying all these. When his elder children made an early start to return to school after their first holiday at Balmacara, a post card followed them, addressed to, "Margaret, Fred, Janet, and Aird, 7 Charlotte Square, Edinburgh," and headed, "Tuesday, 7 a.m."—"Your whistle wakened me at 4.20. I rose and looked out, and knelt down for you all. Ps. cxix. 47.—A. W." Some time before, in November 1896, he had come up to their room to tell them of the birth of their youngest brother (whose name, Lancelot Law, showed his devotion to two of his Anglican masters), and added, "He is lying down there with every comfort, and our Saviour was laid in a manger." The same note appeared in the grace at table with which he sometimes began the day—"Thou hadst not where to lay Thy head!" Or some other brief sentence might be used which related the common things of life to its master-interest.

"It was a revelation to hear him say grace at table," one friend has written. "It was seldom more than a single sentence, but no one who heard it would easily forget the moment's silence followed by such words as, 'My cup runneth over,' or, 'Thy word is more to me than my necessary food.' One had the impression of great depth of reality and sincerity. It was the same at family prayers; the passage of scripture chosen was as a rule very brief; if a word of exposition was added, it was also brief, but extraordinarily searching, bringing one into the Presence of the most High God." [1]

[1] Rev. Tissington Tatlow, in the *Student Movement*, May 1921.

Sometimes, however, on special occasions which remain vividly in the memories of those who were present, he would speak with greater fulness at family worship. Such was the evening when, at the close of a gathering of relatives to celebrate the twenty-first birthday of one of his nephews, he stood on the hearthrug, Bible in hand, read one or two verses from the Gospel of Luke, and then spoke for perhaps a quarter of an hour with extraordinary simplicity and beauty on our Lord's young manhood during the silent years at Nazareth. There were also quiet Sunday evenings in the country, when the household numbered but four or five in all, and he expounded such a text as, " Take My yoke upon you," with a tenderness and a depth of experience which he never surpassed in addressing the largest congregation.

On this subject it is not easy—nor perhaps is it needful—to write much. Yet it may be said with confidence that here lay a privilege which was gratefully realised and eagerly looked forward to by guests and servants alike. To some at least of the latter the opportunity of sharing in family worship led by Dr. Whyte meant more than his words of commendation, brief but long remembered, or the sprigs of edelweiss, which he once brought from Switzerland for each member of his household, or the books which would reach a friend's manse the week after he had stayed there with a request that one should be given to every one beneath its roof. After his death, the nurse of his younger children wrote : " I always think the blessing of his prayers has followed me."

Dr. Whyte's desire that his children should share his own deepest interests and impressions received a notable illustration in the summer of 1900. Twice within two months he travelled half across Europe in order to see the Passion-Play of that year at Oberammergau—first with Dr. Sutherland Black, and then with Mrs. Whyte and their three eldest children. He and Dr. Black set out from London

late in July, and spent a few restful days visiting
Augsburg and the beautiful country on the border of
Bavaria and the Western Tirol, round Neuschwanstein
and the Plansee — scenes which are closely inter-
twined with the legends of Lohengrin and Parsifal.
As they read over the text of the Passion-Play in the
quiet of this mountain retreat, its narrative caught
a fresh light from their memories of the *Parsifal*.
Then they went on to Oberammergau, and were able
to see the Play twice—at a regular, and also at a
supplementary, performance.   After the former, Dr.
Whyte wrote to his wife :

" Sabbath Night.

" This has been a great and memorable day.
The deep-toned church bell woke me at 4.15.
At six, Dr. Black and I attended Mass, along
with 800 of our fellow-tourists and the devout
people of the village.   We breakfasted at seven,
and were in our places in the great auditorium by
eight.   It was a glorious morning and worthy
of the glorious day.   I shall not attempt to
describe the day in writing.   I shall leave it to
Dr. Black's enthusiastic conversation when we
all meet. . . . A great Alpine thunderstorm came
over just as the Play was at its darkest to-day,
and it has just burst over us again as I write."

The two friends then travelled swiftly westward,
making only short stops at Innsbruck and Chartres,
and found Mrs. Whyte and the children established
in a cottage near St. Quay, on the Breton coast,
whose granite headlands reminded them of the
rockbound coast of Aberdeenshire.   The discussions
on Oberammergau which followed led to a second
journey thither, and in mid - September the little
party found themselves established in the " presbytery."   They had secured rooms with Mgr. Schroeder,
who had for some years been priest in the village ;
and, on this occasion, Dr. Whyte highly appreciated
not only the Play itself, but the discussions with his
host, in which Mrs. Whyte acted as interpreter.

Three years later a spring holiday was spent above Grenoble, in the Alps of Dauphiny, and Dr. Whyte's meditations among the vineyards prompted two letters, one, to his son Robert, which was afterwards quoted in the sermon already mentioned on the True Vine, and the other to his friend of the Dean Bridge cab office :

" DEAR MR. STEWART,—It's worth all a minister's and a poor believer's trouble coming out here just to see the vineyards at present. If you would see Isa. liii. 2–3 and John xv. illustrated in all nature, come and see a vineyard. For all the vines at present are so many roots in a dry ground. Black, dry, twisted, gnarled, hacked at their roots with axes, and all hacked up their stems and branches with the frosts of winter : there is no tree, or plant, or bush in all the land so unpromising, so almost forbidding to look at, as just the vine. No language could describe to one who had not seen it with his own astonished eyes, the picture of death that all the vineyards are at present. The apple trees, and the plum trees, and the cherry trees are all radiant with white and gold and purple blossom : but the vines all around—there is no beauty that we should desire them. Read Isa. xi. 1–2 and Isa. liii. and John xv. and meditate and pray. And, when, at any time, you despair of your own bringing forth fruit unto holiness, come and see all the vines and all their branches that cover the vineyards of France ! Be sure that in spite of all appearances at present, this land will in a few months be covered with grapes : and then the faith, and the labour, and the poverty of the vine-dresser here will all be rewarded and crowned with a miraculous harvest from all his vines. Think of how unpromising CHRIST looked to the carnal eye ! But under all outside appearances to the contrary, He was all the time the *Son of God*. Under all the death-

like appearances of the vine at present, it *is* a
Vine : and it will prove itself to be a vine in
due time. As the ' True Vine ' did : and all
His branches will : each in their season. And
James Stewart among them : and, I hope and
trust,   ALEXANDER WHYTE."

Dr. Whyte's presence near the Grande Chartreuse
this spring enabled him to see the departure of the
monks from the famous monastery when they were
compelled to leave France by the recently passed law
separating Church and State. He afterwards described the scene to the Rev. George Dodds—the
wagons standing at the monastery gate, ready to
leave, piled up with such of the Fathers' belongings
and the treasures of their Order as they were able
to take with them. In reply to a question whether
they had looked sad amid the bustle of departure,
Dr. Whyte answered :

" Yes, of course they were sad ; *and I was
sad too*. Though their faith was somewhat
different from mine, I could not but feel what
it must mean to leave what had been the home
of their Order through so many centuries."

During these years one great happiness to Dr.
Whyte was the more frequent converse which the
circle of five intimate friends enjoyed as the passing
years brought some increase of leisure. Dr. Dods
and Dr. Taylor Innes had been resident in Edinburgh
for many years ; but Dr. Webster Thomson's retirement in 1902 from his church in Aberdeen brought
him within more easy reach of the other friends, and
Dr. Sutherland Black also was able regularly to join
the circle. The range of learning represented by the
five was remarkable—not in theology alone, but in
classics, literature, law, and some departments of
science. Dr. Whyte, borrowing a phrase from
Coleridge, spoke of Dr. Taylor Innes's " oceanic
reading," and the phrase might fitly have been

applied to the others as well. The contributions of Dr. Dods and Dr. Black to the common fund have already been indicated. That of Dr. Webster Thomson lay largely in a singularly sympathetic temper, a mature wisdom, and a wide knowledge of religious art. When his active ministry reached its close, Dr. Whyte wrote the following letter :

" VERY DEAR THOMSON,—This is a great milestone to you and me. But, then, it is only a milestone. The end of the Journey will be all joy.

> ' When the shore is won at last,
> Who will count the billows past ? '

You say you have been an ' unprofitable servant.' Who has not ? Who but One ? And, for that also, we are complete in Him. ' What would I do as a minister,' said Thomas Boston, one of the most profitable servants of Christ in Scotland—' What would I do, but for the " Imputed Righteousness " ? ' And one of Chalmers' last entries in his Journal was this : ' What would I do, if God did not justify the ungodly ? ' Dear Friend, you have been of great profit to us, your favoured friends, at any rate. It is not given you to know or believe what you have been to us. What a strong pillar, beside broken reeds. What a strength of judgment, beside our weakness of character and will. You cannot know how we all have leaned on you, and looked up to you,—and everybody knows it. Chatting to old Mrs. Raleigh in her room on Saturday, and turning to you, I said, what I often say, ' I have able men among my friends, and good men—but I have no one like Dr. Thomson, for soundness of judgment, and warmth of heart combined.' She drew her chair nearer me, and threw a kiss at me for her answer.

" Dear Thomson : As Chalmers said also, about Loch Lomond—I hope there will be a

Cruden Bay in heaven : and two or three times
yet on the way !

    " Salute your children and your doctor for

" A. W."

Of Dr. Taylor Innes Dr. Whyte said, when preaching his funeral sermon :

> " To the praise of God in His servant, I will
> say that I never knew a man so just, so fair,
> so honourable, so scrupulously generous, and
> so universally considerate and kind in all his
> criticisms and characterisations of friend and
> foe as Dr. Innes was."

Dr. Taylor Innes had a graciousness and dignity of
manner which were in part due to the Highland
strain in his blood and upbringing, but were chiefly
the expression of a spirit finely tempered by the
double school of study and suffering—his married
life had lasted but a single year: He carried his
learning lightly, and seemed little anxious to secure
success at the Scottish Bar or to apply his exceptional command of English prose to the writing of
such a notable book as his friends never ceased to
look for. It is true that he was recognised as the
greatest authority on Scottish Church Law, and his
few books are still valued by men whose judgment
counts for much ; [1] but his friends had in view a work
of wider appeal. " Dr. Dods and I," said Dr. Whyte,
" were wont to quote Dr. Johnson against our
friend, and to say to him, ' Sit down doggedly, sir !
And sit down at once ! ' " Two written exhorta-
tions may also be quoted to the same effect :

> " If this summer you would write a ' reminis-
> cence ' every day, of your life and of your
> college friends, like Mozley's *Reminiscences*, and
> publish anonymously next winter, you would

[1] Mr. H. J. Laski is among those who have given high praise to his
Law of Creeds in Scotland. (See *Studies in the Problem of Sovereignty*,
p. 29 n.)

do us a great service, and create a great sensation for good. You could write a brilliant book of such sketches which would save the next generation of students from many mistakes and stumbles—intellectual, moral, theological, and religious. Think of it, and lay it to heart.

" A. W." [1]

" Thank you, dear Innes, you have done more than you will ever know to make these thirty-five years bright for me. And no one will rejoice more to see this great book of yours than will your devoted friend,

" A. WHYTE."

On one memorable occasion in 1906 " the five Cardinals," as Dr. Whyte's children sometimes called them, met in conclave at Balmacara. In Edinburgh they commonly spent Saturday afternoon together, when Dr. Whyte's preparation for Sunday was already accomplished, and his mind was free for the discussion of their many common interests. They met for lunch, sometimes at Dr. Dods's house in Great King Street, more often at 7 Charlotte Square. A long walk followed, while the others maintained their power of walking far, and it often ended round Miss Innes's tea-table in Morningside. She noted that, on these occasions, although Dr. Whyte usually spoke less than the others, he was always the inspiring spirit of the group, leading the conversation to fresh fields, and drawing out the interest and information of the others. His own joy in these Saturdays is expressed in a note to Dr. Innes, written on a Saturday at the end of a holiday in Mull :

" MY VERY DEAR INNES,—I look to see you this day week for a walk. You must not talk of shortening or sacrificing our walk for golf or anything else. One of the bright things of my

[1] The hope here expressed was partially fulfilled by the publication of Dr. Innes's *Chapters of Reminiscence* after his death.

life will die out if you ever give up our long
Saturday walk as long as we are able to take it.
Conceive, if you can, our Saturday walks in
heaven !—Love to you and all,   A. W."

A letter to Miss Innes at the close of a summer
at Balmacara contains the sentence : " We have had
a rich succession of dear friends, and what has this
life better to give ? "   And a later note to the same
friend shows how the writer looked even on the
lesser events of life, such as a holiday plan broken
into by illness, in the light of Eternity :

> " Let me honestly and truly express my
> feeling for you in this ' crook in your lot '—
> that you are not in the Highlands by this time.
> I can well imagine what a disappointment this
> is to you and Dr. Innes. But, cheer up ! ' In
> His Will is our tranquillity.' I share my deepest
> thoughts with you as I meditate this week-end
> on, ' In Thy Presence is fulness of Joy.' Pray
> that I may speak with truth and power on
> these words on Sabbath."

The same characteristic is shown in a long letter
to his wife describing a journey from Balmacara to
Edinburgh with a visit to the dentist as one of his
objects. Owing to the carelessness of a porter at
Inverness, the bag which contained all the fruits of
his preparation for the following winter was lost ;
but the following day saw its recovery, and the letter
concludes :

> " The dentist and everything has seemed full
> of hope and comfort since I got my little bag.
> I had consoled myself all the way from Inverness
> with the 32nd Paraphrase,[1] and such-like, and
> with the assurance that God knew where my
> bag was, and that if He had need of its con-
> tents and of me He could preserve it, and if

---

[1] " What though no flowers the fig tree clothe "—a rendering of
Hab. iii. 17, 18.

He had no need of it and me then it were better I never saw it again."

Literature and politics filled a large place in the talk of the five friends, but the chief place belonged to the Bible and its interpretation and to the Church and her work. No difference of judgment broke the harmony of their talks, yet there was undoubtedly a wide divergence between the advancing critical radicalism of Dr. Sutherland Black and the open-minded but guarded outlook of the other four. Some years before, Dr. Whyte had written regarding an article on the Second Gospel by Dr. Black: " I think your Mark exceptionally good : in its clearness, reasonableness, and reverence. Go on with such work : and grow in such virtues : is the prayer of—Yours, A. W." His attitude to his friend's later work as joint-editor of the *Encyclopædia Biblica*, and sponsor of the advanced Swiss and Dutch critical theories which that work brought to the notice of British readers, is shown by the following letter—written from Bonskeid in April 1901 to his eldest son, then taking a year in Germany between school and college :

" DEAR FRED,—Your mother has just read to me your delightful letter from Dresden. It is a letter after her own heart, and she read it to me with the most appreciative emphasis. You must have had a delightful time. As we have had here. . . .

" Our first visitor here was Dr. Sutherland Black. We had a time of great enjoyment with him. Dr. Black is naturally full of his *Biblica*, which is being severely handled by all the critics, especially the article ' Gospels ' by Professor Schmiedel of Zurich. He is a critic himself of extraordinary boldness, not to say anything more. He applies to the Gospels the disintegrating method which has for so long been applied to the Old Testament. The result

is startling enough to the student of the Gospels.
Dr. Black wholly goes with his contributor, but
scarce anyone else in England or Scotland goes
with him. Of course Dr. Black is outside the
jurisdiction of the Churches, but there is some
fear of trouble at the Assembly over George
Smith's last book,[1] as well as over the book
of a young and very able scholar of our Church,
Mr. Moffatt. He has published an *Historical
New Testament* full of the new learning, and
sufficiently disconcerting even to such liberals
as Dr. Dods. But it is much to be hoped that
the controversy will be fought out in the critical
journals, and not in the Church courts. I have
been led into this page by the mention of Dr.
Black's name. For we talked about nothing
else but Biblical criticism all the time he was
here. We walked one day to Tummel Bridge
and back : and, literally, every foot of the way
talked of these new and great questions. . . .

" I have read a good deal while here for my
class-work next winter, *D.V.* Chiefly Wesley's
Journals, a remarkable book. I shall probably
have four lessons out of the two Wesleys and
Whitefield. *Your* next winter is much in our
thoughts. But He who has the keys at His
girdle will take that matter in hand, as He has
so wisely and graciously taken us and all our
affairs hitherto."

This letter should be read in the light of the
admiration which Dr. Whyte often expressed in later
years for Dr. Moffatt's work, and of a friendship which
grew steadily stronger with more frequent meetings.
Once when Dr. Moffatt's claim to a certain theological
chair was being discussed, and the suggestion was
made that it might be wise for the Church to choose

---

[1] *Modern Criticism and the Preaching of the Old Testament.* Sir
George Adam Smith's book was made the subject of a " heresy " case
a year later, but he was acquitted by a large majority of the General
Assembly of his Church.

a less daring scholar, Dr. Whyte broke in with, " I put all my money on Moffatt ! "

In these years, as at all periods of his life, Dr. Whyte's absorption in theological and devotional reading and in the practical work of the ministry never interfered with his watchful observation of public events, or with what Sir William Robertson Nicoll called " his unnatural interest in the Press." To meet or to correspond with men who were taking a large share of the world's burden always gave him pleasure. Lord Morley sent the following graciously phrased message on the last day of the year 1901 :

" I thank you sincerely for being so kind as to send me your beautiful book on Newman, which I have read with refreshed interest.

" I venture humbly to enclose, χάλκεα ἀντὶ χρυσεῶν,[1] a small piece of brass in return for gold."

Two years later he wrote again in acknowledgment of a letter from Dr. Whyte regarding the *Life of Gladstone* :

" FLOWERMEAD, WIMBLEDON PARK, S.W.,
November 8, 1903.

" DEAR DR. WHYTE,—I thank you for your kind letter, and for the vivacious way in which it conveys pleasant and friendly notions. My task was really impossible, and yet somehow it has been performed.

" To me almost more interesting than the general approval of the book is the question how many people will have eyes for the host of delicate issues lurking under a prosaic surface. Of these people you are pretty sure to be one.— Yours sincerely, JOHN MORLEY."

During the following winter, 1903–4, Dr. and Mrs. Whyte had especial pleasure in welcoming two distinguished public men who stayed with them during short visits to Edinburgh, Viscount Peel and Mr.

[1] *Iliad*, vi. 236.

Joseph H. Choate. The ex-Speaker of the House of Commons came as leader of the Temperance movement, which grew out of his celebrated Minority Report on Licensing Reform, and which for a time drew together an unexampled number of leading men and women from very different parties and churches. For two or three years, 7 Charlotte Square became a kind of glorified committee-room from which the activities of the " Peel movement " in Scotland radiated out. The stir and noise of the movement were, indeed, arrested outside the door of " the Study " ; nor did Dr. Whyte at this time speak in public on questions which had a political bearing. But he followed with warm interest this attempt to bring fresh forces into the temperance movement, and gave his own support both by his presence at meetings addressed by Lord Peel, Lady Henry Somerset, and others, and by signing the manifestoes of their campaign. It gave him great satisfaction to welcome as his guest the dignified statesman who, at the end of a long life of public service, had sacrificed his years of leisure to head this new crusade.

A few months after Lord Peel's visit, Mr. Joseph H. Choate, then American Ambassador in London, visited Edinburgh to deliver an address as President of the " Associated Societies " in the University. At this time Dr. Whyte's eldest son was President of the University Union, and Mr. Choate stayed with the Whytes. He proved a gracious and charming guest, and his own impressions were recorded in a letter written on his return to London, in which he said :

> " I look back upon my two days and four hours in Edinburgh as among the richest of my life, and the best part of it all was that I was permitted to have a glimpse of your own family life—so unique and so interesting—and to enjoy your generous and cordial hospitality."

Much has been said of the concentration of Dr. Whyte's energies on the vocation which he so steadily

pursued. This cannot be overstressed ; yet these
records show, too, the other side of his nature, and
make it clear at how many points he touched life
and to how many interests his mind and heart were
hospitable. So this chapter may fittingly end with
three or four brief letters illustrating different interests
of this period :

To Professor Saintsbury he wrote :

> " I am an old admirer of your work and you
> must not think this line an intrusion or an
> impertinence. I thank you for your letter in
> to-day's *Times.* Such a letter sweetens the air
> and will do good. My heart warmed to you
> again when I read it.—Your indebted reader,
>
> " A. W."

A wholly different side of his various reading is
indicated by a post card to his nephew, Dr. J. Y.
Simpson, who had recently been appointed Professor
of Natural Science in New College, Edinburgh :
" Be sure to order Waggett's *Scientific Temper in
Religion* (' in the Press '). The contents make me
think of you." And when a younger brother of the
same family, to whom the counsel already quoted on
the use of an interleaved Bible had been sent, was
about to preach his trial discourse before Dr. Dods
in United Free St. Luke's Church, Dr. Whyte wrote :

> " *Saturday Night.*
>
> " DEAR HUBERT,—I shall think of you to-
> morrow forenoon. I wish I could have heard
> you preach in the dear old pulpit, from which
> I have heard so many sermons of grace and
> genius and scholarship. For dear old Moody
> Stuart had all three. We look to you young
> fellows to take up the tradition of scholarship,
> and deep, tender, experimental preaching. From
> the moment you enter the pulpit think of nobody :
> neither yourself, nor Dods, nor anybody else.
> When you give out your text say—aloud, if you
> feel moved—but in any case say with Newman :

' May the motive of the preacher be the salvation of the hearer, and may the hearer's motive
be his own salvation.'   A. W."

Another friend of these years, whom Dr. Whyte
knew through correspondence before they met face
to face, was Mr. John Owen of Wellington. Dr.
Whyte's reply to his first letter began : "You have
a great name—John Owen " ; and a few months
later this letter followed :

> " MY DEAR FRIEND,—God has given you a
> warm and a gracious heart : and what better
> blessing can He give to any man ? Your truly
> noble letter came into my hands this morning
> when I much needed such a word of comfort.
> The Lord will reward you.
> " I go from home less and less. Years gather
> on me : and my work here is never done. It
> accumulates on my heart and conscience as the
> years pass. But I lean on a gracious Arm, and
> I am supported by the great kindness of such
> men as yourself.—With high regard,
> " A. WHYTE."

On Dr. Whyte's sixty-ninth birthday, a letter of
congratulation from Dr. and Mrs. Barbour called
forth this reply :

> " *January* 13 [1905].
> " VERY DEAR BROTHER AND SISTER,—If there
> is any man living who can say, and who ought
> to say, without ceasing, ' Bless the Lord, O my
> Soul, and forget not all His benefits ! '—I am
> that man. All that fills my heart as I write the
> above date, I can tell to no one.
> " Dearest Hugh and Margaret, God more and
> more bless you.
> " ALEXANDER WHYTE."

CHAPTER XXIV

FREE ST. GEORGE'S AND FOUNTAIN-
BRIDGE : CALL TO DR. KELMAN

1901–1907

" Come, my friends,
'Tis not too late to seek a newer world."
TENNYSON.

" If the ministers of the Church to-day go out among the poor
and needy, they are not by any means going into dark and heathen
places, but into places where the response of the human spirit and its
sense of infinity are as much to be reached as in the mansions of the
rich."—LORD HALDANE.

THE last three chapters have been occupied with an
account of Dr. Whyte's wider interests and of his
service to the Church in the more remote parts of
Scotland ; but all through these years the central
work of his life went on for eight months in each
year in harmonious co-operation with his junior
colleague, Mr. Hugh Black. Its main features have
already been described, but certain activities deserve
mention which especially marked this period. Three
books were added at this time to the list of his
published writings. The renewed study of Bishop
Butler in his Classes, where the great Anglican was
treated as the last of the Stoic moralists, led to
the publication in 1903 of a volume containing an
Appreciation and extracts from the *Analogy* and the
Sermons. A further volume of evening addresses
also appeared—the last of the six volumes of *Bible
Characters*—which bore the title, *Our Lord's Characters*, and contained for the most part studies in the
Parables.

In 1905, Dr. Whyte's long-looked-for study of the
Life of our Lord was published. In the judgment of
many this was his greatest book. Its full title, *The
Walk, Conversation, and Character of Jesus Christ
our Lord*, in itself foreshadows the treatment of
its great subject. It is the least subjective, and

at the same time one of the most practical, of Dr. Whyte's books. It shows the gentler rather than the more daring side of his imagination—his imagination in its sympathetic and interpretative use; and nowhere in his writings are there more frequent touches of quiet yet penetrating insight, or more unexpected applications of incidents from the Gospel story to the life of every day. These qualities stand out especially in the studies in the Youth of Jesus in the earlier part of the book, and in the later sermons on, " A Teacher come from God," and " The Son of Man hath not where to lay His Head"; and, if there are any sermons of which it may be said more truly than of the rest that no other preacher could even have conceived their outline, they are three which occur in sequence—" Our Lord at Table," " Our Lord's Holidays and ours," and " How our Lord and His Disciples would read their Newspapers."

Throughout these years Dr. Whyte's love for the Mystics was undiminished, and it gave him real happiness to note how the classics of the devotional life were being brought steadily within the reach of the ordinary reader. One of a series of post cards to Mr. H. R. Allenson, whose small edition of the Mystics had then begun to appear, bears the inscription, " Happy man to be able to spread abroad such spiritual gems ! ", and another reads :

" *Sabbath Morning.*
" Thank you sacredly for your beautiful *Brother Lawrence.* I carry a little copy in my vest pocket continually. Your choice and cheap edition will give him a new lease of his fruitful life.   A. W."

Other messages refer to Tauler's Sermons ; and once, when Dr. Whyte came upon Luther's glowing tribute to Tauler in preparing his class-work for the following winter, he forthwith sent a post card from Balmacara to Mr. Allenson with the passage transcribed in his own hand.

He had ere this become the preacher of preachers to not a few who knew his sermons only from the printed page, and it was not less true that he was a pastor and friend to many outside his own congregation and Church. For they found that his sympathy surmounted barriers, theological and other, which other men lacked imagination to pass over. On one stormy Sunday night, late in March of the year 1903, all the household at 7 Charlotte Square had already retired, save that a circle of young people were still talking in the " schoolroom " to the right of the front door. They heard the door-bell ring, and the eldest son went to the door, where he found a man waiting on the doorstep while a cab stood in the rain with a dimly seen figure inside it. The visitor asked for an immediate interview with Dr. Whyte; and when it was suggested that it was now too late for an interview, but that a message would be given to him in the morning, he replied that his business was so urgent that no message would serve, but that he must see Dr. Whyte at once. His son went to fetch him from his bedroom, and then left him in the study with the mysterious visitor.

About twenty minutes later the stranger left, and Dr. Whyte came to the schoolroom saying, " Fred, I want to speak to you." When they were alone in the study he said that his visitor was the legal adviser of General Sir Hector Macdonald, who had been the hero of the Highland regiments—and, indeed, of the whole Highland people—since the Sudan campaign five years earlier, and whose tragic death in Paris had become known a day or two before. His body had just been brought home to Scotland, and the funeral was to take place at the Dean Cemetery early on Monday morning. The solicitor had begged Dr. Whyte to conduct the funeral service. He had at once consented, and he asked his son to be ready to accompany him six hours later, for it was now close on midnight. The service at the grave was very simple, but it was conducted with all the tenderness and the deep note of human sympathy which Dr.

Whyte brought to such an occasion as this ; while his son shared with Lady Macdonald and one or two others the sad privilege of laying the remains of the Highland soldier in their final resting-place. Not far off was the spot where Dr. Whyte had laid the body of his little son eighteen years before, and where his own body now rests.

The most noteworthy event in Dr. Whyte's ministry on its practical side during the years following his moderatorship was the new departure made in the work at Fountainbridge.[1] Twice before, the congregation in the mission-church there had become strong enough to emerge from the state of pupilage and to make a new and independent beginning. In the year 1899 the time was felt to be ripe for this process to be repeated ; and the colleagues in Free St. George's appealed to their people to furnish £4000 to enable the Fountainbridge congregation to start afresh in the growing district of North Merchiston. In effect, the parent congregation thus bought back for the third time the buildings in Fountainbridge which they had originally erected ; and by so doing they did much to make it possible for the Rev. George Low and his people to break fresh ground in the " Candlish Memorial Church." The way was thus made clear for a new venture in Home Mission work. About a hundred of the former congregation remained in Fountainbridge as a nucleus, and the office-bearers of Free St. George's were called upon to give very special help, as a new Kirk-Session and Deacons' Court began to be built up in the new congregation.

In Dr. Whyte's view the choice of a minister to undertake such a task as that now opening in Fountainbridge was of the greatest importance. High as was his estimate of the work done by the Church's scholars, he reckoned such service in the Home Mission field as at least on an equality with it. Thus he once wrote of the Rev. William Ross, who

[1] Cf. pp. 168, 255 f. above.

had toiled for many years in one of the most difficult
fields in Glasgow : " Noble fellow !   There is no man
in all Scotland doing better work. I would rather
have his record than that of any minister I know."
And during a later vacancy in Fountainbridge, after
the death of this old friend, he wrote :

> " I could wish it were possible to get Ross
> of Cowcaddens sent back to earth for twenty
> years : he would be the man.   But even he
> was not Ross of the Cowcaddens when he came
> to it.   Cowcaddens, and much of the grace of
> God, made him."

Fountainbridge did, however, secure two successive missionaries—Harry M. Ross and T. Struthers
Symington—very different in their gifts, but alike
in the devotion with which they placed these gifts at
the service of the men and women and children around
them. It was to the former that the task fell of in-
augurating the new work. He was a native of Inverness, possessed of all the Highland softness of voice
and more than the traditional Highland enthusiasm.
No man could have given himself to his work with a
more unreserved dedication ; and when he died in
Aberdeen in the last days of 1922, worn out before
his time by the intensity of his self-giving, but
radiantly happy to the end, he was described as
" the most Franciscan man whom his Church has
ever produced."   The tribute was anticipated by the
boys of a class in a neighbouring school during his
ministry in Fountainbridge, whose teacher was seeking to explain what a saint was.   At first they looked
perplexed, but as her description advanced, a light
broke, and they shouted, almost with one voice,
" I ken yin : Harry Ross ! "
     Dr. Whyte's estimate of his young friend's work
was given in a letter written when he went to
Aberdeen :

> " Fountainbridge has had a splendid succes-
> sion of Missionary-Ministers from James Wilson's

day [1] down to the present day; and Mr. Ross's
name shines out among them with a lustre all
its own.   In personal character, and in spiritual
genius, Mr. Ross stood quite by himself.   And
for many a day he will be remembered in Fountainbridge with the highest honour and with the
warmest love."

Mr. Ross, in his turn, said of Dr. Whyte : " In
days of doubt and misgiving, when I am not far
from doubt and despair, I find in the tokens of his
faith and love the key of the prison."   When the
young missionary took possession of the old manse
close to the church, he found evidence that while
Mrs. Whyte and others had planned to provide for
his outward needs, Dr. Whyte had taken thought
for his intellectual equipment.   A revolving bookcase sent from the study in Charlotte Square was
waiting, with eight volumes of Newman's Sermons.
Some time after, when Mr. Ross was ordained to the
full charge of the congregation, these were joined
by a selection of Puritan divines, with the recommendation, " The Puritans are an inestimable
treasure to those who will use them aright."   But
more than such gifts were the unfailing interest and
sympathy shown by Dr. Whyte towards his work,
and that of his like-minded sister and wife—as
towards all who grappled with the problems of
Fountainbridge both at this and at other times.
When the whole district was torn by a strike in the
rubber works, in which many hundreds of men and
girls were employed, Dr. Whyte took the question
deeply to heart, and gave his best counsel to Mr. Ross,
who was striving to help in securing a just settlement.   He was unwearied in his endeavour to maintain a close contact between Fountainbridge and the
whole membership of St. George's, and to enlist as
many active workers as possible.   He would set
aside a precious half-hour of his Classes' time in order
that the missionary might plead for volunteers for

[1] Dr. James Hood Wilson of the Barclay Church.

the many activities under his care ; and Communion seasons were always kept as times when the claims of Fountainbridge, both on the gifts and the prayers of the congregation, were especially remembered. It was also a well-understood arrangement that this work claimed all the time that Dr. Whyte's assistant could spare from his congregational duties.

Dr. and Mrs. Whyte were at one in the conviction that a mission church deserved the best service that could be given to it, and made a steady effort—in which they were supported by a band of workers too numerous to name here—to break away from the idea that such a church provides a fitting repository in which backless hymn-books and chairs of doubtful stability may end their career. In summer, successful flower shows were carried through ; but the most notable enterprises in this direction were two loan exhibitions held in the church hall in Fountainbridge. The first was an Art Exhibition which was open for ten days in the summer of 1902. The Committee of Management included the then President of the Royal Scottish Academy and his successor in office, the present King's Sculptor for Scotland, the Professor of Fine Art in Edinburgh University, and the Director of the Scottish National Gallery ;[1] and the exhibits ranged from Raeburn's portrait of Sir Walter Scott to works by Watts and Rodin and by several of the leading Scottish artists of the day. This exhibition was so warmly appreciated and the lectures given on the pictures and other exhibits were so intelligently followed, that somewhat later an historical exhibition was organised on the same lines. Again the committee included the most expert men and women in Edinburgh in the field covered by the exhibition, and the objects lent showed Scottish history in miniature from early times, through its heroic age (represented by the spurs of Robert the Bruce) to examples of the primitive culture still sur-

[1] Sir James Guthrie, *P.R.S.A.* ; Sir J. Lawton Wingate, *P.R.S.A.* ; Pittendrigh Macgillivray, R.S.A.; Professor Baldwin Brown; and James L. Caw, F.S.A.Scot. Mrs. Traquair was also a member.

viving in the Western Isles. Still later, Dr. Whyte
took part in the dedication of a memorial window in
Fountainbridge Church, given by Miss Grace Warrack,
and executed by a young artist in stained glass—Miss
Una Adamson. The occasion was made memorable
by an address by Mr. D. Y. Cameron, in which he
spoke of Art as " that ceaseless music which linked up
all the centuries—a great spiritual language, which
could move where no other influence moved," and
pled that once more " the Church should be the great
home of Art, as it was in other days."

Dr. Whyte's own share in the varied activities in
Fountainbridge took up no small part of his time and
strength.   One letter refers to a " mothers' strawberry
feast " there, and in another he tells his colleague
who was absent at the moment, that, in spite of a
severe cold, he must go to a " soiree," as the disappointment would be too great if neither colleague
appeared.   His deepest interest, however, always lay
on the personal and evangelistic side ; and in the
midst of the New Year Temperance campaign, or,
as it was tactfully named, " Holiday Festival," he
sometimes gave the address at the Watchnight service.
At one such service he gave a deeply impressive
address on the words, " Hold Thou Thy cross before
my closing eyes."   But his help took many different
forms, and ranged from his presence and counsel at
the Advisory Board to an address given during the
midday meal hour at the slaughter-house to such of
the employees as cared to gather in the " jobbers'
room."   On one occasion he and Mrs. Whyte arranged for their too hard-working friend, the missionary, to take a journey to the United States, and
on another sent him for a fortnight to study the
methods of the London settlements. When they
were at Bonskeid one summer, and he was camping
with a band of lads from his club some twenty miles
away, they arranged that the party should come
over for an afternoon.   Mr. Ross always retained a
memory of Dr. Whyte showing the beauties of the
Falls of Tummel to one of the party, whose drinking

habits had given great concern to all his friends, though he was a good-hearted lad in his sober hours.

No account of Dr. Whyte's work for Fountainbridge could approach completeness if it failed to mention his relation to two other bodies—the Men's Brotherhood and the Children's Choir. The former had its origin early in Mr. Ross's ministry, when the " Pleasant Sunday Afternoon " movement was new, and therefore somewhat suspect, in Edinburgh. He went to Leeds and other English cities to see the P.S.A.'s in operation there ; and on his return he and Mr. William Cairns, who had accompanied him and became secretary of the new Brotherhood, started the venture in Fountainbridge. The central activity, there as elsewhere, was the religious meeting on Sunday ; and the accessories of Book Club and Holiday Club were soon at work. As these developed, Dr. Whyte followed them closely and gave the full weight of his influence to support the Brotherhood against its critics. When it had been fully established, he arranged for a type of service new to Free St. George's, over which he himself presided — a Brotherhood demonstration in which organ and orchestra harmoniously joined. The Book Club made an especial appeal to him ; and at the half-yearly book-distributions, when the volumes (over 150 in number) purchased with the weekly pennies of the members were handed out, he either attended and spoke himself or sent a message of encouragement. But his chief reason for supporting the Brotherhood movement was that he looked upon it " as a door to the Communion Table." That it did in an important degree fulfil this function in Fountainbridge was shown by the concurrent growth of the rolls of the Brotherhood and the Congregation ; for, while the former was quadrupled in two years, the latter more than doubled.[1] These results confirmed Dr. Whyte's

[1] The increases between 1903 and 1905 were : Brotherhood membership, 207 to 794 ; Communicant membership, 186 to 400. A considerable part of the latter increase was attributable to the work of the Brotherhood.

estimate of the work done by Mr. Ross and his fellow-workers. What he on his side contributed was indicated by Mr. Cairns's statement, as President of the Edinburgh Brotherhood Council, on the Sunday after his death, that " the memory of that great-minded and large-hearted preacher and friend would live long to encourage and hearten and inspire them. A son of the people, Dr. Whyte knew instinctively what labouring toil meant."

The Children's Choir, conducted by Mr. Cairns in Fountainbridge, lay quite as near to Dr. Whyte's heart. He often presided at its concerts, and on his way to the platform he would pause to say a word of encouragement to the expectant children gathered in their best array behind the scenes. One of his opening speeches contained a special word of praise for the joiners who had set up the stage for the concert ; he said he would prefer to speak of them as *carpenters*, thus, in Harry Ross's words, " lifting their work into the divine atmosphere." Another occasion in Fountainbridge when he rejoiced to be present and to speak, was the service at which the boys and girls who had attended the children's meeting in the church hall were, at the age of fourteen, presented with illuminated certificates of transfer, and were intro-duced to the congregation, of which it was hoped they would soon become members.

After Mr. Ross left Fountainbridge, Dr. Whyte more than once visited him at Bainsford, near Falkirk. In the manse there, Dr. Whyte showed a special interest in his little boy, and, patting his head, said, " A Shakespeare head ! " Nor did it really spoil the parents' delight when they learned from another minister's wife, a few months after, that the same compliment had been paid to *her* boy ! The services of this Bainsford Communion Sunday were indeed a rich spiritual feast, for Dr. Whyte preached on " Who is a God like unto Thee ? " in the morning ; on " The Lord's my Shepherd," and William Law on Prayer in the afternoon ; and on Psalm ciii., the post-Com-munion psalm, at night. On another Sunday he

31

found time between services to visit the senior elder
of Bainsford Kirk, who was seriously ill, and greatly
strengthened the sick man by the prayer that " the
Name of the Lord might be as medicine unto him."
Another saying which remained firmly in Harry
Ross's memory was this : " If we cannot have Christ's
arm, we can have His heart."

It was inevitable that, as Dr. Whyte's ministry
in Free St. George's lengthened, many of those who
had supported him longest and most faithfully should
pass from his side.   The winter of 1905–6, which
completed his thirty-fifth year as minister, brought
a succession of particularly heavy losses.   At New
Year, Mr. A. W. Black, M.P., brother of Dr. Sutherland Black, died of injuries received in the Elliot
Junction railway accident during the great snow-
storm of that winter.   Within a few months, Professor J. P. Wood, Professor Laidlaw, Mr. Hately,
Mr. James Simson, and more than one other leading
elder passed away.   Professor Wood was one of Dr.
Whyte's many trusted friends in the legal profession,
and was, in words used by Dr. Whyte after his death,
" a great lover of our Church and of our Lord."

The same winter brought warning of an approaching loss of a different kind.   It was, indeed, foreshadowed in a letter from Norway to Dr. Taylor
Innes in August 1905, in which Dr. Whyte said :

> " After three weeks on the heights above the
> capital [Christiania] I will return home to let
> Mr. Black off to America.   He has been having
> amazing congregations all these past Sabbaths.
> What a spell he holds over the people ! "

This visit to the United States resulted in Mr.
Black's being called to a chair in Union Theological
Seminary, New York.   In addition to his work in
this famous college, the appointment gave him many
opportunities of preaching and meeting with students
elsewhere.   Two years earlier he had declined a
similar call ; but he had now completed ten years'

service in St. George's, so it was no surprise when he decided to accept the renewed offer of the chair in New York. Dr. Whyte was kept informed at every step of the negotiations, and entirely understood the reasons for his colleague's resignation, so they parted with the same cordiality with which they had worked together ; yet the resulting vacancy in the junior pastorate of Free St. George's was a serious blow to him, for, as he characteristically said of Mr. Black, " He helped me in every way—rather, it was I who helped him." So now, at the age of seventy, Dr. Whyte again found himself faced with the prospect of bearing for some considerable time a burden which he had found well-nigh crushing when he was a much younger man. In May he wrote to his nephew, J. Y. Simpson, then recovering from a serious illness in the South of France, telling him of Mr. Black's probable departure, and adding :

> " What am I to do ? Resign also, and make it a clean and clear vacancy ? Give me your mind and your father's mind when you are able. And be able soon !—Most affectionately,
>
> " A. W."

On the back of this letter are pencilled notes of a possible reply in Sir Alexander Simpson's hand.[1] Several reasons in favour of resignation are suggested —the strain and anxiety of a new vacancy for a man of seventy, the desire that " Scotland and the world " should hear Dr. Whyte's message, and not Edinburgh alone ; and the possibilities that a lectureship in Evangelistic Theology might be found for him, that he might have more leisure for writing, or might visit America. These were the thoughts of one of the most loyal elders of Free St. George's, who had special opportunities of gauging the relative importance of the narrower and the wider claims upon Dr. Whyte's time and service. There is no record

---

[1] Professor Simpson had received the honour of knighthood a year earlier on his retirement from the Chair of Midwifery in Edinburgh University after thirty-five years' service.

whether a letter on these lines was ever sent; but by the end of the year such thoughts became familiar to many of Dr. Whyte's friends, and even began to gain public utterance. In particular, the religious need of the Highlands, where he had done such unique service a year before, was felt to constitute a strong claim on his future energies. What, it was asked, might he not do to repair the breaches in the Church of the North if he were set free from regular congregational duties, and could work from Balmacara or elsewhere as a " Superintendent " after John Knox's own heart?

For several months Dr. Whyte himself watched with eagerness and some anxiety the effort made by the congregational committee to persuade the Rev. John Kelman of the New North Church, Edinburgh, to follow Mr. Black as colleague in St. George's. Mr. Kelman was the son and namesake of Dr. Whyte's old friend and ally of the Revival of 1874; and for ten years his eloquence, his freshness of outlook, and his power of drawing young men and women into a new sympathy with religion, had made a deep mark on the city, while his students' meetings in the Operetta House had been as sustained in their attractive power as those of Henry Drummond fifteen years before. It was natural that Free St. George's should look to him as the ideal successor to Mr. Black, but the question at once arose whether he would feel justified in leaving a vigorous, attached, and growing congregation to go to another in the same city, and whether, if he did so, his unique work among the students of the University could go on. Dr. Whyte confined himself to urging Mr. Kelman, in a letter from Balmacara on 14th August 1906, not to reach a final decision until he had heard all that the representatives of Free St. George's had to urge in support of their request. It was a severe disappointment when Mr. Kelman stated that he felt his duty still lay in the New North; nor did requests to three other well-known preachers, made before the end of the year, reach a more fortunate issue.

In the autumn, Dr. Whyte wrote to Mrs. Robert Simson :

> " Thank you for your kind and beautiful letter. Thank you very much. This business is tearing me to pieces : but I feel it to be my best duty to the congregation to leave the work to a younger and a fitter man."

It was the belief indicated in the last sentence which chiefly prompted the resignation which Dr. Whyte placed in the hands of the Kirk-Session on 9th January 1907. However much he may have desired either relief from the burden of responsibility or leisure for other work, he would not have resigned unless he had been at the moment convinced that the congregation would profit from " a clean and clear vacancy." This appears from more than one letter. A few hours before Dr. Whyte met with the Session, his wife wrote to Mrs. Robert Barbour, telling how the decision had been reached—and reached with the approval of Dr. Barbour, who, like Sir Alexander Simpson, united the characters of elder in St. George's, brother-in-law, physician, and trusted counsellor. The letter continues :

> " We believe St. George's will call Mr. Kelman, and that under his guidance it will go forward with renewed energy to fuller service than ever before. For my husband I believe the decision is also right, and his mind is at peace. His health is excellent, but the strain has been great for many years, and I believe that with release from anxiety he will go forward to new and happy work, whether in his study among his dear old Mystics, or among our friends in the Highlands."

Two days later Dr. Whyte wrote to Dr. Taylor Innes :

> " As you know, my mind has for a long time been settling toward my resignation. It has been a painful process, but it is over now. My

immediate resignation is my clear and imperative duty to the congregation : and that apart
from any question of colleagueship. In my
clear judgment my time of usefulness to the
congregation is at an end, and hence my decision.
What this decision is costing me I shall not
attempt to put on paper even to you."

But the congregation by no means agreed with
this view of their minister's " clear and imperative
duty," nor did they admit that he had no further
work to do for them. Even before they met on
21st January, in order to beg him to remain with
them, he had himself begun to waver. Four days
earlier he wrote to Dr. Webster Thomson, thanking
him for the support of his friendship and counsel,
and saying that " not a few fresh and powerful considerations " had been pressed home upon him, and
that he had asked for a week's delay before he reached
a final decision. " I am full of fear," he concluded,
" lest I take a wrong and irretrievable step ; or do
not take the right step."

Before the week thus asked for elapsed, a resolution was passed with enthusiasm at the congregational
meeting. It expressed the gratitude of his people
for Dr. Whyte's long ministry, their sense that his
power had never been greater than during the months
when the whole weight of the pastorate had again
rested upon him, and their earnest hope that he would
retain the senior pastorate, and so help in every way
the colleague whom they hoped speedily to obtain.[1]
This resolution and the report of the speeches of Mr.
Howden, Mr. Stuart Fraser, and Sheriff Campbell
Lorimer, three of the elders who had supported it,
further influenced Dr. Whyte's mind towards a
continuance of his ministry in Free St. George's ; and

[1] A first draft of the resolution exists in Dr. Taylor Innes's handwriting, from which one sentence may be quoted : " They recognise
especially that Dr. Whyte, while preaching always the everlasting
Gospel, has taken upon him the burden of the changing times, and has
been enabled in a singular degree to unite the hearts of the fathers to
the children and of the children to the fathers."

he wrote to Mr. Scott Ireland, who had become
Session-clerk not long before : "Thank you, in pen
and ink, for the *Resolution* of Monday night. I would
have a heart of stone not to be moved by such extraordinary kindness." But a still more decisive factor
was a frank talk with Mr. Kelman, whom the congregation were again preparing to call, on the understanding that, if he came to Free St. George's, he
would have full opportunity to continue his students'
meetings. At the outset Dr. Whyte urged the view
which had been so much in his mind—that it would be
easier for a new minister to start work as sole pastor of
Free St. George's than as junior colleague ; but the
younger man blew this argument into thin air by
stating emphatically that, while he might give fresh
consideration to a call to be Dr. Whyte's colleague, he
could not even consider a call on other terms. Once
persuaded that this was Mr. Kelman's real mind,
Dr. Whyte wrote a letter to be read at the next meeting of Kirk-Session :

"DEAR MR. SESSION-CLERK,—If you agree
and resolve this evening to call Mr. Kelman, I
would like to tell you how long I was beforehand
with you in my discovery and in my appreciation
of our friend. I was beforehand with you by
some fifteen or sixteen years. For when I was
looking out for the best assistant I could lay my
hands on all these years back, I selected Dr.
Kelman's son, then newly licensed. But I was
just a day too late. For when I went to invite
young Mr. Kelman to come to my help, I found
that he had been engaged only the day before
to go to Aberdeen to assist Dr. George Adam
Smith. But for that day's delay of mine Mr.
Kelman might have been first my assistant, and
then my colleague, all this time. Only in that
case we would never have had Mr. Black. But
Mr. Black came and remained with us till Mr.
Kelman is at his best. . . . If you secure Mr.
Kelman for yourselves and for me, we shall feel,

and we shall say, with the Psalmist, ' What shall we render unto the Lord for all His benefits towards us ? '

"Loaded with His benefits, I am most truly yours, ALEXANDER WHYTE."

The rest of the story can be briefly told. After Dr. Whyte withdrew his resignation, the call to Dr. Kelman (as he soon after became) was vigorously pressed forward ; and after some weeks of intense conflict between the claims of the old sphere and of the new, he agreed to come to St. George's. This happy issue for the congregation was largely due to two men—the Rev. W. M. Falconer who had guided their deliberations with singular wisdom as Moderator in the vacancy, and Mr. Scott Ireland, to whom Dr. Whyte wrote during his Easter vacation at Borrow-dale : " Above all men, it is to *you* we owe this great settlement. *I*, at any rate, look on it so. God bless you for all your labour of love."

With Dr. Kelman's induction as colleague, the last period of Dr. Whyte's long ministry began. To this fruit-bearing, autumnal season of his life belong also his principalship of the New College and his greatest work for the cause of Christian unity, which will together introduce the last division of this record.

PART FIVE—"UNTIL THE EVENING"
1907–1921

CHAPTER XXV   PRINCIPALSHIP OF NEW COLLEGE,
                                     EDINBURGH
1909–1916

> " If I live yet, it is for love, more good
> Through me to men."
> BROWNING.

> " The perseverance of the saints is made up of ever new beginnings."

DR. WHYTE's interest in the theological colleges of
his Church, and especially in New College and its
students, had never flagged. He gave signal proof
of it, as we have seen, by devoting the presentation
made by his congregation at his semi-jubilee to found
a Theological Literature Prize. Sometimes he himself gave copies of a book which he admired to all the
students in one year or in the whole college ; or if,
as he confessed on one occasion, he " was quite run
down in his bank-book," he would stir up the generous
mind of some friend to take his place, that he might
present a new book of Dr. Denney's or a new edition
of a Puritan divine to the students of one of the
theological halls.

He greatly appreciated, too, the opportunity of
addressing gatherings of divinity students. But these
opportunities came only at intervals, until, when he
was already an old man, a closer bond was formed.
A reference has already been made to the death of
Principal Rainy at the close of 1906 ; and during
the somewhat troubled two months that followed,
when the questions of the St. George's colleagueship
and Dr. Whyte's own resignation were still unsettled,
he was further embarrassed by a proposal that he
should be appointed to the vacant principalship.

It was argued that this post, which the distinction of its occupants from Chalmers to Rainy had made the most conspicuous in the Church, would give him a fitting platform from which to do wider work, especially in the Highlands ; and it was hinted that the alternative choice of Dr. Marcus Dods would not be acceptable to the more conservative section of the Church in the North. But this proposal, good as were the intentions that prompted it, was most unacceptable to Dr. Whyte himself. It seemed, indeed, to involve something not far short of treachery to a friendship of more than forty years ; for, as long as Dr. Dods held his chair in the New College, his great work as an interpreter of the New Testament and the qualities which had bound his students to him in an affectionate regard, both as a teacher and as a man, gave him an incontestable claim to the principalship. It was a real distress to Dr. Whyte that he should be placed in even apparent opposition to his friend, and his satisfaction was all the greater when, after he himself had most emphatically refused nomination, the General Assembly of 1907 unanimously appointed Dr. Dods Principal.

Unfortunately, the new Principal's tenure of office was brief, and was shadowed both by his own increasing ill-health and by the death of Dr. Webster Thomson, which made the first break in the circle of the five friends. At this time Dr. Whyte wrote to Miss Innes :

" If you can spare your brother at all at lunch to-morrow, do send him in to me. It is the first time that he, Dr. Dods, and I will meet after the removal of our friend. And I would like much that we all break bread together— both in remembrance, and in anticipation."

In April 1909, Dr. Dods died after a lingering illness, and the principalship of the New College again became vacant. Again Dr. Whyte's name was mentioned, and on this occasion many who had considered Dr. Dods's claim incontestable two years before, were foremost in urging Dr. Whyte's appointment.   The precedent of Dr. Candlish's principalship was quoted, since he had held the post with distinction while he was senior minister of Free St. George's.   At first, Dr. Whyte's unwillingness to accept nomination was hardly less pronounced than two years before.   He wrote to the Convener of the College Committee (Dr. A. C. Welch, who became his colleague in the New College not many years later) stating that he could not accept the post ; and he prepared a letter to the Moderator of Edinburgh Presbytery, setting forth his reasons :

> "I have neither the classical scholarship, nor the theological learning, nor the intimacy with academical matters, nor the clearheadedness, nor the surefootedness, nor the talent nor the taste for leadership, nor any gift for dealing with such theological and academical and ecclesiastical problems as are pressing for solution, and all of which endowments and attainments ought, in my judgment, to be conspicuously possessed by the Principal of the New College. I do not possess even one of those endowments : and the things I have not received, nor have been enabled to attain, must not be demanded of me nor expected from me.—Believe me to be dutifully and affectionately yours,
> "ALEXANDER WHYTE."

His private letters at this time were hardly less emphatic.   Yet the Church took a different view both of the qualities required by a Principal and of those possessed by her distinguished son, and the opinion that Dr. Whyte should be called to take up the honourable succession grew in strength until the Assembly met.   Meanwhile Dr. and Mrs. Whyte went to St. Mary's Loch to avoid the strain of its meetings. But many messages continued to reach him, and an incident may be recorded which shows how his sense of humour came to his rescue in these perplexing days.   A letter arrived from Edinburgh which made it needful to communicate with one of his advisers there.   The one post of the day had already gone, so he and his wife walked along the lovely road from Rodono to the little post office of Capper-cleugh, where the telephone had recently been installed.   Dr. Whyte always left the task of tele-phoning to some deputy, and on this occasion he sat with a peaceful smile in the corner of the little office while his wife wrestled for twenty minutes with a dilatory and not too audible telephone.   She finally emerged from the contest, hot and somewhat out of temper, remarking, " It is working very badly."   He replied, " The astonishing thing is that it works at all !   Don't you remember ' Bozzy ' and the dancing dogs ? "   On the way home he told the story, as he remembered it—how Boswell had once complained to Dr. Johnson that he had wasted five shillings in seeing an exhibition by a troupe of dancing dogs, which, he said, had *danced very badly*; so he asked whether Dr. Johnson did not consider that he had been defrauded. "Not at all, sir ! " Dr. Johnson replied; " *the marvel is that they danced at all !* "   The dancing dogs became a family proverb from that time forth.

During these days of retreat a change came over Dr. Whyte's mind regarding the principalship. Quite suddenly, it would appear, the counsel of the inward Monitor which had so steadily forbidden him to accept the position was changed, and when the call of the Church came, he found himself free to obey. On Sunday, 23rd May, he conducted a little service at Cappercleugh, and at the close of a quiet day said to his wife, " If it is God's will, He will put something in my heart, to turn my judgment in that direction." Next morning, he came down saying, " I cannot explain ; but He has turned me towards it." On Tuesday, Dr. Barbour — now, as ever, at hand in moments of perplexity—arrived in a taxi from Edinburgh, bringing the latest reports of feeling in the Assembly.   Later in the afternoon a sheaf of telegrams of congratulation arrived, from which it appeared that the Assembly had not only been unanimous, but that no other name had been brought forward, and that Dr. Whyte was requested to meet a deputation in Edinburgh next day. When they met, his friends in the deputation urged him to accept the principalship, but there was little need of urging, since the *vox ecclesiæ* and the interior Voice were now at one. At the evening session of the Assembly he was introduced to the House, wearing the grey overcoat familiar to his fellow-citizens, and stood facing the chair as the Moderator (Dr. Archibald Henderson) asked if he accepted the office to which the Assembly believed that Christ, through His Church, was calling him. The applause amid which he had entered was hushed as he replied in memorable words :

" I think, sir, in the morning, when we were conversing about this, I said that my feelings were such that I could not employ many words, and I fell back on these words which sprang to my mind, *Secretum meum est*—my feelings are my own. My thoughts about myself, and my estimation of myself—these are all my own. No man here who knows me, or anything about me, will doubt that my feelings are very deep, indeed indescribable and incommunicable, and therefore I will not dwell upon them. For the past two or three years, whenever my name came up—and I could not shut my eyes and my ears—whenever my name came up about the principalship, I felt it was the most preposterous thing, and the most impossible thing, that could be suggested. In all sincerity that was my feeling. As the months went on this grew upon me—I have to apologise to some friends here in the House and others for the way that I repelled them sometimes when they came to press this upon me. I sometimes said—and they could not answer that—I sometimes said that, if ' He in whom will and power are one ' had designed me for this office, He would have spoken to my judgment, and would have led my heart. That was my feeling and judgment for months and years. But last week, sir, unaccountable as it may seem—I am not trying to account for it, because there is nothing unaccountable in the ways of Christ towards His servants, if I may say I am one of them—as I was not a member of the Assembly, I went to the country to get some quiet rest and reading. And, in a way I will not attempt to describe—I do not understand it myself—a hand seemed to take hold of my heart and turn me towards some aspects of this office—as much towards those aspects, as my heart had been at one time turned from them. It is my own secret. I need not attempt to justify the change, or to explain it : I cannot do it. And when, after a week's thought . . . your overpowering message came to me last night, this scripture came with it : ' A certain man had two sons. He said to the first, " Son, go work to-day in my vineyard." The son said, " I will not," but he afterwards repented and went.'

" Fathers and brethren, I am not making jest of the Lord's words. I can sincerely say that that came home to me with remarkable power and, shall I say, confidence. And if I was for two or three years saying, ' No, I will never do that,' I come now to say, ' If you have any work for me to do, I have repented of these things, and I am willing to take it up.' I will only add, fathers and brethren, that when you are near God in the pulpit, and at the family altar, and especially in secret, you will remember the New College, and the students and the Professors, and especially the poor Principal."

The news that " Dr. Whyte of Free St. George's " had become " Principal Whyte of the New College " as well, brought joy to many hearts and congratulations from many hands. His replies had in every case an individual touch—the unmistakable sign-manual of the writer. Two may be quoted which relate this new honour to old friendships. To Mrs. Alexander Barrie he wrote :

> " I wish your husband had been in the Assembly last week. There is no man I would like to share all this with me more than ' Barrie.' Assure him that his name is written among the deepest in my heart, and indelibly.—God bless you both, and all yours."

And, acknowledging a letter from Mr. Longair, brother-in-law of Dr. Webster Thomson, he said :

> " My post-bag would not have been complete without your letter. For it connects my beloved friend, Dr. Thomson, with this new situation in which I find myself. Had he been in life he would have been the first man I would have consulted about it. And, how his sound judgment, and pure heart, would have supported me ! "

If there was an inevitable backward look, Dr. Whyte now also showed an exhilaration of spirit and power of entering into contact with the minds of his students which surprised some even among his friends. The prospect of association with young men who were preparing for the Christian ministry, the sense that his own hard struggle for knowledge had been thus vindicated in the day's end, and the relief of a decision made clear after long perplexity, must all have had their share in raising his spirits to a glow which could not be quenched even by the task of acknowledging seventy-six letters of congratulation which arrived in one morning. Now that he had passed the threescore years and ten, a vein of playfulness came to the surface which had found little outlet during his arduous middle years. At meals he chaffed his wife and daughters continuously. When mushrooms appeared, he feigned suspicion: " You're sure they're all right ? . . . Ah,

well, I'll just escape the principalship ! " And when
a letter of congratulation was opened from a man
twenty years his junior, who explained that he himself was already on the shelf, Dr. Whyte looked across
the table : " I think, Mother, if you'll have a shelf
put up, I'll just get onto it ! "

A few days later he wrote in more serious vein to
his son, Fred, in London : " I am reading, I suppose
for the dozenth time, Hanna's *Chalmers*. He was the
first Principal of the New College. Oh ! what a falling
off is here ! Be sure you read *Chalmers* carefully."

Another letter to his son, written on 12th October,
refers to the actual beginning of his work as Principal :

> " New College opens to-morrow. The thought
> of the opening has given me a multitude of
> thoughts, such as no man in Scotland can
> possibly have the like. And I hope I may
> have courage and wisdom to give expression to
> some of them in a way that may be encouraging
> and strengthening to those students who have
> been ordained to begin life as I began it."

The Inaugural Address here alluded to is that on
Former Principals of the New College, which furnished
so many vivid reminiscences for the earlier chapters
of this book. The closing passage in particular,
in which Dr. Whyte unlocked the treasure-house of
memories of his boyhood and student days as he
had never done before, made a deep impression on
the large gathering in the Assembly Hall which was
privileged to hear it. To these days also belong
the address in Aberdeen on the Revival of 1859,
which gives the clearest picture of another side of
his youth,[1] and a letter to John Dickson—the last
of a series which extends over fifty years.

> " You may have heard," it says, " that the
> Assembly took the amazing step of making your
> old friend Principal of the New College last May.
> And now the time has come for me to open the

[1] Chapter V., above.

Session. I will have occasion to mention your name in my opening address, and I wish you to come over and be present. Will you do me that great favour for the sake of the old Kirry times? Do come! "

In Dr. Whyte's hands the principalship gained a somewhat new significance. The Principal of New College was no longer the recognised leader in the polity of the Church, as each successive Principal from Chalmers to Rainy had been; but Dr. Whyte was singularly successful both in winning the personal confidence and love of the students, and in relating the life of the College to that of the community and the Church. His doubts as to his own " surefooted-ness and clearheadedness " in the conduct of college business were soon set at rest, or proved irrelevant; for he used to say that no Principal could have failed to perform that part of his work with credit who had a Secretary of Senatus like Dr. Alexander Martin at his right hand. At Senatus meetings, as at every other board over which he was called to preside, Dr. Whyte's great contribution was his own presence, and the atmosphere of dignity, charity, and utter humility and disinterestedness which that presence brought. Yet he brought also a store of ripe wisdom garnered from his long experience of the virtues and the mistakes of his fellow-men. With his colleagues in the Senatus, his relation from first to last was one of entire confidence, and their work together was a delight to him as to them. As one of their number wrote after his death:

" It has been a joy and honour to have him for years as Principal of New College. In most ways he was younger than any of us. Nature itself taught us to revere him: and what we revered was a character that became nobler every year."

For the rest, he attended the college dinner from time to time, and on special occasions, such as the

32

opening or close of the session, either presided or
gave an address himself. The " Appreciations " of
Goodwin and Wesley, afterwards published, were
originally delivered in this form.[1]

The burden of the principalship was not in itself
heavy for one who had performed so many arduous
tasks as Dr. Whyte. Yet it came to a man of seventy-
three, who was still responsible for half the pulpit
work and much of the pastoral care of St. George's,
and was bearing the whole weight of his two Classes ;
and so it contributed to the first breakdown of his
health at the end of 1909, less than two months
after the delivery of his Inaugural Address. As
we have noted, he had already become a venerable
figure before he reached the age of sixty. Then, for
fifteen years, age seemed to make little further mark,
save that it added a perfect whiteness to the silver
hair and constantly increased the beauty of his
expression. During this long period his energy
showed no failure, and, apart from recurrent attacks
of rheumatism in one shoulder, his health was the
envy of many younger men. But at this point a
sudden heart attack gave warning that even his
strength had limits, and that a measure of rest was
necessary if his working life were to be prolonged.
Happily the needed relief was gained. His physicians
(Dr. Joseph Bell and Dr. G. A. Gibson) felt considerable anxiety during this winter and the following
summer when a second heart attack followed the
World Missionary Conference ; but gradually his
health was re-established, and those who leant upon
him, in congregation and college and far beyond, were
enabled to hear his voice for full seven years more.

The beginning of Dr. Whyte's illness came at an
unfortunate moment—a few hours before he was to
receive one of the greatest honours of his life, the
Freedom of the City of Edinburgh. This was without
doubt the rarest distinction conferred upon him, for
it had not been granted to any minister of religion
for generations, if, indeed, any minister had received

[1] *Thirteen Appreciations*, pp. 157 ff., 361 ff.

it since the Reformation.[1] It was thus a unique
proof of the confidence and regard of all classes of his
fellow-citizens, and showed how high an estimate
they set upon his service to the community as a
whole. The Freedom of the City was at the same
time offered to Mr. Asquith, who was unable to
receive it till a later date, and to Sir William Turner,
who had been Principal of Edinburgh University
since 1903. Thus the University, and the New
College, were honoured together in the person of their
respective heads. In some ways no two Principals
could have been more different than the great
preacher and the great educational administrator
and teacher of anatomy. Yet there was a certain
resemblance between the careers of Sir William
Turner and Dr. Whyte which made their association
seem wholly appropriate. Each had been a citizen of
Edinburgh for so long that even men in middle life
could scarcely remember the time when their citizen-
ship began. Each had been appointed Principal
when over seventy years of age, and lived to justify
his appointment by years of fruitful work. Each in
his own way had been a great teacher ; and each
retained in old age a power of vigorous speech and
a dignity of bearing which recalled an earlier and
more stately epoch.

It was a sharp disappointment to Dr. Whyte's
friends, as to himself, that he could not receive the
Freedom of the City with Sir William Turner in the
Synod Hall on 10th December 1909. But two months
later, immediate anxiety as to his health had been
relieved ; and the Lord Provost, Sir William S.
Brown, arranged a special and less exacting ceremony
in the Council Chamber on 8th February 1910, at
which Dr. Whyte was enrolled as an Honorary
Burgess. In acknowledging the honour which the
City had conferred, he spoke of the great citizens and
preachers in the far-off days when he had first known
Edinburgh, and of the greater future that awaited
a re-united Scottish Church.

[1] I am indebted to Mr. F. H. Deas for verifying this statement.

During the following year, Dr. Whyte was one of the select company who were present at the Inauguration by Their Majesties, King George and Queen Mary, of the Thistle Chapel, which had been added to St. Giles Cathedral. In the same year, the last of his academic honours came to him when he received the degree of Doctor of Laws from his own *Alma Mater*. It gave him no ordinary pleasure to receive it at the hands of Dr. (now Sir) George Adam Smith, who had become Principal of the University of Aberdeen less than two years before. During the days which he spent at Chanonry Lodge as the guest of his old friend, he recounted many student memories of King's College, to which he now returned after forty-nine years amid circumstances so greatly altered. The student-audience greeted him with " a popular ovation " when he came forward to receive the degree of LL.D. from the friend who, in Scots phrase, had " sat under him " in Free St. George's long before.

It is easier to describe these outward landmarks in Dr. Whyte's life at this period than to give an impression of his day-to-day influence on the life and work of the New College. This influence was felt on the side of practice not less than on that of study. In Chapter VI. we saw that he had been a leader in the " Missionary Society " of his own student days ; and his principalship coincided with a time of expansion in the work for social betterment with which that Society had been especially charged. The scene of their work was now the Pleasance—a district of Edinburgh which had long ceased to deserve a name given centuries before, when it contained the houses and gardens of the wealthy, overlooking the eastern wall of the old city. For some twenty years, settlement work had been carried on there by the students, and had steadily grown in effectiveness. In 1908 the Rev. J. Harry Miller was appointed Warden, and left a church in the western part of Edinburgh in order to take up this work. Mr. Miller was one of Dr. and Mrs. Whyte's most intimate friends among the younger ministers of the Church, and Dr. Whyte on becoming Principal readily entered into his plans for the development of the Settlement's activities. It is not needful to tell in detail the story of Dr. Whyte's association with the Pleasance Settlement, since in several ways it repeated his part in the forward movement in Fountainbridge less than ten years earlier. Here, also, his wisdom proved a strength to the Advisory Council, he spoke with a gracious geniality at such social meetings as he was able to attend, and he dispensed the Lord's Supper or the Sacrament of Baptism with a solemnity and a tenderness which no other could approach. But in this new field there was another side of the work which he steadily kept in view. It afforded the practical training-ground of students preparing for the ministry; so he used the whole weight of his influence to make this training effective, and to secure full recognition for the Warden as a member of the teaching staff of the College. He often asserted that it was not so much by the study of generalised " problems " as by seeking to help this and that burdened life that true ministers were made. When the progress of the work made it needful for a Kirk-Session to be formed from the Advisory Council, he warmly supported this scheme in the Presbytery, so that the company gathered in from the mean streets around might advance towards a true congregational life.

The material needs of the work were also much on his mind; and it was a great satisfaction to him when a small group of generous business men joined to purchase a derelict brewery adjoining the somewhat cramped settlement buildings, and to convert it into buildings for the extension of the Settlement, and for other agencies aiming at social betterment in the district. A further scheme to which Dr. and Mrs. Whyte gave much thought was that of forming a residence for theological students out of the two lofty houses in Mound Place, immediately to the west of New College. It was their ideal thus to provide a place of welcome for the many foreign students who came to take classes there ; but Dr. Whyte also laid stress on the social gain for "regular " students from other parts of Scotland.   Information was gathered as to the working of residential theological colleges in the United States and elsewhere ; and, though the full scheme could not then be completed, two important results were achieved, thanks to the generous support of Sir Michael Nairn and other friends.   The new quadrangle, originally suggested by Professor Patrick Geddes, was formed out of the waste ground in front of the Rainy Hall and made into a terraced, stone-flagged garden ; and a Warden's Lodge was provided, which brought its occupant into closer touch than before both with the College itself and with the Pleasance Settlement.

Dr. Whyte was ever on the watch for opportunities of coming into personal contact with his students, and two gatherings stand out conspicuously in his first two years of office.   Before the war, the theological course of the United Free Church extended to four winters, the summers being left free for other work, as they had been when Dr. Whyte was a student.   Thus " the Fourth Year " completed their course in spring.   A letter to his eldest son in March 1910 shows how Dr. Whyte planned to meet such an outgoing group of students in four days of friendly converse in the island of Arran :

" Our arrangements for April are completed. The Fourth Year New College men all come to us from the 8th to the 12th.   And Dr. Moffatt comes to speak to them on Richard Baxter, and Mr. Macaulay on Phillips Brooks.   We intend two hours of such work in the forenoon : and then the long afternoon for walking and climbing, etc., and the evening for social enjoyment.   This is a new experiment, and the smallness of the Fourth Year class enables us to make the experiment under the best conditions.   The plan would be perfect if *you* could be with us.   Is that likely ?"

The experiment yielded so rich a harvest of profit and enjoyment that it was repeated with some variations in autumn. On this occasion the party was composed of the students who were about to enter the New College Settlement as residents, and included Dr. Herbert Gray and the sub-warden of the Settlement, Frank W. Scougal, a son of Dr. Whyte's old friend, afterwards a missionary in Manchuria, who gave his life on the Salonica front during the great war. From 26th to 30th September, Dr. Whyte was at Bonskeid, accompanied by his devoted daughter, Margaret—he had still to be carefully guarded against over-exertion—while Mr. and Mrs. Harry Miller entertained the eight prospective residents less than half an hour's walk away. Several hours every day were spent at Bonskeid, and Dr. Whyte talked with the men in twos and threes, walking near the house and watching the first gold and crimson of autumn stealing over the trees in the valley. Then the company of twelve or fourteen gathered in the dining-room, and he spoke for over half an hour, giving of his best, as he often did when he had fewest hearers, and encouraging free discussion after he had spoken. On the first day his topic was the place of the Settlement and of the practical work carried on there in the life of the College ; on the second he gave lessons from the lives of his own college friends, naming no one, but describing in swift, vivid touches how one man of brilliant parts had proved a failure in the testing work of his vocation, while another, of far less natural ability and academic distinction, had built up an effective and attached congregation by using to the utmost the powers which he possessed and by unremitting pastoral effort. But the third day's talk was the most memorable, as Dr. Whyte opened the secret of his own perennial freshness of spiritual vision. His subject was that on which he had often enlarged—*Nulla dies sine linea*—the vital importance for the preacher, of industry, method, and constant application. Towards the close he said that his

hearers might perchance wonder why he, an old man
whose working days were now drawing near their
end, should still continue the toil of study instead of
seeking for rest. His answer was that the call still
came to him to use his days, however few they might
be, to find in the best writers fresh truths and lessons
which might, by God's grace, bring some further
inspiration to his congregation and to the young
men and women of his Classes.

Another " Retreat," of which Dr. Whyte acted
as leader not long after, was held in the Women's
Missionary College of the United Free Church in
Edinburgh by a number of its former students, who
had returned from widely scattered spheres of work
for a further course. Dr. and Mrs. Whyte were
keenly interested in the growth of this College for
the training, in biblical studies and the psychology of
religion, as well as through educational and social
work, of women preparing to serve in the foreign
field or at home. They watched with admiration
the guidance of its activities by its first Principal,
Miss A. H. Small ; and on this occasion they gladly
took part in a brief reunion of those who had passed
through it. One of those present, a missionary on
furlough from India, thus described the gathering,
and the way in which Dr. Whyte stamped his own
devotional spirit on every action, from the brief but
memorable words of thanksgiving before each meal
to the Lord's Supper celebrated before they parted :

> " We spent three profitable hours with Santa
> Teresa, John Bunyan, and William Law, but it
> is difficult to give you even a breath of the air
> which has restored our souls. It was just the
> atmosphere, the atmosphere of Heaven, which
> our leader lives in continually."

Only a few of the students who passed through
the New College during Dr. Whyte's principalship
took part in the gatherings in Arran or at Bonskeid,
but each student spent at least one long evening in
Dr. Whyte's study. Sometimes he asked Dr. Denney

or Dr. Kelman to speak on a minister's work to the men of "the Fourth Year," gathered at 7 Charlotte Square; but more often he talked himself, and his students had the inspiration of hearing him in his own library, surrounded by the battalions of his books. "The First Year," as well as the senior men, had their own evening, and one of his later students, the Rev. J. N. Dick, has thus described it :

> "As Principal of the New College, he was the most beloved man within its walls. His was no mere academic interest, but a personal care for the individual student. . . . One memorable night he showed us his interleaved Bible, open at the preface to John's Gospel, and well worn, well annotated, well fingered it was. Countless notebooks, filled each holiday (as he told us) with material for his famous Bible Classes, were also produced. And so the evening passed on, until the favourite hymn was sung and the favourite benediction pronounced. Then Law's *Serious Call* was put into each man's hand, and, as he bade us ' Goodnight,' we were assured of ' an ever-open door at Charlotte Square.' "

The "non-regular" students, gathered from beyond the Atlantic, from Hungary and other continental lands, and even from Armenia, were not forgotten, and Dr. Whyte set aside an evening each winter to spend with them. Every session before the war brought one or more young American graduates to take a post-graduate theological course in Edinburgh before they began ministerial work in their own land. One of these (the Rev. Charles W. Gilkey, now of Chicago), who came to know Dr. Whyte well during the second winter of his principalship, sends this extract from his Edinburgh notebook:

> "*Alexander Whyte :* the incarnation of all that is noblest and finest in the old type of Scotch preacher and in the Puritan divine.

Careful, faithful, original : a mystic, given to rhapsody, contemplation, vision even ; preaching the unsearchable riches of Christ as revealed in Christian experience. Not speaking or thinking in modern terms, he nevertheless fastens with surprising accuracy on the eternal elements of ' experimental ' religion. An *individual* in character, personality, even style ; whom to know is to love and never to forget : a demonstration to us young radicals of what the ministry has been and may be, and a preacher to age, if not to youth, of Christian perseverance."

Seldom if ever did any Scottish disciple of Dr. Whyte's so unerringly analyse the nature of the tie which bound young men, speaking a wholly different theological language, to their revered master. Yet their respect for his message was hardly greater than his appreciation of work produced by the " young radicals " themselves. Thus he wrote to Lady Simpson after her son had delivered the opening address of one session at the New College :

" OUR DEAR SISTER,—Jim was simply firstrate this afternoon. I was proud of him. He made a great impression on us all, and gained for himself a great place in every thinking mind and loving heart present.—Believe me, your brother,   A. W."

During his principalship the Cunningham Theological Lectureship was held by two scholars born and bred in the Free Church—James Strahan and James Moffatt. Dr. Whyte's delight in presiding at these lectures comes out in postscripts to two letters to Dr. Kelman : " You have no idea of the brilliancy of the lectures Strahan is giving." " We had a simply brilliant lecture from Moffatt this forenoon. He is a wonderful fellow." One of the last meetings at which he presided as Principal—and one of those which most filled him with admiration—was a small gathering at which Dr. A. J. Carlyle of Oxford unfolded with equal enthusiasm and learning a scheme under which the scholars of various churches should combine to trace through the centuries the intricate and ever-changing relations of Church and State.

It afforded Dr. Whyte the keenest pleasure also to transmit to Dr. Denney the invitation to give the Cunningham Lectures in the New College—those lectures on *The Christian Doctrine of Reconciliation*, which Denney lived to write, but was not spared to deliver. The two men first came to know one another well shortly before Dr. Whyte's appointment as Principal; and in 1907 we find Dr. Denney sending him a letter of seven closely written pages on St. Paul and some of his modern interpreters. It is easy to imagine how heartily Dr. Whyte must have assented to such a sentence as—" The Calvinists and the Puritans, I am quite sure, and the simplest evangelical preachers, are right in their instinct for what is vital "; for his openness of mind towards the newer theology had never detracted from his loyalty to the old. From this time forth the friendship grew steadily more close until Dr. Denney's last illness began. Two notes from Dr. Whyte in 1911 ran:

> " Thank you much for your choicely conceived and choicely worded letter. You will not believe how much I value your friendship, and how much I feel honoured and strengthened by it."
>
> " I can honestly say that the writings of no living man restore me and reassure me more than yours nor so much."

In June of the same year Dr. Whyte sent the following post card from Rodono to the Rev. A. B. Macaulay:

> " I have come out here for a few days' ' retreat ' alone. I have read *Jesus and the Gospel* again since I came. A book to be read again and again, and to be proud of, and to pray over.   A. W."

Three years later he wrote from the same quiet retreat to Dr. Denney himself regarding another of his books :

"Bear with me, and let me say what I cannot fully say—how much I have again enjoyed and got good from your *Death of Christ*. I brought the book to this place with me, and, after I had read it again, still I could not lay it down. And I have got enjoyment and good from the book only second to the enjoyment and the good you must have got in writing it. What an honour and what a service to be able to write such a book ! Pardon me for saying how proud I am of you, as so many are, and how much this and all your books make me love you. Go on with such matchless work. Is the report true that you are engaged on a book on Paul ? I devoutly hope it is so.

"Believe me, with more honour and love than you will accept,   ALEXANDER WHYTE."

To this Dr. Denney replied :

"I do not know what to say to your letter, except what you yourself say, that in every way it is far more than I can accept. To think of your reading what I have written at all gives me searchings of heart, but to have you read it twice and then write of it as you do can only come out of your own goodness and generosity and not out of anything in the book. I am more grateful for your kindness than I can tell, and if it makes me proud it makes me humble too.

"How I wish I were able to write a book on St. Paul. If I were free, I might try a chapter or two, but in the meantime I have left the Word of God to serve tables,[1] and am beginning to fear I will soon lose the power either to write or read. The unintelligent and inexperienced books

---

[1] Dr. Denney was giving much of his strength at this time to the convenership of the Central Fund Committee of his Church.

about Paul are dreadful—all done by just men who need no repentance and therefore have no glimmerings of what was vital to the apostle. It is always a marvel to me that the street preacher goes straight to the point in Paul, and finds all his answers where the ninety-and-nine just men find all their difficulties."

The last letter in the series dates from the time when Dr. Whyte resigned his pastorate in St. George's :

"*January* 4 [1916].

"MY DEAR DENNEY,—What can I say in answer to such a letter as yours, but God bless and reward you for writing it ! I lay it at His feet.

"Always, and more than you know, yours,
"ALEXANDER WHYTE."

CHAPTER XXVI

CHRISTIAN UNITY IN SCOTLAND
AND BEYOND

1907–1913

"Love to each plant, that in the garden grows
Of the eternal Gardener, I prove,
Proportioned to the goodness He bestows."

DANTE.

IN the years which followed Dr. Kelman's induction
as colleague in Free St. George's, the story of Dr.
Whyte's work for the New College and for his own
congregation is closely interwoven with that of his
advocacy of Christian Unity—of which he became,
indeed, rather a great exemplar than a mere advocate.
His efforts on behalf of unity were in a true sense a
sequel to his conflict for the freedom of his own
Church described in Chapter XXII. His interest in
other Churches and his desire to enter into fellowship
with them have, indeed, appeared at many points in
this record ; and for many years he had taken an
appreciative part in the meetings of the Christian
Unity Association, where he especially valued the
friendship of the late Dr. Wilkinson, Bishop of St.
Andrews. But his conviction of the evil of ecclesiastical strife was given a sharper edge by what he saw
in the Highlands between 1900 and 1905, and especially in the latter year.

" The sad cleft," he wrote, " that has been
driven through so many of our congregations
in the North during these past years is seen at
its saddest at the Communion season. What
a pain it was to me to see the state of things
in congregation after congregation during these
otherwise heavenly seasons. And what a heavy
cross must lie on the hearts of our ministers, who
have to live and work all the year round among

such divisions and alienations and bitterness as
burdened my own heart even as a sojourner for
a short season among such scenes of sorrow." [1]

The sense, also, that much stiff soil throughout the
Scottish Churches had been turned over by the House
of Lords' decision prompted him, and many more,
to ask whether it was indeed needful to rest satisfied
with existing divisions, or whether a wider union
might not soon be attained.

Even in the Highlands there were signs of hope.
A brotherly feeling was beginning to grow up between
the congregations of the United Free Church and their
neighbours of the Church of Scotland. Just five
years after the judgment of 1904, Dr. Whyte conducted a memorable Communion service at Plockton,
the parish in which Kyle of Lochalsh is situated. On
this occasion the little United Free Church could by
no means contain those who came by boat or by road
from the glens around Lochcarron to join in the Sacrament services, and the weather forbade an open-air
Communion. So the Parish Church was offered and
accepted, and Dr. Whyte dispensed the Lord's Supper
to the united congregations there.

In his own pulpit, also, he kept the question of
unity in its widest bearings steadily before his people.
When a Whitsunday call to prayer for unity was issued
by the leaders of the English and Scottish Churches,[2]
he responded eagerly. On that Sunday he preached
a sermon entitled "That they all may be One," in
which he began by reading the letter which had been
sent out to the Churches of Britain, and continued :

" Along with that so influentially signed letter
let this still more influentially signed letter be
read, which was addressed to the Church at
Philippi, and which was brought to Philippi from
Rome by Epaphroditus. And especially let this

[1] Quoted in the *Daily Record*, 18th January 1907.
[2] The signatories were, the Archbishops of Canterbury and York
(Drs. Davidson and Maclagan) ; Dr. J. H. Jowett and other Free
Church leaders ; and Dr. Rainy, Dr. A. J. Milne, and Bishop Wilkinson
representing the larger Scottish Churches.

peacemaking passage in this apostolic epistle "—
the opening verses of the second chapter—" be
well pondered in our day and by ourselves."

Towards the close of the sermon, Dr. Whyte used
these far-reaching words :

> " The first step to a real union of Christendom
> will be taken when we come to admit and to
> realise that the Greek Church was the original
> mother of us all ; that the Latin Church was her
> first child ; and that through both those Churches
> we ourselves have our religious existence ;
> through them we have the universal foundations
> of our Creeds and Confessions and Catechisms ;
> our public worship also ; our Christian character
> and our Christian civilisation ; and everything
> indeed that is essential to our salvation. . . .
> When we have humbled ourselves to admit that
> some other Churches have things of no small
> moment to teach us and to share with us, and
> things it will greatly enrich us to receive and to
> assimilate ; when we are of a Christian mind
> enough to admit and even to welcome thoughts
> and views and feelings like these—then the day
> of a reconstructed Christendom will have begun
> to dawn, at least for ourselves."

This message was one which Dr. Whyte never
ceased to repeat in varied forms during his ministry.
He was content to leave it to others to define doctrinal
statements or adjust constitutional difficulties, for
his faith never wavered that all these problems
would be solved in due time, if only Christian men
dealt honestly with their own failures and honestly
sought to understand the beliefs and appreciate the
achievements of others. This Whitsunday sermon
was circulated in two forms : it was first sent to
friends of Dr. and Mrs. Whyte as a reminiscence of
their Silver Wedding ; and shortly after, it was
published by Messrs. Dent with a Foreword by Dr.
Cameron Lees, the minister of St. Giles' Cathedral,

Edinburgh, who had proved himself a loyal friend
both to Dr. Whyte personally and to the United
Free Church in her days of trial. Another leader of
the Church of Scotland, the late Lord Balfour of
Burleigh, who did unique service of many kinds for
the Scottish people as a whole as well as for the
national Church, also expressed his whole-hearted
approval. In his letter of thanks to Dr. Whyte he
paid a tribute—all the more generous in that it came
from a former opponent—to Principal Rainy, who
had just died at Melbourne :

KENNET, ALLOA,
" December 22, evg. [1906].

" DEAR DR. WHYTE,—I do not know whether
or not I am actually indebted to you personally
for the copy of your sermon on Unity, which I
have received, with the prefatory note by Dr. Lees.
Whether I am or not I should like to thank you
very warmly for the sermon itself. If we can
all only be got to think of the *difficulties* as well
as of the advantages and duty of peace in a
Christian spirit it will be for our discipline and
health.

" I hope we are all trying and in some ways
really drawing somewhat together.

" In any case I acknowledge your service
in the cause, the greatest to my mind in which
anyone in Scotland can enlist at the present
time.

" You will all be thinking to-day of the loss
you have sustained in the death of your great
protagonist, a notable Scotsman and one who
has made his mark in the history of our time.

" My own personal relationship with him was
always of the pleasantest, and I mourn the loss
of a friend if not in quite so intimate a way as
will be the case with many others.

" With sincere good wishes for the season,
I am, very faithfully yours,

" BALFOUR OF BURLEIGH."

In the six years that followed the receipt of this letter, Dr. Whyte's figure became more and more a rallying-point for those in the Churches of his native land who sought after a closer fellowship and a wider comprehension. Thus the minister of an Edinburgh Parish Church said, " There is no man like him in Edinburgh—just to be in the same room with him is a benediction "; and the organ of the Scottish Episcopal Church referred to him as " a glorious possession, a personality whose influence extends far beyond the borders of his own communion, a character whom we all delight to honour." But while Dr. Whyte's influence extended ever more widely after he had passed the threescore years and ten, he worked as earnestly for brotherhood in the more restricted as in the wider sphere. It may tend to clearness if we now seek to trace, not the exact sequence of events in the years under review, but rather the expanding circles of his endeavour after unity.

Few events in these years gratified him more than the steadily growing co-operation between his own congregation and that of St. George's Parish Church, where the long and fruitful ministry of Dr. Archibald Scott was drawing near its close. Dr. Whyte's feeling had, indeed, greatly changed since he first spoke beneath the dome of old St. George's twenty years before. In 1886, Mr. George Clarke was conducting a series of evangelistic services in the west end of Edinburgh. The meetings in Free St. George's were over, and Dr. Whyte had agreed to introduce him at the first of those held in St. George's Parish Church. Mr. Clarke records how, as they approached together the broad flight of steps leading up to the lofty columns of the portico, his companion withdrew the arm linked in his own and shrank back with a troubled look, while the words broke from him : " I cannot do it : I cannot do it." Mr. Clarke looked inquiringly, and Dr. Whyte added : " You do not understand ; but I cannot do it : no minister of Free St. George's has gone up those steps since

Dr. Candlish came down them in 1843." Then, overcoming his hesitation, he ascended the steps and entered the church. But before the end of Dr. Scott's ministry, this shadow cast by "old, unhappy, far-off things, and battles long ago," had passed away, and it was an unmixed pleasure to Dr. Whyte to enter the sister church. Early in the year 1909, an exchange of pulpits was arranged. Dr. Scott was too ill, when the time came, to preach in Free St. George's, and his place was taken by Dr. James Mitchell of South Leith. In 1911 Dr. Whyte preached in the Parish Church one of his greatest sermons on unity, again choosing the title, "That they all may be one," and driving home the lesson that it was all-important to read the books and the journals written by men of other Churches, and to endeavour to understand their principles. "Because," he said, "all the Churches, and all their ecclesiastical parties, as well as all the nations, and all their political parties, are all appointed and ordained of God not to be an end in themselves, but to be His appointed means of making all men to grow, amid all these things, in truth and in love."

The day on which this sermon was preached was marked by a fierce gale which prevented many from attending, and Mr. M'Kerrell Brown—the elder of St. George's Parish Church who was named in an earlier chapter — expressed his disappointment at the smallness of the congregation. Dr. Whyte's reply showed an outcrop of the Calvinism which lay deep in his nature: " Never mind : those that were ordained to be there, were there." Some years later, as the centenary meeting of the congregation approached, the same friend asked Dr. Whyte if he was bearing it in mind. " Yes," he replied, " I am dreaming about it night and day." At this meeting, on 4th June 1914, the chair was taken by Dr. Scott's successor, the Rev. G. L. Pagan, who not many months after gave his life in the war. Dr. Whyte began his address by recalling Dr. Scott's habitual, cheerful greeting: " How are you, good neighbour ? " and went on to speak of the men who had given the congregation its mould and character in the early days.   Next he compared the separation in 1843 to the going forth of a daughter from her mother's house to form a home of her own, and referred to the other congregations which had sprung from the parent stem :

> " That," he went on, " gives me courage to face you—to know that we have brought the honour and love of five or six congregations besides Free St. George's, who claim you as their great mother, and who look to you to be brought under your great wing at no distant day.   You remember, sir, the Preacher in one of his sermons says there is a time to build and a time to pull down, a time of war and a time of peace.   When I read that, and think of that, I thank God I did not live in the time of rending. . . . I look forward to the day—standing on this coign of vantage, surrounded by such men as I am, it is not very far away—when I see your Church, the Church of Scotland, and the Free Church of Scotland united."

This last vision he steadily sought to keep before the eyes of his fellow-countrymen—and that not only in sermons or addresses directly concerned with the movement towards Union, but on such other occasions as the closing of the long course on " The Makers of Scotland " in his Classes, or when he returned thanks to the Lord Provost and magistrates of Edinburgh after he had received the Freedom of the City.[1]

Meantime, the increasing sympathy between the Church of Scotland and the United Free Church had begun to take practical shape.   The same General Assembly of 1909 which appointed Dr. Whyte Principal of the New College received from the General Assembly of the Church of Scotland an invitation to enter into conference on the causes of their separation.   The acceptance of this suggestion

[1] See pp. 335, 499 above.

by the United Free Church, on the sole condition that the conference should be unrestricted in its scope, and the cordial words in which this acceptance was announced by Dr. Archibald Henderson, the Moderator, gave to many in both Churches a new hope for the religious future of Scotland ; and some of those who had the longest memory of past divisions were among the most hopeful. Such were Dr. Whyte himself, and, in the Church of Scotland, the octogenarian Dr. William Mair of Earlston, who had been working for many years to secure such an advance. Each Church appointed a Committee of a hundred— composed in the Presbyterian fashion of ministers and elders equally—to confer together, under the joint-convenership of Dr. Norman Macleod and Lord Balfour of Burleigh from the Church of Scotland, and Dr. Henderson and Dr. Robson from the United Free Church. Thirty years before Dr. Whyte had supported the Disestablishment movement, believing that it was the first step towards reunion in Scotland ; but now he rejoiced to see a better way open, and to take his place in the Conference. He afterwards confessed to having been a silent member — as, indeed, he was in the Presbytery and Assembly of his own Church, where he was the most assiduous of listeners, but seldom spoke. But when, on 9th November 1909, the Conference on Union held its first meeting, he was asked to lead the gathering in prayer, and his prayer is still remembered by some who heard it :

" Our eyes are filled with a great vision. We pray that it may come, and come soon ; and if the vision tarry, we will wait for it ; and when it cometh we will say, ' This is the Lord, we have waited for Him, and we will be glad in His salvation.' "

Shortly before the General Assemblies met in 1912 a definite milestone was reached in these negotiations. A document, afterwards known as " The Memorandum," was submitted by the representatives

of the Church of Scotland. It was in the main the
work of Lord Sands ; [1] and it gave clear expression
to the claim for Spiritual Independence, which had
always been at the heart of the contendings of the
Free and United Free Church, as well as to that of
the National Recognition of Religion which was a
primary tenet of the Church of Scotland. It further
outlined the steps by which the measure of agree-
ment on these fundamental positions might be made
fully manifest, and other lesser divergences and
difficulties might be removed. After the first discussion of the Memorandum by the United Free
Church section of the Conference, Dr. Whyte wrote
to his son, who had now become Member of Parliament for Perth City :

" MY DEAR FRED,—I was so impressed to-
day with the ability and high tone of the discussion of the Established Church proposals to
our Church, that you will have seen—so impressed, that I am moved to write you to say
that, unless there is something of commanding
importance in Parliament on the day of the
Church-Union discussion in our Assembly, I will
send you a railway ticket so that you may see
and hear that great question discussed in a
worthy way ; as, judging from the committee
discussions, it will be in the Assembly. Not
because you have only an academic interest in
the discussion ; but because you are bound to
have a hand, and, perhaps, a deep hand, in the
parliamentary settlement of this great question.

" Pentland gave a capital speech this afternoon on getting the Freedom of the City presented to him.[2] Both Lady Pentland and he
were full of interest in you and yours.—Your
ever loving Father,   A. W."

---

[1] Then Sheriff C. N. Johnston, Procurator of the Church of Scotland.
[2] Lord Pentland had just retired from the office of Secretary for
Scotland to become Governor of Madras. Dr. Whyte offered the
opening prayer at the ceremony.

Two months later, during the week after the General Assemblies closed, there appeared in the *British Weekly* a long article with the heading, " United Free Church Assembly, May 28, 1912 "— the date of the debate on Union—" *Church Union in Scotland*, An Undelivered Speech by Principal Alexander Whyte." This was the fullest, and most mature, as well as the most imaginative, of all his pleas for Union.

" Having tasted," he said at the outset, " during these past months and years not a little of the sweetness, and the strength, and the exhilaration |of loving friendship with brethren of the Church of Scotland, I constantly regale myself with the vision and the anticipation of the great time that is soon coming to the Church of Christ in Scotland and to the beloved people of Scotland. And while your able and experienced engineers are intently studying how to tunnel this Alp, and how to scale that other Alp, I am weakly leaving all that to far abler and more capable men than myself ; and am dwelling already in luxurious imagination, and in full assurance, on the sunny side of all our Alps of separation."

Then he pictured what would follow the first united General Assembly :

" Just as the famous statue of Memnon was wont, in some miraculous way, to give out sweet sounds every morning as soon as the first rays of the rising sun fell upon it ; even so, it demands no great flight of imagination to see and to hear John Knox, who is the father of us all, lifting up his strong hands of benediction over the gathering and departing members of that great Assembly, and pronouncing over them this captivity-returning psalm of national thanksgiving :

    ' God doth build up Jerusalem ;
      And He it is alone
    That the dispersed of Israel
      Doth gather into one.' "

The "undelivered speech" goes on, in the same strain of impassioned prophecy, to picture the spiritual blessings which will follow the accomplished Union.

> "On the first Sabbath after that greatest of Scottish Assemblies there will be a universal exchange of pulpits from John o' Groats to Maidenkirk. And our Highland brethren especially will hold a perfect jubilee of rejoicing over a faithful, a prayerful, and a reunited people."

Many grave questions will await consideration in the United Church, and will be faced and solved as neither Church alone can face them—questions bearing upon the education of the ministry, the spiritual efficiency of the eldership, the right use of the Lord's Day. "Devotional and liturgical questions also will arise ; indeed, as everybody knows, they are arisen already." And the greatest openness of mind and readiness to learn from other Christian bodies will be needed in this regard. Again, "the Church of Christ in Scotland and the newspaper press of Scotland will work together in the future for the true and the universal good of Scotland, in the good time to come." But, before this Land of Promise can be reached, there is one "insurmountable Alp" that stands in the way—the question of endowments. Dr. Whyte confessed that, for him, this was no more than " a subordinate principle," and characteristically turned the thoughts of his imagined audience to a closely related and positive duty.

> "The ablest speeches, for and against, in this controversy always leave me cold. My passions will not kindle either way. But I will tell you, sir, something that more and more touches and awakens my conscience, and more and more kindles my imagination in this matter of church finance and ministerial support. And that is the great Scriptural principle and the noble practice of proportionate giving. . . . And,

since I am in the vein of prophecy at any rate, I will take it upon me to foretell that there will be such a thankful response to that appeal from that Assembly, that, to employ the prophetical hyperbole, there will not be room to receive it. O yes ! O yes ! Good old Malachi ! There are thousands of poor manses in Scotland where there will be plenty of room found to receive an adequate dividend ; and, along with it, the divine blessing that the Lord hath promised shall always accompany it."

By way of commentary on the reference to liturgical and devotional questions in this vision of the future of the Scottish Kirk, there may be added a remark with which Dr. Whyte closed a long talk on a moor above St. Mary's Loch about this time. He and his wife had been discussing these things, and she asked why he did not give public utterance to his ideals. His reply was : " The time is not yet. Only a united Church would be strong enough to do what I hope for—the recovery of the Christian Year, an optional Liturgy, the simplification of the Standards, Superintendents who will have all the virtues and none of the faults of Bishops."

After the Union discussions in the Assemblies of 1913, Dr. Whyte sent a post card to his son in London : —" Both Assemblies unanimous. The end is sure." Two days later, on 29th May, there occurred one of the brightest moments of his long life. He had been deputed to ask for the support of the Church of Scotland in the evangelistic campaign which was to be conducted during the following winter by Dr. Chapman and Mr. Alexander. On this errand he was accompanied by Sir Alexander Simpson, Dr. James Wells, and Mr. Alexander Sloan. When the deputation entered the Church of Scotland Assembly, and especially when the Moderator, Dr. Wallace Williamson, shook hands with Dr. Whyte, there was a scene of intense enthusiasm, the whole Assembly rising and cheering again and again. As Dr. Whyte addressed the House, carrying them along in his glowing appeal first for union and then for the spirit of revival, and telling of his own experiences of the Revivals of '59 and '74, the Moderator of the United Free Church, Principal Iverach, entered to make the first of those visits of courtesy and brotherhood which have been exchanged year by year since. And he remarked how familiar it seemed, on his first visit to the Church of Scotland Assembly, to find it swept by the tide of Dr. Whyte's eloquence, as the gatherings of his own Church had so often been. It was, indeed, another foretaste and omen of the future—that united future whose accomplishment Dr. Whyte always connected with the divine purpose and the divine guidance. For, after describing the thrill which had gone through his own Assembly two days before, when it was announced that both they and their brethren of the Church of Scotland had decided unanimously to go forward, he spoke of that decision as one that would make "the moderatorship of Dr. Williamson a red-letter day"—though "such aged and withered men as he could not expect to see the day that would crown all their labour with Christ's blessing"—and concluded: "What the Lord has begun, He will surely finish in His good time."

While these steps were being taken towards Presbyterian reunion in Scotland, wider horizons were opening, and here the year 1910 had a special significance. In January, while Dr. Whyte was recovering strength after his illness of the previous month, he had the satisfaction of welcoming to the pulpit of Free St. George's the present Bishop of Durham (then Canon Henson). Next came the approach of the World Missionary Conference, held in the United Free Assembly Hall in June. Dr. and Mrs. Whyte were in close touch with the preparations for the great gathering through their friend, Mr. J. H. Oldham, its secretary. Mr. Oldham, who had been compelled by a breakdown in health to give up the educational work in India to which his life had been dedicated, acted

as assistant in St. George's during the year before Dr.
Kelman came to share the burden of the pastorate,
and his support greatly helped Dr. Whyte throughout
those arduous months. He then showed the same
zeal and thoroughness in dealing with the problems
of Fountainbridge Sunday School as he showed four
years later on the great field of the World Conference,
and so Dr. Whyte followed his work in helping Dr.
John R. Mott to guide its deliberations with all the
closer interest. Much of the practical organisation
in preparing the New College for use during the
Conference was done from 7 Charlotte Square; and
Dr. Whyte's eldest daughter brought to this—as she
brought to countless other tasks during those years—
an energy which was only equalled by her method
and watchful care for detail.

It is not possible to describe here that unique
gathering of twelve hundred delegates from every
continent—men and women who had worked strenuously in their separate fields, and now found themselves members of an international and catholic
brotherhood, for a few days made visible to mankind.
Dr. Whyte felt its full exhilaration, and wrote at the
end: "We have had a week here past all praise."
His own personality and character made an efface-
able impression on many who now saw him for the
first, or the only, time.

The first public session was held on the evening of
14th June. Lord Balfour of Burleigh presided, and
on his right, beside the Archbishop of Canterbury,
was Dr. Whyte, who offered the opening prayer.

"Who that heard it," the late Dr. Alexander
Smellie wrote after Dr. Whyte's death, "will
ever forget that wonderful prayer? . . . There
were thanksgivings for the churches of East
and West, for the contributions to Christian
thought and character and achievement of Anglican and Nonconformist and Presbyterian,
for ' saints of the early dawn of Christ ' and
' saints of the cloistered Middle Age ' and ' saints

of the modern home.' We saw, as in a vivid picture, the procession of mighty souls whom our conquering Lord had been leading through the centuries behind the wheels of His chariot, and turning to His own purposes for the conversion and spiritual education of men ; and our foolish fears were rebuked, and we felt that, with such a Captain and under such a banner, defeat should be inconceivable. It was just one instance of Dr. Whyte's sweep of imagination, his catholicity of heart, and his assurance that doubt and despair are criminal, *Christo duce et auspice Christo.*"

Through the business sessions of the Conference Dr. Whyte sat intent, glad at heart, but silent. One most congenial duty, however, fell to his share. During the second week of the Conference, a dinner was given by the Senatus of New College to a hundred representative Foreign Missionary delegates, and he welcomed them in the Rainy Hall in a speech which was described by those who heard it as one of his greatest utterances. Unfortunately, amid the press of larger meetings, it passed unreported; but Dr. Mott wrote four days later : " He made a truly wonderful address at the New College reception. I have attended countless functions of that kind, but never heard a welcome address that would compare with his on that occasion." A further echo is found in the following letter from the then Bishop of Southwark, afterwards Bishop of Winchester :

" BISHOP'S HOUSE,
KENNINGTON PARK, S.E.,
July 5, 1910.
" MY DEAR DR. WHYTE,—In your charming speech at the banquet you talked of how we must exchange the knowledge of each other's literature. I have very little material upon which to act, but if I send you this little book into which I compressed some thoughts that I

rather care about, and if I add that I have given my wife as her present for her fortieth wedding day your *Bunyan's Characters*, I think you will say that I have not been altogether unmindful of your friendly injunctions.

" It was one of the true pleasures of my Edinburgh visit—so pleasant but so exhausting —to have the honour of making your own acquaintance. Believe me,—Yours very sincerely,
"EDW. SOUTHWARK."

Another exchange took place between 7 Charlotte Square and Kelham ; for a few weeks later Father Kelly of the Sacred Mission, who had been one of Dr. and Mrs. Whyte's guests during the Conference, wrote a most appreciative letter of thanks for a copy of the *Commentary on the Shorter Catechism* which his host had sent. But the most remarkable proof of the width of Dr. Whyte's influence was given in Rome a year later. Its origin was as follows. One of the leading figures of the Conference was Mr. Silas M'Bee, an American layman, the editor of the *Constructive Quarterly*. On the last day of the Conference Mr. M'Bee wrote that he and his wife were returning to their home, " Locust Cove, N.Y.," to put it in order for the next spring, that Dr. Whyte might have " a home in America " when he went to take the messages of the Edinburgh Conference to the people of the United States. This warmhearted scheme never reached its accomplishment : instead, in the spring of 1911, Mr. M'Bee engaged in what he somewhat quaintly called " an eirenic itinerary," embracing a great part of Europe and the Near East. On this journey he sought to gather in fruit from the seed sown at the Edinburgh Conference. After visiting Palestine and Syria, he returned to Rome, where he was graciously received by Cardinal Merry del Val, then the Cardinal Secretary of State, and their conversation turned to a remarkable letter, written before the Conference, by the Archbishop of Bologna (Bonomelli), which had caused a deep impression when it was read there. Mr. M'Bee's letter to Dr. Whyte telling of the interview continues :

" We were later speaking of the letter of Bonomelli at Edinburgh (and you will rejoice to know that I have been unable to find any opposition from any source in Italy to that letter), when I mentioned your name—and immediately the Cardinal exclaimed with enthusiasm, ' But Dr. Whyte is a rare man and his writings are beautiful—wonderful.' This letter is written to have you and your family know that the Cardinal Secretary of State of the Vatican has not escaped your influence." [1]

Some years after, Mr. Basil Mathews was attending an Armenian service in the city of Tarsus. He was informed that the text of the sermon was John iii. 16, but of the sermon itself he understood just three words, " Dr. Alexander Whyte." It may have been through some New College student that the name had been carried so far ; but it is not without significance that the message of the Scottish interpreter of St. Paul should have been received and valued both in the Apostle's birthplace and in the Eternal City where he met a martyr's death.

[1] Letter dated 10th April 1911. Later in the year Mr. M'Bee published an account of the incident in practically the same words in *An Eirenic Itinerary*, p. 104. The fact that the first of Dr. Whyte's writings that travelled outside the Protestant world was his appreciation of the great Spanish saint, Teresa, probably helped to win the admiration of the Spanish Cardinal.

" That which should accompany old age,
As, honour, love, obedience, troops of friends."
SHAKESPEARE.

πρὸς γὰρ Διός εἰσιν ἅπαντες, ξεῖνοί τε, πτωχοί τε.

HOMER.

MANY of the sayings and letters quoted in earlier chapters have shown Dr. Whyte as a bringer of encouragement. This side of his nature was secure from the dulling influences of old age : rather it grew stronger to the end ; nor was it ever more strikingly exemplified than during his last colleague-ship. During these years, seldom a week passed— or, when both colleagues were in Edinburgh, seldom a day—on which Dr. Whyte and Dr. Kelman did not exchange some fragment of congregational news or discuss some question bearing on the work which they shared ; and the numberless messages from the senior to the junior colleague which the patient church-officer—or postman—delivered at 52 Melville Street, constantly ended with a sentence, or a brief but pregnant phrase, of appreciation.

Only a few of these messages, which show how the smallest not less than the most far-reaching problems were settled by the colleagues together, can be given here. Nor is it needful to quote from the large number which deal with the needs and perplexities of individuals, since to do so could but reinforce impressions of Dr. Whyte as a pastor already recorded. But one post card strikes a quite distinctive note. It gives a list of six members whom Dr. Whyte had seen during a Monday afternoon's visiting, and adds the comment :

" No. 1, I found in a strait betwixt two : she could not make up her mind which of her ministers to love most.   But No. 6 is the spiritual *genius* of them all.—A. W."

A post card from Switzerland on Christmas Day, 1908, contains the following self-reproach :

" ——'s death sent a pang of remorse into my conscience for my neglect of him.   Did you know him ?   It took all the Lord's Supper this Christmas morning to allay the pain.   Live for your people !   Christmas blessings !—A. W."

And again :

" Nothing will make up for a bad pastorate. The blood of Christ itself does not speak peace in my conscience in respect of a bad pastorate. Set every invitation and opportunity aside in the interest of a good conscience toward the homes of your people."

On the first New Year's Day after Dr. Kelman came to St. George's, Dr. Whyte writes :

" MY DEAR COLLEAGUE,—I cannot tell you what a joy it is to me so to address you.   Where would I have been without you ?   The peace of mind I enjoy because of you cannot be told. But our Master knows it ; and He will not forget to reward you for it all.

" As to my holiday, I will only say,—Next Christmas, *D.V.*, go out to such a rest and refreshment as I experienced."

Two other messages greet Dr. Kelman on his return from different holidays :

" In the Name of your Master : Welcome ! "
" Most welcome home to the helm.   There is a great sense as of a drifting ship when you are away."

The following note referring to a congregational meeting shows how Dr. Whyte was ever anxious to

set his colleague in the foremost place; and also
bears testimony to his warm regard for Mrs. Kelman
senior, whose strong nature and deep piety had been
nurtured, like his own, in the north-east of Scotland
in the stirring days which followed the Disruption :

> " DEAR DR. KELMAN,—You will take the
> Chair to-night, and I will sit beside you for
> reference and consultations—if required.
> " Could your mother possibly come with you
> to-night from 7 to 8 to receive the ladies ? Your
> wife will be away, and my wife is in her room
> with the remains of a bad cold. If your mother
> and sister are able to be out, they would greatly
> make up for the other absences. But I am
> afraid that we ask too much of your dear mother.
> At the same time, how good it would be if she
> could come ! "

When Dr. Kelman published his volume of essays,
Among Famous Books, Dr. Whyte wrote :

> " I have spent a long evening over your
> extraordinarily illuminating and impressive book.
> 'Marius' is a really first-rate piece of work.
> 'Bunyan' also is as delightful as it is able. But
> 'Pagan Reactions' is your special message, and it
> is a masterpiece. And many whose blessing is
> the blessing of God will bless you for it. I lay
> down your book with a great exhilaration of
> spirit : and with a deepened gratitude to God
> for my colleague."

It was natural that one who habitually related
even the small events of life to the thought of the
divine Providence, should so interpret this comradeship in the work of the Kingdom. Thus one " Monday
morning " he writes :

> " VERY DEAR DR. KELMAN,—I took your
> brilliant evening as an answer to prayer.—
> Believe me,   A. W.
>   " Rest and recruit ! "

34

A " Saturday night " note runs : " I send enclosed
to-night lest I may not be out [at church] to-morrow
morning. Whether I am out or no, you shall not
be forgotten before God." And one on " Sabbath
afternoon " : " I know one man whom you sent
home this forenoon consenting to his cross—for a
time at any rate. You will have many such to your
account on that Day." Another slip of paper, which
probably accompanied the gift of a book, bears the
following :

> " With daily gratitude to God that He sent
> you to cheer and to uphold my poor old age.
> You will never know, such is the straitened
> language of this life, how true that is. But try
> to believe it from me,   **A. W.**"

Beside these may be placed a message on a post
card to Dr. Taylor Innes—probably the last sent by
Dr. Whyte before his friend's death : " You have
made my colleague very happy by your letter, and
they who make him happy are my valued friends."
Dr. Whyte in his turn greatly welcomed the letters
or words of gratitude which often came to him from
Dr. Kelman and from other friends, near at hand or
at a distance.

Through this eighth decade of Dr. Whyte's life,
while he seldom spoke directly to the children of
Free St. George's, he had by no means lost his gift of
awakening the interest of young hearers. This was
shown at a Memorial Service after the death of King
Edward the Seventh, to which the senior pupils were
gathered from eight elementary schools within a mile
of the church. After " The Flowers of the Forest "
had been played as a voluntary, and the " Happy
Land " had been sung, Dr. Whyte told the children
that the service was held because the King of kings
had summoned to His presence King Edward, His
servant, whose name was written in Heaven as
" Edward the Peacemaker " ; and who had been a
peacemaker all his life—among his companions in
boyhood and youth and among kings and statesmen

in later years.   He then pointed out how marvellously
changed Edinburgh would be if every boy and girl
would try to be a peacemaker at home and in school ;
and he closed by urging all his hearers to resolve to do
this, and to climb the Mount, as Dante did, sur-
mounting sin after sin, till they also were summoned
to the presence of the King.

But if a true account is to be given of this portion
of Dr. Whyte's ministry, some reference must be made
to the shadow which was not wholly dispersed even
by these bright features, or by the widening contacts
with new forms of Christian activity described in the
two preceding chapters.   Now as always, his spirit
was oppressed less by any outward happening than
by the keenly felt burden of sinfulness within.   For
several years after 1907 much of his preaching was
coloured by an experience at Balmacara which he
himself looked on as a turning-point in his ministry.
The summer had been persistently cold and wet—
one of the most inclement of the last twenty years ;
and in the middle of September most of the large
party left Balmacara to return to school or to work.
Then, at last, summer came, as Dr. Whyte was
left with four, and finally with two, of his young
companions.   For ten days the loch and the late
harvest-fields lay steeped in quiet sunshine, and the
great hills towered higher in the faint haze.   Twice
within a week he disappeared for five hours, and on
his return reported that he had walked some seventeen
or eighteen miles over beautiful but mountainous
roads.   " Not bad for a man," he wrote to Dr. Black,
" who is past the Psalmist's limit.   I remembered your
walk with me at every turn.   A splendid autumn
afternoon."   It was on one of these walks—by the
Strome Ferry road to where it overlooks Lochcarron,
and then round by Plockton—that Dr. Whyte found
himself wrestling with the question whether he should
not, for the remainder of his ministry, preach more
than he had been wont to do on the gentler and more
hopeful aspects of Christian truth, and less on sin and

its fruits.   But, as he told his congregation when he
returned to Edinburgh a fortnight later :

> " what seemed to me to be a Divine Voice spoke
> with all-commanding power in my conscience,
> and said to me as clear as clear could be : ' No !
> Go on, and flinch not !   Go back and boldly
> finish the work that has been given you to do.
> Speak out and fear not.   Make them at any cost
> to see themselves in God's holy Law as in a glass.
> Do you that, for no one else will do it.   No one
> else will so risk his life and his reputation as to do
> it.   And you have not much of either left to risk.
> Go home and spend what is left of your life in
> your appointed task of showing My people their
> sin and their need of My salvation.'   I shall
> never forget the exact spot where that clear
> command came to me, and where I got fresh
> authority and fresh encouragement to finish this
> part of my work."

None could fail to be deeply moved by this
announcement, given forth with all the preacher's
burning intensity of conviction ; but different hearers
reacted very differently to it.   One wrote of this
" powerful but gloomy sermon on Original Sin " ; a
second said long after : " My heart sank as I listened
to these words " ; but a third before retiring to rest
that night pencilled a note thanking her minister for a
message which met her most urgent need and which
no other preacher could give.   Yet, as we recall those
intense passages regarding the sinfulness of sin, it
must not be forgotten that they rested upon a deeper
and a positive conviction regarding the holiness of
God.   Three years later a young Anglican clergyman
spent some hours with Dr. Whyte on the West Coast ;
and the following is his most sharply cut recollection
of their talk together.   He asked whether it was not
possible here and now to be sanctified and kept free
from sin, and quoted the testimony of a friend whose
surrender had been so complete as to enable him to
say that sometimes for days together he had not

consciously disobeyed God. " No, sir," was Dr.
Whyte's reply, " no man who knows what God is
would say a thing like that—no man who has seen the
exquisite holiness of God would say a thing like that."
The speaker's eyes seemed to open with intense clearness and certainty as he spoke of that " exquisite
holiness of God."

The solemn injunction of the Divine Voice, as he
unhesitatingly considered it, heard by Dr. Whyte on
that Ross-shire hillside, sent him back to the Puritans
for his evening subjects ; and a series of letters to
Sir William Robertson Nicoll showed how his
thought turned to Fraser of Brea, Thomas Shepard,
Halyburton, and Goodwin. But now, and not for
the first time, he suggested that the opportunity of
sending a message forth through the *British Weekly*
should pass to a younger man.

> " I never can be thankful enough," he had
> written some years before, " for the splendid
> pulpit your journal has been to me, and for the
> friends it has secured to me among people whose
> faces I have never seen. At the same time,
> there is a limit to the continual appearance of the
> same man with the same set of ideas in a paper
> such as yours is."

How the editor replied to his friend's self-effacing
suggestion, both at the earlier and the later time, may
be inferred from another of Dr. Whyte's letters :

> " MY DEAR NICOLL,—If the half, or the
> quarter, of what you say is true—it leaves
> me no choice. I had intended to retire from
> the *British Weekly* and leave room for some
> younger man. But your letter is such that it
> has given me some thought the last twenty-four
> hours.
> " Well—how will this do ? I am preaching
> on a series—*Some Experimental and Autobio-*
> *graphic Psalms*. I fear you may find that I am
> harping on some strings of which your readers

have had enough already : but, if the title and the line of thing suits you, I shall try to put the lectures into as good a shape as I can for your pages. Only—will you send me a proof faithfully ? My hand is so barbarous sometimes that I must see a proof. . . . You are a continual marvel to us all here : the amount of work you get through, and the quality of it : not to speak of no end of things we only dimly realise. —Believe me, A. WHYTE."

Extracts from two other letters to Sir W. Robertson Nicoll, written during the courses on Thomas Shepard and Fraser of Brea, reveal something of the hesitation in Dr. Whyte's mind, as he was drawn hither and thither, now by the inclination of his own spirit, and now by the perception of what the hearer or reader of the twentieth century was prepared to receive. In one, he says that there may prove to be " more of Whyte than of Shepard " in his lectures on the New England divine. (As a matter of fact, the complaint of some of his best friends was that there was too much of Thomas Shepard, and not enough of Alexander Whyte.) But he then tells how, on a night of lashing rain, when he feared that not more than twenty people would come to hear about Shepard, the church had been two-thirds full, and continues :

" I cannot tell you how cheered I honestly and purely was, after purging out the vanity of my heart. At the same time, I do not wonder at a considerable class of people coming out to Shepard : he has been such a blessing to myself."

The other letter states the opposite point of view :

" I have had far more than my proper share of your widespread pages for my old-fashioned lucubrations. Even our own case-hardened people may take their own way of showing me that

they are dead tired of my ancient men and me.
But in any case, if I live, I intend to write two
little books on the above autobiographers."

The two volumes, on the Covenanter, Fraser of
Brea, and on Thomas Shepard, appeared in 1911 and
1912. Their predecessor among Dr. Whyte's published books was the last volume of *Bunyan Characters*, on Bunyan himself as portrayed in *Grace
Abounding*; and they were followed in 1913 by
Thirteen Appreciations. Many of these Appreciations
had been published earlier, along with passages
chosen from the works of the authors described.
But now they were gathered, and several others
added to the number—such as the New College
addresses on Goodwin and Wesley. One which now
appeared for the first time was on William Guthrie,
a character who appealed to Dr. Whyte from many
points of view. He was a Forfarshire laird who
resigned his patrimony, not far from Kirriemuir, to
become a preacher in the days of the Covenant; he
was a famed shepherd of sick souls; and his devotion
to the angler's art never deserted him. These things
join to make the paper on William Guthrie the
most charming of the shorter appreciations. But
the whole book is full of charm. The origin of all
the papers lay in " the Classes "; and if, as we
have seen, Dr. Whyte's talks to his audience of
young men and women represented the concentrated
essence of much study, the *Thirteen Appreciations*
give the *quintessence*—or, to use a homelier metaphor,
the *crême de la crême*—of a lifetime's constant and
varied reading.

The same conflict, which appeared in Dr. Whyte's
letters to the editor of the *British Weekly* regarding
the continued publication of his sermons there, could
also be traced in his communications with Dr. Kelman
regarding the pulpit of Free St. George's and the
Classes. At a comparatively early stage in their
colleagueship, Dr. Whyte proposed to hand over the

Classes to his colleague ; but Dr. Kelman's negative was as decided as that of Sir William Robertson Nicoll—perhaps more decided, for he realised what the Classes meant to his colleague and to the hundreds who attended them.　Indeed, Dr. Whyte himself confessed : " My class-work has been the great delight of my holidays for thirty years past."

Then came the illness already described ; and in the autumn of 1910 Dr. Whyte wrote to Dr. Kelman before he returned from the Highlands :

> " But for my years, I never felt better, or went home with more desire and love for my work.　But I am warned not to go by my feelings.　At any rate I will always go by my feelings toward you, which are warmer and more loving than you can know."

After consultation, Dr. Whyte's advisers allowed him to resume work on condition that he should only preach once on alternate Sundays.　But, on some occasions at least, he revenged himself by increasing the length of his sermons from thirty-five to forty-five minutes or more.　When he had only the opportunity of writing one sermon in a fortnight it naturally extended to more than the former length. One of the greatest sermons which the present writer ever heard in Free St. George's was preached one Sunday morning in November 1910, on one of Dr. Whyte's favourite texts—" I will stand upon my watch, and set me upon the tower," and the words that follow ; [1] and the closing passage showed how graciously the preacher could bring hope to those who were burdened by their slow progress in the spiritual life.　After Christmas of this year he shared the Young Men's Class with Dr. Kelman, conducting it only on the Sundays when he had not preached ; and with the end of this winter, the long history of his Classes quietly closed.

With the relief thus gained, Dr. Whyte's health

---

[1] Hab. ii. 1 ff.　The sermon is the last of those in *James Fraser of Brea.*

gradually but steadily improved, and he was able
to maintain, or even increase, his other activities.
Yet he was greatly bent on obtaining support for
Dr. Kelman in the form of a third colleague—" a
man," he wrote to a friend at a distance, " who
would be already on the spot and in harness, before I
drop out of harness." He looked upon the question as an urgent one, but, after several efforts
in this direction had been made without success, he
was obliged to let his plan be placed on one side.
On one occasion, when the chance of securing a third
colleague hung in the balance, he wrote to Dr.
Kelman from Switzerland : " My very absence from
home this past week has thrown me more than usual
upon prayer and faith and hope and assurance that
all will issue well for our dear people."

Later in the same year (1912) he wrote again :

> " My continual and anxious thought is, how
> far, and how long, I can, in any way, continue
> to assist you. Sometimes I feel as if I could
> be of some use to you yet : but at other times
> I feel that my time and use are done."

Another letter concludes :

> " I have so much that I would like to say
> to our people that I shrink from facing what
> cannot be far away : leaving pulpit and every-
> thing in your strong hands. Meantime — the
> deepest thanks for all your goodness to me,
> " MR. LOTH-TO-STOOP."

Still another letter expresses regret that he has
occupied the pulpit so often, and adds :

> " But I can mend my ways, in this matter,
> in the time to come : and I intend to do so. I
> shall, most willingly, and most thankfully, *D.V.*,
> take the prayer-meeting till Christmas : and I
> shall give my afternoons to the visitation of the
> sick and aged people. But I shall only take
> the forenoon pulpit when you are absolutely

unable to take it.   And, accordingly, in your programme for October, November, and December,
set ' J. K.' down as often as you possibly can,
and ' A. W.' as seldom as you possibly can."

Once, during the series of discourses on Shepard,
Dr. Whyte admitted his disappointment at the falling
off in interest in the evening services which he conducted : in the morning, when he preached from
whatever text had been borne in on his own spirit,
the interest was undiminished.   His colleague saw an
opening, and, summoning all his courage, told him
that the congregation at times felt weary of the
Puritans and longed for Dr. Whyte's own message,
delivered with the freedom which he used in speaking to humbler audiences.   Dr. Whyte said little in
reply—he was slow to admit that the more introspective Puritans were unsuited for " human nature's
daily food "—but a day or two later a note reached
Dr. Kelman, in which he promised to refrain from
following Thomas Shepard by Thomas Goodwin,
Thomas Boston, and Thomas Halyburton,[1] and suggested instead a course of Sunday evening addresses
" (not read) " on such psalms and hymns as " The
Lord's my Shepherd " and " Rock of Ages," under the
general heading, " I will sing with the Spirit, and with
the Understanding also."   These, along with " Just
as I am " and " The Sands of Time," formed the
texts of not a few of Dr. Whyte's greatest and most
moving addresses to smaller congregations during the
later years of his ministry.   Yet he felt the limitation of his advancing years, which forbade him to
help friends at a distance as he had been wont to
do.   When his nephew, Hubert Simpson, was inducted to Westbourne Church, Glasgow, at the end
of 1912, he wrote that his doctors would not grant
him permission to preach an introductory sermon
there, and added : " But I must not complain.   I
have had a long day's work : and I must not at its

---

[1] For the sermons on Goodwin which appeared later, cf. pp. 563, 599
below.

end enact the ignoble part of 'Mr. Loth-to-Stoop.'"
A few months later he sent this message on a post
card to Harry Ross at Bainsford :

> " You don't know how old and frail I am.
> Nor how I am bound up here to give every re-
> maining atom of my strength to my home work.
> The arrears of my home work overwhelm me.
> Believe me, I would, if I could. I was talking
> to the men [at New College] to-day about John
> Wesley's *Journal*. Accept a copy.
>
> " A. W."

While Dr. Kelman was thus striving, consistently
and not without success, to prolong the active
ministry of his venerated colleague, the home at
7 Charlotte Square continued to be a centre of manifold interests. Indeed, the interest in public affairs
became stronger as the thoughts of the eldest son
began to turn to political life. But first, he spent a
year as Warden of Edinburgh University Settlement ;
and, when he left Balmacara in September 1907 to
take up this work, his father placed the following
letter in his hands :

> " *Sabbath Night.*
>
> " VERY DEAR FRED,—You leave us to-morrow
> to enter on a great honour and a great oppor-
> tunity. Your own heart will be speaking to you
> to-day about all that far better than I can do.
> But there are one or two things that my long
> life has taught me that I would like to share
> with you to-night. Be humble, be genial, be
> affable ; respect and honour all your fellows.
> Never be sullen or gruff or hot, however men
> may worry you or weary you. Keep all kinds
> of debate, as far as may be, away from your table.
> Write Augustine's motto on your table : ' Let
> no back-biting or tale-bearing man sit here.'
> And if debate will sometimes arise, keep you
> well out of it. Rather let error live than love
> die. And always, all your days, let your most

silent and unobtrusive guest speak more than yourself. . . .

"Learn Newman's 'Gentleman' by heart, and practise the character every hour of your day. Spite of the sub-tone of irony that is in it, see yourself as in a glass in it. I am not afraid that your intellect or your industry shall come short : but watch well your heart and your manners.—I am,

"Your Chiefest Well-wisher."

Some months later, Dr. Whyte wrote regarding one of those evenings in the House of Commons Gallery of which he never grew weary :

"Dear Fred,—I came home last night at half-past eleven, having been in the House eight hours. The debate was instructive and impressive. I often thought of you ; and wondered if you would ever sit on those benches, and if ever I would live to see it. And this kept continually coming to my mind : Impress on him, with all your might, the absolute necessity of incessant work. The men who made an impression on the House, and who made real contributions to the debate, were the men who had mastered the whole situation by hard work, and who spoke out of a full and stored mind. No one impressed me more than Samuel.[1] He looks young : he looks younger probably than he really is ; but at the end of a long and exhausting debate, his mastery of his subject, and his stores of knowledge, greatly impressed both sides of the House. . . .

"Go on with your good work. . . . My work lies in a very different field. I am busy every day with the Apostolic and Sub-Apostolic ages of the Church : under the guidance and inspiration of

---

[1] Sir Herbert Samuel, the present High Commissioner in Palestine, was then Under-Secretary for Home Affairs. The debate was on the Licensing Bill, referred to below.

Lightfoot and Rainy. Lightfoot has the reading and the learning; but Rainy has the masterful grasp of the principles and the deep appreciation of the evangelical life."

Dr. Whyte still cherished another hope for his son, as a letter written in the summer of 1908 shows :

"VERY DEAR FRED,—It is not too late for you to look at the Church. Have you given this your full and final consideration ? Your generation is to see great openings for service in the Church—Union, Subscription, recasting of the Confession, great social questions : besides the Gospel itself, to the preacher himself, and to those to whom he speaks. You are not too late, and I might be able to convey over to you some of my experiences and some lessons of my life before I depart."

But an incident occurred between the dates of these two letters which had a definite bearing on the son's career, while it proved of great interest to the father. The Scottish Temperance Societies had organised a series of meetings in support of the English Licensing Bill which the Liberal Government of that day was striving to carry through Parliament; and in May 1908, Mr. Lloyd George came to Edinburgh to address a demonstration in the King's Theatre in favour of the Bill. He was the guest of Dr. and Mrs. Whyte, and, short as his visit was, it laid the foundation of a warm mutual regard between the preacher and the statesman. In the following years, Mr. Lloyd George never heard of Dr. Whyte's presence in London without inviting him to 11 Downing Street. After one such meeting the guest returned home, as many others have done, full of praise of the captivating courtesy of his host. "And," he added, with a touch of shrewd observation, "it was at breakfast, mind you, *at breakfast* ! " Urbanity at the breakfast-table was an achievement worthy of remark.

Some months later, Mr. Lloyd George required information as to the Austrian system of State Insurance against sickness, in view of the preparation of his own Insurance Bill, and asked A. F. Whyte to go to Austria for six weeks and prepare the desired report.   Soon after, Whyte became political secretary to the late Lord Lucas, and a year later he was invited to stand as Liberal candidate for Perth City, then a separate and compact constituency with an almost unbroken Liberal record.   Dr. Whyte was interested in and gratified by this new prospect, though he maintained his strict rule never himself to attend a political meeting.   But much counsel passed from one to the other—some of it such as few young politicians can have received.   A post card, when A. F. Whyte was at the Settlement, ran : " Always glance at the *Times*.   There is scarcely a number of it that does not contain something that makes me think of you and your work."   And a note from Beatenburg at the same period read as follows :

> " DEAR FRED,—' A dream cometh through the multiplicity of business.'   Well, I dreamed last night that you had got a post as leader-writer on the *Glasgow Herald*.   In the great days of the *Times* leaders, when they made and unmade ministries, it was wont to be said that you could always know a *Times* leader by its felicitous opening.   The first sentence was always so attractive, so pat, and so epitomic of its contents. And Pascal said that it was the beginning that was so difficult to him.   Leader-writing or no— remember the Psalmist's faith and confession : ' My times are in Thy Hand.'   A. W."

When Dr. Whyte's son left for Perth to start his campaign, a pencilled note followed him :

> " DEAR M.P.,—Be sure to read, and read again, and pencil in hand, Jowett's Introduction to the *Republic*.   A. W."

After the dissolution, when the campaign of January 1910 was in full progress, Dr Whyte set down the

outcome of his own meditations during a wakeful night,
linking the contest in Perth with the history of the
city during the Reformation. The letter ended :

> " A noble word about John Knox as the great
> Scottish Commoner of those days, fighting Crown
> and Lords for the freedom of the people, would
> fire the hearts of the men of the East End.
> Your own heart fired at the end of a speech, and
> a passage prepared out of such material, would
> not only do much for the present situation, but
> would tend to mould and ennoble your speaking
> all through life. Best success !   A. W."

The good wishes with which this letter closed were
justified by the result—a majority of over 700 on an
electoral roll of 5000. The following day, Dr. Whyte
wrote :

> " VERY DEAR FRED,—I was pacing up and
> down in my study late last night, occupied with
> my own thoughts, when Aird rushed in with the
> great news : for great news it is. But the best of
> it all to me, is the way you have conducted your-
> self through this trying contest. . . . All taken
> together, this event has made me very proud
> and very glad. It gives you such an opportunity
> for great service : and that at such an early
> period of your life. I was reading the Life of
> William Wilberforce, the great Abolitionist, last
> night ; and as I read of his youthful entrance
> into the House of Commons, and went on to his
> splendid services there, it seemed to me a token
> for good that I was absorbed in such a noble Life
> at the very hour when you were being proclaimed
> a member of the same great House. You will
> read Wilberforce's Life some day. . . .
> " God bless you with every gift and grace
> necessary for a public life of great usefulness,
> and for a personal life of great faith and prayer
> and love.—Believe me, your thankful father,
> " ALEXANDER WHYTE."

A letter of the following autumn shows how Dr. Whyte found a political as well as a religious use in the History of Words, which he now studied with unwearied delight in Sir James Murray's great *Oxford Dictionary* :

" Some day you should prepare a speech on your nickname, RADICAL. See ' nickname ' in Sir James Murray. Go to the root of the word, *radix*, and then apply it, illustrating, to your world of things—to all questions of legislation, and government, and finance, etc. Accept the nickname as your pride and your ornament, and as the universal principle of all your statesmanship. Set down the term, RADICAL, in your notebook when you receive this note, and every day add illustrations and suggestions, and, in time, you will have material for a paper or a speech that will make its mark for good on all who read or hear. Let others scamp and skin the surface of questions : be it yours to go to the *root* of them. ' Make the tree good,' said our Lord : *i.e.* Make the *root* good, and the goodness of the root will pass up into all the branches and all the leaves and all the fruit. And be ' radical ' in your style : that is to say, a clear thinker, and a hard worker, always, in the shortest speech or paper, doing your very best."

Dr. Whyte was again greatly delighted when the election of December 1910 added two hundred to his son's majority, and wrote to his third son, who had also been hard at work in Perth :

"DEAR AIRD,— . . . When your telephone came it sent a thrill through the whole house from kitchen to garret. Fred deserved it all, for he has fought nobly. . . .

" I had ' the Evangelical Prophet ' in the Class this afternoon. If any one throws Lloyd George in Fred's face, tell him to ask them if they have read Isaiah : for instance, chap. v. 7,

8, and 9,[1] and all up and down his book. The
Chancellor could not hold the candle to the
prophet for fearless invective."

Even Dr. Whyte's long self-discipline in refraining
from controversy had not wholly dulled his pleasure
in the shrewd blows dealt by others in a cause which
he approved.

During this autumn a visit to Mrs. Haldane—
whose son had recently carried through the re-
organisation of the Territorial Army—was a great
refreshment to Dr. and Mrs. Whyte. After their
return from Cloan, Mrs. Whyte wrote to their hostess
that she and Dr. Whyte must be looked on as " the
most stalwart Radicals in Scotland," adding : " One
morning at 4 a.m. he had a great concern that Mr.
John Redmond be invited to Edinburgh to make a
great exposition of Home Rule, and it was with
difficulty we persuaded him of the lions in the path.
He thought us very lukewarm." But Dr. Whyte
and Mrs. Haldane had a community of interest even
deeper than their common political enthusiasm.
Both belonged to a generation whose representatives
became fewer year by year ; and they rejoiced alike
to recall the great days following the Disruption,
with their unbounded devotion and generosity, and
to welcome the coming of a new spirit into the life
of the Scottish Churches in which the old contentions were steadily disappearing in a new unity.

During this year the old acquaintance of Dr.
Whyte and Lord Esher, which had begun on the
Sunday evening at Lochearnhead described in
Chapter XI., ripened into friendship. Over a generation separated their first from their second meeting,
which occurred when Lord Esher found himself
suddenly taken ill in Edinburgh, and let Dr. Whyte
know of his presence there. During his convales-
cence they had more than one long talk, and on his
return to London, Lord Esher wrote :

[1] The passage regarding those who " join house to house and lay
field to field."

" *March* 31, 1910.

" My dear Principal,—After all these years it is a great pleasure, and a deep lesson, to find myself once more brought into contact with you.

" One cannot measure the value of impressions, but that evening at Lochearnhead has never ceased to count for much in my life. I have just republished a volume of Essays. They are concerned with matters which would not interest you much ; but one of them is the enclosed, which I venture to beg of you to accept, in its magazine form, as a token of profound regard and gratitude.—I remain, yours very sincerely,   Esher."

Two years later, Mrs. Whyte wrote to ask if Lord Esher would give his signature to a memorial in which she and her husband were greatly interested on behalf of the persecuted Armenian people. He replied that, although he had never signed a petition in his life, he would do anything for Dr. Whyte— " the best man I have ever known " ; and the signed memorial accompanied the letter. A few months later he returned to Edinburgh and addressed a meeting of heads of colleges and schools, in the study at 7 Charlotte Square, on the European situation and the means of averting war. During this year (1912) Mr. Norman Angell also paid two visits to Dr. and Mrs. Whyte, and enlisted their warm sympathy in his endeavour to arouse public opinion on the danger into which Europe was fast drifting.

During these years Dr. Whyte's holidays were of two kinds—those in which he and his wife, or sometimes he alone, went away to gain time for quiet meditation, and those family expeditions in which hours of meditation were varied by hours with a large circle of young people. A retreat of the former type is referred to in a letter from Edinburgh to his wife :

" DEAR COUNSELLOR,—After a Senatus meeting to-morrow afternoon I have nothing in my
book till the Communion morning, Sabbath
week. . . . How shall I put in these days best ?
—going to St. Mary's Loch—*Solus cum Solo*.[1]
You will not be disposed to leave home the day
after you arrive ?—but I will spend the days
not unprofitably in solitary meditation. My
mind may change before I see you, but meantime my thoughts run as above. The solitude of
St. Mary's Loch and the walks draw me much."

But, whatever the degree of solitude on a holiday, reading always occupied many hours. Thus he
writes to Dr. Kelman from Brodick : " Rest is sweet :
rest and good books." And a post card from Balmacara conveys this suggestion to his colleague, who
had several well-read ministers within reach of his
summer quarters at Ballantrae :

" When Matthew Arnold comes to hand
collect a clerical symposium and get the best
reader in the party to read aloud the last essay,
' The Jewish Church,' while the ladies sew, and
the men smoke.—Love to you all,   A. W."

The literature of the day finds its place also :
a post card to Dr. Macaulay calls his attention
to two articles dealing with Bergson ; and a note
to Dr. Kelman thanks him for an introduction to
Chesterton's writings :

" I have literally and etymologically had a
debauch of Chesterton this week. . . . [His]
Browning made a very deep impression on me :
very deep.—Gratefully yours,   A. W."

But it should, perhaps, be added that Dr. Kelman's
essays in this direction were not always so successful ;
for once, when he had given Dr. Whyte a volume
of Francis Thompson's Poems at the beginning of a

[1] " Alone with the Alone "—a phrase originally derived from
Plotinus, the greatest of the Greek Mystics.

holiday, with a special recommendation to study the
Hound of Heaven, Dr. Whyte, on his return to Edinburgh, confessed, " with a curious half-ashamed and
half-exultant glance," that he had been so occupied
by eleven volumes of Shepard that the *Hound of
Heaven* had returned unread !

In 1910 Dr. Whyte spent his last West Highland
holiday on Eilean Shona, an island in the Macdonald
country, not far from the scene of Prince Charlie's
first landing in the '45. The situation was more
open than that of Balmacara, and the views of
mountain and sea were not less beautiful. The
surroundings are described in two letters to Dr.
Taylor Innes :

> " Now that I have been three or four days
> here, I can write with confidence and with
> urgency : Come and see ! We are on an island,
> some five miles in rugged circumference . . .
> and a motor-launch takes us to the mainland in
> two minutes. . . . Yesterday it took us up to
> the top of Loch Moidart : after which some of
> our party walked on for a mile or two on a most
> charming Highland road, and then returned to
> the launch, which then took us round our
> island. When out on the heaving Atlantic, we
> saw the Western Isles towering up in the distance,
> with Skye, with her steel-blue peaks, in the far
> north. But come and see for yourself ! Arrange
> with Black and come together ! "

A further note next day explains that Dr. Sutherland Black is unable to visit Eilean Shona, but
concludes :

> " There are these points also in our island
> home : there is a hill on it as high as Arthur's
> Seat, from which there is a splendid view. The
> engineer of our motor - launch is a son of an
> Edinburgh goldsmith, and our helmsman is a
> Catholic crofter. Come and make their acquaint-
> ance ! "

The holidays of the two following summers were
spent in the Dolomites. On both occasions the
numbers and the pleasure of the party were augmented
by the presence of Dr. Sutherland Black, his niece,
and two nephews; and in the intervening spring of
1912 his niece, Margaret Emily Fairweather, had
married Alexander Frederick Whyte. Dr. Whyte
rejoiced greatly both in his son's happiness and in
the new link which now united him to his long-
valued friend. Of Dr. Black he wrote to his daughter-
in-law : " You know—or, rather, you do not know—
what he is to me. Even this new tie can scarcely
bind us closer than we already are bound together."

Swift glances at these Dolomite scenes are given
in a series of post cards from Dr. Whyte to his
colleague. One refers to a motor run over the
Dolomitenstrasse—motoring, both in Scotland and
in the Alps, gave especial pleasure in these years—in
the brief phrase: " I shall not attempt to describe the
indescribable." Another post card from Cortina is
headed, " Feast of the Assumption," and depicts it as
a " universal holiday : holy day. From 4 a.m. Mass
has been performed in the churches . . . a Highland
Communion in Dolomiteland." In a post card at the
close of the second visit he quotes the reported saying
of a Scots shepherd after a spell of rainy weather :

> " To the carnal mind very disappointing
> weather : but let us remember that it ' saftens
> the sod, and slockens the ewes, and is the will
> o' God.'
> " But our company makes up for much.
> Our party breaks up this day week—Dr. Black
> and his division to go to Venice, and I and mine
> to go to the Luther and Behmen country for a
> week or two."

Dr. Whyte was again disappointed of his desire
to visit the home of Behmen, but he and his wife
spent several days of great peace and quiet contemplation in the pine-woods around Eisenach and
the Wartburg.

During the five years before the outbreak of the war, one or more of his children took him every winter to one of the high Swiss stations, in order to give an effective break in his winter's work. The following letter, describing the journey to Waldhaus-Flims, and his occupations there just after his first illness, was sent to Mr. G. Elmslie Troup, then assistant in Free St. George's and editor of the congregational "Notes":

"DEAR MR. EDITOR,—My journey? Yes: we had Mr. Devine"—headmaster of Clayesmore School—"all the way to London. And the eight hours looked like one, such was his wit and his wisdom. After a good night's rest . . . Margaret and Aird and I started for this place *via* Paris. The caves of Neptune were not entirely closed around the Channel, but my attentive children got me comfortably seated in a corner of the smoking-saloon, which was soon filled with clouds of fragrant smoke. And I set down my escape from sea-sickness to the tonic effects of the exhilarating atmosphere. When Sir Thomas Barlow was putting me through my catechism on Monday evening, he asked me if I smoked much. 'None at all,' I answered. 'Did you ever smoke?' he asked. 'No,' I replied. He then tapped over my heart before and behind, and smiled to himself and said, 'Good!' All which I took as a token for good. But to give the weed its due, I really think it had something to do with my successful crossing of the tossing Channel.

"Where am I now? . . . A cup of a valley, 4500 feet above the level of the sea: filled with a little Protestant village, and a number of hotels and summer residences. The sides of the cup are covered with woods and snow, and the rocky rim of the cup is made up of serrated peaks of rock and snow and ice. A sight only to be seen in Switzerland. . . .

" My occupations ? I am in the open air most of the day. My companions *ski* and skate and toboggan, and I walk alone—*nunquam minus solus quam cum solus*.[1] In the long evenings I read, and write a little. My colleague [2] instigated me, and indeed as good as commanded me, to bring out with me Baur and Pfleiderer and David Somerville ; and, at my own instance, I brought Reuss and Bruce and Goodwin. I never travel without having a volume of Goodwin with me. Give him a chance yourself some day. I note the marks on the margin that I made as I first read him in 1861. . . .

" My newspapers these days ? The *Times, Scotsman, [Edinburgh Evening] News, Dundee Advertiser, Perth Courier, Westminster, Daily News, Nation, British Weekly*, etc. Jonathan Edwards read his news-letters in order to see how the second petition of the Lord's Prayer was being answered in New England in his day.

" The weather ? At this moment I am sitting with my window open to the southern sun, and feel him almost too hot. The snow that fell three weeks ago lies still three feet deep all over, just as it fell. There was not a breath of wind as the snow fell, and there has not been a breath of wind since. A steel-blue sky all day, with a sun of molten silver : and a deep-blue sky all night, with a universe of studding stars. . . . Three weeks of such weather amid such scenery is my full justification for coming so far. Three weeks of such rest and such recuperation for three days of a somewhat assumed indisposition ! For all of which I must try to make up after my return home."

---

[1] " Never less alone than when alone."
[2] The reference may be to one of his colleagues in New College. Dr. Kelman has no recollection of recommending the two German divines.

On the same occasion he wrote to Dr. Kelman :

"The weather is as soft and warm as spring :
too soft and too warm for the sports-people, but
it suits me to perfection. . . . When, at any time,
I count up my benefits, as I sometimes try to
do, my incomparable colleague has a high and a
shining place among them. Let him not over-
task himself doing so much of his old colleague's
work for him ! "

Mr. Tatlow, the General Secretary of the Student
Christian Movement, has thus recorded his memory
of this Christmas :

"I shall never forget the first time I saw
Dr. Whyte. He was seated at the head of a
table in the dining-room of the Grand Hotel at
Waldhaus-Flims. . . . I think I expected him
to be rather grave and abstracted, a little ' dour,'
and interested chiefly in theological ' shop.'
Here was a distinguished-looking man, with
massive features, clean-shaved, ruddy com-
plexion, a full head of snow-white hair, twinkling
blue eyes, a quick, eager way of speaking in a
broad Scots accent, who beamed upon us, and
went on beaming all dinner-time. During the
fortnight that followed we talked each evening
after dinner about every conceivable subject :
politics, the Swiss method of Government,
preaching, journalism, the Student Movement,
foreign missions, theology, books, and Church
Unity are among the topics I remember being
discussed."

Dr. Whyte's eldest daughter always accompanied
him on these winter journeys. On one of the earlier
she made such unusually rapid progress in the art
of ski-ing, that he had the experience, which he
thoroughly enjoyed, of hearing himself pointed out
as "Miss Whyte's father." In the years from 1912
to 1914 Sir Alexander Simpson and his daughter
joined the party, and a letter from Dr. Whyte told

of their drive from Chur to Lenzerheide, first in a carriage through deep mud, and then in an open sleigh through yet deeper snow. A little later he wrote to his nephews describing their father, who, like Dr. Whyte himself, was in his seventy-seventh year :

> " Sir Alexander is confounding his home doctors, and is getting up an appetite for the curlers' bacon and greens—as I write, I see him, in his shirt-sleeves, the most youthful of the group. In all seriousness, he is full of life and interest and enjoyment, and gathers us all around him as the head of the party. . . . Be sure he will come home twenty years younger : and ready to take another chair."

But amid all these interests the central things were never far away from Dr. Whyte's mind. On one occasion he sent a post card to Mr. Hollins with this inscription : " When Boots knocked on me between four and five this morning, I was deep in a dream of grace about *you*. Whenever we awake, we are still with the God of all grace." On the last of these expeditions, to Engelberg at Christmas 1913, Mr. and Mrs. J. C. B. Geddes were among the party ; and, as the English chaplain had had a serious accident on the rink, the two Scots ministers took his place. " Jack and I," Dr. Whyte reported on a post card, " gave the Anglicans a Scotch service : not without acceptance." And two post cards to his wife on another Christmas Day show how his own heart welcomed the sacred season :

> " *Christmas Morning*.
> " My first thoughts are of HIM and of you all. Divine Service with His body and blood at 11."

> " *Christmas Day*, 1 p.m.
> " Been at service and [the Lord's] Supper. My heart was broken with sin and grace : as it might well be ! The day is past belief for beauty : past description. Would you were all here."

In the months following October 1911, several of
Dr. Whyte's oldest friends passed away, among them
Dr. Taylor Innes, Lady Simpson, Dr. Joseph Bell,
and Dr. Simeon Macphail. Of the last, he wrote:
" Mac is home where there are no murky mornings.
He had many such here : but when the shore is won
at last, who will count the billows past ? "

Yet this period brought many bright gleams as well.
Dr. Whyte's health was better than for long, and one
day in July 1913 he could chronicle a walk with Dr.
Sutherland Black of a quite old-time length : " He and
I walked three hours and a half, over Corstorphine
Hill and round by Cramond. I feel that I have
earned my dinner, and two hours of Goodwin after
dinner. I preach from him on Sabbath night."

The two following months—months of almost
unbroken sunshine—were spent at Bonskeid. The
party which gathered to enjoy the last weeks of an
unusually perfect summer was even larger than in
former years. A year earlier Dr. and Mrs. Whyte's
second daughter, Janet, had married Clinton Chance of
Birmingham, so they had with them for a time both
a son-in-law and a daughter-in-law ; and two of their
younger children, Rhoda and Robert, who had just
completed their courses at Somerville and Balliol,
brought Oxford friends whose presence added fresh
interests. A further satisfaction to Dr. Whyte was
that for these two months Sir James Barrie was near
at hand at Killiecrankie Cottage. Thus for his
family, as for so many others, the summer of 1913
stood out in the retrospect of the years that followed
as a time of varied activity and much happiness.

Earlier in the year, Dr. Whyte gave perhaps the
most signal proof of his breadth of sympathy when
he received at 7 Charlotte Square Abdul Baha Abbas,
the leader of the Persian Bahai movement.[1] Bitter

---

[1] There have been three outstanding leaders among the Bahai.
The Bab, or Forerunner, began to preach in Persia in 1844, and met a
martyr's death. After him came Baha 'Ullah, the great teacher and
lawgiver of the movement. On his death in 1892, his son, Abdul Baha,
succeeded him, and continued to inspire the movement till his death in
1921.

persecution in Persia had driven him with his father
into exile, first at Adrianople and then in the fortress of
Acre (Akka). The Turkish revolution set him free to
visit the western world, and after travelling in the
United States he came to London, where he spoke to
large audiences in the churches of Archdeacon Wilber-
force and Dr. R. J. Campbell. In private he said that,
foreseeing the wars and troubles that threatened to
sweep over Europe, he had come to draw together the
friends of peace.

In January 1913, Dr. and Mrs. Whyte received
him as an honoured guest in Edinburgh. Dr. Whyte
attended a public meeting, presided over by Dr.
Kelman, at which the venerable teacher pleaded for a
universal language as one means of securing peace.
Next day, Dr. Whyte presided at a meeting in his own
study of students from the Orient, including Hindus,
Moslems, Parsees, and Jews. His opening words,
addressed to Abdul Baha, were :

> " Dear and honoured Sir, I have had many
> meetings in this house, but never have I seen such
> a meeting It reminds me of what St. Paul said,
> ' God hath made of one blood all nations of men,'
> and of what our Lord said, ' They shall come
> from the East and the West, from the North and
> the South, and shall sit down in the Kingdom of
> God.' "

The teaching of the Bahai leader, and the fidelity
to the ideals of their faith which his followers had
shown through much persecution—especially to that
of world-brotherhood and the application of the law
of love throughout all human affairs—appealed to
Dr. Whyte as a significant manifestation of the Christian spirit outside the bounds of Christendom.

A tribute to the catholicity of outlook which
marked Dr. Whyte's home, notwithstanding his own
firmness and intensity of belief, may be quoted from
a very different source. One of his friends—a man
of science, whose religious interest remained strong
although he had long lost contact with Christian

belief and with the activities of organised Christianity
—was known to say, " 7 Charlotte Square is my
church now." Dr. Whyte's whole personality, and
especially his width of sympathy, won the confidence
of not a few whose intellectual life had carried them
far from his creed.

The variety of interests which marked the year
1913 continued through the winter and spring that
followed. Dr. and Mrs. Whyte still sought to forward
the fuller mutual understanding of men and women
belonging to different Churches by gatherings in
their own home. On these occasions the doors
between the drawing-room and the study were
thrown open, and in the large room thus formed a
company of eighty or ninety friends assembled to
hear an address from one who came with a distinctive
religious message. The subject of one such meeting
was "The Fellowship of Silence"; and two members
of the Society of Friends, Mrs. Marsh and Miss
Violet Hodgkin, told of the spiritual quickening
found by little groups of Friends and Anglo-Catholics,
first in New Zealand and later in England, as they
shared a form of worship generally associated with
Quakerism alone.[1]

Dr. Whyte entered with great zest into the evangelistic campaign which was carried on in the early
months of 1914 by Dr. Chapman, the American
preacher, and his fellow-worker, the singer, Mr. Charles
M. Alexander. For long he had looked forward to
their visit, and soon after their arrival he was suddenly called upon to take the place of Dr. Chapman,
who was unable through illness to address a great
meeting in the United Free Assembly Hall. Dr.
Whyte spoke on the hymn " Just as I am "—his
favourite subject during those months—with an
eloquence, a pathos, and a home-coming power
which made this address stand out in the memory of
some who knew him well as among the very greatest
of his utterances. The later meetings of the campaign were held every afternoon and evening in the

[1] See *The Fellowship of Silence*, edited by the Rev. Cyril Hepher.

large building then known as Olympia. Dr. Whyte attended constantly, and his presence, with that of his still more venerable friend, Dr. George Wilson of St. Michael's Parish Church, linked the movement with that of Moody and Sankey forty years before. When Dr. Whyte was asked how he could spare time and strength to be present so often, his reply came swiftly, " I simply can't stay away."

Just as this mission closed, in March 1914, news came of the birth in London of his first grandchild, Joan Elizabeth Fairweather Whyte. Later in the spring the little girl was brought north to be baptized by her grandfather in the quiet of his study among his treasured portraits and books.

During the General Assemblies of 1914 the movement for Presbyterian reunion received a new expression, when a large congregation of women belonging to the conferring Churches gathered for a Communion service within the venerable walls of St. Giles'. Dr. Whyte dispensed the Sacrament, and the occasion was a joyful one for him, since his interest in the growing share of women in the Churches' life was only second to his longing for unity.

This chapter may close with a little sheaf of stories and impressions—differing in their gravity and import, but all in their measure characteristic —gleaned from the rich harvest - field of these years.

We have seen that Dr. Whyte's humour, which had been tinged by a certain grimness in middle life, had become quaint and almost playful as he grew old. This appeared, as in the case of Martin Luther, in the unconventional addresses of some of his letters. His brother-in-law was several times indicated simply by—" Sir Alexander, 52 Queen Street." But once, when Dr. Whyte had received from him a paper on " Life and its Epiphanies," delivered as a Presidential Address to the Harveian

Society of Edinburgh,[1] the post card of acknowledgment bore a more elaborate address :

> " TO THAT TRUE HARVEIAN,
>   SIR ALEXANDER R. SIMPSON, M.D., &c." ;

and an inscription :

> " A paper of genius : of true genius sanctified.—Believe me,   A. W."

Once, in response to a birthday greeting, Dr. Whyte sent a post card to Mr. and Mrs. Hollins with the short hymn, " O Saviour, I have nought to plead," typed over his signature. The address, in his own hand, was, " The Organist and his Wife, 3 Grosvenor St." Another post card, addressed to a friend who had received an honorary degree, ran : " Well-earned! Signed, Alexander Whyte."

Neither Dr. Whyte's independence nor his considerateness for others deserted him with the onset of old age ; and both were shown by the way in which, at least down to the time of his illness, he would venture out on foot for an afternoon's visiting, or to attend an evening meeting, in face of the slanting rain driven before an Edinburgh gale. On one occasion, when he had walked across the town to a meeting through lashing rain, and was asked why he had not taken a cab, he replied that he saw no use in two men getting wet !

There was another side to his independence, noted by a friend who wrote :

> " He would not ingratiate himself ; he had not a trace of that insincerity which is perhaps the class sin of clergymen. He neither could nor would be all things to all men ; he never said or did anything because it was desired or expected, no matter by whom, that he should

[1] Named in honour of William Harvey, discoverer of the circulation of the blood.

say or do it. . . . That is why, had he been of
the Episcopal Church, he would never have been
a bishop." [1]

It ought perhaps to be added that the writer of
these words is not a prejudiced Presbyterian. As he
indicates, Dr. Whyte was never " a master in the
science of exigencies." Yet he possessed both wisdom
and sympathy; and his wisdom came to light in such
incidents as the following: A young minister, whose
first church was in a small country town, came to ask
advice as to whether he should accept a call to a large
and exacting city charge. Dr. Whyte put the laconic
question to him, " Can you clarify your thought, sir ? "
—not the question which might have been expected
from him, but one which showed that he had measured
both his friend and the needs of the congregation
calling him. After a few moments of thought his
visitor replied, " I think I can " ; and Dr. Whyte
said, " Then you need not fear to accept the call."

His often unsuspected power of observation was
shown when another young friend came hot-foot to
announce his engagement. Instead of expressing
surprise, Dr. Whyte somewhat disconcerted his
visitor by asking, " Why didn't you tell me this
months ago ? " " *Months ago ?* " " Yes ; in June,
at ——" " But it has only happened *now*." " Ah !
well," said the old man, " perhaps *then*, the wish was
father to the thought."

In spite of all his love of solitude, he delighted
also—and especially as the years went on—to watch
the ways of humankind. Once he spent several days
with a party of young people on the outskirts of Paris,
at Neuilly, whence they made expeditions to the sights
in and around the capital. They spent one day walking through the salons and bedchambers of Versailles,
and next morning, when a similar programme was suggested, he begged : " Just leave me on the boulevards.
What are other people's chests-of-drawers to me ? "

His family continued to guard the door of his

[1] Rev. Alfred Fawkes in the *Expositor*, March 1921, p. 192.

study against needless intrusion, but there were some favoured individuals who gained ready access. Among them at this period was one four-footed friend —a greyhound, who was allowed to wander in when he liked, and for whom the owner of the study would save fragments from his frugal lunch, because he loved the dog's mistress.

A scene at Dr. Whyte's table has been depicted by Mr. Tatlow in most lifelike miniature :

" One night at dinner the maid came in with a visiting-card and something written upon it. A question from his family, a quick answer, and then a general family appeal not to help the man, that he had been helped too often. Dr. Whyte had no money, his family it was clear would provide none ; he entered upon no discussion, but turned to me. ' Lend me a sovereign,' was all he said. I produced one amid the amused protests of the family. Dr. Whyte turned to the maid and handed her the sovereign with the words, ' My compliments.' He looked at me and smiled as he said, ' He's a poor man.' The three remarks quoted record everything said by Dr. Whyte during the episode."

His sympathy, not less than his generosity, often found expression with the utmost economy of words. Near the end of his life in Edinburgh, a friend came to see him who had been passing through very deep waters. When Dr. Whyte entered the room, he came up to her, took her hand, and very slowly repeated the four words, " *Out of great tribulation.*"

An incident told by Dr. Kelman brings out that other central characteristic, his humility :

" On one occasion, when a prominent citizen had been imprisoned, and the whole city was aghast at the scandal, as Dr. Whyte came into the vestry on Sunday morning the bells were

Drummond Young, Photographer, Edinburgh

IN THE STUDY AT
JOAN'S BAPTISM

ringing for church.   He turned to me and said :
' Do you hear those bells ?   He hears them in his
prison cell this morning.   Man, it might have
been me ! ' "

Generosity, sympathy, humility, are but three
cumbrous names representing diverse facets of the
one, simply named, virtue of Love.

" . . . Salute the sacred dead,
    Who went and who return not.—Say not so ! . . .
    We rather seem the dead, that stayed behind.
    Blow, trumpets, all your exultations blow !
    For never shall their aureoled presence lack . . .
      They come transfigured back,
    Secure from change in their high-hearted ways,
    Beautiful evermore, and with the rays
    Of morn on their white shields of Expectation."
                                          LOWELL.

THE last of those gatherings in Dr. Whyte's study
of men and women holding many divergent opinions,
which had begun in the days of Henry Drummond's
student meetings nearly thirty years before, took place
on the afternoon of 7th July 1914.   The speaker
was Baron Friedrich von Hügel, and the title of his
address, finally adjusted after much correspondence,
was, " On certain central requirements of Religion,
and the difficulties special to Liberal Movements in
face of these needs—as experienced from within the
Roman Catholic Church."   The great scholar and
thinker gave an address in which learning and
originality were lit up by occasional flashes of
quaint humour.   He set out from the Protestant
theology of Troeltsch ; but, as he afterwards did in his
Essays and Addresses on the Philosophy of Religion,
he developed from it certain of the positions of Liberal
Catholicism.   Professor W. P. Paterson   thanked
Baron von Hügel in one of his scintillating little
speeches, and so brought to a close the last meeting
of a remarkable series—a meeting in which an
Austrian Catholic, who had made England his home
for forty years, interpreted to a Scottish audience
the thought of the profoundest German Protestant

theologian of the age then swiftly approaching its close.

During the fortnight that followed, Dr. and Mrs. Whyte prepared for a journey which cut them off from their own country for the first critical weeks of the war. How it appeared in prospect is shown by a letter to Sir William Robertson Nicoll, in which Dr. Whyte said that he hoped, while spending a few weeks in Switzerland, to go over the sermons which he had preached during the three previous years on subjects suggested by Thomas Goodwin, and to shape them into book form. With this plan in mind, he set out from Edinburgh. In London, on 28th July, he and his wife lunched with Dr. Suther-land Black, Professor J. H. Morgan, Mr. Norman Angell, and Mr. Robert Donald of the *Daily Chronicle* ; and he sat, as a silent listener, while an eager discussion went on regarding the acute crisis in Ireland, which was being hourly overshadowed by the infinitely darker war clouds then rolling up over Europe. The dangers latent in the international situation were not indeed unfamiliar to him, for he had given his warm support to more than one move-ment for the preservation of peace. Yet, even at this stage, the nearness and vastness of the peril were not fully understood, and Dr. and Mrs. Whyte were advised that they could safely proceed to Arveyes-sur-Bex on the mountain slopes above the Rhone valley. Their daughter - in - law and little granddaughter and also their daughter, Margaret, were among the party.

They had reached this quiet Swiss retreat just before the first week of August involved all the nations of Western Europe in the war, either as com-batants or as sufferers through its effects. They were much impressed by the calm and courageous bearing of the Swiss people during this crisis, and by the forethought with which every needful measure had been taken by the Federal Government—the calling out of the national defence force to guard the neutrality of their country ; the provision that, when the men were not drilling, they should work in the harvest fields in the district where they were stationed ; the regulation of food supplies, and of the movements of nationals and strangers alike ; the spirit of self-restraint and mutual helpfulness shown on all hands ; and the calm yet eloquent words addressed by a young pastor to gatherings in his wide mountain parish before he left to take up Red Cross work on the frontier. But, while all this went on around, Dr. Whyte's mind was constantly strained by anxiety for news of his children and of the course of events in Britain—when news came slowly and in most contradictory form. He wrote to his son, Robert :

" *Sabbath, August* 9, 1914.

" VERY DEAR ROBERT,—Yesterday being your birthday, I thought much about you. . . . You can judge, or rather, you cannot, what a time we are having up here : what a time of suspense and anxiety. Think of it ! Such a week as last week was at home and abroad, and not a letter, nor an English newspaper, coming into our hands ! Everything is ' held up ' at the French frontier. Oh ! how we long for news, true news—for what we get one hour is contradicted the next hour. But we hope soon now to get our big post : and then what a time we look to having as we read up consecutively the *Times* and the *Westminster* and the *Chronicle* ! And also the letters which you and the others have written and posted.

" We are all well, and as merry as it is possible to be during such a tragical time. We have every comfort in this excellently managed house, and with such glorious Alpine surroundings. Joan is the joy of the whole chalet.

" I am taking some hours every day to prepare a volume of pulpit work for the printers.

" To Aird and you—your father's present love and warmest prayers.

" ALEXANDER WHYTE."

On the same day a telegram reached Dr. and Mrs. Whyte from three of their older children, " *Robert est soldat . . . il a bien fait* " ; and two days later a letter came from Robert, written from Edinburgh on Sunday, 2nd August. In it he told of the rumours and the preparations proceeding around him, expressed his confident hope that his parents would suffer nothing more than inconvenience though war might soon surround them on all sides, and said of himself : " Sitting looking at the rain on the streets of Edinburgh is rather a disconsolate business at this time : and if there turns out to be any call for untrained men, well, I suppose I shall respond to it." On the day after Britain's entry into the war, he responded, enlisting as a private in the 9th Royal Scots, a kilted battalion proudly known in Edinburgh as " the Dandy Ninth." A few days later his brother, Aird, joined the Scottish Horse near Perth.

Meanwhile the days passed slowly at Arveyes, until the time when the French mobilisation and military requirements allowed civilian trains to carry British subjects across France to one of the Channel ports. On 25th August, Dr. Whyte wrote to Dr. Kelman :

" DEAR DR. KELMAN,—Prince of letter-writers as of other good things — your most welcome and delightful letter has just come into my hands. We are all packed up, and are waiting our orders to go down to Lausanne to join the train appointed us to carry us through France. ' Us ' being Fred's wife and baby, her sister, Mary, Miss Young, my wife's secretary, Mr. Graham of Dalton Hall Residence [Manchester], and Mrs. Whyte and myself.[1] There has been a committee at Lausanne working at these preparations, night and day, for some time past, and presided over by our minister there, Rev. Mr. Sutherland : and, if we get off with any comfort, it will largely be due to him.

[1] Miss Whyte was at Lausanne preparing for the journey.

" But for the war our first fortnight here
would have been a surpassing delight : but the
war ! Ah me ! And then such tragic events,
and no news coming to us : sometimes the suspense was too terrible. We have nothing to be
called a post. . . . The poor sheets that came
to hand from day to day were filled with the
most contradictory reports.

" We expect to start immediately ; but when,
and where, we shall arrive is known to nobody.
Only, we will be travelling through a friendly
country, and, that being so, we have very little
to fear."

Yet it was an anxious task, this crossing of France
by a train sent by circuitous ways and liable to delays
at every turn, followed by a crossing of the Channel,
when an old man of seventy-eight and a baby of less
than six months were in the party. But, now as
always, Dr. Whyte's eldest daughter proved the
most capable of couriers, and she was well seconded
by the other ladies. He left himself in their hands ;
and sat through the night in a crowded second-class
carriage with the same expression of serenity which
his companions had noted in the storm-tossed boat on
Lochmaddy years before. Nor did he suffer seriously
from the absence of rest during two nights on train
and steamer. Within three days he was able to
communicate again with Dr. Kelman—this time on a
post card :

" St. James's Court, London,
Friday [August 28].
" Dear, dear Colleague,—Here I am—safe
and sound on English soil again : after experiences. We remain here for a few days to look
around and ahead and make family plans. You
will have heard before us of the enlistment of Aird
and Robert.—In love and trust,   A. W."

On reaching London he learned that his colleague
had been summoned to undertake very responsible

service as one of the senior chaplains with the Expeditionary Force ; and the following day he wired : " You have my consent and with it my benediction." A week later he sent this message to Dr. Macaulay from Gerrard's Cross in Buckinghamshire : " Thank you for your so good letter. We are in a little paradise here for ten days : then home. But what a pandemonium is so-called Christendom ! " He had just dispatched a letter to Dr. Kelman, encouraging him in the service to which he was about to go, when news came that his colleague's health had suddenly broken down, and that there could be no thought for several months of his working, either as a chaplain or at his accustomed post in Free St. George's. Two letters to Mrs. Kelman follow :

> " When your letter was delivered to me I was walking alone in the fine old garden of this house, and was picturing to myself how my princely colleague and I would soon walk and talk together with the ripe apples falling all around us. I was forecasting the story he would tell me of his appointment to his great post, and, then, the plans he had laid for St. George's in his absence : plans that I felt sure would show all his incomparable power of forethought and wise management. And my distress when I read your sad letter was greater than I can tell you. I will only say that my distress was but his distress and yours over again. . . . I and my household here are praying and hoping for the best of messages to-morrow morning.
>
> " You cannot know, dear Mrs. Kelman, how much I love and trust and lean upon your noble husband.—Do believe me,
>
> " ALEXANDER WHYTE."

The second letter begins : " You are never out of my thoughts. How could it be otherwise ? We return home to-morrow. I will see Mr. Ireland to-morrow evening. And we will take such counsel together as we are able. Mrs. Whyte and I go to the camp at Scone on Friday to see Aird."

By this time hope was held out that a voyage to Australia would suffice to restore Dr. Kelman's health ; and Dr. Whyte wrote on his return to Edinburgh, expressing warm approval of the project, and promising to do his part to " keep things going " while his colleague was away. He added : " For my part, I would most earnestly deprecate a premature return " ; and ended with the words : " Rest in the Lord, and wait patiently for Him." His promise to " carry on " in Free St. George's was most amply fulfilled. Like many others who had more than earned entire rest, he returned at the call of 1914 into full harness. He was no longer forbidden to preach in the evening ; and for the first three winters of the war he preached as a rule either morning or evening in his own pulpit, and from time to time in the Pleasance or Fountainbridge. After Dr. Kelman's return from Australia, and in the intervals of his subsequent war service, Dr. Whyte gained some respite. Yet he worked steadily on throughout more than half of the war years, and brought comfort to many, even in the midst of the sorrow which came to his own home.

At this time his debt, and that of the congregation, to his assistants was unusually great. From 1912 to 1914 they had among them a man of outstanding spiritual power in the Rev. George S. Stewart, formerly a missionary in South Africa, whose profoundly devotional spirit and love of mystical theology brought him into close contact with Dr. Whyte. His successor, the Rev. John Macrae, who remained at Free St. George's throughout the difficult war years, had been for some time minister of the Scottish congregation in Calcutta, and thus brought to his work in Edinburgh a mature judgment and exceptional experience. Admirable work was also done by a succession of junior assistants, including the Rev. J. O. Ritchie, and at later periods two young Americans, John Hayes and Evan Thomas, who had come to Scotland to take post-graduate courses in theology. One development of the first winter of the war was the expansion of the monthly congregational " Notes " into a small weekly magazine bearing a reproduction of Dürer's St. George on its cover. Week by week the proofs were corrected in Dr. Whyte's study and passed under his minutest scrutiny ; and then the paper went forth on its great errand, to maintain as intimate a contact as possible between the old minister and his people who remained in Edinburgh, and all those at a distance — the absent colleague and especially the young men and women on service.

Free St. George's, like other congregations, was soon engaged in war work of many kinds. Early in the autumn a telegram arrived from Dr. Matthys Rooseboom, a Dutch friend of Dr. and Mrs. Whyte's, who had often worshipped in Free St. George's when he was a student in Edinburgh. He told of the thousands of Belgian refugees pouring over the frontier into Holland, and of the efforts of the Dutch to help them. Dr. Whyte read the message from the pulpit, and before long the congregation had contributed several hundred pounds for Dr. Rooseboom's work. Soon after the young people of " the Order of St. George " resolved to send a special gift of comforts to the Indian sappers and miners in France ; and Dr. Whyte presided when Sir Andrew Fraser, a former Governor of Bengal, told them of the hardships suffered by the Indians in the course of their service on the Western Front. Nor was Dr. Whyte interested only in efforts on a wide scale : among the individuals whom he helped was M. Paul Wissaert, a Belgian sculptor, who found himself stranded in Edinburgh without the means to carry on his profession. Dr. Whyte gave sittings himself for the medallion now placed in the Scottish National Portrait Gallery,[1] and afterwards approached over twenty friends to secure a fund by which M. Wissaert

[1] For this and its companion medallion, see Appendix IV., where the impression made by Dr. Whyte's personality during these sittings is recounted in the sculptor's own words.

was enabled to execute the medallion of Principal
Rainy which now occupies the central place in the
Rainy Hall at New College.

Towards the end of 1914, Dr. Whyte was called
to the sick-bed of Professor Campbell Fraser, the
editor of Berkeley and author of *The Philosophy of
Theism*, the last link with the Edinburgh of Chalmers
and Sir William Hamilton. Professor Fraser, who
had been a member of Free St. George's during his
early ministry but joined the Scottish Episcopal
Church in later years, retained his mental power to
the great age of ninety-five ; and Dr. Whyte wrote
not long after : " I had the happiness to recite an old
Scottish paraphrase to him shortly before he passed
away." It also fell to Dr. Whyte to take part in a
memorial service in St. Giles', at which the Bishop
of Edinburgh was present with members of the
two Presbyterian churches and the professors of
the University and New College. The Rev. A.
Campbell Fraser afterwards wrote to tell Dr. Whyte
how greatly his presence had been valued, and added
that his father would have regarded the service " as
a visible token of the drawing together of the broken
fragments of theological Scotland."

As Christmas approached, Dr. and Mrs. Whyte
felt more and more acutely, as countless others felt,
the tragedy of the far greater breach of unity in
Christendom revealed by the war. They suggested,
and the Kirk-Session at once concurred, that an open
Communion service should be held on Christmas
morning, thus bringing, in a way new to the experience of their Church, the thought of the Cross right
into the heart of the Christmas season. During
these months Dr. Whyte also sought to gain the
widest support for the daily service of intercession
held in St. George's Parish Church ; and a card was
circulated commending the example of the medieval
" Pax bell " which was rung daily at noon while
war lasted, as a summons to all—" whether in church
or at home, in street or workshop "—to share in
united intercession for peace.

In the last days of 1914 he sent this message to the " Weekly Notes " :

" DEAR MR. EDITOR,—Aristotle, 'the Master of all who know,' as Dante calls him, and 'the Secretary of Nature,' as Bacon calls him, says that happiness is the bloom that the gods make to lie on a life of goodness. Well, I wish you and all your readers a truly Aristotelian Christmas ; a Christmas that is happy with all the happiness that always lies in a life of true goodness. Say, therefore, to all your readers that if they would enjoy a truly happy Christmas, let them and their children go about all this Christmas season doing good. And, then, the city is full of divine opportunities of doing good, and, thus, of both an Aristotelian and a Christian happiness. Also I congratulate both you and your co-editor with a Christmas congratulation on the great success of your ' Weekly Notes.' For I hear on all hands of how much your ' Notes ' are enjoyed by all who read them ; but especially by the women who remain at home. And then, all this Christmas and New Year season, depending on the good providence of our God, we all count the days till we get Dr. Kelman home again : brought to his desired haven, filled with all the fulness of God, and with his youth renewed like the eagle's.—Believe me, his old colleague, ALEXANDER WHYTE."

How Dr. Whyte applied his own precept at one war-time Christmas was described to the writer by the late Miss Joan Cameron. She was one of a group of women, connected with the Edinburgh Young Women's Christian Association, who arranged to invite the girls forming the chorus at one of the Christmas pantomimes to a small At Home in the Association's rooms. The question arose who should be asked to address the gathering before it dispersed, and Dr. Whyte's name was suggested. At first the proposal seemed a somewhat daring one, but Dr. Whyte was duly asked, and agreed to come. He began his speech by saying that it could hardly be thought that an aged minister could have anything to say that would interest his hearers, but that he had been asked to come and felt he could not refuse. The old man's noble appearance, his radiant smile, and the half-humorous humility of his opening sentences, so captured his unaccustomed audience, that they listened breathlessly while he talked for twenty minutes on John Bunyan; and at the end one of them rose and expressed the warm and spontaneous thanks of the whole company for his presence and his words.

By the beginning of 1915, two more of Dr. Whyte's children were absent on service. His eldest son had received an honorary commission in the Royal Naval Volunteer Reserve, and was engaged as a King's Messenger to the Fleet, carrying dispatches sometimes to the Mediterranean and sometimes to northern waters ; while his youngest daughter was about to sail for Egypt to nurse in a Red Cross hospital in Alexandria. At one meeting which he addressed with Dr. Kelman he mentioned the part that his children had taken, and exclaimed, " If I had twenty, I would give them all." He was fully persuaded of the absolute necessity of the Allies' stand against the menace of German militarism, and both spoke and encouraged his colleague to speak on " the righteousness of our part in this awful war." He had, indeed, previously held the belief that the Kaiser was genuinely working for peace, and the reaction in his mind after war broke out was all the stronger. One sermon on Satan tempting David to number the people was heard of in very high quarters in Berlin. In it he said that, little as he would like to have the keeping of the Kaiser's conscience, he would still less wish to bear such a moral responsibility as rested upon the Kaiser's court preacher.[1]

[1] Dr. Stalker informs me that the sermon is referred to in *Erinnerungen aus meinem Leben*, by Dr. Ernst von Dryander (1922), p. 278.

At the end of February, Mr. Lloyd George had occasion to address a meeting at Bangor before the departure of a Welsh contingent for the Front. The meeting took place on Sunday, and he began his speech as follows:

" Before I decided to come down here I met one of the most eminent Scottish divines, a great and old friend of mine, Dr. Whyte of Edinburgh. We were discussing what I have to say to-day. I remarked to him: ' I have only one day on which to say it, and as that is Sunday I am very much afraid that my constituents won't listen to me.' He replied: ' If they won't have you, come to Scotland, and we will give you the best Sunday afternoon meeting you ever had.' But I thought I would try Wales first. Dr. Whyte told me, in the Shorter Catechism, you are allowed to do works of charity and necessity on the Sabbath, and those who tell me that this is not a work of necessity do not know the need, the dire need, of their country at this hour." [1]

Dr. Whyte fully realised, also, the place of what might appear to be subsidiary activities in the prosecution of the war ; and at a later period, when Sir George Paish and Mr. Stewart, the Public Trustee, came to Scotland on the request of the Treasury to urge upon business men and other special audiences the pressing need for economy, he specially interested himself in bringing his fellow-ministers together to hear their appeal.

But much closer to his own heart was his relation to the young men who had gone forth from the congregation to active service. He signed letters of greeting to all at the Christmas season, and among the papers of this period are some rough pencilled notes of a message to those on active service :

" GENTLEMEN,—In your absence from us, and in your unparalleled circumstances, try to

[1] *British Weekly*, 10th February 1921.

believe how much you are on our minds and in our hearts, Sabbath day and week day : in the pulpit, in the prayer meeting, and in family worship, you are always with us. And the love and the honour that go out to you from the whole congregation is a great joy to us your ministers, as it is a great blessing to all those who so think of you. ' Then sang Deborah and Barak in that day and said, Praise ye the Lord for the avenging of Israel when the people so willingly offered themselves. My heart is toward the men of Israel who offered themselves so willingly.' And we are proud to think that your names will be written with the names of Zebulon and Naphtali, a people who jeoparded their lives on the high places of the field. For you have jeoparded your lives in a way every whit as holy as was the way of Israel. . . . And, by the blessing of the God of Peace when He arises to be the God of Battles, you, like the men of Israel, will lead captivity captive."

Although Dr. Whyte was now entering his eightieth year, he delighted in visiting the Y.M.C.A. huts at Duddingston and other camps near Edinburgh to speak to the men in training, and once at least went as far afield as Stobs. In the unconventional surroundings of these gatherings, and in face of the stern facts of life and death, duty and sacrifice, he spoke with especial force and freedom to these soldier audiences. He also followed closely the sustained effort of the women of his congregation, who had undertaken to maintain at full strength the staff of fourteen or fifteen women workers needed by the two Y.M.C.A. huts in the remote camp of Nigg in Easter Ross.

Yet in the midst of this patriotic effort he had thoughts to spare for the wider international issues raised by the war and for the peace that lay beyond it. In April 1915 he and his wife were again at Gerrard's Cross, when an invitation reached her to go

to the Hague as one of twenty women delegates from
Great Britain to a conference called by the Women's
International League, which was to meet under the
presidency of Miss Jane Addams of Chicago, one of
the greatest social reformers of her time.   Dr. Whyte
thoroughly approved of his wife's acceptance ; and
she was in London ready to start when the war
conditions of the moment caused the whole delegation
to be turned back.

From this time onward Dr. and Mrs. Whyte were
seldom without a son in the fighting line.   Robert,
after several months as a private in the Royal Scots,
obtained a commission in the Black Watch.   He had
a further period of training at Nigg, and by the end
of May 1915 was with the First Battalion on the
Western Front.   Through June and July he was in
the trenches near La Bassée or farther north, with
intervals in rest billets behind Béthune, where he
spent a week in hospital early in August.   Then followed a brief leave, spent with his parents at St. Mary's
Loch.   When he returned to his unit they knew that
he would soon be in the heart of the offensive which
had been in preparation for months.   On 25th
September the First Division, which included his
battalion, was on the left of the main attack in the
Battle of Loos, advancing from a point near Vermelles in the direction of Hulluch.   On the morning
of that day he led his men from point to point, finding
such cover for them as he could, until, as they began
an attack at close quarters on a little wood, he fell,
killed instantaneously by a shell.   Earlier in the
advance, and only a few hundred yards away, his
friend George Smith, Sir George Adam Smith's eldest
son, met the same swift death while advancing with
the 2nd Gordons.

Robert Whyte's body now lies in the British
cemetery at Dud Corner, beside the Béthune-Lens
road, where it crosses the high ground to the west of
Vermelles.   He had just entered his twenty-third
year when he gave up his life for his country—the
country which, like his eldest brother, he had hoped

to serve in another field. Had the opportunity been granted him, he would have achieved a service of no common kind ; for he had remarkable gifts both of intellect and personality. He had already gained a wide knowledge of English literature and of political thought, and had shown a true vein both of poetic and of critical talent, while his power of drawing other men to himself in close friendship was singularly strong. These qualities, and his delight in nature, were never more clearly shown than in the letters and poems which he sent home from France.

The news of Robert's death first reached his parents on 1st October, in a letter from his devoted servant, J. M. Small. All who saw Dr. Whyte in the days that followed noted the courage with which he met this sorrow. The deepest secret of his courage lay in his consciousness of a Divine Companion as he faced it : among his first sermons after he returned to his pulpit was one of great impressiveness on the words, " Lo ! I am with you always." To the many friends who expressed their sympathy, he sent a card bearing the words, " Our consolations abound by Christ, and you have added to them." His own sorrow enabled him but the better to minister to those of his congregation and friends who passed through the same trial during the following years. He gave to one such a copy of his lectures on Bunyan's *Holy War*, with the inscription, " To ―― in memory of his son and mine." And at a later stage of the war he wrote to an old friend in St. George's :

" DEAR MRS. SIMSON,―Our soldier boys are not dead : they are already with Christ, the Captain of Salvation, which is far better than the longest and the best life on this earth. Let us never think of them without singing :

' How bright these glorious spirits shine ! '

" Dear Mrs. Simson, I cannot tell you how dear and honoured your family name is, and

will always be, to me. Nor can I assure you enough how all who bear that name will always be loved and prayed for by your old minister,
" ALEXANDER WHYTE."

On 31st January 1916, he wrote from 7 Charlotte Square to Baron Friedrich von Hügel, who had also been recently bereaved :

"MY DEAR FRIEND,—Your rich and generous letter has been read by us over and over again, but has not been answered as it ought to have been. It is not easy answering such a letter : and I am not to attempt to do that. Only to assure you how much we feel with you in your domestic bereavement, and to tell you that the loss of our boy Robert in the war has opened our hearts much to all who are at present in the same family distress. I shall carefully preserve your letter also for what it contains about your friend, the Abbé Bremond ; and if any message comes from him, be sure it will be greatly valued both for your sake and his. Also I note, with warm thanks, your invitation to come to see you, should we be back in London again.

" Mrs. Whyte may have told you that I have resigned my charge of St. George's Church here. It is our way to take our charge from the hands of the Presbytery of the bounds, and to return our charge when we are no longer able to discharge the duties. I am 80 years old, and it is high time I were removing out of sight, and letting young and able men take my place. I have had a long and happy life in my charge here : but many humbling thoughts crowd my mind during these days. But—' His mercy endureth for ever.'

" Your true and indebted friends here never forget you.—Believe me,
" ALEXANDER WHYTE."

The first intimation of the step referred to in this letter had been given some seven weeks before in a letter to Dr. Kelman marked "Thrice private," which began :

"Not for one reason nor two nor three, but beset behind and before with compelling reasons, I had taken up my pen last night to tell you that I have made up my mind that the time is overdue for me to resign and retire from my share of the pulpit and pastorate of St. George's. But as I lay in my bed and thought and thought the whole matter over and over again last night, the thought of how this step of mine might affect *you*, makes me hesitate this morning to write as I had intended to write. That my retirement would affect both you and the congregation beneficially, and in more ways than one, I clearly see. But there are other possible effects it might have on *you* that I cannot put out of my mind. And why I write to you to-day is to put before you what is continually in my thoughts : and to prepare you for the step that I must take soon, and without postponement or retractation."

Such was the humility, and such also the spirit of considerateness, in which Dr. Whyte prepared to lay down the burden which he had borne for forty-five years. His decision was intimated in the following letter sent to the Kirk-Session in the last days of 1915 :

"DEAREST OF BRETHREN,—The time has fully come, indeed, it is long overdue, for me to resign the Senior Pastorate of St. George's, and to retire from all active service connected therewith. For years now I have not been able nearly to perform my part of the work, and it is time that all the work should pass over into hands able for it all. . . .

"And what can I say more but this ? I

am not Samuel : but I will say to you what
Samuel said to the elders of Israel when he laid
down his prophetical office : ' As for me, God
forbid that I should sin against the Lord in
ceasing to pray for you.' And you will not
forget me when you are near God.—Believe me,
My Beloved Brethren,

" ALEXANDER WHYTE."

When the Session called the congregation together
to consider this letter, Dr. Kelman spoke of the
world-wide influence of Dr. Whyte's ministry, and
of the contrasted qualities in his personal character :
" Erudite and yet passionate . . . he has been the
most scathing prophet of sin in our generation, and
the tenderest friend of sinners." Lord Rosebery
wrote that his resignation meant " the disappearance, or partial disappearance, of a great light and
glory of Edinburgh, and indeed of the Christian
faith." Of the expressions of love and admiration
from the Kirk-Session, Deacons' Court, and the
congregation as a whole, it is needless to write
here — save to quote Dr. Whyte's characterisation
of the Minute passed by the Kirk-Session : " It
does not measure me : it measures and blesses
those who wrote and adopted it." At the meeting
of the Presbytery of Edinburgh, which dealt with
his resignation, a letter was read from Dr. Whyte's
colleague in the New College, Dr. A. R. MacEwen,
the historian of the Scottish Church—then stricken
down by fatal illness half-way through his year as
Moderator :

" Now, after more than forty years of un-
flagging service, he [Dr. Whyte] is by universal
consent our foremost minister, held in honour
everywhere. . . . His great powers have been
broadened by his incessant study and deepened
by his devotion to the Church of God. At a
time when many have been tempted to religious
trivialities and vagueness, he has made the
teaching office of the Church his first concern,

and has commended evangelical truth to multitudes with picturesque vigour and searching realism. As a pastor he has set before the community a high ideal of efficiency ; and in the Presbytery it will be remembered that his wide sympathies have seemed only to increase his love for our own Church, and his generous estimate of his brethren in the ministry."

How the congregation gave further expression to their gratitude, and how Dr. Whyte felt unable to face the pain of a formal parting, may be gathered from the following letter sent to every member :

" *To the Congregation of*
    St. George's United Free Church.

" *May* 1916.

" DEAREST OF PEOPLE,—This is my continual song in these days concerning you and myself :

> ' If Thou shouldst call me to resign
> What most I prize, it ne'er was mine.
> I only yield Thee what was Thine :
> Thy will be done.'

For years past God has been preparing me for my resignation by my decaying strength, by His voice in my judgment and in my conscience, and by many conspiring providences of His around me and toward me. I was not precipitate to resign, because He had made His work among you very dear to my heart ; and if my resignation has been at all a wrench and a pain to me He will forgive me all that and will still uphold and accept me. Above everything else, what has borne me up, and has reposed and rejoiced my heart, is this, that He has in His extraordinary goodness given me such a colleague and successor, and you such a minister, as Dr. Kelman : a man of such splendid endowments, of such ardent love for his Master's work, and of such universal acceptance. Now, my dear friends, when you at all realise what I have been passing through you will easily

understand how impossible it is for me to face
the Congregation or even the Committee, in
the way that it was wished I should do. I know
that the suggestion of a Congregational Meeting
was made in the kindest of minds toward myself,
but I could not face such a meeting at present :
it is to me impossible. I had been falling upon
some devices of my own to deaden somewhat the
pain of my resignation feelings ; but when the
knowledge of your extraordinary kindness came
to me my reawakened emotion completely over-
came me. The wisest man I ever knew said to
me in a dream the other night : ' No,' he said,
' do not attempt to speak to them ; you will be
sure to break down.' And in saying that he
showed both his knowledge and his wisdom, for
I break down as often as I again think of you.

  " As to your noble gift after my resignation,
there were some things very dear to me, from
which I would have had somewhat to withdraw
my former support, but you have greatly lessened
that distress by your munificent generosity.
The most fitting words I can find anywhere to
express my present mind are contained in the
Apostle's thankful message to the elders and
deacons and people of his beloved Philippi. ' I
rejoice in the Lord greatly,' he wrote, ' in that
your care of me has flourished again. Not
because I desire a gift ; but I desire that much
fruit may abound to your account.'

  " As to the exquisitely beautiful Book of Congregational Names, and every name ' written not
with ink,' over and above what that Book will
be to me all my days, it will be a precious heir-
loom in our family for generations to come.

  " And now, Mr. Ireland—speaking of Philippi,
in this present matter as in so many other
matters—you have been a perfect Epaphroditus
to me. As Paul said of his friend, you have
always behaved as a brother to me. You have
all along, from the beginning, been my com-

panion in service and my fellow-soldier in Jesus
Christ. Like Paul's fellow-soldier, you have not
regarded your life if you could serve this Congregation and all its Ministers, but especially
me. May you always be held in the high reputation that the Apostle pronounced on your
Philippian forerunner because of his so many
and so self-denying services.

" In his old-age diary Thomas Boston has a
heart-touching entry about his ' silent Sabbaths.'
But, after making that entry, Boston soon came
to see that his silent Sabbaths were all ordained,
both to his people and to himself, with divine
wisdom and with divine love : To his people,
in order that the Ettrick pulpit might gain a
freshness and an attractiveness that it sorely
needed after his too long and too monotonous
ministry ; and to himself, in order that he might
attend to his own soul, all the remaining Sabbaths
of his life, as he had been wont to attend to the
souls of his people. Also, on those silent
Sabbaths he learned to pray for the comfort and
the prosperity of his successor in the pulpit as
he had been wont to labour and to pray for his
own comfort and prosperity. His silent Sabbaths
gave Boston time also to read his Bible, and that
not in search for pulpit texts, as formerly, but
to read it as all ' written to himself,' as he now
saw, for his own salvation. In short, Thomas
Boston came to see with Thomas Chalmers that
some years of silent Sabbaths are a good way
of winding up a pulpit and pastoral life, and a
good opportunity of making preparation for the
better life and the better services in the Upper
Sanctuary.—Believe me, in all this,

"ALEXANDER WHYTE."

In spite of Dr. Whyte's formal resignation, his
work in St. George's continued for another year.
Indeed, the chief outward and visible sign of the
change was that he was now referred to as Minister-

Emeritus instead of as Senior Minister. He preached
as often in 1916 as during the previous year. Once
when Dr. Kelman was absent from a meeting of the
Deacons' Court, he sent him a copy of the agenda,
with the note : " A specially genial and happy meeting :
with blessings on you.—A. W." ; and he even offered
to break his summer holiday, if need were, in order
to undertake any particularly urgent pastoral duty.

The spring of 1916 brought another loss, as directly
due to the war as if it had taken place on the field of
battle. The first Zeppelin raid in Scotland had taken
place a few days before, and Sir Alexander Simpson
was returning from a meeting in support of war-time
prohibition through the darkened streets of Edinburgh,
when he was knocked down and rendered unconscious
by a motor which his partial deafness had prevented him from hearing. He was taken to a ward
in the Royal Infirmary, where he had worked for
so long, and tended with all care, but he passed
away the same night. It was such a passing as he
would have chosen, with no weakness or long waiting ; and the friends who gathered for the funeral
service at 52 Queen Street still remember the beauty
of Dr. Whyte's prayer, and the note of thankfulness
which ran through it. Yet the loss was great ; for
the two men had come from Glasgow to Edinburgh
in the same month (October 1870), and they had been
bound together not only by the tie of marriage but
by forty-five years of fellowship in the Kirk-Session of
Free St. George's and in many of the religious movements of the time. Never had Sir Alexander Simpson
done more for his minister and his greatly loved Church
than during his last years of comparative leisure ;
and only a few months before he had taken a morning
service for Dr. Whyte, speaking on the missions to
the Jews which lay very near his heart.

In the same month of April, Dr. and Mrs. Whyte
visited Exeter to see their youngest boy, Lance, who
had now left school, and was in training for the R.F.A.
at a camp in South Devon. A letter from Exeter to

Dr. Kelman closed : " We go to London in the hope of seeing all our children once more together : before they scatter—when to return ? " A post card to Dr. Macaulay, with a photograph of the statue of Richard Hooker beside the Cathedral, showed how Dr. Whyte found consolation in the Puritan divines in those anxious days :

> " I have often felt remorse for having spoken to you too lightly about Thomas Boston's works. I am reading his *Crook in the Lot* to-day with honour and admiration and benefit. Hooker is under my window. Nobody speaks lightly of *him*."

Anxiety as to the progress and issue of the war often weighed heavily upon his mind. Once, walking back from St. George's, he suddenly stopped on entering Charlotte Square, and turning to Mr. Macrae, who was with him, said, " Will we win through ? " His companion tried to give reasons for the hope that was in him, and then Dr. Whyte said : " Yes, I want to hear you argue it, and I think you're right. But I'm sometimes not sure—not sure." On Saturday, 3rd June 1916, it had been announced in the morning's paper that Dr. Whyte would give some memories of his long ministry in his sermon on the following day ; but the first news—more disquieting than that which followed—of the Battle of Jutland had come in, and he wrote the following letter :

> " *Saturday : private.*
>
> " DEAR DR. KELMAN,—I do not know how you feel about this disastrous naval battle. Our papers are all trying to belittle the loss to our nation and to our great cause. But it cannot be belittled. . . . So profoundly am I impressed with that, that I feel strongly that *you should be in your own pulpit to-morrow morning to comfort and strengthen your many sad and depressed people* : advertisements notwithstanding. Five minutes after the service begins the advertisements will be all forgotten. . . .

" I have prepared a service with a view to the present circumstances of the congregation and my own, and somewhat such a sermon as might have been my speech, had a congregational meeting been held in connection with my jubilee; but I cannot intrude a discourse full of congregational and personal reminiscences on the people to-morrow. If I must be in the pulpit, which I do hope not, I will make the whole service praise and prayer and scripture. With my present feelings I could do nothing else. Think over all this, and let me hear what your feelings are. . . . To-morrow will be a great opportunity for you if you take my counsel."

Through these months, in spite of such anxieties, both his sympathy with aged friends and his delight in children's voices kept all their freshness. In May, he wrote from Edinburgh to Mrs. Haldane, then in her ninety-second year :

" Meditate much with me on that great Scripture, 1 Cor. i. 30. It is one of the Apostle's greatest passages. I had hoped to give you this message to-morrow in person, but have been kept here."

And Mrs. Haldane replied :

" I will meditate on your passage. There is nothing so invigorating, especially at present, as the Scripture itself. This war has taken possession of all our lives, but we can look with confidence to Him who is King of kings and Lord of lords. . . . I have been with you in spirit in sorrow, as you have been with me."

At the other end of the ladder of the years, he maintained his interest in the Children's Choir, finding time to preside at more than one of their concerts, even during the years of war. On the last of these occasions he arrived on foot and remained for the whole concert—refusing the offer of a cab to bring him to the hall and the suggestion that he might be glad

to leave half-way through the programme ; and all
the evening the hearts of those present were gladdened
by his smile.

Dr. Whyte found another source of cheer in the
growing spirit of unity among the Churches. Some
months before, he had called the attention of his people,
through the congregational " Notes," to a little book of
prayers for war-time by the Rev. Ronald Knox.

> " *An Hour at the Front*," he wrote, " is the best
> prayer - book that this war has produced. The
> author of the little book is not of our divinity school,
> but he is of a great school, and if you come on some
> small offences as you read and pray, step over them
> and pass on to something safer and better."

In proof of his appreciation of these prayers, he
sent Father Knox a copy of his own book on Newman,
and received a reply of cordial thanks.

The united daily service of intercession in St.
George's Parish Church, and the arrangement by
which the congregations of the two St. Georges'
worshipped together during the summer vacation,
were sources of satisfaction and of comfort ; and yet
more, the united Communion service referred to in a
letter addressed to the writer of these pages from
Bonskeid on the first Saturday of August 1916 :

> " We arrived here late last night, but safe
> and full of comfort and thanksgiving. We had
> a remarkable Communion service in St. George's
> yesterday at noon. Ministers and elders from
> all the neighbouring congregations took part,
> and altogether it was a uniting and a refreshing
> hour. . . . Your dear mother comes to tea this
> brilliant afternoon, and I take the Chapel to-
> morrow : ' Thou shalt call *His name* JESUS.' "

Dr. and Mrs. A. H. F. Barbour and their younger
children were already at Bonskeid to welcome Dr.
Whyte's party, and together they formed a large
and united circle during the following weeks. He
was cheered by the presence of those of his children

whom war activities allowed to reach Perthshire,
and of two little grandchildren, Joan Whyte and
Michael Chance. He enjoyed the quiet of the hills,
and even now he was seldom idle. His Sundays,
indeed, were far from idle. On the last three Sundays
of September he gave of his best, as his manner was,
to small country congregations, and on two of these
occasions he spoke for nearly an hour—at Blair-
Atholl on " Just as I am," and in Fincastle Chapel
on " Lord, teach us to pray." In his address on
this favourite text (Luke xi. 1) he spoke with bold,
imaginative vision, telling of the infinitely distant
point to which astronomers say that all the stars
are moving, and asking whether heaven itself might
not lie in that region whither all the worlds are
irresistibly drawn. On the evening of 24th September, in the same little building, he dispensed the
the Lord's Supper, being assisted by the ministers of
the nearest Church of Scotland and United Free
Church. At this, his last Highland Communion, there
was no sermon ; but he " fenced the tables " in the old
Scottish fashion, though with a simplicity and a charity
that were wholly his own, describing some of the marks
of the true believer—love for the Lord's Day, for the
Bible, for good books, and for family worship.

Soon after his return to Edinburgh, Dr. Kelman
was asked to preach and lecture to the British troops
on the Western Front, and Dr. Whyte wrote :

> " After looking as well as I can at the whole
> situation, and at myself, I now offer to take
> the pulpit for one service each Sabbath during
> your absence : morning or evening, *pace* Dr.
> Barbour ! I am quite well : and I am never so
> well or so happy as when I am preaching or
> preparing to preach."

In December 1916 he reached his jubilee as a
minister, but set his face against any public celebration. Some months before, when a rumour of
such a celebration reached him, he wrote to Dr.
Kelman, " I write at once to beseech you to deliver

me from any such cross." But more than his personal shrinking from such a function was the sense that it would strike a discordant note after more than two years had been passed in the agony of the war. So four members of the Presbytery of Edinburgh, which Dr. Whyte had attended so long and faithfully, came to his study as messengers from their brethren; and Dr. Robert S. Simpson of the Free High Church expressed, with his delicate insight, the affection and reverence with which his fellow-ministers looked up to Dr. Whyte. The scene is described in the later sentences of a letter sent just afterwards to the colleague in France :

"NEW YEAR'S DAY [1917].

"DEAR DR. KELMAN,—Just home from a most excellent service. Symington, Macrae, and Thomas each read their own scripture and offered prayer. A very good congregation. Things struggle on in your absence : but in everything we miss you. But the two assistants do their work splendidly : willingly, devotedly, acceptably.

"The Christmas Communion service was particularly helpful—I believe, to us all.

"You may have seen or heard that the Presbytery sent a deputation of the brethren to me with a Jubilee Address. Dr. Simpson, Dr. Martin, Dr. Drummond, and Mr. Henderson, elder, came with the Address. Dr. Simpson read it, he having composed it. The Address was very generously conceived, and was very eloquently worded : altogether it was a function that, I think, did good to all concerned. . . .

"You were remembered this forenoon amid deep and sympathetic silence.—Always yours,

"A. W."

So quiet was the gathering which marked the fiftieth year of one of the most outstanding ministries ever accomplished in the Scottish Kirk.

1917–1919

> " The soul's dark cottage, batter'd and decay'd,
>   Lets in new light through chinks that Time hath made :
> Stronger by weakness, wiser men become
> As they draw near to their eternal home:
> Leaving the old, both worlds at once they view
> That stand upon the threshold of the new."
>   E. WALLER.
> " Love, like wine, the older the better."—GOODWIN, quoted by A. W.

TOWARDS the end of January 1917 the United Free Church Presbytery of Edinburgh, like others throughout the Church, gathered those of its ministers who were within call for conference and prayer. A brief retreat was held in the Library of the New College, and the Lord's Supper was dispensed in the High Church by Dr. Simpson and Dr. Hastings. The first session of the retreat dealt with personal and devotional themes, the second with some of a minister's responsibilities, and the third related these subjects to the needs of the hour, and especially to the needs of the men on service. At the first, after Dr. W. M. Macgregor had spoken on Repentance and Dr. H. R. Mackintosh on Hope, Dr. Whyte closed the session. Had he foreseen that this would prove his last address within his beloved College and to his fellow-ministers, he could not more fittingly have chosen his subject. It was called simply " A Review," but this somewhat colourless title covered a speech which was nothing less than a *consummatio totius vitæ*, a gathering together of the experience of his lifetime as a preacher since "his mouth had been opened to preach the Gospel " in the schoolhouse of Buchanty fifty-eight years before. The whole utterance was steeped in autobiography, and the method of preaching which he commended to his

sons in the ministry was the personal and experimental method. One passage may be quoted, in
which he told that he never read a portion of Scripture
alone or at family worship that texts did not " leap
out " at him as if they had been written expressly
for him.

" I select," he went on, " the most home-
coming of these texts, and I write upon it every
forenoon : even though I have, nowadays, no
pulpit use for what I write : no pulpit use, only
my own paramount and pressing use. And I
am, to this day, making such rich and manifold
gain by that method, that I am bold to recommend it : aye, and to urge it on every old and
effete preacher like myself. And for an instance, my text this very forenoon was this,
' Your life is hid with Christ in God.' "

A few days after this gathering Dr. Whyte was
confronted by a new call. Dr. Kelman's work for
the Y.M.C.A. had been so greatly valued in France
that he was asked to return for a longer period ; but
before he did so an even more responsible task was
laid upon him. He was asked to go to the United
States on a semi-official errand, to lecture on the
war aims of the Allies, at the critical moment when
the American people were still undecided, though
on the brink of their final resolve to enter the war.
Dr. Whyte was not less anxious than four months
earlier that his colleague should be set free, and wrote
to Dr. Barbour :

" With your consent and Dr. Russell's I
would offer Dr. Kelman one service each Sabbath
during his absence. I never was better in
health than at this moment : and I never enjoyed
my desk and the pulpit more. As a matter of
fact, I write every forenoon for three or four
hours for my own edification."

So matters were arranged, and Dr. Kelman sailed
for the United States on 24th February, taking with

him one of Dr. Whyte's books, as a tribute of admiration from the author to President Wilson, with an inscription telling how his father, John Whyte, had suffered for the cause of American unity in the Civil War. President Wilson acknowledged the gift not long after through his secretary, Mr. Tumulty.

Just before this Dr. Whyte travelled to Clayesmore School, near Winchester, to be present at the dedication of a memorial window in the School Chapel. He and his wife had given this window to the School, in memory of Robert, who had spent there the years before he went to Balliol; and the service of dedication was conducted by the Bishop of Winchester, whose friendship Dr. Whyte had gained at the World Missionary Conference seven years before, and who had also lost a son on the Western Front. Bishop Talbot spoke of the good that had already arisen out of the war, and traced its origin to " the one great principle running through life—that giving was better than getting—the divine principle of sacrifice for others." Those who were present carried away a lasting memory of the two great Christians of different communions, as they " stood side by side in their sorrow and pride, and in mutual regard and affection for each other."

On 25th February, the day after Dr. Kelman sailed for America, Dr. Whyte preached on the words, " I am come that they might have life," closing with a most impressive evangelical appeal. He then told his people that, during the coming months, he and others would assist his " gifted colleague," Professor H. R. Mackintosh, who had promised, not for the first time, to help the congregation in their time of stress. But on this occasion Dr. Whyte soon began to be conscious of the strain placed upon him, his courageous words to Dr. Barbour notwithstanding. On the following day he replied thus to a request from Dr. Macaulay :

" I would like much to do it : but, really, I am not able. My remaining strength ebbs away

fast. And every moment of my time, and
every atom of my strength, will be needed
to keep things right here till Dr. Kelman's
return."

On the following Sunday evening he presided for
the last time at the Lord's Table, in the Hall of the
Pleasance Settlement ; for he had made a point of
taking the Warden's place at Communion seasons,
while Dr. Miller was absent as a chaplain in France.
At such a service a few months earlier Dr. Whyte
had thus announced the theme of his action sermon :
" The last time I was here we took Ps. ciii. 1–5 (' O
thou my soul, bless God the Lord '), and we enjoyed
ourselves so much that we shall just take the same
again." " But," adds one of his hearers, " it was all
new, fresh from his great, loving heart." Before
the Sacrament on 4th March 1917, he took as his text
the question asked by the children in every pious
Jewish family at the beginning of the Passover,
" What mean ye by this service ? " [1]   In his address
he took up in succession the words, " Passover,"
" Eucharist," " Sacrament," " Communion," and
" Lord's Supper," explaining each, and drawing out
its meaning so simply that none of his unlettered
audience could fail to understand, but with a spiritual
depth that none of them could plumb or exhaust.
But the most remarkable fact regarding this sermon
was the way in which it linked the close of Dr. Whyte's
ministry with its beginning, for he had used the
same headings forty-six years before, in instruct-
ing his first class of young people in St. George's
regarding the nature and meaning of the rite of
which some were preparing to partake for the first
time.

Early in the morning of the following Sunday
some six or eight inches of snow fell—an unusual fall
in Edinburgh. A rapid thaw followed, and by the
hour of service the streets were only passable to those
who were prepared to struggle through deep melting

[1] Ex. xii. 26.

snow along unswept streets and side-walks. So it happened that the congregation in St. George's was one of the smallest to which Dr. Whyte had ever preached there. His subject was taken from a familiar phrase in Jeremiah—" A Study in the Swelling of Jordan " is the title on the manuscript. He first sketched the rapid, treacherous course of the Jordan, which had made its crossing a symbol of the last great ordeal awaiting every human soul. Next he told in the words of Scripture how the dread River had been crossed by our Lord, by the Penitent Thief, by Stephen, and by Paul. Then, following John Bunyan, he described the crossings of Christian, Christiana, and certain of her companions; and after he had told of the last hours of Augustine, of Luther, and of Butler, he applied all this to the experience awaiting his hearers, repeated three verses of " Just as I am " and the summons, " Come, ye blessed of My Father," and closed with these—his last words from the pulpit of St. George's :

> " And to all who so come to Him, who keep so coming, He will surely say, ' When thou passest through the waters, I will be with thee, and through the rivers they shall not overflow thee : till the redeemed of the Lord shall return, and shall come to Zion with songs, and with everlasting joy upon their heads. They shall obtain joy and gladness, and sorrow and sighing shall flee away.' "

The Communion Sunday came a fortnight later, and on Saturday, 24th March, Dr. Whyte's post cards giving the subject and order of service had been dispatched to the aged and bedridden members of his congregation and to Dr. Kelman in America, while his action sermon lay ready on his desk. Its title was, " A Study in the Hebrew Children's Question at the Passover Supper " ; and its earlier pages followed the line of his address at the Pleasance three weeks before, but the later part was entirely new. That afternoon he attended the preparatory service, which

38

was conducted by Mr. Macrae, who noticed that he was looking flushed and tired. Shortly after returning to his study he had a sudden and acute heart-attack. As it passed over, and the pain abated, he began to talk to Mr. Macrae, who had called to see him, of preaching on the morrow ; and it was only when he was urged to consider how disastrous it would be if he broke down during the Communion service next day that he consented to see Dr. Barbour. So his active ministry ended ; for, although the heart-weakness was in itself no more alarming than that of seven years before, those seven years—including two and a half years of the war—had inevitably reduced that power of recuperation which had served him so well until he had passed fourscore. At first he was very prostrate in body and had many attacks of sharp pain, especially at night. Yet the activity of his mind was so little impaired that, when a friend called ten days later and offered to read aloud to him, nothing would satisfy him but that an article in the April number of the *Hibbert Journal*, which had been begun in his hearing, should be completed.

When his bodily vigour had returned sufficiently to allow him to be taken thirty miles by motor, he and Mrs. Whyte went to Merlindale, a house by the Upper Tweed, which had been lent by their warm friends, the late Dr. J. G. Bartholomew and his wife.[1] There, amid the grass-clad Border hills, in a country rich in legends from the fabled days of Merlin onward, the early summer was spent ; and Dr. Whyte enjoyed sitting for hours in a shelter, surrounded by masses of papers and magazines, listening to the ripple of the Tweed near by, and now and then walking in the garden. Dr. Cairns, who found him in these surroundings, has described the pleasure he took in the doings of a mother-partridge, who led her little brood through the long grass near the shelter where he could observe her quietly. At the end of May he wrote to his congregation, through the " Monthly Notes " :

[1] The great cartographer had been an elder of Free St. George's for several years.

" Merlindale, Broughton.

" Dear Mr. Editor,—You ask me how I am. I am not so young as I once was, but I never was better in my general health. And, otherwise, I have never had two better, nor indeed two such months all my life as April and May have been. . . . When you visit my aged and infirm friends, assure them of the abiding love of their old minister, " Alexander Whyte.

" P.S.—I would like all my friends to know of Dr. Bartholomew's great goodness in giving me his beautiful country house, Merlindale, for these divine weeks—all so full of the singing of birds, the blossoming of trees, and the springing of corn. By the Divine Word all these things were made at the first, and by Him they all consist to this present, and blessed be His Holy Name. " A. W."

Soon after midsummer Mrs. Whyte and he went south, and his next letter to the congregation was sent from the quiet village which became his home for the next two years, in a district with abundant memories of Milton, Cromwell, and William Penn.

" Watercroft,
Penn, Buckinghamshire,
July 25, 1917.

" Dear Mr. Macrae,—You ask a line or two for your summer number. But before all these spring Sabbaths are left behind, I must testify to the intense delight with which I have heard of the great edification and enjoyment you have all had at the hands of my New College colleague. I always felt sure it would be so. For both in the pulpit and in the chair, and through the press, Dr. Mackintosh is a very rich possession to our own Church and to all the Churches. And now I look forward to hearing often of a similar edification and enjoyment during the happy Sabbaths when the two congregations of the same name shall worship together in the same church.   For there is a time, says the Preacher, to break down, and a time to build up ; a time to rend, and a time to sew ; a time of disruption, and a time of reconstruction :   and   on   all   these   autumnal Sabbaths our Lord will look down and see His prayer for the mutual love and the inward and outward union of His disciples fulfilled in you."

Then, after quoting 1 Cor. i. 10, Phil. ii. 2, and Eph. ii. 14 and 21 as the interpretation of this prayer by " the apostle who had most of his Master's mind," the writer continued :

" For myself, I left Merlindale, that Peebles-shire paradise, only for this one compelling reason. As you know, Fred is working very hard in London at present, and that in more spheres of national service than one ; so hard that he has no prospect of a proper holiday at all this summer.   That being so, we were led to think of looking for a house for a month or two in some place to which he could run out in the evening after his day's work is over and return to his post in the morning.   And besides, Penn being near London, our other children could far more easily visit us than they could were we all the summer in Scotland. . . . Believe me,
                    " ALEXANDER WHYTE."

The desire to be within reach of his children, so as to see them readily in their brief leisure, was the strong magnet which drew Dr. Whyte away from the land which he had served with so steady a de-votion to spend his last three and a half years in the South of England.   For at this time his married daughter,   Janet,   was   living   in   Worcestershire; Margaret soon after took up the arduous work of organising recreation huts for American soldiers and sailors in various parts of Britain ; Rhoda had returned from Egypt, and after being on duty in a war hospital at Chelsea, went on to further service near Boulogne and at Genoa ; Aird was with the K.O.S.B. on the Western Front ; and Lance was preparing to return thither after having been wounded in April in the advance between the Vimy Ridge and Arras. But while this was Dr. Whyte's single motive, those who watched over his now slender strength wished to find for him a spot where freedom from needless interruption could be combined with the opportunity to see friends often and easily, and where he could sit in the open air for a greater part of the year than is possible in Scotland.

His tranquil life at Penn was varied by several short journeys, on one of which he wrote to the people of St. George's (at the end of October 1917) :

" LONDON, S.W.,
Communion Sabbath afternoon.
" Here I am surrounded by every attention and comfort, no man could possibly be more so, and the stillness and quiet and perfect peace in the heart of London is past belief to you. I am as quiet and peaceful as if I were spending the Sabbath at Balmacara, or Bonskeid, or Merlindale. Literally, there was not a sound all this morning but that of the trumpeter announcing the change of guard at Buckingham Palace far across St. James's Park.

" At eleven o'clock I entered into fellowship with the Congregation. I said to myself the opening psalms, ' This is the day God made,' and ' Thou hast, O Lord, most glorious,' and the paraphrase, ' 'Twas on that night.' Then, when Dr. Mackintosh was delivering his action sermon, .I read ' that blessed sixth of John,' as Bunyan called it, in John's Gospel — 'that spiritual Gospel,' as Luther called it ; then I saw the Elders bringing forward the elements ; and then I felt the great peace that fell on the great Congregation ; and then I heard Mr. Hollins leading you in David's perfect post-communion Psalm ;

and then I saw the people going down to their own homes, full, as the Catechism says, of 'spiritual nourishment and growth in grace.' In the afternoon and in the evening I will be with you again. . . .

"We expect to return to Penn next week, this time to Troutwells, the beautiful home of Sir Courtenay Ilbert, the Clerk of the House of Commons. Sir Courtenay and Lady Ilbert have been kindness itself to Fred's family and to us. They have put their country-house at our disposal in the most thoughtful and generous-hearted way. I will write you soon from Trout-wells.—Meantime, as always,

"ALEXANDER WHYTE.

"P.S.—Join with me continually in the appeal—

"Father of Peace and God of Love,
We own Thy power to save."

A few days later the peace of his London retreat was broken by an air raid, and " at sunrise " next morning he rose to write down the reflections which it had awakened. He named the resulting paper, "A Raid Night Reverie in London "; [1] and in it, beginning from Socrates and the Stoics, and coming down to some of the masters of Christian thought in modern days, he set forth the counsel which the wise and good man will follow when faced by the immediate imminency of the great change.

A visit to Oxford some months later was thus described on a post card to Dr. Barbour :

"Rhoda gave me her arm through the grounds of Magdalen College this forenoon. Magnificent ! At the same time I felt a certain freedom in the great College, over which Good-win was 'sometime President.'—Always and everywhere yours, A. W."

[1] Published in the *British Weekly*, 8th November 1917.

Dr. Whyte's Gladstonian use of post cards was maintained to the end, and many of them, as well as of his later letters, ended with the same characteristic conclusion as that just quoted. His devotion to the writings of Goodwin was also maintained ; and the first task which he accomplished in the autumn of 1917, as his health became somewhat restored, was the final revision of his last book. Its full title is *The Spiritual Life—The Teaching of Thomas Goodwin, as received and reissued by Alexander Whyte.* He had been working upon it from the year 1911 onward, and had taken the manuscript of the greater part to Switzerland in July 1914 ; and now that leisure had come to him it was completed and published. It is full of autobiographic fragments, some of which have been reproduced in the earlier part of this book ; but it has also the special interest that, as Dr. Sutherland Black wrote after Dr. Whyte's death, " it reflects without addition or subtraction (almost) all that he had ever said." Yet in one sense there was both subtraction and addition. The sermons in this book show a less daring imagination than those of the author's prime, but they have an added mellowness and tenderness ; nor can a passage of more urgent and winning appeal be found in any of his writings than that which closes the sermon on the words, " The Son of Man had not where to lay His head."

As Dr. Whyte was now severed from most of his own books—many of which were given to the New College when 7 Charlotte Square was dismantled at the end of 1918—and as he could no longer visit other libraries, he became more dependent than ever upon the skilled and ungrudging researches of Dr. Sutherland Black. Both before and after Dr. Whyte left Scotland, his friend sent him many letters elucidating such points as Goodwin's place of burial in Bunhill Fields and the Latin quotations embedded in his works. A little anthology of fragments of curious learning might well be culled from these letters, which range from Ovid to writers on the

Roman Breviary, and from Thomas Traherne and " Coke upon Littleton " to a current astronomical text-book. Thus Dr. Black tells on a post card that he has been reading " Dryden's translation of Ovid's (splendid) 15th Book," and continues : " I find myself wondering whether perhaps Goodwin's interest in the *Metamorphoses* may not have been stimulated by Dryden ? Or, contrariwise, Dryden stimulated by Goodwin ? "   And on 15th June 1917, he asks whether Dr. Whyte had ever offered, or joined in, the prayer beginning, " O God, who art meek and lowly in heart," which had been offered by millions of Catholics that day.

Two brief phrases are worthy of note at the beginning of *The Spiritual Life*—the dedication, " To John Kelman," and the legend, " Vol. I.," on the title-page.   A second volume on Goodwin was, indeed, planned, but never proceeded beyond the stage of preliminary notes.   Other projects for writing filled many days during Dr. Whyte's sojourn at Penn ; and the following, among the headings inscribed on covering sheets or envelopes containing notes, show the regions in which his thought moved : " A Study in Wisdom," " As for David, Prayer,"—a variant is, " David and his X-rays " — " John Newton's Approaching Soul," " A Study in that Great Love wherewith God hath loved us," " A Study in Death." But the project to which he gave most time and reflection was that of bringing the thought of the Abbé de Tourville to the knowledge of English readers.   De Tourville wielded a wide influence in France as a singularly sensitive spiritual director, who knew how to state the truths of inward and personal religion in modern language.   He wrote little, but his teaching is enshrined in the *Piété Confiante*,[1] a series of letters to two novices, which " touch on many aspects of education, on the social studies in which he had collaborated with Leplay, and on the place of America in the further evolution of society."

[1] Published at Paris in 1905.

" The core of the Abbé's doctrine," says Mrs. Whyte, who twice read his book to Dr. Whyte in a free translation while they were at Penn, " lay in a passionate devotion to Jesus Christ, who, as guerdon of the travail of His soul and of His sufferings, receives the power to become the spiritual centre of every human soul ; so that, whenever we so desire, we can come into inward contact with Him, and receive direct from Him the spiritual nourishment and daily guidance that we need. ' Lay aside all scruples,' pled the Abbé, ' throw away your account-books of debit and credit in the spiritual life, launch out into the deeps of the great ocean of the love of God with Jesus as your pilot.' Very simple, old, evangelical teaching—but in the hands of the Abbé de Tourville it received a new charm, and a new adaptation to the needs of the modern soul seeking its way over un-charted seas ; and Dr. Whyte wished to make it available where the French edition might not come without his introduction. But the plan was never carried out."

There do, however, remain some sheets of pencilled notes with a draft title-page in Dr. Whyte's hand— " The Pastoral Letters of l'Abbé de Tourville, con-densed and Englished by Alexander Whyte "; and these show how deeply his heart was engaged in this his last literary plan.

The two years at Penn were enriched by new friendships as well as old, and especially by the friendship of Sir Courtenay Ilbert, whose name is associated with one of the first steps in the granting of self-government in India, and who was Clerk of the House of Commons from 1902 to 1921. Dr. Whyte felt it a rare privilege to hear him talk on men and books and affairs out of his wide knowledge, and to have the use of his books at Troutwells, during the winter of 1917–18 ; and the pleasure of occasional visits from Sir Courtenay and Lady

Ilbert was continued during the two subsequent years.

Many of the newest books continued to find their way to Dr. Whyte's table, and he spent much of his time reading or hearing them read. Thus a friend from Scotland was asked in an Oxford Street book-shop if he knew the old Scots clergyman at Penn to whom Sir James Frazer's *Folk-Lore in the Old Testament* had just been sent. Dr. Whyte's letter to his friends in St. George's, dated " Troutwells, Christmas Day, 1917," consists of an enthusiastic appreciation of three books then newly published— Lord Morley's *Recollections*, Dr. Denney's *Christian Doctrine of Reconciliation*, and the Rev. (now Pro-fessor) James Robertson's *Spiritual Pilgrimage of Jesus*. Dr. Denney's book he calls " by far the best book of the past year . . . in the best world of books " ; and, notwithstanding his own devotion to the older theology, he concludes his account of it by saying: " No old book, however true and powerful, will speak to preacher and hearer in our days as Dr. Denney's *Reconciliation* will speak." Passing on to Mr. Robertson's book, he continues: " Elisha was not Elijah : nevertheless the mantle of the ascending prophet fell upon his youthful successor." [1] Soon after, he wrote to Dr. Macaulay, then on war service in France :

> " I have just finished my second reading of Denney's *Reconciliation*. I began my second reading with the intention of sending you some selected sentences of Denney's. But Hazlitt's saying about Burke came into my mind: ' The only specimen of Burke is all that he ever wrote.' Have you time and mind to read Denney at present ? If so, send by return your safe name and address.
>
> " What a contrast in my comfort and peace compared with that of you and your con-gregations ! "

[1] Dr. Denney had passed away six months earlier.

Then, by way of postscript, he added one quotation :

"Even if no man should say—'Thou, O Christ, art all I want, More than all in Thee I find'—God says it" (p. 235).

To one who was arranging for the republication of a little book entitled *Christ in You*, he wrote: "I am not able, I am not worthy, to write a 'foreword' to such a book. I have not attained to its teachings : nor am I within a thousand miles of them. But I follow after." Thus to the end he showed the same spirit which made him declare himself, in one of his great sermons on "Luke eleven and one," to be "but a raw beginner in the art of prayer." Soon after his arrival at Penn, he wrote to Mr. John Owen :

"MY DEAR AND OLD AND TRUE FRIEND (I had almost written, dearest and oldest and truest of friends : and, even if I had, it would have been no exaggeration), — I am giving myself up wholly to devotional and experimental reading and meditation. My pulpit and pastoral work is closed, and I am more free to give attention to my own soul, which much needs all my attention. At the present moment I am reading, I rather suppose for the tenth or twelfth time, Marshall on *Sanctification*. Have you ever read the Puritan classic ? It is not easily read : but even when but partially grasped it is one of the most blessed of the great books of the soul. If you do not possess it, I would be honoured and delighted to send you a copy. As to Goodwin, vol. i. [his own *Spiritual Life*, already referred to], it is already in the printer's hands. Do not trouble to look for it : you shall get one of the first copies that comes from the press.—Believe me, Always and everywhere, Yours,

"ALEXANDER WHYTE."

But other letters show that this statement as to the limitation of Dr. Whyte's reading must not be taken in too literal a way. Thus a post card to Miss Innes reads :

> " How we—Dr. Innes, Dr. Dods, Dr. Thomson, and I—would have enjoyed Raleigh's *Six Essays on Johnson*, when on our spring holiday ! Get this fine book of criticism out of the Club, and read it thinking of them and of me."

A letter in the same vein tells how the writer and Dr. Black had enjoyed *Dr. Johnson and his Circle*, and ends, " with constant thoughts of the ' three just men made perfect.' " Another letter is dated from " The Good Shelter " in the spring of 1918 :

> " Dear Miss Innes,—I often think of you, and wonder how you are, and how things are with you. Things are so different, both with you and me, than they were not so long ago. We have been in this beautiful English valley now for nearly a year. . . . I write a little daily, if only by force of an old habit, and I read little but the papers, and some old divinity. I find that, for me, the old books are the best. Only —what led me to take up my pen this moment was my having finished the only novel I have read for years, *The Setons*, by O. Douglas. . . . As I read it I often thought of you, and of our old Glasgow life. I think you will enjoy some of its chapters much. . . . If you read the homely story, and like it, drop me a card. Anyhow, drop a card now and then, about yourself, to your old and abiding friend,
> " Alexander Whyte."

That this appeal was not disregarded is shown by two subsequent post cards, one of which reads :

> " Thank you. For it was of such letters as yours that Dr. Johnson said that they ' kept old friendships in repair.' "

And the other :

" One word of best thanks and warmest good-will.—Believe me, always and everywhere yours, as of old, and for so long,   A. W."

A letter written in October 1918 may be added :

" VERY DEAR MISS INNES,—I have shared your most welcome letter with Dr. Black, who is with us here.   Fred has been laid up at Perth, but is so much better that we expect him here in the end of the week.   We have his wife and children with us.   Our two sons, Aird and Lance, are at the front, but are both hitherto safe and well and in good spirits.   Rhoda is nursing in Italy. . . .

" We are deeply anxious about where our future home is to be, now that ' No. 7 ' is out of our hands.   What brought us south is like to keep us south, in the meantime—to be near Fred, and to be within a short journey of our other children when they come home.   Could I be with you as of old, I might have much to say of my inward life : here I will only say that what I preached so long to you is now the one stay and strength of my life.—Believe me, with abiding love,   ALEXANDER WHYTE."

A few months earlier, when Aird Whyte was con-valescent after being seriously injured in a mustard-gas attack during the German advance in the spring, Dr. Whyte wrote to his sister-in-law, Mrs. A. H. F. Barbour :

" Thank you most warmly for all your kind remembrance of us.   We have had Aird out for some hours. . . . He is looking well : though not free from hospital care as yet. . . . All around here is sunlight and garden beauty.

" Let us thank God continually for all His abounding gifts, and for His unspeakable Gift."

Two post cards to Dr. Macaulay, one of which describes the melancholy dispersal of Dr. Whyte's mighty library, belong to the autumn of 1918, and are written in the minute handwriting of his last years :

> " In dissolving and distributing my library —painful job !—I did not well know what I could ask you to accept, that you do not already possess. Fred, who is superintending the process that I was not permitted to attempt, will send you a book not unworthy of your kind acceptance.   " A. W."

> " Thank you for your tonic letters. Your letters are always such. And for your tonic examination paper. May you be spared and used to set many such.[1] Fred arrived here last night, looking wonderfully well. He rests and recruits here for a week before returning to his London duties. Aird is wounded in a London hospital, but is fast getting well.
> " Write a tonic letter again soon to yours,
> " A. W."

After Dr. Whyte had spent six months at Penn, he realised that his work in Scotland could not be resumed even in part ; and this prompted him to resign the principalship of the New College, which he had held for nearly nine years, and in which he had found so much happiness, and given so much both to his colleagues and to the students. When he first wrote to Dr. Martin on the subject, his former colleagues sought to dissuade him from resigning ; but he saw his way clearly, and his decision was intimated through the College Committee to the General Assembly of 1918, of which Dr. R. J. Drummond was Moderator, and was reluctantly accepted by the Assembly. None of Dr. Whyte's letters breathes more of the spirit which irradiated

---

[1] Dr. Macaulay was at this time an examiner in theology, and soon after became Professor of Apologetics and Systematic Theology in the United Free Church College, Glasgow.

his later years than that which he addressed to the
Moderator at this time :

> " GOOD SHELTER, PENN, BUCKS,
> *May 24, 1918.*

" DEAR DR. DRUMMOND,—My much-loved
and much-honoured friend, thank you for your
so generous and so beautiful letter. But what
am I to say in reply to it ? What but just this
—nothing has at all changed with me since I
sent my resignation of the Principalship to the
Convener of the College Committee. My advanced age and the whole state of my health
and the advice of my doctor all make it impossible
for me to hope ever to take up the delightful
duties of the Principalship again with any
expectation of being able to perform these
duties in any really efficient way. Not that I
resign my happy post without a sore pang.
Between ourselves, all through these past
months I have been doing my utmost to imitate
the conduct and character of Mr. Humble-Mind
in the *Holy War*, and to avoid the conduct and
character of stiff Mr. Loth-to-Stoop, and I
really think I have at last learned to be content
and more than content—indeed, in everything
to be thankful. And well I may be. For I
have had a long life allotted me, and it has been
a life full to the brim of unparalleled mercies.
All of which has made me both able and willing
to stand aside and give place to some other man
who will be much younger than I am, and I hope
much abler than I have ever been for the important duties of this post.

" But, sir, though the General Assembly
permits me to leave the New College, I shall
never, as long as I live, leave the dear and close
friendship of my beloved colleagues. Nor shall
I ever neglect to do all that lies in my power
for the comfort and the encouragement and the
whole well-being of our beloved students.

"And now, Sir, as I sit here and pen these lines, I look up and see you all. Indeed, every day and every hour I look up and see the great Hall filled with dearly beloved Fathers and Brethren. And as often as I again see you all, I again commend you all to our blessed Lord, in whom all fulness dwells, and in whose fulness we are all complete.

"And in all this, my dear Brother,—Believe me,   ALEXANDER WHYTE."

Two other letters may be added, written in the same connection—one to Sir Robert Simpson, for over forty years the Depute-Clerk of the General Assembly ; the other to the Rev. George Macaulay, who had forwarded a resolution of sympathy and regard from the Presbytery of Edinburgh :

"DEAR SIR ROBERT,—I cannot thank you enough for the Assembly and personal messages you have so kindly sent me. Only I am not so foolish as to accept, in all their fulness, the too-generous words spoken and written concerning myself. These words are much more the measure of your goodness of heart than they are any measure of any merits of mine, and ever I shall treasure them as a happy memory of a happy time.

"My love and honour to your dear wife, and my old age blessing to yourself.—Believe me,
                    "ALEXANDER WHYTE."

"DEAR MR. MACAULAY,—How shall I thank you enough for your kind and heartsome message ? By these things men live : both by sending such things and by receiving them. I cannot tell you how I was wont to enjoy the Presbytery. It was one of the true delights of my life to see the business of the House put through as you and the other brethren did it. And now it is my delight to follow you in imagination and prayer. What a solace it is to me in my banishment to receive such a message from such honoured and beloved brethren : and from yourself.—Believe me,

"ALEXANDER WHYTE."

During the same spring he sent this message to Miss Evelyn Simson, the first woman in the United Free Church to be appointed an assistant for pastoral work, who had sent him the Free St. George's "Notes" containing the annual report of the congregation's work :

"Thank you for your incomparable ' Notes ' for April. For never since St. George's was, could such a record of prosperity have been issued. . . . It makes me feel somewhat like Emeritus Simeon in the Temple."

And he sent for inclusion in the May number "the best passage in the best sermon of the best divine in the English Church — Richard Hooker " — the passage beginning : " Christ hath merited righteousness for as many as are found in Him." Again, in the last year of his life he used the same classical passage in the same way.

Some months before he had written to Mr. Scott Ireland, who was making a brave fight against a serious illness.

"DEAR MR. IRELAND,—Thank you for your reassuring letter telling me that you are back in your native air, and that your journey was accomplished without difficulty or fatigue. . . . We had all our children with us on Sabbath, which made me think of David's words, ' God setteth the solitary in families.' And as I thought of you, I recollected the words of a greater than David : ' The Father hath not left me alone : for I always do those things that please Him.'

" Believe me, always and everywhere, your old minister and true friend,

"ALEXANDER WHYTE."

In January 1918, Mr. Scott Ireland died ; and his place as Session-clerk was taken by the late Dr. J. W. Ballantyne, whose pioneer work in the field of ante-natal hygiene has won recognition throughout the English-speaking world. Shortly before this, Dr. Whyte had written to Dr. Ballantyne from Penn :

> " VERY DEAR FRIEND,—Thank you warmly for your fine letter. Mrs. Whyte read it to me as I breakfasted in bed. It was the best ' kitchen ' [*Anglice*, ' relish '] to my morning meal. Write another like it every month or so, as long as I still am in Dante's ' opaque and palpable flesh.'
> " In the flesh or out of it, always and every-where, yours,   A. W."

From the time that Dr. Ballantyne took up the duties of Session-clerk, he spent an hour every Sunday even-ing in writing a full account of the doings of the day, and of the preceding week, in Free St. George's for the benefit of his old minister. No words could exaggerate the happiness which these letters brought to Dr. Whyte ; and one of them is referred to in the following letter to Dr. Kelman, who had just declined a call to the United States :

> " HAPPIEST OF MEN !—After many messages about you, and the great Session meeting—a letter of four quarto pages from Dr. Ballantyne crowned the record. I propose to keep it for insertion in the new edition of the *History of St. George's* long overdue. What a meeting it must have been ! We were wont to say that no minister in the world had such a Session around him as Dr. Candlish had : but I feel sure they never sent him home with such a strong, proud, re-devoted heart as you went home with last Monday. Yes : the happiest of men and the most to be envied of ministers ! "

Dr. Ballantyne had his reward for his informative weekly letters in a long series of post cards from Penn,

and later from Hampstead. One bore the inscription :
" Prince of letter-writers ! Thank you : Thank
you." The legend on another was of the briefest :
" Believe me, A. W." ; but its real message was
found in the pencilled address :

> " Dr. Ballantyne,
>   (The Best of Correspondents),
>   19 Rothesay Terrace,
>   Edinburgh."

Another, regarding an election of elders, ran :

> " When I read your splendid list of potential
> elders my heart sang :
>
>> " ' And ever may thy palaces
>>   Prosperity retain ! '
>
> A. W."

Another post card shows that Dr. Whyte did not forget
his correspondent's professional interests, nor fail to
follow the literary work of those who had formerly
been among the young men of Free St. George's :

> " You will have read ' Lens ' in this morn-
> ing's *New Statesman*."

On one occasion when Dr. Ballantyne's letter
failed to arrive by the expected post, Dr. Whyte
sent by return an anxious — almost an agitated —
inquiry as to the cause of the delay, beginning,
" Dearest of Correspondents."

His interest in other good causes was unabated,
whether those which he had helped in the past, or
others arising out of war conditions. Thus he sent
to a friend working in a club for soldiers and sailors
in a French Base a large parcel of the little Bagster
edition of the *Pilgrim's Progress*, with thumbnail
illustrations. Forty years before, he had recognised
the anonymous preface as the work of Robert Louis
Stevenson, and his booksellers say that he had given
away more copies of this than of any other book. It

was given to the choir-boys of Penn ; and another copy went to an invalid member of Free St. George's, with a reference on the fly-leaf to the song in the Valley of Humiliation, for she had been fond of singing. On the occasion of a congregational meeting in Fountainbridge, a parcel of books arrived beforehand from Dr. Whyte's publishers for distribution by the Rev. Ian Neilson who had just been inducted as minister ; and on the same occasion (14th August 1918) Dr. Ballantyne received a post card regarding the books, with the single word, " Speed," written above the address, and also the following letter :

" DEAR SESSION-CLERK, — I shall be with you in spirit on Thursday evening. How glad I would have been to be with you bodily ! Fountainbridge has a great history. It was a great day for St. George's, as well as for Fountainbridge, when Dr. Candlish appointed James Hood Wilson to that work. And the dear old saint showed his fine generosity in telling off so many of his elders to work along with Wilson. The same generous and brotherly mind still dwells in the minister of St. George's and in the eldership.

" Assure the congregation of my abiding love for them and for their children. My special benediction for Mr. Neilson."

He wrote to Mr. Cairns in acknowledgment of an address signed by all the children in the Children's Choir :

" Words absolutely fail me to express my surprise and delight as I read and reread your fine letter. . . . Assure the young people that their names will be handed down to my children and children's children. As your own name, sir, will be with love and honour."

Not long before his death, when he heard of the success of the Children's Choir in raising a total sum of £4000 in two years for war charities, he wrote again: " Rely upon it—that noble figure is recorded in heaven "; and sent at the same time this message to the Edinburgh Brotherhood Movement: " I shall always be glad and proud to see my name as in any way connected with your noble Brotherhood."

The joy in meeting with Christian leaders from other lands and other branches of the Church, which had marked Dr. Whyte's years of activity, followed him through these years of rest. Two of those with whom he came in contact at this time were Fra Elizondo and Father Nicholas Velimirovic, now Bishop of Ochrida. Fra Elizondo was one of the little Basque people, among whom he did his life-work and by whom he was greatly beloved. But, while he lived the ascetic life and wore the plain habit of a simple Capuchin friar, he had travelled widely and had become the friend of men belonging to very various schools of religious thought.[1] Dr. Whyte had several long talks with him, and the Scottish minister and the Basque friar found a strong bond of sympathy in their common debt to the works of Santa Teresa.

Among the many Serbians who visited Britain during the war none exerted an influence comparable to that of Father Nicholas Velimirovic. He came as a patriot representing a country desolated by the invaders who then held its soil, but—far more than this—as one who sought after the widest reconciliation both between nations and churches. It was in part due to Dr. Whyte that he visited Edinburgh in November 1916, and preached in St. Giles' and in Free St. George's. Six months later, when Dr. Whyte was slowly gaining strength after his illness, he received a letter from Father Nicholas which closed with the words: " This war is because of the Church. It can't be finished until the Church awakens. Everything that happened after our Lord was in connection with Him. This war concerns

---

[1] Cf. the memorial appreciation by Sir Alfred Davies in the *British Weekly*, 16th November 1922.

Him more than anything during [the] last 1900 years."
Later in the year, when the writer worked out this
thought more fully in a little volume, *The Agony of
the Church*, published by the Student Christian
Movement, Dr. Whyte commended it in a Foreword,
beginning : " The Eastern Church, the Church of the
Apostles and the Mother of us all, in this book speaks
to her children in all lands and in all languages, and
to us, with an authority, and a wisdom, and a tenderness all its own."   In this book the writer contended
that the war was due to the de-christianisation of
Europe and of the Church in Europe.   His appeal
was that the message of reconciliation should be
proclaimed afresh in its integrity, by a Church walking
in " the way of saintliness," as " the common good
of mankind, destined for all continents and all races,"
and so as the one " guarantee of a godlike peace
profitable for the whole of mankind."   This teaching
made a strong appeal to Dr. Whyte, who was cheered
two years later by the account sent by Father
Nicholas of the support given by the Churches of
south-eastern Europe to the movement for a World
Conference on Faith and Order.

The practical sympathy which Dr. Whyte had
shown with the Serbian people in their day of distress
was recognised after the Jugoslav kingdom came
into being, when, by the command of the King of
Greater Serbia, he received the Order of St. Sava.
This honour reached him in May 1919, not long after
he left Penn.   But throughout these years his interest
in the oppressed peoples of the Near East remained
constant.   At a critical stage in the Russian Revolution he took a keen interest in the preparation of a
" Message from the Christian People of Great Britain
to the Christian People of Russia."   It was printed
in English and Russian, and expressed not only the
sympathy of those who sent it with the much-tried
Russian Church, but their trust that out of these
distresses a new conviction would emerge among the
nations that the highest values are to be found in
Christ.   The signatures included those of Earl Beatty,

and of many leaders in the Church, in Labour, in literature and the arts. Among the last-named were those of two friends of Dr. Whyte's later years, Miss Lena Ashwell and Mr. D. Y. Cameron.

He joined, too, for the last time in an appeal on behalf of the Armenian Christians, whose tragic fortunes he had followed for forty years ; [1] nor did he ever cease to give his warmest sympathy to the efforts of Lord Bryce and his fellow-workers on their behalf. A few months before his death, when the troubles in Ireland were at their height, he joined in an Appeal for Prayer on behalf of Ireland, addressed to " all the Christian Churches and Fellowships in Great Britain and Ireland." Only through prayer, he was convinced, could such troubles find a peaceful issue ; and there remains a pencilled suggestion in his own handwriting for an addition to this Appeal :

" *Postscript to Irish Letter.*

" Truth often separates :
" Love always unites.
" ' Love me,' says Augustine, ' and then say anything to me and about me you like.'
" And Richard Baxter's people were wont to say, ' We take all things well from one who always and wholly loves us.'
" ALEXANDER WHYTE."

Those among whom Dr. Whyte spent these two years were not unconscious of his greatness. After his death, in a little magazine published in Penn in the interests of Church unity, there was applied to him Dante's noble phrase, " That spiritual splendour." And this chapter may conclude with some impressions placed on record by friends who saw him there. The Rev. D. Macrae Stewart, a chaplain of the Australian

---

[1] The appeal appeared in the *Times* of 2nd May 1919. The other signatories were, Lord Bryce, Cardinal Bourne, the Bishops of Oxford and Winchester, Lady Frederick Cavendish, Dr. Scott Lidgett, and Mr. Aneurin Williams.

Forces who had known him in Scotland long before, wrote :

> " One who stayed with him in his home was filled with wonder at the way in which, without seeming effort, he gave the impression of undying freshness. His grace at table was different for every meal, his way of conducting family worship varied constantly—sometimes a few words of Scripture and nothing else ; sometimes a prayer ; sometimes a hymn and benediction. Every slightest, single act of worship had been thought of before it was offered, and came from his heart."

Dr. Kelman wrote to the members of Free St. George's :

> " Dr. Whyte is reading insatiably, and being read to.   In the silence of the country he is often alone, and Penn is deep in the heart of rural England.   Friends run up for a night from town, or spend a week or two in the abundant hospitality of that household.   Then they depart again, leaving him to his quiet thoughts.   But books are friends that never depart, and in their perpetual and blessed company he spends the calm and bright evening of his days.   Now and again temptation masters him, for even the most experienced saint is not beyond its bow-shot. Dr. Whyte's temptation stands only a few paces down the road.   It is the Methodist Chapel wherein, in moments of weakness, he disobeys all orders and preaches to an astonished and delighted congregation.   Then, they say, his eye gleams, and his voice gathers strength, and he sends forth winged words, as he used to do among us.   It has not happened often, and has not done him any harm.   From the pulpit he returns to the garden and the gentle ministry of those beloved ones who are around him, and Thomas Goodwin."

Principal Cairns has preserved another impression in miniature :

" I asked him how the political leaders of the day compared with Gladstone and his own contemporaries. ' They're a different race,' he said, and I inferred, ' a smaller ! ' I like to think of him as I saw him when he came to the gate with us, and stood in the village street looking after as we went down the road, smiling, bareheaded, silver-haired, the very picture of noble, venerable, and happy old age."

One of Dr. Whyte's chief delights were the frequent visits of his eldest son, Fred, who for a time occupied another house in Penn, where, one Christmas Day, Dr. Whyte baptized a little granddaughter under the Christmas Tree. His son's diary for that day proceeds :

" For Christmas dinner we went to Troutwells, where A. W. seemed to drop twenty years. He said, in fact, that in sleeping, eating, and enjoying his friends' company, he was as young as ever— which is true : but when he walked or worked, the years found him out. He talked of the past, but his reminiscent vein never had enough detail to be caught and preserved—which is, and always has been, his tantalising way."

A series of further extracts under dates during May 1918 show how fresh were his political interests. One passage describes his walking up and down the lawn for an hour, his arm linked in his son's, " punctuating the talk with constant questions," about his companion's journalistic work, or regarding " the Maurice affair, Ireland, whether Haig has the confidence of the Government, and so on." And again :

" He grows no more conservative with age. His interest in the Labour programme is most alert. He challenges me to say how much of it I would accept, and whether the Liberal Party

could not take up most of it.   He is in the true
line of the Kirriemuir Chartists with whom he
began seventy-five years ago ; and he manages
to combine his admiration for Lloyd George with
it all : is genuinely distressed to read the attacks
this week in the *Spectator*, *Nation*, and *New
Statesman*.   He urged me to make ' a great
speech ' in Perth on the lines of the Labour
manifesto."

The following day's entry describes him " still
ruminating on the political future—as an old
Home Ruler, distressed about the Irish situation.
He sits there in his chair, more lion-like than
ever, his white hair long and shaggy, his
shoulders squarely drawn up against the chair-
back, his long thin hands striking out in
emphatic gestures, and his face growing young
and animated in the warmth of his argument.
At such moments the melancholy of his nature
falls away, and his unquenchable zest in affairs
and still more in persons is that of a man in his
prime.   I could imagine men coming from all
parts to catch a glimpse of the old veteran in his
evening years and going away marvelling at his
youth.   To grow more liberal with time, and at
eighty to warm himself with the promise of the
new world that is being designed by the Labour
Party, is a fate any man may envy."